CRIME AND PUNISHMENT IN EARLY MODERN RUSSIA

This is a magisterial new account of the day-to-day practice of Russian criminal justice in the seventeenth and early eighteenth centuries. Nancy Kollmann contrasts Russian written law with its pragmatic application by local judges, arguing that this combination of formal law and legal institutions with informal, flexible practice contributed to the country's social and political stability. She also places Russian developments in the broader context of early modern European state-building strategies of governance and legal practice. She compares Russia's rituals of execution to the "spectacles of suffering" of contemporary European capital punishment, and uncovers the dramatic ways in which even the tsar himself, complying with Moscow's ideologies of legitimacy, bent to the moral economy of the crowd in moments of uprising. Throughout, the book assesses how criminal legal practice used violence strategically, administering horrific punishments in some cases and in others accommodating with local communities and popular concepts of justice.

NANCY SHIELDS KOLLMANN is William H. Bonsall Professor in History at Stanford University. Her previous publications include *By Honor Bound. State and Society in Early Modern Russia* (1999).

NEW STUDIES IN EUROPEAN HISTORY

Edited by

PETER BALDWIN, *University of California, Los Angeles*

CHRISTOPHER CLARK, *University of Cambridge*

JAMES B. COLLINS, *Georgetown University*

MIA RODRÍGUEZ-SALGADO, *London School of Economics and Political Science*

LYNDAL ROPER, *University of Oxford*

TIMOTHY SNYDER, *Yale University*

The aim of this series in early modern and modern European history is to publish outstanding works of research, addressed to important themes across a wide geographical range, from southern and central Europe, to Scandinavia and Russia, from the time of the Renaissance to the Second World War. As it develops the series will comprise focused works of wide contextual range and intellectual ambition.

A full list of titles published in the series can be found at:
www.cambridge.org/newstudiesineuropeanhistory

CRIME AND PUNISHMENT IN EARLY MODERN RUSSIA

NANCY SHIELDS KOLLMANN

CAMBRIDGE
UNIVERSITY PRESS

CAMBRIDGE
UNIVERSITY PRESS

University Printing House, Cambridge CB2 8BS, United Kingdom

Cambridge University Press is part of the University of Cambridge.

It furthers the University's mission by disseminating knowledge in the pursuit of education, learning and research at the highest international levels of excellence.

www.cambridge.org
Information on this title: www.cambridge.org/9781107025134

First published 2012
First paperback edition 2015

A catalogue record for this publication is available from the British Library

Library of Congress Cataloguing in Publication data

Kollmann, Nancy Shields, 1950–
Crime and punishment in early modern Russia / Nancy Shields Kollmann.
p. cm. – (New studies in European history)
Includes bibliographical references.
ISBN 978-1-107-02513-4 (Hardback)
1. Criminal law–Russia (Federation) 2. Punishment–Russia (Federation) I. Title.
KLB3946.K65 2012
364.94709′03–dc23 2012008943

ISBN 978-1-107-02513-4 Hardback
ISBN 978-1-107-69976-2 Paperback

To Linda and Ron

Contents

Acknowledgments

It is humbling, and a great honor, to spend so much time immersed in the lives of people who lived hundreds of years ago. This project took me to the archives, where I read case after case of murder, assault and other dire moments in the lives of ordinary Muscovite people. While trial transcripts have their formulaic limitations, it is still possible to hear in them real people's voices and to engage in the tiny slices of their lives exposed when they brought their problems to court, or when their problems brought them to court. Of course, their sensibilities and ways of life were radically different than our own, but they aren't completely alien. In these cases I found the same range of human emotion – love and lust, anger and revenge, conscientiousness and corruption – that drives human behavior today. Thanks to generations of archivists, we have these people's stories to share.

Perhaps in part because it is so satisfying to read primary sources detailing the course of criminal litigations from crime to arrest to trial to punishment, this project took a long time. I have accumulated many debts along the way. I am very grateful for financial support for research and writing from many sources, including a Fulbright–Hays Faculty Research Abroad Fellowship (summers 1998 and 1999), two wonderful stints at the Stanford Humanities Center – one in 1998–9 when I sorted through piles of materials and one in 2007–8 when I wrote most of the book – and a residential fellowship at the Center for Advanced Study in the Behavioral Sciences at Stanford in 2011–12 where I wrapped it up. Generous grants from the National Endowment for Humanities, the American Philosophical Society and the Stanford Institute for International Studies (now the Freeman–Spogli Institute), from Stanford's sabbatical program and from Stanford's Dean of Humanities and Sciences also provided time off for writing. I am humbled and gratified by all of this support.

I am grateful for permission to publish some material previously included in these articles: "Marking the Body in Early Modern Judicial Punishment," *Harvard Ukrainian Studies* 28, nos. 1–4 (2006): 557–65 (reprinted with permission © 2009 by the President and Fellows of Harvard College); "27 October 1698: Peter Punishes the *Strel'tsy*," in *Days from the Reigns of Eighteenth-Century Russian Rulers. Newsletter of the Study Group on Eighteenth-Century Russia*, Cambridge: Study Group on Eighteenth-Century Russia (2007), 1: 23–36; and "Torture in Early Modern Russia," in Kivelson, Valerie A., Petrone, K., Kollmann, Nancy Shields, and Flier, Michael S. (eds.), *The New Muscovite Cultural History*, Bloomington, Ind.: Slavica, 2009, 159–70.

I have greatly benefitted from the help of colleagues here and in Russia. At the Russian State Archive of Ancient Acts (RGADA) Iurii Moiseevich Eskin and Svetlana Romanovna Dolgova were immensely helpful, as was the staff of the Reading Room, led by Alexander Ivanovich Gamaiunov (aided in my day by the charm of the Reading Room's resident cats). My colleague Alexander Borisovich Kamenskii, of the Russian State Humanities University and now the Higher School of Economics in Moscow, has generously given me archival advice, translation tips and collegial support for which I'm very grateful. My colleague Mikhail Markovich Krom of the European University in St. Petersburg also offered intriguing questions and unfailing interest in my project. Also here in the US I am particularly appreciative of three close friends and great scholars who have been constantly stimulating in discussions and who at key moments provided me new perspectives on important issues: Jane Burbank on empire, Valerie Kivelson on citizenship and Elise Wirtschafter on moral philosophy. Val Kivelson also generously shared with me her notes on a dozen witchcraft cases – many thanks! I've also received terrific feedback from many other colleagues who have read parts of this book or discussed it with me at conferences or informally over the years. A list of them that I am sure is incomplete includes Daniel Rowland, Paul Bushkovitch, Michael Flier, Gary Marker, Ned Keenan, Bob Crummey, Don Ostrowski, Russell Martin, Richard Roberts, Aron Rodrigue, Bissera Pentcheva, Bob Crews and Laura Stokes. Profuse thanks must go to the anonymous peer reviewers of the manuscript. They generously gave of their time to provide detailed and insightful commentary on issues large and small. Jack Kollmann, as always, provided an assiduous editorial red pencil, consistent encouragement and depth of knowledge on any issue regarding religion, art, architecture and the visual. Colleagues in the Study Group on Eighteenth-Century Russia in two conferences provided great critiques. Rather late in the game, in Autumn 2010 when I was resident faculty at Stanford's Overseas Studies Program in Moscow, I received energy and enlightenment from two disparate sources: first, the audiences at three institutions where I spoke – the Higher School of Economics in Moscow, the European University in St. Petersburg and the National University of Kyiv-Mohyla Academy – and, second, Stanford students who peppered me with questions that made me think through and sharpen the "big picture" argument. Finally, revisions were completed in the rich atmosphere of collegial interaction of the Center for Advanced Study in the Behavioral Sciences at Stanford. It is feedback from colleagues like these that keeps us going and growing as scholars, although, of course, the responsibility for the final product is all mine.

Finally, I'm particularly grateful to some friends, totally out of academia, who helped keep me grounded. In the last stretch of writing. Peter Newsom calmly and mindfully reassured me that, yes indeed, there would be an end to this project. Throughout the process Linda and Ron Henry recharged my batteries on many a long walk on the beach and surrounded me and my family with warmth and love.

Abbreviations

AAE	*Akty, sobrannye v bibliotekakh i arkhivakh Rossiiskoi imperii Arkheograficheskoiu ekspeditsieiu Imp. akademii nauk*, 4 vols. and index, St. Petersburg: Tip. 2-ogo Otd. sobstvennoi E. I. V. Kantseliiarii, 1836, 1838.
AI	*Akty istoricheskie, sobrannye i izdannye Arkheograficheskoiu kommissieiu*, 5 vols., St. Petersburg: Tip. Ekspeditsii zagotovleniia gosud. bumag, 1841–2.
AIu	*Akty iuridicheskie*, St. Petersburg: Tip. 2-ogo Otd. sobstvennoi E. I. V. Kantseliiarii, 1838.
AIuB	*Akty, otnosiashchiesia do iuridicheskogo byta drevnei Rossii*, 3 vols. and index, St. Petersburg: Tip. Imperatorskoi Akademii nauk, 1857–1901.
AMG	*Akty Moskovskogo gosudarstva*, 3 vols., St. Petersburg: Tip. Imperatorskoi Akademii nauk, 1890–1901.
DAI	*Dopolneniia k Aktam istoricheskskim*, 12 vols. and index, St. Petersburg: Tip. Ekspeditsii zagotovleniia gosud. bumag, 1846–75.
f.	*fond* (collection)
Kurbskii, *History*	Fennell, John L. I. (ed. and trans.), *Prince A. M. Kurbsky's History of Ivan IV*, Cambridge University Press, 1965.
KV	*Krest'ianskaia voina pod predvoditel'stvom Stepana Razina. Sbornik dokumentov*, 4 vols. in 5 pts., Moscow: Izd. Akademii nauk SSSR, 1954–76.
MDBP	*Moskovskaia delovaia i bytovaia pis'mennost' XVII veka*, Moscow: Nauka, 1968.

Novombergskii, *Koldovstvo*	Novombergskii, N. Ia., *Slovo i delo gosudarevy. Vol. 2. Materialy. Prilozhenie. Koldovstvo v Moskovskoi Rusi XVII-go stoletiia*, Moscow: Iazyki slavianskoi kul'tury, 2004.
ODB	*Opisanie dokumentov i bumag, khran. v Moskovskom arkhive Ministerstva iustitsii*, 21 vols., St. Petersburg and Moscow: Tip. Pravitel'stvuiushchago Senata, 1869–1921.
op.	*opis'*, *opisi* (catalog)
Postnikov	Tikhomirov, M. N., "Zapiski o regentstve Eleny Glinskoi i boiarskom pravlenii 1533–1547 gg.," *Istoricheskie zapiski* 46 (1954): 278–88.
PDP	*Pamiatniki delovoi pis'mennosti XVII veka. Vladimirskii krai*, Moscow: Nauka, 1984.
PRP	*Pamiatniki russkogo prava*, 8 vols., Moscow: Gosudarstvennoe izd. iuridicheskoi literatury, 1952–63.
PSRL	*Polnoe sobranie russkikh letopisei*, 43 vols. to date, St. Petersburg and Moscow: Akademiia nauk SSSR, 1841– .
PSZ	*Polnoe sobranie zakonov Rossiiskoi imperii*, Series 1, 1649–1825, 45 vols., St. Petersburg: Tip. II Otd. Sobstv. Ego Imp. Vel. Kantseliarii, 1830.
RGADA	Rossiiskii gosudarstvennyi arkhiv drevnikh aktov
RIB	*Russkaia istoricheskaia biblioteka*, 39 vols., St. Petersburg and Leningrad: Arkheograficheskaia komissiia, 1872–1929.
RZ	*Rossiiskoe zakonodatel'stvo X–XX vekov*, 9 vols., Chistiakov, O. I. (ed.), Moscow: Iuridicheskaia literatura, 1984–94.
SbRIO	*Sbornik Imp. russkogo istoricheskogo obshchestva*, 148 vols., St. Petersburg and Petrograd: Imp. Russkogo istoricheskogo obshchestva, 1867–1916.
Schlichting	Graham, Hugh F. (trans. and ed.), "'A Brief Account of the Character and Brutal Rule of Vasil'evich, Tyrant of Muscovy' (Albert Schlichting on Ivan Groznyi)," *Canadian-American Slavic Studies* 9 (1975), 2: 204–72.

SGGD	*Sobranie gosudarstvennykh gramot i dogovorov*, 5 pts., Moscow: Tip. N. S. Vsevolozhskago, 1813–94.
SIDG	Novombergskii, N. Ia., *Slovo i delo gosudarevy.* Vol. 1. *Protsessy do izdaniia Ulozheniia Alekseiia Mikhailovicha 1649 g.* Moscow: Iazyki slavianskoi kul'tury, 2004.
SRIa	*Slovar' russkogo iazyka IX–XVII vv.*, 29 vols. to date, Moscow: Nauka, 1975– .
stol	Office in Military Service Chancery
Taube and Kruze	Roginskii, M. G., "Poslanie Ioganna Taube i Elerta Kruze," *Russkii istoricheskii zhurnal* 8 (1922): 29–59.
VBDM	*Vosstanie I. Bolotnikova. Dokumenty i materialy*, Moscow: Izd. Sotsial'no-ekonomicheskoi literatury, 1959.
ZA	*Zakonodatel'nye akty Russkogo gosudarstva vtoroi poloviny XVI-pervoi poloviny XVII veka*, Leningrad: Nauka, Leningradskoe otd., 1987.
ZA Petra	*Zakonodatel'nye akty Petra I*, Voskresenskii, N. A. (ed.), Moscow: Izd. Akademii nauk, 1945.

Introduction

This book analyzes the criminal law in Russia in the context of early modern state-building in Europe and Eurasia. It focuses primarily on the seventeenth and early eighteenth centuries (for which case law exists) but begins in the "long" sixteenth century (starting from the late fifteenth) when Russia's laws and judicial institutions were founded. It analyzes how courts handled serious crime (felony theft, robbery and murder; state crime), pursuing various themes: how written law compared to practice, how the courts were structured and staffed, how trials progressed, how evidence was gathered, how judges reached verdicts, how communities and individuals participated in the judicial system. Particular attention is given to punishment – exile, corporal and capital sanctions – not only as evidence of judicial practice but also as a reflection of the state's legitimizing ideology. Such a study of legal practice is warranted in Russian historiography because most previous work on Russian legal history has focused on the letter of the law, not practice. More boldly, the study provides historians of other early modern states a case study of law and adjudication in a centralizing empire. Russia has often been regarded as a peripheral outsider employing unique forms of governance and development; this book shows that its state-building experience was part of a broader early modern continuum of change.

Since about the 1970s, historians and philosophers have explored how the early modern state came into being across Europe and in the Ottoman Empire, analyzing strategies of governance, of centralization and empire, and of the formation of sovereignty from roughly 1500 to 1800. Those strategies in turn are applicable to the Russian experience. One avenue of research has chronicled the "sinews of power" – states' creation of infrastructure to support military reform and territorial expansion. "Sinews" embodied new taxes and bureaucratic institutions to administer territory, collect revenues and mobilize human and material resources; they took the form of colonial administration for expanding multi-ethnic empires.

"Sinews of power" were represented by new codifications of the law and new centralized judicial systems, particularly criminal venues. Another fruitful avenue of research explores how confessionalization in post-Reformation Europe – movements in Catholicism and Protestant denominations to define the faith and discipline members – complemented states' efforts to consolidate society around state and church; to some extent, toleration of religious diversity worked to that effect in the Ottoman and Russian empires. Yet another approach examines the use of ideology and visual symbolism based on dominant religious discourses to legitimize power.[1] Russia paralleled its contemporaries in all these strategies.

At the same time scholars of early modern Europe caution against exaggerating the power of the centralizing state, a point particularly useful for Russian historians. Several tacks complicate the picture described above, one analyzing local governance. R. W. Scribner, for example, in a study of local policing in early modern Germany, cautioned against concentrating "on the observable structures of the state and its prescriptive legislation at the expense of close examination of the practical difficulties the state encountered in the pursuit of its own goals." He showed that "at the grass-roots, where policing really mattered," the early modern state was "far more fragile."[2] John Brewer and Eckhart Hellmuth echo such a conclusion where it seems least expected, that is, in reassessing the early modern English and Prussian states. They suggest that an overly Weberian focus on what Michael Mann called the "despotic" (formal and legal) power of early modern states has obscured the problems that such states encountered in creating "infrastructural" power, that is, building administrative institutions and relationships with society to execute state demands. Early modern states regularly relied on intermediary bodies including nobles, bureaucrats, municipal guilds and town councils to execute policy. Thus, like Scribner, Brewer and Hellmuth recommend an approach that "looks neither from the top down, nor from the bottom up, but at the points of contact . . . Negotiation not coercion is the key concept." Similarly, Michael Breen declares that in early modern France the law was neither "autonomous in the modern, Weberian sense" nor "façade," but was "one part of a much larger legal system of dispute resolution that incorporated mediators, arbitrators and other parties who

[1] Europe: Tilly and Ardant, *Formation*; Brewer, *Sinews*; Weisser, *Crime and Punishment*, ch. 6. Ottoman Empire: Imber, *Ottoman Empire*.

[2] Scribner, "Police and the Territorial State," 103, 116. Jason Coy also contrasts official displays of power in sixteenth-century German towns with officials' "negotiation and compromise with their communities": *Strangers and Misfits*, 97–128.

brokered, negotiated, or otherwise helped to bring about informal settlements."[3] Early modern states became modern, in other words, by seamlessly integrating what in social theory have often been seen as opposing categories: centralized/decentralized, personal/public, legal/customary. Exposing the misguidedness of those theoretical binaries, early modern legal cultures took their strength from a rich bricolage of social and political interaction.

Looking at state organization complicates the implicit narrative that early modern state-building leads to the nation state. It might have eventually, but in these centuries, states were pluralistic. European states ran a continuum from fairly unitary monarchies in which kings still had to cooperate with parliamentary, noble and other social institutions (England and France), to what Charles Tilly calls states with "fragmented sovereignty" (Switzerland, northern Italy and some of the Holy Roman Empire), where power was shared among loose confederations of city states, principalities and the like. Many others were land-bound empires: the Ottomans in an arc to the south, Poland–Lithuania, Russia from the Baltic to Siberia, the Habsburgs from Spain to the Netherlands to Hungary. As in their heartlands, rulers of multi-religious, multi-ethnic empires were forced, according to Karen Barkey, to "share control with a variety of intermediary organizations and with local elites, religious and local governing bodies, and numerous other privileged institutions." They unified their empires primarily around a supranational religious ideology; they controlled by strategies from toleration of difference, to co-optation of elites, to measures to prevent regional elites from building local power, to coercion. So implicated were imperial governments in negotiating with local communities to accomplish extraction and control that scholars call imperial sovereignty "layered," "divided" or "delegated": "Sovereignty is often more myth than reality, more a story that polities tell about their own power than a definite quality they possess."[4]

A further perspective on early modern state-building explores the relationship of power to violence. Michel Foucault argued that early modern European rulers governed by terror through "spectacles of suffering" – mass public executions and punishments – until in the seventeenth and eighteenth centuries they were able gradually to substitute discourses of conformity internalized by individuals, inculcated with

[3] Brewer and Hellmuth, "Introduction," 11–12. Breen, "Patronage, Politics."

[4] Tilly, *Coercion, Capital*, 20–31; Barkey, *Empire of Difference*, 9–15, quote on 10; Benton, *Search for Sovereignty*, 30–3, "myth" quote on 279. Burbank and Cooper on empire and nation: *Empires*, 1–3.

better means of communication and institutions such as the prison, the asylum and public schools. But, Foucault contended, such discourses were no less violent. A parallel school inspired by the work of Norbert Elias countered with a bottom-up vision of these processes: Pieter Spierenburg, Richard van Dülmen, Richard Evans and others contrasted spectacles of execution to the emergence of "civilizing" trends that gradually obviated the need for rule by terror. Etiquette, learning and court culture became standards for aspiring individuals and groups, societal violence decreased and society stabilized from within.[5]

Lest the emphasis of these theories on internalized discourses lull one into seeing state power as progressively more subtle, philosophers and theorists such as René Girard and Giorgio Agamben, among many others, draw attention back to the foundational role of violence in maintaining sovereignty in any state. Paralleling Max Weber's comment that sovereignty is the monopolization of the means of violence, this philosophical approach contends that all human groups create society and state power by coalescing around a ritualized, controlled use of violence. The sovereign exists in an "exceptional" space, permitted to kill for the greater good of the community, whether by leading armies against foreign enemies or domestically by executing traitors and criminals. Scholars develop this argument from different angles: Girard drew on literature and social anthropology to develop a theory of mimetic violence and scapegoating as the essence of sovereignty; Walter Burkert drew on the study of ancient religions; Giorgio Agamben traced such ideas to classical Greek political philosophy.[6] These theories suggest that all governance involves violence, no society escapes it, no state does without it. The challenge for rulers was how to control and use violence – how to deploy it symbolically, how to legitimize it, how to avoid destabilizing excess and how to balance it with less coercive strategies of power.

These approaches to early modern state-building provide the theoretical context for this study of the practice of the criminal law in Russia. Even more than its European and Ottoman counterparts, early modern Russia exhibited a striking tension between claims of centralization and

[5] Foucault, *Discipline and Punish*; Evans, *Rituals*; Spierenburg, *Spectacle*; van Dülmen, *Theatre of Horror*; Briggs et al., *Crime and Punishment*; Schrader, *Languages*, 18, 188–9; Rousseaux, "Crime, Justice and Society"; Muchembled and Birrell, *History of Violence*. Elias wrote in the 1930s but was not popularly known until the 1960s.

[6] Weber, "Politics as a Vocation," 78; Girard, *Violence and the Sacred*, ch. 1; Burkert, *Homo Necans*; Agamben, *Homo Sacer*. Reflections in this vein regarding Russia: Geyer, "Some Hesitant Observations."

the challenges of governance. Russia from 1500 to 1800 was certainly building the "sinews of power": it was pursuing military reform to expand empire from Eastern Europe to the Pacific and building the bureaucratic apparatus and social institutions (such as serfdom) to administer and pay for that expansion. It was broadcasting its legitimacy through an ideological discourse of autocracy, disseminated in league with the Orthodox Church through imagery, architecture, ritual, proclamations and the formulas of official documents.

But, as in other early modern empires, Moscow's claims to central power were "more myth than reality." Moscow as imperial center deployed what Jane Burbank and Frederick Cooper have called a Eurasian approach to empire, a "politics of difference,"[7] one that allowed broad swaths of social and political life to be managed by local communities, except for key powers claimed by rulers. In Russia, those were criminal justice, resource mobilization (human and material), and military recruitment and control, and even in the criminal law, the center's power to enforce the law as written was informally limited by the local situation. As in Europe, governance united formalized law and institutions with flexible practice and popular concepts of justice. On the ground, European "rationalizing" states look less rational and Muscovy's proclaimed "autocracy" looks less autocratic.

Clearly this approach is intended to counter a historiography that draws sharp distinctions between Europe's "rule of law" and rationality and Russia's "despotism" and brutality.[8] Such a normative approach goes back to sixteenth- through eighteenth-century European visitors to Russia who arrived attuned to markers of European change. Members of Europe's elite, they embodied new standards in education, civility and political engagement; many had deeply felt religious convictions, honed in confessional struggles. Their classical educations gave them categories of freedom and despotism with which to process Russian reality. Comparing Muscovy (a term emanating from foreigners' accounts now used to refer to Russia before 1700) to the phenomena they were experiencing at home – waxing state power, enfranchised elites and emerging middle classes, rising literacy and civility, confessionalization – they declared Russia less civilized, less religiously sophisticated, more despotic

[7] Burbank and Cooper, *Empires*, ch. 1.

[8] See this clash of categories in Richard Pipes' Weberian focus on Russia's lack of "rule by law" versus George Weickhardt's lawyerly view of Russia's legal complexity: Pipes, *Russia under the Old Regime*, xxi–xxii; Weickhardt, "Due Process and Equal Justice"; their polemic on property: Weickhardt, "Pre-Petrine Law of Property"; Pipes, "Was There Private Property?"; Weickhardt, "Response."

and more violent than a proper European state. These travelers were not necessarily wrong about what they described: Muscovy was indeed less socially and economically developed, less culturally diverse and certainly less politically pluralistic than the leading states of contemporary Europe. But these travelers established tropes that reified Russia's differences as they exaggerated what came to be seen as "modern" elements of their own societies.[9]

By the nineteenth century, when Europe had developed greater political pluralism, bureaucratic transparency and even some civil rights, Russian historians themselves advanced this binary opposition in a "statist" paradigm that focused on Muscovite tsars' claims to unlimited power unbalanced by any social or institutional legal rights. Regarding the law, they applied what would become Weberian "ideal types," condemning Russia's legal system as lacking predictability and rationality, riddled with corruption and inefficiency.[10] While twentieth-century Soviet historians rejected these polarities and rewrote Russian history around class struggle, their approach also affirmed "centralization" and "absolutism" and in spite of themselves perpetuated an image of Russia as unique and different from the West.[11]

More recent historiography in Europe, America and Russia on early modern Russian law and governance has both echoed and contested old tropes: Horace Dewey and Ann Kleimola undermined a monolithic, despotic model with studies of Muscovite law in the late fifteenth and sixteenth centuries; George Weickhardt argued that Muscovite law de facto provided "due process." V. A. Rogov presented Muscovy's legal system as rational and not despotic. Others offered less positive interpretations: Evgenii Anisimov pronounced the Russian legal system endemically ridden with brutality and a culture of denunciation; Georg Michels and Chester Dunning have argued that state and society were brutal and violent; Richard Hellie alternately asserted that Muscovite law was orderly and enforced in practice and that its society was more brutal and violent than what he considered the European standard.[12] But a binary opposition

[9] Poe, *'A People Born to Slavery'*; Wolff, *Inventing Eastern Europe.* Debate on these tropes: Poe, "Truth about Muscovy"; Kivelson, "On Words, Sources."

[10] Bogoslovskii, "Zemskoe samoupravlenie"; Chicherin, *Oblastnye uchrezhdeniia*; Got'e, *Istoriia oblastnogo upravleniia*; Sergeevich, *Lektsii i issledovaniia.*

[11] They did, meanwhile, produce excellent source publications and studies of legal codes. A few examples: PRP; RZ; ZA; Man'kov, *Ulozhenie* and *Zakonodatel'stvo;* Nersesiants (ed.), *Razvitie*; Skripilev (ed.), *Razvitie.*

[12] Rogov, *Istoriia.* Representative of Dewey's work are "1550 *Sudebnik*" and "Muscovite *Guba* Charters"; Kleimola, *Justice in Medieval Russia.* Weickhardt, "Due Process." Anisimov, *Dyba i*

of rational/despotic whether applied to law or society is being complicated by micro-historical works. Studies on law and administration across the empire – in the north, on the southern steppe frontier and in Siberia – and on such social groups as townsmen, gentry and bureaucrats demonstrate the pluralism of early modern governance described above. Among them, major monographs on the practice of the criminal law in the eighteenth century (by Christoph Schmidt) and on litigations about lese-majesty (by Angela Rustemeyer) are particularly valuable complements to this book.[13]

Following this lead, this book takes as "bottom-up" an approach as possible. Echoing early modern European and Ottoman practice, it shows how the formal procedures and strictures of law were shaped by such factors as community and individual interests, extra-legal procedures such as settlement and flexible interpretations of the law in judicial pardon. It argues that Russia's practice of the criminal law should be seen as an integration of "public" and "private," and that, indeed, these oppositions are irrelevant. Russia in these centuries was not moving from a personalized judicial system to a more rational one; the formalized legislative and institutional reforms that are tracked here into the eighteenth century did not undermine the system's flexibility in process and adjudication.

While laws asserted the primacy of the tsar's justice, adjudication and judicial practice responded to local concepts of justice that were oriented towards preserving the integrity and stability of communities. For their part, communities respected the tsar's legitimacy, acquiesced in the authority of courts and officials, adhered to the moral authority of their oaths to the tsar and accepted the judiciary's monopoly on prosecuting serious crime. They did so with the expectation that courts and officials would provide them with security and protection from crime, would punish evil and would not be excessively corrupt, arbitrary or brutal. When the balance tilted towards too much corruption or too little responsiveness, people complained, petitioned, even revolted. Thus, judges had and used significant leeway in sentencing, balancing their

knut; Michels, "Violent Old Belief" and "Ruling without Mercy"; Dunning, "Terror." Compare Hellie, "*Ulozhenie*: Preamble," 185 with "Late Medieval and Early Modern Russian Civilization."

13 North: Shveikovskaia, *Gosudarstvo i krestiane*. Steppe frontier: Glaz′ev, *Vlast′ i obshchestvennost′*; Davies, *State Power*. Siberia: Anan′ev, "Voevodskoe upravlenie"; Redin, *Administrativnye struktury*; Vershinin, *Voevodskoe upravlenie*. Townsmen: Bulgakov, *Gosudarstvennye sluzhby*. Gentry: Kivelson, *Cartographies*; Lapteva, *Provintsial′noe dvorianstvo*. Bureaucrats: Rybalko, *Rossiiskaia prikaznaia biurokratiia;* Pisar′kova, *Gosudarstvennoe upravlenie*. Schmidt, *Sozialkontrolle;* Rustemeyer, *Dissens und Ehre*.

obligations to the law with their personal judgment. Communities cooperated with courts and manipulated them. That sentences varied from the written law was not, in other words, evidence of an arbitrary or "illegal" judicial culture, but indication that a balanced judicial culture was functioning well. Such local governance practices were typical in early modern governance across the board.

These conclusions emerge through study of several themes. One is Muscovy's efforts to construct and maintain a centralized bureaucratic and judicial apparatus with limited finances, manpower and judicial expertise. A related concern is how the center depended upon local communities: how judicial institutions were staffed, how communities cooperated with, manipulated and resisted the tsar's judicial power. A third is the development of judicial expertise: lacking law schools and universities, lacking a legal profession, Muscovy had to inculcate judicial expertise somehow. This work explores where that knowledge resided. A fourth theme is the use of violence – in judicial torture, in executions and punishments. Here Muscovy's practice of state-sanctioned violence is compared to the paradigm of "spectacles of suffering." The symbolic use of violence is explored, particularly the violence at the heart of sovereignty revealed by the profound interactions of tsar and people in moments of state crisis. This study extends to the reign of the reforming Tsar Peter I "the Great" (ruled 1682–1725) in order to problematize claims of a radical break in Russian history by this admittedly radical ruler.

SOURCES OF POSITIVE LAW AND LEGAL PRACTICE

For the non-specialist reader, a brief chronological sketch. This book begins in the late fifteenth century with the reign of Ivan III (ruled 1462–1505), who accomplished significant territorial expansion, founded the bureaucracy (military, land and foreign affairs chanceries, treasury), expanded the gentry-based army and issued a short law code in 1497. Thereafter, under his son Vasilii III (1505–33), grandson Ivan IV ("the Terrible," 1533–84) and great-grandson Fedor Ivanovich (1584–98), these processes of state-building and imperial expansion progressed, marked by high points in the conquests of the Volga trading emporia, Kazan (1552) and Astrakhan (1556). Two eras of political turmoil – Ivan IV's Oprichnina (1564–72) and the "Time of Troubles" (1598–1613) (discussed in Chapter 14) – interrupted but did not divert these trends. The new Romanov dynasty (Mikhail Fedorovich, ruled 1613–45; Aleksei Mikhailovich 1645–76; Fedor Alekseevich, 1676–82) accomplished immense expansion to Siberia and some movement into the Black Sea steppe and modern-day Ukraine and Belarus. Peter I (ruled 1682–1725) accelerated all these state-building processes with aggressive military reform, territorial expansion and administrative-judicial changes.[14]

The criminal law system grew in response not only to rulers' ideological claims to power over the whole realm, but also to the social instability caused by their actions. As Moscow raised old taxes and invented new ones, people suffered, culminating in Russia's most important non-cash fiscal strategy of state-building, enserfment (gradually fixing to their social status tax-paying urban and rural populations from the sixteenth century to 1649). Geographical (let alone social) mobility was frozen for the majority of the population, in legal theory; in practice, thousands fled into Siberian forests or to the steppe where paradoxically local governors, desperate for manpower to defend the borders, often recruited into service. Declaring flight a crime, Muscovy's rulers multiplied the burden on criminal courts. Crippling tax rates also spurred crime; from the mid sixteenth century robbery and brigandage were endemic on the few major highways of Muscovy's huge empire.[15] Theft and robbery were banes of town and village life, even though Muscovy had far less wealth, consumer goods and social inequality than had Europe to attract property crime. Spontaneous violence, in Muscovy as in Europe, was also common: strangers in a tavern get into a brawl; knives, ubiquitous in a peasant society, quickly appear; dead bodies fall on the barroom floor. Occasionally social unrest erupted into peasant or urban rebellion. All this created demand for an effective criminal law apparatus.

That apparatus was documented by the state in codes, decrees and cases, and this study builds up from those sources. It should be noted, however, that looking for state–society interaction in early modern Russian legal practice is difficult, since virtually all indigenous sources were produced by government offices. Even direct address by litigants in petitions to the court or in testimony was filtered through formulaic prose, scribal expertise and litigants' need to speak to the law's standards. Nevertheless, court records open up a rich canvas of governance in action.

[14] Until this point, scholars often call early modern Russia "Muscovy," but "Russia" is also accurate; starting with Peter, who declared himself "Emperor of *Rossiia*," "Muscovy" is not used.

[15] Keep, "Bandits and the Law"; Got'e, *Istoriia oblastnogo upravleniia*, 1: 334–45; Michels, *At War*, 130; Eeckaute, "Les brigands en Russie"; Dewey, "Muscovite *Guba* Charters."

Positive law starts with codes that asserted the state's authority and regulated officialdom. A fifteenth-century Writ on Homicide, two regional administrative charters and the 1497 Law Code (*sudebnik*) demonstrate a transition from the "dyadic" law of earlier centuries (embodied in the Rus′ Law [*Russkaia pravda*]) to a triadic model wherein law not only provided compensation to victims of injury but also recognized the state's interest. The 1497 code was primarily a handbook for judges, defining fees for services, describing procedure, establishing capital punishment for highest crime (theft of church property, treason, arson, kidnapping and recidivist theft) and corporal punishment for lesser crime, as well as compensatory fines for injury.[16] In 1550 a slightly longer law code developed the law in sanctions, procedures and punishment for official corruption. Charters from the 1530s for brigandage felony boards (*guba* institutions) heightened corporal and capital punishment and the use of torture.[17] A regionally specific 1589 Law Code supplemented the 1550 code with some harsher sanctions, decrees of the second half of the sixteenth century intensified social control, and a 1606 code that softened norms on encroaching enserfment was not adopted into use.[18]

As bureaucracy grew with empire into the seventeenth century, the Felony Chancery encoded the criminal law in handbooks, much of which content was integrated into the 1649 Ulozhenie. This massive compendium developed judicial procedure, introduced Russia's first formal treatment of state crime and greatly expanded the use of corporal and capital punishment.[19] The 1669 Criminal Articles intensified some sanctions and shifted administrative authority among rival officials and chanceries, but their influence was never as great as that of the Ulozhenie in procedure and sentencing because the latter was printed and widely disseminated, while the 1669 Articles were not. Tellingly, a 1714 decree required that the Ulozhenie be preferred to all intervening legislation until a new code was completed (it never was). While the Military Articles of 1715 were not

[16] Writ: RZ II: 187–9. 1397–8 Dvina Charter: RZ II: 181–2. 1488 Beloozero: RZ II: 192–5. 1423 immunity charter: PRP III: 98–9. Dyadic and triadic: Kaiser, *Growth*, ch. 1. Early Muscovite criminal decree: Alekseev, "'Zapis′ chto tianet.'"

[17] 1550 Law Code: RZ II: 97–120. 1539 Beloozero Charter: RZ II: 213–15. 1555 Medyn Charter, RZ II: 218–23. 1555–6 Felony Handbook: PRP IV: 356–70. Regional brigandage charters: Iakovlev (ed.), *Namestnichie*; RZ II: 227–34.

[18] 1589 Law Code: PRP IV: 413–43. Late sixteenth-century decrees: ZA. 1606 Law Code: PRP IV: 482–542; Weickhardt, "Composite Law Code."

[19] Felony Handbook 1616–36: PRP V: 188–220; Felony Handbook 1635–48: PRP V: 221–39. Ulozhenie: RZ III: 83–257. English translation of Ulozhenie: Hellie (trans. and ed.), *Muscovite Law Code*. 1669 Criminal Articles: PRP VII: 396–434.

used in civil law, myriad other Petrine decrees provide the remainder of the positive law used in this work.[20]

Legal practice is illuminated by case law, which survives beginning in the seventeenth century. Cases were gathered from about fifty archival collections, initially with a focus on two regions, Beloozero and Arzamas. North of Moscow, Beloozero was historically closely integrated into Muscovite governance, although bordering the more autonomous Far North (Primor′e, Northern Dvina basin). Arzamas was an administrative town in the Middle Volga, integrated into Muscovite control in the first half of the sixteenth century. Both areas' archives (located in Russian State Archive for Ancient Documents, RGADA) are rich, starting in the early seventeenth century for Beloozero and in the late century for the Arzamas area; they extend into copious eighteenth-century holdings. Because records are voluminous, research focused on homicide cases, where process, punishment and state power are most sharply defined. Many cases of felony and misdemeanor assault and theft, from the earliest records into the 1720s, were also surveyed.

For Beloozero and its region, ten collections from Beloozero, Ustiuzhna Zheleznopol′skaia, Kargopol′ and the St. Cyril Beloozero Monastery were surveyed, identifying 128 litigations primarily from the Beloozero and Ustiuzhna Zheleznopol′skaia region. They included fifty-three homicide and seventy-seven other serious cases. The chronological distribution was about forty cases in the first half of the seventeenth century, about seventy-five in the second half and about fifteen in the first half of the eighteenth. Of these 128 cases, only 23 are complete, that is, including a verdict, sentence and punishment (13 homicide, 10 others). For the Arzamas region, surveyed archival collections included thirty-seven collections from Arzamas, Temnikov, Kadom, Shatsk, Nizhnii Novgorod, Alatyr′ and a few other towns. All told, 100 litigations (57 homicide, 43 lesser cases) were identified, of which only 8 homicides and only 4 other cases were complete with verdict. Chronologically, Arzamas-area cases clustered in the early eighteenth century: only about seventeen before 1700, and most from about 1718 to the 1730s.[21]

[20] 1649 more influential: Man′kov, *Zakonodatel′stvo*, 203. Governors in Belgorod reported that the 1669 Articles did not reach their frontier town until 1675: Glaz′ev, *Vlast′ i obshchestvennost′*, 139. PSZ v: no. 2828 (1714); Romashkin, *Osnovnye nachala*, 14. Military Articles not used in civil courts: RZ IV: 317–18; Romashkin, *Osnovnye nachala*, 26–31; Serov, *Sudebnaia reforma*, 386, n. 2. Many Petrine laws are included in PSZ III–VII and ZA Petra. Ulozhenie finally replaced with PSZ (1830) and subsequent legal codifications.

[21] A complete list of surveyed archival collections: Bibliography.

To counterbalance the dearth of completed cases in Beloozero and Arzamas archives, research expanded beyond these regions. Many resolved cases were found in RGADA's vast Military Service Chancery collection (f. 210) and in two collections related to the Far North (f. 141, *Prikaznye dela starykh let* and f. 159, *Prikaznye dela novoi rozborki*). Fond 210 has an excellent printed catalog (ODB XI, XII, XV–XX). Cataloging is less accessible for the other two collections; only a few volumes of a printed catalog for f. 141 have appeared, covering into the 1620s.[22] But fonds 141 and 159 are amply described in in-house catalogs. All in all, 152 cases in these three collections (72 homicide, 80 lesser crimes) were read, with a chronological range spread evenly over the seventeenth century, clustering in its second half (these collections do not extend much into the eighteenth century). Of the 152 cases surveyed, 97 (30 homicide cases and 67 lesser crimes) were complete with verdict.

Published sources – excerpts of cases, decrees, official correspondence – supplemented archival documents, including all the usual suspects: AI, DAI, AAE, AIu, AIuB, AMG, PSZ, ZA and other collections. Flagged were items concerning judicial punishment, court procedure and staffing, brigandage officials and the involvement of church institutions with secular courts. Many narrative accounts have been used, particularly in Part II, and attention is given to the challenges of working critically with chronicles, memoirs and particularly foreign travel accounts. Normative judgment certainly shaped foreigners' accounts, but many were astute observers, often delegated by their governments to convey factual information. If used critically, recognizing their biases and identifying their access to Russian society, commentary by foreigners can provide valuable eyewitness testimony.[23]

The result is a rich source base of laws and mostly incomplete litigations from the early seventeenth century through about the 1720s, with the heaviest chronological representation from 1650 to 1690. Beloozero and Arzamas evidence is filled out by judicial records from the Muscovite heartland, the southern frontier and Siberia. The entire empire is not covered, nor is every up and down of legislative change demonstrated in the cases. But these archival and printed primary sources amply demonstrate how the state defined crime, established and executed procedure and levied sanctions; how individuals and communities interacted

[22] ODB; Voskoboinikova (ed.), *Opisanie*.

[23] Envoys' attempts to be accurate: Poe, *'A People Born to Slavery'*, ch. 2.

with courts and used them to their own benefit; how state and society each in their own ways mobilized violence.

The book is divided into two parts. Eight chapters survey "Judicial Culture" (Part I). Chapter 1 examines the structure of Russian governance in comparison to European and Ottoman practice, showing how the pursuit of centralization was common to all. To suggest the challenges in centralizing criminal adjudication in Russia, it examines venues of criminal law in the sixteenth and seventeenth centuries – brigandage boards, local governors and even (improperly) church and landlords' courts. Chapter 2 demonstrates that courts were staffed by recruiting locals, pausing on the case of executioners. It addresses the problem of where legal expertise resided, given that Russia had no notaries, lawyers or professional legal scholars. Chapter 3 pursues the consequences of recruiting staff locally by exploring how communities interacted with the court in the initial stages of arrest and in detention. Chapter 4 explores the perennial problem of policing official corruption. The second half of Part I analyzes trial procedure. Chapter 5 shows that Russia used, as did early modern Europe, inquisitory trial process and similar forms of evidence such as interrogation and community surveys; like its European counterparts, it also used judicial torture, the topic of Chapter 6. Chapter 7 considers adjudication, examining judges' autonomy in sentencing and individuals' and communities' ability to shape trial process and outcomes, including various forms of appeal by litigants and judges. Here too Russia's practices of local adjudication resemble European courts' willingness to shape verdicts to local circumstances. Chapter 8 concludes by examining early eighteenth-century reforms of judicial institutions and chancery practices in the context of Peter I's introduction of the European model of the "well-ordered police state."

Part II explores "Punishment," beginning with two chronological chapters on corporal punishment from the late fifteenth through the seventeenth century (Chapters 9 and 10), showing that courts gave some deference to elites. Some forms of punishment, such as shaming "marketplace" beatings, were common to European practice. Chapter 11 takes a thematic approach, exploring bodily mutilation and branding in the context of the growth of the exile system. In early modern conditions of communication, marking the body was one of the few available forms of establishing the identity of exiles whom the state wanted to control. Supplementing these three chapters, the Appendix tracks the evolution of laws on capital punishment and exile, showing in particular the expansion of the number of felonies allowed before the death penalty was invoked. Chapter 12 concludes the discussion of corporal punishment by analyzing early eighteenth-century norms on punishment and by showcasing the excellent work of a group of Arzamas judges from 1718 into the 1720s.

The concluding chapters of Part II explore capital punishment under two rubrics – executions for felony crime and those for political or state crime, which might be called more generally "highest" crime, since this category also included the religious crimes of witchcraft and heresy. These chapters focus on the symbolic language of rituals of capital punishment and assess the conditions and constraints on the use of the death penalty. Chapter 13 assembles what little can be known about Muscovite rituals of execution for felony crime; most of this evidence is from local court cases. Turning to highest crime, the European paradigm of "spectacle of suffering" provides a provocative comparative model. To assess whether Russia used capital punishment in so theatrical a way, to cases are added a mixed palette of narrative sources including chronicles, travel accounts and memoirs. Chapter 14 explores the prosecution of treason and religious crime in the "long" sixteenth century, exploring whether Ivan IV's violent Oprichnina (1564–72) and the chaotic Time of Troubles (1598–1613) changed judicial practice. Chapter 15 examines the first systematic definition of highest crime, included in the 1649 Ulozhenie and examines seventeenth-century prosecution of such cases. The next two chapters flip the perspective and analyze the "moral economy" of popular violence. Chapter 16 assesses the interaction of judicial policy, ideology and popular beliefs about justice by exploring patterns of rebellion and state punishment of urban and peasant rioters (1648, 1662, 1682) and of cossack and peasant rebels in the Stepan Razin revolt (1670–1). Chapter 17 explores the symbolism of crowd violence in some of these uprisings, exploring the relationship of sovereignty and violence and uncovering the excruciating obligations thereby imposed on the sovereign. Here the specifics of Russia's legitimizing ideology – the vision of the tsar as a pious and just ruler who personally rectifies injustice – perhaps contrasts to contemporary European more secular ideologies of monarchy and absolutism. Chapter 18 returns to the "spectacle of suffering" paradigm, exploring how Peter I rejected traditional Muscovite ideologies of legitimacy and asserted his sovereign right to wield exemplary violence to punish highest crime. The Conclusion opens a broader discussion of judicial violence in criminal law, contrasting Russia's later development of capital punishment to that of its European peers.

PART I

Judicial culture

CHAPTER 1

Foundations of the criminal law

In 1666 Grigorii Kotoshikhin, a high-ranking Kremlin bureaucrat in the Foreign Affairs Chancery, defected to Sweden and wrote a treatise on Muscovite government to ingratiate himself with the Swedish king. On Russia's judicial system, he remarked that "nowhere is trial and justice given for any person in any case except in the tsar's chanceries . . . and in the towns, in the villages and districts of the tsar's estates, and in the chanceries of the patriarch, metropolitans, archbishops and bishops." To our modern eyes, this description might seem hopelessly medieval – so many courts, such fragmentation of authority. Yet to Kotoshikhin and readers in his day,[1] this statement might seem remarkable for its brevity: Kotoshikhin was underscoring the tsar's control over the judiciary when most states of Muscovy's size and ilk struggled with more fragmented judicial institutions.

Kotoshikhin informs us that adjudication took place in only two jurisdictions: the tsar's courts in chanceries, towns and his own estates, and in courts of the church. Furthermore, Kotoshikhin goes on to note that "the religious authorities do not inflict corporal or capital punishment without the tsar's knowledge on anyone for anything." Rather, they transferred those so sentenced to the tsar's courts.[2] Muscovy's judicial centralization was paralleled by centralization of other major government functions – revenue collection, military recruitment and mobilization, administration. This chapter addresses the issue of Muscovy's centralization in comparative context, before turning to definitions and venues of the criminal law.

[1] Kotoshikhin, *O Rossii*, ch. 7, art. 45, p. 122. The "towns" Kotoshikhin refers to were administrative-military centers that did not have urban autonomies: Hittle, *Service City*. The text circulated in Swedish translation in the seventeenth century: Kotoshikhin, "'On Russia'", 5.

[2] Kotoshikhin, *O Rossii*, 122.

CHIMERAS OF CENTRALIZATION

Muscovy was a centralized, bureaucratic empire, to be sure. Historians have derided its centralization as oppressive and "hypertrophic," ridiculing the efforts of Kremlin-based bureaucrats to control the most mundane decision-making by provincial governors, such as purchasing office supplies.[3] The implication is that Muscovy was either backward or despotic to exert such central control. But the picture is more complicated and more interesting than that.

Russian government from the Muscovite period into the modern era did indeed exert as strong centralized control as it could over society and officialdom. It did so to capture all possible resources in a setting where resources were scarce. But the state's reach exceeded its grasp and in the end Russian rulers fell short of homogeneous control. In all of this, reach and grasp, they resembled their peers. Across Europe and in the Ottoman Empire from the sixteenth through eighteenth centuries, rulers were trying to concentrate authority and falling short. Even as European monarchs strove to unify fiscal systems, create national bureaucracies, strengthen the ruler's courts and codify the law,[4] they made concessions to local interests – social estates, municipalities, religious and ethnic minorities. Pluralistic approaches to governance were all the more called for in multi-ethnic, multi-religious empires. Thus, early modern rulers faced a tension between centralizing power and devolving it. In this context, Russia's centralization can be seen in a continuum of normal early modern state-building. A brief survey of goals of centralization and practice, particularly in the legal realm, among Muscovy's peers might help to blur the binary oppositions often alleged between Europe and Russia.

Muscovy's European peers who were most successful in building a unified monarchical state, such as England and France, faced challenges in the form of privileged social groups – enfranchised estates, privileged municipalities, religious, linguistic or ethnic communities – and great judicial diversity. For the majority Christian population, canon law and *ius commune* created a common legal foundation, alongside which regional codes and customs (*ius proprium*) shaped local practice.[5] In France,

[3] Hypertrophic: Hellie, "Structure," 22 and "The Law." Starr calls such practices in Imperial Russia "inadequate bureaucratization": *Decentralization*, 27–9. Muscovite administration: Poe, "Central Government"; Davies, "Local Government."

[4] European judicial reforms: Schneider, "Courts"; Shaffern, *Law and Justice*, 191–200; Lenman and Parker, "State, Community."

[5] Bellomo, *Common Legal Past*, esp. ch. 4 on *ius proprium*.

powerful discourses of absolutism and dissemination of court culture established the foundation of the king's centralized power, as in Muscovy. But France's vaunted absolutism was accomplished by skillful accommodation with provincial nobilities, guilds, municipalities and other intermediary bodies, and by recognition of regional languages, over 300 provincial and local customary law codes and age-old seigneurial privileges. The French king codified the criminal law in the Villers-Cotterets Statute of 1539 and nominally presided over a network of sovereign courts – thirteen in the late eighteenth century – which were in practice controlled by a professional, hereditary officialdom whose purchased positions were beyond the king's direct control. Below them stretched at least two levels of regional and local courts, staffed with local nobles and functionaries. By the seventeenth century French judicial professionals, the *noblesse de robe*, had risen to a position of power and status equal to that of the ancient nobility of military origin; they became a leading force for political pluralism and legal transparency by the eighteenth century. Stuart Carroll calls early modern France "a composite polity, a state which imperfectly melded together regions with distinctive and varying identities."[6] France's judicial diversity empowered society and presented French kings with much greater political challenges by communities and elites than Muscovy ever faced.

In England, judicial centralization was also balanced with local institutions. Criminal law was firmly in the hands of the king's justice, with superior courts in London (the King's Bench for serious crime and the Star Chamber for "riot") and twice-annual assizes by the king's judges and lawyers in the countryside in six circuits. The Marian Statues of 1554–5 codified criminal judicial procedure, introducing written dossiers but not the inquisitory mode. Local participation was intensive: criminal law investigation and local policing were done by elected justices of the peace, constables and coroners, involving thousands in counties across the realm; juries and grand juries engaged landed gentry and local values in adjudication. Lawyers provided counsel.[7] England's model of interaction between society and state in legal practice, although based on very

[6] Carroll, *Blood and Violence*, 331. French kings' accommodations with society: Beik, *Absolutism and Society*, chs. 4 and 7; Henshall, *Myth of Absolutism.* Franklin L. Ford's classic on *noblesse de robe*: *Robe and Sword.* Composite state: Nexon, "State and Bureaucracy," 511 (citing H. G. Koenigsberger); Tilly, *Coercion*, 20–31.

[7] Briggs et al., *Crime and Punishment*, 25–31, quote on 3. Schneider, "Courts," 449–50. Marian Statutes: Weisser, *Crime and Punishment*, 96–8; Langbein, *Prosecuting*, chs. 1–5. English system compared to Muscovy: Kivelson, "Muscovite 'Citizenship'."

different assumptions of legal "rights," was in structural ways similar to Muscovy's local judicial practice.

Sprawling, multi-ethnic territories, such as the Commonwealth of Polande–Lithuania and the Habsburg and Ottoman empires, resembled Muscovy even more: all three realms faced problems of controlling a large, contiguous realm with great diversity of ethnicity, religion, language, culture and historical traditions. Pushed by a strong nobility, the Polish-Lithuanian state developed a federative model over the fifteenth and sixteenth centuries. The Union of Lublin creating the Commonwealth in 1569 allowed Crown Poland and the Grand Duchy of Lithuania separate systems of local government, landholding, military organization and law. Polish law governed Crown Poland; the Lithuanian Statute, the Grand Duchy. Within the Commonwealth "politics of difference" abounded: ethnic and religious groups (Armenians, Tatars, Jews) enjoyed judicial autonomies; towns used Magdeburg law, including criminal law jurisdiction. Although in principle the king's courts adjudicated criminal cases for non-urban populations, the nobility enjoyed so much privilege and local control that they and their lands were virtually immune from state punishment.[8]

Habsburg Emperors faced similar challenges in asserting centralized authority over their growing Central European realm from the sixteenth century on, inasmuch as they ruled over two sovereign monarchies (Habsburg Emperors were simultaneously kings of Bohemia and Hungary) and other states claiming political autonomies (Croatia, Transylvania, German principalities). One scholar, abjuring the label "empire," calls the Habsburg realm a "relatively confederal dynastic agglomeration," but the strategies of governance were essentially the same. All the Habsburgs' constituent lands featured strong nobilities, towns and urban classes that enjoyed their own law codes and institutions of self-governance (noble assemblies, urban town councils using Magdeburg law). Towns and even noble latifundia enjoyed immunities from the emperor's justice, extending sometimes even to capital punishment (the *Blutbann*). Habsburg Emperors Maximilian I and Ferdinand I asserted claims to centralized power beginning in the late fifteenth and sixteenth centuries by creating three central privy chanceries, housed in Vienna, for administration, finance

[8] Diversity of jurisdictions: Bardach et al., *Historia państwa*, 123–8, 244–8. Town jurisdictions: Kamler, "Penalties"; Maisel, "Torture"; Uruszczak, "Torture in Practice." Norman Davies colorfully characterizes Polish nobility's legal untouchability: *God's Playground*, 1: 348–55, based on Łoziński's classic *Prawem i lewem.*

and military affairs. To standardize the criminal law for the Holy Roman Empire, Charles V issued the *Carolina* in 1532. But, as Ulinka Rublack remarks: "The Imperial law code of 1532 served only as a guideline in regard to basic questions of evidence, procedure, and punishment; every territory composed and updated its own law codes." Not only the plethora of regional privileges stymied Habsburg efforts to centralize; so also did historical circumstances. To the end of the seventeenth century, religious war, Turkish invasion and noble or proto-national resistance to central control foiled their attempts, particularly in Hungary and Transylvania.[9]

The Habsburgs settled into a governing strategy that tolerated such local differences. Paula Sutter Fichter observed that as long as income kept coming in and military defense was secured, early modern Habsburgs were satisfied: "neither Ferdinand II nor his seventeenth-century successors had command control over legal or fiscal affairs in any part of the monarchy. Nor did they apparently want it." The law provided only a minimal unifying network over the realm; more effective were the culture and ritual practices of Baroque Counter-Reformation Catholicism.[10]

The Ottoman Empire also relied upon such "imperial imaginaries," that is, ritual, ideological and symbolic discourse to assert overarching power. Ottoman sultans used the rhetoric of Islam, the visual power of imperial architecture and the seductive sophistication of court culture to broadcast imperial claims across the realm. The sultan's legal system joined in this discourse, grounding the sultan's legitimacy in much the same terms as in Muscovy: the ruler provided justice, protected his people from harm and patronized the church. Ottoman sultans physically constructed empire-wide unity by creating a network of Islamic courts with oversight over both religious and secular issues; they codified sultanic law around Islamic law; they created a juridical and scribal bureaucracy whose professionalism reached a peak in the sixteenth century.[11]

9 Confederal dynastic: Nexon, "State and Bureaucracy," 518. *Blutbann*: Kann, *History of Habsburg Empire*, 131–2. Rublack, *Crimes of Women*, 52. Other towns in the Holy Roman Empire: Boes, "Public Appearance," 260; Coy, *Strangers and Misfits*, 24–30. Brian Levack notes "local and regional courts were allowed to operate without much interference from central or national judicial control": *Witch-Hunt*, 69. Michael Weisser shows that Habsburg courts in early modern Spain used both the *Carolina* and a harsh 1567 Spanish criminal code, but local codes and local practice moderated their application: "Crime and Punishment," 77–8.

10 Fichtner, *Habsburg Monarchy*, 38; also Evans, *Making of Habsburg Monarchy*.

11 Imperial imaginaries: Burbank and Cooper, *Empires*, 15–16. Ottoman courts: Imber, *Ottoman Empire*, ch. 6.

At the same time, Ottoman legal centralization derived strength from accommodation with regional diversity. Daniel Goffman notes: "The state chose not to impose a uniform and rigid legal system upon its territories. Instead, by compiling a series of provincial law books (*kanunname*) that incorporated many local customs and statutes, in the fifteenth century the government constructed a flexible system of jurisprudence at the local level." Meanwhile, other groups enjoyed their own courts and laws – Orthodox Greeks, Armenians, Jews and resident foreign merchants. Administrative practice integrated local elites by selling local offices, a policy that by the eighteenth century undermined central authority with the rise of regional notables. Nevertheless, Ottoman imperial strategy created great stability: "The secret to Ottoman longevity and the empire's ability to rule over a vast and mixed collection of territories was not its legendary military, its loyal bureaucracy, its series of competent rulers, or a particular system of land tenure. Rather, it was simply its flexibility in dealing with this diverse society."[12]

Like Habsburg emperors, Ottoman sultans and Polish kings, Muscovy's tsars faced an empire of great ethnic and religious diversity as it grew from 1500 to 1800.[13] But the challenges it faced were different. In contrast to the elites, institutions and historical customs created by the powerful historical conjunction of Roman heritage, Germanic tribes and the Catholic Church in Europe, and in contrast to the highly articulated societies of the Mediterranean and Middle East presided over by the Ottomans, Muscovy extended its authority over East Slavic principalities and steppe peoples who were less politically organized. Skillfully manipulating subjects' cultural practices, Muscovy integrated new areas by co-opting elites, forging reciprocal relations and tolerating local custom. They put down colonial uprisings coercively, to be sure, but they minimized resistance with a laissez-faire colonial policy and minimal definitions of the state's central aims. Despite the necessity of such flexibility, the state insisted on local performance of its few basic goals: resource extraction in a realm of scarcity, military control and the criminal law.[14]

[12] Goffman, *Ottoman Empire*, 75–7, 91–2. Judicial diversity: Imber, *Ottoman Empire*, 204–5. Ideology, law, institutions: Inalcik, *Ottoman Empire*, chs. 9–10, 12–13. Administration and courts: Khoury, *State and Provincial Society*; Imber, *Ottoman Empire*, chs. 5–6; Jennings, "Kadi, Court"; Barkey, *Empire of Difference*.

[13] Muscovy's state-building project: Hellie, "Russia"; Hartley, "Russia as Fiscal-Military State"; Dunning and Smith, "Moving beyond Absolutism"; Kollmann, "Russia" and "Muscovite Russia, 1450–1598."

[14] Sixteenth-century expansion and administrative centralization: Zimin, *Rossiia na rubezhe*, *Rossiia na poroge* and *Reformy Ivana Groznogo*. Imperial strategies: Khodarkovsky, *Russia's Steppe Frontier*;

In the law the early modern Russian state was able to impose uniform codes and practice more effectively than its peers because, as it expanded, it moved into territories with minimal formal judicial traditions. Among East Slavs, Moscow encountered a few monasteries and hierarchs' courts using Byzantine church law, princely courts using the Germanic-type "Rus′ Law" and colonial peoples with indigenous legal norms and institutions.[15] For all, the state was successful in enforcing its claim to criminal law authority, allowing lesser-level adjudication to remain in those communities. Muscovite law was practical, focused on establishing a single procedure and policing officialdom. Visiting foreigners, often trained lawyers or scholars and steeped in tropes of Muscovy as a despotism, disparaged it. Giles Fletcher, writing in 1590, characterized the 1550 Law Code fairly accurately while dismissing it: "Their only law is their *speaking law*, that is, the pleasure of the prince and of his magistrates and officers . . . They have no written law, save only a small book that containeth the time and manner of their sitting, order in proceeding, and such other judicial forms and circumstances, but nothing to direct them to give sentence upon right or wrong." Adam Olearius, writing in the mid seventeenth century, admitted that the 1649 Ulozhenie improved on its predecessors ("formerly there were very few written laws and customs"), but still underscored the state's discretion: "As all of this [resolving suits] is done in His Tsarist Majesty's name, it is incontrovertible, and no appeal is permitted." The German diplomat, Johann-Georg Korb, writing early in Peter I's reign, wrote: "Except a little index upon which are the judicial forms, and some legal axioms that have the force of precedent, they have no written law, the will of the monarch and the *ukase* of the senate being the supreme law . . . For in a country governed despotically, nothing but the sovereign's pleasure has force of law."[16]

Lacking Europe's lawyers, learned law faculties and universities, traditions of jurisprudence, articulated hierarchies of judicial venues and codes

Romaniello, *Elusive Empire*. Hittle emphasizes resource scarcity in Russia's urban development: *Service City*, chs. 1–4.

15 Rus′ Law: Feldbrugge, *Law*, ch. 2; Kaiser, *Growth*. Canon law: Weickhardt, "Pre-Petrine Law and Western Law" and "Canon Law."

16 Fletcher, "Of the Russe," 177; Robert Crummey notes that Fletcher ignores many substantive provisions of the law (ibid., 177, n. 7). Olearius, *Travels*, 227–8 (his first trip to and from Holstein was 1634–5; his second in 1636 took him through Russia via Moscow to Persia and back through Russia in 1638–9; his third was in 1643; he expanded the first edition of his *Travels* [1647] in 1656). Korb, *Diary*, II: 186. Similarly, in the early eighteenth century, John Perry: "there being no Juries in that Countrey, nor Counsel admitted to plead as in England, but the Will of the Judge": *State of Russia*, 143.

particular to communities, Muscovite law undoubtedly seemed to these travelers sorely lacking in the judicial protections of a civilized society. In disdaining Muscovy as despotic, they missed the point of Muscovy's practical legal handbooks and bare-bones judicial structures, which established consistent procedure and norms across the realm with amateur judges and inadequate resources; they were applied and pragmatic, not learned.

Moscow's rulers also accomplished centralization by gradually eliminating pockets of political and judicial autonomies, such as those in conquered principalities, demesnes of eminent families or appanages for dynastic kin; in the seventeenth century non-ruling male members of the dynasty were not allowed territorial holdings at all. Giles Fletcher wrote in 1590: "Some there have been of late of the ancient nobility that have held divers provinces by right of inheritance, with an absolute authority and jurisdiction . . . But this was all annulled and wrung clean from them by Ivan Vasil′evich [Ivan IV, ruled 1533–84], father to this emperor."[17] They allowed an exception to this approach in westward expansion, where Muscovy permitted European-style legal estates (including noble, cossack and burgher privileges in Belarus and Ukraine) to retain corporate institutions and rights, sometimes even including the criminal law.[18] In the Middle Volga and for other Muslim communities, Muscovy tolerated Islamic courts for religious and petty crime, but not for criminal law. Elsewhere as well, indigenous communities used local traditions for issues below criminal law. The primacy of the tsar's courts in the criminal law was almost uniform.

Another strategy by which Moscow accomplished centralization with greater success than its peers involved service and dependence on the ruler. No human resource was untapped; everyone had to serve. Peasants and urban people paid taxes; a privileged cavalry class served as military officers and secular officials; less privileged military units provided specialized skills (musketeers, artillery, infantry); bureaucrats staffed chanceries and local offices. Exactly how Muscovy imposed the service principle is not evident in surviving sources. Coercion certainly played a role. A dynastic war in the fifteenth century demonstrated that Moscow's grand princes would use force to enforce the loyalty of regional elites; coercion,

[17] Sixteenth-century absorption of autonomous regions: Zimin, *Rossiia na poroge* and *Reformy Ivana Groznogo*; Kashtanov, "Iz istorii poslednikh udelov." Fletcher, "Of the Russe," 135.

[18] Mal′tsev, *Rossiia i Belorussiia*, 173–4; Nikitin, *Istoriia goroda Smolenska*, 197, 215. Kovno privileges: AMG II: no. 876 (1656).

sometimes in the form of mass population transfers, subdued landholders of newly conquered principalities in the late fifteenth and sixteenth centuries. But Moscow's relative poverty also played a role: no one could make money from land ownership in this cold, northern clime; winning wealth in warfare was a better option. Those who in better locations might have developed into local power elites joined the service of the Moscow grand princes and benefitted from the state's expansion from the late fifteenth through eighteenth centuries. Grand princes and tsars generously compensated such boyar clans and provincial gentry with land, peasants, booty and prestige. These elites in turn provided the leadership – in military offices or domestic estates – to control enserfed peasants, townsmen and other productive social groups.[19]

Moscow's rulers also secured one of the key goals of state-building, expressed in Max Weber's familiar dictum that the essence of sovereignty is the monopolization of violence.[20] In the late fifteenth and sixteenth centuries they integrated private military retinues into their own centralized army; they also made the state the exclusive agent of sanctioned violence (corporal and capital punishment, judicial torture) and eliminated private blood violence. Given that the elite organized itself in factions dominated by clans and that family honor was paramount, one might expect to see the sort of blood vengeance over honor that undermined public authority in early modern Italy, France and Spain. But in Muscovy insult to honor was co-opted into state courts. All social groups could litigate for vindication and monetary fines for verbal insult; litigations over precedence (*mestnichestvo*) provided protection to elite clans' honor in the assignment of military offices.[21]

Centralized control was also built on a network of offices across the realm; in the sixteenth and seventeenth centuries Muscovite rulers created offices for state monopolies, other specialized services and for general administration, all interacting with the populace but tightly linked with the center. In creating this system, Moscow encountered little institutional opposition: towns and regions with traditions of self-government and church institutions used to running their own affairs accepted the

19 The importance of war in solidifying French monarchical power: Innes, "Charlemagne's Government"; Carroll, *Blood and Violence.* Marshall Poe emphasizes redistribution of wealth to the elite as the Russian state's key objective: "Central Government."

20 Weber, "Politics as a Vocation," 78. On violence and state formation: Lewis, *Sanctioned Violence*, 1–5.

21 Honor and precedence: Kollmann, *By Honor Bound*, ch. 4; Eskin, *Ocherki istorii mestnichestva.* European blood feuds: Carroll, *Blood and Violence*; Muir, *Mad Blood Stirring.*

tsar's claim to supreme power and retained autonomy at lower levels of governance. Administrative strategies such as not allowing local offices to be sold as venalities (foregoing short-term income for long-term control) and rotating governors quickly through local positions to prevent their setting down roots maintained central control; coercion was visited upon those failing to pay taxes, to serve or to accept Muscovite authority.

Moscow's rulers and elite primarily pursued self-interest in all this central control. Nevertheless, society benefitted. Creating a strong judiciary responded to Muscovy's ideological dictate that the tsar be a pious shepherd and Old Testament judge to his people; he was supposed to protect the innocent and punish the wicked. In ideological and visual sources the tsar's role as just judge was highlighted far more than his military leadership.[22] Thus Muscovite rulers were expected to provide a functional judicial system. Furthermore, Moscow's pursuit of single-minded control in the criminal law responded to rising crime. Wars and crippling taxation in the sixteenth century caused depopulation, vagrancy and disorder. Sixteenth-century charters establishing local boards for the pursuit of brigands frankly described the situation: "You have petitioned us to say that in your districts brigands are attacking many villages and hamlets and stealing your property and burning your villages and hamlets, and assaulting and robbing many people on the roads and murdering many. And many other people in your districts are harboring brigands in their homes, and the brigands bring to them their booty."[23] Communities benefitted from the establishment of criminal courts.

In all these motivations for central control, the Muscovite government shared common goals with its European and Ottoman peers; its ideological justifications were, however, very different. Already in the sixteenth century European state-building was shaped by powerful discourses, some contesting monarchical authority in favor of greater political pluralism, others redefining monarchy around concepts of the public good and an impersonal concept of the state. Concepts of absolutism and *Polizeistaat* argued that monarchical power should work towards the creation of a more orderly society, the "common good," higher public morality and the creation of wealth for the benefit of state and society. Such a comprehensive ideology of social unity and discipline did not animate Muscovy's centralization efforts in the late fifteenth through seventeenth centuries, as

[22] Rowland, "Did Muscovite Literary Ideology?" and "Muscovy"; Flier, "Political Ideas and Rituals."
[23] 1539 Beloozero Charter, art. 2: RZ II: 213–14. See also 1555 Medyn Charter: RZ II: 218.

Angela Rustemeyer has remarked.[24] Before Peter I (ruled 1682–1725) there was no explicit rhetoric of the "*Polizeistaat*." Muscovy's legal codifications, even the great 1649 Ulozhenie, were starkly instrumental: charters of local government to the Dvina lands in 1397–8 and to Beloozero in 1488, for example, both begin with straightforward declarations that governors should enforce the grand prince's laws, as enumerated therein. The 1497 and 1550 Law Codes similarly begin with no goals beyond defining "how boyars and *okol'nichie* are to judge." The most philosophical that the 1649 Ulozhenie gets is in mandating that "judgment and procedure would be the same in all cases." The 1669 Criminal Articles dispense with introduction and justification entirely.[25] Some moral disciplining and confessionalizing emerged in the first half of the seventeenth century, and the concept of "common good" began to circulate at court in the late seventeenth century from Ukraine, but these ideas did not generate a vibrant, applied program of energized state power. Russia awaited Peter the Great for a more proactive vision of the state.

Centralization claimed is not centralization achieved, of course. Here Muscovy ends up looking much like its European and Ottoman counterparts. In practice, central bureaucratic control was often stymied: communication was impeded by climate, distance and lack of roads, as well as by lack of literacy, education and printing. Russia suffered a dearth of manpower and income, forcing the state to understaff and underpay the bureaucracy in favor of military costs and benefits bestowed on the highest elite. Serfdom entrusted to landlords a wide sphere of petty crime and daily law and order. Ethnic and religious diversity demanded different governing strategies and institutions. And, most significantly, the officials of the formal legal system worked with communities whose concepts of justice were oriented not to enforcing the letter of the law but to maintaining social equilibrium. For all these reasons, officials in practice ruled with flexibility. Muscovy's centralization in the end functioned as an integration of personalized strategies of rule with formalized procedure, institutions and law. Muscovy's bureaucratic empire might look "hypertrophic" in its single-minded quest to control resources, but its practice was diverse and even practical.

[24] Raeff, *Well-Ordered Police State*, 167–79; Scribner, "Police and Territorial State." Rustemeyer, "Systems and Senses."

[25] 1397–8 Dvina Charter: PRP III: 163. 1488 Beloozero Charter: PRP III: 170. 1497 Law Code: RZ II: 54. 1550 Law Code: RZ II: 97. 1649 Ulozhenie: RZ III: 84. 1669 Criminal Articles: PRP VII: 396.

DEFINING THE CRIMINAL SPHERE IN THE LAW

Muscovite law had no theoretical jurisprudence. There were no law schools or university juridical faculties until the late eighteenth century and no legal bar until the mid nineteenth. Thus, Muscovy's legal corpus was utilitarian. One searches in vain for definitions of the criminal sphere. There was no single term for a "criminal" or "crime" until Peter the Great's time; a term denoting the "criminal" law (*ugolovnoe*) is later still, dating to the end of the eighteenth century.[26] Further, no formal distinction was made between civil and criminal law, although this was not unique to Muscovy. As Bruce Lenman and Geoffrey Parker note, "the modern distinction between the criminal and the civil aspects of a wrongful act, and thus between punishment and compensation, was foreign to almost all European legal systems before 1800."[27] At the same time, all these legal systems reflected the distinction in practice. Venues also do not clearly demarcate different spheres of the law since Muscovy treated virtually all crime in a simple juridical hierarchy of local governor's and chancery courts and local boards for brigandage felonies, as discussed below.

Procedure and punishment are the best guides for distinguishing spheres of the law in Muscovy. Three related areas can be discerned: misdemeanors; felonies; the highest crime, which in Muscovy was regarded broadly to include treason, revolt and spiritual crimes such as witchcraft and religious dissent.[28] Misdemeanor crime – assault, petty theft with battery, loan fraud done by non-professionals – was tried by accusatory mode and generally punished by fines to the court and compensation of injury or corporal sanctions. As for felony crime, the 1497 Law Code distinguished it from misdemeanor by introducing what might be called state's interest: even if a person convicted of capital crime had no property with which to compensate his victims, he was not to be given to them in slavery as compensation. He was still to be executed.[29]

[26] *Prestupnik, prestuplenie*: RZ IV: 320–1; Romashkin, *Osnovnye nachala*, 32–61; PSZ V: no. 2673, point 3 (1713); Military Articles: ch. 1, art. 6: RZ IV: 329; ch. 3, art. 35: RZ IV: 334 (1715). *Ugolovnoe*: *Slovar' Akademii rossiiskoi* II (1790): 183.

[27] Lenman and Parker, "State, Community," 12. Man'kov says the same for Muscovy: *Ulozhenie*, 311–12.

[28] Man'kov sees a distinction in terminology and institutions in the 1649 Ulozhenie between crimes against property and person and crimes against the state: *Ulozhenie*, 295, 330–41. Weisser notes a similar distinction in early modern France: *Crime and Punishment*, 11–13.

[29] Still execute: 1497 Law Code, arts. 11, 39: RZ II: 55, 59. 1550 code on accusatory format, arts. 15–18, 29–31, 62: RZ II: 99–100, 102, 108–9.

A cumbersome triad of "theft, robbery and murder" (*tat'ba, razboi, dushegubstvo*) to denote the felony sphere is evident as early as fifteenth-century immunity charters and the 1497 Law Code; brigandage felony received particular definition in charters of the sixteenth century that established boards of local landowners to pursue professional brigands (the *guba* system). Felonies can be distinguished by several characteristics: they were tried by inquisitorial procedure with torture (see Chapters 5 and 6); they were susceptible to corporal and capital punishment; unlike misdemeanors, they could not be amicably settled; finally, as in prosecuting brigands in Europe, reputation for criminality elevated an act from misdemeanor to felony.[30]

Initially Felony Chancery and brigandage officers had jurisdiction over only theft with material evidence and robbery, while murder was handled by governors, but by the seventeenth century their duties had de facto expanded to include homicide and other serious cases, as well as a variety of local duties – surveying, settling land disputes, collecting taxes and fees.[31] At the turn into the seventeenth century, when the Felony Chancery more clearly defined justifications for torture, it thereby defined the criminal sphere more clearly; thus seventeenth-century sources sometimes call felonies "torture cases" (*pytochnye*). The 1649 Ulozhenie developed the law on felony crime by adding a chapter on capital punishment and by expanding discussion of brigandage felonies; it also gave significant attention to the more common accusatory trial model.[32]

The prosecution of highest crime varied only in intensity, not in venue, procedure or law. The 1497 Law Code's list of capital crimes included crimes against state and church ("church thief," "rebel") along with common felonies ("killer of one's landlord," "kidnapper," "arsonist"). Not until the 1649 Ulozhenie did the law explicitly identify a sphere of state crime, devoting its first three chapters to blasphemy and insult to the church, assaults on the person of the tsar and political treason and

[30] No single word for felony; one approach referred to "theft and robbery cases" (*tatinye i rozboinye dela*): August 1556 Decree, art. 13: PRP IV: 366; oath: PRP IV: 186 (1550s); 1555 decree: PRP IV: 356–7. Not to settle felonies: August 1556 Decree, art. 17: PRP IV: 367. Criminal reputation: 1539 Beloozero Charter: RZ II: 214; 1589 Law Code, art. 4: PRP IV: 414. Felonies defined in 1550 Law Code, arts. 58–61: RZ II: 107–8. Inquisitorial format, punishments: 1550 Law Code, arts. 52, 56–7: RZ II: 106–7.

[31] Homicide added: PRP V: 216–17 (1631). Definitions of spheres of criminal law: AAE III: no. 37 (1614); AAE III: no. 94 (1618); AMG I: nos. 135 (1621), 202 (1628); Glaz'ev, *Vlast' i obshchestvennost'*, 49, 214–24.

[32] Three criteria for torture: 1616/17 Felony Handbook: PRP V: 193–4, art. 19. Misdemeanor and felony distinguished: Felony Handbook, art. 59: PRP V: 200 (*c.*1619). "Torture case": RGADA f. 210, Sevsk stol, no. 283, fol. 349 (1672).Ulozhenie chs. 21–2: RZ III: 230–51; ch. 10: RZ III: 102–51.

disrespect to the sovereign's palace and properties.[33] In judicial practice, torture, sentences and punishments for state crime (secular or religious) were harsher than for common felonies. In sum, highest crime was that which attacked the foundations of the state, whether its religious institutions and beliefs or secular rulers.

By the mid seventeenth century the law in letter and practice recognized three areas of law in which the state's courts were involved – highest crime, felony and misdemeanor – of which the first two qualified as "criminal law" in their use of inquisitorial procedure, susceptibility to capital punishment and other indicators. But neither terminology nor norms, neither specialized staff nor separate venues, isolated these types of crime from each other. They could all be judged in the same courtroom with the same personnel and the same codes.

CHANCERIES, GOVERNORS AND BRIGANDAGE ELDERS

Moscow's rulers (grand princes until 1547, tsars thereafter) monopolized the criminal law, but several venues carried out criminal cases. Chanceries were the central points of jurisdiction and several wielded authority in the criminal law. Russia's chancery system grew organically as the state expanded – a few chanceries were founded in the late fifteenth century, several were added in the sixteenth, and in the seventeenth century the system grew from 44 chanceries with 656 staff to 55 chanceries and 2,762 staff.[34] Some chanceries were functional (Foreign Affairs, Landholding, Military Service); others were territorial (Siberia, Middle Volga, the North); others dealt with single social groups (Foreign Merchants, Musketeers). Many of these chanceries tried criminal cases of people from their functional or territorial jurisdictions; for example, felony authority for the townsmen of Moscow was exercised by the Moscow Administrative Chancery (*Zemskoi*); new model troops such as artillery, infantry and musketeers around the realm were adjudicated in Moscow by their own designated chanceries; in Moscow chancery employees were adjudicated in-house by their superiors (after 1648 by the Petition Chancery).[35]

[33] 1497 Law Code, art. 9: RZ II: 55; Ulozhenie chs. 1–3: RZ III: 85–91. See Chapter 15.

[34] Statistics: Demidova, *Sluzhilaia biurokratiia*, 23. Overviews: Leont′ev, *Obrazovanie prikaznoi systemy*; Zimin, "O slozhenii prikaznoi systemy"; Brown, "Early Modern Russian Bureaucracy" and "How Muscovy Governed."

[35] Artillery jurisdiction: AAE IV: no. 9 (1646). Petition Chancery: AMG II: no. 371 (1648). Jurisdiction: Chicherin, *Oblastnye uchrezhdeniia*, 171–8; Kuritsyn, "Pravo i sud," 405–8; Kavelin,

So a governor's authority in the countryside did not necessarily apply to all the residents of his area.

On the highest crimes the Military Service Chancery (*Razriad*), specially designated commissions and occasionally other chanceries took the lead, delegating to local governors investigation before verdict. Authority over common felony locally was in the hands of governors (overseen by the Military Service Chancery that assigned them and their scribal staffs) or brigandage boards (overseen by the Felony Chancery).[36] By the seventeenth century governors (*voevody*) in provinces (*uezdy*) were the foundation of local administration and judiciary. Governors worked as part of their service obligation, supported by the land and cash allotments the state provided to all servitors. Major trading centers (Kazan, Novgorod) and frontier towns often had two or more governors of high rank. Smaller provinces sufficed with one, often awarded to retired and injured gentrymen as a sort of sinecure. As military men, governors did not have specialized training for the law and were not required to be literate.

In judicial work governors applied individual tsarist decrees, the Law Codes of 1550, 1589, 1606, 1649 and 1669 and the norms handed down by the Felony Chancery. They used both forms of judicial procedure, accusatory and inquisitory. A governor's job was defined by the charter he received on appointment; some of them extend for dozens of pages, in which judicial duties usually take up less than a paragraph (the format was not standardized until 1719). In a governor's many roles, military, taxation and trade issues were primary.[37]

Governors' autonomy was broad, but limited by various factors. For one, short terms. Governors in the most important towns were limited to short terms of a year, and for lesser towns a term of about two years was maximum. Governors in Siberia had longer terms because of the challenge of communication.[38] Second, they existed in a world of multiple

Osnovnye nachala, 18–27; Dmitriev, *Istoriia sudebnykh instantsii*, chs. 1–3; Mikhailov, *Russkoe grazhdanskoe sudoproizvodstvo*.

[36] Brown, "With All Deliberate Speed," 148 and *passim* and "Military Chancellery."

[37] A selection of such charters includes Viazma: AMG I: nos. 129 (1619), 135 (1621); Toropets: AMG I: no. 202 (1628); Usviat: AMG II: no. 633 (1655); Mogilev: AMG II: no. 739 (1655); Dünaburg: AMG II: no. 867 (1656); Pereiaslavl′: AAE IV: no. 211 (1676); Korsun: AI I: no. 208 (1691); Chernigov: PSZ III: no. 1540 (1696); Tobol′sk: PSZ III: no. 1594 (1697); Terek: PSZ III: no. 1585 (1697); Verkhotur′e: PSZ III: no. 1595 (1697); Iaroslavl′: PSZ III: no. 1650 (1698); Tiumen′: PSZ III: no. 1670 (1699). PSZ V: no. 3294 (1719).

[38] On governors: Schmidt, *Sozialkontrolle*, ch. 2D; Dewey, "Decline of Muscovite *Namestnik*"; Chicherin, *Oblastnye uchrezhdeniia*, 74–354; Crummey, *Aristocrats and Servitors*, 49–51; Kivelson, *Autocracy*, 133–43; Davies, *State Power*, 22–6 and "Local Government"; Bulgakov, "Zemskoe

jurisdictions. Church institutions, landlords and some Moscow chanceries enjoyed judicial and administrative authority over people subject to them or over certain categories of crime, and they often conflicted with governors in the exercise of those powers. Furthermore, in many communities governors had to work with locally elected officials – administrative, judicial – which were only gradually consolidated or eliminated by the end of the seventeenth century. Scholars argue that the state allowed or at least benefitted from the proliferation of all this institutional diversity since it kept governors from amassing personal satrapies of power.[39]

Central here are the brigandage (*guba*) officials with whom governors were expected to work. Brigandage boards were created in the early sixteenth century to engage local communities in the fight against professional criminals and robber bands.[40] All across Europe in the sixteenth century communities looked to municipal and royal courts for help against brigands and for dispute resolution, finding "an attractive spectrum of alternatives to resolve conflicts in the form of a functioning justice system." In England, for example, the medieval system of justices of the peace was expanded in the criminal law; in early modern France, also to combat brigandage and violent crime, a similar system of a vice bailli and constables elected from the local nobility was instituted.[41] In Muscovy, this seemingly decentralizing move benefitted central power, as the Felony Chancery kept tight control and provided no material bases on which communities could turn brigandage institutions into bastions of local power. Some regions never developed brigandage boards, which were strongest where the gentry were plentiful, as in the northwest (the initial model is said to have come from Pskov), northeast and in the heartland around Moscow. They were rare on the southern frontier or Siberia,

sudoproizvodstvo"; Zaozerskii, *Tsarskaia votchina*, 55. Siberian governors were given two-year terms in 1621, four years in 1653 and between four and six in 1695: Gentes, *Exile to Siberia*, 29. On Siberian administration, see Aleksandrov and Pokrovskii, *Vlast' i obshchestvo* and Akishin and Remnev, *Vlast' v Sibiri* (handbook of institutions and brief biographies of Siberian governors); Vershinin, *Voevodskoe upravlenie.*

39 Strategies to curb governors: Glaz'ev, *Vlast' i obshchestvennost'*; Romaniello, *Elusive Empire*, 128–45; Brown, "Early Modern Russian Bureaucracy," 349–55.

40 The first charter dates to 1539, but scholars argue brigandage boards pre-dated it: Dewey, "Muscovite *Guba* Charters," 282. Historiography on brigandage system: Bogatyrev, "Localism and Integration," 65–8; Glaz'ev, *Vlast' i obshchestvennost'*, 3–31. Nosov, *Ocherki*; Chicherin, *Oblastnye uchrezhdeniia*, 449–504; Keep, "Bandits and the Law." Microhistory: Glaz'ev, *Vlast' i obshchestvennost'*; Pashkova, *Mestnoe upravlenie*, 103–24.

41 Schwerhoff, "Criminalized Violence," 35 and "Social Control of Violence," 234–9; Briggs et al., *Crime and Punishment*, 11, 25–7, 47–67; Greenshields, *Economy of Violence*, 46–58; Weisser, *Crime and Punishment*, 91–5.

where gentry and peasant communities were too sparse to support them. In the Far North (Pomor'e) where communes were already strong, they were also not fully implemented. There, as M. M. Bogoslovskii has described, governors and elected "land" (*zemskoe*) officials already existed.[42]

Brigandage boards were composed of locally elected leaders – an elder, a scribe and wardens – who organized posses of locals to chase down, arrest and try criminals. Brigandage elders were expected to be upstanding citizens of the community: in 1627 the Felony Chancery stressed to the residents of Torzhok that if they did not select a candidate from the highest group of townsmen, the Chancery would do so in their place. The 1649 Ulozhenie suggested that elders should be recruited from retired or disabled gentry who were still fit enough for the job. In 1635, for example, a gentryman petitioned Moscow that he was "old, without family, wounded and with a deserted landholding." He sought appointment as a brigandage elder in Beloozero, but was awarded the bigger job of governor instead, with brigandage duties.[43] Where there were no local gentry, peasants and townsmen could be elders. Brigandage elders could stay in the job many years, although occasionally the Felony Chancery mandated a change or the community ousted a particularly corrupt one. Elders were given the authority to punish up through execution, without reference to the governor or the Felony Chancery, guided by Chancery decrees and handbooks (1530s–50s, 1590s, 1610s, 1630s).[44]

The criminal sphere in Muscovy was made more complicated by a third type of criminal justice official, investigators (*syshchiki*) sent specifically to investigate a pressing issue. Investigators were used since at least the mid sixteenth century to root out criminals in particular areas, to investigate complaints of official corruption or, from mid seventeenth century, to track down runaway serfs.[45]

[42] Brigandage system: Chicherin, *Oblastnye uchrezhdeniia*, 481–7; Bogatyrev, "Localism and Integration"; Schmidt, *Sozialkontrolle*, ch. 2D; Glaz'ev, *Vlast' i obshchestvennost'*, chs. 5–6; Bulgakov, *Gosudarstvennye sluzhby*, 140–72. Geographical distribution: Bogatyrev, "Localism and Integration," 68–74; Glaz'ev, *Vlast' i obshchestvennost'*, chs. 1–4; Keep, "Bandits and the Law," 206; Bogoslovskii, "Zemskoe samoupravlenie."

[43] AAE III: no. 171 (1627). Ulozhenie ch. 21, art. 4: RZ III: 230. *Vremennik* III (1849), no. 5, pp. 42–4 (1635).

[44] Felony Chancery Handbooks: PRP IV: 356–83; PRP V: 188–239.

[45] Investigators: Glaz'ev, *Vlast' i obshchestvennost'*, 70–5; Schmidt, *Sozialkontrolle*, ch. 2E; Man'kov, *Zakonodatel'stvo*, 187; Eroshkina, "Prikaz sysknykh del [articles nos.] 1–5"; Gurliand, "Prikaz sysknykh del"; Brown, "Muscovite Government Bureaus." A decree of 1627 ordered brigandage officials to replace investigators (AAE III: no. 171), but they were still cited: AI I: no. 194 (1636); AMG II: no. 448 (1650).

Over the course of the seventeenth century, communities established different balances of power between these various officials.[46] Governors adjudicated day-to-day crime, handling misdemeanor assault and petty crime cases, felonies such as homicide and arson and state crimes such as witchcraft and treason. Brigandage elders were intended to be sheriffs with posses seeking out bands of robbers, but as they were drawn into a wider array of tasks, some functioned as governors. Occasionally communities even petitioned Moscow to have only a brigandage elder or a governor, not both, in order to avoid the double burden of support.[47] Even though they were selected by their peers, brigandage elders were so closely supervised by the Felony Chancery and governors that they were considered government workers – in the language of the time, "chancery" workers (*prikaznye*) as opposed to those elected (*vybornye*) from the community.[48] Gradually over the seventeenth century brigandage boards fell under the authority of governors and the Military Service Chancery, although the Felony Chancery put up a losing battle.[49] In the 1670s and 1680s, Moscow tried to consolidate local institutions, including the criminal law. Brigandage boards and many other locally elected offices were abolished in 1679, as well as investigators for criminal affairs in May 1683, to free up local gentry for new model troops and, according to the officially stated goal, to relieve communities of the burden of supporting so many offices.[50] Governors took over criminal justice and kept it when the Felony Chancery managed to reinstate brigandage boards in 1684. Special investigators re-emerged as well; they were being sent out against criminals and runaway serfs through the 1690s. Both the brigandage system and the Felony Chancery were conclusively abolished in 1701–2, consolidating criminal law in the hands of the Military Service Chancery, local governors and new municipal administrations.[51]

[46] Tensions between brigandage staff and governors: Chicherin, *Oblastnye uchrezhdeniia*, 450–71, 478–86; Glaz'ev, *Vlast' i obshchestvennost'*, chs. 2–4; Torke, *Die staatsbedingte Gesellschaft*, 52, 65–9; 73–5; Keep, "Bandits and the Law," 206, 215; Kolesnikova, "Mestnye organy vlasti."

[47] "Dela ob opredelenii," docs. 1 (1639) and 8 (1644); AMG II: no. 568 (1653); Glaz'ev, *Vlast' i obshchestvennost'*, 102–23.

[48] Glaz'ev, *Vlast' i obshchestvennost'*, 173, 223–4; Chicherin, *Oblastnye uchrezhdeniia*, 482–3. On *vybornye*, see Chapter 2.

[49] Compared to the 1649 Ulozhenie (ch. 21, art. 3: RZ III: 230), the Felony Chancery's 1669 Criminal Articles excluded governors from criminal jurisdiction (1669 Articles, art. 2: PRP VII: 396).

[50] PSZ II: nos. 779 (1679), 1011 (1683); Sedov, *Zakat*, 403–10; Ustiugov, "Evoliutsiia," 159.

[51] PSZ II: no. 1062 (1684). Investigators sent: PSZ II: no. 998 (1683); PSZ III: no. 1625 (1698). Final abolition: PSZ IV: nos. 1874 (1701) and 1900 (1702); Eskin, "Razboinyi prikaz"; Brown, "Muscovite Government Bureaus," 323 and "Early Modern Russian Bureaucracy," ch. 11.

GOVERNOR AND BRIGANDAGE ELDER IN BELOOZERO AND ARZAMAS

Cases from Beloozero and Arzamas illustrate dynamic relationships between brigandage elder and governor. In Beloozero the brigandage administration existed throughout the seventeenth century and enjoyed some autonomy. It had its own office, which served as a repository of records of trials, a prison and a venue for trials.[52] In 1662 the brigandage elder resolved a homicide case himself in these offices: he used his brigandage staff to bring in a man for questioning; he sent the accused off to prison with his brigandage warden (*gubnoi tseloval'nik*) and later released the defendant on surety bond to return for trial before him at a later date. But in most cases, brigandage elders in Beloozero were subordinate to the governor. In a very early case of 1616, for example, the governor, having questioned a man accused of murder, sent him to the brigandage elder for detention; the elder later collected a dead body fee from the defendant and sent it to the governor. In 1663 the Felony Chancery ordered brigandage elder I. I. Voropanov to arrest a defendant and question him, then it ordered Beloozero governor I. I. Perfilev to arrange transport of defendant and case to Moscow for resolution. Responding that he did not have sufficient sworn officers to make the trip, Voropanov delegated a local worker instead. In the following year the brigandage elder delegated his duties to the governor, since he was too ill to continue.[53] By the end of the century, the reinstituted brigandage system in Beloozero had been completely integrated into the governor's office. For example, in 1692, a governor tried a homicide suit in the brigandage office (*gubnaia izba*), while in 1695 and 1696 the next governor tried such a suit probably in the same space, now called the *sysknoi prikaz*.[54] Across the century in Beloozero governors are seen controlling all phases of trials, from ordering the investigation of a dead body and arrest of the accused to carrying out inquisitions to making verdicts.[55]

[52] For more Beloozero and Arzamas cases, see Kollmann, "Judicial Autonomy." As repository: RGADA f. 1107, no. 480, fol. 4 (1628). As prison: RGADA f. 1107, nos. 214, fol. 5 (1616); 3109, fols. 15, 16 (1683); 3187, fols. 4, 5 (1684).

[53] RGADA f. 1596, no. 8 (1662). RGADA f. 1107, no. 214 (1616). RGADA f. 1596, no. 10, esp. fol. 1 (1663); Voropanov's resignation: RGADA f. 1107, no. 1588, fol. 2v (1664).

[54] RGADA f. 1107, nos. 3904, fol. 1 (1692); 4160, fol. 1 (1695); 4133, fol. 2 (1696).

[55] Some of several examples: RGADA f. 1107, nos. 19 (1613), 167 (1615), 214 (1616), 288 (1619), 514 (1620), 369 (1624), 823 (1638), 1100 (1646), 1771 (1669).

The Arzamas area had a brigandage system from at least the early seventeenth century, but case records do not survive until the waning days of brigandage institutions. Here the same patterns as in Beloozero are observed: brigandage staff did logistics, working with governors. Cases show, for example, an elder interviewing the principal witness in a murder case along with the governor, *stol'nik* S. A. Liubavskii, in Kadom in 1685.[56] Governors also used their own undersecretaries, gunners, musketeers and artillerymen to carry out tasks. Throughout the towns of the region, cases were tried in the governor's office. Beloozero and Arzamas cases show that governors and elders carried out procedures and norms that were standardized across the realm; V. N. Glaz'ev's study of Voronezh shows the same. In so doing, this judicial system offered benefits to each side: communities received protection from crime and the state asserted its control over violence.

CHURCH AND LANDLORD

In principle criminal jurisdiction should have been confined to the governors' and brigandage elders' offices. In practice, there was some slippage. The church, for example, since Kievan times, had enjoyed broad immunities, even occasionally for criminal law. Similarly, landlords enjoyed law and order control over their peasants, and they sometimes also crossed the line into the prosecution of felonies.

In the judicial arena the church had the right to judge the population in religious areas, defined according to Byzantine models to include family law, marriage, divorce, rape, inheritance and dowry, as well as heresy.[57] The church also had authority to judge people of clerical rank in disputes. Finally, church institutions possessed wide judicial immunity from the state's officers and court fees for their dependent lay people (peasants, servants) regarding minor crime or other disputes. To serve ecclesiastical courts, the church possessed a body of Byzantine-derived canon law that

[56] Arzamas brigandage elder in 1604: Veselovskii, "Arzamasskie pomestnye akty," 238. Both Beloozero and Arzamas had a governor and two brigandage elders in 1613: "Dela ob opredelenii," 6–9. An Arzamas governor's instructions in 1629 make no mention of brigandage staff (AMG 1: no. 213), but those of 1679 do: Iakovlev (ed.), *Namestnichie*, 94–9. RGADA f. 1122, op. 2, pt. 1, no. 1018, fol. 9 (1685).

[57] Old scholarship on church jurisdiction retains its value, as the topic was ignored in Soviet scholarship: Nevolin, "O prostranstve tserkovnogo suda," 347–80; Dmitriev, *Istoriia sudebnykh instantsii*, 93–115, 324–33; Chicherin, *Oblastnye uchrezhdeniia*, 153–71. More recent work: Efremov and Shtamm, "Osnovnye istochniki prava," 28–32; Shtamm, "Ugolovnoe pravo," in Nersesiants (ed.), *Razvitie*, 161–3; Shtamm, "Sud i protsess," 215–21; Stadnikov, *Tserkovnyi sud*, 4–29, 107–24.

eventually provided procedural models for Muscovy's evolving judicial system. As Moscow's grand princes from the fifteenth century asserted their authority in the criminal realm, church and state worked together in the criminal law, so much so that a major historian of church courts, M. Gorchakov, considers the church judicial apparatus a complement to and extension of tsarist power.[58]

A complicating factor here, however, was that there was never in Muscovite history a single institutional "church." Ecclesiastical institutions from patriarch's to bishops' to monastic lands enjoyed judicial immunities not only from the sovereign's courts but also from each other. Bishops granted monasteries immunities from their own courts and fees, for example.[59] One rule almost without exception, however, was that felonies were excluded from any church institution's judicial authority – in the words of a 1625 immunity charter "excluding robbery, murder, theft with material evidence, and death-producing and bloody cases." Accordingly, church people were required to participate with financial support and manpower in their local brigandage system.[60]

Throughout the Muscovite period, the church in councils (1551, 1667) and the energetic Patriarchs Filaret (1618–33) and Nikon (1652–8) increased the church's power, particularly defending the right of the church to judge ordained clerics in all things. The 1551 Stoglav Church Council, for example, affirmed the right of clergy to be judged only by church courts, attempted to regularize a system of mixed courts for suits involving church and lay people, and tried to establish a hierarchy of church courts centered on the bishop for religious crime and disputes among lay dependents of religious institutions.[61] In the seventeenth century the state created a Monastic Chancery to abolish monastic immunities and to try clerics and their dependents for all but religious crime, but church complaints forced its abolition in 1677. In 1669, parallel to the publication of the 1669 Criminal Articles, the church issued new rules that imposed a layer of church oversight in the secular court process. Clerics or monks accused or involved as witnesses in criminal cases were

[58] Canon law influential on secular law: Kaiser, *Growth*, ch. 6; Weickhardt, "Canon Law Code." Multiplicities of law in Kiev Rus′: Franklin, "On Meanings." Gorchakov, *O zemel′nykh vladeniiakh*, 441–2.

[59] Monasteries valued the right to collect court fees for themselves: Nevolin, "O prostranstve," 369; Dmitriev, *Istoriia sudebnykh instantsii*, 94; Chicherin, *Oblastnye uchrezhdeniia*, 153–4.

[60] PSZ I: nos. 200 and 201, quote on 420 (1625). Monasteries often claimed (usually unsuccessfully) immunity from brigandage obligations: AAE III: no. 152 (1624); AIu nos. 348 (1652), 365 (2) (1656).

[61] Stadnikov, *Tserkovnyi sud*, 21–5; J. Kollmann, "Moscow Stoglav," 472–508.

to be interrogated not by the secular judge of the case, but by a representative of the patriarch. Should a clerical defendant refuse to confess in the face of strong evidence, he would be defrocked before being sent to secular court. Accordingly, the secular 1669 Criminal Articles reflected this provision. In 1697 particularly harsh procedural norms were defined for clerics accused of participating in the schism, to be carried out by the patriarch's courts.[62]

With the death of Patriarch Adrian in 1690, Peter the Great began to consolidate church juridical institutions by reinstating a Monastic Chancery for cases involving clerics and property issues for church lands. In the Spiritual Regulation of 1721, he established the Synod, a centralized authority over the church in the form of a collegial body of twelve bishops. It exercised judicial authority in most traditional areas (authority over clerics, authority in issues of belief and heresy, certain issues of family law) and kept control over the secular dependents of all church lands, including monasteries, in most affairs. Secular courts took criminal jurisdiction for all but clerics, and such previously religious crimes as family law that involved violence (abduction for forced marriage, rape, landlord sexually abusing dependents, incest) were transferred to secular courts.[63]

Monastic, bishops' and patriarchal courts, therefore, could address a wide range of crimes for clerics and lay dependents; archives include cases of misdemeanor assault and theft, divination, horse theft, carousing, theft of fiscal books by a monastic treasurer, a non-fatal knifing between two monastic elders, assault among monastic peasants and collecting a surety bond for a criminal.[64] Hierarchs regularly heard cases of rape, although such cases could also be heard by secular courts.[65] Church courts used procedures and often the law codes of secular courts (except that clerics

[62] Monastic Chancery: Hellie, "Chapters 12 and 13," 186. 1669 church code: PSZ I: no. 442; also erroneously published under 1667: AAE IV: no. 161; Man'kov, *Zakonodatel'stvo*, 204. 1669 Criminal Articles, arts. 28, 119: PRP VII: 406, 432. Affirmation of church immunity: AI I: nos. 65 (1681), 135 (1686), 146 (1687) and 167 (1688). PSZ III: no. 1612 (1697). Seventeenth-century reforms: Hellie, "Chapters 12 and 13"; Nevolin, "O prostranstve," 371–3; Man'kov, *Zakonodatel'stvo*, 203–7.

[63] Petrine decisions in a variety of questions about civil and church jurisdiction: PSZ VI: nos. 3761 and 3854 (1721), 3963 and 4081 (1722). Petrine reforms: Stadnikov, *Tserkovnyi sud*, 107–24; Cracraft, *Church Reform.*

[64] Church trials of misdemeanor and felony: Chicherin, *Oblastnye uchrezhdeniia*, 166; Nevolin, "O prostranstve," 369; Grekov, "Novgorodskii dom sviatoi Sofii" IV: 81–9. Assault and theft: Slatin, "Monastyrskii sud." Divination: AAE III: no. 176 (1628). Horse theft: PRP V: 142–3 (1635). Carousing: AIu no. 301 (II) (1640). Theft of fiscal books by a monastic treasurer: Ivanov, *Bukhgalterskii uchet*, 189–94 (1646). Knifing: AIu no. 70 (1678). Assault: PDP no. 199 (1691). Surety bond: AIu no. 307 (VII) (1693).

[65] Archbishops hear rape case: RIB XII: nos. 199 (1689) and 245 (1694); PDP no. 194 (1691). Secular court: PSZ II: nos. 1266 and 1267 (1687); Kollmann, "Women's Honor."

were forbidden to swear an oath). In a 1609 case from the Nikolai Koriazhemskii Monastery in Sol′ Vychegodsk province, for example, accusatory procedure was followed: litigants testified and agreed to oath-taking, but settled the case before the oath. Conversely the Solovetskii Monastery used inquisitorial format, as in felony crime, in 1646, including interrogations and examination of material evidence in a case of theft from the monastic treasury.[66]

Church courts, despite their aversion to corporal punishment and the state's prohibition on torture outside of state courts, used both. A. P. Dobroklonskii found the monastic court of the Solotchinskii Monastery in the seventeenth century trying felony cases (including murder) and using torture. Georg Michels argues that bishops routinely dealt violently with their subjects, including in judicial cases. But church institutions also settled criminal cases (forbidden by law) to avoid state courts and possible punishment: in 1551/2, for example, the hegumens of two monasteries made a settlement in a murder case involving peasants of their two dominions, "not having gone to trial before the brigandage elder according to the sovereign grand prince's decree." In 1642 a monastic peasant accused of killing a peasant of another monastic village settled specifically to avoid going to the governor's court in Novgorod.[67]

Church courts also turned to secular courts in criminal cases. In 1579, for example, the steward of a village owned by the Suzdal′ Pokrov convent asked the governor to investigate a large-scale assault on their village; in 1625 the Archbishop of Tobol′sk transferred a case between a boyar and gentryman to the Chancery of the Kazan Palace in Moscow; in 1640 two priests settled a homicide case in the governor's court; in the early 1640s the Tobol′sk governor heard cases involving theft of items from a church by a servant of another church and a case of homicide by a monastic peasant.[68]

[66] Church courts using canon and secular law: Efremov and Shtamm, "Osnovnye istochniki prava," 28–32; Shtamm, "Ugolovnoe pravo," in Nersesiants (ed.), *Razvitie*, 161–3. Slatin, "Monastyrskii sud," 119–21 (1609). Ivanov, *Bukhgalterskii uchet*, 189–94 (1646). Accusatory procedure elsewhere: Dobroklonskii, "Solotchinskii monastyr′," 118–20; RGADA f. 1441, op. 6, nos. 173 (1675), 242 (1679), 275 (1681), 330 (1685). Inquisitorial procedure: RGADA f. 1441, op. 6, nos. 237 (1679), 238 (1679), 303 (1683), 482 (1709), 546 (1718).

[67] Dobroklonskii, "Solotchinskii monastyr′," ch. 5; Michels, "Ruling without Mercy." Grekov asserts that the Novgorod archbishop's court sent torture cases to the local governor: "Novgorodskii dom," 109. AIu nos. 270, 281–2 (1551/2). PRP V: 143–4 (1642).

[68] AIu no. 46 (1579). Tobol′skii archiereiskii dom, no. 108 (1625). DAI II: no. 70 (1640). Tobol′sk: Lipinskii (ed.), "Rospis′," pt. 1, nos. 30 and 6 respectively.

The St. Cyril Beloozero Monastery provides good examples of a religious institution's varied judicial practice. The monastery's judicial board of elders managed a great deal of petty crime in-house. In 1675 a case of assault between two peasants of a monastic village used accusatory procedure as in secular courts. Each side gave his version of the incident; they cited and rejected witnesses until they established a "common witness," whose testimony implicated the defendant. The monastic board then sentenced him to beating with bastinadoes and released him on surety bond. All proceeded as a governor's court would have. So also in the Petrine period: in 1718 the St. Cyril brothers heard a case of theft between two monastic workers.[69]

These were misdemeanors. None of these cases crossed the line into the governor's felony jurisdiction, and in the Beloozero area the governor's court generally handled serious cases involving church dependents. In 1676, for example, a local customs officer complained to the governor that he had been beaten by peasants, including some identified as sons of priests. That got the local archbishop involved, who approved the priests' sons' arrest. In an interesting instance of venue shopping, in 1681 a peasant of the St. Cyril Beloozero Monastery complained to the local governor that he had been beaten by a Vologda townsman who hired him to transport goods. The townsman had promised that he would litigate the case at the monastery, but he failed to do so, so the peasant turned to the secular courts.[70]

In Beloozero the governor's courts regularly enlisted local priests and monastic officials for help. In 1616, for example, the Beloozero governor and secretary assigned to a local priest the task of questioning the local community over a recent murder, perhaps because the priest was literate. In 1620 a local governor queried the monastery over who had jurisdiction to punish a peasant of the monastery in a case he had resolved; the monastery claimed the duty and carried out the punishment that had been decreed by the governor (knouting in the marketplace). In 1675 a local monastery sued to the Beloozero governor in a case of assault by the peasants of a local landlord; the governor managed the case until the two parties reached a settlement whereby the landlord agreed to work with "the brothers" at the monastery; if they could not agree, they promised to

[69] RGADA f. 1441, op. 6, nos. 173 (1675) and 546 (1718). Other criminal cases done in-house: RGADA f. 1441, op. 5, no. 78 (1690); op. 6, nos. 656 (1653), 224, 237, 238, 239 (all 1679), 275 (1681), 303 (1683), 330 (1685), 482 (1709), 546 (1718), 656 (1653).

[70] RGADA f. 1107, nos. 2333, fol. 2 (1676) and 2881 (1681). Other such cases: RGADA f. 1107, nos. 2754 (1680), 3109 (1683), 3284 (1686), 3835, fol. 1 (1691).

return the case to the tsar's courts. In 1692, similarly, a peasant was accused of killing his wife and the trial was conducted by the local governor. When he needed testimony from the local priest, he formally requested the archpriest of the Transfiguration Cathedral in Beloozero to witness the questioning, as mandated by 1669 church rules.[71] All in all, church courts rarely heard serious felony cases without recourse to governors, but they did trespass on the governor's jurisdiction.

Like the church, landlords also handled petty crime, as was the case in Europe. Sixteenth-century British manorial courts, for example, met biennially and handled all manner of civil disputes and petty crime; they could involve hundreds of representatives of the manor's population as juries and spectators. From the sixteenth century Muscovite gentry possessed judicial autonomy short of the criminal law, sometimes affirmed by charter. But their actual practice of petty justice can barely be studied for lack of estate records.[72] A few surviving archives provide glimpses of their work.

Large landholders managed their estates with staff who were somewhat educated and knowledgeable. For example, *stol'nik* A. I. Bezobrazov in the mid seventeenth century maintained a staff of four bailiffs to represent him in Moscow. These men were literate, trained in chancery skills and knew how to work the bureaucracy; some were in fact related to chancery scribes. In the countryside, Bezobrazov's bailiffs were typically not so well prepared. He issued them orders in the same way that the state instructed provincial governors, detailing their general responsibilities (collecting taxes and fees, supervising agricultural production) and, as in orders for governors, warning them not to drink or carouse or to abuse the peasants. They and others were, however, allowed to "discipline" peasants for misbehavior, as evident in two memos by the eminent boyar Boris Ivanovich Morozov in which he instructed the elder of one of his villages to beat a peasant "mercilessly with bastinadoes."[73] To judge by Bezobrazov's provincial bailiffs, such bailiffs were rough characters. One bailiff informed him, for example, that when a peasant woman insulted him in a dispute over goose eggs, he beat her with a stick. A. A. Novosel'skii in his study of

[71] RGADA f. 1107, nos. 214 (1616), 514 (1620), 2249 (1675), 3904 (1692).

[72] British manorial courts: Briggs et al., *Crime and Punishment*, 38–42. Muscovite gentry: Antonov, "K voprosu o sudebnom immunitete." Shtamm discusses Russian landlord courts briefly: "Sud i protsess," 221–2.

[73] Bezobrazov: Novosel'skii, *Votchinnik*, 54–90 and appendices I and II; his Moscow bailiffs, 54–65; Novokhatko, "Upravlentsy." Morozov: *Khoziaistvo krupnogo*, no. 2, p. 12 (1648) (verb used was "*smiriat'*," the same used in church records for corporal punishment) and no. 177, p. 139 (1652).

Bezobrazov's estate noted that bailiffs administered corporal punishment for minor infractions, particularly regarding failure to fulfill obligations to the landlord, without any formal process, and peasants frequently complained of their cruelty.[74]

Provincial bailiffs who enjoyed the right of manorial justice over petty crime in their landlords' villages were obligated by tradition to rule in council with village elders and selected representatives of the village. Landlords' judicial agents used procedures like those of the tsar's courts. In 1652 the bailiff of one of Morozov's Zvenigorod estates reported to him in the same way a governor would have reported to his superiors in Moscow: he had investigated a report of a brawl in a village, taking testimony from witnesses and accused, determined the facts, and then turned to his superior for further instructions. In another case of 1652, Morozov ordered a runaway peasant who had been imprisoned "in fetters" at his estate in Viazma province to be released with a surety bond from the community against any future flight, paralleling state courts' use of surety.[75]

Even more than in church lands, landlords' bailiffs crossed the line into the state's claimed judicial sphere. The law was explicit that private individuals should not take the law into their own hands; the Ulozhenie and 1669 Criminal Articles, for example, forbid anyone to torture a suspected criminal. Likewise they rail against individuals who conceal criminals on their estates and obstruct investigations.[76] But landlords handled crimes such as assault and battery, even murder, that should have been brought to state courts. In 1648, for example, Boris Ivanovich Morozov was informed of a bloody melee that had broken out in a land dispute between his villagers and peasants of a neighboring village owned by Prince Vasilii Andreevich Golitsyn. Morozov consulted with Prince Golitsyn, comparing versions of what happened, and then instructed his bailiff to carry out further investigation. Because of the serious injury, this sort of case should have gone to the governor's court. In 1660, similarly, Morozov instructed his local bailiffs to thoroughly investigate allegations that another of his bailiffs had beaten people, even killing some, and had stolen large quantities of grain. He told them to interview the community

74 Novosel'skii, *Votchinnik*, 69; Bezobrazov's attention to complaints against his bailiffs, 88–9. Petitions versus Morozov bailiffs: *Khoziaistvo krupnogo*, nos. 27 (1660), 35 (1660), 59 (1652).

75 *Khoziaistvo krupnogo*, no. 67, p. 66 (1652) and no. 41, p. 53 (1652).

76 No torturing: Ulozhenie 21, art. 88: RZ III: 245; 1669 Criminal Articles, art. 16: PRP VII: 401. No concealing criminals: Ulozhenie ch. 21, arts. 78–9, 81, 87: RZ III: 243–4; 1669 Criminal Articles, arts. 43, 45–7: PRP VII: 413–14.

for facts and to send the principal witness (the bailiff's own slave) to him in Moscow. This is classic judicial process (see Chapter 5). By all evidence, Morozov was intending to handle this case of homicide in-house.[77]

Similarly, in a case of 1670 of a fight at a wedding in one of Bezobrazov's villages, the landlord instructed his bailiff to investigate all the way up to "torture and burning with fire," despite prohibitions on private torture. A board of bailiff, elder and villagers proceeded to conduct a community survey, replete with face-to-face confrontations and torture by knout. Torture by fire was avoided, as the perpetrators confessed their guilt and were punished, again by knouting. Another case also cites torture. A peasant complained to Morozov in 1660 that his wife had been falsely accused of taking in stolen goods. He charged that the bailiff, "favoring" the complainant corruptly, had tortured his wife with a knout. Knowing judicial procedure for secular courts, the husband had demanded that the accuser be brought before the community (*mir*) for a face-to-face confrontation before the next stage of torture, burning with fire. The bailiff complied and in the confrontation the accuser confessed his slander and cleared the wife. In response to the petition, Morozov ordered his bailiff punished and the wife paid a dishonor fee. Without direct reference to the Ulozhenie for procedure or sanctions, this case replicates judicial procedure of the tsar's courts, which was, most likely, the only source from which Morozov and his bailiffs would have learned their craft.[78]

Landlords sometimes turned to the court to solve problems with unruly peasants. In 1653, for example, Treasurer Bogdan Minich Dubrovskii sent to state courts a peasant and his wife whom he accused of stealing from him and absconding. Having caught the couple, he asked the court to exile them. After a cursory trial in which the peasant admitted to the judges of the Military Service Chancery the theft and flight, the court sentenced him to eternal exile to Oleshna. By 1669, the new criminal law code specifically referred to theft by peasants and slaves from their masters as felony theft (*tat' ba*), so indeed this case belonged in state courts.[79]

In judicial procedures on their estates landlords and their staffs liberally wielded violence. In 1648, for example, a gentryman delivered to the court one of his slaves with a suspicious letter, reporting that he had beaten the

[77] *Khoziaistvo krupnogo*, nos. 5 (1648) and 28 (1660).

[78] Novosel'skii, *Votchinnik*, 73 (1670). *Khoziaistvo krupnogo*, no. 24 (1660).

[79] RGADA f. 210, Sevsk stol, no. 147, fols. 209–26 (1653); similar case: RGADA f. 1171, no. 170, fol. 1 (1683). 1669 articles, art. 114: PRP VII: 431.

man before turning him in. Valerie Kivelson has uncovered numerous witchcraft cases in which accused witches testified that their landlords beat them into forced testimony. In another example, in 1639 Prince Aleksei Mikhailovich L′vov petitioned to the court about his wayward nephews, who were constantly in trouble. He reported that he had previously been given permission from the court to knout his nephews for a theft they had committed, and he had done so, but that they continued to disobey. Conversely, in 1645 a man of the high-placed Moscow servitor Mikhail Pushkin was found guilty of falsely accusing his master of treason. The case was heard at the highest level by a panel of chancery judges; they ruled that the man be beaten with bastinadoes and returned to his master. The verdict, however, included a note that Pushkin "was not to punish the man himself." In a settlement document of 1642, two landlords reached a curious agreement that the court accepted: regarding the theft of a horse, they agreed that if the peasant accused of horse theft was discovered in the same crime again by the rival landlord, then his landlord would deliver him to the plaintiff, where he would be knouted mercilessly at the stables. Should the guilty man's landlord fail to deliver him, he would pay a 50 ruble fine to the plaintiff.[80]

Governors occasionally jostled with landlords over criminal jurisdiction. A governor of Sol′ Kamskaia in 1689, for example, reported to Moscow that in a felony suit against two men brought by the powerful Stroganov mining family, he had been ordered to send them to Moscow for trial. He had done so in December 1688 but he reported that the Stroganovs had seized the men on the road and held them for a couple of months. The men made a settlement and the Stroganovs released them, without involving the governor. The governor reported this as if the Stroganovs were acting above the law, and meanwhile he had lost track of two prisoners and a case for which he was responsible.[81]

A Petrine case reveals the world of customary justice on the estate in fascinating detail. On August 20, 1718 in Arzamas a priest reported to the local court that his son had been stabbed to death on the road by men who owed him money; he complained that the accused men had admitted the crime and had been imprisoned in leg irons in the "judicial office" (*sudebnaia izba*) of their landlord, Prince Petr Alekseevich Golitsyn, who

[80] RGADA f. 210, Prikaznyi stol, no. 567, fols. 193, 202–6 (1648). Kivelson, "Coerced Confessions," 173. RGADA f. 210, Sevsk stol, no. 111, fol. 107 (1639). AMG II: no. 264 (1645). AIuB II: no. 155 (v) (1642).

[81] RGADA f. 159, op. 3, no. 3689 (1689).

was then away serving as governor of Riga. While imprisoned in this rudimentary jail, one of the men had escaped. The local Arzamas judge, then, investigated not only the crime but the escape. He sent his staff to Golitsyn's estate to arrest the murder suspects and investigate what had transpired. In interrogation the estate steward laid out the landlord's system for dealing with crime: when the murder was discovered, he himself investigated the death, interrogated the accused and imprisoned them in the estate's jail. He then reported the case to his landlord in Riga, who instructed him to take the men to the governor's court. But they escaped soon thereafter. The governor ended up trying the two men who remained and sending bailiffs out to hunt down the escaped men, but he did not punish Golitsyn's ineffective prison guards, as he would have done if it had been an official jail.[82] All in all, landlords' estates seem more likely than church courts to cross the bounds in jurisdiction and use of judicial violence. For lack of sources one cannot know the full extent of such trespassing on the tsar's felony authority. Given the broad local authority of secular and lay landlords in a society of enserfment, and the scarcity of governors' offices relative to the huge empire, some of this was unavoidable. But state courts did what they could to enforce the tsar's claim to monopolize criminal authority.

Many have remarked on the administrative and judicial diversity reflected here. Hans-Joachim Torke commented in his classic study that there was so much multiplicity in administrative forms in Muscovy that one cannot speak of a single system, while the great nineteenth-century liberal historian Boris Chicherin maligned Muscovy's judicial diversity, calling it "medieval ... lacking all good order and system." It is easy to exaggerate the situation. When it came to major crime, the tsar controlled it. There is no evidence of rampant vigilante violence; in one instance of an alleged lynching, the state sent an investigator immediately.[83] In the same way as the state managed to co-opt disputes over honor into the non-violent framework of the tsar's courts, so also it convinced communities of the necessity of using the tsar's courts for the most violent crime. The government accomplished this task not only by threatening to punish

[82] RGADA f. 1380, no. 30 (1718). Interaction of bailiffs and communal self-government on late eighteenth-century estate: Hoch, *Serfdom and Social Control*, esp. chs. 4–5.

[83] Torke, *Die staatsbedingte Gesellschaft*, 51; Chicherin, *Oblastnye uchrezhdeniia*, 178. Lynchings: Kollmann, "Lynchings."

anyone who took the law into his own hands and any tsarist official who abused his power, but also by providing a corpus of criminal law and judicial institutions. To do so the state surrounded its unprofessional military governor judges with staff who had judicial expertise and it policed officials with threats of severe punishment. That, at least, was the theory. How the state went about these goals, and how well it succeeded, is the concern of the next three chapters.

CHAPTER 2

The problem of professionalism: judicial staff

In May 1635 the Mtsensk governor wrote to Moscow in panic. His undersecretary had been selected by the community to serve as undersecretary for the local brigandage office and he faced disaster if he lost that worker:

> The undersecretary Rodka Olovenikov has worked 15 years without a cash and grain salary, and he administers and writes up all your sovereign affairs ... Without this Rodka there would be no one to administer and to write up your sovereign affairs in the governor's office in Mtsensk ... We receive many orders from the Military Service Chancery and from other chanceries regarding decrees, taxes and lawsuits, and without him, Rodka, all those your sovereign affairs would pile up here in front of me, and in Mtsensk in the governor's office there would be great delay [*motchanie*] in your sovereign affairs.[1]

Even taking into account rhetorical liberties, this governor's plaintive request suggests how central to local administration were the bureaucrats. Governors were the judges, but the linchpin of the system was his scribal assistants, because they were professionally trained. As discussed in Chapter 1, governors were military men of high and middle Moscow ranks whose role as judge was only one of several more pressing responsibilities (military, fiscal, economic, administrative); they received no training in the law. In many communities they worked with brigandage elders who also had no specialized juridical knowledge. Governors recruited other staff from the community, who worked without pay as their service to the tsar. In chanceries that heard criminal cases – primarily the Military Service (*Razriad*) and Felony (*Razboinyi*) – expertise in the law resided in the scribes. In the sixteenth century, judges in chanceries themselves were bureaucrats and that remained the case for the important Military Service and Foreign Affairs Chanceries through the subsequent

[1] AMG II: no. 11 (1635).

century when otherwise military men took over high offices. Such "noble officials" (in Robert Crummey's words) headed chanceries where they had little expertise and "no special training in the exacting routines of chancery work"; they often headed several different chanceries over a career. Governors in the provinces were equally untrained. None of this augured well for efficient local government or justice.

Nevertheless, the state was committed to providing good justice: the two earliest law codes sternly warn judges "not to favor or avenge anyone or to take any bribes." The 1649 Ulozhenie emphatically instructs judges to administer the law "to all people of the Muscovite state, from the high to low ranks, fairly for all." One might dismiss this as mere rhetoric except for the personal engagement of Tsar Aleksei Mikhailovich in the drafting of the 1649 Ulozhenie and in prosecution of other cases. Since, as Crummey observed, a military man as judge "left all of the routine work and most of the thinking to the specialists who served under him," scribes were the best hope of enforcing the law across the realm.[2]

THE PROBLEM OF PROFESSIONALISM: SCRIBES

Foreign visitors to Muscovy immediately noticed the absence of lawyers. Visiting Russia in the early sixteenth century Sigismund von Herberstein remarked, "The testimony of a nobleman carries far more weight than that of the common people, who rarely have an attorney or advocate and must state their case themselves." Jacques Margeret wrote around 1606 that "their laws provide that everyone plead his own case or have some kinsman or servant of his assigned to do this, for they have no lawyers at all," while, writing in 1698, the diplomat Johann-Georg Korb concurred that litigants presented their cases "without the assistance of either attorneys or advocates."[3] To them this was a remarkable lacuna.

The lawyerly profession was well established in Western Europe by the sixteenth century. In England lawyers were attested since medieval times, particularly for the civil law. A textbook for lawyers had been written in 1187–9 and a cadre of professionally trained jurists developed along with

[2] 1497 Law Code, art. 1: RZ II: 54. 1550 Law Code, art. 1: RZ II: 97. Ulozhenie ch. 10, art. 1: RZ III: 102. Hellie, "Early Modern Russian Law" and "*Ulozhenie*: Preamble"; Gurliand, *Prikaz*. Crummey, *Aristocrats and Servitors*, 40–1, 44, 52–7, quote on 41; Ustiugov, "Evoliutsiia," 162.

[3] Herberstein, *Description*, 51. Margeret, *Russian Empire*, 30. Korb, *Diary*, II: 187. Similar comments by Richard Chancellor in 1553 ("no lawyers, but every man is his own advocate": "Voyage," 33) and early eighteenth-century John Perry ("no Juries in that Countrey, nor Counsel admitted to plead": *State of Russia*, 143).

civil courts. Similarly, in Italian universities and towns of the twelfth and thirteenth centuries lawyers and a professional notarial class thrived with the revival of Roman law. Already in the early 1400s in Florence, for example, a powerful guild of "lawyers and notaries" oversaw professional training and standards. Notaries, while not professionally trained in the law, applied legal expertise as they drew up wills, contracts and deeds.[4] In the criminal law in early modern Europe, lawyers were less involved in trial procedure: as a rule, both in England with its jury trials and on the Continent where the inquisitorial technique spread in the sixteenth century, in criminal cases the prosecution used lawyers but defendants were denied counsel. Nevertheless, legal expertise was widely spread and could be procured in preparation for trial.[5]

In Russia, neither notaries nor lawyers existed as a formal profession until the Great Reforms of the 1860s. This reflects how in early modern Russia literacy was compartmentalized and functional. The vast majority of the population was illiterate, and others possessed reading and writing skills appropriate for their work. Merchants and artisans deployed the vernacular to carry out business, keep accounts and write contracts and correspondence. Most parish priests were literate enough to read the liturgy in Slavonic and to sign documents; in the 1649 Ulozhenie priests were the preferred substitute to sign a document when a litigant was illiterate. Large landholders – from patriarch to monasteries to gentry – and even large villages employed scribes to produce needed documents. Functional literacy should have been widespread among the provincial gentry for estate management and official service; studies by David Miller for the sixteenth century and Carol Stevens for the seventeenth showed that about half the members of groups of gentry (donors to a monastery, members of a regiment) could sign their names.[6]

Literary skills primarily resided in the church. At monasteries and bishops' sees, monks composed and copied chronicles and other religious works in a high register of Russian that became suffused with Slavonicisms over the seventeenth century. After the Time of Troubles, under Polish and Ukrainian influence a few noblemen and bureaucrats mastered Russian and Slavonic sufficiently to write poetry, parodies and other

[4] Kim, "Lawyers"; Briggs et al., *Crime and Punishment*, 11; Bouwsma, "Lawyers."

[5] Langbein, *Prosecuting*; Briggs et al., *Crime and Punishment*, 28; Langbein, "Criminal Trial." In England lawyers were not permitted in criminal court until the second half of the eighteenth century.

[6] Priests sign: ZA no. 188, art. 7 (1628); Ulozhenie ch. 10, art. 246: RZ III: 144. Miller, *Saint Sergius*, 239–43 and Table 3; Stevens, "Belgorod"; Glaz′ev, *Vlast′ i obshchestvennost′*, 191.

forms of secular literature.[7] By far the greatest repository of literacy, however, was the tsar's bureaucracy, and here it was functional, secular and nearly vernacular. In all these settings, literacy was learned on the job, not in schools.

Only in the chancery system could someone develop expertise in the law and legal procedure. Nineteenth-century historians disdained the Muscovite chancery system for its overlapping jurisdictions and functions, but now scholars express greater appreciation. They point out that Muscovites had no difficulty figuring out where documents went and who had authority (and, one might add, how to game the system). Ol′ga Novokhatko notes "such a spontaneous and from an accepted point of view irrational approach to administration was in its way intelligent and practical," providing an "organizational mobility" that allowed the chanceries to perform their work quickly, efficiently and accurately. L. A. Pisar′kova declared Muscovy's chancery system a solidly established bureaucracy for its times. Borivoj Plavsic declared that "there is good reason to believe that pre-Petrine Russian administration was organized in a more modern manner than it came to be after Peter's many 'reforms'," and Richard Hellie spoke of "the glorious medieval Muscovite civil service tradition." Several scholars of the judicial system acknowledge that expertise resided in the scribes, not the military-class judges.[8]

Professionalism was created in part by establishing the bureaucratic class as a tight social and professional group, rigorously trained and supervised. Heredity within families provided most of the scribes in Moscow chanceries, but this was not a closed social stratum. Inward mobility was constant as bureaucracy grew. Socially scribes came from some of the pockets of literacy in Muscovy – gentry, priests' sons, townsmen, lower serving ranks such as musketeers – and entrance into the stratum was competitive. It was attractive because Moscow chanceries provided decent salaries, provisions in kind and the ability to own land, a right nearly exclusive to the military servitor class. Regularly the state tried to prevent tax-paying and military men from depleting their ranks by

[7] Muscovite literacy: Marker, "Literacy and Literacy Texts"; Okenfuss, *Discovery of Childhood.* Literature by scribes: Bushkovitch, *Religion and Society*, 140–5.

[8] Critique: Chicherin, *Oblastnye uchrezhdeniia*, 270–89, especially 273, 281. Novokhatko, *Razriad v 185 godu*, 63, 581–7. Pisar′kova, *Gosudarstvennoe upravlenie*, 80. Plavsic, "Seventeenth-Century Chanceries," 23–7, 36–8 (21). Hellie, "Russia," 490–2, quote on 499. Other positive views: Demidova, *Sluzhilaia biurokratiia*, ch. 4; Brown, "Bureaucratic Administration," 67–8; Poe, "Central Government," 453–8; Davies, "Local Government," 466–8; Romaniello, *Elusive Empire*, 130–4. Scribal judicial expertise: Man′kov, *Ulozhenie*, 314; Serov, *Sudebnaia reforma*, 87–8, 266–8.

entering scribal service, as in 1640 when sons of priests and deacons were forbidden to join the bureaucracy; some managed to join anyway and Peter I abolished such restrictions.[9]

The bureaucracy was composed of undersecretaries (*pod'iachie*) in several ranks, secretaries (*d'iaki*) and state secretaries (*dumnye d'iaki*). Even though bureaucrats worked side by side with military servitors (boyars and gentry) in Moscow chanceries and governors' offices, the two social strata did not mix. Even as military men moved into officialdom in the seventeenth century, their social superiority to bureaucrats was affirmed. Bureaucrats were excluded from the clan-based system of precedence (*mestnichestvo*)[10]; gentry and boyar families did not intermarry with scribal clans. At the Kremlin court the bureaucracy's subordinate status was marked symbolically: the Muscovite Grigorii Kotoshikhin in the 1660s reported that state secretaries stood during sessions of the boyar council while the boyars, from military clans, sat. These status distinctions were revealed in rules about entry into the Kremlin: higher ranks were allowed to progress farther before having to dismount or alight from their carriages and walk the rest of the way; undersecretaries of the lowest ranks were prohibited from riding at all in the Kremlin grounds. Not until 1680 were state secretaries allowed the considerable honor of using the patronymic in their names. Nevertheless, bureaucrats enjoyed status and prestige beyond other groups: state secretaries and secretaries received ample dishonor compensation according to the 1649 Ulozhenie.[11]

Novice undersecretaries worked decades to ascend three stages of clerkdom, hoping to be promoted to secretary. Relatively few reached that rank: Natalia Demidova calculated that the number of secretaries in central chanceries and in provincial offices stayed a relatively modest number, rising from 78 to 154 between 1626 and 1698, while between the 1640s and the 1690s undersecretaries proliferated, rising from 1,535 to 4,538. Few rose from secretary to the conciliar (*dumnyi*) rank of state

9 Social background of scribes, efforts to restrict entrance: Brown, "Early Modern Russian Bureaucracy," 86, 91–2, 107; Demidova, *Sluzhilaia biurokratiia*, ch. 2; PRP v: 230 and 358 (1640); Suslova, "Severnoe dukhovenstvo." Growth of the bureaucracy: Demidova, *Sluzhilaia biurokratiia*, ch. 1. Major studies: Brown, "Early Modern Russian Bureaucracy," "Bureaucratic Administration" and "How Muscovy Governed"; Pisar'kova, *Gosudarstvennoe upravlenie*, ch. 1; Demidova, *Sluzhilaia biurokratiia*; Plavsic, "Seventeenth-Century Chanceries"; Likhachev, *Razriadnye diaki*.

10 Precedence claims by state secretaries: Bogoiavlenskii, "Prikaznye d'iaki," 226–8; Eskin, "'I Vasilei skazal'"; Novosel'skii, "Praviashchie gruppy."

11 Kotoshikhin, *O Rossii*, ch. 2, art. 4, p. 24. Entering Kremlin: PSZ I: nos. 116 (1654), 468 (1670); PSZ II: nos. 901–2 (1681), 1064 (1684); Kotoshikhin, *O Rossii*, ch. 2, art. 14, pp. 29–32. PSZ II: no. 851 (1680). Dishonor: Ulozhenie ch. 10, arts. 83, 91, 93: RZ III: 110–11.

secretary: there were about two state secretaries at the beginning of the seventeenth century and about eleven by the end.[12]

State secretaries participated in diplomacy, legislation and counsel side by side with the boyars. Secretaries oversaw the running of their chancery or of a division in a large chancery; statistics show that half of the secretaries in the seventeenth century spent their entire careers working in a single chancery, and another quarter worked only in two chanceries,[13] developing expertise sufficient to resolve many issues without consultation. Some foreign observers appreciated them. Tsar Aleksei Mikhailovich's doctor Samuel Collins, who lived at court for several years in the 1660s, observed: "every Province [has] its *Precause* or Office, wherein is a *Bayor,* or Lord, and a Chancellor call'd a *Diac,* who hath many Clerks under him; He represents the *Boyar,* who is the Representative of his Imperial Majesty." John Perry, writing in the 1710s, depicts senior chancery scribes as de facto sovereign judges:

> A Bench of *Diacks* (or Chancellors) sate as Judges in each of these principal Offices or Courts in *Mosco,* whose Business it was to hear and determine Matters . . . and to make Report from Time to Time of their Proceeding to their respective Lords, under whose Command they acted, and the said Lords seldom coming themselves in person to hear any Causes, the *Diacks* representing Matters to them in such Forms and Colours, as they thought proper.[14]

Collins and Perry got it right: the "boyars" or governors from the ruling class represented the tsar, while the bureaucrats could wield considerable judicial expertise and power.

Judicial knowledge was dispersed from Moscow to the provinces by dispatching secretaries to serve with governors and to train and supervise undersecretaries. Demidova speaks of the "great mobility" of scribes, "transferred to temporary chanceries, sent on administrative assignments to provincial towns, army units and on embassies."[15] Matthew Romaniello chronicled the mobility within a group of over 300 scribes who served in the Kazan area; in the course of their careers most served in several different provincial centers and over half were promoted to Moscow chanceries, where they applied their particular skills (in the military, fiscal

[12] Estimates of ten to fifteen years in each of three undersecretary ranks: Plavsic, "Seventeenth-Century Chanceries," 29–30; Brown, "Service Land Chancellery Clerks," 43. Statistics: Demidova, *Sluzhilaia biurokratiia,* 24, 39.

[13] Brown, "Early Modern Russian Bureaucracy," 89.

[14] Collins, *Present State,* 71; Perry, *State of Russia,* 188.

[15] Demidova, *Sluzhilaia biurokratiia,* 44–5, 59–60, quote on 44. Moscow secretaries sent into the field on assignment, retired or exiled there: Brown, "Service Land Chancellery Clerks," 64–6; "Early Modern Russian Bureaucracy," 333; Demidova, *Sluzhilaia biurokratiia,* 69.

or judical sphere) as much or more than their local knowledge. The cases surveyed here show such mobility: in 1701 an undersecretary in the Military Service Chancery was prosecuted for bribery; investigation revealed that he had begun his career in the governor's office in Belgorod and had been promoted to Moscow in May 1699. As noted in Chapter 1, even the work of officials on landlord's estates demonstrated the dissemination of Muscovite chancery standards, as in a classic formula used by Boris Ivanovich Morozov when he wrote to his bailiff "and when this document arrives to you, you are to . . . ," and in his bailiff's identifying himself humbly in the diminutive.[16]

Bureaucrats in provincial offices provided the legal knowledge that kept a system based on amateur military judges working. Chanceries were committed to having justice delivered speedily at the local level by, on the one hand, providing local judges with the expertise and instruction they needed to render verdicts (see Chapter 7) and, on the other hand, by exerting oversight, insisting on frequent reports and accounting.[17] Specifically in the law, they kept judges in line by several strategies. The first was collegiality. Chancery and local courts were composed of panels of judges, including a military service officer as senior, and bureaucrats. The 1649 Ulozhenie described it as "a boyar or *okol'nichii* or a member of Council with colleagues, three or four men"; S. K. Bogoiavlenskii's index of seventeenth-century Moscow chancery judges shows anywhere from one to three secretaries working alongside men of military rank as judges. In the Felony Chancery, for example, in any given year at least one boyar or *okol'nichii* and two to three secretaries served as judges. In major provincial offices a secretary might join the governor, while in smaller towns governors worked with undersecretaries trained to Moscow standards. In practice, scribes in regional offices served longer in place than did their governor partners, averaging four years in position to the governor's one or two. Even over the turbulent Time of Troubles (1598–1613), scribes remained in place. Thus scribes were in a position to provide expertise and implicit oversight. In Moscow chanceries, secretaries were authoritative enough to dispatch lesser cases by themselves.[18]

16 Demidova, *Sluzhilaia biurokratiia*, 58–60; Romaniello, *Elusive Empire*, 131–3. RGADA f. 210, Prikaznyi stol, no. 965, fols. 152–69 (1701). *Khoziaistvo krupnogo*, nos. 152, 154, 186–7, 190, and *passim*.

17 D. O. Serov sees concern about the competence of judges as early as 1497: *Sudebnaia reforma*, 340–3, 349, 351, 407.

18 Ulozhenie ch. 10: art. 23: RZ III: 104–5; Bogoiavlenskii, *Prikaznye sud'i*, 138–44. Length and continuity of service: Romaniello, *Elusive Empire*, 131–4; Rybalko, *Rossiiskaia prikaznaia*

Provincial offices demonstrate collegial adjudication. In Beloozero in the seventeenth century, for example, governors were generally listed in partnership with a secretary or undersecretary.[19] Scholars have generally argued that social status differences between military and scribal men might have inhibited give and take; in 1680 a decree mandated that only the name of the senior judge (usually a man of military background) be listed in documents along with the phrase "with colleagues." But in practice scribes had the upper hand with judicial expertise. They advised judges on judicial procedure; they made sure that the proper form was used and that all orders had been carried out; they selected excerpts from relevant laws according to which judges resolved cases.[20]

A second strategy whereby proper procedure was ensured was the creation of a uniform model of bureaucratic language and paperwork, an impressive feat in view of the size of the empire.[21] Documents were produced as books or scrolls. Register books were kept of correspondence, but most documents came into the offices as petitions on long narrow sheets of paper. As court cases accumulated documents, they were glued together in long scrolls, described by Olearius: "To make them, they cut up whole sheets of paper in long strips, glue the narrow edges together and roll them up. Some of the scrolls are 20, 30, or even 60 or more ells long. One can see very many of them in the chancelleries, piled one on top of another." Samuel Collins scoffed at the unwieldy format: "They waste abundance of Paper in writing down things at large (as our Common-law Clerks do) all in Rolls of a great length."[22]

By the sixteenth century the formulaic template of key documents was established, as was much chancery practice.[23] The language of official

biurokratiia. Center's "oversight" of governors: Davies, "Local Government." In 1630 a state secretary and secretary resolved a homicide case in the Military Service Chancery: AMG I: no. 259 (IX).

19 Governor and secretaries named together in Beloozero: RGADA f. 1107, nos. 19, fol. 1 (1613); 113, fol. 15 (1614); 167, fol. 3 (1615); 214, fols. 1, 4 (1616); 288 (1619), fol. 1; 514, fol. 1 (1620); 480 (1628), fol. 2; 703, fol. 1 (1635); 823, fol. 1 (1638); 1155, fol. 3 (1648); 1219, fol. 2 (1650); 1451, fol. 4 (1658).

20 PSZ II: no. 820 (1680). Skeptical of collegiality: Brown, "Early Modern Russian Bureaucracy," 122–30; Shtamm, "Sud i protsess," 214. Scribes prepare excerpts of laws for provincial judges: RGADA f. 1122, op. 2, pt. 2, no. 1629, fol. 6 (1674); RGADA f. 1107, no. 3549, fols. 7–9 (1688); RGADA f. 1135, no. 297, fol. 6 (1696); Titov (ed.), *Kungurskie akty*, no. 72 (1697).

21 Chancery paperwork: Novokhatko, *Razriad v 185 godu*, ch. 1; Iliushenko, *Istoriia deloproizvodstsva*, 21–30; Brown, "Early Modern Russian Bureaucracy," ch. 2 and "Bureaucratic Administration," 75–8.

22 Olearius, *Travels*, 227. Collins, *Present State*, 42.

23 The 1550 Law Code describes production and validation of documents; the Ulozhenie's massive tenth chapter expands this theme and threatens harsh sanctions for improper document preparation: 1550 Law Code, art. 28: RZ II: 101–2; Ulozhenie ch. 10, arts. 11–13, 22, 128–9, 246–53: RZ III: 103–5, 119, 144–6.

paperwork was standardized to a chancery Russian close to contemporary vernacular. By the seventeenth century handwriting was standardized as cursive (*skoropis'*); conventions of abbreviation were complex but consistently used. Punctuation and spelling varied, as it also did in printing at this time in Europe. Procedures of assembling, proof-reading, signing off and recording documents were fixed by the mid seventeenth century. Documents of the same genre produced as far apart as Belgorod and Siberia and separated by decades in time show basically the same form and language, bespeaking a remarkably centralized bureaucracy.

A third strategy for providing legal expertise in a situation of amateur judges was to pay close attention to the integrity of records. Historical sociologists have pointed to bureaucratic record-keeping as crucial in early modern state-building; Anthony Giddens calls such practices "surveillance," meaning the systematic written recording of material and human resources.[24] Muscovite laws from the late fifteenth century devote attention to the integrity of legal documents. The 1497 Law Code specifies the need of judges to seal documents and secretaries to sign them and regulates slavery documents; the 1550 Law Code also focuses on fees, seals and signatures and raises other perspectives. It introduces prison and corporal punishment for scribes who corruptly write documents; it expands on the 1497 Law Code's attention to registration of slavery documents; it sets norms for maintaining confidentiality of testimony; it describes in some detail the preparation of trial transcripts by undersecretaries, with approval and signature by secretaries. In the 1570s the mercenary soldier Heinrich von Staden observed some of this, noting how scribes ensured documents against forgery by signing on front and back, particularly on the joints where sheets were glued together.[25]

The 1550 Law Code also included an important rule prohibiting work to be done at home, which was repeated thereafter and was a common complaint in allegations of judicial corruption.[26] The 1649 Ulozhenie's massive tenth chapter on judicial procedure introduced more rules regarding proper signatories, registration of documents and document

[24] Giddens, *Nation-State and Violence*, 41–9.

[25] Sign and seal: 1497 Law Code, arts. 15–18, 22–6, 40: RZ II: 56–7, 59. Slavery documents: 1497 Law Code, arts. 18, 42, 66: RZ II: 56, 59–60, 62. 1550 Law Code, arts. 4–5, 28–9, 76–80: RZ II: 97, 102, 115–16. Staden, *Land and Government*, 14–15.

[26] Forbid taking documents home: 1550 Law Code, art. 28: RZ II: 102; Ulozhenie ch. 10, art. 13: RZ III: 103; Tiumen' governor order: PSZ III: no. 1670, p. 561 (1699). Allegations of officials keeping books at home: RGADA, f. 210, Sevsk stol, no. 294, fols. 311–30 (1676); DAI X: no. 23 (1682).

integrity. Once a secretary had approved a transcript, there were to be no more insertions or removals of text or documents.[27] In the second half of the seventeenth century decrees defined working hours for scribes in the chanceries, issued more instructions on proper composition and signing of documents, instructed scribes not to reveal testimony to litigants and initiated a review of accusatory trial procedure in the wake of widespread complaints about surveyors.[28]

A fourth strategy to ensure that local governors followed proper procedure and applied the law correctly was supervising them and their staffs, requiring that they report to central chanceries at key stages in important cases or defer to the center for verdicts.[29] For some serious cases chanceries would send judges lists of questions to pose to witnesses. When it came to the death penalty, judges themselves often turned to Moscow for verdicts, even when they were not required to do so (see Chapter 7). As Peter the Great later said, oversight from the center was needed lest "from ignorance" a judge mistakenly punished someone too harshly, even unto death. A response to the Sevsk governor regarding a witchcraft case by the Military Service Chancery in 1677 demonstrates careful oversight: "investigate this dragoon Emel′ko in Sevsk, interrogate him according to his petition, give him a face-to-face confrontation and thoroughly investigate. If it comes to torture, then order him Emel′ko tortured and burned with fire. Whatever emerges in the investigation, write to us, the sovereign, and send the report to the Military Service Chancery." Similarly, in a case of 1649, the judge in Elets was instructed to orally interrogate the two accused in sight of instruments of torture, and if they did not confess, then he was to proceed to torture and report the results to Moscow.[30]

The center also supervised its judges with the repetitive wording of bureaucratic documents, a characteristic of Muscovite chancery documents that has caused modern scholars to dismiss the bureaucracy as

27 Ulozhenie ch. 10, arts. 11, 12, 21, 22, 137 (composition and recording), 128–9 (record books), 246–50 (signatories): RZ III: 103, 105, 119, 121, 144–5.

28 Scribes' working hours: PSZ I: nos. 237 (1658), 462 (1669), 477 (1670); PSZ II: no. 839 (1680); PSZ III: no. 1393 (1691). Judges and boyars' hours: PSZ II: nos. 621 (1676), 777 (1679). Instructions: PSZ II: nos. 742 (1678), 964 (1682), 1241 (1687), 820 and 826 (1680); PSZ III: nos. 1576 (1697), 1608 (1697). Surveyors: PSZ II: no. 1140 (1685).

29 Muscovy had regular couriers and a fast pony express that governors were not to use for routine correspondence: PSZ I: no. 18 (1649); AMG III: no. 465 (1661). Micro-managing from the center: Kivelson, *Autocracy*, 134–8.

30 PSZ VI: no. 3847 (1721). Novombergskii, *Koldovstvo*, no. 30, p. 111 (1677); RGADA f. 210, Belgorod stol, no 270, fol. 474 (1649).

childlike and backward.[31] Documents repeated – word for word – previous communications and orders. Court transcripts grew to tremendous length, much of it verbatim repetition, in which the historian, and undoubtedly local officials as well, searches for a new element, namely the order of what to do next. In responding to local governors, central chanceries were painstakingly literate. Seeking a confession to treason from one recalcitrant witness, for example, the Military Service Chancery in 1664 instructed one provincial governor in systematic steps: ask him to write down his accusation, seal it and give it to you; if he is illiterate, have him ask his father confessor to write it down; send the letter to Moscow. If he refuses to tell his father confessor, then ask him to tell you only, individually. If he still refuses, then take him to torture. When a governor responded to Moscow, his scribe composed the document as a verbatim summary of orders and then a point-by-point response to each order.[32] The result seems mindlessly mechanical, but it served important purposes.

First and foremost, such repetition instructed the judges in the law. Case transcripts are unremittingly consistent in describing scribes reading information to judges and judges making a rule (even if the scribe, like any good assistant to an executive, essentially told him what to do); there is no reason to consider such descriptions of process empty words. If judges were paying attention at all, they were repeatedly confronted with descriptions of basic judicial procedures (how to carry out interrogations and community surveys, when to proceed to torture) and standards for taking action. By drumming judicial procedures and norms into their governors' heads so repetitively, the center was teaching them. This is an old response to such a situation. Matthew Innes argues that Charlemagne's capitularies were similarly intended to inform local judges of the law and proper procedure; in some criminal cases Ottoman military judges oversaw the work of provincial judges with documentation in exactly this redundant format; even in modern colonial experience the British faced a two-fold problem of infusing native African justice with fundamental concepts of "Rule of Law" and doing so with colonial administrators who were not trained in the law. So, they

[31] Starr, *Decentralization*, 27–9. Alexander V. Issatschenko derides the "simplicity" and "awkwardness" of legal texts of the Kievan period and ignores Muscovite chancery language, other than calling the prose of Grigorii Kotoshikhin, a professional Kremlin scribe, "readable and instructive": "Russian," 122, 128.

[32] SIDG no. 274, pp. 518–19 (1664). Daniel Collins describes a typical transcript: "Speech Reporting," 271–3.

wrote painstakingly detailed descriptions of British law for these administrators, who were then to teach their African charges.[33]

Writing trial transcripts so thoroughly accomplished another goal as well. It filled in the gaps in knowledge that could result from frequent change of personnel or delays in trials. Daniel Collins, in his study of the use of direct speech in Muscovite trial transcripts, observed that new scribes and new judges needed to be informed and that even the original scribes and judges would have had trouble recalling all the details of a trial that had dragged on over time. When a trial reached the stage of verdict, the scribe would prepare a transcript of the entire case with all documents in full and citations from the law to inform the verdict. He would then read it aloud, although perhaps in what would be an interminable reading they skipped to the most relevant new material. But cases are clear that only on the basis of "hearing" the case and excerpts of the law could verdicts be rendered. Collins notes: "By hearing (and sometimes also reading) reports of the testimony presented in the comparatively non-analytic mode of Direct Speech, the judges became, in effect, witnesses of the trial proceedings."[34]

Other early modern court systems supervised judges in similar ways. Ulinka Rublack depicts the "extraordinarily tight" interaction between the professional jurists at the duke's court in early modern Württemberg and local judges, amateurs who held their positions as sinecures, some hereditarily. Particularly in criminal cases, Württemberg judges were required to submit minutes of court proceedings, seek permission for torture and executions and obtain legal referrals from University jurists; "the questions for the interrogation of suspects were also often pre-formulated by the supreme council or the Tübingen lawyers."[35] Muscovite governors did not have universities to turn to, but secretaries in the chanceries played the same role.

Threat and punishment also encouraged provincial governors and their staffs to use uniform procedure and application of the law. Communications between local judges and the center did not always enumerate the

[33] Innes, "Charlemagne's Government," 81–2; Ottoman documents, Imber, *Ottoman Empire*, 226–7, 236–7; Kaya Sahin, Tulane University, personal communication; Moore, "Treating Law as Knowledge."

[34] Collins, *Reanimated Voices*, 179, 73 and "Speech Reporting," 271, 273. Read aloud to tsar or chancery judges: ZA no. 233 (1636); AMG II: no. 444 (1650); RGADA f. 159, op. 3, Novgorod chetvert, no. 1618, fol. 53v (1682); PSZ II: nos. 1140 (1685), 1174 (1686). Read aloud to governors: AMG II: no. 264 (1645); RGADA f. 1122, op. 2, pt. 2, no. 1629, fol. 11 (1674); RGADA f. 210, Prikaznyi stol, no. 793, fol. 258 (1681); RGADA f. 1107, no. 3284, fol. 1 (1686).

[35] Rublack, *Crimes of Women*, 52.

consequences of not following proper procedure, but governors heard plenty of that elsewhere. The 1497, 1550 and 1589 Law Codes were to a great extent concerned with defining court procedure, setting fees for services, disciplining judges and scribes for corruption, and punishing litigants for abuse of the judicial process. The 1649 Ulozhenie's massive tenth chapter (with 287 articles, it constitutes about a third of the entire code of 967 articles) continues this policing role. Furthermore, in the orders governors were given at the start of their appointments, they were warned that failure to obey the tsar's orders and any official corruption would yield "great disgrace," "destruction," confiscation of lands, fines or worse, "as the tsar decrees." Individual decrees and law codes spelled out such consequences as well. As Chapter 4 details, the state made good on these threats, punishing corrupt officials and, in so doing, deterring others.

Governors as judges got the point. In correspondence with the center justifying their actions when accused of wrongdoing, the first thing they referred to was "the tsar's order": they did nothing not covered in their "orders." Conversely, when litigants accused an official of corruption, they charged him with acting "without the tsar's order." One litigant in 1670 claimed that his wife was wrongly tortured, "without the tsar's order and without investigation."[36] Officials accused of improper procedure fiercely defended themselves: in 1655, for example, a governor appealed to the center, saying he had been wrongfully accused and imprisoned for failing to muster the troops. He explained how he had indeed done his job and asked them to clear his name. In 1672 in the Tula area, the governor vociferously objected to the allegation that he had not sufficiently supported the work of an investigator (*syshchik*); so energetically had he himself sought out criminals, he said, that he brought one defendant to torture four times![37] These local officials, after all, lived on the edge; they needed the lands, cash and in-kind support that service provided.

The state did not hesitate to punish infractions by officials from scribes to governors. For obvious malfeasance, punishment was harsh, as when in 1605/6 an undersecretary's hand was cut off for doctoring land records and in 1676/7 when the Military Service Chancery not only ordered an undersecretary knouted and dismissed from his job, but also ordered all other chanceries not to hire him. His crime: altering a verdict after the

36 Novombergskii, *Koldovstvo*, no. 22 (1670).

37 RGADA f. 210, Sevsk stol, no. 148, fols. 504–15 (1655); RGADA f. 210, Sevsk stol, no. 283, fols. 335–49, 378–80 (1672). Three times was the usual limit for torture; see Chapter 6.

transcript had been signed off by the secretary. Similarly, in 1690 a local undersecretary in the Chuvash territory swindled locals by having them affix their seals to blank documents on which he then wrote false loan agreements. He was fired and brought to Moscow for further investigation. In 1701 two other undersecretaries were ordered knouted for composing fake documents and seeking bribes. Moscow also policed its officials for less egregious offenses, such as mistakes in official paperwork. In-house, layers of approval generally kept chanceries from issuing documents with mistakes in them, but when it happened, punishment was swift. In 1658, for example, an undersecretary in the Patriarch's Court Chancery was knouted at the Military Service Chancery before his assembled compatriots for a mistake in the tsar's title.[38]

In the provinces, punishment could befall both judges and scribes, although with deference to social rank. In 1663, for example, the Orel brigandage elder was imprisoned for a week for sending a document with a mistake in the tsar's name to the Felony Chancery, and his scribe who had read it aloud to Chancery judges in Moscow was ordered beaten "mercilessly with bastinadoes, instead of the knout" with his shirt removed to intensify the punishment. Similarly, in 1666 a governor in Sapozhok sent to Moscow a memo in which the tsar's title was written incorrectly. The Military Service Chancery threatened to knout him and dismiss him from his job, but "for your simpleness and lack of understanding," it pardoned him and reduced the punishment to a token two days in prison. The undersecretary who wrote the document, however, was to be beaten mercilessly with bastinadoes. In 1669 the Mozhaisk governor unwittingly sent to Moscow reports that had been written by his undersecretary with unnamed "inappropriate words." For that, the Military Service Chancery fired off a stern rebuke: the governor was ordered imprisoned for a day simply for accepting the reports, and his undersecretary was ordered beaten with bastinadoes mercilessly. Even sterner was the rebuke sent to a general and his undersecretary in 1670 for using the wrong terminology to describe the greetings that an emissary from the tsar had expressed when he arrived at their unit ("you were supposed to report that he had given you the tsar's *merciful message* but you said that he *had asked for your health*"). For this incorrect turn of phrase the Military Service

[38] *Opis' arkhiva 1626*, pt. 1, 263–4 (1605/6); Novokhatko, *Razriad v 185 godu*, 359–60 (1676/7). PSZ III: no. 1387 (1690); RGADA f. 210, Prikaznyi stol, no. 965, fols. 43–8 and 152–69 (two cases 1701). PSZ I: no. 233 (1658).

Chancery labeled the responsible scribe "a petty undersecretary, a field laborer and a field laborer's son and a little cheat" and decreed harsh corporal punishment.[39]

Chancery staffs internalized these rules, as is clear from an incident in Moscow in 1669. An undersecretary of the Military Service Chancery recognized official documents in the stall of a silk merchant in Moscow and went straightaway to an undersecretary in the Chancery responsible for the market neighborhood and explained the breach of security. They immediately went to the market and found the merchant and documents, which they identified as drafts of chancery paperwork. In interrogation the merchant testified that he had taken the documents in exchange for silk from a widow and was using them to wrap merchandise. He claimed he did not know it was wrong to have such documents. Chancery judges responded not only by punishing him, but also by issuing a decree to the elders of all the merchant rows, making it their responsibility to inform merchants that they are forbidden to buy paper with writing on it "if it is chancery writing and not students' writing"; the elders would be held responsible and given "harsh marketplace punishment" for breaking this rule.[40]

These might seem like petty infractions; ideally legal culture (respect for the law, the tsar's sovereignty) would be internalized enough for small mistakes to be tolerated. But they evidence the determination with which Moscow tried to enforce a single bureaucratic culture and law. The centralized Muscovite state leaned on its bureaucrats to provide consistent judicial expertise. The military elite provided symbolic leadership, but the bureaucrats had behind-the-scenes authority. A dramatic statement of this relationship is presented in 1634 in the treason verdict of General Mikhail Borisovich Shein. Addressing the two secretaries on his staff, the verdict noted: General Shein "did not listen to you in anything, he insulted you and treated you worse than prison guards, and gave you no authority, and you did everything at his orders unwillingly." The secretaries were released, but the general was executed.[41]

39 PSZ I: no. 351 (1663). RGADA f. 210, Prikaznyi stol, no. 985, fols. 507–9 (1666). PSZ I: nos. 458 (1669), 485 (1670). Similar cases: RGADA f. 210, Prikaznyi stol, no. 655, fols. 48–56 (1671); no. 872, fols. 293–4 (1685); no. 898, fols. 188–9 (1685); no. 1867, fols. 143–6 (1695); RGADA f. 210, Sevsk stol, no. 294, fols. 269–71 (1677). On social deference in punishment, see Chapters 9–10.

40 RGADA f. 210, Prikaznyi stol, no. 786, fols. 305–12 (1669).

41 AAE III: no. 251 (1634). On Shein's execution, see Chapter 15.

A LAWYERLY CLASS?

Clearly scribes provided judicial expertise to military men in local and chancery courts. But who provided legal advice to litigants? Cases show that plaintiffs of all social origins – no matter how lowly, even litigants who could not sign their own names – filed cases with proper terminology and properly cited law. For example, reflecting their own or their scribes' knowledge of the law, litigants specifically included in their petitions the request that a "bailiff" be sent out to inspect a dead body or arrest a suspect;[42] in 1649 a gentryman petitioned that his son had been tortured "without a trial and without an inquisitory confrontation and without any material evidence," citing some of the preconditions for the use of torture. A case of 1651 includes a soldier's request that the sentence levied on two men for homicide be carried out. His petition uses legal phraseology (calling the men "known criminals") and a stock phrase ("so that they in the future will find it ill-advised [*nepovadno*] to commit crime and lay in wait and kill people on the roads"). A knowledgeable scribe clearly shaped this prose. Also in 1651, a defendant first pleaded self-defense to a charge of homicide (which would have reduced his guilt). In face-to-face confrontation with his accusers, however, he dropped the claim. The first plea smacks of shaping his testimony to suit the law, perhaps on professional advice.[43]

Where did litigants get such lawyerly advice? A few sources come to mind, starting with undersecretaries themselves and assistants to whom litigants entrusted their cases. The latter, however, seems less likely. For criminal trials no intermediaries were allowed; the judge and scribe investigated directly. In the accusatory form of trial (see Chapter 5), litigants were allowed to send substitutes if they were called away to service or were otherwise unable to attend a trial: the law recognizes "fathers sending sons, brothers brothers, uncles nephews." The law also allowed litigants, again in non-criminal trials, to bring their case to third-party mediators, although it also expressed concern about mediators testifying falsely for bribes.[44] There is no indication that such substitutes

42 Send a bailiff: RGADA f. 1107, nos. 600, fol. 1 (1632); 774, fol. 1 (1637), 1155, fol. 2 (1648); 1219, fol. 1 (1650); 1423, fol. 1 (1657); 1926, fol. 1 (1671); 2340, fol. 3 (1676); 2249, fol. 1 (1675); 2454, fol. 2 (1677); 2758, fol. 1 (1680).

43 RGADA f. 210, Prikaznyi stol, no. 263, fols. 512–13 (1649). Soldier: RGADA f. 141 1651, no. 58, pt. 2, fols. 196–214, 280 (1651). Self-defense: RGADA f. 141 1651, no. 58, pt. 1, fols. 1–4 (1651).

44 Send substitutes: ZA no. 188, art. 1, p. 149 (1628); Ulozhenie ch. 10, arts. 108–9, 156, 157: RZ III: 113–14, 126; PSZ II: no. 1158 (1686); PSZ III: no. 1363 (1690). Agreements to use a mediator (*tretie*): AAE III: no. 277 (1637); AIuB I: nos. 123 (I) (1679), 123 (II) (1688), 123 (III) (1691). Process defined: Ulozhenie ch. 15, art. 5: RZ III: 163. This sort of trial: Kavelin, *Osnovnye nachala*, 147–51, 345;

or mediators were professionals with legal training; people selected friends or community members for such roles.

A third likely locus of legal advocacy was the trained staffs that large landholders employed. For secular and clerical landlords, specialized individuals were assigned to "take care of cases." They lobbied chanceries, worked their landlord's patronage networks and presented cases in court. The scurrilous rogue Frol Skobeev was said to make his living as a "great cheat, who looked after other people's legal affairs."[45] One other repository of judicial knowledge might have played a lawyerly role: the "town-square" scribes in major centers.

In every community there were professional scribes who wrote petitions, contracts and other documents for litigants to present to the governor's court, a chancery, a customs office or other establishments. Known as town-square scribes (*ploshchadnye podiachie*), they are an elusive group, not included in enumerations of social ranks but cited often enough to show that they performed vital functions.

Town-square scribes are noted from the 1540s or so, although the practice is probably older than that. They are cited in the sixteenth century in towns such as Novgorod, Tver′, Pereiaslavl′ Zalesskii, Pskov and Ivangorod, in addition to Moscow. They were not employees of the state; they "lived from the pen" by charging per document. They organized as a guild, limiting membership to maintain good income. Self-imposed limits of ten such scribes working for one chancery in Moscow in 1691 and sixteen in Kostroma in 1685–97 are recorded, while the number of such scribes in Ivanov Square in Moscow averaged about thirty from 1649 to the early 1680s. Town-square scribes selected an elder who kept registers of their work and oversaw its accuracy.[46]

As just suggested, Moscow had several groups of town-square scribes. The Military Service, Musketeer, Slavery and Foreign Affairs Chanceries, as well as patriarchal chanceries, sponsored collectives of such notaries to serve petitioners to their offices. Important squares around town also hosted them, the most important being Ivanov Square by the Kremlin

Shtamm, "Sud i protsess," 222–4; Hellie, *Slavery*, 275–80. Concern about false testimony: ZA no. 42 (1582).

45 Frol Skobeev: *Pamiatniki literatury XVII vek*, I: 59. References to such staff (*striapchie* in church institutions): ZA no. 42 (1582); PSZ II: no. 857 (1681); Sedov, "Podnoshenia"; Novokhatko, "Upravlentsy."

46 Zlotnikov, "Podiachie Ivanovskoi ploshchadi," 95, 102–3, 119–20. A town-square scribe is depicted in Act I, Scene I of Modest Mussorsky's opera *Khovanshchina*. Instruction to elder: AI I: no. 149 (1687). Selling such services as a monopoly was forbidden at mid century: AAE III: no. 295 (1640).

"Ivan" Belltower. These men served the busy traffic of litigants to the many chanceries that did not have their own coterie of notaries. Across the realm, all documents – petitions, wills, loan and slavery contracts, deeds, rental contracts for shops and contracts for hiring workers – could be written by non-state notaries. They were considered trusted professionals in their own right; when Moscow burned in 1626, not only chancery scribes but also "those who write on the squares, village and church clerks" were recruited to help restore records. In a case of 1636 in Novgorod the governor called in local town-square scribes to identify the handwriting and signature of a contested document. The Ulozhenie of 1649 went further in recognizing them: it considered authentic only documents affirmed by town-square scribes in towns and Moscow; documents written by village or estate scribes were not to be accepted and those written by literate people should be witnessed and registered by town-square scribes.[47]

Why is the existence of these various cadres of people literate in the law important? First, some, such as the town-square scribes, served as a recruitment pool for the state, particularly in the countryside.[48] Second, they provided expertise to litigants. They knew the proper form of a petition; they knew enough to suggest to litigants what to ask for or how to plead. Natalie Zemon Davis eloquently showed how French notaries who wrote appeals for pardon to the king shaped petitioners' stories. Notaries knew the formulary, the law and the turns of phrase to win mercy for their client.[49] They also thereby shaped how one sees the law in practice. In the cases surveyed here, knowledgeable scribes seem to have had similar influence. In 1699, for example, a townsman from Lukh requested that the defendants in his misdemeanor assault case be questioned "separately," an element in the inquisitorial form of court procedure that had only two years earlier been extended to misdemeanor trials. A petition in 1694 filed by the Greek scholars of the Likhud family deftly mobilizes the terminology and practice of Muscovite procedure. Ioannikii Likhud sued that his son had been falsely accused of rape; the son, Nikolai, also petitioned, charging a court official with trying to extort a false confession from him and charging his accusers with lying. Although

47 Zlotnikov, "Podiachie Ivanovskoi ploshchadi," 100 (1626). SIDG no. 60, p. 81 (1636); similar case: PSZ III: no. 1387 (1690). Ulozhenie ch. 10, arts. 246–53: RZ III: 144–6. Kathryn Burns on the nature of "truth" embodied in notarial records: "Notaries, Truth."

48 Demidova, *Sluzhilaia biurokratiia*, 63–4.

49 Davis, *Fiction in the Archives*, 15–25. Critical opinion on the veracity of court depositions: Gaskill, "Reporting Murder," 2–3.

affecting the humble prose typical of petitions (an ignorant foreigner, "I do not know trials and face-to-face confrontations and how transcripts are written"), Ioanniki Likhud's petition knowledgeably noted that although his son had been threatened with torture, grounds for torture had not been met (no accusations by felons, no material evidence and no confession). The son not only cited chapter and verse of the Ulozhenie but also identified the proper jurisdiction for his case.[50] The state was apparently distrustful of spreading such knowledge, even as it insisted on proper formulas in documents: the 1669 Criminal Articles forbid court personnel to distribute to litigants or to witnesses in community surveys "model letters (*obraztsovye pisma*)" for petitions and testimony.[51] The Articles' anxiety over "model letters" suggests the court's wishful desire to hear litigants' authentic voices (even though a good scribe would know how to craft it); modern students of Muscovite judicial paperwork should keep in mind that they were filtered by scribal voices.

These various literate people, particularly town-square scribes, could play the role of de facto lawyers. Notaries in other early modern settings certainly functioned in this way, giving individuals access to the legal system at the same time as they acted as extralegal arms of enforcing the king's law.[52] Not until 1864 was the legal profession created in Russia, but these pockets of expertise provided the knowledge people needed to make the system work for them.

ELECTED COMMUNITY OFFICIALS

Supported by knowledgeable bureaucratic staff, governors still faced challenges in finding police and judicial staff, as exemplified by a complaint from the governor in Oskol in 1635. When the town executioner died, the governor recruited a new one from among the guards of the town gates. Other such guards then began to leave that service rather than be next in line for the unpleasant job. Petitioning to Moscow, the gate watchmen appealed to the state's purse strings: they advised that an executioner should be recruited from among people who had no work, not from people like themselves who served and paid taxes. The governor consulted Moscow and the Military Service Chancery supported the

50 RGADA f. 210, Prikaznyi stol, no. 1378, fol. 44 (1699). RGADA f. 210, Prikaznyi stol, no. 1710, fols. 162, 237–42, 332–5, quote fols. 333–333v (1694).

51 1669 Criminal Articles, arts. 28 and 120: PRP VII: 408, 433. 1679 charter to governor of Arzamas repeated this prohibition: Iakovlev (ed.), *Namestnichie*, 97.

52 Burns, "Notaries, Truth."

watchmen: "for the work of torturing" the governor is "to order a man selected from the unregistered ["wandering people" or *guliashchie liudi*] . . . not in [state] service, and who do not pay taxes."[53] In this case, the governor's ability to staff his office conflicted with other municipal tasks such as gate watch. In other cases the very mode of recruitment posed unwelcome burdens on communities and undermined judicial work.

Governors had at their disposal only a small paid staff; they included undersecretaries, bailiffs (*nedel'shchiki, pristavy*) and couriers (*rozsylshchiki*). Bailiffs, according to an oath from 1568, did such duties as collecting fees, overseeing convicts and participating in trials. Also under the governor's command were regiments of musketeers, cossacks or artillerymen who could be sent on assignment. In 1638, for example, in Beloozero, artillerymen arrested and brought in a man who had been accused of stabbing another; in another case, they arrested the wife of a man implicated in a murder when he himself could not be found.[54]

Much of a governor's or brigandage elder's staff, however, were not supported by an annual stipend but were selected by their community to serve as part of the community's and individual's service obligation to the tsar (*vybornye*). This includes brigandage wardens (*tseloval'niki*, second in command to the elder; they also oversaw the prison), brigandage scribes, prison guards, executioners and town criers (*birichi*). In addition, gentrymen were expected to help the brigandage elder or governor hunt down criminals; where there were few gentry, townsmen and peasants, cossacks and musketeers were mobilized. Villages fought neighborhood crime by designating officials: hundredmen (*sotskie*), fifty-men (*piatidesiatskie*) and decurions (*desiatskie*).[55] Hundredmen's oaths confirm that their work was fundamentally criminal justice: in 1699 in the northwest, for example, hundredmen were to ensure that in their community there would be no "fighting, theft, murder, illegal alcohol, sex crimes, gambling and libel, arson, tobacco, any criminality (*vorovstvo*)" and that "no thieves, robbers,

53 AMG II: no. 4 (1635).

54 Oath: AIu no. 289 (1568). Annual salary: AIu no. 44 (1568). Bailiffs: 1497 Law Code, arts. 28–31, 34–5, 44: RZ II: 57–8, 60. 1550 Law Code, arts. 32, 47–9, 53–4, 99: RZ II: 102, 105–7, 120; Ulozhenie ch. 10, arts. 142–8: RZ III: 123–4. RGADA f. 1107, no. 823, fol. 1 and no. 824, fol. 2 (both 1638).

55 Selection was mandated from sixteenth-century brigandage charters to 1669 Criminal Articles: Iakovlev (ed.), *Namestnichie*, no. 9, p. 80 (1586); 1669 Criminal Articles, art. 116: PRP VII: 431. Officers in action: AAE I: no. 244 (1555); RGADA f. 1107, no. 1423, fol. 1 (1657); RGADA f. 1107, no. 1548, fol. 3 (1662); RGADA f. 1596, no. 8, fols. 1, 2 and RGADA f. 210, Prikaznyi stol, no. 959, fol. 9 (both 1662). Hundredmen and other village police officials in the North: Bogoslovskii, "Zemskoe samoupravlenie," vol. 1, *Chteniia* (1910), bk. 1, p. 314; Chicherin, *Oblastnye uchrezhdeniia*, 469–70, 486–7. Elected service: Bulgakov, *Gosudarstvennye sluzhby* and "Struktury posadskogo samoupravleniia"; Glaz'ev, *Vlast' i obshchestvennost'*, 38.

traitors, runaway serfs, religious dissenters, foreigners, Germans, Poles, Tatars and spies" should live in the region. They were to arrest criminals and bring them into the brigandage office, suffering "fines and harsh corporal punishment" for dereliction of duty. One sees such police officials throughout the realm: in 1701 the Nerchinsk governor was instructed to have his peasant communities select elders and officers to seek out crime.[56]

In these ways the state leaned on local communities to fight crime. One benefit of this practice was that it put responsibility on the people most affected to support state administration. In selecting such officials, communities pledged to obey them, cooperate in posses, do no crime themselves and provide for these officials' upkeep. Appointment charters also warned these officials to do their job honorably and not to favor or seek bribes.[57] Nevertheless, such selected service and upkeep for it were burdensome to individuals and communities. The subvention paid by the town of Shuia for its brigandage office in 1631 included "the salaries of the brigandage scribe and wardens, guards, executioner, town crier, paper, firewood and all the prison-related expenses." Brigandage staff were to use their own horses ("since they are given salary"), not the tsar's or community's horses, an indication of how this system was constructed on the cheapest basis.[58] Sources are full of communities resisting these fees. In 1625, for example, the gentry of Murom complained that a local monastery and the Murom townsmen were claiming immunity from sharing the cost of the brigandage office; the Felony Chancery denied such immunity and ordered them all to share the costs. Eventually a general statement that no immunities from brigandage obligations were to be tolerated was issued in 1637.[59]

Furthermore, the state deployed primarily moral pressure to force selected officials to do a good job. They took oaths of office, swearing before God and to the tsar, which was a serious obligation; sometimes communities put up surety bond as guarantee (on penalty of paying a fee should the person in question not fulfill his obligations). Nevertheless, incentives for working less than energetically were rife, as discussed in the

56 Hundredmen oaths: AI I: no. III (1683); AIuB II: no. 230 (XL) (1699). AIu no. 288 (1690). PSZ IV: no. 1822 (1701).

57 Bogoslovskii, "Zemskoe samoupravlenie," vol. I, *Chteniia* (1910), bk. I, chs. 15–17 and "Mirskoi vybor zemskogo sudeiki, 1659 g." AIu no. 288 (1690).

58 AIuB II: no. 246 (V), col. 749 (1631). Similar list for Serpukhov and Kolomna: AAE II: no. 19 (1601); AIu no. 352, p. 378 (1663). Horses: AAE III: no. 276 (1637), quote on 420; AAE III: no. 163 (1625).

59 AAE III: no. 163 (1625). ZA no. 246 (1637). Communities refuse support: Glaz'ev, *Vlast' i obshchestvennost'*, 193–200; Chicherin, *Oblastnye uchrezhdeniia*, 470–6.

next chapter. Here, in conclusion the example of the executioners showcases the challenges governors faced in staffing their judicial work.

EXECUTIONERS

The executioner (*palach, zaplechnyi master*) administered whippings and other torments for torture and judicial punishment and carried out executions. Unlike some countries, where executioners came from hereditary outcast classes, in Muscovy it was simply another job in the brigandage or governor's office.[60] It was the community's responsibility to select or hire an executioner when they were setting up a brigandage district. A 1601 directive to Serpukhov and Kolomna lists the expectations for staffing: "in those towns we ordered there to be a brigandage warden, a scribe, a prison guard, an executioner and a town crier ... they are to change in this job annually." Numerous documents attest to communities acknowledging this obligation, such as appointment charters for local judges in the Far North and a receipt in which a "town crier and executioner" accepted his annual upkeep (in cash and goods) from the "farming people" of the Vladimir Uspenskii convent.[61] A document from Shuia in 1631 shows the community delivering to the governor funds it had collected for the executioner's upkeep; he then transferred it to the brigandage office. In a provincial town in 1617 the executioner was paid 12 rubles annual salary, while the prison guard received 10.5.[62]

Sometimes communities could not afford these burdens. In 1625 in Murom, for example, local gentry complained that, because they could not collect sufficient funds, most of the governor's staff – the guards, the executioner and the town crier – had left and that they had had to hire prison guards at high prices. The 1649 Ulozhenie instituted salaries for executioners in the city of Moscow to be paid by the Felony Chancery, but local communities were still responsible until September 1680, when provincial executioners were given an annual salary, paid from the income

[60] Executioners in Germany: Stuart, *Defiled Trades*, esp. ch. 3; Roper, *Witch Craze*, 53. Little has been written on Muscovite executioners: Chicherin, *Oblastnye uchrezhdeniia*, 469; Torke, *Die staatsbedingte Gesellschaft*, 56–7.

[61] AAE II: no. 19 (1601). Bogoslovskii, "Zemskoe samoupravlenie," vol. 1, *Chteniia* (1910), bk. 1, pp. 86–7, no. 5 (1652) and "Mirskoi vybor zemskogo sudeiki, 1659 g." Other such payments: AIu no. 352 (1663); AIu no. 223 (VII) (1659).

[62] AIuB II: no. 246 (V) (1631). Bulgakov, *Gosudarstvennye sluzhby*, 157–8 (1617). Other examples: Glaz'ev, *Vlast' i obshchestvennost'*, 201.

of the brigandage office.[63] Salaries seem not to have materialized, however. The Kostensk governor complained in 1696 that his office, home and prison were in disrepair and the executioner had died; he was instructed have an executioner selected from the "unregistered." In response to the persistent governor of Belev, who wrote repeatedly in 1701 and 1702, the Artillery Chancery was ordered to see to the dilapidated town fortifications and the new urban ministry, the Ratusha, was told to have town elders of Belev select an executioner.[64]

The repugnance of the executioner's job made staffing always difficult. Sources are replete with governors complaining that they have no executioner and cannot find one.[65] Some governors simply put cases on hold; others recruited someone close at hand, often over their protests. In 1621 the governor of Dankov recruited a cossack to be an executioner; in 1632 when the governor of Valuiki reported that he had no executioner, Moscow ordered him to "have one selected from the local people." The governor of Evfremov faced a similar quandary in 1649. He reported that he had no executioner and was therefore unable to pursue a homicide case. The previous executioner had been a musketeer who was still living in town, but that man reported that he had been forced to take the role by the previous governor and would not do it again. Another local man had experience as an executioner, but he had taken tonsure as a monk and was therefore not available. Reminding the tsar that he could not recruit an executioner from the army ranks, the governor asked for guidance. In 1682 for the rushed job of executing Princes Ivan and Andrei Khovanskie, no executioner was available, so a musketeer was dragooned for the task. In a homicide case of 1684 in Beloozero, the torture was administered by the brigandage prison guard.[66]

Lacking a hereditary caste for this purpose, ultimately the state needed to clarify where executioners were to come from. The 1649 Ulozhenie decreed that executioners in Moscow should be selected from non-serving people (*volnye liudi*) guaranteed by surety bond by local residents. As for provincial towns, however, the Ulozhenie simply decreed that

[63] AAE III: no. 163 (1625). 1649 Ulozhenie ch. 21, arts. 96–7: RZ III: 246. Provincial executioners: PSZ I: nos. 779 and 780 (1679); PSZ II: no. 836 (1680).

[64] Glaz'ev, *Vlast' i obshchestvennost'*, 159. RGADA f. 210, Sevsk stol, nos. 484, fol. 333 (1701) and 150, fols. 86–9 (1702).

[65] Difficulty staffing: Chicherin, *Oblastnye uchrezhdeniia*, 488; Torke, *Die staatsbedingte Gesellschaft*, ch. 2. Governors' complaints: AMG I: no. 141 (1621); Glaz'ev, *Vlast' i obshchestvennost'*, 196, 213 (1628); AMG I: no. 325 (1632).

[66] AMG I: no. 141 (1621). AMG I: no. 325 (1632). RGADA f. 210, Belgorod stol, no. 270, fol. 478 (1649). Matveev, "Zapiski," 45 (1682). RGADA f. 1107, no. 3187, fols. 4, 5 (1684).

communities should select them. In 1681 the state improved the situation by decreeing that governors should appoint as executioners volunteers from townsmen (*posadskie liudi*) or, lacking volunteers, they should order the urban commune to select someone from their most junior ranks or from unregistered people, "so that no town would not have an executioner."[67]

Shame might have played a role here, but it is not explicitly cited in seventeenth-century Russian sources. A German observer, Adam Olearius, made this assumption: "They formerly did not consider the office of executioner as infamous and dishonorable as they do now. Now no honest or notable person has friendly relations with someone who has been whipped unless false witness was given against him, or unless he was wrongly punished because of the judge's enmity toward him." Nevertheless, he went on to say that Muscovite executioners made good money, taking in bribes from victims and selling prisoners alcohol. Peter I's reforms explicitly introduced the European-style sense of honor and shame that Olearius referred to. On the one hand, Peter declared that individuals who had been touched by the executioner's hands (using the German term *profos*) would no longer be honorable or serve in honorable positions. On the other hand, he tried to dissociate the executioner himself from shame: "no one is to despise a general-provost (*geval'diger*), executioner or other servitors of the court when they are carrying out their duties." But, as Abby Schrader shows in her study of corporal punishment, the position of executioner became so shameful over the course of the eighteenth century that the government was reduced to recruiting them from criminals and to isolating them from society. By contrast, in Schrader's words, in Muscovy "an executioner was just another skilled workman who made an honest living."[68] That might be overstating the case: executioners in Muscovy were not an outcast class, but no one particularly wanted to do the job.

The challenge of staffing the executioner position was symptomatic of the more general problem of staffing in an economy of scarcity. Muscovy was a huge and sparsely settled empire at a latitude and climate that supported only subsistence agriculture. Particularly for local government, Muscovy's centralization efforts were often stymied by these harsh realities.

[67] Ulozhenie ch. 21, art. 96: RZ III: 246; PSZ II: no. 868 (1681).

[68] Olearius, *Travels*, 231–2. Executioner's hands: 1715 Military articles, ch. 24, art. 209: RZ IV: 365. Not to despise: 1715 Military Articles, ch. 23, art. 204: RZ IV: 364. Eighteenth century: Schrader, *Languages*, 38–46, quote on 39; Anisimov, *Dyba i knut*, 537–9.

For executioners, the government eventually offered salary to make sure the job was done. One might ask why the state did not create a salaried officialdom everywhere instead of relying on communities to select staff. The question prompts some general reflections. Tradition and cost probably explain why the centralizing Muscovite state leaned so heavily on community participation. The custom of communities selecting members to perform public service was an old one among the East Slavs. From earliest times through the nineteenth century, family patriarchs constituted village boards of elders to govern and act as liaisons with landlords and state officials. European and Russian social thought of the nineteenth century idealized such communal organization (as well as communal agricultural cooperation) as constituting native roots of democratization and socialism. Russian historians in the late nineteenth and early twentieth centuries, buoyed by the rise of political parties and elected government in the years flanking 1905, looked to the Muscovite period for evidence of Russian roots of democracy and found it in the early modern custom of selecting officials for local self governance. M. M. Bogoslovskii's pioneering studies of institutions of village government in the Russian North in the seventeenth century demonstrated thriving peasant self-government: locally selected judges (*zemskie sudeiki*) carried out most adjudication, working with governors on criminal cases. In this scholars such as Boris Chicherin and Bogoslovskii looked for a political opposition between central authority (*prikaznoe*) and that of elected (*zemskoe*) officials, but more recently, scholars see no such opposition but rather cooperation, or at least compliance with state authority.[69]

It is not surprising that the Muscovite state took advantage of such traditions when setting up local criminal justice. Involving the community in adjudication is attested in Moscow's earliest law codes: communities paid fees for unsolved homicides;[70] the 1497 and 1550 Law Codes mandated that the grand prince's judges work in the presence of

[69] Peasant communal government: Hoch, *Serfdom and Social Control*. Selections of *zemskie* judges: AIu no. 332 (1557–81). Chicherin, *Oblastnye uchrezhdeniia*, 471; Bogoslovskii, "Zemskoe samoupravlenie." Denying opposition, particularly with regard to brigandage elders: Torke, *Die staatsbedingte Gesellschaft*; Glaz'ev, *Vlast' i obshchestvennost'*, 67–8, 135; Keep, "Bandits and the Law," 216; Sedov, *Zakat*, 403–10. Modern studies of communities of the north: Shveikovskaia, *Gosudarstvo i krestiane Rossii*; Torke, *Die staatsbedingte Gesellschaft*; Zhukov, *Upravlenie i samoupravlenie*.

[70] Fees for unidentified bodies cited as early as the Rus' Law: Kaiser (trans. and ed.), *Laws of Rus'*, art. 3, p. 20. Fee in the seventeenth century was four rubles, four *altyn* and one and a half *dengi*: 1669 Criminal Articles, no. 124: PRP VII: 433–4; RGADA f. 1107, nos. 703, fol. 16 (1635) and 1929 (1671); RGADA f. 210, Prikaznyi stol, no. 1151, fols. 107–20 (1676).

community elders and leading members (*starosta, lutshchie liudi*). Even though this practice faded, engagement with the community endured in the custom whereby, for example, locally selected witnesses were called upon (*poniatye*) to witness arrests or inspections of dead bodies and to provide surety bonds (*poruka*) for defendants, witnesses and those convicted in all manner of trials.[71]

Engaging the community in mandatory service was also cheaper for Moscow, a key non-cash fiscal strategy to support the center's state-building project.[72] Historians have termed this aspect of Russian society "patrimonial," "liturgical," or even evidence of a "slave mentality," as if Russians embraced their bondage to the state.[73] But none of these terms is helpful; psychologizing is unnecessary. Moscow's service society was a strategic expedient in a resource-deprived setting to accomplish the state's goals of social control, territorial expansion and enriching the elite.

Given the difficulties of staffing, one wonders why the state would put so much effort into the judicial system. V. N. Glaz′ev commented that the Felony Chancery "worked hard" to ensure that communities selected local brigandage staff and that they served effectively. Peter B. Brown marvels at the "robust spirit of professionalism" and "service ethos" exhibited by chancery scribes whose fees hardly covered the cost of the system or their salaries; he explains these attitudes by reference to scribes' expectation of good remuneration by working to the top of the ladder; fear of punishment or dismissal through frequent job reviews; the prestige of practicing literacy; and the religious basis of their oath of office.[74]

Valerie Kivelson provides perhaps another explanation of why the state and its officers cared about providing a good judiciary. She argues that state legitimacy was predicated on a sort of social contract. People served, knowing that the tsar would take care of them. It was the tsar's obligation

71 Work with local representatives: 1497 Law Code, art. 38: RZ II: 59; 1550 Law Code, arts. 62, 68: RZ II: 109, 112. AAE I: no. 196 (II) (1542); DAI I: no. 87 (1555); Bogoslovskii, "Zemskoe samoupravlenie," *Chteniia* (1912), bk. II, pp. 180–3. Surety: 1550 Law Code, arts. 56–7: RZ II: 107–8. 1555 Medyn Charter, arts. 2, 6: PRP IV: 181–3. 1616/17 Felony Handbook, art. 2: PRP V: 189.

72 Fiscal underpinnings of state-building: Hellie, "Russia"; Hartley, "Russia as a Fiscal-Military State." Enserfment was another such non-cash fiscal strategy.

73 Patrimonial: Pipes, *Russia under the Old Regime*, 22–4. "Liturgical," meaning service, not religious rite: Mousnier, *Social Hierarchies*, ch. 9. Slavery trope: Poe, *'A People Born to Slavery'*; Rancour-Laferriere, *Slave Soul of Russia*, 1–2. Different perspectives on why the elite accepted mandatory service: Pipes, *Russia under the Old Regime*, xxi–xxii; Hellie, "Thoughts on the Absence"; Poe, *'A People Born to Slavery'* and "What Did Russians Mean"; Kollmann, *By Honor Bound*; Kondratieva, *Gouverner et nourrir.*

74 Glaz′ev, *Vlast′ i obshchestvennost′*, 204; Brown, "Service Land Chancellery Clerks," 65–6 and "With All Deliberate Speed," 137, 145.

to protect the innocent, feed the poor and distribute Christian charity and mercy. In the law these expectations resulted in a paradoxical dilemma: studying land disputes, she shows that the Service Land Chancery strove manfully to resolve cases of endless complexity (exacerbated by litigants' clever manipulations), attributing their dogged dedication to the tsar's "inclusive, universal promise of administering justice fairly and mercifully." Such interaction not only affirmed the tsar's legitimacy but also integrated state and society.[75]

One can only agree, citing, for example, numerous tsarist decrees that express solicitude for local communities over the burdens of taxation and service. Decrees ordering the building of a new brigandage office in 1663 in the Novgorod area, for example, instruct officials to requisition the necessary construction, fees and offices from the community, but not to collect more in order to avoid hardship on the community. The order of 1679 abolishing the brigandage system and many other local offices spoke of reducing the burden on communities; a 1678 decree to undersecretaries of the Moscow Judicial Chancery instructed that when they are sent out to do a community survey, they should write up only the survey, not copy the entire case "so that the litigants do not suffer more red tape (*volokita*)."[76] The expressed solicitude might be weak comfort compared to the rigors of service, but it reflects a pragmatic understanding of the limits of the people's ability to support the state and also affirms the tsar's ideological position as shepherd to his people.

At some level, the state's efforts – although undermined by lack of resources and manpower – demonstrated its role of acting out the tsar's ideological obligations. At the same time people's insistent demands that the state rectify injustice – heard in individual and collective petitions from the Far North to Siberia to the southern frontier – testify to their confidence in the state's willingness to respond. The next two chapters examine how well the tsar's government responded to demands for investigations and trials.

[75] Kivelson, *Cartographies*, 53–4 and "Muscovite 'Citizenship'."

[76] AIu no. 352 (1663). PSZ II: nos. 779 and 780 (1679). PSZ II: no. 742 (1678).

CHAPTER 3

Staff and society

In 1676 in Beloozero the governor was investigating a death and the injury of eight men after a melee over disputed land between peasants of two landlords. The governor sent out the brigandage warden and a town square scribe to inspect the dead body and the wounded men, and he sent his bailiff to arrest the accused, who refused to come. But the worst defiance came when the governor instructed the hundredman of one of the villages to gather local people to witness an inspection of the disputed land. The elder of a village involved in the fracas refused to cooperate and tried to prevent them from proceeding. They went anyway and, the hundredman later reported, as they were camped at night across a river, men from that village shot at them.[1]

This case suggests how complicated local involvement in the judicial process could be. When murder struck, neighbors and kinsmen reported the deed and demanded justice. When brigands infested local roads, local people joined the governor or brigandage elder to root them out. But, by the same token, communities and individuals resisted when it served personal or local self-interest, even in the criminal law. Across early modern Europe, policing faced the same tensions, as it often depended upon community cooperation. In early modern England, for example, justices of the peace and coroners leaned on the assistance of locals. As in Muscovy, the discoverer of a dead body was to report it to the constable and summon the "hue and cry" to chase down suspects. In England village women were called upon to examine unwed women suspected of being pregnant or having delivered an illegitimate child. In such instances, people and officers could decide how energetically to cooperate or pursue their tasks. As Malcolm Gaskill comments, "all participants in pre-trial investigations of suspected homicides ... judged their actions according to loyalty to the Crown, state and law on one side, and an affinity with the

[1] RGADA f. 1107, no. 2305, fols. 1, 17 (1676); similar case: RGADA f. 1107, no. 1058, fol. 2 (1645).

political interests of the parish, region or county community on the other . . . If their behaviour seems capricious, inefficient, dishonest or even blatantly corrupt, then one needs to accept that the law and its agents existed as a resource for popular action as much as a constraint on it." Malcolm Greenshields makes the same observation regarding early modern France: the most "effective and numerous police force was unofficial, its investigations and pursuits spontaneous. For it was upon the great mass of the people in the Haute Auvergne that order ultimately depended."[2]

Sixteenth-century European towns displayed similar patterns. Studying Württemberg, R. W. Scribner notes that "the coercive force at the district governor's command was rather meagre." With only one or two constables in a governor's employ, "in great part policing depended on policing by consent, through the co-operation of the community." Reminding community members of their oath of allegiance to the state only went so far; communities withheld support when it suited their interests. People fled summonses, they refused arrest, they ignored officials and even attacked them. Ultimately, he concludes that "the orderly policing of the territorial state depended on the consent of its citizens, although this was often a grudging consent given only conditionally." In delegating police activities to the community, the early modern state weakened its local control.[3]

These challenges of local governance in England, France and the German lands were all paralleled in Muscovy. This chapter looks at communities' interactions with judicial officers in the early stages of a criminal case – initiating suits, carrying out arrests and detaining the accused.

REPORTING AND ARRESTING

As in early modern Europe, criminal cases in Muscovy were initiated by the aggrieved parties, rarely by the state. One foreign observer around 1671 relates that "if a man is murther'd, and no body prosecured his murtherer, the law takes no notice of his death." For brigandage felonies, once a case was initiated with the proper form of evidence, the court took over the investigation. For the highest crimes, cases could be initiated by the state, which actively pursued rebels, religious dissenters and the like. But such cases could also be brought by private accusation, in which case the

[2] Gaskill, *Crime and Mentalities*, ch. 7, 262. Greenshields, *Economy of Violence*, 58.

[3] Scribner, "Police and the Territorial State," 116.

accused had the right to a confrontation with his accuser (called an *izvetchik*), since material evidence might be lacking in allegations of sorcery or plots. Once a case was lodged, the governor's staff and community-based officials carried out the investigation. There were no formal organs of preliminary investigation.[4]

Homicide was the easiest crime for which to get local cooperation. V. N. Glaz′ev reports that in Voronezh, a dead body would be brought to the local church and the community would gather to view it while authorities were summoned. Our cases show various practices: sometimes the body was kept at the place of homicide (as in Beloozero in 1688) and at other times moved. In 1683 a dead body was removed from the scene of the crime to a nearby village; in 1699 one was brought back to the deceased's home; in 1714 a body was removed to a local monastery "under guard."[5]

For serious crime, locally selected police officials – hundredmen, fifty-men and decurions – often took the initiative. In 1657 a village's hundred-man and decurion initiated investigation when a peasant reported that his brother had been badly beaten by a neighbor. They tried to put the suspect on surety bond, but he refused to cooperate. The governor then backed them up by sending out three successive arresting parties, to no avail. In 1688 in Beloozero the fifty-man of a village took the lead in bringing "to the brigandage office to *stol′nik* and governor V. I. Korachagov" a peasant accused of killing another peasant while people were gathered around brewing beer for the upcoming holyday of St. Nicholas the Miracleworker. The fifty-man had already inspected the dead body before witnesses and the local church scribe had written it up.[6]

But generally governors or brigandage elders took the lead in criminal cases. To prepare a trial required manpower: corpses and injuries had to be reviewed, defendants arrested, witnesses brought in. In Moscow chanceries, judges had units of military men to carry out arrests and to staff the court; in the countryside, brigandage elders and governors deployed all possible staff and selected people. Sometimes brigandage staff was sufficient. In 1643, for example, the brigandage elder of Ustiuzhna

[4] Collins, *Present State*, 72. Tel′berg, *Ocherki*, ch. 4; Serov, *Sudebnaia reforma*, 83–5. Pre-trial procedures: Man′kov, *Ulozhenie*, 330–41. Serov credits Peter I with creating independent investigative organs, but they did not endure: *Sudebnaia reforma*, 351–73.

[5] Glaz′ev, *Vlast′ i obshchestvennost′*, 273. RGADA f. 1596, no. 45, fol. 2 (1688). RGADA f. 1107, nos. 3109, fol. 8 (1683) and 4375, fol. 2 (1699). RGADA f. 1441, no. 245, fol. 2 (1714).

[6] RGADA f. 1107, no. 1423 (1657). RGADA f. 1596, no. 45, fol. 1 (1688); similar case: RGADA f. 1107, no. 4375 (1699).

Zheleznopol′skaia sent his warden to inspect a body; the brigandage elder in the same office sent his scribe with the governor's bailiff to arrest a man in 1683. In 1670 the Beloozero brigandage elder sent his warden to inspect a wounded woman and to survey witnesses; here the victim identified the culprits as a band of robbers. Sometimes governors drew on both brigandage and their own staff. In 1687, for example, the governor of Beloozero sent the brigandage warden to arrest a murder suspect; his successor in 1692 sent brigandage scribes to arrest a homicide suspect and inspect the dead body and on his second attempt to arrest the same man, he sent three town-square scribes.[7]

Town-square scribes had the literacy needed to record testimony and write surety bonds and reports on such missions.[8] Governors also sent their own bailiffs, couriers (*rozsylshchiki*), artillerymen, musketeers and even servants from local monasteries.[9] In 1679, for example, the Beloozero governor sent a musketeer to a village to join the local hundredman to inspect a woman beaten by her husband and to arrest the suspect; testimony revealed that the husband's abuse had come to the hundredman's attention before, but that he had always ordered the wife to stay with her spouse. In 1673 a governor sent a servant from a local monastery and the decurion (*desiatskii*) of the local village to arrest a suspect and inspect a body; they reported that the suspect was unable to walk and "carrying him [to the office] was impossible."[10]

Governors and brigandage elders resorted to such a variety of helpers from lack of manpower. In a case in 1662, for example, when the brigandage elder of Beloozero was ordered to send a case and four defendants to Moscow, he reported: "I have no brigandage wardens or bailiffs to send with them, there are only two brigandage wardens in

[7] RGADA f. 1171, nos. 75, fol. 1 (1643) and 170, fol. 1–2 (1683). RGADA f. 1107, no. 1849, fol. 1 (1670). RGADA f. 1596, no. 39, fol. 3 (1687). RGADA f. 1107, no. 3906, fols. 3, 18 (1692); similar case, using a brigandage scribe and a courier: RGADA f. 1107, no. 4438, fol. 2 (1700).

[8] Town-square scribes as staff, all in RGADA f. 1107: to arrest two men accused of assault, no. 1926, fol. 3 (1671); to manage a community survey in Beloozero, no. 2100, fol. 1 (1673); to inspect a wounded body, no. 2560, fol. 1 and no. 2475, fol. 1 (1678); to inspect and interview a seriously beaten man, no. 2555, fol. 2 (1678).

[9] Governors' staff, all in RGADA f. 1107: courier makes an arrest, no. 74, fol. 2 (1613); two undersecretaries inspect a wounded man, no. 823, fol. 3 (1638); bailiff pursues a thief and collects stolen goods, no. 1058, fol. 1 (1645); bailiff arrests suspects, no. 1219, fol. 2 (1650).

[10] RGADA f. 1107, nos. 2655, fols. 2, 6 (1679) and 2099, fols. 1–2 (1673). Other examples, all in RGADA f. 1107: artillerymen in 1624 (no. 369, fol. 3), in 1628 (no. 482, fol. 1), in 1637 (no. 774, fol. 2), in 1638 (no. 823, fol. 1) and in 1639 (no. 871, fol. 1); musketeer sent from Beloozero to arrest men accused of assault and theft in 1672 (no. 2004, fol. 469); monastic servant sent in similar case in 1678 (no. 2547, fols. 2–3).

Beloozero, and they work at the prison all the time, night and day, and there are very few bailiffs in the governor's office (*s'ezzhaia izba*), and they have already been sent out on tasks to Beloozero province in the tsar's affairs." He sent some "Beloozero brick makers" instead.[11]

Other aspects of criminal trials demanded the participation of the community. When governors sent someone to inspect a body or make an arrest, for example, they instructed their officers to gather witnesses from the local village, described in a 1596 case as "local and nearby priests, deacons, elders, wardens, and the leading peasants." In one case of 1683 where the suspect was a gentryman, the order instructed the bailiff and town-square scribe to collect the following as witnesses: "from various districts hundredmen and fifty-men and decurions and from various service lands and hereditary estates elders and wardens and peasants, many people."[12] Such community representatives could attest that abuses had not occurred in the arrest.

Governors' struggles to find the help they needed are evident in an exchange between Moscow and the governor of Shuia in 1645. The governor had been ordered to take a party of 100 Suzdal′ and Lukh gentrymen to pursue local bands of criminals, but the Shuia governor reported there were only 60 local gentry and they were already assigned to frontier guard duty. He could call on only "monastic servants, townsmen, peasants, hundredmen, fifty-men and decurions, but the monastic servants are poorly prepared and without horses." Moscow ordered him to recruit all the local retired gentry, but not to disturb the gentry already assigned to border duty.[13] This case in a nutshell shows the conflicts governors faced between their military, administrative and judicial responsibilities.

Communities often refused to cooperate, despite Moscow's sternest orders. In 1664 the Military Service Chancery ordered Pereiaslavl′ Zalesskii to chase down an escaped prisoner. "You are to seek him out everywhere . . . have town criers announce on many days that no one is to take in any visitors or strangers." All newcomers should be brought to the governor's office and whoever captures the convict will receive a reward. But should anyone hide him or not turn him in, they will face a "merciless death penalty"; furthermore, the governor will be

[11] RGADA f. 1596, no. 10, fols. 1–iv (1662).

[12] AI i: no. 249 (1596). RGADA f. 1107, no. 3109, fol. 3 (1683); similar case: RGADA f. 1107, no. 288, fol. 1 (1619).

[13] AAE iii: no. 325 (1645).

punished for failing to enforce the order. The governor was instructed to send this notice to estate managers, village elders and sworn wardens (*tseloval'niki*) as well as to monasteries and even to hermit monks. Nevertheless, as often as the cases surveyed here reflect success in bringing in suspects, they also show frequent resistance by individuals, families or whole communities. The problem was recognized: in 1687, for example, Felony Chancery warned its staff that if it sent men out to a Moscow suburb to arrest someone in a felony, it should not inform any other chancery to which the accused person might be subordinate, lest the accused person be informed and flee or hide material evidence.[14]

One can understand a community's point of view. Across Europe and in Muscovy in pre-modern times, people tried to avoid the courts. As Robin Briggs noted, "Peasants were very generous with mutual assistance within certain limits, but these definitely excluded taking sides in other people's quarrels, or giving damaging evidence on behalf of anyone who was not a relative or close associate." People in small communities do not want to rile up animosities or get on the wrong side of a quarrel that they would have to live with for years. They resisted where necessary or offered other expedients, such as providing surety guarantees for neighbors and friends, urging quarreling couples to settle a case, or calling in priests or local leaders to mediate. As J. A. Sharpe notes, going to court was "a last resort."[15]

Muscovy demonstrates a full range of resistance. Sometimes communities resisted passively – bailiffs returned empty-handed, reporting that "everyone had fled," tipped off in advance. In 1683 in Beloozero, for example, the town-square scribe and bailiffs reported that when they reached the village of a gentryman suspect, "he and all his people and peasants and their wives and children had all fled and his home and all his peasants' homes were empty." In this case, it took three arrest warrants over several months to bring in the suspects. Multiple efforts were made in a 1692 Beloozero case: a party of undersecretaries sent out to arrest a homicide suspect reported that "he has fled us and is in hiding." They seized his father, brother and wife in his place. They made a second attempt in March 1694, but he was still in hiding and nowhere to be

[14] Rumiantseva (ed.), *Dokumenty Razriadnogo*, sect. III: no. 41 (1664). PSZ II: no. 1265 (1687). Glaz'ev notes such resistance: *Vlast' i obshchestvennost'*, 247.

[15] Briggs quoted by Lenman and Parker, "State, Community," 22, with broader discussion 20–2; Sharpe, "Enforcing the Law," 107–17, quote on 107.

found. In 1695 an arresting party reported that "when they saw us, a whole group of peasants fled their homes."[16]

Aware that resisting arrest was a crime, sometimes individuals were careful to specify that they were not "refusing" to comply (*uchinilsia sil'no*), but that they would come in on their own on the appointed day. Often they did, as in 1669 when a bailiff tried to arrest a man in Beloozero. The accused man's son reported that his father was out surveying his villages but would come to the trial date. Subsequently he did. Conversely, in a 1675 case of assault a landlord outside of Beloozero refused to turn over his peasants to the bailiff, but declared he was not acting in defiance (*sil'no*). He would bring in the men the following week. But he failed to appear and eventually settled the case with the landlord of the wounded men.[17]

Sometimes suspects simply refused arrest, as in 1613 when a courier reported that the drinking companions of a murder suspect refused to gather surety bond and come into Beloozero for testimony. Two men accused of homicide in 1693 locked themselves in their home when the arresting party came; "having listened through the window as we read aloud the summons ... they refused (*uchinilis' sil'ni*) the sovereigns' order."[18] Sometimes resistance was violent – kinsmen, neighbors, large bodies of people often refused the emissaries, insulted and even physically attacked them. When in 1683 the brigandage elder of Ustiuzhna Zheleznopol'skaia sent his warden, scribe and the governor's bailiff to arrest a peasant, the opposition was even more deadly. The landlord's wife, "having gathered her people and peasants, with guns and halberds chased them across the field," recovered the arrested man and beat the officers bloody. Such problems persisted into Petrine times.[19]

In cases of resistance, bailiffs often arrested kinsmen or neighbors as hostages until the suspect turned himself in. A Beloozero artilleryman sent to arrest two gentry in 1624 was told to arrest household staff (*dvorniki*) if they themselves could not be found. In a case of 1687 in Kadom, the landlord's wife refused to yield an accused peasant to the arresting party,

16 RGADA f. 1107, nos. 3109, fols. 7, 11–15, quote on fol. 8 (1683); 3906, fols. 4, 18 (1692); 4160, fol. 1 (1695).

17 RGADA f. 1107, nos. 1771, fol. 11 (1669) and 2249, fol. 2 (1675); similar case: AIuB I: no. 80 (XIV) (1698).

18 RGADA f. 1107, no. 19, fols. 2–5 (1613). RGADA f. 1596, no. 55, fol. 2 (1693) (at the time there were two "sovereigns": Ioann and Peter Alekseevichi). Other such resistance or flight: RGADA f. 1107, nos. 74, fol. 2 (1613); 1926, fol. 3 (1671); 2093, fol. 2 (1673); 2454, fol. 5 (1677); 758, fol. 3 (1680); 4133, fol. 3 and 4151, fol. 4 (both 1695).

19 RGADA f. 1171, no. 170, fols. 1–2 (1683). Petrine examples: AIuB II: no. 213 (1697); RGADA f. 1107, no. 4438, fols. 6, 14 (1700); RGADA f. 1380, no. 52, fol. 5 (1719).

so they took the suspect's mother instead; in testimony she professed ignorance. Finally, the landlord brought his peasant to court.[20]

Even local officials could be recalcitrant, as cited in the beginning of this chapter and as occurred in 1684 in Siberia. The fifty-man of the Moscow musketeers who were delivering a prisoner to Tobol′sk reported insubordination: as ordered in their travel documents, he had asked a village steward for sleds and escorts, but the steward scorned the documents and urged the villagers to attack the group with sticks. One musketeer was beaten in the face. Finally, the community provided escorts and carts, but on the way the escorts allowed the prisoner to escape,[21] perhaps encouraged by bribes.

Resisting arrest, refusing to provide a surety bond or to give evidence, and escaping custody were so common that sixteenth- and early seventeenth-century law punished such behavior with strict fines; the 1649 Ulozhenie and later decrees added corporal punishment. Communities were also punished for failing to help track down criminals with sufficient energy or for hiding criminals in their midst.[22]

Resistance is a built-in liability of a criminal justice system that relies on local staff. Certainly, the state tried to avoid such conflicts of interest. Governors were not supposed to be appointed to serve in their home communities and bailiffs were not supposed to serve summonses in their home towns. But locally selected staffs could not escape local ties. Arresting professional criminals who preyed on the community was welcome, but arresting, guarding and participating in the prosecution of their neighbors gave pause. The scholar of Late Antiquity Peter Brown makes a relevant observation regarding the late Roman Empire, where centrally appointed governors also dealt with locally provided staff: "A governor was as effective as his staff allowed him to be, and the venality and inertia of the *officia* were legendary."[23] Using locally selected staff bound only by loyalty oaths and surety bonds and relying on other forms of community involvement made local government vulnerable to community sentiment and weakened policing.

[20] RGADA f. 1107, no. 369, fol. 5 (1624). RGADA f. 1122, op. 2, pt. 2, no. 1424 (1687).

[21] DAI XI: no. 35 (1684).

[22] Jan. 1555 Felony Handbook, arts. 9, 10: PRP IV: 358; ZA no. 229 (1635); Ulozhenie ch. 10, arts. 119–20, 122, 138–42, 229: RZ III: 116–17, 121–3, 140–1. PSZ II: no. 740 (1678). PSZ II: no. 1265 (1687). AMG I: no. 140 (1621). 1669 Criminal Articles, art. 28: PRP VII: 406–8. Punished for failing: Chicherin, *Oblastnye uchrezhdeniia*, 498–502.

[23] Brown, *Power and Persuasion*, 22. Jason Coy makes the same point about seventeenth-century Ulm's policing practices: *Strangers and Misfits*, 24–30, 51, 97–104, 127–35.

BOND AND CUSTODY

When bailiffs succeeded in arresting suspects, they had several options for custody. In principle, prison was the preserve of the brigandage staff and was intended for professional criminals. For misdemeanors, other options were available. One was to use a surety bond (*poruka*) guaranteeing that defendants, plaintiffs and witnesses would show up throughout the trial. A decree of 1664, for example, instructed the governor of Kadom to release from prison on surety bond three defendants in a misdemeanor case of assault and petty theft; prison was inappropriate because "they were not put in prison in a case of theft, robbery or homicide," citing the triad that defined felonies. Providing bonds could be risky for communities: guarantors were held liable if their subject absconded, as happened in a 1648 case in Kursk.[24]

Placing a suspect in custody with a guard (*za pristava*) was the next more secure confinement after surety bond. A decree of 1637 mandated that custody should be used for people arrested in non-criminal cases rather than putting them in prison with felons and because the overcrowding in prison causes "hunger" and they die from "bad air." In homicide cases that did not seem to be professional crime, defendants were given into custody, as in a 1656 case of a woman accused of killing her husband.[25]

Resources were always short and the responsibility of custody onerous. In a case of July 1626, for example, the governor of Mozhaisk put a man in custody with some local musketeers, paying them for the upkeep. By August he had run out of money to pay them and Moscow ordered him to put the man in prison where he was responsible for his own upkeep. By 1658 a decree put the cost of prison on those confined. A case of April 1647 shows other problems with custody: the governor of Kozlov reported to Moscow that he had placed several arrested people with custodians and now they were complaining of the burden. It was "plowing time" (*pashennaia pora*) and they needed to be out in the fields to work. Custody with a guard also entailed risks should the captives "walk away." In 1629 in Meshchevsk, the governor reported that several prisoners accused of treason had been given into custody since there were no prison guards

[24] AMG III: no. 674 (1664). RGADA f. 210, Belgorod stol, no. 338, fols. 915–16 (1648). Other examples: RGADA f. 1107, nos. 2305, fol. 17 (1676) and 19, fols. 1–2 (1613); RGADA f. 1596, no. 8, fol. 5 (1662); RGADA f. 1107, nos. 1771, fol. 4 (1669) and 2099, fol. 1 (1673); RGADA f. 1122, op. 2, pt. 2, no. 2083, fol. 2 (1676); RGADA f. 210, Prikaznyi stol, no. 1549, fol. 138 (1692).

[25] ZA no. 248 (1637). RGADA f. 210, Sevsk stol, no. 187, fol. 454 (1656).

available; they had promptly fled custody and the custodian had been tortured to see if he had cooperated with them.[26]

Prison was sometimes used to confine criminals, even in non-felony cases. Considerations of cost and gravity of crime came into it, and even perhaps social rank. For those charged with very serious crimes – political and religious crime, brigandage felonies – prison was their fate. For example, in a case of 1640, a priest accused of having said treasonous words against the tsar was initially given into custody, but once he was tortured in the case, he was imprisoned; a decree of 1653 categorically denies custody for such serious crime.[27] Other uses of prison were more discretionary: in one case a governor was chastised for imprisoning without an order a gentryman for insulting him, while in a precedence case of 1657 a high-level servitor was sentenced to be imprisoned to exacerbate his humiliation. Prison in Muscovy was, nevertheless, hardly a foolproof form of confinement.

PRISON

Muscovy used prison in the same ways that many other states did. Prison was generally a jail, a place of confinement for awaiting trial, rather than a sanction in and of itself, as in Ancient Greece and Rome. For some crimes monastic prison was a sanction. Since Christian churches avoided capital or corporal punishment and believed in the possibility of repentance and forgiveness, monasteries, bishops and other hierarchs in the medieval West and in Muscovy maintained prisons to discipline and correct. Terms were usually short but conditions were harsh, sometimes focusing on darkness and isolation to inspire reflection. Rulers often used monastic prison in political struggles as an alternative to executing a rival and sparking further violence; in such a case, the conditions of captivity were generally less severe.[28]

Kings and towns in medieval and early modern Europe, as in Muscovy, kept secular prisons for the highest crimes; for lesser crimes, prisons could be private monopolies whose custodians made money on entrance fees paid by prisoners or on taverns and other services they provided inside the enclosure. As this suggests, unlike modern prisons, pre-modern prisons

[26] SIDG no. 30, p. 40 (1626). PSZ I: no. 221 (1658). RGADA f. 210, Prikaznyi stol, no. 172, fols. 254, 257 (1647). AMG I: no. 259 (1629). Other instances of fleeing custody: RGADA f. 1107, no. 480, fol. 2 (1628); RGADA f. 210, Prikaznyi stol, no. 1824, fol. 148 (1698).

[27] SIDG no. 203 (1640). PSZ I: no. 105 (1653). AMG II: no. 18 (1635). AMG II: no. 950 (1657).

[28] Peters, "Prison before the Prison"; De Jong, "Monastic Prisoners."

allowed considerable freedom of movement: prisoners could be released daily to beg alms or work for income; visitors were welcome; family members could accompany; social elites were treated better (for a price) than lower-class prisoners. But conditions were by no means easy: disease and hunger decimated prison populations.[29]

As a rule, in Muscovite law and practice prison was rarely used as long-term judicial punishment; codes often decree short terms, meant to have exemplary and deterrent effect on others.[30] Prisons emerge in law codes in the mid sixteenth century, reflecting the development of triadic judicial relations. Brigandage charters and the 1550 Law Code decreed brief prison terms for criminals for whom there was well-based suspicion or who refuse to confess and for crimes against the state (false accusation of court officials, corruption of officials below the level of judge).[31] In the 1649 Ulozhenie, prison was assigned more often, generally for short terms, but felonies included two to four years in prison; the phrase "imprison until the tsar's decree" also occurs frequently.[32] But the 1669 Criminal Articles by and large dropped prison as a sanction in favor of surety bond or exile.[33]

From the late fifteenth century various places in Moscow were used for incarceration. When several male kinsmen of the grand prince were imprisoned, for example, Kremlin buildings and homes were used. Ivan III's brother Andrei was imprisoned in the Treasury in 1491. Prince Vasilii Ivanovich Shemiachich, Vasilii III's second cousin once removed, was imprisoned "in the palace on the riverbank" in 1524; Prince Iurii

[29] Peters, "Prison before the Prison," 31–43; McConville, "Local Justice," 271–2.

[30] Rogov argues that the intent was for short stays on the monastic model: *Istoriia*, 255. Little is written about Muscovite prisons, and it starts around the mid seventeenth century: Rogov, *Istoriia*, 230–60; Chicherin, *Oblastnye uchrezhdeniia*, 494–7; Anisimov, *Dyba i knut*, 589–614; Gernet, *Istoriia tsarskoi tiur'my*. Brief surveys: Shtamm, "Ugolovnoe pravo," in Nersesiants (ed.), *Razvitie*, 196–7; Shtamm, "Ugolovnoe pravo," in Skripilev (ed.), *Razvitie*, 210–11.

[31] 1550 Law Code, arts. 4, 6–13, 33–4, 42, 47, 52, 54–6, 58, 71: RZ II: 97–113. Jan. 1555 Felony Handbook, arts. 2–3, 8, PRP IV: 356–8. 1555 Medyn Charter, arts. 5, 7–8, 11: PRP IV: 182–4. 1589 Law Code, arts. 6, 8, 11–12, 103, 107–8, 111, 126: PRP IV: 414–29.

[32] Prison for insulting or falsely accusing officials: Ulozhenie ch. 1, arts. 7, 9: RZ III: 85–6: ch. 3, arts. 1–2, 5, 7, 9: RZ III: 89–90; ch. 10, arts. 30–1, 92, 105, 142: RZ III: 107, 111, 113, 123. Until the tsar decrees: ch. 10, arts. 8–9, 186–8: RZ III: 103, 132–3; ch. 21, arts. 43–4, 71: RZ III: 237, 242; ch. 25, arts. 2, 6: RZ III: 252–3. For corrupt officials: ch. 10, arts. 20, 148: RZ III: 105, 124; ch. 21, arts. 83, 86: RZ III: 244. For threatening or committing crime: ch. 10, arts. 135, 139, 141, 202, 231, 251–2: RZ III: 121–3, 135, 141, 145–6; ch. 11, art. 27: RZ III: 156; ch. 21, arts. 9–10, 16, 21, 28: RZ III: 231–3; ch. 22, arts. 3, 11, 17: RZ III: 248–9; ch. 25, art. 3: RZ III : 252–3. Until surety bond: ch. 21, arts. 64, 92: RZ III: 241, 245. Custodial: ch. 6, art. 6: RZ III: 92.

[33] 1669 Criminal Articles do not prescribe prison: arts. 8, 9, 17, 24 and commentary: PRP VII: 398–9, 402, 404. The 1669 code ends by mandating inventories of prisoners and prompt resolution of their cases (arts. 126–8): PRP VII: 434.

Ivanovich and Prince Andrei Staritskii were also held there, in 1533 and 1537 successively. Ivan IV's uncle Prince M. L. Glinskii was imprisoned "in the stone palace behind the tsar's palace" in 1534, and in 1538 Prince Ivan Fedorovich Telepnev Obolenskii followed him there.[34] Prince Ivan Bel'skii was imprisoned in October 1538 at the Kremlin home of Prince Fedor Mstislavskii, a brother-in-law of the current leading boyar, Prince Vasilii Shuiskii. The mercenary Heinrich von Staden reported in the 1560s that prisons and a torture chamber were located inside the Kremlin by the north gate. As court favorite and then as tsar, Boris Godunov imprisoned rivals such as the Shuiskie and Romanovy in separate households, even with servants.[35]

Sixteenth-century decrees required brigandage offices to maintain prisons, replacing, according to a 1555 decree, notoriously corrupt private prisons. Felony prisoners were to be separated from others.[36] Monasteries were used as prisons for clerics, for persons guilty of religious or moral offenses, and for political rivals.[37] Seventeenth-century sources reveal more of the conditions in prisons. In monasteries repentance was to be inspired by horrific conditions, as described for a monk exiled to the Tikhvin Monastery in 1687: "it was ordered that his prison and its doors and windows be blocked up with brick, leaving only one small window for giving bread and water, and that he be guarded severely."[38] Less stringent measures applied to the archbishop of Suzdal, who was exiled to the Siiskii Monastery in 1634 for his unruly life; he was to be allowed a cook, a servant and his own cell, but was not to be allowed to attend

[34] Years of imprisonment and death: Prince Andrei Vasil'evich, 1491–d. 1493: Shmidt, "Prodolzhenie," 263, 269 (7000, 7002). Prince V. I. Shemiachich, 1524–30: Shmidt, "Prodolzhenie," 281, 284 (7032, 7038); PSRL IV, pt. 1: 541 (7031); *Novgorodskie letopisi*, 124 (7037). Prince M. L. Glinskii, 1534–6: Zimin, "Kratkie letopistsy," 13, 14 (7042, 7045); PSRL XIII: 79, 115 (7042, 7045); Postnikov, 283 (7042). Prince Iurii Ivanovich, 1533–6: Shmidt, "Prodolzhenie," 285, 287 (7042, 7044); Zimin, "Kratkie letopistsy," 14 (7044). Prince Andrei Staritskii, April–Dec. 1537: Shmidt, "Prodolzhenie," 288 (7045, 7046); PSRL XIII: 97, 121 (7045, 7046); Postnikov, 284 (7045). Obolenskii: Postnikov, 282 (7046).

[35] Bel'skii: PSRL XIII: 126 (7047). See Chapter 14 on minority struggles. Godunov: Rogov, *Istoriia*, 251–2; Pavlov, *Gosudarev dvor*, 73–5. Staden, *Land and Government*, 45.

[36] Jan. 1555 Felony Handbook, arts. 9, 13: PRP IV: 358–9. A 1591 decree distinguishes between felony (*tatinye, rozboinye*) and general prisons (*opal'nye*): PRP V: 227–8.

[37] See Chapter 14 on monastic imprisonment of political rivals. The St. Cyril Beloozero Monastery received many such prisoners: RGADA f. 1441, op. 2, nos. 53, 54, 57, 89, 90, 152, 170, 172 (1701–11); op. 5, nos. 64, 65, 69, 70, 71, 73, 91, 93, 94 (1662–78); op. 6, nos. 176, 342, 351, 448 (1676–1700). The Novgorod Archbishop's court in the seventeenth century kept a prison: Grekov, "Novgorodskii dom," 110. Solovetskii Monastery as prison: Kolchin, *Ssyl'nye i zatochennye*. Eighteenth-century monastic prisons: Anisimov, *Dyba i knut*, 597–605.

[38] AIu no. 307, doc. 6 (1687).

church, was to be deprived of the Eucharist unless he were dying, and was not to be allowed paper or ink.[39]

Lay prisoners in monasteries suffered similar conditions. A woman incarcerated in 1676 for killing her husband was to be "kept in shackles under the harshest possible guard" and made to attend services daily. A gentryman sent in 1628 to the St. Nicholas Monastery in Karelia for sexual misconduct (fathering illegitimate children with his second cousin) was to be kept in leg irons and required to join in daily monastic labor, "sowing grain and shoveling ashes from the oven." He was to be given half-food rations, denied liturgy and allowed confession and communion only if he were at death's door. On the other hand, a Siberian tsarevich exiled to a monastery in 1667 for drunkenness was explicitly to be brought to church daily, "once he has become sober." At the end of the century, particularly for schismatics, decrees also instructed monasteries not to allow such prisoners access to reading and writing materials.[40]

By the seventeenth century in the city of Moscow secular prisons were more formalized. Grigorii Kotoshikhin remarked that in Moscow there were "prisons for all manner of criminals" and that fifty executioners were employed in Moscow, presumably in chancery courts and prisons. Chanceries such as Military Service, Felony and Slavery maintained prisons in their own offices, thus separating different types of prisoners. The Military Service Chancery prison is cited in 1672, when it put a man arrested for illegal tobacco possession "behind bars" (*za reshotku*); in the same year the Felony Chancery prison was referred to as the "black chamber" and in the 1670s it was so overcrowded that it was turning away new prisoners. The Foreign Affairs Chancery prison is attested in 1672 by a surety bond for its bailiff.[41] Chanceries could also transfer prisoners to the "prison court" (*tiuremnoi dvor*) in the Kremlin or nearby. The great historian of the Kremlin, Ivan Zabelin, identified two Kremlin prisons in the sixteenth and seventeenth centuries – by the Trinity gate

[39] AAE III: no. 249 (1634); other examples: Michels, *At War*, 145; RGADA f. 1441, op. 6, no. 448, fols. 1, 2, 6 (1700).

[40] RGADA f. 1441, op. 5, no. 71, fol. 1 (1676). AAE III: no. 177 (1628). AAE IV: no. 154 (1667). RGADA f. 1441, op. 2, no. 57, fol. 4 (1701); PSZ VIII: no. 5353 (1728). Another example: RGADA f. 1441, op. 5, no. 73 (1658).

[41] Kotoshikhin, *O Rossii*, ch. 7, art. 34, p. 114. RGADA f. 210, Sevsk stol, no. 283, fol. 372 (1672). Other references to "behind bars" in Military Service Chancery: MDBP pt. II, no. 54 (1656); RGADA f. 210, Prikaznyi stol, no. 970, fol. 123 (1665); RGADA f. 210, Sevsk stol, no. 416, fol. 471 (1688). Felony Chancery: PSZ I: nos. 328 (1662), 527 (1672), 538 (1673); PSZ II: no. 626 (1676). Foreign Affairs: AIuB II: no. 262 (IV) (1672). Slavery Chancery: ZA no. 199 (1630).

and just outside the Kremlin near the Konstantinov gate; they are cited from the 1630s through the 1680s.[42]

In the countryside, confinement choices were the same: surety bond, custody, being kept "behind bars" in the governor's office or prison. Here limited resources made it harder to separate criminals between felony and misdemeanor criminals. In Cherdyn′ the governor reported in 1630 that he did not have such two prisons; in the same year in Beloozero brigandage officials were criticized for imprisoning together felony criminals, drunks and Tatars accused of treason. In September 1637 the brigandage elder of Murom was criticized for holding in the "felony" prison people arrested in minor suits, including runaway slaves and serfs, which caused overcrowding and hunger. He was ordered to place lesser prisoners in custody, saving prison for people accused of felonies.[43] Local governors often separated male and female prisoners; in 1635, for example, a woman accused of killing her husband was given into custody, while her male accomplice was put in prison. In a 1688 case where a married couple was accused of murder, the judge imprisoned them in separate cells, she with other women.[44]

Staffing prisons cost communities manpower and upkeep in money and food. The 1555 Felony Chancery Handbook mandated that communities elect as prison guards sixteen people to serve in rotation through the year, living at the prison, in the words of a 1591 decree, "day and night without a break." These mandates continued in seventeenth-century law codes and communities provided funds as required. A governor reported in 1654 that the Ustiug community paid nine prison guards 113 rubles total per year; for the new prison, 20 new guards were elected and were to be paid one ruble each per month. Secretaries elected to work at the brigandage office were also paid a ruble per month.[45]

Locals considered prison service an onerous burden. Moscow addressed the situation in 1666 by decreeing that wardens and guards for the large

[42] Zabelin, *Istoriia goroda Moskvy*, 420–2, 652. "Prison court": AMG I: no. 459 (1632); PSZ I: no. 336 (1663); PSZ II: nos. 669 (1676), 691 (1677), 845 (1670), 1032 (1683); PSZ III: no. 1345 (1689). "Large" prison in Moscow: AMG I: no. 176 (1624); PRP V: 228–30 (1641); AMG III: no. 319 (1661); PSZ I: nos. 336 (1663) and 384 (1666); Anisimov, *Dyba i knut*, 589.

[43] Chicherin, *Oblastnye uchrezhdeniia*, 474. Cherdyn′: AI III: no. 163, p. 29 (1630). Beloozero: RGADA f. 1107, no. 544 (1630). AAE III: no. 272 (1637). Vologda prison for prisoners of war: AIu no. 223 (1) (1607).

[44] RGADA f. 210, Belgorod stol, no. 83, fol. 260 (1635); similar case: RGADA f. 210, Belgorod stol, no. 83, fols. 369, 371 (1637). RGADA f. 1107, no. 3549, fol. 6 (1688).

[45] Jan. 1555 Felony Handbook, art. 13: PRP IV: 359. 1591 decree: PRP V: 227–8. 1616/17 Felony Handbook, art. 54: PRP V: 199. Ulozhenie ch. 21, arts. 4, 95, 97: RZ III: 230–1, 246; 1669 Criminal Articles, art. 3: PRP VII: 397; DAI III: no. 115 (1654).

Moscow prisons were no longer to be selected, but that the Felony Chancery should hire eight guards per year from the urban populace in Moscow. The problem of staffing prisons in the countryside, however, continued. Another burden on communities was building prisons. Disputes were numerous over who was responsible to pay for construction, as, for example, when the schismatic Avvakum and three others were exiled to Pustoozero. Local communities so heatedly disputed who should pay to build their prison that construction was delayed for more than two years. Other decrees, anticipating resistance, specified that for prison construction, all communities in the brigandage district were to participate, with no immunities recognized. As a rule, communities cooperated; on rare occasions the state paid for prison construction.[46]

Provincial prisons were to be surrounded by a fortified fence and often a ravine; horizontal log construction made it easy to divide them into cells assigned according to crime or gender. Several documents provide architectural details. With a prison population of 350 in 1654, Ustiug built two new prisons, each 18 and a half fathoms long (about 130 feet) and 11 fathoms and 3 hand-spans (*chetverti*) across (about 89 feet); inside each were four cells (*izby*) of four fathoms (28 feet) and two guard posts (*karaulni*), all at a cost to the community of "285 rubles 12 *altyn* and 2 *dengi* for lumber, carpenters, iron fittings" and all other parts (this at a time when the median cost of a horse was well less than ten rubles). They moved the wives and families who were accompanying male exiles into the old, broken-down prison. Other documents recording the costs of prison construction depict some prisons as "earthen," dug into the ground, producing dark, damp and terrifying conditions.[47]

Such prisons were vulnerable to escape. Investigation into a foiled escape in Mosal'sk in 1630 found that the prisoners had been able to dig under the foundation since the beams were "rotten." The prisoners testified they had abandoned their plan when they realized that once outside they would be caught: "around the fortress there are strong guards at night and they guard all around the prison and the musketeers and

[46] Onerous burden: Bulgakov, *Gosudarstvennye sluzhby*, 151–5. PSZ I: no. 384 (1666). PSZ II: no. 780 (1679). Pustoozero: Barskov, *Pamiatniki*, no. 3. Communities building, or refusing to build, prisons: AAE III: no. 163 (1625); AMG I: no. 272 (1630); AAE III: no. 271 (1637); ZA no. 246 (1637); AIuB II: no. 246 (IX), col. 751 (1641); AAE IV: no. 72 (1654); PSZ II: no. 1271 (1687). AAE II: no. 19 (1601).

[47] DAI III: no. 115 (1654). A *sazhen* was 7 feet. Cost of horse: Hellie, *Economy and Material Culture*, 39–40. Other prisons: Shuia DAI VI: no. 99 (1674); Beloozero DAI X: no. 43 (1682). Earthen prisons: SIDG no. 268 (1659); AMG II: no. 843 (1656); RGADA f. 1441, op. 2, no. 57, fol. 3 (1701).

cossacks who stand at the city gates pace back and forth without stop all night." A defrocked priest who had been arrested in the Stepan Razin uprising and imprisoned in the Tikhvin Monastery managed such an escape in 1671 by cutting through the wall. He climbed out when he heard the guard snoring and scaled the monastery wall, using implements and rope that had come to hand during his captivity. He was soon caught and the Novgorod metropolitan ordered the monastery to build a much stronger prison for him, to shackle him hands and feet and guard him continuously. Nevertheless, he escaped again in August 1673.[48]

Something of the laxness of prison security is suggested by documents recruiting prison guards. Decrees consistently mandated that prison guards and wardens be selected from among the most propertied residents; one document specifies in 1654 that the residents should not select "criminals or drunkards," while another details the qualities and duties of guards and wardens: "They are to do no crime, not play at dice or cards, not drink and carouse; they are to keep no prostitutes or alcohol; they will not leave town before this year's work is over, and they will always watch over the prisoners carefully, and will not release the prisoners at night or day to the tavern. At night they will lock them in their prison cells and they will not let the prisoners have iron, knives, axes, files, rasps, pitchforks or any weapons, and they will not bring any sharp metal items to them baked into bread, a fish dish, cakes or pies. They are not to free any prisoner because of their own favoritism or corruption."[49] One can doubt whether such ideal guards were ever located.

Even if the ideal prison guard stood on duty, daily routines provided opportunity for escape. Although at night prisoners returned to their locked cells and prisons, during the day there was much coming and going. Kotoshikhin around 1666 reported that felony prisoners' "fathers and mothers, or other kinsmen and wives and children" provide them food. Those without kinsmen and those imprisoned for lesser crime, he reported, were allowed to leave the prison daily in groups of two, shackled, to beg for bread and money. A decree of 1669 mandated that prisoners could accept no clothing or equipment on loan from visitors, on penalty of knouting.[50] There is plenty of evidence of prisoners begging for alms. In 1641, for example, prisoners in the "big Moscow prisons"

[48] AMG I: no. 269 (1630). KV III: nos. 147, 158 and 258 (1671).

[49] Jan. 1555 Felony Handbook, art. 13, PRP IV: 359. DAI III: no. 115 (1654); AIu no. 280 (1641); AAE IV: no. 72 (1654). Sureties for Siberian prisons: AIuB II: no. 262 (III) (1669); Verkhotur'e AIuB I: nos. 3–4 (1671); RGADA f. 210, Prikaznyi stol, no. 1130, fols. 46–7 (1689).

[50] Kotoshikhin, *O Rossii*, ch. 7, art. 47, p. 122. PSZ I: no. 448 (1669). AIuB II: no. 262 (III) (1669).

complained that they had not been allowed to stand at their usual spots at busy gates: they were standing with more than 500 beggars at the Nikolskie gates and were dying of hunger from lack of donations. In 1660 a Tatar woman imprisoned in the Musketeer Chancery in place of her sons, who were accused of stealing 1,000 rubles, died hours after returning from town, where she had gone to beg and to purchase the bread and honey that she consumed sitting in front of the Chancery just before she expired.[51]

As the Tatar woman's story reveals, prisoners could walk in the courtyard of a prison in the day, chat, eat and even drink with the guards. A few remarkable cases of escape reveal something of this. A man accused in 1688 of murder escaped one morning while the prison warden was off in the tavern, buying beer for himself and the prisoners for breakfast. This followed a day and evening when the guard had taken several prisoners into town, going to the bath and taverns. In interrogation, he asserted that the other prison guards knew what he was doing, as if it were not unusual. Another story of escape comes from an accused schismatic named Samoila; imprisoned in the Chancery of Foreign Affairs in January 1688, he escaped when his guard fell asleep next to him, leaving unattended his cap in which lay the keys to Samoila's fetters. Samoila took them, unlocked himself and fled. Eventually captured, he reported that not only had his guard been sleeping, but also the "bailiff and the translators on duty and the undersecretary" and the guards at the doors. He opened both the iron and wooden doors of the Chancery, which had been left unlocked, and exited through the Kremlin Spasskii Gates and the city gate going across the river, pretending to be a priest. He walked from Moscow to Elets on the southern frontier before being apprehended in February by a suspicious gentryman. Once he was returned to Moscow, greater care was ordered. He was to be held in fetters and irons "with great caution," two guards were to be stationed with him day and night without a break, and when shifts changed, written documentation was to be exchanged hand to hand.[52]

In the event of an escape, guilt had to be apportioned. Guards were interrogated, including with torture; decrees from the sixteenth century to the 1649 Ulozhenie made communities liable for poorly constructed prisons and lax guarding. A monk prison guard at the Tikhvin

[51] 1641 Felony Handbook: PRP v: 228–30. AMG iii: no. 88 (1660).

[52] RGADA f. 1107, no. 3549, fols. 18–22 (1688). DAI xii: no. 17 (1688). Other escapes: AMG ii: no. 667 (1655); RGADA f. 1107, no. 3835, fol. 4 (1691); RGADA f. 409, op. 4, no. 336, fol. 2 (1729).

Monastery helped a prisoner escape in 1687 by giving him a bag of food and a hunting spear; the guard's guarantors (4 monks and 8 monastic servants) had to pay the surety bond. Arzamas judge Ia. G. Chertkov interrogated his prison guards in 1719 before the instruments of torture and even while hoisted up in strappado, but did not proceed to torture; in a similar case, the guards were tortured.[53]

Non-felony prisoners were required to support themselves in prison awaiting trial. Fees for guards and for entrance into prison are cited as early as 1550 and through the seventeenth century, paid by prisoners or plaintiffs. A 1630 decree established norms of upkeep as two *dengi* a day, paid to the Chancery directly.[54] Ultimately the state took upon itself prison upkeep: in 1662 the tsar established upkeep for the chancery prisons, the Moscow prisons and all towns, two *altyn* per day per person from the tsar's treasury. But this did not stop begging and complaints by prisoners that they were "dying of hunger." Petrine legislation set upkeep fees at twice as much per day in St. Petersburg as in Moscow prisons, to be paid by the petitioners.[55]

Even before then the state apparently paid for felony prisoners, as is implicit in the 1649 Ulozhenie's mandate that the Treasury pay for prisons built in Moscow by the Felony Chancery, and in queries from governors about how to pay for felony prisoners. In 1658 the state took upon itself to pay the costs of custodians when people were given in custody in "word and deed" cases. A Petrine law that required accusers in felony crimes to pay upkeep costs stands out as a change. The fact that chanceries required local governors regularly to submit lists of their prisoners and urged them to resolve cases and release prisoners, suggests not only a desire to render justice but also most likely an attempt to cut costs.[56]

[53] Jan. 1555 Felony Handbook, art. 9: PRP IV: 358. 1616/17 Felony Handbook, art. 62: PRP V: 200. Ulozhenie ch. 21, art. 101: RZ III: 246–7. AIu no. 307 (VI) (1687). RGADA f. 1380, no. 52 (1719); RGADA f. 1380, no. 52, fol. 11 (1719).

[54] Fees called *pozheleznoe* and *prokorm*: 1550 Law Code, art. 3: RZ II: 97; 1649 Ulozhenie ch. 20: arts. 94, 102, 112: RZ III: 225–6, 228; 1630 ZA no. 199; 1653 PSZ I: no. 105; 1680 PSZ II: no. 845. Decrees establish who is to pay: PSZ I: no. 221 (1658); PSZ II: no. 998 (1683). Man'kov, *Zakonodatel'stvo*, 176–7; Hellie, *Economy and Material Culture*. Difficulty of feeding prisoners in seventeenth-century Germany: Rublack, *Crimes of Women*, 69–77.

[55] PSZ I: no. 328 (1662). Hunger: AMG I: no. 675 (1634); RGADA f. 210, Prikaznyi stol, no. 592, fol. 1 (1650); PDP no. 156 (1657); RGADA f. 210, Prikaznyi stol, no. 970, fol. 148 (1665). Petrine norms: PSZ VI: no. 3685 (1720), 3940, 4091, 4094 and 4111 (1722).

[56] Ulozhenie ch. 21, art. 94: RZ III: 246. PSZ I: no. 221 (1658). Accusers pay: PSZ VI: no. 4091 (1722). Lists: AMG I: no. 265 (1629); RGADA f. 210, Prikaznyi stol, no. 1431, fols. 428–9 (1695); PSZ IV: no. 1822, art. 59, p. 126 (1701).

Nevertheless, as seen in Chapter 7, cases could drag on for years and prisoners languished in prison. The Ulozhenie called for criminal cases to be resolved within six months, and the 1669 Criminal Articles specified "immediately, so that they do not sit in prison for no reason"; the Ulozhenie also decreed that anyone in prison for debts should be released on surety bond after five years. Nevertheless, prisoners languished in jail. A prisoner in Belev complained in 1622 that he had been in prison for five years and had no one locally to post surety bond or to petition to resolve his case.[57] Other cases cite prisoners still incarcerated, before or after their case had been resolved, for anywhere from a few months to seven years.[58] Relief might be found when landlords petitioned or in cases of illness; seriously ill prisoners could be released on surety bond, to recover or to die.[59]

As already seen in passing, in the second half of the seventeenth century the state confronted overcrowding and staffing problems in prisons. The 1669 Criminal Articles put prisons in the charge of musketeers, paid by the treasury. This may not have been put into effect, however, since, when the brigandage system was abolished in November 1679, the burden of providing prison guards was cited and nothing was said about musketeers.[60] A flurry of decrees following the 1679 abolition of brigandage offices aimed at clearing the prisons. In June 1679, for example, runaway peasants turned in to the Moscow Judicial Chancery were to be released on surety bond immediately. In early 1680 Moscow chanceries instructed all local offices to submit lists of prisoners, to resolve their cases promptly and to release on custody or surety bond as many as possible. Convicts who lacked money to pay court fees and plaintiffs' claims were sent to

57 Decrees cite multiple years in prison: 1616/17 Felony Handbook, art. 44: PRP v: 197; Ulozhenie ch. 21, art. 21: RZ III: 233; 1669 Criminal Articles, art. 20: PRP VII: 402–3. Resolve promptly: Ulozhenie ch. 21, arts. 92, 104: RZ III: 245, 247; 1669 Criminal Articles, arts. 8, 128: PRP VII: 398–9, 434. SIDG no. 9, p. 9 (1662).

58 Two months: RGADA f. 210, Prikaznyi stol, no. 162, fol. 416 (1645). 12 weeks: AMG I: no. 675 (1634). One year: AMG I: no. 263 (1629); RGADA f. 210, Prikaznyi stol, no. 1539, fol. 290 (1693). Two years: RGADA f. 210, Sevsk stol, no. 187, fols. 452–7 (1656); AMG I: no. 266 (1629). Three years: 1647 AIuB I: no. 55 (XI) (1647); RGADA f. 1122, op. 2, pt. 1, no. 1195, fols. 8–9 (1696); RGADA f. 1122, op. 2, pt. 2, no. 1629, fols. 10–11 (1674). Four: RGADA f. 1122, op. 2, pt. 2, no. 1424, fol. 14 (1687). Seven: RGADA f. 1103, no. 2808, fol. 4 (1714). Many years: ZA no. 192 (1629).

59 SIDG no. 203 (1640); RGADA f. 210, Prikaznyi stol, no. 592, fols. 1–IV (1650); RGADA f. 1135, no. 297, fols. 7–7v (1696); RGADA f. 1107, no. 4303, fol. 8 (1698).

60 1669 Criminal Articles, art. 3: PRP VII: 397; PSZ II: nos. 779 and 780 (1679). Glaz'ev cites this reversal: *Vlast' i obshchestvennost'*, 207. Documents (surety bonds, fees) suggest elections continued after 1669: RGADA f. 210, Prikaznyi stol, no. 1130, fols. 46–7 (1689); AIuB II: no. 262 (VII) (1688); PSZ III: no. 1360 (1689); PSZ III: no. 1557 (1696). Nevertheless, some historians see a gradual shift to hired guards: Chicherin, *Oblastnye uchrezhdeniia*, 467–9; Man'kov, *Zakonodatel'tsvo*, 188.

work in exile in 1683 rather than sit in prison, while in 1690 runaways brought to the Slavery Chancery were to be released after a month if their landlords had not initiated suit. Orders to resolve prisoners' cases promptly continued into the Petrine period.[61]

This survey of Muscovite criminal law officers has described a system challenged to do an immense job with inadequate resources. Communities were hard pressed to support the many people they were called upon to select (criminal law staff were only some of the positions provided by communities). Communities and locally selected staff faced conflicting loyalties in cooperating with the judicial apparatus; they had difficulty supporting local prisons and the state struggled with various approaches to pay for prisons. Even governors, scribes and others on annual salary had difficulty accomplishing their jobs, with too many non-judicial responsibilities and overall low pay. Not surprisingly, complaints were rampant that officials abused their power to increase their income.

61 PSZ II: no. 768 (1679). Abolition: PSZ II: nos. 779 and 780 (1679); PSZ II: no. 815 (1680); AI V: no. 55 (1680). PSZ II: no. 1055 (1683). PSZ III: no. 1368 (1690). Petrine laws on prisoners: PSZ V: no. 3319 (1719); PSZ VI: no. 3928 (1722); PSZ VII: no. 4989 (1726). Petrine-era investigations into prison conditions: Kosheleva, *Liudi*, 316–17.

CHAPTER 4

Policing officialdom

Foreigners were appalled by the corruption of the Muscovite bureaucracy. Sigismund von Herberstein in the early sixteenth century, for example, wrote that "a verdict can none the less be bought and this is no secret," remarking astutely that "perhaps the great poverty is one cause of such avarice and injustice, and because the prince knows this he winks at it." A generation later Giles Fletcher saw corruption up and down the hierarchy of local government: the governors

> are men of themselves of no credit nor favor with the people where they govern, being neither born nor brought up among them . . . being so bare and coming fresh and hungry upon them lightly every year, they rack and spoil [their communities] without all regard of justice or conscience, which is easily tolerated by the chief officers [of the chanceries] to the end that they may rob them again and have a better booty when they call them to account, which commonly they do at the end of [the governors'] service.

A century later nothing had changed. Aleksei Mikhailovich's doctor in the 1660s, Samuel Collins, noted that all scribes had to be bribed to get a petition accepted, while Johann-Georg Korb, writing in 1698, alleged: "Their custom is to prove their statement by witnesses, whom they bribe at a trifling rate . . . Presents, too, and gifts, and largesses, are a great help to a suit: nothing is expedited in a *Pricas* [chancery], unless the diaks and scribes have first been put in good humour with gold or silver."[1]

These colorful and most likely exaggerated quotes could probably be replicated for most early modern states, but even so they do remind us that a perennial problem of empire is the policing of officialdom. Russia in the sixteenth through eighteenth centuries proved the wisdom of Ferdnand Braudel's apt phrase – "'Distance – the First Enemy' of all

[1] Herberstein, *Description*, 51–2; Fletcher, "Of the Russe," 150; Collins, *Present State*, 44; Korb, *Diary* II: 188–9.

extended empires."[2] Huge distances and skeletal communication networks challenged Moscow's ability to control; so also did the realm's relative poverty and the strategies of governance adopted to deal with these problems. Corruption was a real problem – it deprived the state of resources, it deprived the people of fair justice. But the issue is not as black and white as these Europeans, with a more legalistic worldview, and certainly as moderns might think: corruption was but the extreme end of the personalized relationships that officials forged with subjects – personalized because of forms of compensation, personalized because concepts of justice expected officials to bend to community needs. With officialdom and communities deeply interdependent, the step from gift-giving to abuse was not far.

STRATEGIES OF COMPENSATION

As Moscow rose from regional principality to east European and Eurasian power (1500–1800), its rulers exponentially extended demand for resources: costly armaments, foreign military expertise, colonial administration, etc. At the same time revenues were scarce. Russia's rulers responded by scrimping on officialdom. The center's highest priority was compensating the elite (Moscow's boyars) and military class (provincial gentry). Both were in principle supported with land and cash grants; beginning in the sixteenth century the state restricted peasant mobility to provide labor for its gentry fighters; by 1649 enserfment was fixed. Men in the highest ranks were favored lavishly, but for most there was never enough land, peasants or cash to go around. Provincial gentry constantly complained of not receiving their full allotments.[3] Since military men in theory were paid in land and cash, they did not receive salary for work as governors, but bureaucrats did (high bureaucratic ranks could also receive land). While Borivoj Plavsic called salaries for secretaries in Moscow chanceries "quite generous," Peter B. Brown, studying undersecretaries of the Moscow Service Land Chancery, marvels that any of them survived on their salaries and estimates that in the second half of the seventeenth century at least half of them earned under a poverty line of 2.5 rubles per year. Natalia Demidova, showing how scribe's land and cash allotments

[2] Official corruption as endemic to all societies: Meny and de Sousa, "Corruption: Political and Public Aspects"; Venkatappiah, "Misuse of Office." Peter Brown paraphrases Braudel in *Power and Persuasion*, 17.

[3] "Only from 25 to 60 percent of the demand for inhabited land created by the nominal grants could be satisfied": Hellie, *Enserfment*, 37. See also Kozliakov, *Sluzhilyi gorod*, ch. 2.

shrank as the bureaucracy ballooned in the seventeenth century, concluded that undersecretaries needed to live off fees and gifts to make ends meet.[4]

Land grants and serfdom were the privilege of the few; as new military formations on the European model were introduced (artillerymen and engineers, musketeers, infantry and dragoons), different compensation strategies emerged. Between privileged and tax-paying strata, members of these ranks did not pay taxes and they could not own populated land. They supported themselves by farming plots granted communally to their units and also by trade (on which they did pay taxes).[5] A third form of compensation to officials was service duties: communities provided cartage, municipal repairs, construction. None of the above provided a comfortable living except to the highest elite. Everywhere one encounters complaints, whether it be decrees cautioning officials not to put fiscal burdens on the people or individuals petitioning for better salary. The governor of Mtsensk reported in 1635, for example, that his undersecretary had worked for fifteen years "without a cash and grain allotment." The state often tried to economize at the expense of scribes, instructing them in 1646 to be armed and on call for military service, cutting their pay in half in 1678, or paying them from fees rather than from community contributions in 1679, for example.[6]

Thus, the state supported another form of compensation for public service: "living from one's work" (*kormit'sia ot del*). This phrase had two meanings. Most directly, it referred to officials' ability to collect fees for services; many were defined in law codes since 1497. Other court fees went directly to state coffers, and both sorts of fees rose in response to the constant wars of the seventeenth century. The significance of such fees is demonstrated by the fact that in chanceries that did not deal with litigation, scribal salaries were three to five times higher than in those that did, to compensate those scribes who would not earn extra income from litigation fees.[7]

"Living from one's work" also referred to the obligation of communities to provide upkeep for officials sent from Moscow. Governors, surveyors, criminal law officers and customs officials were supported by communities. Sometimes letters of appointment specified the amounts; in

[4] Plavsic, "Seventeenth-Century Chanceries," 36–8. Brown, "Service Land Chancellery Clerks," 49–53; Demidova, *Sluzhilaia biurokratiia*, ch. 3.

[5] Hellie, *Enserfment*, 151–265; Stevens, *Russia's Wars*, chs. 4–8.

[6] AMG II: no. 11 (1635). ZA no. 319 (1646); DAI VIII: no. 22 (1678). PSZ II: no. 779 (1679).

[7] Hellie, *Economy and Material Culture*, 513–18; Demidova, *Sluzhilaia biurokratiia*, 141–5.

most cases amounts were determined by local circumstances. The practice could be lucrative: a gentryman complained to the Military Service Chancery in 1653, for example, that he had been awarded the governorship of the town of Ruza but the community had refused to accept him, preferring to keep its brigandage elder. He protested that he had assumed great debts to go there, and he had no intention of sharing duties (and gifts) with the brigandage elder. Moscow affirmed that he should be the town governor.[8]

When an official arrived, representatives of the community greeted him with a home stocked with bushels of food, animals and staff. In addition to regular provisioning, throughout his tenure an official received gifts on holydays and other public occasions. Research has overturned a common presumption that such provisioning in kind, also called "feeding" (*kormlenie*), was abolished in the mid sixteenth century; it was robustly practiced well into the eighteenth century.[9] The system of upkeep and gift-giving undoubtedly led to corruption, but it could also create durable governance because of the interdependent, personal obligations associated with gift-giving.

As Marcel Mauss and others have argued, it was an ancient tradition in European government, and elsewhere, that public servants be supported by gifts. In early modern Europe, Seneca's and Cicero's texts on gifts for public officials were translated and widely reprinted as communities struggled to figure out what was proper and what crossed the line into bribery. In classical texts, what distinguished gifts from bribes was in part the publicity of the gift (secrecy was to be avoided) and in part its value (overly expensive items smacked of bribery). The range of acceptable public gifts was remarkably similar across Europe. Food and wine were appropriate, as were articles of clothing as long as they were not too fancy. Luxury items – silver goblets, jewel-studded bound books – were more suspect.[10]

Gift-giving in Muscovy paralleled these norms. There, proper gifts – called *pominki* or *pochesti* – were given not only to bureaucrats, but also exchanged between client and patron to acknowledge relationships of

[8] AMG II: no. 568 (1653). Office as sinecure: Kivelson, *Autocracy*, 135–6; Givens, "Eighteenth-Century Nobiliary."

[9] Davies, *State Power*, ch. 5 and "Politics of Give and Take"; Enin, *Voevodskoe kormlenie* and "Voevodskoe prazdnichnoe kormlenie"; Glaz′ev, *Vlast′ i obshchestvennost′*, 191–3; Kivelson, *Autocracy*, 139. Tamara Kondratieva construed "feeding" broadly to include the tsar's bestowing food to his men at banquets, as well as gifts supporting local officials: *Gouverner et nourrir*, 29–63.

[10] Davis (*Gift*, "Introduction") critiques Mauss's concept; Groebner, *Liquid Assets*.

dependence. Gifts of food and drink were given on three holydays (Christmas, Easter and St. Peter's Day in early summer) and on the name day of the recipient, his key kinsmen and his wife. Special attention was given to gifts for women, since they were seen as acceptable intercessors. In local communities, everyone who had a stake in government gave such routinized gifts. Monasteries, for example, budgeted a generous amount annually for gifts to the local governor, officials of the alcohol monopoly and customs office, and other officials with whom they had legal and fiscal dealings. They made sure to give these gifts publically before witnesses, in a ceremonial fashion, often to the wives and daughters of the officials at their homes, underscoring personal respect rather than influence peddling. Individual litigators also gave gifts. Jacques Margeret, a French mercenary who served at court for several years in the early seventeenth century, observed these customs: "It is also somewhat permissible for them during the week after Easter to accept some little thing when they meet, kiss each other, and exchange eggs . . . However, they may not take any gift if it be presented to them in hope thereby of gaining favor." All told, communities bore quite a burden from such exactions: one community in the seventeenth century recorded spending 1,857 rubles in one year for such provisioning![11]

Gift-giving had reciprocal effect, understood by all. Brian Davies uncovered a fascinating case of 1647 in which the townsmen of the frontier town of Kozlov greeted their new governor with generous provisions and ceremonial gifts, but he refused to take anything. In response, they drove him out of town, reasoning that if he failed to accept their gifts, they could not do business with him. The Kozlov community's action underscores that gift-giving created a working relationship between community or individual and an official. Givers expected a judge to move a case along expeditiously, a tax collector to grant a delay in payment or a surveyor to do his job fairly.[12]

Distinguishing gift-giving from corruption depended upon the local moral economy. Popular petitions and official investigations suggest that in Muscovy the transition from gift to bribe (*posul*) involved (1) extorting excessive provisions or gifts; (2) not following through on implicit reciprocal obligations; (3) abusing power, such as releasing prisoners for bribes,

[11] Patron–client relations: Kivelson, *Autocracy*, ch. 5; Krom, "Private Service." Margeret, *Russian Empire*, 28–9. Enin, "Voevodskoe prazdnichnoe," 104.

[12] Davies, "Politics of Give and Take," 57. Economy of gifts: Sedov, "Podnoshenia v moskovskikh prikazakh," 143–5; Brown, "Neither Fish nor Fowl"; Potter, "Payment, Gift or Bribery"; Hellie, *Economy and Material Culture*, 519, 530; Novokhatko, "Upravlentsy."

using physical violence, monopolizing trade, unjustly arresting; (4) imbalancing the benefits, that is, favoring one faction to the exclusion of others.[13] A new concern arose in the context of early modern empire: graft. Across Europe, as the amounts of pounds, francs and rubles expended on state projects increased, officials, often very high-ranking ones, found it tempting to rake off some benefits. Particularly after Peter I inaugurated so many public works, this became a major problem in Russia.

The likelihood of official corruption grew out of Muscovy's own choices about governance. Had sixteenth-century tsars created a well-salaried, well-trained, and disciplined officialdom based on a cash economy, many of the temptations could have been avoided. But such an expectation of modern, Weberian bureaucracy is wildly irrelevant to Muscovy and to most early modern European countries as well. Not only did Muscovy lack the resources for transparent salaries, it also lacked the conceptual framework for impersonal governance, which took centuries to develop even in Europe. In Muscovy, as "bureaucratic" as the state was, it was also inextricably personalized: all communications to the state by private individuals, and all communications among officials as well, were construed in a stylized language of petitioning personally to the tsar in submission and supplication; the tsar responded by granting his "favor." As in early modern Europe, personal networks among clan-based factions structured politics.[14] The language and practice of "feeding," "gifts" and tsarist "favor," and the politics of patronage and clientelism, coexisted with legal definitions of law and procedure. When relations with officials were based on gift-giving, people expected that officials would bend the law to their circumstances. Officials had to apportion their interaction to avoid excesses.

PREVENTING CORRUPTION

Russian rulers tried to police their officials with several strategies. First was the preventative measure of not appointing men to governorships in communities where they held land, in the words of a 1672 decree, "so that they will not oppress with enmity any servitor or lower rank people or peasants, or that in friendship they do give the guilty any indulgence." But

[13] Complaints against local officials: Glaz'ev, *Vlast' i obshchestvennost'*, 286–92.

[14] Petitioning: Kollmann, *By Honor Bound*, ch. 5, esp. 199–201; Rowland, "Problem of Advice." Clan-based patronage: Kivelson, *Autocracy*, ch. 5; Harding, "Corruption."

in practice, by the early seventeenth century, as Valerie Kivelson has shown, the rule was being broken, potentially favoring one local faction over another. Keeping the terms of office short, a year or two at a time was remarked by foreigners: the English diplomat Fletcher noted "These dukes and *d'iaki* . . . are changed ordinarily at every year's end," while the German scholar Olearius noted approvingly: "so that a locality may not be subjected too long to an unjust administration, and, on the other, so that the *namestnik* [governor] may not become too friendly with the inhabitants and be tempted to neglect his duty." Nevertheless, the problem was vexed. When Siberian governors were given longer terms in 1695, the rationale was that short terms intensified officials' exploitation and graft. Nevertheless, Siberian governors continued to be notorious for corruption.[15]

As discussed in Chapter 2, the state policed officials by tracking their work closely, but this provided only relatively weak oversight. A more effective policy, already noted in Chapter 1, was that Russian tsars avoided the sale of office to private bidders. France and England notoriously used this device for short-term income in the seventeenth and eighteenth centuries, as did the Ottoman Empire. Historians have tried to see the positive in this practice. When venality became formalized in France in the early seventeenth century, for example, onlookers in England considered it progressive compared to their situation whereby the dominant faction distributed offices. Historians of the Ottoman Empire argue that sale of offices fostered loyalty to the regime among local elites. In the long run, however, the purchase, heritability and often subdivision of offices undermined central power. Russian rulers resisted this expedient, insisting on centralized control despite the huge expanses and social diversity of its empire.[16]

The state tried other means to stop corruption. One was its willingness to accept and pursue complaints. The Petition Chancery was established in the reign of Mikhail Fedorovich (ruled 1613–45) to field complaints against officials in a very corrupt time; two Moscow judicial chanceries

[15] PSZ I: no. 508 (1672). Kivelson, *Autocracy*, 141–3. Fletcher, "Of the Russe," 150; Olearius, *Travels*, 177. PSZ III: no. 1511 (1695). Siberian corruption: PSZ III: no. 1670, p. 552 (1699 citing 1611 situation); DAI XII: no. 2 (1684); Aleksandrov and Pokrovskii, *Vlast' i obshchestvo*, 134–40; Witzenrath, *Cossacks*, 127 (a revisionist view).

[16] Peck, "Court Patronage." Khoury, *State and Provincial Society*, chs. 4–5. Plavsic notes that although venality was never practiced, Muscovite scribal offices were often hereditary: "Seventeenth-Century Chanceries," 33–6; Hellie, "Russia," 491. Certain monopolies forbidden to limit abuse: AAE III: no. 295 (1640 notarial); DAI V: no. 96 (1669 gambling).

(*Moskovskii* and *Vladimirskii*) accepted appeals of judicial corruption. In the countryside when a new governor was appointed, he was instructed to summon the community and seek out their complaints; occasionally the tsar summoned representatives of the highest social groups in consultative ritual assemblies (*zemskie sobory*).[17] Litigants could seek transfer of a case if they felt the assigned judge had enmity towards them (see Chapter 7).

The state also leaned on collective responsibility and moral obligation. Surety bonds for elected judicial officials included harsh penalties to the guarantors should the official abuse or neglect his responsibilities. The 1589 code required the community to post surety bonds for men they selected to serve. Surety bonds for a bailiff in the Foreign Affairs Chancery in 1672 and for a brigandage warden in Pereiaslavl′ Riazanskii in 1688 threatened fines for the guarantors if they should release prisoners or shirk duties. The state also leaned on the spiritual power of oaths: officials swore loyalty to the tsar on a cross when they took office and were often reminded of this weighty obligation.[18]

The state also tried to prevent conflict of interest. For example, the state ruled in 1648 that cases against secretaries and undersecretaries could not be heard in the chanceries where they were employed, because, in the words of a collective petition from gentrymen, "we cannot have a just trial with the secretaries in the chanceries since the others who work in those chanceries are their brothers, nephews and children." Such cases were to be sent to the Petition Chancery, although Peter B. Brown argues that chanceries persisted in trying their own personnel in-house. Another step towards judicial transparency was taken in 1681 when boyar judges in the Appeals Court (*Raspravnaia palata*) were instructed to recuse themselves in cases involving themselves or their kinsmen and associates (*svoistvenniki*).[19]

Moscow's rulers also tried to curb official corruption through the law. In Muscovy's first law code (1497), at least 40 of its 68 articles set fees for judicial services, defined proper behavior for judicial and administrative personnel, and condemned bribery and false testimony. While it did not threaten corporal punishment, mid-sixteenth-century laws did. Brigandage charters from 1539 through the 1550s required corporal punishment up to

[17] Brown, "Guarding the Gate Keepers," 226–30, 237–40; Sedov, *Zakat*, 463–5. Councils of the Land: Kollmann, *By Honor Bound*, 200–1.

[18] 1589, arts. 4, 6: PRP IV: 414; Davies, *State Power*, 119; Kivelson, *Autocracy*, 139. AIuB II: nos. 262 (IV) (1672) and 262 (VII) (1688).

[19] AMG II: no. 371 (1648). Brown, "Guarding the Gate Keepers." PSZ II: no. 885 (1681); Sedov, "'On mne svoi . . .'."

execution for bribery and dereliction of duty,[20] as did the 1550 and 1589 Law Codes; they also recommended corporal punishment for false accusation of judges and for frivolous suits. Such codes culminated in the 1649 Ulozhenie's ample attention to official malfeasance.[21] Similarly, the oath of brigandage elders from the 1550s required that they take "no bribes and gifts" (*posuly, pominki*), while that in 1656 of a governor prescribed the death penalty for taking bribes. A charter to a Siberian governor in 1611 threatens him with knouting for engaging in illegal trade, while the judicial charter to Ustiuzhna Zheleznopol'skaia of 1614 threatens execution and confiscation of property for judicial officials – brigandage elder, land judge and land scribe – who sign off on a corruptly composed document.[22] A decree of around 1620 threatened fines for corrupt governors and officials, while an appointment order in 1646 to a hundredman in the Artillery Neighborhood cited corporal punishment and fines, as did those for village hundredmen in Beloozero in 1683, in the Novgorod area in 1699 and for land judges in the North. Charters of appointment for investigators (*syshchiki*) also decreed harsh punishments for malfeasance.[23] These varying sanctions, supplementing or contradicting law codes, suggest the variety of standards available around the realm.

Threats of punishment abounded in correspondence between governors and the center. In 1638, for example, the governor of Dedilov was sternly reminded that he had no jurisdiction over artillerymen and cossacks, who had judicial venue in their respective Moscow chanceries. If he persisted in bringing them to trial, he would be transferred from his post and suffer "great corporal punishment." Governors on the southern frontier were threatened in 1651 with "great disgrace and corporal punishment without mercy" and a fine of 100 rubles for not submitting court fees twice a year on time.[24]

20 1497 Law Code, arts. 1, 67: RZ II: 54, 62. 1539 brigandage charter: PRP IV: 178 (art. 8). Jan. 1555 Felony Handbook: PRP IV: 358–9 (arts. 7–8, 13). August 1556 Decree: PRP IV: 367 (art. 15).

21 1550 Law Code, arts. 3–5, 7–11, 28, 33, 34, 42: RZ II: 97–9, 101–4. 1589 Law Code, arts. 3–5, 105–6: PRP IV: 414, 425–6. Similar provision: ZA no. 42 (1582). 1649 Ulozhenie ch. 10, arts. 5–6, 8, 123, 143, 146, 148: RZ III: 102–3, 117–18, 123, 124; ch. 21, arts. 83–4, 104: 244, 247. On corruption: Man'kov, *Ulozhenie*, 295–8.

22 PRP IV: 186–8 (1550s). AMG II: no. 867 (1656). PSZ III: no. 1670, p. 554 (1611). AAE III: no. 36, p. 75 (1614). Other oaths: PSZ III: no. 1540, p. 231 (1696); AMG II: no. 817 (1656).

23 ZA no. 98 (1620). AAE IV: no. 9 (1646). AI V: no. 111 (1683). AIuB II: no. 230 (XL) (1699). In the North: Bogoslovskii, "Zemskoe samoupravlenie," *Chteniia* (1910), bk. 1, nos. 1–15, 22, pp. 82–101, 105, esp. nos. 7 (1652), 22 (1643) and "Mirskoi vybor zemskogo sudeiki, 1659 g." Investigators: 1669 Criminal Articles, art. 2: PRP VII: 396; PSZ I: no. 220 (1658); PRP VII: art. 6, p. 189 (1683); Glaz'ev, *Vlast' i obshchestvennost'*, chs. 2 and 3.

24 AMG II: no. 105 (1638); PSZ I: no. 66 (1651).

As with accusations of shirking service (see Chapter 2), officials defended themselves vociferously when accused of corruption. In 1612 in the midst of the Time of Troubles, for example, a military officer protested that he had been falsely accused of not obeying orders to defend Vologda; he explained that his orders had been different and called this slander. A governor in Briansk, accused in 1628 of not obeying an order to execute two criminals, explained in painstaking detail how the original orders had never been received. Similarly, the governor of Lebedian point by point refuted charges that he had not allowed musketeer and cossack officers to take up their posts in 1629. Another claimed in 1634 to have been slandered because of enmity by a mill official and by the governor who had replaced him regarding his oversight of a local saltpeter works. He declared to the tsar, "my service to you, just sovereign, was good," bragging that under his direction the works were far more productive and efficient than saltpeter mills in Temnikov, Pereiaslavl′ and Meshchersk.[25]

Officials also often headed off accusations of corruption by rushing to explain away any failures. The governor of Shuia explained to the Military Service Chancery in 1618 that he was unable to try a case of assault and battery because the defendants were a powerful gang of local bullies against whom he was helpless. "They are people with many kinsmen and many clients and allies and they disobey me." He therefore sent the case and plaintiff to Moscow for adjudication. Similarly, the governor of Beloozero reported in 1628 that his colleague, secretary Mikhail Svetnikov, refused to come to work, despite his many entreaties, justifying why he, the governor, was carrying out a criminal investigation on his own. The documentary form of a "notice" (*iavka*) often functioned to allege one's innocence – for example, the brigandage elder of Shuia informed the state in 1626 of allegations of illegal wine trade and theft of tavern income that he had heard from the tavern scribe and another townsman.[26] Similarly, the Mtsensk governor cited at the head of Chapter 2 in 1635 reported that the community had selected his office clerk as brigandage scribe, and he feared falling into "disgrace" if the tsar's work suffered because he had lost his scribe. More dramatically, the governor of Briansk summoned all the local elite when his undersecretary accused him of treason in 1641. He publically refuted the accusation and thrust the keys to the governor's office to the assembled crowd, threatening to leave rather than tolerate

[25] DAI 1: no. 165 (1612). RGADA f. 210, Prikaznyi stol, no. 36, fols. 467–6, 485–91 (1628). AMG 1: nos. 241 (1629) and 620 (1634).

[26] PDP no. 206 (1618). SIDG no. 218 (1628). PDP no. 127 (1626).

such slander. They questioned the undersecretary, who admitted he fabricated the charge of treason because he feared being beaten by his boss. He called the governor "a harsh man, who beats you without mercy." The Military Service Chancery, investigating this donnybrook, kept the governor in place and chastised the undersecretary for false accusation, a rather modest punishment. Examples of such self-defense can be multiplied.[27]

Servitors declared themselves so aggressively for many reasons: they feared the corporal punishment, fines, confiscation of lands and loss of income which had been threatened. They also cherished personal honor: being falsely accused of disobedience to the tsar (which is how corruption was construed) was a great insult requiring response. The state also had high stakes in punishing corruption: doing so protected scarce resources and delivered on the tsar's duty to protect his people. It punished when it could, but there were structural impediments to truly effective policing of officialdom.

ATTACKING CORRUPTION

In 1620 Tsar Mikhail Romanov decried corruption: "in the towns governors and chancery officials conduct our various affairs not by our decrees, and cause violence, damages and great extortion to all people – monastics, servitors, townsmen, peasants, visitors – and take many bribes and gifts and goods for upkeep." His reign was particularly notorious for the emergence of so-called "powerful" (*sil'nye)* people against whom collective petitions were lodged for their ability to manipulate local courts.[28] Similarly, Grigorii Kotoshikhin, with perhaps some rancor at his erstwhile colleagues, condemned chancery judges:

> their oath and vowing is nothing to them and they do not fear punishment; they cannot make their eyes and thoughts resist temptations and they immediately reach out their hands to take, if not actually themselves, then on the back staircase, through their wives or daughters ... by such temptation their evil taking draws their souls into the depths of unquenchable fire and not only damages their souls but also the tsar's.

[27] AMG II: no. 11 (1635). SIDG no. 204 (1641), quote on 361. Further examples: Novombergskii, *Koldovstvo*, nos. 5 (1630), 6 (1636), 20 (1664); RGADA f. 210, Prikaznyi stol, no. 567, fols. 190–3 (1648); RGADA f. 210, Sevsk stol, no. 158, fols. 504–15 (1655).

[28] ZA no. 98 (1620). Corruption in Muscovy: Torke, *Die staatsbedingte Gesellschaft*, 76–81; Brown, "Early Modern Russian Bureaucracy," 247, 264–80; Glaz'ev, *Vlast' i obshchestvennost'*, 286–92. Collective petitions: Kivelson, *Autocracy*, 224–7, 234–40; Torke, *Die staatsbedingte Gesellschaft*, ch. 3.

Foreigners agreed, including Adam Olearius: "although the taking of bribes is forbidden under threat of punishment with the knout, nevertheless it occurs surreptitiously. The scribes in particular are ready to accept pledges or presents."[29]

Russian folklore and satirical literature gleefully skewered bureaucratic and judicial corruption. Popular from the late sixteenth or early seventeenth century was the Tale of Ersh Ershovich, a parody of accusatory court procedure and scurrilous litigants in which fish go to court over possession of Lake Rostov. In another tale, Frol Skobeev was a consummate schemer who earned his living "looking after other people's legal affairs"; this satirical tale dates to the early eighteenth century. Finally, the Tale of Shemiaka's Judgment adapted to Russia the theme of corrupt judges and wily peasant litigators found in many societies. Here a feckless young man escapes numerous deserved court convictions by bribing a vain and foolish judge. The tale spread widely in prose, verse and woodblock versions and is even referenced in the cases surveyed here: in 1642 the governor of Tobol′sk ordered a man beaten with bastinadoes for calling the governor's court a "Shemiakin's court" (*shemiakovskoi sud*)."[30]

Moscow had reason to worry about provincial officials. They were far from the capital, their communication with the center could be slow, they had too much to do with too little staff. They could be insolent, apparently weighing the likelihood of punishment against the short-term gain of fees from services. The Riazhsk governor was sent numerous orders to transfer a case around 1678 because the plaintiff had accused him of enmity, but he refused to cooperate. In 1680 the Ustiuzhna Zheleznopol′skaia governor was harshly criticized (but not punished) for refusing to yield jurisdiction over the people of a prominent local landholder. Moscow fulminated at him: "You are acting disobediently, forcing his people to serve in your staff and causing them burden and losses, imprisoning and destroying his estate for your own law-scoffing greed (*bezdel′noi korysti*)."[31] Governors sometimes left their positions in disarray, even absconding before their replacements had arrived in order not to admit to negligence. They ignored orders: in 1695 an order to

[29] Kotoshikhin, *O Rossii*, ch. 7, art. 38, p. 118; see also art. 9; Olearius, *Travels*, 226.

[30] Ersh, Shemiakin: *Pamiatniki literatury XVII vek*, II: 176–84. Skobeev: *Pamiatniki literatury XVII vek*, I: 59. Semiachko and Smirnov, "Povest′ o Ershe Ershoviche"; Ingham, "Muscovite Law"; Panchenko, "Povest′ o Frole Skobeeve"; Bobrov and Vasil′eva, "Povest′ o Shemiakinom sude"; Sedov, *Zakat*, 542–8. Lipinskii (ed.), "Rospis′," no. 116, p. 35 (1642).

[31] AIuB I: no. 58 (I) (1678). RGADA f. 1171, no. 210, fol. 2 (1680). Similar cases: RGADA f. 1441, op. 6, no. 263 (1681); RGADA f. 1171, no. 221 (1684).

governors to send all felons to Moscow for trial at the Musketeer Chancery was repeated; it noted that none had initially responded, that criminality was rising and that governors were being bribed to protect the criminals; it did not, however, specify punishment for failure to comply.[32] These cases suggest the state's relative weakness – governors risked being punished, assuming that the state did not have the manpower to replace them and would turn a blind eye.

Governors were not the only problematic local officials. From the beginning of the brigandage system, laws anticipated suits against brigandage staff for abuse of power. The earliest charters threatened fines, prison and harsh corporal punishment for corrupt elders or their staff. The 1669 Criminal Articles put the prosecution of brigandage staff in the hands of the investigators that the code introduced. Indeed, V. N. Glaz′ev notes that communities often complained of corrupt brigandage elders.[33] In 1622 the brigandage scribe of Shuia submitted a complaint against his colleagues, alleging that the elders and wardens of Shuia were taking bribes to protect criminals and that they had threatened him: "And one of the wardens grabbed me by the throat and cast me out and threatened me with murder on the roads or home and everywhere, saying 'We will not leave you alive, because you are not in league (*soveten*) with us and do not do things as we do (*po nashemu*).'" The community of Uglich reported in 1641 that their brigandage elder was elected inappropriately: "he is young and has a small salary, whereas by the tsar's orders brigandage elders are to be from among the most prosperous gentry." They accused him of drinking, wasting resources, beating his staff and dismissing staff without the tsar's order. They recommended a replacement; the central government promptly dismissed the old and appointed a new brigandage elder.[34]

Expecting that the tsar as just judge would rectify injustices, communities and individuals did not hesitate to complain, and they got results. The abbot and brothers of the St. Cyril Beloozero Monastery in 1582, for example, complained about a brigandage elder who was surveying their lands. They accused him of forcing them illegally to pay taxes on deserted

[32] AMG III: no. 210 (1660); Chicherin, *Oblastnye uchrezhdeniia*, 476–8. PSZ III: no. 1515 (1695).

[33] 1539 Beloozero Charter, arts. 7–8: RZ II: 215; 1555 Medyn Charter, arts. 12, 13: RZ II: 222; PRP IV: 186–7 (1550s); Jan. 1555 Felony Handbook, arts. 7, 8, 11, 13: PRP IV: 358–9; August 1556 Decree, arts. 13, 15: PRP IV: 366–7; 1616/17 Felony Handbook, art. 55: PRP V: 199. 1669 Criminal Articles, art. 5–6: PRP VII: 397.

[34] PDP no. 115, p. 155 (1622). "Dela ob opredelenii," no. IV, pp. 38–41 (1641). Other complaints: AMG II: no. 279 (1647); PDP no. 153 (1651); Glaz′ev, *Vlast′ i obshchestvennost′*, 210.

plots, of imprisoning their men and demanding gifts.[35] In 1639 the gentrymen and peasants of Kashira complained that tax collectors sent from Moscow were extorting bribes and excess taxes. When the tax collectors were given a face-to-face confrontation with their accusers, they responded that the extra money was an acceptable gift (*v pochest'*), not a bribe (*posula*). They were, however, found guilty and ordered to be knouted and to pay back the money. Their commanding officers, two men of Moscow rank, were initially ordered executed and their property confiscated because, as the verdict reminded them, their orders of appointment and oath of office explicitly forbade such behavior. They were then pardoned and were instead knouted in the marketplace in Tula "mercilessly" as a deterrent to all. The publicity of the punishment, and the initially harsher sentence, demonstrated both the state's commitment to punish corruption and the tsar's mercy. A group of Karelians who had joined Muscovite service complained in 1657 of being abused by local Russian landlords; the Chancery invited them to submit more detailed complaints and instructed the governor to investigate all allegations "seriously" and to satisfy their complaints "so they will never again need to complain like this." Even officials complained about other officials – the governor of Kursk reported in 1648 that the local brigandage elder had improperly released prisoners.[36]

Moscow often responded promptly. The Tatar community of Perm Velikii and Cherdyn' complained in 1621, for example, about excessive taxation, abuse and even murder of two of their number by tax collectors. They boldly identified the culprits as "men of Andrei and Petr Stroganovy," a powerful family that enjoyed mining monopolies in the Urals. The Military Service Chancery ordered the local governor to do a full investigation, to "protect them [community members] in the future from such abuses" and to order the tax officials to obey the law. In 1636 the state responded with alacrity to a charge against the brigandage scribe of Kursk, accused of torturing a gentryman without official permission and of scoffing at Moscow's authority. The scribe was arrested that same day and denied all, charging both that the gentryman had been tortured properly and that he had insulted and threatened the scribe in court.

[35] Suing governors: Aleksandrov and Pokrovskii, "Mirskie organizatsii"; Pokrovskii, *Tomsk. 1648–49 g.*, ch. 2; Aleksandrov and Pokrovskii, *Vlast' i obshchestvo*, ch. 5; Davies, *State Power*, ch. 5. Barsov, "Akty, otn. k istorii Belozerskogo kraia," 14–15 (1582). In 1687 the Patriarch complained to the Tsar about governors ignoring his immunity and abusing his people: AI v: no. 157.

[36] RGADA f. 210, Sevsk stol, no. 111, fols. 186–95 (1639), quote on fol. 188. Another example: AAE III: no. 150 (1623). AAE IV: no. 94 (1657). RGADA f. 210, Belgorod stol, no. 338, fols. 914–16 (1648).

When hundreds of landlords protested the work of surveyors in Moscow province and the surveyors counter-sued in 1686, the state sent out a new set of surveyors and promised face-to-face confrontations with all the litigants.[37] An investigator was sent in 1660 to respond to community complaints about the governor of Kaluga, who vociferously defended himself in over 244 face-to-face confrontations with his accusers. Investigations were not a panacea: in 1639 in Shuia Moscow was forced to start an inquiry into an investigator who himself had been sent to look into local corruption; the community was charging him with bad behavior.[38]

One reason why many of these cases are unresolved might have been the complexity of the judicial process: defendants often responded with countercharges. For example, both sides in a corruption dispute in Nizhnii Novgorod appealed to Moscow in 1682: the land (*zemskii*) judge of the town had been accused in 1677 of drinking, carousing and writing documents at his home "without the counsel of the townsmen and his fellow elders, colluding with his compatriots." The complainants alleged that he admitted his bad behavior and that his father confessor had succeeded in getting him sent to a local monastery to dry out and repent. But the accused man sued, calling it slander and claiming that he had been condemned "without trial and without a face-to-face confrontation and without an investigation." He ended up, according to his account, stranded half way to exile, ill and poverty-stricken in Ustiug Velikii; he won a proper trial and was vindicated. Cases often developed this way, with charge and countercharge, as in a case of 1684 in which a man accused of shirking taxes counter-sued the local land judge for falsely accusing him in order to cover up his own thefts from the treasury. When false accusation was proven, the courts provided compensation for injured honor. In a case of 1667, for example, a townsman of Tula accused his local governor and a judge in the Felony Chancery of ruling corruptly against him. He lost his suit, had to pay dishonor compensation and was beaten for dishonor to a social superior.[39]

As seen, in cases that were resolved, Moscow did not spare the rod. For example, the Military Service Chancery in 1628 ordered a brigandage

[37] AAE III: no. 118 (1621). SIDG no. 259 (1636). PSZ II: no. 1215 (1686); Sedov, *Zakat*, 479–90. Other examples: DAI III: no. 68 (1650 governor punishes colleague); PSZ I: nos. 123 (1654 boyar guilty of bribes) and 170 (1655 corruption).

[38] AMG III: no. 4 (1660). PDP no. 139 (1639); see also no. 143 (1640). Shuia corruption: Kivelson, *Autocracy*, 138–40, 146–8, 160–7. Similar self-defense: AMG I: no. 241 (1629).

[39] DAI X: no. 23 (1682). Lipinskii (ed.), "Rospis'," no. 7 (1684). RGADA f. 210, Prikaznyi stol, no. 787, fols. 25–33 (1667).

warden to be beaten with bastinadoes "mercilessly" because he had failed to report a treason case immediately; in 1676 a tavern chief who had stolen money from the till was ordered beaten and fined. In 1687 a tax official from the Kola Peninsula was ordered beaten with bastinadoes and exiled to Pustoozero for stealing money from the treasury and abusing the people; a governor, because of his higher status, was fined in 1700 rather than beaten for disobeying orders to transfer a case.[40] But the state had a harder time changing the structural bases of corruption.

THE PERSISTENCE OF CORRUPTION

The underpinnings of corruption were several. Lack of manpower was a serious problem. The bureaucratic apparatus grew steadily, but numbers of staff did not keep up: governors' offices increased from 185 to 302 from the 1620s to the 1690s, but only 1,918 staff were divided among those 302 provincial offices by the end of the century. In these conditions, courts might have been loath to fire corrupt chancery staff. As Borivoj Plavsic shows, many secretaries and undersecretaries convicted of corruption easily found employment elsewhere because of "a perennial shortage of trained administrators."[41] Perhaps something of that is at stake in a surprising ruling in a murder case of 1635. Two Beloozero undersecretaries had conspired to murder a third to prevent his being promoted above them; they were found guilty. The crime was all the more regrettable since, as the case reports, the murdered undersecretary had been a good, honest scribe, while the murderers came from a local scribal family known for corruption. But the men, who admitted premeditated murder under torture, were only fined by chancery judges, when the death penalty should have been prescribed. Perhaps the Chancery was protecting its own, or simply trying to preserve some trained scribal personnel. Similarly, governors could be treated leniently. The St. Cyril Beloozero Monastery complained in 1658 that the Beloozero governor had protected a local gentryman from prosecution for assault and sexual crimes. The Moscow chancery deprived the governor of jurisdiction in the case, but did not further investigate or punish him. Similarly, in 1660 a Tatar dignitary (*murza*) in Temnikov complained that the local governor had judged two cases unjustly "for his scofflaw greed, not according to the

[40] SIDG no. 218 (1628). RGADA f. 210, Sevsk stol, no. 294, fols. 311–30 (1676). RGADA f. 159, op. 3, Novgorod chetvert, no. 2470, fols. 128–33 (1687). AIuB 1: no. 58 (IV) (1700).

[41] Demidova, *Sluzhilaia biurokratiia*, ch. 1, esp. 48, 72–4; Plavsic, "Seventeenth-Century Chanceries," 32.

[1649] Conciliar Ulozhenie, bypassing the law." The tsar granted the *murza*'s request to transfer the cases to Moscow for reconsideration, but did not chastise or investigate the governor.[42]

Efforts at quality control were few and not well enforced. In modern bureaucracies they include such strategies as appointment by merit-based tests, regular checking of account books, frequent on-site inspections, regular transfer to different postings to keep officials in line. In our period, chancery staffs in Moscow had regular oversight, but in the provinces it was ineffective.[43] Although governors were required to keep annual reports and to make inventories at the beginning and end of their tenures, these moments of control did not prevent officials from depleting reserves and neglecting equipment. The government did periodically try to clear the decks of officials who had become entrenched. In 1632 the brigandage elder of Murom was told to have new brigandage wardens elected in place of those who had been serving "five, six, ten or more years"; the new ones were to serve no more than a year. In 1661 in a reform that went nowhere, all governors and their staffs were to be replaced by brigandage elders and their staffs.[44] Moscow generally did not have the capacity to carry out such country-wide initiatives and reforms.

Furthermore, tough prosecution was inhibited by the law's social inequities. The 1649 Ulozhenie promised uncorrupt justice – "all judicial cases are to be rendered to all people of the Muscovite State, from the greatest to the least rank, according to the law" – but not a law uniform for all. Far from it. Rather, social groups enjoyed differential relations to the law – for example, the highest ranks enjoyed de facto immunity from corporal punishment except in the most serious crimes (see Chapters 9–10). The practice of dealing differently with different social groups was part and parcel of what Jane Burbank has called an "imperial rights regime," namely, that groups identified by social class, ethnicity, region or religion were governed according to a combination of local customs and overarching imperial law.[45] Such a policy was in place for social groups from the earliest law codes and for non-Russian, non-Orthodox peoples of the realm from

[42] RGADA f. 1107, nos. 703 (1635) and 1429 (1658). RGADA f. 1167, op. 1, pt. 2, no. 1371, fols. 4–5 (1660).

[43] The eighteenth-century English Excise introduced such measures (Brewer, *Sinews of Power*, 101–14), but see Brewer and Hellmuth's comments on the weaknesses of even this strong state: "Introduction." Annual reviews: Demidova, *Sluzhilaia biurokratiia*, 61–2.

[44] Oversight: Davies, *State Power*, 119; Kivelson, *Autocracy*, 139; Demidova, *Sluzhilaia biurokratiia*, 62–75. AAE III: no. 210 (1632). PSZ I: no. 313 (1661).

[45] Ulozhenie ch. 10, art. 1: RZ III: 286–7. Burbank, "Imperial Rights."

the foundation of the Russian empire in the sixteenth century. The policy promoted stability, but its social deference could stand in the way of punishing high-ranking officials.

So also could the written law's relative weakness in defining official corruption. The 1649 Ulozhenie's first three chapters on crimes against the state significantly did not include a crime of dereliction of official duty. Furthermore, professionalization that might have militated against corruption never occurred. For Russian elites, military service was all that mattered, not administrative. Muscovy certainly never developed a civil service elite, a *noblesse de robe* or other professional cadres that might have brought into being, as they did elsewhere, higher professional standards, social prestige and political capital.[46]

The imbrications of legal and personal in Muscovite governance also created a culture open to excess and abuse. Attitudes expressed in collective petitions from the seventeenth into the nineteenth centuries – while deploring official inefficiency and corruption – perceived civil service in personal terms. Communities did not seek impartial rule by law but rather requested locally based courts staffed by local judges who would rule according to local circumstances and knowledge of communities and their norms. This opened the door to favoritism.[47] Muscovites also lacked institutional avenues to report and punish corruption. When the state decreed punishment for local officials, it had no independent police force to enforce it, but had to enlist a neighboring official. For example, in a case of 1650 in Iur′ev Polskoi a brigandage elder was ordered to punish a governor by levying a fine and reading the tsar's denunciation to him in front of a crowd. Similarly, in a case of 1669 the governor of Vereia was ordered to carry out a punishment on the governor of Mozhaisk and his undersecretary. Glaz′ev cites cases where a local brigandage elder was asked to investigate the local governor for corruption, and vice versa.[48] The situation was ripe for abuse when peers were called upon to punish peers.

Finally, Muscovy lacked venues to report corruption. In principle, litigants could sue against a judge for enmity, but in the absence of a special envoy from Moscow, local people had no one to complain to against a local official; they had to submit their complaints against the

[46] Ulozhenie, chs. 1–3: RZ III: 85–91. Early modern French and English judges advocated for better courts: Sawyer, "Judicial Corruption"; Prest, "Judicial Corruption."

[47] Kivelson, *Autocracy*, 224–7, 234–40; Wortman, *Development*, 21; Torke, *Die staatsbedingte Gesellschaft*, ch. 3.

[48] AMG II: no. 452 (1650). PSZ I: no. 458 (1669); Glaz′ev, *Vlast′ i obshchestvennost′*, 222–3.

governor or his staff to that very office. Petitions indeed mention that a corrupt governor "refused to let us sue" him. The only recourse available to such litigants was to travel to Moscow, but even there a gentryman or townsman would be complaining to a chancery official reluctant to prosecute a social peer or connected through patronage networks with the accused official. The most successful petitions were collective ones presented by communities, which usually came together only in times of great stress.[49]

A noted innovation in the seventeenth century paradoxically exacerbated the difficulty of appeal. In pursuit of a more impersonal, bureaucratic model of officialdom, laws from 1649 on tried to restrict the ability of individuals and groups to appeal directly to the ruler. Individuals were to present their complaint up a line of judicial venues instead.[50] The frequency with which this injunction was repeated testifies not only to the ideology of the tsar's benevolence but also to the absence of other means to appeal injustice.

Only adequate resources would have combated the structural foundations of corruption in Russia's judicial and administrative system: personalized dependence between community and officials, inadequate salaries, the reliance on community support for upkeep; absence of strong professions (law, officialdom), a dearth of practices and institutions of systematic oversight. The judicial system worked only when the balance between personalized interaction of community and society and legal norms was maintained; too often it went awry.

49 PSZ III: no. 1511 (1695). Difficulty of filing grievances: Davies, *State Power*, 216–25; Kivelson, *Autocracy*, 140.

50 Prohibiting petitioning the tsar: 1649 Ulozhenie ch. 10, art. 20: RZ III: 104–5; ch. 1, arts. 8–9: RZ III: 86; PSZ II: no. 1092 (1684): PSZ III: no. 1707 (1699); PSZ IV: no. 1748 (1700); PSZ V: no. 3261 (1718); PSZ VI: nos. 3838 and 3947 (1721, 1722).

CHAPTER 5

Procedure and evidence

On November 30, 1636 in the southern frontier town of Oskol a party of four local men – two gentry and two cossacks – brought the dead body of Tikhonka Gorianov, son of one of them, to the governor's office, alleging murder. Governor Konstantin Mikhailovich Pushchin launched the case by questioning them. They charged that the young man's wife Donka had killed him in the forest. Pushchin ordered Donka brought in, questioned her and, upon her confession, to affirm it ordered her interrogated in sight of the instruments of torture and then tortured. He then put her in custody and wrote to Moscow seeking instructions; it was, by then, February. The Military Service Chancery responded on March 8, 1637, ordering him to carry out a second torture session to ask about prior planning or co-conspirators. Anyone she implicated should be arrested. Receiving these instructions on March 24, Pushchin proceeded to two more oral interrogations (one in sight of the instruments of torture), followed by a second torture session, in each of which she testified that she had killed her husband on her own initiative because he "beat her constantly." Reporting this back to Moscow, the Chancery instructed him in June to execute her if she were not pregnant. If she were, he was to wait until she gave birth, according to the law. Assuming time for this resolution to reach Oskol, total time between reporting the crime and conclusion of the case was about seven months.[1]

Most criminal cases were not resolved as expeditiously as Donka Gorianova's murder trial. But this case displays key elements of the trial process – the governor as judge controlled the case, interrogating, torturing to confirm a confession, corresponding with Moscow. He used, in other words, the inquisitory process. This chapter will examine trial procedures.

[1] RGADA f. 210, Belgorod stol, no. 83, fols. 369–71 and 584–5 (1636). Oskol is approximately 475 miles from Moscow.

ACCUSATORY AND INQUISITORY PROCEDURES

In Muscovy inquisitory procedure often contained elements of the accusatory trial, so both processes will be briefly examined. Each had deep roots across Europe. The accusatory mode was known throughout medieval Europe as well as in the East Slavic lands. Used for everything from dishonor cases to misdemeanor injury, accusatory trials were dyadic and litigant-driven. Plaintiffs initiated the suit: both sides presented and rejected each other's witnesses; they could settle the case. The judge's role was honest broker and renderer of the verdict; the scribe wrote up a trial transcript that "reanimated" the oral proceedings when he read the transcript to the judge for verdict. Most litigation used this form, and law codes provide ample description (the 1497, 1550, 1589 Codes, the huge tenth chapter of the 1649 Ulozhenie); even Grigorii Kotoshikhin describes it in his account of chancery courts.[2]

The accusatory format (*sud*) was suited to small-scale communities, urban or rural, and its goal was usually restitution. Proof in an accusatory trial was primarily witness evidence or documents, but as Johann-Georg Korb related around 1698, "If the case cannot be cleared up by evidence, it is terminated by swearing." Taking an oath by kissing the cross was so serious a ritual in Muscovy that the law allowed individuals to do it only three times in their lives; in practice people settled cases before reaching that point. Olearius in the mid seventeenth century declared that anyone who took an oath in a trial, even if he spoke the truth, was "driven from the church in which he had executed the oath, and was thereafter held in contempt" – probably an exaggeration but Olearius captures how grave was this encounter with the divine.[3] The accusatory mode reflects a more personalized concept of justice and judicial procedure than does the inquisitory.

The inquisitorial procedure (*sysk, rozysk*), on the other hand, is judge-centered, representing the interests of the public or state, and uses torture to seek proof. It cannot be settled, reflecting the primacy of state's

[2] Collins, *Reanimated Voices*, 27–34. Accusatory mode: Shtamm, "Sud i protsess," 224–44. Ulozhenie ch. 21, arts. 49, 51–4, 88, 91: RZ III: 238–9, 245; Kotoshikhin, *O Rossii*, ch. 7, arts. 40–2, pp. 118–21. Dyadic and triadic: Kaiser, *Growth*, ch. 1.

[3] Korb, *Diary*, II: 187; Olearius, *Travels*, 228; see also Herberstein, *Description*, 74–5; Fletcher, "Of the Russe," 174–5. Judicial duel, while cited in sixteenth-century codes, was no longer used: Dewey, "Trial by Combat"; Weickhardt, "Muscovite Judicial Duels"; 1550 Law Code, arts. 9–14, 62: RZ II: 98–9, 108–9; 1589 Law Code, arts. 12–22, 27, 30: PRP IV: 415–18. Oath-taking: Kollmann, *By Honor Bound*, 119–21. Its antiquity: Mikhailova and Prestel, "Cross Kissing."

interests over popular calculations of the social harm caused by punishment. Known in Roman law, the procedure had fallen into disuse in Europe until a twelfth-century revival by secular jurists and canon lawyers seeking to standardize procedure and stop abuses associated with oaths and ordeals (the Catholic Church abolished the judicial ordeal in 1215). Confession (which was being instituted for Catholics at the same time) was considered the supreme proof and torture became the centerpiece of inquisitorial procedure to achieve it.[4]

In the fifteenth and sixteenth centuries two processes coalesced to further develop the inquisitory process in Europe. Kings and municipalities were asserting greater social, political and moral discipline, but growing population, rising crime and the impersonality of urban life made the accusatory format less effective. Applied to criminal cases, the inquisitory mode was driven by systematic interrogation and torture rather than litigants' give and take. Inquisitors assembled a dossier for submission to a judge for verdict. Codifications of criminal law promoting the inquisitory mode, or introducing some aspects of it to the British jury-based system, proliferated in sixteenth-century Europe.[5]

These codifications put a strong emphasis on transparency of procedure and rationality of proof. Charles V's 1532 *Carolina* is a particularly good example. Written to instruct a local judiciary that was not as highly trained as the Emperor's professional jurists, it is didactic and prescriptive; John Langbein calls it a "primer for laymen." It painstakingly prescribes stages of procedure and standards of evidence and repeatedly exhorts judges to use their judgment in assessing evidence and justifying the use of torture.[6] The challenge that Charles V faced of imposing uniform justice in a diverse empire with judges who were not trained jurists paralleled that facing Muscovy's rulers, although Muscovy lacked the jurisprudential background to produce a code like the *Carolina.*

The inquisitorial process is encountered from the late fifteenth century in Muscovy. The 1497 Law Code refers to three crucial elements of inquisitorial procedure: investigation by judges (*obysk*), testimony about an accused man's reputation and torture.[7] Where Muscovite codes received the inquisitorial method from is unclear. It was unlikely to have

[4] Langbein, *Prosecuting*, chs. 7–8; Langbein, *Torture and the Law*; Pihlajmaki, "Torture"; A. K., "Torture"; Peters, *Torture*, ch. 2.

[5] Inquisitory mode in Europe and England: Langbein, *Prosecuting*; Weisser, *Crime and Punishment*, chs. 2 and 4; Briggs et al., *Crime and Punishment*, chs. 1–2; Boes, "Public Appearance," 260–1.

[6] Langbein, *Prosecuting*, 157, 173–5, 207.

[7] Some see it even earlier: Shtamm, "Sud i protsess," 244–5. 1497 Code, arts. 12–14, 34: RZ II: 56, 58.

come to the East Slavs in Byzantine legal codes (excerpts from Justinian) imported after the 988 Christianization, because those preceded the European revivals that modified original Roman legal process.[8] Nor would Muscovy have taken it from the Grand Duchy of Lithuania. There, urban communities based on Magdeburg law used the inquisitory mode based on the *Carolina*, but such urban codes per se were not influential in Muscovy. Those that were – the sixteenth-century Statutes of the Grand Duchy of Lithuania – on the other hand, were weak on inquisitorial procedure. They mention torture only rarely and do not dwell at all on procedure.[9] George Weickhardt argues that inquisitorial procedure came to Muscovy through the *Carolina* (1532) by the seventeenth century in its intensive interactions with Poland (but admits that it might have come even in the sixteenth century). He based his argument on strong similarities between it and Felony Chancery norms of the 1610s and 1620s regarding procedure and probable cause for torture, arguing that "without law schools or universities, Muscovy is unlikely to have developed this concept [probable cause] on its own."[10]

Weickhardt is insightful to look for Western influence in this process. By the late fifteenth century Moscow's jurists in the Foreign Affairs and other chanceries had established contact with Europe and were facing some of the same issues that prompted the inquisitorial revival in Europe – namely, a desire to control crime and to enhance political control. At the same time, Muscovite inquisitorial procedure was adapted to local conditions: it did not include key features such as judicial appeal to learned universities (there were none) or the role of the procurator, a juridically trained middleman who investigates and interrogates behind closed doors to assemble a written dossier. In Muscovy the inquisitorial court was an open one. Judges actively interrogated and scribes read aloud the court transcript in preparation for making a verdict as in accusatory cases.[11]

[8] Langbein, *Prosecuting*, 138–9.

[9] Maisel, "Torture"; Uruszczak, "Torture." In the 1529 Lithuanian Statute, torture is mentioned only regarding theft (sect. 13, art. 14); the accusatory process is dominant: Lazutka et al., *Pervyi litovskii statut*, 244, 315. The 1588 Statute mentions torture only a few more times (Stat′ia 14, glavy 17, 18, 21): Lappo, *Litovskii statut.*

[10] Weickhardt, "Probable Western Origins." The *Carolina* was widely published in French, English, Swedish, Polish and other translations. Weickhardt notes that pre-Revolutionary Russian historiography denied foreign influence: ibid., 56, citing Sergeevich, *Lektsii i issledovaniia*, 617–25. A modern Russian translation of the *Carolina* does not link it with Muscovite practice: Bulatov (trans. and ed.), *Karolina.*

[11] Mixing of accusatory and inquisitory procedures throughout the 1649 Ulozhenie: Man′kov, *Ulozhenie*, 310–12, 322–3. Inquisitory mode: Shtamm, "Sud i protsess," 244–51.

The 1550 Law Code and brigandage charters from 1539 and the 1550s developed the inquisitory procedure with significant attention to issues of testimony, eyewitness evidence, material proof and community report of reputation. Judges collected evidence proactively: in oral interrogation of defendant, plaintiff and witnesses; in face-to-face confrontations to resolve disputed testimony (a practice also used in the accusatory mode, but here managed by the judge); in torture. Investigation was supposed to proceed from benign to coercive: the oath for brigandage elders of the 1550s, for example, specified that interrogation, face-to-face confrontations and community inquests had to affirm criminal reputation before proceeding to torture.[12]

The inquisitorial procedure was used for serious criminal cases – murder, felony theft and robbery, arson, high political and religious crime. In cases of theft or robbery, three conditions divided accusatory and inquisitor formats: material evidence, witnesses or community knowledge of felonious character. Without at least one of them a case would be tried in accusatory mode.[13] In practice, inquisitorial mode was used widely for cases including breaking fire safety laws, riding a horse into the Kremlin instead of dismounting, fleeing military service and land disputes.[14] But the open form of Muscovite inquisitory cases evidences the influence of accusatory procedure. In a striking case in the Far North in 1642, for example, a peasant sued a group of men for the stabbing death of his brother and the poisoning of his uncle, plus losses totaling 100 rubles. Such a criminal case should have used inquisitorial method, but at first accusatory procedure was used. The plaintiff and defendant were put on surety bond to be available for the trial process and the principal defendant stated his version in court, denying all and noting that the local judge had already examined the dead body (an inquisitorial practice) and a settlement agreement had been submitted (accusatory). But the plaintiff

[12] 1539 Beloozero Charter, arts. 3–5: RZ II: 214. 1555 Medyn Charter, arts. 2–3, 6–9: RZ II: 219–21. Criminal reputation as probable cause in the *Carolina* (arts. 25–6): Langbein, *Prosecuting*, 274. Reputation in seventeenth-century Württemberg criminal trials: Rublack, *Crimes of Women*, 44. PRP IV: 186–8 (1550s).

[13] 1616/17 Felony Handbook, art. 19: PRP V: 193–4; repeated in Ulozhenie ch. 21, art. 49: RZ III: 238. 1669 Criminal Articles, art. 72: PRP VII: 421. Inquisitory mode was also used when an individual had exhausted his three chances to swear an oath: Ulozhenie 14: art. 2: RZ III: 159.

[14] Fire: RGADA f. 210, Prikaznyi stol, no. 2513, fols. 1–10 (1674); RGADA f. 210, Prikaznyi stol, no. 674, fols. 53–5 and fols. 165–95 (1675 two cases); RGADA f. 210, Prikaznyi stol, no. 710, fols. 82, 119–25 (1676); RGADA f. 210, Prikaznyi stol, no. 1049, fols. 77–8, 123–5, 210–12 (1686 three cases). Riding in Kremlin: RGADA f. 210, Prikaznyi stol, no. 1039, fols. 11–13 (1680). Fleeing service: RGADA f. 210, Prikaznyi stol, no. 786, fols. 67–70 (1669). Land disputes: Kivelson, *Cartographies*, 36–7, 46–55.

objected and the trial continued in accusatory mode: the plaintiff presented lists of witnesses, whom the defendant promptly rejected as biased; documents were disputed; eventually the two men agreed to take an oath to resolve their differences. They also used inquisitory procedures: each demanded that the other be tortured for evidence. The admixture of accusatory elements with inquisitory in so serious a case reflects either ill-trained officials or a local culture of adapting the law, or both.[15]

Other cases also illustrate courts' application of both forms, as in a murder investigation in 1651 in which the governor of Olonets resolutely used inquisitorial procedure – oral interrogation, face-to-face confrontations and torture – but the scribe reported testimony using phrases characteristic of witness dispute in accusatory trials (*ssylki, slat'sia iz vinovatykh*). In a witchcraft case of 1648 the judge consciously shifted from accusatory to inquisitorial mode as the seriousness of the charges mounted.[16]

Over the course of the seventeenth century inquisitory format became preferred even for misdemeanor cases.[17] In Beloozero, for example, in the first half of the century judges used accusatory form in such cases, but when the case involved officials, they used inquisitory technique (generally without torture); increasingly in the second half of the century, inquisitory became the norm in Beloozero.[18] Over the century the St. Cyril Beloozero Monastery clerical judges used both accusatory and inquisitory formats in cases of assault and theft. In the cases from around the realm studied here, as the century progressed inquisitory approach was more often used for non-felony injury than accusatory.[19] Muscovy's inquisitorial procedure shared much in common with accusatory trials in oral interrogation and forms of evidence; torture distinguished it. Before reaching torture, judges considered several other kinds of evidence in the pursuit of probable cause.

[15] RGADA f. 141 1642, no. 59 (1642); see also Bogoslovskii: "Zemskoe samoupravlenie," *Chteniia* (1912), bk. II, p. 186.

[16] RGADA f. 141 1651, pt. 2, no. 58, fols. 198, 201 (1651). Novombergskii, *Koldovstvo*, no. 10 (1648).

[17] Man'kov, *Zakonodatel'stvo*, 175; Kuritsyn, "Pravo i sud," 409. Ulozhenie on accusatory form (*sud*) for misdemeanor assault: ch. 10, art. 136, ch. 13, art. 4: RZ III: 121, 159.

[18] Accusatory in Beloozero: RGADA f. 1107, nos. 74 (1613), 113 (1614), 266 (1618), 425 (1626), 480 (1628), 509, fols. 1–11 (1629), 510 (1629), 509, fols. 12–13 (1630), 544 (1630), 600 (1632), 815 (1638), 817 (1638), 871 (1639), 909 (1640), 977 (1642), 1059 (1645), 1219 (1650), 2998 (1682), 4156 (1695). Inquisitory in Beloozero: RGADA f. 1107, nos. 1059 (1645), 1429 (1658), 1451 (1658), 1716 (1668), 1849 (1670), 2249 (1675), 2881 (1681).

[19] Accusatory at St. Cyril: RGADA f. 1441, nos. 173 (1675), 275 (1681). Inquisitory: RGADA f. 1441, nos. 237–8, 224 (1679), 330 (1683). Around the realm, accusatory: MDBP pt. 2, no. 13 (1634); AIuB I: no. 87 (1680); inquisitory: MDBP pt. 2, nos. 32 (1639), 63 (1668), 129 (1688); PDP no. 165 (1668).

MATERIAL EVIDENCE

In 1685 a group of local Tatars – "*murzy* and village elders Kuska Alymov syn and colleagues" representing the "whole villege of Azeev and all the landholders of Kadom province" – reported to the governor of Kadom a brutal fight between brothers in which one man lay seriously wounded. The governor sent out an inspecting party to interview the wounded man. They arrived too late and examined his corpse instead: on the dead man were "beaten places, on his head two wounds under the right ear, and a bit higher it is a bit beaten as well." The governor had ordered that, should the man die, they were to seal his property and arrest the suspect, so they secured his home, seized the suspect's wife since he had fled, and the case was underway.[20]

Often the first piece of evidence that a judge confronted was dire injury – a corpse brought in, an injured man displaying his wounds. Governors' first duty was to order an inspection of such material evidence (*osmotr*), usually sending out a party to do so. Parties might also be charged with arresting suspects and bringing in witnesses. They gathered witnesses (*poniatye*) to the inspection from the surrounding community. Since examinations were scrupulously recorded, the participants always included a literate person.

Muscovite courts did not have the benefit of medical expertise in evaluating such evidence. In England starting in the fifteenth century coroners, while not medical doctors, provided a modicum of expertise; on the Continent trained medical experts began carrying out examinations and autopsies on victims of homicide and violent crime in the sixteenth century.[21] Professional police began to appear in Europe in the eighteenth century. In our cases the inspecting party's role was to establish the gravity of the injury and to collect whatever evidence was immediately observable by common sense investigation.

Examinations were thorough. In a murder case of 1692 in Mosal′sk, for example, the party of the Mosal′sk undersecretary, musketeers and local witnesses observed the place of the death, where they reported that "human brains from the head and a pool of blood were standing under the birch tree"; they observed the dead body in the village to which it had been brought, reporting that "he was about ten years old, his head was all smashed, you could see that brains had issued from the head and the dead

[20] RGADA f. 1122, op. 2, pt. 1, no. 1018, fols. 3–4 (1685).

[21] Gaskill, *Crime and Mentalities*, 254–6, 260–2, 266; Greenshields, *Economy of Violence*, 186.

body was all bloody; it lies in blood in peasant Ivashko's courtyard." In another case of 1692, the description was equally gruesome:

> his forehead was cut open and bloody, on the right cheek it was cut with a whirl-bat [a cudgel with lead pieces attached] and bloody, on the left hand his two middle fingers were crushed and bloody, on this right arm the elbow was beaten with a whirl-bat and bloody, on his spine opposite the heart it was blue and swollen and his waist was deeply scratched and bloody.

In a 1690s case, the examination confirmed death by drowning: the witnesses observed "no wounds from beating." Even a horse involved in a crime in 1680 was inspected to identify it: "and by examination the horse is a gelding, a brown bay with dark mane, on the right a mark, its right ear cut." Examinations also took place in chambers. A high-ranking gentryman was brought directly to the Moscow Judicial Chancery in 1673, where his wounds were examined by the principal judge, a second high-ranking official and the chancery secretary: he was "stabbed with a knife in the left shoulder, the wound being small but deep."[22]

Judges also accepted documentary evidence, although this occurred relatively rarely given the nature of criminal activity. In a 1657 case of rape that resulted in death, the judge in the Moscow Administrative Chancery (*Zemskoi prikaz*) asked the Musketeer Chancery (Moscow's police force) to verify a defendant's allegation that the dead woman had been knouted there for prostitution. The Musketeer Chancery confirmed that it was true. Cases reveal governors and Moscow police asking the Military Service Chancery to check muster lists for gentrymen involved in crime; a governor consulted local slavery records in a 1682 case of runaway serfs. When a woman requested in June 1692 that she not be forced to accompany her husband into exile, the governor in Galich sent her petition to the Military Service Chancery, which approved her request.[23]

Muscovite judges held that law trumped written precedent, as evident when in the 1680s the Chamber of Appeals overturned a case because it had been decided "according to precedent, not according to the Ulozhenie [of 1649]." But judges did use precedent. In a memo of 1629

[22] RGADA f. 210, Prikaznyi stol, no. 1549, fol. 136 (1692). Whirl-bat (*kisten'*): AIuB 1: no. 78 (1692). RGADA f. 1122, op. 2, pt. 1, no. 1195, fol. 5 (1690s). RGADA f. 210, Prikaznyi stol, no. 1039, fol. 11 (1680). RGADA f. 210, Prikaznyi stol, no. 669, fol. 9 (1673). Other examples: RGADA f. 1107, no. 1451 (1658); RGADA f. 210, Prikaznyi stol, no. 710, fol. 122 (1676).

[23] MDBP pt. 5, no. 19, p. 282 (1657). Military Service Chancery consulted: RGADA f. 210, Sevsk stol, no. 416, fols. 471–5, 584–7 and 593–7 (three cases 1688). AIuB 1: no. 51 (1682). RGADA f. 210, Prikaznyi stol, no. 1532, fols. 58–63 (1692). Horse purchase registers used: AIuB 1: no. 55 (XXXI) (1) (1669).

regarding peasants who had killed their masters and then fled across the western border, the Military Service Chancery asked the Felony Chancery to identify precedents for such cases, including punishment and their treatment of dependent children. The Chancery found about six such cases. In 1681 chanceries were directed to compile lists of cases that had been resolved in the absence of specific clauses in the Ulozhenie and 1669 Criminal Articles; such cases were to be used as precedent. In a case in Livni in 1698 a plaintiff asked that his case be resolved "according to the Ulozhenie and New Articles and by the examples of resolved cases."[24] By far the greatest source of evidence in Muscovite inquisitorial cases, however, was interrogation.

ORAL INTERROGATION

Oral interrogation (*rospros, dopros*) of litigants, witnesses and other involved parties was the most commonly used investigative technique. Codes mention the process regularly,[25] but provide only a few guidelines for procedure, such as judges being told to question witnesses separately and scribes being enjoined not to read the results of a community survey in front of the litigants. Individuals, according to the Ulozhenie, testified under their oath to the sovereign, before an icon, so that "they will speak truthfully, as they will stand on the judgment day of Christ." Codes since 1497 exhorted witnesses, outside of those being asked about an accused person's criminal reputation, to testify to what they saw, not hearsay.[26] Throughout, the focus was on testimony, not emotion; no attention is given to psychological factors such as facial expression or body movement as indication of guilt or repentance, as was becoming common in post-Reformation Europe.[27]

[24] Chamber of Appeals: Sedov, *Zakat*, 415. AMG I: no. 259 (IX) (1629). PSZ II: no. 900 (1681). RGADA f. 210, Prikaznyi stol, no. 1824, fol. 147 (1698). The Slavery Chancery 1620s–30s using legal precedents: Hellie, *Slavery*, 96–7, 144, 235. Precedents from 1686–8 cited in 1701 case: RGADA f. 210, Prikaznyi stol, no. 965, fols. 165–6.

[25] Oral interrogation: Ulozhenie ch. 2, art. 16; ch. 10: arts. 7, 251; ch. 21: arts. 35, 38, 44–7, 63: RZ III: 88, 102, 145, 234, 236–8, 240. The Ulozhenie generally associates *dopros* with accusatory trials and *rospros* with investigatory. East Slavic church codes included the Byzantine "On Witnesses" text, but it was not used in Muscovy: Kaiser (trans. and ed.), *Laws of Rus'*, li, 118–21.

[26] Not read community survey aloud: ZA no. 30 (1558); speak truthfully: Ulozhenie ch. 10, art. 173: RZ III: 130; testify to eyewitness: 1497 Law Code, art. 67: RZ II: 62; 1550 Law Code, art. 99: RZ II: 120; 1589 Law Code, art. 203: PRP IV: 439; Ulozhenie, ch. 10, arts. 161, 172–3: RZ III: 127, 130.

[27] Rublack, *Crimes of Women*, 44–5; Royer, "Dead Men Talking." Rustemeyer notes that with the decline of torture in the eighteenth century, interrogators in Russia became more interested in "conscience": *Dissens und Ehre*, 353–4.

In practice, judges appropriately interviewed witnesses one by one (*porozn'*). This was particularly stressed in political crime cases, where the investigative process was kept as secret as possible.[28] Unlike the back and forth between litigants in accusatory trials, judges maintained control, directing specific questions at defendant or witness. Often instructions from Moscow specified questions to ask, or governors reported exactly what questions they posed.[29]

There were few exemptions from testifying. The Ulozhenie held that wives should not testify against their husbands, but even that rule was broken in practice, and other relationships did not provide immunity. For example, a wife testified on behalf of her husband in a case of murder in 1635, saying that he killed defending her. After the Stepan Razin uprising, a wife was questioned in July 1672 about her husband; the two were put into a face-to-face confrontation, where he denied her allegations of his involvement in the rebellion.[30] An accused man's mother was seized and interrogated about her son in 1687 after he fled an arresting party. In high stakes cases like witchcraft, families were pitted against one another: spouses testified against each other, mothers against daughters, other family members against kin.[31]

Neither ethnic identity nor gender nor social class were obstacles to giving evidence. Women, serfs and slaves testified, as did non-Russians. In a database of about 250 (mostly unresolved) criminal cases from the Arzamas, Kadom and Temnikov areas into the early eighteenth century, about 30 cases identifiably include Mordva or Tatars (others might be masked by Russianized surnames).[32] In a case in Kadom of a man accused

[28] AMG I: nos. 55 (1614), 259, p. 276 (1629), 527 (1633); AMG II: no. 444 (1650); RGADA f. 210, Sevsk stol, no. 263, fol. 254 (1663); RGADA f. 210, Sevsk stol, no. 294, fols. 189, 196 (1676); RGADA f. 1107, no. 3906, fol. 12 (1691); RGADA f. 210, Prikaznyi stol, no. 1378, fol. 44 (1699). Political crime: Tel'berg, *Ocherki*, 175–7. Secrecy also the norm in inquisitorial procedure in Europe: Peters, *Torture*, 63–4.

[29] Questions sent from Moscow: RGADA f. 210, Belgorod stol, no. 83, fol. 259 (1635); RGADA f. 210, Belgorod stol, no. 83, fols. 582–3 (1637); RGADA f. 210, Prikaznyi stol, no. 567, fol. 393 (1648). Governors reporting what they asked: RGADA f. 141 1651, pt. 2, no. 58, fol. 197 (1651) and fol. 263 (two cases 1651); RGADA f. 210, Sevsk stol, no. 187, fol. 454 (1656).

[30] Wives and husbands: Ulozhenie ch. 10, arts. 176–7: RZ III: 130. RGADA f. 210, Belgorod stol, no. 83, fols. 258–67, 708–9 (1635). KV III: no. 210, p. 236 (1672); similar case: RGADA f. 1107, no. 4310 (1698).

[31] RGADA f. 1122, op. 2, pt. 2, no. 1424, fols. 2–3 (1687). Kinsmen in witchcraft: RGADA f. 210, Prikaznyi stol, no. 564, fols. 196–7 (1647); Novombergskii, *Koldovstvo*, nos. 1 (1622), 6 (1636), 11 (1647), 21 (1664), 26 (1676).

[32] Russians or their literate substitutes signed court records in Cyrillic; Tatars and Mordva signed in Arabic or with a "mark": RGADA f. 1167, op. 1, pt. 1, no. 7, fols. 5v, 6v, 7v, 10v, 11v, 12v, 13v (1675); RGADA f. 1122, op. 2, pt. 1, no. 1018, fol. 9v. (1685); RGADA f. 1380, no. 164, fol. 10 (1720). See Kollmann, "Russian Law in a Eurasian Setting."

of murdering his brother in 1685, witnesses at the inspection of the body included Tatars and Russians; when a Russian peasant listed witnesses to be interviewed in his trial in 1680, he included non-Russians (*murzy i tatarovia*). Tatar women participated in trials and gave evidence: in 1685, for example, an accused murderer fled arrest, so the deputies arrested his wife and took testimony from her.[33]

Face-to-face confrontation of litigants and witnesses (*ochnaia stavka*) played an important part in the inquisitory process. For highest crime, it was mandatory that the accused person confront his accuser (*izvetchik*), since in allegations of sorcery, plots and threats, material evidence was often hard to come by.[34] In brigandage trials, it was used when a defendant accused another man of criminal activity and that person rejected the accusation. Such procedures could take the form of simple oral questioning, or they could take place at the next stage of coercion, which was questioning in the presence of the instruments of torture, or they could even be done with one or both of the parties in the process of being tortured.

In all these forms of oral interrogation, judges strove to control their courtrooms. Rarely do cases cite disruption, but it could occur. For example, the governor of Rostov reported in 1663 that, as he was trying to carry out an interrogation of two brothers, one "sat down in the governor's office rudely and leaned out the window on both elbows." When the governor ordered him beaten with bastinadoes for such impudence, he and "his brother ran out of the office and rang the church bell, summoning a big crowd to the town square." The governor put them both in prison and asked Moscow for advice. Similarly, the landlord of a murdered peasant requested in 1680 that his case be resumed after a face-to-face confrontation had descended into a melee of name-calling. Such reports call to mind legal provisions ordering litigants to behave politely in court or risk punishment and the obligation of paying dishonor fines to insulted judges.[35]

Governors also often encountered accused who were in no condition to testify. A 1645 case involving allegations of treason was deemed so serious that the accuser was questioned upon arrest even while drunk (where he

[33] RGADA f. 1122, op. 2, pt. 1, no. 1018, fol. 3 (1685). RGADA f. 1167, op. 1, pt. 1, no. 626, fol. 2 (1680). RGADA f. 1122, op. 2, pt. 1, no. 1018, fols. 4, 7 (1685). Women in trials: Kollmann, *By Honor Bound*, chs. 2–3.

[34] Tel′berg, *Ocherki*, 179–98.

[35] AIuB II: no. 197 (1663). RGADA f. 1167, op. 1, pt. 1, no. 626, fol. 2 (1680). Ulozhenie ch. 10, arts. 105–6: RZ III: 113.

accused his landlord of treason) and again when he had sobered up the next day (when he recanted it all). In a 1676 case the governor simply reported that the accused was too drunk to be interrogated; the governor imprisoned him to sleep it off and questioned him the next day.[36] Codified law did not spell out procedures for interrogation. More problematic for the law were community surveys and torture, and to at least the former topic the law devoted significant attention.

COMMUNITY SURVEYS AS EVIDENCE

From the mid sixteenth century on in brigandage charters, Muscovite law struggled with the problem of community participation. On the one hand, as in Western Europe, reputation was taken seriously as evidence. Brigandage elders were instructed to assemble their community and gather information on people suspected of crime; in a trial, if the community spoke against the accused, or did not know him, he could be brought immediately to torture or verdict.[37] On the other hand, jurists knew that people would dissemble if it suited individual or community needs. Thus, law codes regulated the community survey, called *poval'nyi obysk*, by demanding a high number of participants to make a community survey valid or by weighting the evidence by social class.[38] Codes forbade groups to testify as one, mandated individual questioning and required a high degree of agreement. Communities were held responsible for their testimony: if a majority of people approved an accused man, they would have to put up surety for him. If he were later caught in crime, they were to be fined or flogged.[39]

Already by the end of the century laws evidenced skepticism about community surveys: the 1589 Law Code exhorted those surveyed to testify truthfully and allowed a person labeled "criminal" to seek a second survey if he felt the first was perjured. The 1649 Ulozhenie demanded that testimony should be written on the spot, not later, and signed by all

36 AMG II: no. 264 (1645). MDBP pt. 5, no. 8, p. 226 (1676).

37 Criminal reputation: 1497 Law Code, arts. 12–13: RZ II: 55–6; 1539 Beloozero Charter, arts. 3, 5: RZ II: 214. Elders assemble: 1552 Dvina Charter, art. 22, RZ II: 231–2; PDP no. 106 (1616). Immediate verdict: Jan. 1555 Felony Handbook, arts. 1–3: PRP IV: 356.

38 1555 Medyn Charter (arts. 1–2: RZ II: 218–19) and Jan. 1555 Felony Handbook (arts 4–5: PRP IV: 357) required fifteen to twenty people. August 1556 Decree (art. 4) mandated fifty or sixty people: PRP IV: 364. The 1550 Law Code (art. 58) equated the testimony of ten gentrymen to that of many lower-ranking people: RZ II: 108.

39 August 1556 Decree, arts. 1, 5, 10, 13–14: PRP IV: 363–7; 1555 Medyn Charter, arts. 2, 6–7: RZ II: 219, 221. Surety bonds for criminals: AIu nos. 290 (VI and VII) (1615, 1617) and 307 (IV) (1674).

witnesses.[40] The 1669 Criminal Articles reduced community surveys to individual questioning on eyewitness evidence only and put more pressure on communities and officials to watch over individuals exonerated by such surveys.[41]

By the end of the seventeenth century the procedure had almost been transformed into simple oral interrogation. In 1688 the Felony Chancery declared that "large community surveys" should no longer be given, since people use them vengefully to promote "quarrels among neighbors" or are suborned by one of the litigants to testify falsely. Two years later, an order from the Moscow Judicial Chancery instructed investigators in Pereiaslavl' Zalesskii to question community members separately, to forbid the plaintiff and defendant from attending the proceedings and not to question people from the villages of the litigants. The latter were to be sent instead to Moscow for interrogation, a seemingly impractical measure that was nevertheless regularly ordered.[42] The inquisitorial procedure had revised community surveys into a more controlled form of evidence. Nevertheless, the survey of community opinion and evidence played a regular role in our criminal cases, often requested by litigants to clear their name. In practice, it produced mixed results.

COMMUNITY SURVEYS IN PRACTICE

Judges turned to community surveys in a wide array of cases; communities and individuals varied in their participation, depending upon their relationship to the case. Sometimes it worked in their interest. In Kaluga in 1660, for example, the entire community submitted a list of complaints against its governor and then willingly participated in a survey of 244 people. Sometimes, litigants requested surveys, as in 1651 when a defendant escaped torture by requesting a community survey that supported his plea of self-defense. In a case of 1664, a man suffered 30 blows of the knout in torture, but when he was led to the fire to contemplate further torture, he petitioned, as allowed by law, for a community survey to prove his innocence.[43]

40 Testify truthfully: 1589 Law Code, arts. 110–11, 205–20: PRP IV: 426–7, 439–42; 1616/17 Felony Handbook, art. 1: PRP V: 188; Felony Handbook 1619, art. 65: PRP V: 201; Felony Handbook 1631: PRP V: 216–17; Ulozhenie ch. 10, arts. 161–6, 167; ch. 21, art. 76: RZ III: 127–9, 242–3.

41 1669 Criminal Articles, arts. 24–5, 28, 33–5: PRP VII: 404–10 and commentary, 462–9.

42 PSZ II: no. 1294 (1688). AIuB II: no. 230 (XXXIV) (1690); see also PSZ III: no. 1412 (1691); Man'kov, *Zakonodatel'stvo*, 174–5, 195–6.

43 AMG III: no. 4 (1660). RGADA f. 141 1651, no. 58, pt. 2, fols. 201–5, 213–14 (1651). RGADA f. 210, Prikaznyi stol, no. 383, fols. 126–7v (1664).

Otherwise, judges called for such surveys. They could be huge. In a 1573 case of murder on the estates of the powerful Romanov family, brigandage wardens and scribes were sent to Kolomna and its province to do a community survey in a radius of "two, three, five, six, ten, fifteen, twenty, twenty-five, thirty *versty* on all sides." All people, if the document is to be believed literally, in nine expanding concentric circles were to be questioned, not a selection, including monastic officials, priests and all laymen. Those who testified should sign the document or have it signed in their place by their father confessors, and anyone incriminated was to be arrested and brought to the Felony Chancery. Escorts for such arrestees were to be dragooned from local people. On the other hand, in some places, such as frontier communities, it could be difficult to gather enough people for a proper survey.[44]

Orders to carry out a community survey were often accompanied by questions to verify allegations made in petitions and testimony. One from 1641 includes two published pages of questions and instructs investigators to remind the participants that they are to "tell the truth and not lie" on pain of "disgrace, corporal punishment and fines." Although the Ulozhenie required individual testimony, transcripts of community surveys routinely present the testimony of several people together, as if they had testified together. All members of communities, men and women, Russian and Tatar, participated. Christians swore an oath on the Gospel, the non-Christians on their faith and on their oath to the tsar (*po ikh vere po sherte*).[45]

Often communities cooperated when their interests were engaged. The governor of Kola Peninsula in 1622 received a report that the customs collectors had so abused local people that one man had died from their beating. The governor sent musketeers to carry out a survey of several neighborhoods of Lapps, many of whom testified to seeing the beatings and others to hearing report of them. On the basis of the survey, the Moscow Chancery found the defendants guilty. In 1651 the governor of Olonets was presented with a settlement document in a case of a brawl that resulted in a death. Not trusting it, he launched an investigation, including interrogation of the defendant with torture, interrogation of at least 15 other witnesses, and a survey of the community around Lake

[44] AIuB II: no. 230 (II) (1573). A *versta* equals two-thirds of a mile. Surveys on frontier: Glaz'ev, *Vlast' i obshchestvennost'*, 240–1.

[45] AIu no. 345 (1641); other examples: AMG I: no. 221 (1629); AIuB I: no. 55 (XII) (1647). Testify together, on oath: RGADA f. 1167, op. 1, pt. 1, no. 7 (1675).

Onega where the death had occurred. One village – its elder and 151 peasants – said that they saw the fight and the murder, and various individuals added details: one alleged there had been prior threats and enmity, several heard the defendant urging his compatriots to kill the victim. Several added that the defendant was "a known criminal" who had assaulted people and seduced women in the past. The court found the defendant guilty of premeditated murder.[46] Where communities were directly affected by abusive officials or murder, they respected the process.

In other cases, they clammed up. Sometimes, no one wanted to go on record against a neighbor. A 1636 case is a blatant example. A special investigator had been sent to Sol′ Vychegodsk to investigate scandalous charges: the community declared that their governor was abusive and corrupt and was favoring local bands of criminals, while the governor reported that a crowd had stormed the jail, seized several prisoners and executed them vigilante style. The investigator struggled to get the community to cooperate. He sent musketeers for people and they refused to come; people refused to testify; landlords refused to submit lists of their people; even the archimandrite of the local monastery refused to cooperate. Although the inspector managed eventually to interview hundreds of people, only a very few admitted to knowing anything at all. Most said they knew nothing, saw nothing and had been told nothing.[47] The community rallied to protect its own.

For crimes lesser than capital crimes, judges could proceed to verdict after having collected information in these formats. For capital and other serious crimes, they needed to obtain a confession and so turned to torture. Because the topic is so complex in law and practice, torture will be treated in the next chapter. This chapter concludes with the process of adjudication once evidence had been gathered.

THE COURSE OF A TRIAL

It is tempting to depict Muscovite criminal practice as hopelessly caught up in delay and dead ends. Certainly that has been the trend of much

[46] RGADA f. 141 1624, no. 31, pt. 1, fols. 110–15 (1622). RGADA f. 141 1651, no. 58, pt. 2, fols. 196–214, 280 (1651). Other examples: RGADA f. 210, Prikaznyi stol, nos. 674, fols. 165–95 (1675); 710, fols. 82, 119–25 (1676); 1049, fols. 17–18 (1686); no. 1049, fols. 93–5 (1686); RGADA f. 1107, no. 2101 (1673); RGADA f. 1167, op. 1, pt. 1, no. 7, fols. 4–13 (1675).

[47] RGADA f. 141 1636, no. 25 (1636); Kollmann, "Lynchings and Legality." Other examples of recalcitrance: PDP nos. 131 (1628) and 145 (1642); AMG 1: no. 140 (1621). A 1628 decree reminded landholders of their obligation to participate, on pain of fine: ZA no. 186.

historiography, and our cases can supply ample evidence. But they also demonstrate the system functioning relatively smoothly, so a balance in assessing how trials progressed has to be struck.[48]

One aspect of the judicial process is illustrated by the fragmentary source record: many surviving cases break off in midstream. Records might have been lost over time, or litigants might have abandoned a case as too expensive or burdensome, or governors might have became too consumed by other duties to pursue. Perhaps simply filing a case helped focus the parties to find an out-of-court solution. Furthermore, our cases demonstrate delay, despite admonitions in the law to carry out trials "quickly, so that in court cases there will be no unnecessary red tape and losses for anyone." A decree of 1648 held that if a plaintiff brings a criminal suit and then does not pursue it within a week, he loses the case.[49] Nevertheless, delays were endemic, for many reasons.

The annual reassignment of governors frequently interrupted trials. A case of murder of a Tatar woman in Kadom that started in August 1674 was pursued energetically by governor S. V. Shamshev the very same day that the dead body was found. He had the body inspected and questioned the accused murderer, Boris Antipin, who admitted guilt. Antipin then sat in prison for six months until February 1675, when the husband of the murdered woman petitioned the court to move the case along. Nevertheless, the next step was not taken until June 1, 1675, after a new governor, S. S. Ushakov, had been assigned to Kadom. After a torture session, Antipin was returned to prison and awaited the resolution of his case, which came only two years later, in November 1677. Yet another governor, Prince I. N. Bol′shoi Belosel′skii, reviewed the testimony, consulted the relevant law code and ruled that Antipin was guilty of premeditated murder and should be executed. The following day, December 1, 1677, Antipin was beheaded in Kadom. In this case, spurts of efficiency, sometimes spurred on by intervening kinsmen and plaintiffs, were separated by long periods of inaction, explained by transfer of personnel, the press of governors' other duties and perhaps time taken to communicate with the center. Moscow anticipated this problem: the instructions to the Arzamas governor in 1679,

[48] Inefficiencies and delays: Bogoslovskii, "Zemskoe samoupravlenie" and *Oblastnaia reforma*; Kivelson, *Cartographies*, 46 and ch. 2, n. 40; Shtamm, "Sud i protsess," 231–2; Hellie, *Slavery*, 219. Fictionalized account of a trial: Kollmann, "Provincial Landowners."

[49] Unresolved cases: Kollmann, *By Honor Bound*, 114–21. Resolve speedily: Ulozhenie ch. 10: art. 22: RZ III: 105; ZA no. 330, p. 222 (1648).

for example, told him to review cases of men in prison and to resolve them promptly as soon as he arrived at his post.[50]

Corruption could be the culprit as well. A Mordvinian peasant Aleksei Vedeniapin in Shatsk district was killed in October 1675 by unnamed Mordva men, who were arrested and brought to the governor of Temnikov. Given that the governor released them after they admitted guilt, one suspects bribery. Almost seven years later in January 1682, the next governor of Kadom was ordered to re-open the case and resolve it.[51]

The process of investigation took time as well. Tracking down evidence and accused criminals could consume months and years. For example, in an investigation of stolen property in April 1687, an incriminating piece of evidence (a fur coat soaked with blood) was discovered in a peasant's hut. Investigation into the theft yielded no result and the case went nowhere. Not until a year later in August 1688 was a connection made between the bloody fur coat and an accused murderer, a friend of the man originally accused of theft. The case record breaks off with the accused murderer released on recognizance pending resolution.[52] Distance in communicating with Moscow also created delay. For example, in Tobol′sk (approximately 1,160 miles away in Siberia) a murder that occurred in 1639/40 involved three torture sessions separated by long intervals – 1639/40, 1640/1 and 1643/4. Then the family of the murdered man petitioned for a settlement in 1643/4 and Moscow approved it on March 17, 1644. Several months later the verdict reached Siberia. In Iarensk (400 miles away in the Urals) a murder was reported on July 13, 1683 and the governor immediately carried out interrogations and torture. But the case surfaced again only in mid October 1686, with the defendant still in prison with no verdict. Notified, Moscow made a ruling on November 12, 1686 and sent it to Iarensk at the end of the month. Communication difficulties delayed everything in so large an empire.[53]

Litigants themselves delayed trials, sometimes by flight, sometimes by legal maneuver. In a 1675 case of one brother killing another in a quarrel, villagers joined in obstruction. The accused murderer fled and when the governor ordered local landholders to send one man per household to the district offices to be interviewed, they sent only a fraction of those requested. Legal maneuvers created delays as well. For example, on

[50] RGADA f. 1122, op. 2, pt. 2, no. 1629, 12 fols. (1674). 1679: Iakovlev (ed.), *Namestnichie*, 97.

[51] RGADA f. 1122, op. 2, pt. 2, no. 1548, 3 fols. (1682).

[52] RGADA f. 1122, op. 2, pt. 2, no. 1424, 15 fols. (1688).

[53] "Uboistvennye dela," 4 (1639/40). RGADA f. 159, pt. 3, Novgorod chetvert′, no. 2466, fols. 77–83 (1683).

February 9, 1628 a murder was discovered in Briansk and investigated in the next few days. On March 12, the governor sent his report to Moscow, and in Moscow the death penalty was ordered on March 14. The defendants immediately appealed to Patriarch Filaret, saying that they had intentionally slandered themselves, unable to bear torture; they professed their innocence. A year later in July 1629, Filaret interceded for them. Nevertheless, in December 1630, they were still in jail in Briansk with no court record and the new governor and his Moscow superiors trying to figure out how the men had been neglected so long.[54] Sometimes governors were at fault. When a woman murdered her husband with the aid of her son-in-law in Kozlov in January 1647, the case started expeditiously. It was investigated promptly and by April the Military Service Chancery had advised a guilty verdict. Meanwhile community members had journeyed to Moscow to plead on their behalf and Moscow ordered a community survey regarding the defendants' reputations. Villagers supported them as "good people" and sought mercy. Then the case languished until spring 1650 when a new governor found the defendants still in custody. Since court records were in disarray, he had to consult with Moscow, which returned a merciful verdict of corporal punishment in June 1650. The punishment was administered a month later. The case had taken three and a half years.[55]

As these cases suggest, judges opened cases promptly, but litigation was often bogged down in process. Nevertheless, the system was capable of efficiency. In a group of about fifty resolved cases surveyed here, the vast majority were concluded within a year. Some cases were resolved on the spot – for example, when night watchmen in Moscow arrested someone for trespassing in the Kremlin, violating fire safety laws or other minor offenses. The accused were brought to the head of the Musketeer Chancery (the city police), interrogated and usually sentenced immediately. This was the case with a potter accused of firing his ovens at night in 1676, a man who rode a horse illegally into the Kremlin in 1680 and another man caught wandering in the Kremlin at night in 1686.[56] In 1688,

[54] RGADA f. 1122, op. 2, pt. 1, no. 1018, 11 fols. (1675). RGADA f. 1135, no. 359, fol. 6 (1700). RGADA f. 210, Prikaznyi stol, no. 36, fols. 467–76, 485–91 (1628); similar case: RGADA f. 1122, op. 2, pt. 2, no. 2083, 9 fols. (1672).

[55] RGADA f. 210, Prikaznyi stol, no. 172, fols. 253–8 and no. 265, fols. 59–60, 67–9 (1647); Kollmann, "Extremes of Patriarchy." Other examples of delay after auspicious beginnings: RGADA f. 210, Prikaznyi stol, no. 77, fols. 330–2 (1640); RGADA f. 1107, no. 2305 (1676).

[56] RGADA f. 210, Prikaznyi stol, nos. 710, fols. 82, 119–25 (1676); 1039, fols. 11–13 (1680); 935, fols. 854–7 (1686).

the Military Service Chancery took two days to investigate a case of a military man arrested in Moscow for carousing and having fled his unit. Some cases considered in the central chanceries were more complex, but were dispatched promptly. In 1663 a case of theft by guards within the Chancery took one month to investigate and resolve; in 1701, the Military Service Chancery judge took a week to investigate a corrupt undersecretary, pausing to order research into his career. A similar case of that same year took two months as the Chancery corresponded with the provinces to learn of the accused's previous service. Conversely, in the provincial outpost of Dobroe in 1681, the governor ruled the same day in a case of two military men found on the road without proper travel documents.[57]

Many cases moved along expeditiously, often thanks to litigants' initiative in settling criminal suits, despite prohibitions on this (see Chapter 7). A homicide case in Beloozero started on August 3, 1638, but arrests were not accomplished until early October. The parties came to settlement on January 25, 1639; total time, five months. Here, the delays might have to do with harvest season and the onset of winter. A murderer in Livni was questioned on March 24, 1648 and in May the governor asked Moscow's advice. On June 30, 1648 Moscow ordered torture, which order was apparently received by July 20. On that date the family of the dead man interceded to settle and the request was approved on July 30. Elapsed time, four months. Another case took a bit longer: two landlords in Luki Velikie sued each other in mid July 1658 over a murder and injuries to their peasants that occurred during a melee over a disputed rye field. Investigation, including torture, ensued promptly, then the case languished over the winter. On March 23, 1659, the litigants submitted a settlement; total time, nine months.[58]

Local judges could be efficient, as was the case with some judges in Beloozero. A murder case of 1613 took six weeks (August 8 to September 17) for the governor to resolve; in 1688 the Beloozero judge resolved in one month (January 12 to February 15) the case of a woman involved in a homicide; four years later a case that started around April reached a verdict in July. In other cases, even when governors referred to Moscow for a verdict,

[57] RGADA f. 210, Sevsk stol, no. 416, fols. 580–92, 785–6, 847–8 (1688). RGADA f. 210, Sevsk stol, no. 263, fols. 251–60 (1663). One week: RGADA f. 210, Prikaznyi stol, no. 965, fols. 43–8 (1701). Two months: RGADA f. 210, Prikaznyi stol, no. 965, fols. 152–69 (1701). RGADA f. 210, Prikaznyi stol, no. 793, fols. 236–40 (1681).

[58] RGADA f. 1107, no. 824 (1638). RGADA f. 210, Prikaznyi stol, no. 567, fols. 391–4, 519–21 (1648). RGADA f. 210, Prikaznyi stol, no. 267, fols. 223–4 (1658).

the case proceeded quickly. In a case of 1647, for example, a son killed his father in Livni (about 275 miles south of Moscow) on November 17; Moscow handed down a death sentence on December 27 and notified Livni on January 29. After an unexplained delay, the execution took place on April 11, 1648. Total time between crime and execution: five months. Another case took two years to resolve: three men were arrested on January 15, 1690, on the basis of a collective community petition accusing them of crime. The governor of Galich subjected the three to repeated tortures, carried out witness interviews and a community survey and consulted Moscow. The process took two years, but by January 8, 1692 a verdict of exile had been received.[59]

The judicial system's obligation to respond to litigants' petitions embroiled it in ways that officials and litigants could manipulate, but good work toiled on. Judges launched investigations, bailiffs captured evildoers; judicial staffs followed cases, ideally all the way to punishment. Litigants and communities manipulated the process as they were able: some could afford to offer bribes; some dared to defy court instructions; many cooperated with courts to the extent that they respected the authority of the tsar and their oaths to him and to the extent that they believed the judicial system could serve their interests. There were limits to the judges' flexibility, however, moments when they used all the power in the law. One of those moments was when a case came to torture.

[59] RGADA f. 1107, nos. 19 (1613), 3549 (1688) and 3904 (1692). RGADA f. 210, Prikaznyi stol, no. 567, fols. 159–64, 276 (1647). RGADA f. 210, Prikaznyi stol, no. 1532, fols. 58–63 (1690). Other examples: eight months: RGADA f. 210, Belgorod stol, no. 83, fols. 369–71, 582–5 (1636); two weeks: RGADA f. 210, Stolbtsy Pomestnogo stola, no. 194, fols. 11–12 (1654); six weeks: RGADA f. 210, Sevsk stol, no. 246, fols. 384–7, 404–7 (1640).

CHAPTER 6

Torture

Muscovite torture was horrific, although deceptively simple – generally done by blows of the knout. No exquisite medieval instruments of torture here. Knouting was done in the strappado position, with the accused raised by his or her arms on a beam (*dyba, brevno*). Weights could be hung on the feet to increase the torment; the weighted person could be shaken while hanging (*vstriaski*). As a further torment the person could be scorched with fire or pinched with hot pinchers (*kleshchmi*).[1] Even water torture could be used, as clinically described by Aleksei Mikhailovich's doctor, Samuel Collins: "they will then shave the crown of his Head and drop cold water upon the bare place, which some that have felt, acknowledge to be the quintessence of all Torments; for every drop strikes like a dart to the very heart."[2] All this was done in pursuit of confession, the "queen of proofs" in the inquisitorial procedure. So confident in torture's ability to get results, Muscovite jurists even allowed torture on holydays and other days of celebration, since, as a 1639 decree noted, "robbers and thieves kill and torment Orthodox peasants and commit arson and beat people up on all days."[3]

Early modern jurisprudence believed that physical pain could penetrate to the truth. It was used in Europe as well as in Muscovy.[4] This chapter examines Muscovite torture in law and practice.

[1] Kotoshikhin, *O Rossii*, ch. 7, art. 34, p. 115; Anisimov, *Russkaia pytka*, 195–207. Strappado in Europe: Levack, *Witch-Hunt*, 78–9; Rublack, *Crimes of Women*, 54–5; Roper, *Witch Craze*, 44–8. See Valerie Kivelson's impassioned analysis of torture in witchcraft cases: "Desperate Magic," ch. 7 and "Torture, Truth."

[2] Collins, *Present State*, 73; also Neuville, *Curious and New Account*, 44; Korb, *Diary*, II: 204. On torture: Olearius, *Travels*, 229; Reitenfels, *Skazaniia*, 117; Fletcher, "Of the Russe," 176.

[3] PRP V: 226 (1639). Repeated in Ulozhenie ch. 21, art. 32: RZ III: 234 and 1669 Criminal Articles, art. 67: PRP VII: 420.

[4] Langbein, *Prosecuting* and *Torture and the Law*; Peters, *Torture*; Silverman, *Tortured Subjects*.

TORTURE IN THE LAW

Muscovite law was maddeningly laconic on this topic. Torture simply appears in the 1497 code; whether it came in with European inquisitorial mode or was taken from church codes is unclear. Sixteenth-century codes and charters provide more information about torture, but not in a systematic way. This is in sharp contrast to contemporary European jurisprudence, where jurists devoted extensive attention to what Roman law had called the "difficult and dangerous business" of torture.[5] Even its defenders understood that the human intolerance of pain made evidence gained under torture circumspect. Thus, authors of codes such as the 1532 *Carolina* of the Holy Roman Empire and the French Criminal Code of 1539 surrounded torture with safeguards. The sixteenth-century Spanish Inquisition, for example, allowed only one torture session and ordered judges not to maim or injure under torture. Not only witnesses but also medical personnel were present, and confessions were not accepted unless affirmed at least a day later. The French Criminal Code of 1539 similarly limited the number of sessions and their duration, required witnesses and expected affirmation of confession at some remove from the torture. The *Carolina* generally allowed two sessions and prescribed lengthy lists of probable cause; at least four witnesses were to be present – the judge, two court officials and a scribe. The accused should be questioned before the instruments of torture preceding their actual use, and once an accused confessed, he was to verify his confession two or more days after the torture.[6]

Judicial torture in the inquisitory mode was first and foremost intended to elicit confession. In Muscovite law if an accused withstood torture without confessing, his testimony was believed and he was spared severe punishment (although often sent to prison); if someone said something in interrogation and denied it in torture, the latter was to be believed.[7] Another goal was to gather further information: even if a defendant confessed without torture, he was tortured to reveal other criminal activity

[5] Church courts using torture: Zimin, *Krupnaia feodal'naia*, 154; Dobroklonskii, "Solotchinskii monastyr'," ch. 5. Torture: Shtamm, "Sud i protsess," 248–50; Man'kov, *Ulozhenie*, 322–3, 333–8. In Europe: Peters, *Torture*, chs. 1–2; Langbein, *Torture and the Law*.

[6] Kamen, *Spanish Inquisition*, 187–91. French Ordinance, art. 141: Langbein, *Prosecuting*, 310; Silverman, *Tortured Subjects*, 42–5. *Carolina*, arts. 18, 25–44, 46, 54–6: Langbein, *Prosecuting*, 272–83.

[7] Withstand: 1616/17 Felony Handbook, no. 9: PRP v: 191; Ulozhenie ch. 10, art. 202; ch. 20, art. 25; ch. 21, arts. 28, 42, 44; ch. 25, art. 14: RZ III: 135, 212, 233, 236–7, 256. Denies in torture: Ulozhenie ch. 21, art. 100: RZ III: 246.

or identify accomplices. A final goal was to establish intent, following a 1625 law that distinguished intent in punishing homicide. Not only defendants could be tortured; witnesses and third parties implicated by the defendant could also be tortured.[8]

In Muscovy torture was used for the highest political and religious crime, as well as for brigandage felonies.[9] The Ulozhenie of 1649 lists myriad other applications, including to investigate false loan documents, to force runaway serfs and slaves to reveal their identity, to investigate whether a community that failed to track down criminals was in collusion with them and many others. With such diversity, it is hard to see how judges decided whether or not to use it. Safeguards against abuse were important, but Muscovy provided fewer of them than in Europe.[10]

Most important was the state's claim to monopolize this sort of violence. Law prohibited private citizens from torturing a criminal they apprehended: "the thief should not be tortured outside of the Chancery," indicating the Felony Chancery.[11] Next, most safeguards were preconditions before turning to torture. The 1497 Law Code defined two of what became three probable causes: when a person was accused by another criminal being tortured (*iazychnaia molka*) or when caught in the act or with material evidence.[12] Brigandage charters added a third probable cause – when called

[8] Confess without torture: 1616/17 Felony Handbook, art. 25: PRP v: 194; Ulozhenie ch. 21, arts. 9, 58 and 64: RZ III: 231, 239, 241. Identify accomplices: Ulozhenie ch. 21, arts. 9, 10, 12, 16–18, 58, 62, 64 and ch. 22, arts. 12, 23: RZ III: 231–2, 239–41, 249–50. Torture to identify accomplices in Europe: Kamen, *Spanish Inquisition*, 188. 1625 intent: PRP v: 204–5; Ulozhenie ch. 21, arts. 69, 71, 73: RZ III: 241–2.

[9] Brigandage charters on torture: 1555 Medyn Charter, arts. 2–3, 5–9: RZ II: 219–22; PRP IV: 187 (oath, 1550s); Jan. 1555 Felony Handbook, arts. 1–3: PRP IV: 356; regional charters: Iakovlev (ed.), *Namestnichie*, 54 (1539), 56 (1540), 59 (1540), 61 and 63 (1541), 66 (1549), 70 (1556), 75 (1571), 81 and 83 (1586), 89 (1595).

[10] Arson, heresy: Ulozhenie ch. 1, arts. 1–3: RZ III: 85; ch. 2, arts. 1–4: RZ III: 86; ch. 10, art. 228: RZ III: 140 and *passim*. False loans: Ulozhenie ch. 10, art. 251; RZ III: 145. Runaway serfs: ch. 11, art. 22; ch. 20, art. 25: RZ III: 155, 212. Community colluding: 1616/17 Felony Handbook, no. 27: PRP v: 195; Ulozhenie ch. 21, art. 60: RZ III: 240. Investigate stolen property: PRP v: 206–7 and ZA no. 182 (1628); Ulozhenie ch. 21, arts. 51, 57, 75: RZ III: 238–39, 242. Question guards on escape: Ulozhenie ch. 21, art. 101; ch. 25, art. 18: RZ III: 246, 256. Illegal alcohol, tobacco: AMG I: no. 146 (1622); Ulozhenie ch. 25, arts. 3, 5, 6, 9, 12–16: RZ III: 252–6. Resolve a deadlocked survey: Ulozhenie ch. 10, art. 163: RZ III: 129. If individual had used up three judicial oaths: Ulozhenie ch. 14, art. 2: RZ III: 159. Felons recanting accusations of others: Ulozhenie ch. 21, art. 44: RZ III: 237; 1669 Criminal Articles, art. 38: PRP VII: 411. No one could vouch for reputation: 1555 Medyn Charter, art. 8: RZ II: 221; 1616/17 Felony Handbook, art. 11: PRP v: 191; Ulozhenie ch. 21, art. 38: RZ III: 236.

[11] Ulozhenie ch. 21, arts. 49 and 88: RZ III: 238, 244–5; 1669 Criminal Articles, art. 16: PRP VII: 401.

[12] The 1497 Law Code's term (*opytati, pytati*) has been interpreted as torture: arts. 14, 34: RZ II: 56, 58. A fourteenth-century note on theft mandated corporal punishment for theft, using the rarely encountered word *muka*, which Kaiser translates as "to torture": Kaiser (trans. and ed.), *Laws of Rus'*, 117. But the context – giving the court a choice between a fine or *muka* – suggests punishment, not torture.

"a known criminal" (*likhoi*) by community opinion.[13] Such surveys were a potent means of limiting torture. According to the 1550 Law Code, if a man were accused by another felon, the judge was to carry out interrogation and community survey to establish criminal reputation before proceeding to torture. The 1550 Law Code also gave judges discretion in using torture: if a first-time thief had no other crime, the judge could proceed to verdict without torture.[14] Seventeenth-century codes affirmed these three probable causes, associating torture with inquisitory procedure (inquisitor trials, then, were sometimes simply called "torture" cases [*pytochnye*]). Otherwise, seventeenth-century laws added little on torture (it is not even mentioned in the Ulozhenie's three chapters on highest crime[15]).

Another important safeguard involved the number of torture sessions allowed. There was no hard-and-fast rule, but Muscovite law since the sixteenth century suggested three times as a limit.[16] Grigorii Kotoshikhin, writing in 1666, often associated torture with three sessions, and a law of *c.*1684 regarding punishment of schismatics specified that suspects should be "tortured severely" three times. Three sessions were not mandatory: the Ulozhenie cites several instances in which two could be sufficient to reach a verdict.[17] As noted, contemporary European practice often called for fewer sessions.

Further safeguard was in the hierarchy of investigative techniques. In some circumstances torture could be used without prior investigation – when a person was brought in with material evidence, when more than one felon accused a person, when a master accused his serf or slave, or when a crime occurred that someone had previously threatened to do.[18]

13 Reputation: RZ II: 214 (arts. 3–5, 1539); Iakovlev (ed.), *Namestnichie*, 54 (1539), 56–7, 59 (both 1540), 59, 61, 63 (both 1541); 66 (1549); Jan. 1555 Felony Handbook, arts. 1 and 2: PRP IV: 356. Community survey: August 1556 Decree: PRP IV: 363–7; Iakovlev (ed.), *Namestnichie*, 69–73 (1556); 1589 Law Code, arts. 205–20: PRP IV: 439–42.

14 1550 Law Code, arts. 55–7: RZ II: 107–8; Ulozhenie ch. 21, art. 28: RZ III: 233.

15 Accusatory/inquisitory mode: 1616/17 Felony Handbook, no. 19: PRP V: 193; Ulozhenie ch. 21, art. 49: RZ III: 238; 1669 Criminal Articles, art. 72: PRP VII: 421. Torture case: RGADA f. 210, Sevsk stol, no. 283, fol. 349 (1672). First three chapters: Tel'berg, *Ocherki*, 198.

16 Three times: 1555 Medyn Charter, art. 3: RZ II: 219–20; 1556 Zubtsovskii uezd: Iakovlev (ed.), *Namestnichie*, 70 (1556), 75 (1571), 84 (1586); 1616/17 Felony Handbook, art. 5: PRP V: 189–90; Ulozhenie ch. 21, arts. 39, 93, 100: RZ III: 236, 245–6.

17 Kotoshikhin, *O Rossii*, ch. 2, art. 14, p. 30; ch. 7, art. 34, p. 115. 1684: PSZ II: no. 1102. Two sessions: Ulozhenie ch. 20, art. 25; ch. 21, art. 28; ch. 25, arts. 9, 12: RZ III: 212, 233, 254.

18 Material evidence: 1616/17 Felony Handbook, nos. 19, 22–5: PRP V: 193–5; Ulozhenie ch. 21, arts. 28, 49–50, 58, 74: RZ III: 233, 238–9, 242. Accusation by a felon: 1616/17 Felony Handbook, arts. 1, 4, 5, 7, 31–6: PRP V: 188–90, 196; Ulozhenie ch. 21, arts. 21, 38, 40, 43–4, 58, 64, 100: RZ III: 233, 236–7, 239–41, 246. Accused by master: 1616/17 Felony Handbook, no. 17: PRP V: 193; Ulozhenie ch. 21, art. 48: RZ III: 238. Reputation: 1616/17 Felony Handbook, nos. 1–11: PRP V: 188–91; Ulozhenie ch. 21, arts. 28, 29, 35, 36, 39, 42–4, 49, 58, 76: RZ III: 233–9, 243. Threaten crime: Ulozhenie ch. 10, art. 202: RZ III: 135.

But generally, before proceeding to torture judges were required to do oral interrogation, face-to-face confrontations, inspection of material evidence and community surveys to establish reputation. Even if this produced probable cause, a final step before physical torture was interrogation in the presence of its instruments.[19]

The law is frustratingly lacking in cautionary statements to judges, but one instruction of 1628 to a governor in Toropets warned him to "do no torture without cause" (*naprosno ne pytat'*). Another cautionary approach is seen in the readiness of authorities to accept appeals; in 1628, for example, they accepted the petition of two musketeers who alleged that they had confessed falsely in torture to escape the pain. Moscow suspended their ordered execution and started an investigation. In Pskov in 1689 a schismatic recanted heresy in testimony and under torture alleged that he had returned to church attendance. Moscow instructed the governor to investigate among the local population to verify this claim, and not to subject him to further torture if he truly turned out to have left the schism.[20] The law also forbade torture in a few circumstances: people who harbored criminals but did not themselves commit crime; defendants if the plaintiffs against them for stolen property had not properly reported the theft; bailiffs if people they had arrested fled. A rule rejecting accusations or recantations made only while awaiting execution limited potentially abusive use of torture, as did a ruling that accusations spoken after a significant period in prison were not to be believed. The Ulozhenie also included harsh punishments for planting material evidence, since such evidence could readily send someone to torture.[21]

The multiplied dishonor fee given to anyone tortured on a false accusation can be considered a safeguard. Such compensation for illegal torturing is also included in numerous European codes.[22] But deference to social rank is not consistent in the law. For example, a landlord would be

[19] Questioning at the instruments first cited in law: 1669 Criminal Articles, arts. 8, 53: PRP VII: 398, 416.

[20] AMG I: no. 202 (1628). Musketeers: RGADA f. 210, Prikaznyi stol, no. 36, fols. 467–76 and 485–91 (1628). Barsov, "Sudnye protsessy," no. 8 (1689).

[21] Harbor criminals: Ulozhenie ch. 21, art. 63: RZ III: 240. Stolen property: Ulozhenie ch. 21, art. 51: RZ III: 238. Bailiffs: Ulozhenie ch. 10, art. 271: RZ III: 148. Recantations: 1616/17 Felony Handbook, nos. 20–1: PRP V: 194; 1619 Felony Handbook, no. 57: PRP V: 199; Ulozhenie ch. 21, arts. 33, 93: RZ III: 234, 245–6. Significant time in prison: PRP V: 207–8 (1629). Planting evidence: Ulozhenie ch. 21, arts. 54, 56: RZ III: 239; 1669 Criminal Articles, art. 55: PRP VII: 416–17.

[22] Two-fold: PRP IV: 365 (1556); four-fold: Ulozhenie ch. 10, arts. 162–3: RZ III: 129; 1669 Criminal Articles, art. 28: PRP VII: 407. *Carolina*, art. 20: Langbein, *Prosecuting*, 273; French Ordinance 1539, art. 164: ibid., 313.

tortured only if his people first incriminated him under torture, but he would be tortured if they did. The law also explicitly allowed torture for people of high rank (*znatnye liudi*) if community investigation called them criminals.[23] Similarly, the law said nothing about excusing individuals on the basis of age, gender, physical or mental infirmity, illness and the like until 1669, and then only implicitly. Reflecting Roman law, the 1669 Criminal Articles raised the issue of incapacity – minor age (under 7), insanity, deafness – excusing such people of criminal responsibility and disallowing their testimony, which one assumes included torture. Ethnic identity was not a barrier. In a case of 1682, for example, a group of Mordva accused of murder was tortured. When Siberian governors were ordered to use torture only on Russians in December 1695, the intent was to preserve the loyalty and thus revenue from tax-paying natives. But natives could be subjected to torture and capital punishment, if permission were received from Moscow.[24]

That the state policed executioners provided safeguards as well. In August 1684, for example, a worker of the St. Cyril Beloozero Monastery accused of murder, Matvei Nikiforov, complained that during torture the executioner had beaten him in the body with his fists and hit him with a noose (*petlia*); the executioner denied this when first questioned. In face-to-face confrontation, however, the executioner admitted that he did not recall how he had behaved, since he had been drunk, and he admitted that he had lied in his oral interrogation. The governor ordered him beaten publically before the governor's office with bastinadoes, instead of the knout, because he had lied in testimony and "so that in the future he will not come to the torture chamber drunk."[25]

Litigants could sue for improper procedure regarding torture. In two cases of 1636, for example, defendants accused officials of torturing them "without the tsar's order." A litigant in 1670 defined proper procedure even more fully when he claimed that his wife had been wrongly tortured "without the tsar's order and without investigation." Others alleged lack of probable cause: a litigant in 1645 complained that he had been arrested and destined for torture "without material evidence and without

[23] Dependents incriminate: Ulozhenie ch. 21, art. 47: RZ III: 238; 1616/17 Felony Handbook, no. 16: PRP V: 193. Elite tortured: Ulozhenie ch. 21, art. 39: RZ III: 236; 1669 Criminal Articles, art. 31: PRP VII: 409. Slaves and others tortured: PRP V: 204–5 (1625); Ulozhenie ch. 21, arts. 69, 71, 73: RZ III: 241–2; 1669 Criminal Articles, arts. 76–8: PRP VII: 422–3.

[24] 1669 Criminal Articles, arts. 28, 108: PRP VII: 408, 429. RGADA f. 1122, op. 2, pt. 2, no. 1548, 3 fols. (1682). PSZ III: no. 1526 (1695).

[25] RGADA f. 1107, no. 3187, 28 fols. (1684).

accusation by other felons."[26] Similarly, in December 1692 a Sevsk gentryman Efrem Lomov was killed in a fight and his sons took the law into their own hands and went after the suspects, beating them and turning them over to the Sevsk governor, who proceeded to interrogation and torture, despite the inappropriate process. The accused then sued, pointing out that the Lomov boys had acted "without reporting the crime to the tsar, without an inquisitory trial, or face-to-face confrontation, or witnesses, or accusations under torture." In 1649 a gentryman complained that his son had been falsely accused of horse theft and had been tortured "without an accusatory trial and without an inquisitory trial confrontation and without any material evidence." He sued for dishonor and injury resulting from the torture.[27]

Two potential safeguards commonly seen in West European practice were weakly developed in Muscovy. One is witnesses. Here, Muscovite law was almost completely silent, and practice provides little evidence. That witnesses were present is suggested by a decree of 1683 that allows a plaintiff to waive his right to come to the torture session. M. M. Bogoslovskii says that a customary privilege in the North, where local self-government was strong, was to be present at torture sessions. A case in 1621 explicitly mandates that a man of high rank (*okol'nichii*) and two secretaries be present at a torture session. But actual cases do not record litigants or neutral witnesses at torture sessions, citing only the executioner and his helpers, the judge who did the questioning, and the scribe who recorded the proceedings. Jacob Reutenfels, at the Kremlin court in the early 1670s, depicts these attendees in passing when he related how, while a man was being tortured with knouting while held across the back of the executioner's helper, "with every blow the judge yells to him 'Speak!,' that is, 'Admit!'"[28]

Another area in which Muscovite law provided weaker safeguards than in European practice was in the thoroughness of the judicial record. In Spanish inquisition practice, in early modern France, in the *Carolina*, scribes recorded every exchange of questions, every facial movement, every turn of the executioner's screw. Katherine Royer describes how, in late medieval England, bodily gesture and facial expression were read for evidence of contrition and guilt, while Ulinka Rublack finds that in seventeenth-century German trials, women's emotions were carefully

[26] SIDG no. 259 (1636); RGADA f. 141 1636, no. 25, fol. 36 (1636). Novombergskii, *Koldovstvo*, no. 22 (1670). SIDG no. 80, p. 139 (1645).

[27] RGADA f. 210, Prikaznyi stol, nos. 1539, fol. 290 (1692) and 263, fols. 512–13 (1649).

[28] PSZ II: no. 1032 (1683). Bogoslovskii, "Zemskoe samoupravlenie," vol. 1, in *Chteniia* (1910), bk. 1, p. 195. AMG I: no. 137 (1621). Reitenfels, *Skazaniia*, 117.

monitored and recorded as evidence. Written transcripts provided judges with information on the victim's psychological state, and could also be used to justify appeal on the grounds of cruelty. By contrast, Muscovite law mandates only that the transcript of the trial be written during interrogation and does not specify its content.[29] In practice, scribes recorded only the briefest answers to questions, usually in summary form, rather than in question-by-question or descriptive format.

Towards the end of the seventeenth century, some judges began to record legal justification before proceeding to torture; the practice became more common in Peter the Great's time (see Chapter 8). In a case in Kadom in 1674, for example, the staff provided the appropriate Ulozhenie article regarding intent, and the governor proceeded to torture. In a similar situation in 1696 in Kurmysh, the staff accurately provided the Ulozhenie article allowing torture to collect further information.[30]

Such relative lack of focus on safeguards for torture opened the door to abuse, particularly since laws neither defined techniques of torture nor specified degrees of severity. A 1539 brigandage charter introduces the idea of torture being done "severely" (*nakrepko*), without defining what that meant; the 1589 Law Code suggested an unrealistically high number of blows for torture (100); a decree of 1673 was the first since 1589 to address the issue, establishing the number of blows for the first, second and third torture sessions for various crimes, ranging from 20 to 100.[31]

In practice, the number of blows varied greatly without evident pattern. Cases record the number of blows from at least the 1640s in highest crime, later for cases of common crime. A man arrested for a tobacco offense in 1640 was given forty-six blows; a cossack accused in Kadom in 1674 of murdering a Tatar woman was given twenty. In February 1684 the Iakutsk governor administered three torture sessions to a peasant accused of killing his own brother. For the first, on February 2, no details survive. In the second session on February 9 he received eighty blows of the knout with four weights added to his body and was pinched with hot pincers (*kleshchami*). Then he was led to the site of the fire to reconsider his testimony, and then interrogated while being scorched with fire.

[29] Silverman, *Tortured Subjects*, 60–2; Kamen, *Spanish Inquisition*, 191; *Carolina*, arts. 181–9: Langbein, *Prosecuting*, 300–2; Royer, "Dead Men Talking," 74–5; Rublack, *Crimes of Women*, 58–60. Ulozhenie ch. 10, art. 11: RZ III: 103.

[30] RGADA f. 1122, op. 2, pt. 2, no. 1629 (1674) (article on intent cited: ch. 21: art. 69). Similar case: RGADA f. 1107, no. 3549 (1688). RGADA f. 1135, no. 297 (1696) (article on torture cited: ch. 21: art. 58).

[31] 1539 Beloozero Charter, art. 4: RZ II: 214. 1589 Law Code, art. 103: PRP IV: 425. PSZ I: no. 561 (1573). Glaz′ev found twenty-five to eighty blows in Voronezh cases: *Vlast′ i obshchestvennost′*, 256–7.

Throughout these torments, he held to his story. His third torture session, on February 19, consisted of fifty blows and five weights and burning with fire. He still held to his story. In 1697, on the other hand, three defendants in a case of assault were each given only five blows, and a fourth defendant received six. In the 1684 case cited above in which the executioner was punished for being drunk, the defendant in the case was put to three torture sessions. The first was in August; the number of blows is not recorded. The second took place on September 29, with twenty-six blows; the third, on January 21, 1685, with twenty-five blows. Then the two parties settled the case.[32] One cannot know how severe were these "blows" nor why judges varied so much in the duration of sessions. The key point is that practice was inconsistent starting with the law itself; the first real legal regulation of torture in Russia came only in the mid eighteenth century.[33] In Muscovite courts, the best hope accused criminals had for good treatment were the various safeguards suggested here and the discretion of judges.

TORTURE IN BRIGANDAGE FELONIES

Simply because the law provided some safeguards does not diminish the horrific experience of being tortured. Disturbingly often, defendants died under torture. A collection of thirty-three witchcraft cases saw deaths from torture in two cases: in 1622 two women died, while in 1629 a man died, two others fled custody "fearing torture" and another was said to have accused others slanderously "unable to bear torture." Two men who were tortured with fire in 1637 about looting and arson in Moscow both later died. In 1664, two men accused of witchcraft, who were subjected to torture by knout and by fire, died in prison within days of their ordeal. Studying witchcraft, Russell Zguta found that of forty-seven trials he collected between 1622 and 1700, three of ninety-nine accused people died in torture.[34]

Even if not fatal, torture was debilitating. Knouting – for torture or punishment – so lacerated the flesh that scars were visible years later.

32 Number of blows: SIDG nos. 33 and 38 (1627), 133 (1647). PRP no. 143 (1640). RGADA f. 1122, op. 2, pt. 2, no. 1629, fol. 7 (1674). DAI XI: no. 11 (1) (1684). Titov (ed.), *Kungurskie akty*, no. 72 (1697). RGADA f. 1107, no. 3187, 28 fols. (1684).

33 Caroli, "La Torture dans la Russie," 811–13.

34 Novombergskii, *Koldovstvo*, nos. 1 (1622), 4 (1629). RGADA f. 141 1637, no. 59 (1637). RGADA f. 210, Belgorod stol, no. 599, fols. 565–71, 654–5, 658 (1664); repeated in Novombergskii, *Koldovstvo*, no. 21. Zguta, "Witchcraft Trials," 1196–7. Another case: RGADA f. 210, Prikaznyi stol, no. 1106, fol. 30 (1686).

Doctor Samuel Collins reflected on the effects of a knouting: "I have seen some whose backs have been scarifi'd like the bark of a Tree, which afterwards were healed, but they could never wear out the scars and marks thereof." A man petitioned the tsar in 1670 that his wife had been tortured wrongly and so harshly that she now lies "on her deathbed," unable to move her arms from the severe knouting. Intervals for healing between sessions could be as short as a week or as long as months; Doctor Collins expected 20 days. Petitioners often interceded for more time to heal. A 1648 petition to settle a suit specifically referred to wanting the defendant to avoid the rigors of torture. All depended upon the judges' instructions and the executioner, whom foreigners suggested could be bribed: Collins said "All this is done where the Hangman is not brib'd, for he will then cut deep," while Olearius alleged that executioners made good money from bribes.[35]

The myth of the "incomparable stubbornness" of the Russian peasant blinds us to the physical suffering involved. This trope was common to foreign travelers, similar to another assertion, seen since the sixteenth century, that Russian women appreciate being beaten by their husbands. Olearius rejected that tale, but he perpetuated the broader trope in his disparaging tale of a woman who withstood torture in order to falsely accuse her husband and thus condemn him to conviction. Johann-Georg Korb gives an extended anecdote on the theme of Russian imperviousness to pain. Reportedly in 1696 Peter the Great, astonished at the ability of a prisoner to withstand torture, engaged him in conversation. "The Czar asked him how he withstood knout and fire, and he said he belonged to an association of men who'd been tortured, that the one who withstood the most was held in highest esteem and had more privileges; he had been himself tortured six times, and was the president of the whole society." He went on to assert "that the knout was a mere nothing; that the roasting of the flesh after knouting was nothing; that he had had to go through far more cruel pains among his associates." Korb followed up with yet more anecdotes of Russians withstanding beatings.[36] These tropes notwithstanding, the torments of torture in the normal judicial process were severe.

It is small comfort that, as horrific as it was, torture was an exceptional procedure in the criminal law, reserved for the gravest of crimes. In legal

[35] Collins, *Present State*, 73. Novombergskii, *Koldovstvo*, no. 22 (1670). RGADA f. 210, Prikaznyi stol, no. 567, fols. 391–4, 519–21 (1648). Olearius, *Travels*, 231–2.

[36] Women like being beaten: Herberstein, *Description*, 41; Olearius, *Travels*, 170, 136. Korb, *Diary*, II: 202–6.

practice judges avoided torture unless completely necessary. In a case of bribery it was avoided, for example, when the gentry and peasants of the Kashira area complained in 1639 about rapacious tax collectors. The Military Service Chancery sent out investigators, who interrogated the complainants and set up face-to-face confrontations. The accused – two gentry, a military escort and a scribe – alleged the money was "gifts," not bribes. Satisfied with oral testimony, the court proceeded to verdict without torture: corporal punishment for the two lower-class men, but execution for the two gentrymen, since they had violated their oath of office. Immediately upon announcing the death sentence, the judges mitigated it to a knouting.[37]

Cases of serious bodily harm or theft also did not always merit torture. In 1651 near Viatka a peasant stabbed another in a fight; he argued that they were fighting over an "old enmity" and he claimed self-defense. The governor placed the accused in face-to-face confrontations with witnesses, who did not describe a situation of self-defense. When so confronted, the defendant admitted that he had acted in anger. This could imply premeditation, but since it was not a homicide case, torture was not used. While the Ulozhenie allowed torture in the case of tobacco possession, a judge in 1672 did not go that far. A Moscow landlord had confiscated tobacco from a Ukrainian merchant who was renting rooms from him; the judge interviewed both. The merchant alleged he did not understand that tobacco was illegal in Muscovy and promised to return home with it; satisfied with his story, the judge resolved to deport him to the Ukrainian Hetman with instructions to better supervise export of tobacco.[38]

Even when it came to murder and felony crime, some judges dispensed with torture completely. Even in such serious cases as homicide, a small group of resolved cases in the database used here (thirty-six) shows torture in only twenty-four (66 percent). In a homicide case of 1613, the Beloozero governor interrogated a suspected murderer, who confessed that he had done the crime with no other conspirators. Satisfied with this confession, the judge proceeded to a verdict of knouting. In late 1622 in the Kola Peninsula a man reported that his brother had died from a beating by a tax collector and scribe. The governor interviewed witnesses, who confirmed that the two men did it. Moscow instructed the governors on the

[37] RGADA f. 210, Sevsk stol, no. 111, fols. 186–95 and 223–4 (1639). Other examples: RGADA f. 210, Sevsk stol, nos. 246, fols. 384–7 and 404–7 (1640) and 263, fols. 251–60 (1663).

[38] RGADA f. 141 1651, no. 58, pt. 1, fols. 1–4 (1651). RGADA f. 210, Sevsk stol, no. 283, fols. 251–2 and 369–77 (1672).

basis of the community survey to knout and imprison the two men, without going to torture. This is a remarkably lenient sentence for a murder by two officials.[39]

With the 1625 decree considering lack of premeditation in homicide a mitigating factor, torture might seem to have been more necessary. But even after then, many homicide cases were resolved without torture. In Belgorod in 1645 a man brought in his brother, a low-ranking officer, for having stabbed a musketeer to death at his home. The governor launched an investigation, inspecting the body, interviewing all the witnesses at the gathering and interrogated brother against brother. The accused man denied the knifing, while ten witnesses said they saw the knifing itself, or said that they heard the fight, saw the man fall and saw the accused with a bloody knife; two said they were not close enough to see. The governor sent this testimony to Moscow before using torture. Without ordering torture, the Military Service Chancery instructed him to execute the accused, then immediately mitigated the sentence to a severe knouting and prison.[40]

Similarly, in 1647 in Livni the governor investigated a case in which the son of a gentryman axed his father to death. In oral questioning the father confessor of the dead man testified that he ran to the site of the fight and gave the dying man confession. The dying man told him they had quarreled over the father's beating the son's wife and that he forgave his son the crime. In oral interrogation, the son admitted the crime and pointed out that his father had forgiven him. Consulting with Moscow, the governor received instructions to execute the man for killing his father. With a confession and witness evidence, they did not use torture to confirm or obtain more details.[41]

Torture was also side-stepped by settling a murder case. For example, in 1648, the dead body of a Crimean in the tsar's service was brought into Livni, along with a local gentryman accused of killing him. The governor interviewed the seven men who brought them in, who all said they saw the beating but did not know the cause of the fight. The accused in oral interrogation admitted he killed the man, having found him trying to rape his wife. The governor asked the Military Service Chancery for further instructions, and it responded that he should torture the defendant "severely" to confirm the story and make sure no one else was involved,

[39] RGADA f. 1107, no. 19 (1613). RGADA f. 141, no. 31 (1622).
[40] PRP v: 204–5 (1625). RGADA f. 210, Prikaznyi stol, no. 162, fols. 264–72 and 416–18 (1645).
[41] RGADA f. 210, Prikaznyi stol, no. 567, fols. 159–64 and 276 (1647).

and then report back. But the victim's family interceded, asking that the defendant be spared torture and punishment and be made to support the orphaned family financially instead.[42]

Judges deferred to individuals for special circumstances, such as pregnancy. In a case of 1688 a peasant in the Beloozero area was accused of killing another peasant in a fight. He admitted that he had fought with the other man over a girl who had been living with the two of them as they wandered the countryside, seeking food and work in a time of famine. He denied any prior intent to kill. In testimony the girl herself confirmed their relationship, but denied knowledge of the murder. Reviewing excerpts from the Ulozhenie and the 1669 Articles justifying torture, the governor ordered the accused man brought to torture to determine intent. He received forty-three blows and held to his story. But the girl was not tortured, "because she is pregnant." That condition did not prevent her from being ordered beaten with bastinadoes, in place of a knout, "mercilessly" for her lewd living. She was sentenced to be released on surety bond, but as a stranger she could find no one willing to sponsor her, so she was simply released. Deference to pregnancy is expressed in a 1637 decree establishing that pregnant women could not be executed until six weeks after birth.[43]

Social class only occasionally won exemption from torture. In 1683 Ivan Iurlov was accused of beating and tormenting his peasants, from which one died. Called in to interrogation, he denied all and said the peasants were attacking him. The governor believed his story and let him off, with no torture. In a case of January 1686, the boyar judges of the Felony Chancery (*Prikaz sysknykh del*) accorded a gentryman only a modicum of deference. They heard the testimony of Vasilii Gavrilov syn Levashov, a gentryman of Riazhsk, who denied ordering his sons to beat up and break the arms and legs of his neighbor, suspected of burning Levashov's fields. But in face-to-face confrontation, other witnesses contradicted him. The judges made their decision based on testimony without torture. They chided him for denying his guilt, for seeking a needless change of venue, and for taking the law into his own hands, when he should have reported the arson to the authorities. Sparing him torture, they sentenced him to execution for premeditated murder. Other cases show that gentrymen

[42] RGADA f. 210, Prikaznyi stol, no. 567, fols. 391–4, 519–21 (1648).

[43] RGADA f. 1107, no. 3549, quote on fol. 10 (1688). ZA no. 244 (1637). Korb related that in 1698 a woman condemned to death was spared knouting when discovered to be pregnant, but he implies that she was promptly executed nonetheless: *Diary*, II: 93–4.

could be tortured – in one case of 1672 regarding rampant criminal activity around Tula, the Felony Chancery investigator claimed to have done four torture sessions on suspects, including at least one gentryman. Shockingly, deference does not seem to have been given for age, young or old. A case of 1674 identifies the defendant as a "child," yet he was brought to torture and eventually executed for murder.[44]

Criminal practice shows that judges or their scribes were knowledgeable and discriminating about torture, using it sparingly and according to the law. A rare record of a single judge's work – that of Iakutsk governor Matvei Osipovich Krovkov from February to August 1684 – shows him navigating torture and non-torture cases. In August, for example, the governor questioned a man about intent: he had beaten another to death in the tavern, but argued self-defense with no premeditation. He held to this story under torture with the knout. In numerous cases Krovkov did not proceed to torture. In February he interrogated a man accused of living with a woman in sin and participating with her in shamanism; the man denied any sexual relation with the girl and denied engaging in shamanism. The surviving case ends there, so if it is not fragmentary, the governor apparently believed his denial and did not consider this a case of witchcraft, which would have merited torture. In May the governor orally questioned an elder of the local monastery about his allegations of a "word and deed" (treason) crime. Krovkov questioned the people named by the elder and was about to put them to torture when the elder recanted, admitting that he had made it all up while drunk. This governor reserved torture for capital crimes. Similarly, in a group of more than 120 misdemeanor and felony cases from Tobol′sk *c.*1639–43, torture was used in only about 20 serious cases.[45]

Intentional murder, with its automatic death sentence, called for torture. In 1644 the governor of Verkhotur′e confronted a grisly murder: a local unregistered man, Ivashko, had had an affair with another man's wife, and her husband Fedko had threatened him. So Ivashko had crept into Fedko's house and killed him in his bed next to his sleeping wife. After interrogation, the governor put both Ivashko and the wife up to torture. Ivashko

[44] RGADA f. 1107, no. 3109, 23 fols. (1683). PSZ II: no. 1154 (1686). RGADA f. 210, Sevsk stol, no. 283, fols. 335–49 and 378–80 (1672). RGADA f. 1122, op. 2, pt. 2, no. 1629 (1674).

[45] DAI XI: no. 11, cases III (tavern beating), II (shamanism), IV (word and deed) (all 1684). Tobol′sk: Lipinskii (ed.), "Rospis′," 17–41. In Tobol′sk, cases with torture included homicide (pt. 1: nos. 6, 26, 35, 76), recidivist theft (pt. 1: nos. 29, 54, 92), church theft (pt. 1: no. 30), stabbing (pt. 1: nos. 73, 93), theft (pt. 1: nos. 44, 52), arson (pt. 1: no. 117), witchcraft (pt. 1: nos. 64, 103), or alcohol or tobacco sale or purchase (pt. 1: nos. 4, 60, 77, 108).

admitted to the crime and denied that the wife had any part in it. She denied not only having a role, but also any sexual relationship with Ivashko. The Siberian Chancery in Moscow ordered the Verkhotur′e governor to torture them both a second time, "severely," in order to establish co-conspirators and prior intent in the crime. The case record ends there. In a similar case in 1644 the Siberian Chancery was satisfied with one torture session: in Tobol′sk an indentured Tatar was interrogated and then tortured "severely" for the murder of another Tatar; he admitted the crime, but said it was done in a fight with no prior intent to kill and no one else was involved. The Siberian Chancery accepted this story and sentenced him to having his left hand severed. In Efremov a woman admitted after interrogation and under torture in June 1649 that she had murdered her husband on the instigation of her lover. Upon consulting with Moscow, the Efremov governor was ordered to ask the neighboring governor in Elets to arrest and send the implicated lover to Efremov for a face-to-face confrontation before the instruments of torture, and if the two parties did not confess, to proceed to severe torture. Their testimonies under torture were to be sent to Moscow.[46]

In these cases Moscow's role varied from providing guiding questions to rendering a verdict, its oversight constituting another safeguard for proper procedure. But judges were ordered to work autonomously (Chapter 7), and case upon case shows them working systematically through the hierarchy of interrogation procedures without central oversight. In Kadom in 1674 the local judge carried out a full inquisitorial process – examination of the dead body, oral interrogation, one torture session of twenty blows and excerpts of the 1669 Criminal Articles – before handing down a verdict for execution, without recourse to Moscow for permission to torture or for a verdict. In a case of 1684 in Beloozero, the judge proceeded to three torture sessions and a verdict, documenting procedure with dates and number of blows of each torture session and justifying the verdict with excerpts from the Ulozhenie and 1669 Criminal Articles. Here, scrupulous attention to procedure legitimized the process.[47]

Judges rarely used three sessions if fewer confirmed a confession and revealed no compatriots. When a mounted cossack in Tobol′sk was tortured in 1643 in the murder of his wife, he pleaded drunkenness, admitting he had stabbed her but alleging that he had had no prior intent

[46] Ivashko: "Uboistvennye dela," 4–5 (1644). Tatar: "Uboistvennye dela," 3 (1644). RGADA f. 210, Belgorod stol, no. 270, fols. 473–5, 478–80 (1649).

[47] RGADA f. 1122, op. 2, pt. 2, no. 1629 (1674). RGADA f. 1107, no. 3187 (1684).

and even had no memory of it. Moscow sent a resolution ordering him knouted for unintentional homicide. Similarly, a Beloozero peasant was accused of beating his wife to death in 1692; in oral investigation he countered that such beating was acceptable discipline for her disobedience, and he noted that the local priest had buried her knowing she had died of his blows. He repeated this testimony under torture (twenty-three blows plus weights). The governor tried to get corroborating information from the neighbors, but they had all fled, so he resolved the case without consulting Moscow, sentencing the man to a knouting for killing his wife unintentionally. Four men were accused of beating a man to death in 1697; on the basis of interrogation, eyewitness testimony and one torture session, the judge rendered a verdict.[48]

On the other hand, cases could go to three torture sessions to convince a recalcitrant defendant to talk, to get more information, to clarify testimony or to affirm a recantation. For example, the governor in Sol′ Kamskaia had subjected three Cherdyn′ townsmen accused of murder to interrogation and three tortures with fire in June 1683. They admitted they had sexually assaulted a woman and beaten her, but denied that they had murdered her intentionally, pleading drunkenness. In a case of 1672, one governor reported that he had used four torture sessions to investigate a band of robbers around Tula, an excessive amount in a case short of political crime.[49]

Judges routinely used torture to determine intent and the circumstances of a crime, even if they had a confession in hand. In April 1649, the Iakutsk governor received a response from Moscow regarding a murder by a Tunguz of another Tunguz. He had interrogated the accused man and followed up with torture to affirm the plea of self-defense. The Siberian Chancery rejected the plea, but agreed that it was unintentional and sentenced him to be knouted, rather than executed, even though the community was demanding blood.[50]

These examples show that procedure guided the use of torture, but its use was not consistent on whether to use torture, how often or how severely. Given that judges and scribes moved positions frequently, they

[48] "Uboistvennye dela," 3 (1643). RGADA f. 1107, no. 3904, 7 fols. (1692). Titov (ed.), *Kungurskie akty*, no. 72 (1697). Another case with only one torture: PSZ II: no. 1102 (1684). Although the 1669 Criminal Articles punished drunkenness associated with homicide more harshly than had the Ulozhenie (Ulozhenie ch. 22, art. 17 [RZ III: 249–50]; 1669 Article, no. 103 [PRP VII: 428]), it was still an effective way to argue lack of intent.

[49] DAI X: no. 87 (1683). RGADA f. 210, Sevsk stol, no. 283, fol. 342 (1672).

[50] DAI III: no. 52 (1649).

carried such practices of judicial flexibility around the realm. In some cases, judicial discretion worked for litigants; regarding torture, it could work against them. This conclusion has the direst implication regarding highest crime – treason, heresy and religious crime, and witchcraft – where torture was almost inescapable.

TORTURE IN CASES OF HIGHEST CRIME

When it came to highest crime, the restraints and safeguards discussed here stood sharply in tension with the government's obsession with rooting out opposition. On the one hand, judges could be restrained if cases turned out to be weak: Mark Lapman found, for example, that only 15 percent of a group of "word and deed" cases (which often turned out to be groundless) between 1600 and 1649 used torture; another small number included the threat of torture.[51] On the other hand, when important cases prompted claustrophobic oversight, a chilling lack of restraint in the use of coercive pain drove prosecution.

Cases of witchcraft called forth great excesses, probably because it was believed that only pain would conquer the devils inhabiting a witch.[52] In the spring of 1647 a suspected male witch was subjected to forty-two blows of the knout, then his head was shaved and water was poured on his head and he was "burned hard" with fire. This case ends with the accused petitioning from prison to be released since he was "oozing pus from his wounds." Similarly, in a dramatic case of possession and witchcraft allegations in Lukh that extended from 1656 to 1660, one man's second torture session included knouting, burning with hot pincers and slow water torture. In 1690 two men accused of hexing many people were tortured with knout and fire. [53]

Neither gender nor status greatly inhibited the maw of torture. In one witchcraft case of 1647, an old woman accused of witchcraft was tortured with blows and water torture, but the judge stopped at eleven blows "since

[51] Lapman, "Political Denunciations," 35–6. Torture used infrequently in Europe: Kamen finds it in only 7 percent of Inquisition cases in Granada 1573–7, 11 percent in Seville 1606–12: *Spanish Inquisition*, 188–9.

[52] Case law starts *c.*1630s. Fire mentioned with torture: RGADA f. 210, Belgorod stol, no. 284, fols. 391–418 (1647/8); RGADA f. 210, Prikaznyi stol, no. 383, fols. 126–7v (1664); Novombergskii, *Koldovstvo*, nos. 11 (1647), 21 (1664), 30 (1677), 33 (1638); RGADA f. 210, Prikaznyi stol, nos. 565, fols. 6–21 (1647); 564, fols. 154–234 (1647); 567, fols. 539–49 (1648); RGADA f. 210, Belgorod stol, no. 599, fols. 565–71, 654–5, 658 (1664).

[53] RGADA f. 210, Prikaznyi stol, no. 565, fols. 6–21 (1647). Lukh: Kivelson, "Through the Prism." Semevskii, *Istoriko-iuridicheskie akty*, no. 7, pp. 70–1 (1690).

she is old"; that did not deter him from proceeding later to a second session of twelve blows and fire. Two younger female defendants – a mother and daughter – in the same case suffered thirty and twenty-five blows, respectively, in their first session, as well as water torture and burning. In their second session, mother and daughter received thirty-five and thirty-one blows, respectively, and burning. Similarly, in a case of 1649, the judge reported that the accused witch was "old and blind" and had fainted under torture. He hesitated to give her more so that she "would not die during torture." Although more men than women were accused of witchcraft, judges did not hesitate to torture women. In a disturbing case of alleged witchcraft perpetrated against the tsar's wife in 1638–9, ten women who worked in the Kremlin artisan workshops were tortured, several with fire; six of them suffered one session, two suffered two sessions, one was put to torture three times, and one four times.[54]

Central chanceries kept a tight rein on such cases, more from interest in the testimony than from fear of injuring the defendants. For example, a Kozlov man was found with a suspicious letter in 1693–4; in questioning and under torture he admitted that he had had it a good ten years and that he had kept it with him as a talisman, not knowing what it said since he was illiterate. Reporting this to Moscow in August 1693, the governor was ordered (in January 1694) to torture the man "once, twice or three times, according to the Ulozhenie" about where he got the letter, and to report back not only his testimony but the number of blows given. They dutifully wrote back that he had already been tortured twice, on July 11, 1693 (twenty blows) and July 23 (fifty blows). They proceeded with his third torture, of sixty blows and fire, and he told the same story. In March of 1694 Moscow handed down a ruling with yet more torment: they were to burn the text of the evil letter on to the back of the accused, knout him mercilessly (destroying the words, undoubtedly), and send the man to eternal exile.[55]

Like accused witches, religious dissenters also merited harsh methods to extirpate the devils inside. Our earliest references to prosecutions of heretics are late fifteenth- and sixteenth-century church heresy trials, for which David Goldfrank suggests that the church, relying on codes infused

[54] RGADA f. 210, Prikaznyi stol, nos. 564, fols. 154–234 (1647) and 567, fols. 539–49 (1649). Novombergskii, *Koldovstvo*, no. 33 (1638). Other cases in which women were tortured: ibid., nos. 1 (1622), 3 (1628), 4 (1629), 11 (1647), 20 (1664), 22 (1670), 26 (1676), 29 (1677), 32 (1690). Torture of a priest: ibid., no. 8 (1640).

[55] RGADA f. 210, Prikaznyi stol, no. 679, fols. 297–300 (1693).

with Roman law, did not hesitate to use torture.[56] In some cases of religious crime, torture did not go beyond knouting. In 1657 a man in Rostov Velikii was accused of preaching heretical ideas; he and two of his students were subjected to torture, but it was relatively mild for a religious case – seven, eight, ten blows of the knout. Conversely, Archpriest Avvakum received seventy blows in torture during one of his many interrogations, but not fire. Most torture in these cases included more than strappado's torments. Around 1666 in a case associated with the Kapitonovshchina, investigators isolated a principal suspect, Vavilo; when he refused to talk, he was tortured with knout and burning with hot pincers. So also were several witnesses against him. The most horrific torture was reserved for the leaders of the group and those with the most significant information. Similarly, in a 1683 case, two men suspected of proselytizing for the schism were subjected to torture, each suffering 100 blows, burning with fire and burning with hot pincers "many times." One of them also had "many weights" placed on his feet, intensifying the strappado.[57]

Secular crime against the state also called forth torture. A cluster of cases – from 1581, 1613, 1614, 1621 and others – regarding individuals caught at the western border and accused of spying or defecting include torture to gain information. In one case, for example, the governor of Kholmogory in the North reported in December 1613 that he had questioned under torture a captured Ukrainian musketeer (Cherkashenin) about his unit's role in the war (the ongoing "Time of Troubles"); in January 1614, he reported the testimony under torture of some captured Lithuanian soldiers, and added that one of the Lithuanians and the Ukrainian had both died from the torture. One case of 1621 included the interesting detail: "if [the defendant] is not seriously hurt from torture (*bol'no pytan*)," then he should be tortured [again] to confirm his recanting, and then hanged for treason. In this case, he was tortured, a third time, "severely" with burning by fire, and then executed.[58]

In serious "word and deed" cases, multiple forms of torture were routinely used – knouting, weights in the strappado position and burning with fire – and, as in witchcraft, some judges tortured beyond the usual

[56] Goldfrank, "Theocratic Imperatives." Church reforms and schism: Bushkovitch, *Religion and Society*, ch. 3.

[57] Rumiantseva (ed.), *Dokumenty Razriadnogo*, sect. II: nos. 14–16 (1657). Avvakum: Esipov (ed.), *Raskol'nichie dela*, I: 116. Vavilo: *Narodnoe antitserkovnoe dvizhenie*, nos. 17, 19–32. Barsov, "Sudnye protsessy," 16–17 (1683).

[58] AAE I: no. 310 (1581). AMG I: nos. 46 and 59 (1613), 63 (1614) and 144 (1521).

three sessions. In a case of 1627, for example, it is recorded that the defendant suffered 100 blows of the knout with ten weights and was raised over fire three times, and still did not testify to the satisfaction of the judges. Burned a fourth time, he confessed. In 1626 a defendant suffered five torture sessions, including knouting, burning with hot pincers and having a toe burned on one foot. In a case that extended from 1638 through 1639, a man suffered eight torture sessions, three with burning. One governor reported in 1659 that he had put a particularly recalcitrant prisoner through eight torture sessions, three with fire.[59]

These cases are full of the terror and pathos of torture. One defendant in a criminal case confessed that he had concocted a "word and deed" case "fearing more severe torture"; another falsely accused someone else to escape more torture. Often torture yielded little. In 1635 a high-powered team of investigators from Moscow traveled to Novgorod to investigate allegations of collusion with the Lithuanian enemy by churchmen in the archbishop's office and a nearby monastery. In the course of a few months of interrogation, they orally questioned dozens of people and subjected several to torture. Clerical rank did not protect anyone from the knout. The interrogators inflicted multiple torture sessions on two monastic servants, two church deacons, two monastic elders and even the archimandrite of the monastery. They used torture by knout, fire and heavy weights. They did so despite the fact that two of the accused were elderly monks – eighty years old – blind and weak. They tortured one man thinking he was feigning unconsciousness, but he remained that way through the torments. The investigators reported back to Moscow that one man had died from torture. They did not uncover treason.[60]

Nevertheless, investigations of "word and deed" cases were not randomly abusive. The Moscow center carefully instructed their investigators or local judges on progressive judicial procedure, demanding to be informed between stages. So, in 1627 and 1629 two governors reported oral testimony and awaited permission to go to torture. In another case of 1629, the governor of Bolkhov interrogated a prisoner who had claimed to have a "word and deed" case; he sent the testimony to Moscow, and received instructions to move to torture regarding treason, other crime and compatriots.[61] Similarly, in a case of 1629 involving peasants who had

[59] Word and deed: SIDG nos. 50 (1629), 32 (1627), 67 (1623), 80 (1645), 148 (1650), 200 (1625). More than three: SIDG nos. 33 and 38 (1627). 1626: SIDG no. 30 (1626). SIDG no. 268 (1638–9). SIDG no. 268, p. 503 (1659).

[60] SIDG nos. 146, p. 241 (1648) and 150, p. 252 (1649). SIDG nos. 60 and 160 (1635).

[61] PRP v: 156–8 (1627). AMG I: no. 257 (1629). Bolkhov: AMG I: no. 257 (1629).

repeatedly crossed the western border and returned, the local governors questioned them and awaited instruction: Moscow ordered them to question the men separately "at torture" (in sight of the instruments) and then to torture them. The prime suspects were summoned to Moscow, questioned in the Military Service Chancery and then the tsar was consulted. Only with his instruction did they move on to a second torture of the suspect. In 1644 one regional governor reported difficulty in getting a defendant to talk in oral questioning and when "raised up" for torture, but informed the center, "without the tsar's order I cannot proceed to torture." The center instructed the judge to have the defendant write down his story. If he refuses to do so, the governor should proceed to confrontation with instruments of torture; if that doesn't work, then he had permission to move on to torture. The judge followed these steps and reported the results of the first torture session; then he received permission to proceed to a second session. One case of 1638 reveals that when confronting a defendant at the instruments of torture, the judge read the tsar's orders to him verbatim.[62]

Given that the state resorted to such brutality when so many "word and deed" cases proved trivial, it is not surprising that courts became all the more abusive when investigating outright political uprising. Punishment for these uprisings is discussed in Chapter 16, but here the use of torture is examined. In a collection of documents regarding urban uprisings around the realm in the summer of 1648, torture was used extensively. Tsar Aleksei Mikhailovich ordered that all the boyars should attend the torture sessions in Moscow; two ringleaders were tortured at least twice, with face-to-face confrontations, knouting and burning with fire. One received thirty-three and sixteen blows in two sessions. In Kursk at least forty accused – including twenty peasants, ten musketeers, a gentryman, a brigandage elder and others – were questioned under torture by knouting and fire. In Ustiug Velikii, over seventy-five men and women were questioned under torture (many others were simply interrogated); one peasant, one townsman and two musketeers died from the torture.[63]

V. I. Buganov's study of the 1662 uprisings in various cities showed that the tsar ordered investigators to "question and torture with all manner of harsh tortures severely." Investigations included knout and burning with fire. Interrogations took place in several sessions with large groups of men,

62 AMG 1: no. 259, pp. 276, 280 (1629). SIDG nos. 274 and 277, pp. 517, 519, 522 (1644). SIDG no. 268, p. 499 (1638).

63 Bazilevich (ed.), *Gorodskie vosstaniia*, 83–92 (Moscow), 124–34 (Kursk), 141–65 (Ustiug Velikii).

ignoring the custom of separate interrogation. In all, over 800 people were investigated in three locations – the Ugresh monastery, Moscow and Kolomenskoe. The most serious suspects were sent to Moscow, where the harshest torture was done – of the 707 people questioned there, 39 were brought to torture (about 5.5 percent), one of them three times, five twice and the rest once. Sessions for most averaged twenty-five blows, but reached as high as fifty and sixty for some. Taking into account broader investigations, Buganov calculated that of more than 1,700 people questioned, 196 were tortured, or about 11 percent, but they were subjected to multiple sessions with many blows. These numbers suggest that torture was reserved for the most recalcitrant or significant defendants and witnesses and that it was relatively unrestrained for highest crime.[64]

Great brutality was used on rebels against the tsar, if contemporary foreign accounts are to be believed. One reports that in April to June 1671 Stepan Razin was put through hideous tortures – beating with a knout, strappado such that his limbs were pulled out of his joints, a hot iron passed over his body, the crown of his head shaved and cold water poured on it by drops, "which they say causeth very great pain." In the prosecution of supporters of Regent Sofiia in 1689, torture by strappado was used on a man of conciliar rank, Fedor Shaklovityi; at least fifteen musketeers allied with him were also tortured, some by water torture according to one account.[65] By 1696–8, Peter the Great was more firmly taking over day-to-day rule. When he confronted serious challenges in the form of the traitor Jansen, the conspirator Tsykler and the musketeer uprising of 1698, he had available to him established patterns of interrogation and execution. How he wielded and changed them is discussed in Chapter 18.

REFLECTIONS ON TORTURE

Muscovite law strove to prevent abuses, as did other early modern European criminal codes. But, as Edward Peters wryly remarks, "Precise, limited and highly regulated in law and legal theory, torture became quickly roughened in the hard world of applied law among the hardened personnel of the court system."[66] Greek and Roman jurists scorned torture, arguing that it is easy to make an innocent man confess with

[64] Buganov, *Moskovskoe vosstanie 1662 g.*, 97–132.

[65] Konovalov, "Razin's Execution." DAI XII: no. 59 (1690). Shaklovityi: PSZ II: nos. 1349, 1352, 1359, 1362 (all 1689) and 1395 (1691); Foy de la Neuville describes the tortures: *Curious and New Account*, 42–4.

[66] Peters, *Torture*, 69.

pain; such critiques were echoed in medieval and early modern reforms as well. Early modern critics argued that if a person could withstand such pain, it must be the work of the Devil.[67] Historically and now, defense of torture takes two approaches. One balances the brutality of the process against the severity of the crime and justifies torture to protect society from evil. Another sees torture in relation to other cultural practices regarding pain in a given society. Lisa Silverman links early modern French practice of torture with the multiple meanings of pain in Western Christianity: pain was an ennobling imitation of Christ's sufferings; God will protect the innocent. At the same time, Christianity taught that pain was the human condition, a result of original sin, and that in the judicial context, it could be used to penetrate man's vanity and willfulness, to force out the truth. Truth was perceived as embodied, as physically resident in the person, and pain was the means to extricate it. André Berelowitch argues that Muscovite judges' recourse to torture even after gathering multiple other indications of guilt reflects a certain irrational belief in the spiritual power of ordeals over mere human evidence.[68]

Muscovites recorded no reflections on why they used state-sanctioned pain, but their use of it suggests that they believed in the veracity of testimony under torture. Should we? Certainly, the cases cited above are so laconically and undramatically written that one can be lulled into thinking that individuals told the truth under torture. This might be the case for those who resisted torture and exonerated themselves, and it might conversely be the case for some hardened felons who really did commit the crimes they confessed to under torture. But the torture process could come down brutally on others – producing ever-widening circles of accusations. Abuses could occur because of Muscovy's lack of systematic procedures of torture and of definitions of torturing "severely" (*nakrepko*). Muscovite law did not provide a systematic handbook on torture like the *Carolina*, and even in Europe, such handbooks only went so far. Citing Peters again: court personnel "were not always academically trained experts, and it is doubtful that the carefully guarded consilia and academic treatises ever had much of an influence except in offering a juridical ideal for actual magistrates and torturers."[69] The absence of

[67] Langbein, *Torture and the Law*, 8–9; Peters, *Torture*, 34, 58, 71.

[68] Peters, *Torture*, 21; Silverman, *Tortured Subjects*, 8–9, 64–8, 80–3; Berelowitch, "De modis demonstrandi." Silverman critiques Elaine Scarry for an exclusively modern definition of torture, but Scarry's passionate meditation on pain, truth and being is essential in any study of the topic: Scarry, *Body in Pain*.

[69] Peters, *Torture*, 62.

regulatory norms in Muscovite law opened broad opportunity for local officials to use torture inconsistently and, at worst, abusively.

Ultimately, the question of why courts used so damaging and coercive a method of interrogation returns us to Muscovite ideology. The world of torture described here is a horrific flip side to the view of the tsar as pious and merciful, namely, the side that obligates the sovereign to use violence against evildoers. Acting on behalf of the tsar, judges protected the common person from crime; they safeguarded the spiritual purity of the realm by torturing heinous heretics and witches in league with evil spirits; they pushed coercive power to bloody extremes in protecting the realm from treason and heresy. One must assume that the practitioners believed that the truth they were getting from torture was real, that the procedures they were following achieved justice and protected the innocent, and that these coercive, brutal measures were necessary. Ultimately, judicial torture preserved Muscovy's "sacred community" and affirmed the justness of the sovereign's use of violence.[70]

[70] Daniel Rowland's phrase: "Problem of Advice," 283.

CHAPTER 7

Resolving a case

In 1660 a Tatar prince, Nurmamet Murza Kniaz Kulumchakov, accused the Temnikov governor, Kirill Poluekhtovich Naryshkin, of corruptly resolving a case involving disputed land, hay fields and oxen, "guided by his unlawful greed, not by the Ulozhenie." Kulumchakov appealed for reconsideration, and his case was sent to the Chancery of the Kazan Palace. Naryshkin did not suffer punishment for this charge; in fact he later made a brilliant career.[1] But the incident shows how litigants played active roles in resolving their cases. Plaintiffs, defendants, their kin and communities, in addition to judges, were involved in the resolution of suits. Litigants could intercede in the process of a trial; judges could act autonomously or turn to chanceries for advice. This chapter examines judges' autonomy and litigants' use of appeal and settlements.

JUDGES' AUTONOMY

Foreigners painted a mixed picture of judges. Giles Fletcher wrote in 1590:

> there is none that hath any authority or public jurisdiction that goeth by descent or is held by charter, but all at the appointment and pleasure of the emperor, and the same practiced by the judges with such awe and restraint as that they dare not determine upon any special matter, but must refer the same wholly up to Moscow to the emperor's council.

Others construed local governors or chancery officials as satraps with complete power. Jodocus Crull, writing in the very end of the seventeenth century, declared that the tsar "creates and deposes Magistrates . . . , they have a Diack or Secretary, and sometimes another Assessor join'd with them, and take Cognisance of all Matters, giving a final and absolute

[1] RGADA f. 1167, op. 1, pt. 2, no. 1371, fols. 4–5 (1660). Naryshkin's daughter married Tsar Aleksei Mikhailovich in 1671 and Naryshkin was promoted to boyar by the next year. In 1682 he barely escaped murder in urban riots: see Chapter 17 and Crummey, *Aristocrats and Servitors*, 152, 197.

Judgment in all Causes, and have full Power to see their Sentences put in Execution, without any Appeal." John Perry, writing in the 1710s, considered the only law "the Will of the Judge, pretending to take some Statute for his Guide, [he] decides the Law as he pleases." Even when local governors must refer a death penalty to Moscow, Perry noted cynically, "they never failed so to represent [the case], as to make the Punishment fall as they would have it." Many observers underscored the tsar's power by recognizing that suits could always be appealed to the tsar.[2]

Belying the trope of despotism, these foreigners captured the dynamism of Muscovite trials: judges had autonomy, the center had oversight and litigants could sometimes appeal. Eager to empower judges to deliver justice promptly, the law was emphatic that judges should rule on their own.[3] The 1497, 1550 and 1589 Law Codes all direct senior judges to render verdicts and punish up through execution, advising lesser judges to refer to them (historians see no evidence that they did); brigandage elders received similar powers: "And elders and wardens are not to send transcripts of criminal cases to Moscow to the boyars as a report for resolution (*doklad*), but they are to resolve those criminal cases themselves according to this instruction" (Medyn Charter of 1555). Another charter adds that the responsibility to execute the guilty "has been placed on your souls."[4] Regional judicial charters from 1488 (to Beloozero) and 1614 (to Ustiuzhna Zheleznopol'skaia) and instructions to governors as a rule instruct judges to punish those guilty of major crime without recourse to the center, with some regional variation; instructions remind governors that being appointed "by the tsar's order" gave them authority and that law codes should be their guides in executing it. V. N. Glaz'ev observed that "the breadth of autonomy of the brigandage elders varied according to their instructions from the Felony Chancery, as it was with the governor." Decrees often instructed judges to rule "as you see fit," but that meant within the constraints of the law.[5]

2 Fletcher, "Of the Russe," 134; Crull, *Ancient and Present State*, 172; Perry, *State of Russia*, 143, 189. Appealed: Fletcher, "Of the Russe," 173; Margeret, *Russian Empire*, 29.

3 See Kollmann, "Judicial Autonomy."

4 Judge's autonomy: 1497 Law Code, arts. 8, 38: RZ II: 54, 59; 1550 Law Code, arts. 59, 60, 62: RZ II: 108–9; 1589 Law Code, art. 114: PRP IV: 427. Lesser judges: 1497 Law Code, art. 43: RZ II: 60; 1550 Law Code, art. 71: RZ II; 113; Alekseev, *Sudebnik Ivana III*, 313–16; Serov, *Sudebnaia reforma*, 340–4. 1539 Beloozero Charter, arts. 3–5, 9: PRP IV: 176–8; 1555 Medyn Charter, arts. 2, 3, 5, 9, 12: RZ II: 219–22; Jan.1555 Felony Handbook, arts. 1, 2: PRP IV: 356.

5 Beloozero, art. 10: PRP III: 172 (1488). AAE III: no. 36 (1614). Glaz'ev, *Vlast' i obshchestvennost'*, 254, 83–8. Governors' "instructions": AMG I nos. 129, 135 (Viazma 1619, 1621); AMG I: no. 202 (Toropets 1628); AMG II: no. 633 (Usviat 1655); AMG I: no. 323 (Uglich 1632); AAE III: no. 236 (Rzhev 1633); "Dela ob opredelenii," docs. 5 and 7 (Beloozero 1635, 1641); ibid., no. 6 (Bezhetskii

In the Thirteen Years War (1654–67) with the Polish–Lithuanian Commonwealth, decrees reinforced judges' power. On May 25, 1654, for example, criminal law officers in Moscow were directed to arrest, try and hang criminals "without writing to the tsar" for permission. With similar severity, in September 1655 military commanders were instructed to hang "without any delay" troops who commit crimes against populations of territory they are occupying or traveling through. Instructions to local officials intensified with rising social unrest in the 1660s. A decree of 1661 sending an investigator to Smolensk province to look into a murder of soldiers requisitioning grain empowered him to make a verdict and give punishment "according to our order and the Ulozhenie." A 1667 instruction to Moscow town watchmen empowered them to arrest, try and punish people of the lower classes (*chernye i obyshnye liudi*), but to consult with their superior chancery regarding people in military servitor ranks.[6] The 1669 Criminal Articles explicitly underscore the autonomy of investigators and brigandage elders in capital punishment: "If someone by his guilt, acting against the law of the great sovereign and the Ulozhenie and the Byzantine codes (*gradskie zakony*), is sentenced to death, execute those criminals immediately, not requesting about it to the Great Sovereign in Moscow." In 1679 a governor assuming brigandage duties in Arzamas was instructed with similar words: "If they deserve the death penalty by our laws, then execute them right away, not writing to us."[7] The general order to investigators of runaway serfs of March 1683 instructed them to hang immediately as an example to others any runaways who had committed major crimes such as murder and arson. An August 1683 order to Kazan adds that if investigators cannot resolve a case, they are to refer to the center; otherwise, they are to handle cases on the spot.[8]

By the end of the seventeenth century instructions to governors were particularly explicit about their responsibility to carry out justice locally, especially in Siberia. The Tiumen' governor, for example, was ordered in 1699 to punish even unto death exiles caught in serious crime. Siberian

Verkh 1637); Iakovlev (ed.), *Namestnichie*, no. 12 (Arzamas 1679); AI I: no. 240 (Iakutsk 1694); PSZ III: no. 1542 (Nerchinsk 1696); PSZ III: no. 1579 (Kazan 1697); PSZ III: no. 1594 (Tobol'sk 1697); PSZ III: no. 1595 (Verkhotur'e 1697). As you see fit: Halperin, "Administrative Discretion."

[6] PSZ I: nos. 126 (1654) and 166 (1655). AMG III: no. 364 (1661). PSZ I: no. 407 (1667).

[7] 1669 Criminal Articles, art. 123: PRP IV: 433. Iakovlev (ed.), *Namestnichie*, no. 12, p. 98 (1679). Judicial autonomy up to death penalty: DAI VII: no. 59 (1679): PRP VII: 201–3 (1683); AIuB I: no. 55 (XLIX) (1690). General order, art. 40: PRP VII: 197 (1683); cited in PSZ III: nos. 1594, 1595, 1579 (1697); *Vremennik*, XXIV: 41–7 (1696/7); PSZ III: nos. 1625, 1644, 1645, art. 2; PRP VII: 206 and 372–9 (all 1698); PSZ III: no. 1670 (1699); PSZ IV: no. 1792 (1700).

[8] AAE IV: no. 279 (1683 Kazan).

governors were told to establish brigandage boards for far-flung communities, where locally elected bailiffs could investigate, resolve and punish crime including felony (*vorovstvo*). Instructions to Tobol′sk decreed that if judges in its subordinate towns could not reach a verdict, they were to appeal to the Tobol′sk governor, not to Moscow.[9]

Charters limit governors' judicial autonomy in only a few instances, one of them being, not surprisingly, highest crime. Governors on the western frontiers were to watch out for spying, defection and suspicious newcomers; they were instructed to investigate "harshly," using torture, then report the testimony to Moscow. Siberian governors were to do the same and were also to be on the watch for violations of trading laws.[10] Charters acknowledged judicial autonomies of some communities – noblemen and bourgeois in territories captured from the Grand Duchy of Lithuania, Ukrainian Cossacks; Moscow's judges were not to interfere unless those judicial systems broke down.[11]

Throughout is evident an effort to give judges discretion in order to render speedy justice, even as the state over the seventeenth century also asserted greater bureaucratic control over society. The tension between central control and empowering officials imposed a fine balancing act but one that was embraced even by the domineering Peter the Great. Charters to governors from his time show even more confidence in judges; from 1706 they encourage governors to rule according to law codes, "the instructions to previous governors and by your own best judgment." The instruction to the governor of Ingermanland in 1707 adds to this same list that the governor should "consult with the commanders of other towns" if need be.[12] The centralized state needed officials on the ground to do their work.

RESOLUTIONS IN PRACTICE

In practice, Muscovite judges embraced the power they were given to resolve cases using their best judgment within the law.[13] Beloozero judges

[9] PSZ III: no. 1670 (1699). Bailiffs: PSZ III: no. 1670, art. 13 (Tiumen′ 1699); PSZ IV: no. 1822, art. 42 (Nerchinsk 1701). Refer to Tobol′sk: PSZ III: no. 1594, art. 30 (1697).

[10] AMG I: nos. 129 (1619), 135 (1621), 202 (1628), 323 (1632); "Dela ob opredelenii," no. 7 (1641); AMG II: nos. 331 (1648), 739 (1655); AAE IV, no. 211 (1676); PSZ III: no. 1595 (1697); PSZ IV, no. 1836 (1701).

[11] AMG II: nos. 633 (Usviat 1655), 739 (Mogilev 1655), 920 (Minsk 1656); AAE IV, no. 211 (Pereiaslov 1676); PSZ III: no. 1540 (Chernigov 1696). A few charters to small jurisdictions instructed governors to handle only minor cases and to refer more serious cases to Moscow or to a neighboring large-town governor: Pechernikov: AMG I: no. 249 (1629); Dünaburg: AMG II: no. 867 (1656); Olshansk: AI I: no. 161 (1687).

[12] PSZ IV: no. 2067, art. 3 (1706). PSZ V: no. 3294, pt. 6 (1707).

[13] Judges' ideosyncratic judgments: Kivelson, "'Sovereign Have Pity'."

provide good examples, as they worked confidently without much reference to Moscow. So, for example, in a 1628 Beloozero case of misdemeanor theft, assault and battery, the governor questioned the litigants in accusatory format, consulted with his colleagues in the brigandage office and found the defendant guilty of lying in his testimony. They resolved many homicide cases: in 1613, a Beloozero judge carried out such a trial with inquisitory format and found the defendant guilty based on his testimony; in 1615 governor Ivan Vasil′evich Golovin used torture to obtain a confession of homicide and resolved the case; in 1638 a Beloozero judge accepted a settlement in a homicide case. The Beloozero governor in 1692 also decided a case without recourse to Moscow: he heard testimony, including under torture (23 blows and one weight), and even though he failed to uncover witness testimony since all the peasants of the village had fled judicial officials, he found the accused man, a peasant, guilty on the strength of his confession. He was ordered knouted and put on surety bond, because he had killed his wife by excessive beating, without intent to kill.[14]

Governors in the Arzamas region were similarly decisive. They launched cases and ordered the successive steps of investigation (*sysk*): they sent staff to examine dead bodies and arrest suspects; they interrogated with and without torture; they corresponded with neighboring governors for cooperation in investigations.[15] In a case in Kadom that lasted from 1674 to 1677, the governor conducted the entire trial, including questioning and torture justified by reference to the Ulozhenie. Reviewing the evidence, and basing himself on excerpts of "Byzantine codes and New Articles [1669 criminal code]," he sentenced the defendant to death and oversaw the beheading. Similarly, the governor of Dobroe on the steppe frontier resolved several cases in 1681 without reference to Moscow: he punished two gentrymen for leaving the unit without his permission and punished two other gentrymen for taking in runaway serfs.[16]

In specific circumstances governors turned to Moscow for help. One was when an official felt he had not been specifically authorized. For example, the governors of Viatka reported in 1682 that crime was so rampant – a cleric had been stabbed to death "at the gates" of the governor's own courtyard – that they had proceeded to execute criminals

[14] RGADA f. 1107, nos. 19 (1613), 167 (1615), 824 (1638) and 3904 (1692).

[15] RGADA f. 1175, no. 1626 (1670); RGADA f. 1167, op. 1, pt. 1, no. 7 (1675); RGADA f. 1122, op. 2, pt. 1, no. 1018 (1685); op. 2, pt. 2, nos. 1727 (1675) and 1424, fols. 1–6 (1687); RGADA f. 1135, no. 297 (1696).

[16] RGADA f. 1122, op. 2, pt. 2, no. 1629 (1674), excerpts on fols. 6, 11. Travel without permission: RGADA f. 210, Prikaznyi stol, no. 793, fols. 236–40 (1681). Runaways: ibid., fols. 252–60 (1681).

and hang them along the roads as a deterrent to others. They affirmed that their original orders allowed executions, but now they had been told by their chancery (Foreign Affairs) to imprison felons and await verdicts from Moscow. They wrote, nervously, defending their previous executions. Moscow responded by affirming their autonomy, telling them to "make judgments according to the tsar's order and the Ulozhenie and New [Criminal] Articles." The autonomy of the governor in Kozlov, Ivan Menshoi Kolychev, was affirmed in a 1696 case; he had been fined for dishonor to a gentryman whom he had ordered knouted for arriving late to troop muster. The gentryman had argued that Kolychev had beaten him "without the tsar's order," but Kolychev protested that his orders instructed him to punish latecomers. The Military Service Chancery investigated and supported Kolychev: the gentryman had arrived late and Kolychev's instructions told him to act as he did. The unfair dishonor judgment was rescinded.[17]

Governors sought expertise from Moscow, as in a case of 1635, when inquisition and torture secured the confessions of three men to premeditated murder in Beloozero. The governor was soon confronted with a flood of reports of outstanding debts owed by the men. Reluctant to order the death penalty, he turned to the Felony Chancery for advice. It returned a guilty verdict and instructed the governor to assess fees and compensation for the widow of the dead man, but otherwise to refuse debt repayment. In 1656, the Russian governor of temporarily occupied Vilnius felt empowered to try, convict and sentence to hanging an accused murderer. But when the community rallied to mitigate the death penalty since the defendant had not previously been involved in serious crime, the governor turned to Moscow for advice. Moscow granted the mercy.[18]

In a third type of recourse, law codes specifically instructed judges to seek advice when they could not resolve difficult cases (*spornye dela*). Should a chancery be unable to resolve it, it would turn to the tsars and boyars.[19] Grigorii Kotoshikhin, whose account of court politics parallels the Ulozhenie, describes such transfer of venue for difficult cases. Several decrees make reference to this: in 1675, a decree mandated that cases of prisoners languishing in prison were to be decided or presented to the center if they proved to be "impossible to resolve"; so also for a 1683

17 RGADA f. 159, op. 3, Novgorod chetvert′, no. 1618, fols. 53–6 (1682). RGADA f. 210, Prikaznyi stol, no. 2115, fols. 1–9 (1696).

18 RGADA f. 1107, no. 703 (1635). AMG II: no. 902 (1656).

19 Nov. 26, 1555 decree: PRP IV: 361; Bogoslovskii, "Zemskoe samoupravlenie," in *Chteniia* (1910), bk. 1, appendix, p. 105, no. 22 (1642). Ulozhenie ch. 10, art. 2: RZ III: 102.

instruction to an investigator in Kazan. In several instructions to governors at the end of the century, the only grounds on which governors were told to refer to the center in making verdicts was when they could not find a basis in law.[20]

Some cases demonstrate both the possibility of appeal and the center's commitment to judicial autonomy. In 1693 in Sevsk two gentrymen had sued a soldier for killing their brother, but they in turn were accused of taking the law into their own hands. They had pursued the murderer on their own, and failing to find him, had beaten up his wife and two brothers, one of whom had died from the assault. Unsure, the judge sought help. The Military Service Chancery encouraged him to make a ruling, assuring him that if he could not reach a verdict, he could refer the case to the tsar.[21] Similarly, in 1669, the brigandage elder in Pereiaslavl′ Riazanskii had reported to Moscow testimony in a case of horse theft, but the Chancery responded that he should decide the case himself, without sending the defendants to Moscow, ruling on the basis of "our order, the Ulozhenie and Byzantine laws." He was then to inform Moscow of his ruling. The Felony Chancery ordered the Kadom governor in 1682 to resolve a case that had been sitting dormant since 1675 because of the negligence of the Temnikov governors. He was to obtain the case transcripts and the arrested defendants from the negligent official, complete the investigation and "make a verdict according to the tsar's order and the Ulozhenie and Byzantine codes and New [Criminal] Statutes, as appropriate."[22]

Judges often sought help to clarify the law. For example, a woman was convicted of killing her husband in 1656, but her father-in-law requested settlement, forgiving the wife and seeking mercy. The governor of Sevsk asked the Military Service Chancery how to rule, and its judges, in turn, appealed to the tsar, noting that the Ulozhenie explicitly stated that women who killed their husbands were to be buried alive, even if their kinsmen sued for mercy. In 1676, similarly, the governor of Belev presented a case of theft from the treasury to the Military Service Chancery, which instructed the governor on how to question the man under torture. Meanwhile the

[20] Kotoshikhin, *O Rossii*, ch. 7, art. 39, p. 118 and art. 42, p. 121. PSZ II: no. 626 (1675). AAE IV: no. 279 (1683). Instructions: PSZ III: nos. 1594, art. 30 and 1595, art. 6 (both 1697); 1670, art. 5 (1699); PSZ IV: nos. 1836, art. 6 (1701) and 2310, p. 584 (1710).

[21] RGADA f. 210, Prikaznyi stol, no. 1539, fol. 288v (1693).

[22] AIuB I: no. 55 (XXI) (I) (1669). Similar instructions: RGADA f. 141 1651, no. 58, pt. 2, fols. 263–4, 180–4 (two cases 1651); RGADA f. 141 1651, no. 58, pt. 1, fols. 1–4, 132–44 (two cases 1651); RGADA f. 159, op. 3, no. 1618 (1682). RGADA f. 1122, op. 2, pt. 2, no. 1548 (1682), quote on fol. 3.

Chancery also asked the Felony Chancery to rule on a point of law: they found no relevant ruling in the Ulozhenie regarding theft from the tsar's treasury, and wondered whether the law about felony theft would apply. The Felony Chancery took the case to the tsar and, speaking in his name, a panel of boyars ruled that the felony theft rule was appropriate.[23] In all these cases chanceries promoted judges' local autonomy.

As that case demonstrates, boyars and tsar constituted the highest venue for judges' referral. In 1686 the governor of Iarensk presented a difficult case to the Novgorod Chancery. A man had confessed to a murder, but alleged that someone else had instigated the crime. The Chancery judges brought the case to the co-tsars and Sofiia, noting that the Ulozhenie and the 1669 Criminal Articles both mandate execution for premeditated murder and that the 1669 Articles specified beheading. The co-tsars and Sofiia turned the resolution over to "the boyars," who ruled that the convicted man should be executed locally, but did not specify the technique of execution.[24]

Only with homicide were judges more cautious, as a 1655 case in Vilnius demonstrates. The governor had arrested, interrogated and found guilty a group of peasants who had shot his messengers on the road. He put three of them to death immediately "in order to frighten others" and consulted Moscow about what to do with the others; he was instructed to hang them as well. With homicide, judges often sought affirmation from the center. In case after homicide case governors carried out procedure independently, often through torture, but reported their findings to Moscow for verdict, even from as far away as Siberia, despite instructions to governors to rule on their own.[25] This is not surprising: homicide was the apex of the judicial system short of state crime; capital punishment was a great step and governors were probably wise to defer the responsibility. The center did not always deflect governors' requests, often affirming central control by resolving the cases and requiring judges to report when they had carried out the verdict.[26] Judges embraced

[23] RGADA f. 210, Sevsk stol, nos. 187, fols. 452–7 (1656) and 294, fols. 182–212 (1676). Ulozhenie ch. 22: art. 14: RZ III: 249 (on burials); ch. 21: art. 9: RZ III: 231 (on felony theft).

[24] RGADA f. 159, op. 3, no. 2466, fols. 77–83 (1686).

[25] Vilnius: AMG II: no. 752 (1655). Homicide referred: "Uboistvennye dela," 1 (1626), 3 (1643, 1644), 4 (1644); AMG I: no. 141 (1621); RGADA f. 141 1624, no. 31, fols. 110–15 (1622); RGADA f. 210, Prikaznyi stol, no. 36, fols. 467–76 and 485–91 (1628); RGADA f. 141 1651, pt. 1, no. 58, fols. 63–5 (1651); RGADA f. 210, Sevsk stol, no. 294, fols. 182–212 (1676).

[26] RGADA f. 210, Stolbtsy Pomestnogo stola, no. 35, fol. 25 (1640); RGADA f. 210, Prikaznyi stol, nos. 567, fols. 391–4, 519–21 (1648) and 1539, fols. 288–91 (1693); RGADA f. 210, Belgorod stol, no. 298, fols. 342–3 (1650).

their autonomy up through corporal and sometimes capital punishment, without reference to the center, but their anxieties over capital punishment suggest the tensions inherent in Muscovy's centralizing project.

CENTRAL OVERSIGHT IN CASES OF HIGHEST CRIME

With highest political and religious crime, cases were usually controlled from the center. Investigators and commissions were often sent specifically to investigate religious dissent, bypassing local judicial officials. Central oversight is also visible in "word and deed" (*slovo i delo*) cases, often seemingly innocuous cases of insult to the sovereign that were taken very seriously. Judges were carefully instructed to follow the sequence of oral interrogations, community survey and then torture, often being told to report the results of the first two procedures before receiving permission to proceed to torture.[27] Other cases of political crime show provincial governors overseen tightly from the center. For example, the governor in Khlynov in the North reported in 1651 that a Votiak had insulted and hit an icon in the tavern. In interrogation, he admitted doing it while drunk. The governors asked Moscow for guidance and the Chancery ordered them to question the man "harshly" about his intent or other participants in the attack; "if he speaks truthfully, then order him tortured" and report his testimony to Moscow. In the meantime, the Votiak petitioned for conversion, most likely to avoid punishment, which the governors also duly reported to Moscow, but its response is not recorded. In 1686 the governor of Venev encountered a case of a young man who had broken into the prison, beat the guards and freed the convicts. The governor took testimony from all the victims and consulted Moscow. The Military Service Chancery considered it so alarming that they had the neighboring governor of Tula send men to Venev to help investigate (a group of retired Tula gentrymen and undersecretaries). Many cases show governors sending transcripts of testimony to the center to await further instruction.[28] Such constant back and forth was the center's best means of policing its officials to prevent abuses and of making sure that political crime was quashed.

[27] Church crime: Barskov, *Pamiatniki*; Barsov, "Sudnye protsessy"; Rumiantseva (ed.), *Dokumenty Razriadnogo.* Word and deed: Novombergskii, *Koldovstvo*, nos. 20, p. 88 (1664), 27, p. 107 (1676), 32, p. 112 (1690).

[28] RGADA f. 141 1651, no. 58, pt. 1, fols. 23–6 (1651). RGADA f. 210, Prikaznyi stol, no. 872, fols. 151–4 (1686). Transcripts sent, instructions sought: Novombergskii, *Koldovstvo*, no. 30, p. 111 (1677); also ibid., nos. 9, p. 41 (1647); 15, p. 78 (1653); 18, p. 81 (1653). SIDG no. 80, p. 138 (1645). Steps laid out: ibid., no. 118 (1647), p. 193; no. 133 (1647), p. 217; no. 274 (1644), pp. 518–19; no. 301 (1649), pp. 556–7.

LITIGANTS' AUTONOMY: APPEAL AND SETTLING

Litigants also shaped trial proceedings, using such strategies as venue hopping, appeal against a biased judge, prompting the judge and settling the case. On the first, selecting among venues was possible in Muscovy since judicial hierarchy was not firmly defined or enforced. In theory cases should start locally, but gentry felt entitled to be heard in the Military Service Chancery; some groups, such as new model army units, were supposed to be judged in their Moscow chancery. Chanceries often accepted cases that should have been done locally and litigants took advantage of this laxity. So, for example, in 1662 in Beloozero, the governor and brigandage elder, investigating a homicide case together, examined the dead body, arrested and interrogated the accused peasant, and obtained a plea of self-defense. But the defendant's landlord requested that the case be tried in the Felony Chancery, so Beloozero officials sent it to Moscow. In that same year the mother of a murdered new model cavalryman (*reitar*) petitioned directly to the Chancery for such troops, which requested that the Beloozero authorities send the transcript of their investigation and the arrested defendants to Moscow for resolution there. This should have been the Chancery's case from the beginning. Similarly, in 1683 a gentryman accused of abusing and murdering his peasants tried to avoid local prosecution by alleging that he had reported the incidents directly to the Felony Chancery in Moscow. Since he had no supporting documents to prove his story, the case was pursued locally.[29]

A case of 1669 shows how venue-hopping could help a defendant avoid the law. In June 1669 I. P. Trubnikov sued in Beloozero that his brother had been murdered in Sevsk by a Beloozero gentryman named Kopylov. Trubnikov had sued in Sevsk and Kopylov had been investigated. But now, Trubnikov complained, Kopylov had been released and was home in Beloozero. When questioned in Beloozero, Kopylov alleged that he had been released on surety bond and was to appear for trial in Moscow in the Felony Chancery in the autumn. In November and December Trubnikov returned with the complaint that Kopylov was still at large: had he been tried in Moscow or not? Upon a second questioning in Beloozero, Kopylov stated that he had appeared in Moscow but that the case had been dismissed; he had, however, no record of the dismissal. The

[29] Send to Felony: RGADA f. 1107, no. 1548, fol. 8 (1662). *Reitar*: RGADA f. 1596, no. 10 (1662). RGADA f. 1107, no. 3109 (1683).

Beloozero governor, probably exasperated by six months of avoidance, wrote to the Felony Chancery in Moscow asking for clarification and instructions.[30]

One of a litigant's most basic rights was appeal against abusive officials. Plaintiffs could petition to transfer a case from a judge whom they suspected of enmity to them or favoritism to the other side (defendants did not have this right). This was cited as early as mid-sixteenth-century brigandage codes and affirmed by the Ulozhenie and the 1669 Criminal Articles. Only in certain cases were transfers not allowed, as when suing land surveyors.[31] Plaintiffs made liberal use of this right; for example, a gentryman successfully petitioned in 1696 to transfer a murder case against one of his peasants from the Shatsk governor to the neighboring governor of Insar because of his "earlier quarrel" with the former. But governors were loath to give up court fees: the St. Cyril Beloozero Monastery complained in 1681 that criminal law jurisdiction over its properties in the Poshekhon′e district had been removed from that governor because of his "quarrels and enmity" towards the monastery, but that the Poshekhon′e governor refused to obey the order. The Felony Chancery firmly ordered him to desist. In 1690 the governor of Pereiaslavl′ Riazanskii received a case that had been transferred through at least two other governors whom the litigants had rejected as biased.[32]

Both plaintiffs and defendants could appeal directly to the sovereign if they felt a case had been resolved corruptly, a right protected since sixteenth-century codes. A townsman of Tula boldly alleged in 1667 that a local enemy of his had colluded with two judges in the Felony Chancery to summon him in a fabricated criminal case. He argued that the case was not a felony. Here the Chancery responded quickly, but not to the plaintiff's liking, perhaps because the accused men were of high stature: boyar Vasilii Semenovich Volynskoi and *stol′nik* Vikula Feodrovich Izvolskii. The case was transferred to the Military Service Chancery, but it ruled against the townsman and ordered him to pay dishonor to the

30 RGADA f. 1107, no. 1171 (1669).

31 Jan. 1555 Felony Handbook, art. 11: PRP IV: 359; 1616/17 Felony Handbook, art. 55: PRP V: 199; AAE II: no. 225, p. 391 (late sixteenth century); Ulozhenie ch. 10: art. 3, 5–7: RZ III: 102–3; ch. 12, art. 2: RZ III: 157; ch. 21, art. 7: RZ III: 231; 1669 Criminal Articles, art. 6: PRP VII: 397. Defendants lacked ability: Chicherin, *Oblastnye uchrezhdeniia*, 490. Enmity-based transfer affirmed: PSZ I: no. 617 (1675); PSZ II: nos. 656 (1676), 746 (1678), 837 (1680), 838 (1680); PSZ III: nos. 1557 (1696) and 1597 (1697). Surveyors: Man′kov, *Zakonodatel′stvo*, 173.

32 AIuB I: no. 55 (LII) (1696). RGADA f. 1441, no. 263 (1681). AIuB I: no. 55 (XLIX) (1690). Similar cases: RGADA f. 1122, op. 2, pt. 2, nos. 1493 (1686) and 1755 (1693); RGADA f. 1167, op. 1, pt. 2, no. 1546 (1690).

judges for his charges. Sometimes litigants simply expressed disagreement with a verdict. For example, a man in Livni protested in 1647 against having to pay what he considered excessive fines when his peasant killed another man. Peter I affirmed this tradition of appeal when he, in 1699 and 1700, allowed people to petition directly to the tsar on the grounds of unjustly resolved suits.[33]

Plaintiffs even intervened in mid-trial, mixing somewhat their rights to appeal. A priest in Beloozero who charged a townsman with beating him, for example, sought a transfer in 1691 after interrogations had taken place. He charged that the witnesses whom the judge had questioned in inquisitorial format were biased against him (he was behaving as if it were an accusatory trial where he could reject witnesses). Not bothered by mixing genres, the relevant chancery (Palace Judicial) took the transcript, including examination of wounds, orders to arrest the accused and witnesses, oral interrogations and surety bonds. It then ruled for the plaintiff.[34]

Litigants also regularly intervened in court cases to move the process forward. This is a right accorded since the 1555 brigandage charters – "if petitioners request torture, then do so" – but one which would seem to contravene the intent of the inquisitory procedure to give judges control over the process.[35] Nevertheless, examples are frequent. Torture was a common request, suggesting that litigants reflected what bureaucrats prescribed as the next stage or that they believed in the efficacy of the procedure as did the courts, or both. We see requests for torture in a 1644 Siberian murder case and in others in 1687 and 1689. Litigants made other requests as well: in 1647 a landlord asked that the local brigandage elder send the results of a community survey to Moscow, since the case had stalled for more than two years; in 1673 the brother of a murdered man petitioned for a community survey. The landlord of a dead peasant reported in 1680 that an investigation had stalled at the stage of face-to-face confrontations and requested resumption.[36] Sometimes plaintiffs suggested verdicts. For example, the landlord of peasants accused of

33 RGADA f. 210, Prikaznyi stol, nos. 787, fols. 25–33 (1667) and 182, fols. 398–9 (1647). PSZ III: no. 1707 (1699); PSZ IV: no. 1748 (1700).

34 RGADA f. 1107, no. 3835 (1691).

35 1555 Medyn Charter, art. 8: RZ II: 221; Glaz'ev, *Vlast' i obshchestvennost'*, 256; Bogoslovskii, "Zemskoe samoupravlenie," in *Chteniia* (1912), bk. II, pp. 197–8.

36 "Uboistvennye dela," 4 (1644); RGADA f. 1122, op. 2, pt. 2, nos. 1424 (1687) and 1195, fol. 6 (1689). AIuB I: no. 55 (XI) (1647). RGADA f. 210, Prikaznyi stol, no. 669, fols. 12–13 (1673). RGADA f. 1167, op. 1, pt. 1, no. 626 (1680).

treason petitioned in 1629 at the end of an extensive trial that the judge should order them exiled. This intercession seemed to have prompted the court to wrap up the case. Similarly, a husband approached the court in 1686 and asked that his wife be convicted in a suit alleging her lewd behavior, since, he alleged, she was a known loose woman.[37]

Communities could even appeal collectively to Moscow. For example, when a woman was convicted of killing her husband in 1647, eight gentrymen from her town traveled to Moscow to speak on her behalf, explaining that her action was justified given the heinous behavior of her spouse. Moscow listened, ordered up a community survey and eventually reduced her sentence. In a similar case of voluntarism, a community of cossacks in Belev in 1688 sent a representative to Moscow to protest property taxes. Their appeal, however, was not heard sympathetically: the Military Service Chancery found the cossack guilty of deserting duty. He stubbornly appealed about the taxes a second time and was refused. For deserting duty, he was ordered beaten with bastinadoes and sent home.[38]

As noted above, litigants frequently settled cases, even when it was forbidden in the criminal law; such a legal stipulation was reflective of triadic principles in legal structure and even perhaps of Roman law theory that put the letter of the law over subjective conditions.[39] It took centuries in Europe and Muscovy for the sensibility of "rule of law" to sink in; the impetus to settle was observed across the board in pre-modern (and even modern) communities, for pragmatic as well as moral grounds. Everyone wanted to avoid the expense, antagonism and risks of a trial – families and communities pressured quarreling parties to settle. In early modern European legal practice, even where Roman law was making inroads, codes in England and Spain urged judges first to seek reconciliation; sixteenth-century French judges were told to respect settlements even when the law forbade them. Bruce Lenman and Geoffrey Parker, exploring the gradual shift in European law to more modern, literal standards, write nevertheless that in practice only those cases came to trial that were the most rancorous, "in a quarrel which had become either too important or too difficult for the parties to settle in any other way."[40]

37 AMG I: no. 259 (1629). RGADA f. 210, Prikaznyi stol, no. 1049, fols. 123–5 (1686).

38 RGADA f. 210, Prikaznyi stol, no. 172, fol. 255 (1647). RGADA f. 210, Sevsk stol, no. 416, fols. 471–5 (1688).

39 Do not settle: AAE I: no. 150, p. 120 (1509); August 1556 Decree, no. 17: PRP IV: 367; 1616/17 Felony Handbook, no. 42: PRP V: 335–6 (1624); PRP V: 237 (1646); Ulozhenie ch. 21: art. 31: RZ III: 234; 1669 Criminal Articles, art. 71: PRP VII: 421; PSZ II: no. 1289 (1688).

40 Lenman and Parker, "State, Community," 16–22 (19); Sharpe, "Enforcing," 107–14.

Early modern European and Muscovite courts struggled with the tension between rule of law and popular concepts of justice. In the cases surveyed here, even when courts insisted that state interest was involved, as in homicide, some litigants sought and won settlement.

Judges seem to have accepted requests to settle homicide as long as they did not involve professional criminals or premeditation. One would like more detail, but cases often include enough details about shared costs to suggest the back-room negotiations that probably motivated these accords. In an early case of 1560, two monasteries settled a suit about the killing of a monastic servant, with the guilty party paying the dead man's debts and damages to the monastery. Similarly, a homicide case was settled in 1577 with the guilty party paying court fees and, most significantly, compensation to the widow and dead man's kin. The state demanded no interest other than a standard fee (*golovshchina*). Another case also provided for survivors: three men – two undersecretaries and one artilleryman – were found guilty in 1635–6 of murdering another undersecretary in order to steal money from him. Under torture they admitted planning the murder with prior intent. But when the man's widow interceded, pointing out her husband's indebtedness, the governor ordered the guilty men to pay off the dead man's many debts. The three men signed a settlement document with the widow, allowing the tsar whatever punishment (*penia*) he ordered (none was). Here, despite premeditation, the death penalty was averted. The law also held that if a peasant kill another peasant without premeditation, then the guilty party should be given as compensation to the murdered man's landlord; this sort of compensation is included in a case of 1647 in Livni.[41]

Cases admitted the state's interest in such settlements. A Zvenigorod case in October 1693, for example, included the formulaic phrase "we are no longer litigants in this suit, but the tsar is free to act as he wishes concerning the crime." But the judge did not take them up, simply allowing the community to settle its differences: the murderers agreed to pay for the damaged property of the widow of a murdered man, to settle her husband's debts and to provide her a generous sum for her upkeep and that of her children. Sometimes the state did impose punishment. In 1644 in Siberia, the mother and brothers of a murdered cossack

[41] AIu nos. 270 (1560) and 271 (1577). RGADA f. 1107, no. 703 (1635–6). *Penia* a monetary fine: 1550 Law Code, arts. 25 and 69: RZ II: 101, 112–13; 1636 Landholding Decree, art. 12: PRP V: 476; PRP V: 144 (1642), 476 (art. 12, 1636); AAE IV: no. 10 (1646). RGADA f. 210, Prikaznyi stol, no. 182, fols. 398–9 (1647).

reached a settlement with another cossack who admitted to the crime, done while drunk; they asserted they did not want "blood spilled for the blood." The Siberian Chancery accepted the petition (which said nothing about compensation), but ordered the defendant knouted in the marketplace before being released on surety bond. In an even more dramatic case in Livni in March 1648, a local gentryman admitted that he had killed another man in a fight when he found that man trying to rape his wife. The governor of Livni, Fedor Lodyzhenskii, asked the Military Service Chancery for guidance; its judges instructed him to question witnesses, torture the accused for evidence and imprison him. Lodyzhenskii received that order in June, but in July the family of the dead man sued for mercy. They asked that the man not be tortured, but that he be ordered to support the abandoned family and pay off the deceased man's debts. The Chancery granted the request, but ordered a highly symbolic message: the man was to be informed of the death penalty, then he was to be immediately pardoned and given corporal punishment instead. He was to be knouted in the marketplace mercilessly "to deter others" and put on surety bond so that he will "feed [the dead man's] children and pay off his debts."[42] Here the judge skillfully deployed all the verbal and symbolic vocabulary at his disposal to demonstrate the rigor and the mercy of the tsar's justice.

Some cases mentioned few of the terms that probably motivated the settlement. The mother and grandmother of a murdered peasant of Beloozero, for example, settled the case in 1638–9 without any terms cited; one assumes the plaintiffs received compensation. Other such uninformative cases include one of two gentrymen killing two peasants, settled by the peasants' landlord in 1640. The men had been in prison for two years; they were released on surety bond with no reference to corporal punishment or compensation. A priest in the Beloozero area settled with three peasants for the death of his son in 1640 with no provisions enumerated; a case of 1642 in Novgorod of a peasant settled with the monastery whose peasant he had robbed and killed. Here the offending peasant agreed to pay damages as assessed by the monastery.[43]

The fact that judges tolerated settlements reflects, again, the imbrication of centralizing uniformity into pragmatic customs of adjudication.

[42] RGADA f. 210, Prikaznyi stol, no. 1526, fols. 40–1 (1693). "Uboistvennye dela," 4 (1644). RGADA f. 210, Prikaznyi stol, no. 567, fols. 391–4 and 519–21 (1648).

[43] RGADA f. 1107, no. 824, 3 fols. (1638–9). RGADA f. 210, Prikaznyi stol, no. 77, fols. 330–2 (1640). Priest: DAI II: no. 70, p. 172 (1640). AIu no. 275 (1642).

A similar intertwining of formal and informal law is seen in the difficulty of formalizing avenues of appeal. In the sixteenth century, processes of appeal were indeterminate. Appeals against a brigandage elder, for example, might go to a governor or bypass him and go directly to Moscow. The Petitions Chancery, created in the sixteenth century, was a general venue of appeal but not a court: it received petitions, often complaints about corruption and injustice, and disseminated them to the proper chancery.[44] In forbidding litigants to approach the tsar directly, the Ulozhenie suggested hierarchy: litigants were to submit such suits to the Chancery to which they were subordinate. The Ulozhenie also identified an appeals court: regarding cases that were difficult to resolve, "the boyars and *okol'nichie* and conciliar men are to sit in the chamber and they are to administer all the sovereign's affairs according to the sovereign's orders all together." Thereafter references to the boyars meeting "in the chamber," in the "Golden Chamber" and in the "chamber for appeals" (*raspravnye dela*) occur through the 1660s and 1670s. Several foreign travelers also cited the tsar's council of boyars as an appellate court.[45] Peter B. Brown sees it also as a board of governance when the tsar was out of town, while Pavel Sedov underscores its appellate quality: when in 1681 the Chamber of Appeals (*Raspravnaia palata*) was constituted with a formal membership of twelve boyars, none of whom was a chancery judge, their charge was to hear cases of corruption in Moscow chanceries. With the change of administrations in 1682, references to this group become rare and by 1694 all the boyars are depicted as reviewing cases as a group, turning to the tsar for advice if need be.[46] So, appeal for local judges and litigants alike – on grounds of expertise, authority, abuse or self-interest – existed, but institutional formats were not very stable before Peter I.

Litigants' appeal to Moscow was based on the abiding expectation that subjects could turn to the sovereign for relief against abuses and injustice. The alacrity and frequency with which central chanceries transferred cases

[44] Avenues of appeal: Bogoslovskii: "Zemskoe samoupravlenie," vol. II, in *Chteniia* (1912), bk. II, pp. 201–7; Man'kov, *Ulozhenie*, 312. Petition Chancery: Volkov, "Chelobitnoi prikaz"; Kotoshikhin, *O Rossii*, ch. 7, art. 28.

[45] Ulozhenie ch. 10, art. 20: RZ III: 104–5; PSZ II: no. 1092 (1684). Meeting schedules: Ulozhenie ch. 10, art. 2: RZ III: 102; PSZ I: nos. 460 (1670), 582 (1674); PSZ II: nos. 621 (1676), 656 (1676), 838 (1680); Fletcher, "Of the Russe," 134, 149, 175; Margeret, *Russian Empire*, 29–30; Perry, *State of Russia*, 188.

[46] Brown, "Early Modern Russian Bureaucracy," 382–9, 528–31; Sedov, *Zakat*, 410–21 and "Sozdanie Raspravnoi palaty." Chamber of Appeals: Eskin, "Raspravnaia palata"; Bogoiavlenskii, "Raspravnaia palata." PSZ III: no. 1491 (1694).

shows that the judicial system was aware of its fragility – the distance of communication; the lack of professional training, let alone *esprit de corps*, of its corps of judges; the ever-present temptation of corruption; the interplay of local concepts of justice with the written law – all called forth such flexibility. That the courts responded in this way demonstrates a system determined to deliver justice.

PRESENTING THE VERDICT

When judges resolved cases, they did so "according to the tsar's order" that had put them in office and citing written codes. To base their verdicts in the law, they turned to their bureaucratic partners, secretaries and undersecretaries. Litigants expected nothing less. For example, a petitioner asked in 1642 for a ruling "according to the Ulozhenie," undoubtedly referring to Felony Chancery orders kept at the governor's office, and the judge instructed his scribe that he would "resolve the case according to the law in general [*po ukazu*]," seeking relevant citations. Court cases are full of citations to the law on procedure as well as punishment. A 1645 case of gentrymen not showing up for a trial includes an excerpt from a 1627/8 law on the topic; in 1650 a case decided in the Moscow Apothecary Chancery included excerpts from two Ulozhenie chapters on treason.[47] In a 1672 case involving an investigator sent to track down robbers in the Tula area, the transcript correctly cited the Ulozhenie's rule about recanting testimony. In 1674 in a case regarding assault on a night watchman in Kitai-Gorod in Moscow, the court in the Military Service Chancery quoted excerpts of the Ulozhenie regarding witness testimony and dishonor rates.[48]

Muscovite law did not prescribe the form of court transcripts as thoroughly as did some European legislation; the 1532 *Carolina*, for example, provided specific language for verdicts, ordered specific punishments and instructed scribes on how to compile the transcript.[49] In Muscovy as the seventeenth century progressed, however, judges included more full discussions of their work. A verdict in Beloozero in 1613, for example, is typically laconic. It records that the judge resolved a homicide case with marketplace knouting and physical mutilation, justifying the

47 "Dela ob opredelenii," docs. 5–7 (1635–41); RGADA f. 141 1642, no. 59, fol. 1 (1642). RGADA f. 1107, no. 1059 (1645). AMG II: no. 444 (1650).

48 RGADA f. 210, Sevsk stol, no. 283, fol. 344 (1672). RGADA f. 210, Prikaznyi stol, no. 2513, fol. 10 (1674).

49 *Carolina*, arts. 181–203: Langbein, *Prosecuting*, 300–5.

verdict with reference to "the tsar's order and the law code" and to the fact that the defendant confessed; it does not, however, identify chapter and verse of any law code. A case of 1639 sentenced two corrupt officials to death simply by declaring that "by the tsar's order the boyars [chancery judges in Moscow] have decreed"; it justifies the verdict by summarizing the transgressions of the men and reminding them of their oath to the sovereign.[50]

By the 1670s, notarial staff were writing transcripts in greater detail. A good example comes from Beloozero in 1684. The judge, *stol'nik* and governor Ivan Artem'evich Martiukhin, specified that his verdict was based on having "heard" the "authentic case" (*podlinnoe delo*), including initial petition, the oral testimony of the three accused, their face-to-face confrontations, testimony under torture of one of them and excerpts from the laws. Noting that the accused had recanted some of his accusations in his second and third tortures, Martiukhin cited laws governing such recantations. He explained that he was not sentencing the defendant to be given over to the plaintiff to compensate for the dead man, as the law would have allowed, since the plaintiff had submitted a settlement yielding that claim.[51] Such detailed written records improved the quality of justice and protected both litigants and officials.

THE PROVISION OF MERCY

Although judges scrupulously followed the law, they enjoyed flexibility in mitigating sentences in the name of the tsar. In a study of 144 resolved seventeenth-century criminal cases of various sorts, sentences in about a fifth were mitigated in some way, if only with a reduction from beating by knout to bastinadoes. Unlike dishonor cases, where reductions favored the privileged classes by sparing them corporal punishment,[52] in criminal cases mercy affected all social ranks. Often cases did not explain the mercy, but some did. In 1654, for example, a chancery judge reduced the death sentence for the governor of Gorokhovets for corruption to a knouting and demotion, attributing the mercy to the intercession of the tsar's son Aleksei, who at that time was a mere baby. Often, as detailed in

50 RGADA f. 1107, no. 19, fol. 7 (1613). RGADA f. 210, Sevsk stol, no. 111, fols. 189–92 (1639). Other examples: RGADA f. 210, Sevsk stol, no. 246, fols. 404–5 (1640); RGADA f. 141 1651, no. 58, pt. 1, fols. 65–65v (1651).

51 RGADA f. 1107, no. 3187, fols. 23–6 (1684). Similar case: RGADA f. 1122, op. 2, pt. 2, no. 1629, fol. 11 (1674).

52 Kollmann, "Quality of Mercy," 3–5 and *By Honor Bound*, 116–18, 121–7, 165, 190–1.

Chapter 13, the tsar's mercy was theatrically staged, taking the form of a last-minute reprieve on the gallows. Such was the case for a cossack guilty of murdering a gentryman in Kozlov in 1650: the governor was instructed to sentence him to death, lead him to the gallows, ready him for execution and then announce the tsar's mercy. Compassion was often involved, as in a case where the death sentence was averted in 1629 for peasants who testified that they killed trying to defend innocent children from sexual attack.[53] Mitigation of sentence was not the norm, but it occurred frequently enough for litigants to hope for the mercy of the court.

Mercy flowed not only from judges, but also from litigants themselves. In a case that stretched from 1673 to 1676, two young men of high-ranking Moscow-based families, a Streshnev and a Tolbuzin, got into a fight at a roadside inn, and Streshnev seriously wounded his opponent. Wounded but confident of recovering, Tolbuzin had signed a settlement document with Streshnev, absolving him of blame in the fight. But he soon died and his family sued for murder. Nevertheless, after the investigation had gone on for a while, the dead man's widow and brother petitioned to settle the case. Responding to this fraternal mercy, the court sentenced Streshnev to "merciless harsh corporal punishment" but immediately awarded mercy, justified in memory of Tsar Fedor Alekseevich's recently deceased father. Similarly, in a case in Kursk in 1652 a priest argued that he had been falsely accused of murder, had been imprisoned for several years and had become impoverished. Now released from prison, he sought return of his confiscated property. In response the tsar ordered that the recipient of the confiscated property should decide whether to give it back or not.[54] Perhaps families gave mercy because of unmentioned compensation, but nevertheless it is significant that the rhetorical vocabulary used was one of forgiveness and charity.

The tsar's benevolence to his people expressed by judicial mercy reinforced the allegory of the realm as a family in which relations between subject and ruler were governed not by rules of the public order, but by the personal interrelations of private life. That courts dispensed so much mercy suggests the unity of bureaucratizing impulses in the seventeenth

[53] PSZ 1: no. 123 (1654). RGADA f. 210, Prikaznyi stol, no. 592, fols. 1–4 (1650). AMG 1: no. 259, p. 285 (1629).

[54] RGADA f. 210, Prikaznyi stol, no. 669, fols. 1–29 (1673); Kollmann, "Quality of Mercy," 15–16. RGADA f. 210, Belgorod stol, no. 339, fols. 61–2 (1652). Similar case: "Uboistvennye dela," 4 (1644).

century and the rhetoric of a godly community. One sees that unity at work even in the fact that sentences in none of the resolved cases of premeditated homicide were mitigated – the tsar was benevolent in less crucial cases, but enforced his rights to sovereign violence for true evil. As discussed in Chapters 8 and 12, Peter the Great's reforms introduced institutions and rhetoric of more impersonal authority and jurisprudence without undermining the studied inconsistency of even the criminal law in the seventeenth century.

CHAPTER 8

Petrine reforms and the criminal law

Peter I (ruled 1682–1725) worked mightily to improve the law as part of his vision of a more powerful Russia playing a more active role in European and Eurasian geopolitics. His reforms continued trends initiated in the 1680s and 1690s, consolidating institutions, intruding law into daily life, rationalizing court business. But they were couched in a European rhetoric of the "well-ordered police state." In Marc Raeff's words, the vision of the "police state" was "modernization for modernity's sake, production for productivity's sake, and 'progress', rather than the old transcendent and ethical goals." Peter's state would be activist, change-oriented and useful to the people. In characteristic *Polizeistaat* form, Peter ruled by decree, issuing at least 3,314 laws by one estimate on everything from the mundane (not cutting down timber destined for shipbuilding, not setting off rockets in the city) to fundamental institutional change.[1] Didactically, to teach his elite, he and his fellow reformers liberally sprinkled phrases such as "for the general good," justifications for his actions ("since nothing is more necessary to the administration of a state than strict adherence to the civil laws") and "explanation."[2] Pace and scope can obscure how early eighteenth-century reforms continued trends: urban and provincial judicial venues were further developed; judicial hierarchy was enhanced; church judicial administration was narrowed; new law codes and regulations were issued (1715 Military and 1720 Naval codes, 1720 General Regulation); court procedure continued its move

[1] Number of decrees: Eroshkin, *Ocherki*, 88. Mundane decrees: public safety and order (PSZ III: no. 1663 [1698]), looting during a fire (PSZ III: no. 1693 [1699]), rockets in the city (PSZ III: no. 1695 [1699]), regulating the poor (PSZ V: no. 3213 [1718]), illegal alcohol sale (PSZ III: no. 1716 [1699]; PSZ IV: nos. 2064 [1705] and 2074 [1705]); timber (PSZ IV: no. 2607 [1712]; PSZ V: no. 3509 [1720]).

[2] Raeff recognizes that Russia's application of the concept lacked much of the European model, but still considers it a break with Muscovite tradition: *Well-Ordered*, pt. 3, quote on 171; Raeff, *Understanding Imperial Russia*. General good: RZ IV: 166 (1708). Adherence to laws: RZ IV: 186 (1722); justification of law: RZ IV: 295 (1714). Explanation (*tolkovanie*): Table of Ranks: RZ IV: 65–6 (1722); Military Articles of 1715: RZ IV: 327–65.

towards inquisitorial process; paperwork and record-keeping were improved. Foreign models were often applied, but in practice most judicial reforms were adapted to existing institutions and practices.

PETRINE CHANGES IN THE LAW AND INSTITUTIONS

More energetically but less successfully than his Muscovite predecessors, Peter I strove to consolidate Russia's corpus of laws. Three times between 1700 and 1719 Peter charged commissions with codifying laws since the 1649 Ulozhenie. None of the commissions succeeded, in part for lack of judicially trained experts, in part for lack of commitment by his successors. With no new codifications, judges in chanceries and in the countryside continued to rely on the Ulozhenie of 1649, as a 1714 directive instructed: "resolve all cases by the Ulozhenie . . . unless some case is not mentioned in the Ulozhenie. Then resolve by newly issued articles."[3] (Recall that the Ulozhenie had been published and disseminated widely, while the 1669 Criminal Articles had not been.) Better access to the laws was provided by regular publication of decrees. Five handbooks of laws appeared from 1718 to 1725, as well as many individual decrees. But efforts to provide regulatory guidance for new institutions and personnel were inconsistent. Many important regulations did appear, but equally important ones were never issued, including founding charters for the Justice College and the new Superior Courts, definitions of qualifications of judges and definitions of the responsibilities of new judicial officials. Lacking such guidance, officials adapted old practices to new terminology and institutions.[4]

Although much attention has been directed at the 1715 Military Articles as a keystone of Petrine legal reforms, they were not used in the secular courts. Nevertheless, they are of some interest inasmuch as they often provide "explanations" for elements in Muscovite law that had gone

[3] Codification projects: Romashkin, *Osnovnye nachala*, 16, 14–16; Babich, *Gosudarstvennye uchrezhdeniia*, 128–46, 185–7, 214–16, 270–4 and "Komissii kak gosudarstvennye uchrezhdeniia"; Kleandrova, "Istochniki prava," 47; Serov, *Sudebnaia reforma*, 136–8. First codification: PSZ IV: 1765 (1700); second: PSZ V: nos. 2819 and 2828 (1714); third: PSZ VI: nos. 3626 and 3661 (1720), 4128 (1722); PSZ VII: nos. 4483 (1724), 4658 (1725). His successors rejected the 1723–6 codification, but continued to request compilation of a "new Ulozhenie": PSZ VII: nos. 4895 (1726), 5287 and 5348 (1728), 5412 (1729), 5567 and 5577 (1730). ZA Petra 40–1 (1714); PSZ V: no. 3435 (1719). 1714 directive cited only once in surveyed cases: RGADA f. 596, no. 345, fol. 11 (1740). Mrochek-Drozdovskii shows reliance on Ulozhenie: *Oblastnoe upravlenie*, 306.

[4] Publications: Serov, *Sudebnaia reforma*, 138–40, 385–6. Charters: ibid., 201–5, 257–60, 446–7; LeDonne, *Absolutism*, 183, 193.

unexplained, such as intent in commission of crime and standards of competence. In the realm of punishment (see Chapter 12), they perpetuated tradition as much as innovated. Early eighteenth-century judicial reforms made few significant changes in judicial procedure and did not systematize the positive law; rather, they tried to transform the institutional settings in which judges worked. In courts with constantly changing names and spheres of competence, judges persisted in rendering justice in patterns essentially the same as before.[5]

A trilogy of brilliant books by P. Mrochek-Drozdovskii, M. M. Bogoslovskii and Iu. V. Got'e, from the most glittering era of Russian historiography – the turn of the twentieth century – plus impressive modern scholarship chronicle three stages of judicial and administrative reform, replete with archival detail from central and local courts: until about 1710, criminal law institutions were clarified within the Muscovite chancery structure; from 1710 to 1719, government was decentralized into eight large *gubernii*; from 1719 through the end of Peter's reign reforms reasserted centralized authority in the College system.[6]

These reforms simplified jurisdiction over the criminal law. Efforts to consolidate all chanceries in the 1680s had been unsuccessful; at the turn of the century the state tried again.[7] For political crime the role of the Preobrazhenskii Chancery was expanded in 1702; for urban administration, in 1699 a central Ratusha was created to oversee municipal governments (*zemskie izby*) in major cities, which were given authority even over brigandage crimes.[8] Judicial chanceries for the city of Moscow were consolidated, giving authority for non-felony crimes to the new

[5] Not used in secular courts: RZ IV: 317–18; Romashkin, *Osnovnye nachala*, 26–31; Serov, *Sudebnaia reforma*, 386, n. 2. Military Articles: PSZ V: no. 3006. Publications of Articles: RZ IV: 327–65; PRP VIII: 319–69; commentary: RZ IV: 314–27, 365–89; PRP VIII: 263–81, 369–456. New Petrine legal concepts: Shtamm, "Ugolovnoe pravo," in Skripilev, *Razvitie*, 158–201. Procedure not changed fundamentally: Serov, *Sudebnaia reforma*, 336–7.

[6] Mrochek-Drozdovskii, *Oblastnoe upravlenie*; Bogoslovskii, *Oblastnaia reforma;* Got'e, *Istoriia oblastnogo upravleniia*; Peterson, *Peter the Great's Reforms*; Schmidt, *Sozialkontrolle*, ch. 3A–3D; Serov, *Sudebnaia reforma*; Pisar'kova, *Gosudarstvennoe upravlenie*, chs. 2–3; Davies, *Empire and Military Revolution*, ch. 4. General overview: Talina, *Vybor puti*, ch. 3. Useful summaries of Petrine offices: *RGADA. Putevoditel'*, III, pt. 1, 58, 218–22, 243, 276, 304, 466–8, 471–2, 496, 498, 525, 527, 547, 586, 600, 608–9.

[7] From a high of 59 chanceries in 1677, the number fell by 1698 to 55: Demidova, *Sluzhilaia biurokratiia*, ch. 1. This stage: Anisimov, *Gosudarstvennye preobrazovaniia*, 63–7; Eroshkin, *Ocherki*, 110–11; LeDonne, *Absolutism*, 68–74; Brown, "Early Modern Russian Bureaucracy," ch. 11.

[8] Preobrazhenskii: PSZ IV: no. 1918 (1702), 1945 (1703). It had been handling political crime since 1696: Golikova, *Politicheskie protsessy*; Serov, *Sudebnaia reforma*, 94–5, 272–84. Urban reform: PSZ III: nos. 1674 and 1675 (1699); Serov, *Sudebnaia reforma*, 96–7, 99–102.

Judicial Chancery (*Sudnoi prikaz*) and for felonies to the Musketeer Chancery.[9] For local administration, the Felony Chancery and the brigandage system in 1701–2 were abolished and governors received criminal jurisdiction, overseen by the Military Service Chancery. Governors were supposed to be helped by elected gentrymen, like the old brigandage boards, but this effort failed. As in Muscovy, investigators and commissions of soldiers continued to be used to combat crime, chase down runaway serfs and otherwise aid governors in their police duties.[10] This early era, then, attempted to focus criminal law in fewer hands.

As the Great Northern War (1700–21) increased the demand for men and revenue, the government tried decentralization. In 1708 the realm was divided into eight *gubernii*, led by powerful *gubernatory* who were answerable directly to the Senate (created in 1711). Many central chanceries were abolished and their bureaucrats transferred to the *gubernii*, a step that Anisimov calls a "catastrophe" in destroying the professional oversight provided by the chancery apparatus. In cities, the Ratusha was abolished and its local offices were subordinated to governors. Below the *gubernia*, the principal division continued to be the *uezd* led by commandants (*komendanty*), although some large *gubernii* created a middle level of "provinces" (*provintsii*) led by senior commandants (*ober-komendanty*). The judicial hierarchy then stretched up from the commandant courts, to the province if available, to the *gubernia* capital to the Senate.[11]

Despite innovative decentralization, this *gubernia* era of reforms perpetuated many previous practices. First, suggesting that Muscovite collegial panels did not work ("the old judges . . . did what they wanted"), a 1718 decree re-introduced the collegial principle, mandating collective agreement by majority vote. Second, the Muscovite tradition of "selected" service by everyone from noblemen to peasants was continued. A 1713 decree mandated a council of gentry (*landraty*) elected by their peers in each *gubernia* capital; in 1715 *landraty* were extended to the *uezd* level. They were charged initially with poll tax censuses and collections, but in the confusion of rapid reforms, *landraty* also took on judicial and

[9] Consolidation of Moscow judicial chanceries: PSZ III: no. 1713 (1699); PSZ IV: no. 1945 (1703). In 1701 the Musketeer Chancery was renamed the "Chancery of Moscow Administrative Affairs" (*Prikaz zemskikh del*): PSZ IV: no. 1859.

[10] Abolition of Felony, brigandage: PSZ IV: nos. 1874 (1701), 1900 (1702) and no. 2018 (1705). Investigators: PSZ IV: nos. 2169 (1707); 2439 (1711); 2573 (1712); PSZ V: nos. 3334 and 3415 (1719). Investigative commissions: Pisar′kova, *Gosudarstvennoe upravlenie*, 103–6, 150–3.

[11] *Gubernii*: PSZ IV: no. 2218 (1708). Senate: PSZ IV: nos. 2321, 2330 (1711). Anisimov, *Gosudarstvennye preobrazovaniia*, 96; Serov, *Sudebnaia reforma*, 104–6.

administrative functions. Nevertheless, D. O. Serov perceives progress in these reforms, arguing they created a more unified, orderly judicial system on the local level.[12]

The *gubernia* stage of reform laid the foundation for a recentralization and a more sophisticated organization of the judiciary. Around 1718, borrowing from foreign models (generally Swedish and Livonian), twelve functionally defined Colleges, overseen by the Senate, were created; they were to be ruled collegially, each College "*Prezident*" with a staff including elected advisers. The now eleven *gubernii* were each divided into provinces, a total of 45; each province was headed by governors, using the Muscovite term *voevoda*. In 1719 *voevody* were issued an "Instruction" full of ambitious *Polizeistaat* expectations: they should build institutions of public health, welfare and education as well as carry out traditional administrative, judicial, military and fiscal roles. Provinces were divided into districts led by locally elected gentrymen (*zemskie komissary*), who performed a variety of fiscal and police duties as had the old brigandage boards. For cities, the centralized model of the 1699 urban reform was restored when, in 1721, a Central Magistrate was created to supervise municipal governments (*magistraty*) in major cities. These received self-government and broad fiscal, administrative, police and judicial authority.[13]

The boldest ambition of this third stage was to create an independent judicial hierarchy of graduated instances and to separate administrative and judicial authority institutionally and in personnel. D. O. Serov calls this the creation – for the first time in Russia – of "general courts" for all suits for all comers, even though many specialized courts persisted for particular crimes (religious and state crime, land disputes) or social groups. The new Justice College became the center of judicial activity (overseen for appeals by the Senate); incorporated into it were seven old chanceries with juridical functions. Below the College were regional Superior Courts (*nadvornye sudy*), ultimately twelve in all; below them provincial courts, renamed from "*landrat*" courts to "chanceries of civil and criminal affairs" (*kantseliarii sudnykh i rozysknykh del*). Both Russians

[12] Collegial decisions: PSZ v: nos. 3261 (1718), 2791 (1714). *Landraty:* PSZ v: nos. 2673, pt. 3 (1713), 2762 (1714), 2879 (1715); Babich, "Landratskaia kantseliariia"; Eroshkina, "Landrat"; Mrochek-Drozdovskii, *Oblastnoe upravlenie,* 55–65; Eroshkin, *Ocherki istorii,* 111–13; LeDonne, *Absolutism,* 69–74; Schmidt, *Sozialkontrolle,* ch. 3B; Serov, *Sudebnaia reforma,* ch. 2. Half of staff: Pisar'kova, "Rossiiskaia biurokratiia," 2004 no. 1: 29–33. Serov, *Sudebnaia reforma,* 106.

[13] Colleges: PSZ v: nos. 3128 and 3129 (1717) and 3368 (1719). Provinces: PSZ v: no. 3380 (1719). Instruction: PSZ v: nos. 3294 and 3381 (1719). *Zemskie komissary:* PSZ v: no. 3295 (1719); LeDonne, *Absolutism,* 130; Bogoslovskii, *Oblastnaia reforma,* 141–63. Other new provincial offices: Pisar'kova, "Rossiiskaia biurokratiia," 2004 no. 1. PSZ vi: no. 3708, ch. 9 (1721).

and foreigners were named as judges, and foreign and Russian law codes were ordered to be translated so that each judge would know all the relevant law. This system of four instances (local, Superior Courts, Justice College and Senate) was a significant achievement.[14]

Petrine law urged judges and litigants to use this new judicial hierarchy, continuing efforts made in Muscovite-era law. As early as 1700 decrees were directing all suits to lower courts save for two (eventually three) issues for which approach could be made to the ruler: threats to the tsar, treason and theft from state treasury. Appeal to higher courts was allowed, as in the seventeenth century, only for "disputed or very important" cases. A memo to the Beloozero *landrat* of March 1721 ordered him to resolve all cases locally, to refer only those he could not decide to the Superior Court in Iaroslavl and not to approach the Justice College directly. Legislation also tried to solve problems of venue-hopping by forbidding bypassing a lower court for a higher venue and transferring a suit to a different court at the same level except for enmity. Even then, stricter terms were imposed to prove enmity than in the Ulozhenie.[15] Access to the ruler continued to interfere with judicial hierarchy. In 1722, declaring that people still insisted on handing the tsar petitions, "giving him no peace," even after he had provided so thorough a network of "Colleges and chanceries, *gubernii* and provinces and in them lower and Superior Courts," Peter I created the post of *Reketmeister* to receive complaints about unjustly resolved cases or cases tied up in red tape. Peter did allow, however, the Senate to approach him if it encountered a case too difficult to resolve. As late as 1724, Peter was still complaining that people were petitioning directly to him or his courtiers; he threatened harsh corporal punishment, even death, for not respecting judicial hierarchy.[16]

Nevertheless, contemporaries did not respect the new hierarchy any better than before. Although the Justice College was intended as an appeals court, it often accepted cases, even relatively minor ones, as first instance. Litigants continued to bypass provincial courts to bring cases to Moscow. Similarly, the Senate was intended as an appeals

[14] Superior Courts: PSZ v: nos. 3201 and 3202 (1718). Justice College, this stage of reforms: Serov, *Sudebnaia reforma*, ch. 4; Kosheleva, *Liudi*, 46–52. Achievement: Serov, *Sudebnaia reforma*, 208–33; see also Kollmann, "Change," 388–90.

[15] Disputed or important: ZA Petra 369–70 (1718), 381–2 (1721). Beloozero *landrat*: RGADA f. 921, no. 30 (1721). Bypassing and enmity: PSZ v: no. 3403 (1719), vi: no. 3577 (1720).

[16] PSZ vi: no. 394 (1722), vii: no. 4177 (1723); Serov, *Sudebnaia reforma*, 242–5. Senate to tsar: PSZ vi: no. 4003 (1722). ZA Petra 385–6 (1724); PSZ vii: no. 4577 (1724).

court for the Colleges, but did relatively little such work, focusing on administrative issues instead.[17]

Separation of administration and judiciary proved unworkable, and in early 1722 the lowest level courts were incorporated into governors' offices. Serov opines that the new lower courts proved too weak in the face of traditionally strong governors. Some de facto autonomy for the lower courts was maintained by adding two locally elected gentry "assessors" to work collegially with the governor; in practice, busy governors tended to let them handle trials on their own. Furthermore, the governor's courts continued to be under the oversight and review of the Superior Courts and the Justice College, maintaining some independence from the administrative.[18]

One early eighteenth-century reform that endured was the practice of review of capital cases for military and civil courts, complementing the seventeenth-century trend of limiting the use of capital punishment. Justifying this step in a decree of 1721 "so that for lack of knowledge someone is not assigned incorrectly a harsh penalty," Peter mandated that the Superior Courts and General Magistrate were to review all sentences of death and hard labor from courts subordinate to them. Affirmed executions were then to be carried out locally. Crimes of graft and corruption received particular attention; in 1721 Peter insisted that the Senate approve and that he sign off on punishments for major theft from the state treasury. After his death in January 1725, review of capital sentences continued.[19] These judicial reforms, as helter-skelter as they seem to us and seemed to contemporaries, introduced new principles and affirmed some existing practices.

TRANSFORMING JUDICIAL PROCESS

For the Muscovite historian venturing into the Petrine era, the most startling evidence of Petrine judicial changes comes in the very look of documents. In one short generation, the handwriting, format and

[17] Serov, *Sudebnaia reforma*, 223–5, 242–53; Mrochek-Drozdovskii, *Oblastnoe upravlenie*, 302; LeDonne, *Absolutism*, 194.

[18] Assessors: PSZ VI: nos. 3917 and 3935 (1722); ZA Petra 384–5 (1722). This stage of reform: Schmidt, *Sozialkontrolle*, 134–5; Serov, *Sudebnaia reforma*, 205–8, 229–42; Kosheleva, *Liudi*, 46–52, 307–21; Pisar'kova, *Gosudarstvennoe upravlenie*, 166–70; LeDonne, *Absolutism*, 189–90.

[19] PSZ VI: no. 3756 (1721). Other references to review: PSZ V: no. 3294, pt. 6 (1719); PSZ V: no. 3316 (1719); PSZ VI: no. 3708, ch. 9 (1721); PSZ VI: no. 3756 (1721); PSZ VI: no. 3847 (1721). Review affirmed: 1726, 1727: PSZ VII: nos. 4964 (1726), 5026 and 5218 (1727); PSZ VIII: no. 5333, arts. 9, 15–16, pp. 97–100 (1728). Serov, *Sudebnaia reforma*, 338–51, 404–14.

language of court records were transformed. Evgenii Anisimov suggests that the changes were required because the chancery system was too inefficient to support the expanded machine; Richard Wortman sees these reforms in documentation as part of the well-ordered police state project.[20] But these changes also continued established trends of improving record-keeping and documentation and forging a professional bureaucracy – knowledgeable of the law, able to administer the realm consistently and fairly, assisted by rational methods of record-keeping.

In the realm of court procedure, a 1697 decree declared the accusatory trial process (*sud*) ripe for reform, plagued by corrupt litigants, "those chicaners and contrivers, those thieves and despoilers of souls, who force the weak to go through red tape, bribes, losses and ruin." For misdemeanor crimes of "injury and ruin," the accusatory process was modified to prevent such abuses as false testimony, filing of bogus cases, buying witnesses. This decree abolished face-to-face confrontations, set rules for rejecting witnesses and allowed oath-taking.[21] A 1723 law, "On the form of the accusatory trial," changed this mode even further. It mandated that all court testimony be recorded by the court *sekretar'* in an orderly dossier; litigants were to be interviewed according to "points" and their responses written down in parallel notebooks, one for each litigant. As in European inquisitorial procedure, the *sekretar'* took on the role of prosecutor assembling the case for the judge. These reforms pushed all trials closer to the inquisitory model by emphasizing orderly procedure and record-keeping.[22]

These reforms were put into practice with great rapidity. The prescribed form of written questions and answers by "points" appears in suits surveyed here by 1724, sometimes with a grid format isolating question and response and a summary that painstakingly notes defendants' and witnesses' answers, point by point. They used this form for oral interrogation, torture and face-to-face confrontations.[23]

[20] Anisimov, *Gosudarstvennye preobrazovaniia*, 95–6; Wortman, "Peter the Great."

[21] PSZ III: no. 1572 (1697); translation by Wortman: "Peter the Great," 303; Schmidt, *Sozialkontrolle*, ch. 7E; Serov, *Sudebnaia reforma*, 92–3, 95. Preferring inquisitory to accusatory: PSZ III: no. 1643 (1698).

[22] *O forme suda*: RZ IV: 451–61; PSZ VII: no. 4344 (1723). Wortman, "Peter the Great"; Peterson, *Peter the Great's Reforms*, 332–55; Serov, *Sudebnaia reforma*, pp. 335–8. Some historians construed the 1723 decree as abolishing the inquisitorial format, but then argued that the law was ignored: Got'e, *Istoriia oblastnogo upravleniia*, I: 394–407; Evremova, "Sudoistroistvo," 234–7; Eroshkin, *Ocherki*, 115–17; RZ IV: 394–6.

[23] RGADA f. 419, op. 1, pt. 1, nos. 1508, 1509 and 1511 (all 1724). Grid form: RGADA f. 419, op. 1, pt. 2, nos. 237 and 242 (1727).

Other improvements in bureaucratic record-keeping also worked to create more orderly adjudication. From the 1690s they addressed three issues: centralizing production of documents, changing their form and improving work processes and professional behavior in the chanceries and local offices. The first approach was evident in late 1699 when the system of town-square scribes who wrote everything from petitions to wills to purchase agreements for land was dismantled.[24] The stated intent was not to capture income, but to affirm the authenticity of documents, as the decree also spelled out rules about signatures of witnesses and keeping notarial record books. Immediately thereafter, on the first day of the first year using the Julian Calendar, January 1, 1700, Peter I declared that all official documents (*kreposti*) would now be written in the Moscow Town Hall or in governors' offices; he allowed public scribes to write only petitions for appeal.[25] These rulings undoubtedly threw document production into chaos, and a typically Petrine retrenchment followed within a year.

A decree of January 1701 reflected that the result of these steps had been higher prices and more corruption than with the public scribe system. The scribes of the Kremlin Ivanov Square were restored, this time as a state institution composed of twenty-four undersecretaries led by four previous Ivanov Square scribes. The decree mandated that all documents for government business were to be written there and not in the chanceries. In provincial towns, analogous offices or desks (*kontory*) in governor's offices were to be established, with "inspectors" under the governor's oversight to supervise their work. The law vehemently forbade all private individuals to write documents or to hire anyone to do so other than these scribes, thereby increasing state revenue with fees for each of three categories of document. Eventually oversight was consolidated under a Notarial Office (*Krepostnaia kontora*) within the Justice College, which centralized registration of documents, oversaw the collection of fees and administered local notarial offices. By the mid 1720s, there were 230 regional *kontory*, each with an inspector and a handful of scribes.[26] A regulated notarial service had been built on the basis of what had existed before.

[24] L. M. Balakireva notes the neglect of the history of notarial activity: "Sozdanie Krepostnoi kontory," 202–3. Cherepnin, *Russkaia paleografiia*, 434–6; Zlotnikov, "Podiachie," esp. 129–30.

[25] PSZ III: no. 1732 (Dec. 1699); PSZ IV: no. 1740 (Jan. 1, 1700). Some other types of documents were allowed to be written in the Customs Office and Musketeer Chancery: PSZ IV: no. 1831 (1701).

[26] PSZ IV: no. 1833 (1701); initially called the "Office (*Palatka*) of Ivanov Square," later the "Office of Notarial Affairs" (*Palatka krepostnykh del*). Zlotnikov notes that the four senior scribes had stayed loyal to Peter I during the 1698 musketeer uprising: "Podiachie," 130. Notarial Office: PSZ V:

These same years saw a reform of bureaucratic paperwork with the twin goals of securing the authenticity of documents and reaping profit. It started with a lucrative stamp tax in January 1699 on the eve of the Great Northern War. Official paper in three graduated sizes with three prices, all stamped with a double-headed eagle (*gerbovaia bumaga*), was to be used in chanceries and in the towns. With the customary brio of Petrine laws, the decree ordered offices to adopt the new procedures immediately and completely, threatening "harsh corporal punishment," confiscation of land and other forms of "eternal destruction" for officials who dragged their feet or for petitioners who did not use the correct paper. Decrees followed supervising the sale of such paper, setting prices and declaring falsification of stamped paper the equivalent of counterfeiting money, punishable unto death.[27]

Also to improve record-keeping, Muscovite scrolls were replaced with notebooks. With typical didacticism, the decree explained their superiority: cases written as scrolls waste paper, as they are written only on one side; the scrolls unglue themselves in humid weather and mice eat them. In the long run many records are lost. But in notebook form the paper lies flat and can be bound into books that are less susceptible to damage. Each year's documents should be bound into annual volumes, with pages numbered in the corners and books titled by type of document, so that an undersecretary seeking a case could easily find it. Completed documents in notebooks should be signed by the governor, undersecretary or secretary.[28]

These reforms were also enacted rapidly. In cases surveyed here through 1701, plain paper and scroll form continued, understandably, given the difficulty of sending information and paper to the frontiers. But by 1704 cases from Arzamas, Shatsk and elsewhere in the Middle Volga used notebooks.[29]

no. 3307 (1719). Pisar'kova, "Rossiiskaia biurokratiia," 2004 no. 1, p. 30; Balakireva, "Sozdanie Krepostnoi kontory," 202–18. Scattered cites of "town-square scribes" continued (Zlotnikov, "Podiachie," 129).

27 Eagle paper: PSZ III: no. 1673 (Jan. 1699). Price rise: PSZ III: no. 1703 (Oct. 1699). Use of stamped paper: PSZ III: nos. 1717, 1730 (1699); AI V: no. 293 (1699); PSZ IV: nos. 1744 and 1786 (1700), 2006 (1704); PSZ VII: nos. 4193, pt. 8, 4270, 4325 (1723). On stamped paper: Cherepnin, *Russkaia paleografiia*, 466–9.

28 Abolish scrolls: PSZ IV: nos. 1803 and 1817 (1700); PSZ IV: no. 1901 (1702); Avtokratov, "K istorii zameny," 278–84; Chekunova, "Vidovye osobennosti," 163. Already in 1697 scribes were being instructed to store scrolls where they could be easily found: PSZ III: no. 1608.

29 Scroll form: Beloozero: RGADA f. 1107, no. 4375 (1699); RGADA f. 210, Sevsk stol, no. 484, fols. 293–6 and no. 470, fol. 227 (both 1701); RGADA f. 210, Stolbtsy Pomestnogo stola, no. 215, fol. 164 (1701); RGADA f. 210, Belgorod stol, no. 1790, fol. 7 (1701). Notebook form: RGADA f. 1103, nos. 491, 499, 509 (all 1704) and 2809 (1714); RGADA f. 1381, nos. 13 (1706), 35 (1707), 126, 129, 131, 134 (all 1713); RGADA f. 904, no. 810 (1710).

All pages in a notebook were supposed to be written on stamped paper, but in cases surveyed here "eagle" paper does not become predominant until about 1720. One case that stretched from 1714 to 1720 had no eagle paper in it at all, while in another case of 1720, stamped paper appears only on a few pages. Since a 1719 decree allowed plain paper to be used as long as fees were paid, these documents were probably accepted as legitimate.[30]

The very handwriting and language of bureaucratic documentation was also transformed. Arzamas cases from 1704 through 1727 demonstrate what A. E. Chekunova calls a "*polisemiia*" of old and new terminology. Petitions of 1715 and 1718, for example, use old and new terms "*chelobit'ie*" and "*proshenie*" interchangeably to mean "petition." New terms for bureaucratic paperwork such as *donoshenie, protokol, promemorariia, ekstrakt* replaced or joined Muscovite terms such as "*otpiska*" and "*ukaz*." The use of Cyrillic numbers endured, even when the new style of Gregorian years had been adopted; in these cases Arabic numerals to denote the year are first seen in 1727.[31]

By the time the 1720 General Reglament published a glossary of Russian equivalents for foreign chancery terminology, many new titles, terms and turns of phrase had been in use for two decades. Already in 1702 a new form of address for petitions (evidenced in cases by 1704) was defined: whereas Muscovite petitions had begun with the traditional "to the tsar, sovereign and grand prince X of all Rus' and [further regional titles]" in the dative case, Petrine petitions were to begin with a new addressee in the declarative nominative: "The most powerful tsar and sovereign most merciful!" (*derzhavneishii tsar' i gosudar' milostiveishii*).[32] Other titles appeared later: petitions starting in January 1722 through at least 1724 address "Peter the Great, Father of the Fatherland." After Peter's death the salutation became even more florid: "to the very most luminescent most powerful Great Sovereign Empress Ekaterina Alekseevna, all-Rus' autocrat."[33]

30 Stamp all pages: PSZ III: no. 1703 (1699). 1714–20: RGADA f. 1380, no. 53. Stamps only in 1720: RGADA f. 1380, no. 51, fol. 13. Sporadic stamped paper: RGADA f. 1380, no. 163, fols. 22, 52 (1720); RGADA f. 419, op. 1, pt. 2, no. 242 (1727); RGADA, f. 419, op. 1, pt. 2, no. 21 (1729). Plain paper PSZ V: no. 3475 (1719).

31 Chekunova, "Vidovye osobennosti," 163–4; Redin, *Administrativnye struktury*, 476–7. Interchangeable terms: RGADA f. 1380, nos. 6, fol. 3 (1715) and 29, fol. 1v (1718). Arabic numerals: RGADA f. 419, op. 1, pt. 2, no. 242 (1727).

32 Glossary: PSZ VI: no. 3534, p. 160 (1720). New title: PSZ IV: no. 1899 (1702); RGADA f. 1103, no. 499 and 509 (both 1704); RGADA f. 1404, no. 135 (1716).

33 Father of Fatherland: RZ IV: 179 (1721). RGADA f. 978, no. 30 (1723). More florid: RGADA f. 419, op. 1, pt. 2, nos. 237, 238, 242 (all 1727).

A striking aspect of Petrine paperwork is the transformation of handwriting. From the graceful cursive of the seventeenth century (*skoropis'*), over the Petrine period letters become larger, more vertical and boxy. L. V. Cherepnin attributes the change to the influence of civil script, which was a simplified alphabet and letter formation devised for printing secular texts around 1708 by Peter's Amsterdam publisher. At the same time Peter's chancery reformers were creating a new literary language that was not, as often asserted, based on Muscovite bureaucratic language; rather, it was an attempt to create a "simple" language on vernacular roots, according to Victor Zhivov. He shows that bureaucratic documents absorbed the new "simple" literary language as it evolved, such that in a few generations there was no longer need for a separate chancery language, as had existed in Muscovy.[34] "Simple" is a relative term here; the influx of foreign vocabulary made Petrine documents difficult to apprehend.

Reforms also addressed the quality of judicial work by reinforcing Muscovite standards. A decree of December 1703, for example, established the working hours of undersecretaries in the Office of Notarial Affairs and set penalties for absences; it reiterated the Muscovite rule against undersecretaries going to private homes to write documents without permission of their supervising institution, the Armory.[35] Reforms imposed stricter rules on the writing, checking, recording and most importantly signing of documents, so that officials could be traced to their work. A flurry of decrees from 1699 to 1706 mandated the recording of all documents in chancery books within two months, defined how many alterations in a document could be tolerated (if annotated) before the text had to be rewritten, and so on.[36] These norms were put into practice. While Muscovite scrolls had been counter-signed by scribes at the juncture of pages on the reverse, notebook cases put more signatures of more responsible people throughout on the faces of the pages. An Arzamas case of 1727 has the undersecretary (*podkantseliarist*) signing along the bottom of the case, plus numerous signatures

[34] Cherepnin, *Russkaia paleografiia*, 473–7; Zhivov, *Iazyk i kul'tura*, 118–24. Civil script: Cracraft, *Revolution of Peter the Great*, 99–103; *Petrine Revolution in Russian Culture*, ch. 6, esp. 257–76.

[35] Reforms of bureaucratic procedures: Anisimov, *Gosudarstvennye preobrazovaniia*, 75–98; Cherepnin, *Russkaia paleografiia*, 434–6; Lukashevich, "Vidy dokumentov"; Iliushenko, *Istoriia deloproizvodstva*, 38–40. PSZ IV: no. 1953 (1703); affirmations of working hours: PSZ V: no. 3131 (1717), PSZ VI: no. 3534, ch. 18 (1720). Corrupt scribes visiting private homes: RGADA f. 210, Prikaznyi stol, nos. 965, fols. 43–8 and 152–69 (both 1701).

[36] PSZ III: no. 1732 (1699); PSZ IV: nos. 1833 and 1850 (1701) and 2080 (1705). PSZ IV: nos. 2102 and 2116 (1706).

of judges throughout the case as witnessing torture and affirming a verdict. Some have notations that they have been checked and properly recorded: a 1725 case, for example, was annotated by two senior secretaries (*zasekretariia*), Fedor Karaulov and Ivan Karapov.[37]

Commitment to orderly and ethical procedure is evident in the regulations defining various bureaucratic staff positions. The 1720 regulation of the senior scribe (*zemskii diak*) in *guberniia* or provincial offices spelled out his working hours and his responsibility to keep an orderly office with all laws readily at hand for reference, to oversee a small staff of copyists and to publicize the laws to all who engage with the court. Especially interesting are his interactions with his superiors: the senior scribe was allowed, even obligated, to inform the gubernator or *voevoda* of relevant laws and make sure he rules by the law; he was to advise him when a case should be sent to a higher venue. Bogoslovskii noted that such secretaries not only were a governor's "walking memory," but also often made decisions. Pisar'kova adds that since about 85 percent of local governors in Peter's time joined civil service from the military with no legal training, it was all the more important that chancery staff be knowledgeable in the law[38]; such amateur judges and scribal expertise had been the case in the seventeenth century.

The General Regulation in February 1720 was the culmination of attempts to professionalize the bureaucracy. Its goal was to create uniform, consistent bureaucratic practice across central and local administrative and judicial offices. The duties of senior officers of the Colleges and chancery officials from *sekretar'* to *notarius* to *aktuarius* to *kantseliarist* and lesser positions were defined (chs. 28–35); the seating arrangements of offices were described and the creation of archives for documents mandated (chs. 40–4). The Regulation defines punishment for misdeeds by chancery staff (ch. 50); it enjoins all to work politely and professionally together (ch. 55).[39] Until the end of his reign, Peter was lecturing his officials about professional behavior: Shafirov's corruption trial in 1722 was cited as the justification for a January 1724 decree requiring that all civil servants – "in the Senate,

[37] RGADA f. 419, op. 1, pt. 2, no. 242, fols. 6–7, 4, 4v, 5, 5v (1727); see also RGADA f. 419, op. 1, pt. 2, no. 237, fols. 1, 3, 3v, 4, 4v (1727); RGADA f. 1103, no. 6, fol. 7 (1721); RGADA f. 1380, no. 17, fol. 8 (1721). RGADA f. 419, op. 1, pt. 1, no. 767, fol. 20v (1725).

[38] PSZ VI: no. 3571 (1720). Bogoslovskii quoted by Pisar'kova, "Rossiiskaia biurokratiia," 2004 no. 1, p. 27; Mrochek-Drozdovskii, *Oblastnoe upravlenie*, 121–2; Balakireva, "Sozdanie Krepostnoi kontory."

[39] PSZ VI: no. 3534 (1720); PRP VIII: 72–105; Bogoslovskii, *Pamiatniki zakonodatel'stva*, 12–33; Cracraft, *Petrine Revolution in Russian Culture*, 159–67.

Synod, Colleges, Chanceries and all courts" – should know the law, apply it and not plead ignorance, on pain of harsh punishment.[40]

Peter I hoped to create a *noblesse de robe*, a bureaucratic elite composed of men of gentry and chancery background who would be regarded as highly as those in military service. Reforms turned to education to do this. In January 1714 appeared a famous order that men of noble rank should not be allowed to marry without study of "cyphers and geometry"; less noted is that in February 1714 he made the same demand of children (ages 15–20) of chancery families and other lower classes (clergy, urban, monastic), mandating that schools be established throughout the realm. These demands were repeated regularly.[41] A group of undersecretaries was sent to Koenigsburg in 1716 to study German, with other undersecretaries in their chanceries expected to pay their expenses. The General Regulation of 1720 exhorts families to place children in both military and civil service, warning that one cannot rise to high civil ranks without education; the Table of Ranks of 1722 reiterates the point. Through the century, as S. M. Troitskii has chronicled, the state continued, with little success, to try to attract noblemen into schools for civil service.[42]

D. O. Serov acknowledges the shortcomings of this group of reforms: no regulations defined the qualifications and appointment/dismissal process for judges (the draft 1723–6 legal codification simply stated that judges should be "godfearing, prudent and knowledgeable"); in practice, most judges appointed to the Justice College or Superior Courts had no prior judicial experience, almost half coming from the military (47 percent of Superior Court judges, 1719–26). He concludes that the tradition endured that the "most knowledgeable jurists" were chancery bureaucrats, few of whom were appointed as judges in their own right. Nevertheless, Serov praises the steps being made to distinguish the role of judge as an independent service status and to create a corpus of professional jurists.[43]

40 Rule promptly: PSZ v: no. 3298 (1719); General Regulation, ch. 4: PRP VIII: 76. Behave properly: PSZ v: no. 3417 (1719), PSZ VII: no. 4337 (1723). Rule by law: PSZ VI: no. 3510 (1720). No bribes: PSZ VI: no. 6586 (1720). Fines for judges proven on appeal to have ruled unfairly and for litigants proven on appeal to have falsely accused: PSZ v: no. 2879 (1725). PSZ VII: no. 4436 (1724).

41 Pisar′kova, *Gosudarstvennoe upravlenie*, 171–8. PSZ v: nos. 2762 (Jan. 1714), 2778 (Feb. 1714), 2979 (1716), 3447 (1718); PSZ VI: no. 3703 (1721). Townsmen from some northern towns successfully petitioned not to be included: PSZ VI: no. 3575 (1720).

42 PSZ v: no. 2997 (1716). General Regulation, ch. 36: PSZ VI: no. 3534 (1720). Table of Ranks, nos. 13–14: PSZ VI: no. 3890 (1722). Similar decrees: PSZ VI: 3845 (1721); PSZ VI: no. 3896, pt. 2 (1722). Troitskii, *Russkii absoliutizm*, 267–92.

43 Serov, *Sudebnaia reforma*, 253–68.

His optimism is affirmed by the cases surveyed here. Arzamas judicial practice from 1719 to 1726 was stable and competent, supported by an able corps of judges and their staffs.

PETRINE JUDGES AT WORK

The emergence in Arzamas of a competent, even professional, judiciary is indicated, first, by the continuity of judges. Almost without a break from 1716 through 1722, Iakov Gavrilovich Chertkov served as the Arzamas criminal court judge; his colleagues Stefan Kireev and Stefan Afanas′evich Nesterov are also cited regularly (1718 through 1722). Chertkov's title changed with Petrine reforms from *landrat* to "judge and *stol′nik*" but he and his staff kept working all the same.[44] By June 1722 Chertkov's court had been merged with the governor's office and renamed the "provincial chancery." A triumvirate of the local governor and two local elected gentry "assessors" combined administrative and judicial power. Three men filled these roles through the decade: Lieutenant Colonel and Governor Stefan Semenovich Chelishev and majors and assessors Mikhail Timofeevich Kishkin and Fedor Vasil′evich Zasetskoi. After September 1723 the governor is not mentioned and Kishkin and Zasetskoi adjudicated all cases, usually working together, sometimes alone, through at least 1727; Kishkin is cited as late as 1729.[45] Thus, despite name changes, the court in Arzamas remained stable and de facto separate from administrative power. This reflects the development of a professional, experienced judicial staff.

Their work was capable. Even more than in late seventeenth-century cases, Arzamas judges and their staffs composed detailed verdicts that summarized the circumstances of the crime, the logic of the decision and citations of relevant law. Verdicts were not only read aloud to convicted criminals but also posted in written form on the gallows. Modern social theory suggests that such narrative tale-telling – in fiction or in court transcripts – provides a "script" by which individuals can understand,

[44] Chertkov as *landrat* 1716–19: RGADA f. 1380, nos. 17, 54, 55; RGADA f. 1404, nos. 97–8, 229, 667–79, 970, 988. Kireev 1716: RGADA f. 1404, no. 135, fol. 3. Nesterov 1718–20: RGADA f. 1380, nos. 29–30, 52–3, 60, 63. Chertkov as *stol′nik* and judge, 1720–2: RGADA f. 1380, nos. 17, 29–30, 51, 53, 61, 63, 164, 175, 372–4, 575; RGADA f. 419, op. 1, pt. 1, no. 577, 579, 766.

[45] RGADA f. 419, op. 1, pt. 1, nos. 765–7, 1043; RGADA f. 1380, no. 768 (all 1722). Kishkin and Zasetskoi adjudicating together: RGADA f. 419, op. 1, pt. 2, nos. 237–8 (1722), 1509–12 (1724). Kishkin alone: RGADA f. 419, op. 1, pt. 1, no. 1507 (1724); op. 1, pt. 2, nos. 240 and 245 (1727). Zasetskoi alone: RGADA f. 419, op. 1, pt. 2, no. 242 (1727). Kishkin: RGADA f. 419, op. 1, pt. 2, no. 21 (1729).

construct and reconcile with moments of collective or individual trauma.[46] Lengthy Petrine verdicts read aloud may well have played such a role for the assembled audience.

Unencumbered by the myriad duties of Muscovite governors, judges in the 1720s era of separation of judicial and administrative powers did their jobs well. Their work was methodical, accurate and orderly. Take, for example, a case submitted in February 1719 to *landrat* Nesterov involving felony assault and robbery by Ivan Kuzmin and Nikita Zinov′ev, who had been apprehended by villagers. Nesterov immediately began taking testimony and ordering excerpts from relevant law codes. He ordered three torture sessions, each separated by a month (February, March and April 1719). The case then sat without progress for more than a year until September 1720, a delay probably occasioned by the 1719–20 judicial reform. When the case resumed in September 1720, "*stol′nik*" Iakov Gavrilovich Chertkov took over. He responded immediately to Zinov′ev's petition to be released from prison pending resolution, sending him out on recognizance (*rospiska*) on September 19. The next day Chertkov ordered excerpts from the 1649 Ulozhenie on the death penalty, on testimony and on property settlements (ch. 21: arts. 13, 18, 20, 22, 26, 27). A month later (October 17) he issued his decision, in a verdict that is a model of Petrine didactic jurisprudence. Chertkov sentenced Ivan Kuzmin to death for assault, injury and robbery of one man and for the murder of another, noting the sentence's deterrent effect and explicitly citing articles from the Ulozhenie. He explained his verdict by noting that in testimony both Kuzmin and Zinov′ev said separately that Kuzmin alone had done the crime; furthermore, Zinov′ev had withstood torture, proving his innocence. Zinov′ev was exonerated, but Chertkov ordered another villager who might have been complicit to be arrested. The sentence was announced and carried out that day, "outside of the town (*posad*) near the stone store house," with a written version of the verdict posted at the gallows. This murder case lasted one-and-a-half years, but took only about five months of court time.[47]

Another case submitted in February 1719 unfolded similarly expeditiously. At stake was the murder of the peasant Ivan Golovlev. His body was immediately inspected and ordered buried. Then the case sat for a year's worth of judicial reforms. By August 30, 1720 judge Chertkov was in charge. He ordered the accused murderers Semen Gavrilov and Semen

46 Alexander Cook cites Fredric Jameson: Cook, "Unsettling Accounts."
47 RGADA f. 1380, no. 53, verdict on fol. 15 (1719).

Fedotov arrested and their property sealed. They were brought in on September 7 with other witnesses and all were questioned, followed by a face-to-face confrontation of the two accused in early November, two torture sessions in November, and a final one on December 2. They each told the same story: Fedotov had come upon Golovlev stealing from his house, he had called for help, Gavrilov came running and in the fight the murdered man pulled a knife. Gavrilov killed in self-defense, defending Fedotov's home – all factors explicitly cited in law codes as exonerating circumstances. On the same day as the final torture, December 2, Chertkov ordered excerpts of relevant law codes and made his ruling: the accused were acquitted (to be released on recognizance in place of surety bond) because of self-defense and defense of one's home. Since no one was found responsible, the village where the dead body was found paid the "dead body" fees, a practice that dates back to the Rus′ Law. The men were only released on December 23, three weeks' delay, time perhaps needed to pay court fees. The case had lasted just under two years, but took up only about five months' court time.[48]

Finally, two murder cases demonstrate that Arzamas judges effectively used the new institutions of judicial hierarchy. In 1724 a peasant in Arzamas reported that another peasant, Timofei Zakharov syn Drozdov, had killed two swornmen during a robbery of a tavern in their village and that another peasant, Ivan Glatkov, had murdered a dragoon. The peasant who reported the crimes tried to excuse the village bailiffs of knowledge of these crimes, which they should have reported. "Majors and assessors" Kishkin and Zasetskii proceeded to try the two cases simultaneously. They arrested Drozdov and Glatkov, the stewards and witnesses. The judges questioned the accused and brought them to torture, starting in January 1724. Drozdov denied killing; he testified that he and a group of men had planned to steal the tavern money, but that he had stood outside and had only helped to drag the bodies into a cart and throw them behind the threshing barn. In the second case Glatkov admitted his crime: the dragoon had asked to spend the night in his barn, and he and two other men had killed him to steal his clothing. They hid the body in the swamp. Several stewards and village peasants denied knowledge of either crime. In their first torture session neither Drozdov nor Glatkov changed their stories, but Glatkov implicated a soldier, who was then given a face-to-face confrontation with him and a first torture session, in which he denied complicity. All three of the men were sent back for their second torture

[48] RGADA f. 1380, no. 51 (1719).

in March 1724; no one changed his story and the soldier soon died of the torture. In their third sessions in June, Glatkov and Drozdov held to their stories.

The diligent Arzamas judges then appealed to the Senate not for advice but for help with a delay. They reported in 1726 that the local office overseeing the native (*iasak*-paying) population on the tsar's lands near Arzamas was stone-walling. Despite their many requests, from January 1724 to June 1726 that office refused to send summoned witnesses. So on May 3, 1726, the Senate ordered the Arzamas Chancery of the Native Population to cooperate; in June it sent one peasant to judges Kishkin and Zasetskii. Arzamas staff were meanwhile preparing the case for resolution, with legal excerpts noting that a convicted man should be held no more than six months awaiting further accusations before execution and requiring execution for premeditated murder. With yet more turmoil in institutional reforms, the two cases languished until 1728, when Glatkov was sentenced to death by beheading for the dragoon's murder, to which he had confessed. But by that time review of capital sentences had been mandated, so the judges duly dispatched the case to the Nizhnii Novgorod Superior Court. Whether the execution took place is not recorded.[49] Arzamas judges in the 1720s worked with dispatch, supported by competent and knowledgeable scribal staff and freed from other administrative or military duties. As Chapter 12 shows, they used sanctioned violence (torture and punishments) carefully according to the law. Early eighteenth-century judicial reforms produced excellent local jurists, but the problem of corruption continued to threaten the state's overall endeavor.

THE PROBLEM OF CORRUPTION

British engineer John Perry, working in Russia in the early 1700s, condemned bribery in the courts from first-hand knowledge: "the Bribery of the Judge is the first Step to go upon; Money is known to be taken on both Sides; and generally he who bids highest carries the Cause, whilst the Sufferer has no Remedy, but to be content."[50] Over the course of Peter I's reign definitions of highest crime began to include official corruption. In the 1710s decrees declared a distinction between state crime and particular crime, identifying state crime with damage to the "interests of state";

[49] RGADA f. 419, op. 1, pt. 1, nos. 1508 and 1509 (1722).

[50] Perry, *State of Russia*, 189–90; see also Korb, *Diary*, 1: 188–90; Butler, "Foreign Impressions," 65–92.

eventually official corruption was included in the three "points" for which people were permitted to appeal directly to the Tsar.[51]

Petrine legislation in 1714 about corruption railed against venal officials who plead ignorance of the law: "so that in the future all cheats (*pluty*) . . . can have no more excuses, it is forbidden to ALL ranks who are assigned to any tasks, great or small, whether in religious, military, civil, political, merchant, artistic or other services, no matter what office they hold, to take any bribes." In 1720 the 1714 decree was repeated with the comment that "although this his Great Sovereign's decree from the Senate was proclaimed and printed in the books of decrees and sold for all the populace to know and now is still being sold, and the decree was sent to the *gubernii*," nevertheless there was no record in the Senate of the *gubernii* having received it. So the decree against bribery was reissued and confirmation of receipt was demanded. Two more decrees against theft of state revenues and bribery followed in that year alone. Again in 1722 Peter I railed against corrupt judicial staff:

> It is known to us that undersecretaries because of bribes have been releasing many convicts not only in small civil suits but in large crimes and felony, but they report it to the judges as if it were simple escapes and the only ones investigated are the night watch and prison guards. Thus, in the future, if any convict escapes, the undersecretaries need to be investigated too, and they are to be tortured along with the night watch before the litigants of the cases, so that there will be no favoring. If the judges are lenient in this to the undersecretaries, then they are liable, like common criminals, to the death penalty.[52]

The state also introduced preemptive measures to prevent corruption, so much so that historians characterize this as an era of denunciation. As already noted, public scribes in the Office of Notarial Affairs in Moscow and in local *kontory* were overseen both for corruption and for accuracy of work. Commissions led by officers of Peter the Great's trusted Guards regiments investigated corruption; briefly, at the end of his reign, military regiments were given fiscal responsibilities and oversight over governors' fiscal affairs. The procuracy-general was created to oversee the Senate, itself intended to oversee judicial officials. Petrine legislation also created an avenue for reporting corruption, which had been a weak point of Muscovite

[51] Early decrees: PSZ IV, no. 1951 (1703), 1765 and 1957 (both 1704), 2026 (1705). Interests of state: PSZ V, no. 2673, point 4 (1713), 2871 and 2786, point 2 (both 1714). Three points: ZA Petra 362–3 (1715) and 366–8 (1718); PSZ V: nos. 2877 (1715) and 3143 (1718).

[52] PSZ V: no. 2871 (1714) (quote on 135); PSZ VI: nos. 3586 (1720) (quote on 194), 3601 and 3648; similar decree: PSZ V: no. 2707 (1713). PSZ VI: no. 3929, p. 523 (1722).

practice. The new office of fiscals, primarily concerned with tax collection, was intended to receive, investigate and report complaints about official corruption. But since many of these overseers proved venal themselves, these efforts failed to produce a smooth-functioning, honest bureaucracy.[53]

Official corruption was prosecuted mercilessly. In 1702 the Preobrazhenskii Chancery was given authority over cases of official corruption in addition to its docket of treason and rebellion; the last decade of Peter I's life witnessed a "reign of terror" against graft, drawing into his net even his closest colleagues such as Alexander Menshikov and Peter Shafirov (see Chapter 18).[54] Nevertheless, structural weaknesses – some of Peter's own making – undermined these reforms.

THE DEMISE OF JUDICIAL REFORMS

Petrine judicial reforms were intended to separate the judiciary and provide it with a professional cohort and orderly procedure. Only the latter goal was achieved. Institutional reforms were poorly implemented, with spheres of responsibilities of many of the new officials unclear and overlapping. Even though some judges, as in Arzamas, worked with professional dispatch, in the aggregate the judiciary was not provided the wherewithal to perform its tasks. Basic needs such as updated and coordinated law codes, judicial training for judges and scribes, sufficient numbers of secretarial staff and enforcement of the hierarchy of venues were lacking. In an era of regulation, a founding charter was never written for the Justice College nor for the Superior Courts. The bold attempt to centralize the judiciary in the 1720s was undermined early on. Parallel to the hierarchy of courts of general purpose there continued to exist many separate courts with overlapping jurisdiction; they included the Preobrazhenskii Chancery for highest crime and military, naval, urban and monastic courts. Separation of powers was undermined because all courts were dependent on governors, their staffs and military units for help in the police aspects of their business and because regional officials

[53] Denunciation: Pisar′kova, citing M. M. Bogoslovskii and A. D. Gradovskii: "Rossiiskaia biurokratiia," 2004 no. 2, pp. 16–17; Anisimov, *Reforms of Peter the Great*, 235–8; Bogoslovskii, *Oblastnaia reforma*, 295–443; Eroshkin, *Ocherki*, 119–20; Wortman, *Development*, 12–14; Yaney, *Systematization*, ch. 1.

[54] Preobrazhenskii Prikaz: Anisimov, *Dyba i knut*; Golikova, *Politicheskie protsessy*. High-level corruption: Pisar′kova, "Rossiiskaia biurokratiia," 2004 no. 2, pp. 12–14; LeDonne, *Absolutism*, 158–63; Serov, *Stroiteli imperii*. Short-lived "Superior court" for political crimes (1723–6): Serov, "Zabytoe uchrezhdenie." Investigatory commissions: Babich, *Gosudarstvennye uchrezhdeniia*, 102–9, 178–80, 205–7, 216–28, 237–43 and *passim*.

such as *gubernatory* and vice-*gubernatory* themselves worked as Superior Court judges. As noted, as early as 1722 independent lower courts were folded into local *voevoda* courts, with assessors.[55]

Contemporaries rejected the reforms. When Superior Courts were abolished in 1727 (along with many other new offices), the legislation declared "the proliferation of officials and chanceries throughout the realm not only serves as a great burden to the state but also a great hardship to the people." In their place was restored a Muscovite-like three-level administrative-judicial hierarchy: *voevody* at the *uezd* and provincial levels, *gubernatory* above them, reporting to the Justice College.[56] As for cities, in 1727 *gubernia* authorities once again took over urban government, including the magistracies' broad judicial competence. The collegial principle of governance and adjudication was abandoned, which Anisimov labels a tragedy, considering it a bulwark against autocratic domination.[57]

By 1727 the spirit of enlightened change infusing the 1719 "Instruction to Governors" had disappeared. While the 1719 Instruction ordered governors to found schools, hospitals and charitable institutions, its 1728 counterpart restricted governors to a Muscovite-like focus on public order, tax collection and defense. This was a particularly unfortunate situation for criminal adjudication, as no viable administrative structure to carry out judicial work efficiently, promptly and ethically had been provided within a local governor's office. Over Peter the Great's reign the scope of governors' tasks had vastly expanded. Collection of the new poll tax, billeting of troops, recruitment, all other fiscal, military and administrative issues had multiplied in quantum ways, while staffing had been cut. By 1726 the number of central and local offices across the realm had multiplied to around 1,700, from around 360 in 1698; conversely, by 1726 there were half the number of civil servants as in 1698. The government had tried to make up the difference in two ways.

[55] Schmidt, *Sozialkontrolle*, 130–7, 154–5 and ch. 3F; Serov, *Sudebnaia reforma*, 201–5, 257–60, 268–70, 447–7; Anisimov, *Gosudarstvennye preobrazovaniia*, 128–9; Kosheleva, *Liudi*, 51–2, 318–21; Redin, *Administrativnye struktury*, ch. 4; Anan'ev, "Voevodskoe upravlenie," 5–7; LeDonne, *Absolutism*, 63–80; Eroshkin, *Ocherki*, ch. 4.

[56] Initial affirmation of Petrine judicial reforms: PSZ VII: no. 4785 (Sept. 1725); Got'e, *Istoriia oblastnogo upravleniia*, chs. 1–3. Some reforms abolished: PSZ VII: nos. 4929 (July 1726), 5017 (Feb. 1727), 5056 (April 1727) and 5069 (May 1727). PSZ VII: no. 5017, pt. 5 (1727). The 1727 structure consisted of 14 *gubernii*, 47 provinces and over 250 *uezdy*. Eroshkin, *Ocherki*, ch. 4. Bogoslovskii, *Oblastnaia reforma*, 246–56; Anisimov, *Gosudarstvennye preobrazovaniia*, 231–40; Wortman, "Peter the Great," 305–6.

[57] PSZ VII: no. 5142 (1727). Anisimov, *Gosudarstvennye preobrazovaniia*, 232. Separation of judicial and administrative was restored for Moscow in 1730 with the creation of Criminal and General Courts, but not throughout the realm: Schmidt, *Sozialkontrolle*, 168, 361–2.

First, Petrine offices had relied on the tried-and-true custom of recruiting locals into service: noblemen became *landraty* and *zemskie kommissary*, commoners became collection agents.[58] Second, salaried state workers were consistently underpaid. In early reforms, undersecretaries were to be paid annual salaries from chancery income. But at the same time, they were to provide their own ink, candles and sand (for blotting the page) and even firewood. The situation worsened: in 1715 land grants to bureaucrats were abolished, leaving only cash salaries; in turn, salaries stagnated as prices rose and inflation soared. Salaries for civil officials were lower by half or more compared to military pay and were paid irregularly, sometimes not at all. Pisar′kova eloquently describes how governors pleaded with Moscow to send salary for their poverty-stricken scribes. In this environment, adjudication could not compete; Got′e remarked that judicial work was just one of many jobs of the post-Petrine governor, not even distinguished by defined hours for court hearings or record books specifically for court cases.[59]

After Peter's death in 1725 the situation became even worse: cost-cutting measures deprived officials below heads and directors of the Colleges of salary, leaving them only the fees, upkeep and gifts given them by petitioners. Such reforms were accompanied with warnings to undersecretaries not to demand excess gifts and fees that were clearly unrealistic. S. M. Troitskii calls this situation "legalized bribery" and D. A. Redin argued that the government had "programmed the bureaucrats into criminals." He makes the intriguing argument that working in such conditions stimulated the corporate solidarity of local officialdom around their increased dependence on gifts and patronage (compared to Muscovite times). G. P. Enin has shown that gifts for upkeep to local officials – the *kormlenie* system – endured until Catherine the Great's time. Praising Catherine II's judicial reforms, the British traveler William Coxe in the 1790s put his finger on the problem: "she has increased the salaries of the judges, who before, from the narrowness of their income, were necessarily exposed to almost irresistible temptations from bribery."[60]

58 Pisar′kova, "Rossiiskaia biurokratiia," 2004 no. 1, pp. 18–19, 29–39. Reliance on selected: Pisar′kova, *Gosudarstvennoe upravlenie*, 116–23, 205–14.

59 Early reforms: PSZ IV: nos. 1833 and 1838 (1701), 1848 and 1954 (1704). Pay own supplies: PSZ IV: no. 1851 (1701); PSZ V: no. 2879 (1715). Pisar′kova, "Rossiiskaia biurokratiia," 2004 no. 2, pp. 3–10; Troitskii, *Russkii absoliutizm*, 253–67. Pisar′kova, *Gosudarstvennoe upravlenie*, 230–5; Anisimov, *Gosudarstvennye preobrazovaniia*, 83–5, 228–31, 237; Schmidt, *Sozialkontrolle*, 134–6; Bogoslovskii, *Oblastnaia reforma*, 519–20; Eroshkin, *Ocherki*, 143–5. Got′e, *Istoriia oblastnogo*, 388.

60 No more salary: PSZ VII: nos. 4897 (1726), 5039 (1727). Troitskii, *Russkii absoliutizm*, 253–67 (256); Redin, *Administrativnye struktury*, ch. 5; Enin, "Voevodskoe prazdnichnoe kormlenie." Coxe, *Travels into Poland, Russia*, III: 144.

The structure and provisioning of eighteenth-century government defeated the best efforts to govern well. The state was under-governed: while in 1698 there was one state employee for every 2,250 people, in 1726 it was one per 3,400.[61] These proportions continued to worsen as the century developed. Nor did civil service attract the professional cadres Peter had hoped for. The Russian nobility avoided it, especially in local government. No training was provided, and service as governors did not last long enough to develop judicial expertise. So Russia never developed a robust civil service professional elite that would have amassed social status and attendant political capital.[62] In structural foundations the quality of local government declined from Muscovite practice.

The general trend of early eighteenth-century judicial reforms was affirmed by the views of Ivan Pososhkov, a self-made man who presented to Peter the Great a treatise on economic reform in 1724. On the judiciary, Pososhkov ticked through many of the goals that bureaucratic reform had been pursuing since the seventeenth century: justice should be speedy, laws should be codified and composed anew to fit Russia's new circumstances, judges should be knowledgeable and impartial. He considered the role of judge and judicial staff to be a duty "above all other callings" and advocated for a professional, salaried staff, just as had Petrine decrees.[63] But Pososhkov's overall mercantilist goal of increasing Russia's wealth through reform points to the challenges Russia faced. The state did not devote the financial resources needed for the excellent goals devised by Peter's reformist bureaucrats.

Judicial work of the Petrine decades demonstrates the progress being made towards a more rational and orderly judicial process. Documents themselves, in their notebook form, distinctive hand and orderly format, project an image of rational, unemotional investigation. More broadly, by instituting a hierarchy of venues, a progressive appeals process, oversight of officials and review of capital sentences, Petrine reforms were institutionalizing the principle that deviance was punished, that the law was transparent and that it was wielded knowledgeably and equitably. In the 1720s Petrine judges were capable of excellent work. This is not to say

61 Pisar'kova, "Rossiiskaia biurokratiia," 2004 no. 1, p. 38.

62 Nobles' disdain: Givens, "Eighteenth-Century Nobiliary." Serov presents Peter's reforms in the light of later Russian reforms to the present day: *Sudebnaia reforma*, ch. 7.

63 Pososhkov, *Book of Poverty and Wealth*, ch. 3.

that the judicial apparatus was inexorably progressing from "personal" to "rational" justice. Criminal law practice continued to be a balanced mix of defined norms, prescribed procedure and orderly record-keeping with flexible adaptation of those norms and practices, skewed in unpredictable ways by the personalized interaction of governors (or judges in chanceries) with gift-giving communities. However discordant in terms of ideal types, this judicial system suited Russian conditions, and its weaker sides might have been gradually eliminated had the best of Petrine legal reforms endured – separating judicial from administrative, developing a professional judiciary and notarial class, fighting official corruption and strengthening local governance. With the radical retrenchment by 1727, however, that was not to be.

PART II

Punishment

Shifting from judicial procedure to punishment entails to some extent a shift in sources and mode of analysis. These chapters are grouped thematically; the first four (Chapters 9–12) focus on corporal punishment, in law and practice, relying primarily on the surveyed database of local court cases. Chapter 13 inaugurates discussion of capital punishment, establishing the rituals of execution for felony capital crime. Here, too, sources are primarily court cases. The remaining chapters (Chapters 14–18) take up the issue of capital punishment for highest crime – treason, heresy, witchcraft, official corruption – and range widely in sources and method. Mindful of the implicit comparative model of Foucauldian "spectacles of suffering," great attention is paid to the symbolism and ritual of these most serious executions. Court transcripts describing such executions are almost entirely lacking; indigenous accounts are also rare and many are in the form of tendentious and quasi-literary historical chronicles, by no means the equivalent of judicial procedure. They will be read critically. By the end of the seventeenth century foreigners and Russians left memoir accounts of rebellions and executions, which can be valuable sources once one has ascertained the author's stance and his access to the events described.

Exploring executions for riot opens up a new angle on the criminal law, inasmuch as rebels often justified their violence as directed against not the tsar, but on his behalf "lawfully" against "traitors." Rebellions often provide occasions not only of official punishment of rebels, but of the rebels' administering what to them was righteous and justified execution. In the most climactic moments of urban rebellion, crowd and sovereign were locked in a drama of chilling intensity. In surveying capital punishment for highest crime, these chapters do not pretend to chronicle every execution and uprising, but to analyze rituals of execution in the context of Muscovite concepts of justice and legitimacy, as well as in the broader European frame.

CHAPTER 9

Corporal punishment to 1648

Around 1649 a governor in Iakutsk asked guidance from the Siberian Chancery in a homicide case: a Russian had shot a Tunguz prince. In testimony the Russian pleaded self-defense, while the Tunguz community was demanding that he be handed over "to hang or kill" him. The village had rioted, killing eleven Russians. The Siberian Chancery responded that the guilty party should be punished according to Russian law: "he should be beaten on the rack in front of the son of the killed man, mercilessly, and be imprisoned until our order." The Chancery asked the governor to explain to the Tunguz community that "if he had planned this with intent, then he would be killed without mercy. But in an unintentional crime we sentence our Russian people to corporal punishment, we do not execute them. And even among the Tunguz, they don't give people who commit homicide without intent to the other side for execution."[1] Here, the Chancery asserted the state's monopoly of violence, prescribed a public spectacle of corporal punishment and applied the law as written, with one omission. It did not insist on compensation in cash or people to the family of the dead man as the law required. This case demonstrates many of the qualities of Muscovite corporal punishment – state's interest, publicity, flexible application of the law.

WHY PUNISH?

In the most fundamental sense, states punish crime because that is what states are supposed to do; they are the controllers of violence. The sovereign state, through its rulers and representatives, alone has the right to inflict harm on the body of the citizen. Each society decides norms of crime and forms of punishment, as well as other uses of state-sanctioned

[1] DAI III: no. 52 (1649).

violence. For long-term viability, states need to devise regimes of punishment that are socially accepted.

As for how society viewed punishment, in the absence of Muscovite sources, it is helpful to look comparatively. In Europe at this time, political treatises, broadsheets, verdicts, sermons and other narrative texts reflected on the implementation of state-sanctioned violence. From such sources Karl Wegert argued that in the early modern German territories, public punishments functioned as a form of social disciplining, but were accepted by the populace for their stabilizing effects. Punishment of heinous crimes – murder, robbery, witchcraft, infanticide – could be construed as expiatory moments when evil spirits embedded in the criminal were destroyed and God's disapproval of misbehavior was assuaged. In the words of Richard van Dülmen, punishment was justified by the goals of "atonement, reparation and deterrence . . . The punishment had to be equal in ferocity to the terrible damage the offence had inflicted." Punishment allowed the state to maintain the law, victims to be compensated and the community to be rebalanced. Discourses about deviance accustomed communities to accept corporal and capital punishment in the interest of local stability; forms of punishment fit local concepts of justice. As Wegert put it, criminal law imposed by the state "derives its *raison d'être* from society: laws which are in conflict with social norms will not survive."[2]

Such a perspective on punishment is useful to keep in mind in turning to Muscovite punishments. On the one hand, as in Europe, Muscovy's use of corporal punishment bespeaks the state's claim to social control. The 1497 Law Code, for example, did not allow a criminal to escape execution if his property were insufficient to pay his debts and court fees or to support victims of his crime; the state's interest in disciplining violent crime overcame a family's or community's interests. The intent was the same in stipulations forbidding parties to settle suits for capital crimes, even if the community wanted the perpetrator to survive to pay compensation.[3] On the other hand, punishment could serve a community's self-interest in ridding itself of the worst thieves, murderers and offenders.

[2] Wegert, "Social Context," 27–35 (26, 22). Van Dülmen, *Theatre of Horror*, 2–4. Both authors also stress the violence that ensued when communities objected to a public punishment.

[3] 1497 Law Code, arts. 8, 11 and 39: RZ II: 55, 59; repeated and expanded in 1550 Law Code, arts. 56, 59–61: RZ II: 107–8 and 1589 Law Code, arts. 108, 113–15: PRP IV: 426–8. Not settle felonies: August 1556 Decree, no. 17: PRP IV: 367; AAE I: no. 150, p. 120 (1509); PRP V: 335–6 (1624); PRP V: 237 (1646); Ulozhenie ch. 21: art. 31: RZ III: 234; 1669 Criminal Articles, art. 71: PRP VII: 421; PSZ II: no. 1289 (1688).

It is difficult to show empirically that Muscovite communities accepted the state's regime of punishment, since narrative sources are lacking. Arguing from absence, that no mention is made in Muscovy of unruly crowds protesting floggings and executions (as was common in early modern Europe) might suggest social acceptance. The fact that they did riot when state coercion seemed to them excessive suggests that they accepted a degree of state-sanctioned violence. That people of all social status across the realm sought redress in the criminal court might suggest that criminal justice satisfied popular expectations; similarly, that judges and communities reached accord in settlements, even in homicide cases, shows that the system provided justice. In this regard, the legal norm that the only people who were excluded from the community (they were denied "honor") were "thieves, robbers, arsonists and known criminals" because they were "evil people (*likhie liudi*)" is telling – it, too, suggests a convergence of state and people over harmful felonies.[4] Given that judges could not bring notorious local criminals to trial without community-recruited posses, guards and bailiffs, the crowd watching a local execution may well have approved of the punishment of people who had broken moral bonds in Muscovy's small-scale urban or rural communities. State-sanctioned punishment was coercive, of course, but it was carried out in a context of interaction between community and state.

PUNISHMENT IN THE LAW BEFORE 1649

Muscovite law codes until 1649 very gradually incorporated corporal and capital punishment.[5] In circulation in manuscript into the sixteenth century in Muscovy, the dyadic Rus′ Law (*Russkaia pravda*) focused on fines for compensation and did not invoke corporal punishment.[6] Even though the East Slavs were exposed to Roman law through Byzantine secular and canon law after Christianization, they adapted these codes by substituting monetary compensation for many harsh sanctions

4 No honor for thieves: 1589 Law Code, art. 71: PRP IV: 421.

5 In response to arguments that the Mongols imported brutality to Russia, historians note that corporal punishment went back to canon law of the Kievan period: Timofeev, *Istoriia*, pt. 2, ch. 1; Evreinov, *Istoriia*, 17–22. Kaiser describes a centuries-long progression towards physical sanctions: *Growth*, 86–93.

6 Kievan law as dyadic, compensatory: Kaiser, *Growth*, 3–17; Feldbrugge, *Law*, 80. Rare references to corporal punishment in tenth-century Rus′ treaties (using the verb *kaznit′*) show Greek influence: 911 treaty: Kaiser (trans. and ed.), *Laws of Rus′*, arts. 3, 4, p. 5; 944 treaty: arts. 5, 6, 12, pp. 10–11; Feldbrugge, *Law*, 106. Rus′ Law in use to sixteenth century: Hellie, "Russian Law," xviii.

(stoning, bodily mutilation, beheading). Such brutality was not encountered in Muscovite law until the seventeenth century.[7]

As with church codes, late fourteenth- and fifteenth-century codes from the city states of Novgorod and Pskov, which might have influenced Muscovite law, maintained the Rus′ Law's preference for compensating victims for loss or injury, saving corporal punishment for highest crime. The Pskov Judicial Charter, for example, mentioned corporal punishment only for arson, horse theft, treason, stealing from the fortress and a third arrest for theft, applying in these cases brutal norms from Byzantine law (*Procheiros nomos*). Similarly, the 1470s Novgorod Judicial Charter mentioned corporal punishment only once in forty-two articles. Chronicles relate many accounts where early Rus′ princes rejected corporal punishment, all the way up to Ivan III's skepticism about using the death penalty for heretics in 1503.[8]

While they did not make significant use of corporal punishment to assert state's interest, these two charters nevertheless advanced triadic principles, as they asserted their city's claim (and in the case of Novgorod, that of the newly imposed Muscovite governor) to collect fines and judges' fees for serious crimes.[9] From the late fourteenth century Muscovite criminal law also aggressively asserted the ruler's judicial authority, but remained cautious on capital and corporal punishment. Early administrative charters and the 1497 Law Code punished such crimes as wounding, homicide and insult to honor with fines to the victim and to the grand prince and fees for judicial services; they reserved corporal punishment for felonies. A mid-fifteenth-century criminal Writ on Homicide includes both fees for the prince's administration and corporal punishment.[10] The 1497 Law Code provides capital punishment only for the highest crime, using a list already encountered in the Pskov Judicial

[7] Benemanskii, *Zakon gradskii*, 147–57; Kaiser, *Growth*, 19–25; Weickhardt, "Pre-Petrine Law and Western Law" and "Canon Law"; Benemanskii, *Zakon gradskii*, 1–93.

[8] Pskov Judicial Charter, art. 8: Kaiser (trans. and ed.), *Laws of Rus′*, 88. Novgorod Charter, art. 10: ibid., 81. Chronicle accounts: Benemanskii, *Zakon gradskii*, 103–84, esp. 144–5, 152, 161–4; on Ivan III, 163.

[9] Triadic principles in Pskov charter: Kaiser (trans. and ed.), *Laws of Rus′*, arts. 7, 8, 27, 52, 96, 97, 117, 120, pp. 88, 91, 96, 102, 104–5; in Novgorod Charter: arts. 10, 33, 34, pp. 81, 84.

[10] 1397–8 Dvina Charter: Kaiser (trans. and ed.), *Laws of Rus′*, arts. 1–4, 6–8, 10, 12, 14–15, pp. 111–13; 1488 Beloozero Charter: arts. 1–4, 6–7, 9–10, 13–14, 16–19, 22–3, ibid., 122–6. Corporal punishment for felonies: 1397–8 Dvina Charter: ibid., art. 5, p. 112; 1488 Beloozero Charter, arts. 10, 20, 23: ibid., 124–6. "On homicide": ibid., arts. 3, 5, p. 115. In awarding judicial immunity to a monastery in 1423, Grand Prince Vasilii I reserved for himself criminal law ("homicide and robbery with material evidence"): PRP III: 98.

Charter (killing one's landlord, stealing church property, kidnapping, treason, arson, professional crime, perhaps spying and homicide).[11]

The ambiguity and paucity of terminology on corporal punishment also suggest its lesser importance in the law. The mid-fifteenth-century Writ on Homicide, for example, distinguishes between cases involving fines (*penoe delo*) and those involving punishment (*polichnoe*), but subsequent Muscovite law does not maintain this or any other such terminological distinction. Nor does Muscovite law adopt even the minimal specification of the late fourteenth- or early fifteenth-century Pskov Judicial Charter. There degrees of corporal punishment are recognized by mandating that judges should "punish according to the crime" (*kazniti po ego vine*); since the same verb (*kaznit'*) had been used since the tenth century to refer to both capital and corporal punishment, here execution was specified using the phrase "to deprive of life" (*zhivota ne dati*).[12] By contrast, fifteenth-century Muscovite codes provided no guidelines on severity of punishment, and only the 1497 Law Code distinguished the death penalty from corporal punishment by using the phrase "to punish with death-dealing punishment" (*kazniti smertnoiu kazn'iu*). The 1497 Code also added some clarity when it specified that "punishment in the marketplace" (*torgovaia kazn'*) meant "beat with a knout."[13] Nevertheless, the ambiguity in the use of *kaznit'* persisted in Muscovite law codes.

In sum, Muscovite codes until the mid sixteenth century used corporal and capital punishment only for the highest crimes. East Slavs and early Muscovite law rejected most penal standards of Roman law as represented in church codes. Muscovy's adoption of inquisitorial process and torture by the sixteenth century reflects some influence of the European revival of Roman law, but the brutal and mutilating punishments associated with it were not adopted until the seventeenth century. Until then, corporal punishment was balanced with other sanctions.

Brigandage charters of the mid sixteenth century showed the most direct reflection of revived Roman law standards in their prosecution of felonies – homicide and recidivist theft and robbery. They liberally

[11] Highest crime: 1497 Law Code, arts. 8–11, 13, 39: RZ II: 55, 56, 59. See commentary in PRP III: 380–4; Dewey, *Muscovite Judicial Texts*, 10; RZ II: 69–73.

[12] "On homicide": Kaiser (trans. and ed.), *Laws of Rus'*, art. 6, p. 115; Pskov Charter: arts. 7–8, p. 88. Alekseev, "'Zapis' chto tianet," 62.

[13] The mid-fifteenth-century "On homicide" simply speaks of the judge's right to "judge and punish" (*sudit' i kaznit'*); the 1488 Beloozero Charter speaks of corporal punishment as the criminal being "subject to punishment" (*byt' v kazne*): "On homicide," art. 3: Kaiser (trans. and ed.), *Laws of Rus'*, 115; 1488 Beloozero Charter, arts. 10, 20, 23; ibid., pp. 124–6. 1497 Law Code, arts. 8, 9, 11, 13, 39: RZ II: 55–6, 59; knouting: 1497 Law Code, art. 10: RZ II: 55.

prescribed torture and knouting and introduced the qualifier "merciless" in regard to corporal punishment (*kazniti bez milosti*), thereby establishing degrees of severity in flogging. They also applied corporal punishment to collaborators, empowering brigandage elders to knout and execute guilty criminals and those who harbored them. Criminal reputation and material evidence called for execution, but at the same time, as already discussed, the use of torture was safeguarded with graduated procedure.[14]

Policing officialdom was also early on the mind of the state; by the mid sixteenth century corporal punishment was deployed on officials. Whereas the 1497 Law Code had simply exhorted judicial officials to behave, sixteenth-century codes threatened knouting.[15] Using corporal punishment in about a quarter of its 100 articles, the 1550 Law Code focused particularly on the complementary goals of punishing corruption and defending the dignity of the court: those who testified falsely in court would suffer knouting in the marketplace (art. 99), while knouting and/or prison awaited those who falsely accused judges of corruption (art. 6, 8–11, 33, 34, 42) or filed frivolous suits (art. 7). But the 1550 Code also maintained traditions of compensation and flexibility for misdemeanor injury: it provided compensation according to the social status of the victim and the severity of the injury and allowed such suits to be amicably settled.[16] Individual decrees to the end of the sixteenth century threatened corporal punishment for crime affecting state interests, such as shirking military service.[17]

[14] Harsh punishment: 1539 Beloozero Charter, arts. 3–5: RZ II: 214. Material evidence and reputation: Jan. 1555 Felony Handbook, arts. 2–3: PRP IV: 356; 1555 Medyn Charter, art. 3: RZ II: 219–20. There is ambiguity in terminology in brigandage charters: in some, *kazniti* refers to execution: 1555 Medyn Charter, arts. 2, 5, 9: RZ II: 219–22 and commentary in PRP IV: 208, 397. Other usages suggest corporal punishment: 1555 Medyn Charter, art. 13: RZ II: 222; August 1556 Decree, arts. 4, 15: PRP IV: 365, 367; brigandage charters 1539–86: Iakovlev (ed.), *Namestnichie*, 54, 56–7, 59, 61, 63, 66, 72, 75, 81, 84.

[15] 1497 Law Code, arts. 1, 67: RZ II: 54, 62; 1539 Beloozero Charter, art. 8: RZ II: 215; 1555 Medyn Charter, art. 13: RZ II: 222; Jan. 1555 Felony Handbook, arts. 7–8, 13: PRP IV: 358–9; brigandage charters 1539–86: Iakovlev (ed.), *Namestnichie*, pp. 55, 57, 60, 62, 64, 73, 81, 87. "Merciless" introduced: August 1556 Decree, art. 15: PRP IV: 367.

[16] Corporal punishment 1550 Law Code, arts. 6–11, 33, 34, 42, 99: RZ II: 97–9, 102–4, 120. Misdemeanor assault: 1550 Law Code, arts. 25–6: RZ II: 101. Settling suits: 1497 Law Code, art. 53: RZ II: 61; 1550 Law Code, art. 31: RZ II: 102. The 1589 and 1606 Law Codes proposed somewhat harsher corporal punishment for highest crime, felonies and official corruption, but the former was only a northern regional code and the latter was not put into use: 1589 Law Code, arts. 102–3, 211, 217: PRP IV: 425, 440–1; 1606 Law Code, arts. 166, 168: PRP IV: 539–41; Hellie, "Russian Law," xxvii; Weickhardt, "Composite Law Code."

[17] Not reporting for duty: AMG I: no. 20; false customs and slavery documents: ZA, no. 28 (both 1557/8).

Law in the first half of the seventeenth century continued to use corporal punishment for serious crime,[18] but at the same time the Felony Chancery developed more nuanced standards for capital punishment. A law of 1625 declared only premeditated murder worthy of execution; for homicide committed without intent and without prior conspiracy, perhaps while drunk or in a brawl, the punishment was severe corporal punishment, usually knouting and, in the case of serfs, the killer and his family were to be handed over as compensation to the landlord of the murdered peasant. Subsequent law refined compensation for the dead man's debts and established fines instead of physical exchange of peasants. The Felony Chancery also modified corporal sanctions in a way in May 1637, when women condemned to death who were pregnant were allowed to wait out their delivery and nurse the child for six weeks before being executed.[19] Thus, through the mid seventeenth century Muscovite law exhibited a graduated range of punishments, enhancing corporal and capital punishment for crime that seriously injured the state's interest or communities.

CORPORAL PUNISHMENT

Muscovite corporal punishment was generally wielded by the terrible knout.[20] European travelers were fascinated and repelled at the brutality of the ordeal. Adam Olearius's classic description recounts how the victim was stripped to the waist and laid on the back of the executioner's helper. Once he was secured firmly with a rope, the executioner set to work. He

> retired a good three paces behind the offender and flailed as hard as he could with a long thick knout, making the blood gush forth freely after each stroke. To the end of this knout were attached three thongs made of hard, tanned elk hide, each the length of a finger, which cut like knives. (In this manner some persons whose crimes were great were beaten to death ... A servant of the court stood by and read from a paper the number of strokes each was to receive. When the

[18] Against selling taxable property: ZA, nos. 214 (1634), 235 (1636/7). Against selling self as slave: ZA, no. 258 (by 1638). Against gathering to carouse: PRP v: 342 (1627). Against fist fights: PRP v: 359 (1640). Against avoiding fire defense duty: PRP III: 344 (1629). Preceding laws, without corporal punishment: ZA, nos. 103 (1620/1), 115–16 (not before 1621/2), 137 (1624), 158 (by July 19, 1627), 163 (Dec. 19, 1627).

[19] Unintentional: PRP v: 204–5 (1625). Compensation for homicide: PRP v: 217–20 (1636), 228 (1640), 236 (1645), 232–5 (1641), 384–5 (1647); ZA no. 276 (1640). ZA no. 244 (1637).

[20] Knouting cited in 1497 Law Code, art. 10: RZ II: 55. Knouting: Sergeevskii, *Nakazanie*, 149–64; Timofeev, *Istoriia*, 150–63; Evreinov, *Istoriia*, 33–8; Shtamm, "Ugolovnoe pravo," in Nersesiants, *Razvitie*, 193–6; Schmidt, *Sozialkontrolle*, 382–3; Anisimov, *Dyba i knut*, 563–6.

prescribed number had been fulfilled, he cried *Pol'no!*, that is, 'Enough'! ... Their backs retained not so much as a finger's thickness of skin intact.[21]

In addition to the form that Olearius describes, victims could also be knouted "on the rack/trestle" (*na kozle*), a phrase first cited around the 1630s. No description survives, but the implication is that the individual was held immobile against a stand rather than a person.[22]

Punishments were done publically, with the stated intent of deterring onlookers from crime and perhaps to act out a ritual of atonement for the affected community. Both goals might be achieved by linking punishment to the location of the crime, an old tradition.[23] For example, because gentrymen and cossacks of Voronezh refused to obey the local governor in 1648, he was ordered to select the three or four most senior ("best") cossacks and beat them in front of his own office. More ominously, in 1648 in Ustiug and 1662 in Moscow rebels were hanged in these towns near the sites of rioting.[24] While the state was demonstrating impermissible behavior, communities might also have appreciated the exposure of the criminal, both as a way to identify him (one historian says public exposure in punishment was a form of "policing"[25]) and as a way to take satisfaction that deviant behavior was being atoned for and purged.

Exposure was certainly the goal in a common Muscovite criminal practice: flogging a criminal while leading him around the marketplace. First cited in the 1497 Law Code in a way that does not specify walking around (the punishment could have been done in a stationary place), by the 1620s sources refer to "punishment around the marketplace," indicating a procession.[26] Punishments in and around town squares and

[21] Olearius, *Travels*, 230–1. See also Fletcher, "Of the Russe," 176; Reitenfels, *Skazaniia*, 117; Neuville, *Curious and New Account*, 43; Crull, *Ancient and Present State*, 175; Perry, *State of Russia*, 218–19. In the 1790s William Coxe purchased a knout to bring home to England: Coxe, *Travels into Poland, Russia*, III: 120–2.

[22] No descriptions of "*na kozle*": PRP V: 259–60. Verdicts including it: AMG I: no. 531 (1633); Lipinskii (ed.), "Rospis'," nos. 1, 8, 13–14, 22, 32, 74, 86, 115, pp. 17–19, 21–2, 29, 31, 35 (1639–42); DAI III: no. 52 (1649).

[23] Deterrent intent: AAE III: nos. 40, 48 (1614). Benemanskii argues that the concept of deterrence by publicity comes from Byzantine law: *Zakon gradskii*, 200–1. To punish at the crime's location: 911 treaty, art. 4: Kaiser (trans. and ed.), *Laws of Rus'*, 5; Benemanskii, *Zakon gradskii*, 286–8.

[24] Voronezh: AMG II: no. 312 (1648). Ustiug: Chistiakova, *Gorodskie vosstaniia*, 190–202 (1648); Bazilevich, *Gorodskie vosstaniia*, 135–65; Zertsalov, "K istorii miatezha 1648 goda," 32–3. Moscow: *Vosstanie 1662 g.*, no. 82 (1662).

[25] Boes, "Public Appearance," 272–4.

[26] "Marketplace punishment" (*torgovaia kazn'*): 1497 Law Code, art. 10: RZ II: 55; early sixteenth-century chronicle (Sofiia II): PSRL VI: 238 (6996); 1550 Law Code, arts. 5, 6, 8, 32: RZ II: 97–8, 102; PRP IV: 539 (1559); ZA, no. 42 (1582). Moving "through the marketplace": AMG I, nos. 161 (1623), 593 (1633); AAE III, no. 266 (1637).

marketplaces had precedent in medieval and early modern European practice. Jason Coy, describing criminal cases in sixteenth-century Ulm, found mobile floggings common, usually combined with expulsion from the city (a penalty not used in Muscovy): criminals were "beaten through the streets of the town from the town hall to one of the city gates." Paul Griffiths, studying criminal verdicts in early modern Norwich, found public punishments, including "whippings from one end of the market to the other," "usually timetabled to meet a rush of people and traffic into markets in a neat fusion of weekly routine and the correction of anti-civic acts." The paths taken for such whippings, he notes, often paralleled the routes of "major civic parades," or could stop at pubs and city landmarks to maximize the criminal's exposure to the people. In eighteenth-century London, according to Robert Shoemaker, the routes of public whippings often began or ended near the scene of the crime.[27]

The humiliation of such punishments was often, in Europe and in Muscovy, heightened by shaming gestures. In Europe, criminals were displayed in pillories or cages or they were flogged wearing around their necks the objects they stole or something symbolic of them. Placards describing the crimes were often displayed near the spot of a stationary punishment.[28] In Muscovy, foreigners reported the same customs. Olearius reports that "each of the [illegal] tobacco sellers had a paper of tobacco hung around his neck, and the [illegal] traders in vodka a bottle." Jacques Margeret says that when a scribe found guilty of taking bribes was beaten, "a purse full of money is hung around his neck. And it is the same with all other things, for if they have taken furs, pearls, or anything whatsoever, including salted fish, this is usually hung around the guilty one's neck when he is beaten." One should not underestimate the importance of such publicity: Paul Griffiths argues that executions were rare in most small towns, so such punitive displays were the primary locus for the state to broadcast its power.[29]

Muscovite judges took full advantage of the public humiliation involved in leading a victim through a bustling city center, often specifying in verdicts that the punishment should be carried out "on market days."

[27] Coy, *Strangers and Misfits*, 46–8; Griffiths, "Bodies and Souls in Norwich," 91–92; Shoemaker, "Streets of Shame?," 234.

[28] Pillories: Coy, *Strangers and Misfits*, 47–8. Wearing objects: Griffiths, "Bodies and Souls in Norwich," 92. Placards: Shoemaker, "Streets of Shame?," 233–4; Griffiths, "Bodies and Souls in Norwich," 92.

[29] Olearius, *Travels*, 231. Margeret, *Russian Empire*, 28–9. Griffiths, "Bodies and Souls in Norwich," 86–7.

The governors of Tobol′sk in the 1640s used symbolic geography in sentencing criminals to being beaten while being "led through the marketplace" (*po torgom v provodku*); they sometimes extended the route. Two merchants from Bukhara, convicted of theft of property and money in June 1640, for example, were sentenced to be "beaten with a knout while being led through the market stalls and the Tatar yurts"; this route was also prescribed for two Tatar women convicted of sexual crime and assault in May 1641. A man in Tobol′sk sentenced to exile for theft in June 1642 was to be "knouted through the stalls, the marketplace and at the foot of the hill where the boats dock" before he was taken away.[30]

Muscovite law employed a few other types of punishment – public beatings for debtors (*pravezh*) are the closest thing to stocks and pillories. In the early seventeenth century, another form of flogging that flayed the skin less brutally than the knout appeared – bastinadoes (*batogi*).[31] Described by the French mercenary Jacques Margeret, writing around 1606, as "rods the thickness of a finger," bastinadoes could be made harsher by stripping the victim of his shirt. Although when bastinadoes emerged in law codes, they were to be used "mercilessly," in practice they were less damaging. In a case of 1689, for example, the verdict specifically states that being beaten mercilessly by bastinadoes was a mercy in place of a beating by knout "on the rack."[32]

The publicity of corporal punishment also humiliated the victim, even though Muscovy did not have as formal a discourse of shame around corporal punishment and executioners as did Europe. Litigations over insult to honor, for example, rarely involved allegations of past corporal punishment as an insult. Foreigners with first-hand knowledge of Muscovy were scandalized by this. In the early seventeenth century Olearius confidently asserted that "formerly those subjected to such punishment [knout] were afterward treated as well as anyone else; others spoke, ate, and drank with them as they pleased. Now, however, these people are considered

30 "On market day": PSZ II: no. 1192 (1686). Tobol′sk: Lipinskii (ed.), "Rospis′," nos. 37 and 29; Bukhara: no. 25; Tatar women: no. 48; Tobol′sk man: no. 98.

31 Dewey and Kleimola, "Coercion by Righter." Bastinadoes: AAE III: nos. 40, 48 (1614); AMG II: no. 102 (1615); RGADA f. 1107, nos. 514 (1620) and 871, fol. 3 (1639); AAE III: no. 132 (1623); AMG I: nos. 233, 236 (1629). First reference in a decree is 1636/7: ZA no. 235. The singular "*batog*" is cited in Kievan sources: SRIa I: 79.

32 Margeret, *Russian Empire*, 64; see also Olearius, *Travels*, 230. Descriptions: Sergeevskii, *Nakazanie*, 164–8; Anisimov, *Dyba i knut*, 576; Evreinov, *Istoriia*, 38–40; Timofeev, *Istoriia*, 180–4; Shtamm, "Ugolovnoe pravo," in Nersesiants, *Razvitie*, 195; Schmidt, *Sozialkontrolle*, 383. Olearius provides an illustration: *Vermehrte Newe Beschreibung*, 112. Without shirt: AMG I: no. 236 (1629); KV IV: no. 125 (1672). "Bare bastinadoes" probably means bare back: DAI XI: no. 17 (1684). Bastinadoes instead of knout: PSZ II: no. 1359 (1689).

somewhat disgraced." But other foreigners disagree: later in that century Jacob Reutenfels commented with surprise that even a boyar had been knouted for the crime of rape, while John Perry, writing in the first decade of the eighteenth century, observed the same: "After their being beat with the Batoags or Knout, tho done by the Hands of a common Hangman, there is no mark of Infamy set upon them for it; there is nothing more ordinary in Russia than to have them afterwards be again admitted into Places of Honour and Truth."[33] Nevertheless, in Muscovy some shame was clearly involved in public punishments; one sixteenth-century chronicle speaks of "the shame of marketplace punishment,"[34] and social deference in punishment discussed below suggests the same. Corporal punishment was a language that spoke many messages to the observing public.

GRADATIONS: RECIDIVISM AND SOCIAL DEFERENCE

In punishing felony theft and robbery, Muscovite law displayed a three-step graduated scale common to Byzantine law and in European *ius commune*.[35] The Dvina Administrative Charter of 1397–8 suggested monetary compensation for a first theft; for the second arrest, the guilty party is to be sold into slavery; for a third, he is to be hanged. The Pskov Judicial Charter proposed unspecified corporal punishment for two thefts, execution for the third. The 1497 and 1550 Law Codes shortened the ladder to two steps: for a first theft, flogging; for a second, execution. But the Felony Chancery returned to a three-step ladder in mid-sixteenth-century brigandage charters: for a first theft, knouting; for a second, bodily mutilation (severing a hand), prison or banishment and knouting; for a third, execution. The Felony Chancery maintained this ladder in early seventeenth-century handbooks (for references, see Appendix). [36]

Brigandage charters prescribed corporal punishment for corrupt officials regardless of social status, but otherwise laws evidence a de facto deference to social class. In the 1550 Law Code, for example, for taking bribes or

[33] Timofeev, *Istoriia*, 77–9; Kollmann, *By Honor Bound*, 47–8. Olearius, *Travels*, 231; Reitenfels, *Skazaniia*, 117; Perry, *State of Russia*, 218.

[34] Shame (*soromotiti torgovoiu kazn'iu*): PSRL XIII, 1st half, p. 118 (7045).

[35] Byzantine law: Benemanskii, *Zakon gradskii*, 169. *Ius commune*: Bellomo, *Common Legal Past of Europe*. On Russia's expanding "ladder of recidivism," see Appendix.

[36] Influence of Byzantine law: Benemanskii, *Zakon gradskii*, 153; 1555 Medyn Charter, art. 11: RZ II: 222; brigandage charters 1539–86: Iakovlev (ed.), *Namestnichie*, 66–7, 73, 86. Bodily mutilation was not, however, practiced until the second half of the seventeenth century (see Chapter 11). A Polish observer commented on graduated penalties: Floria, "S. Nemoevskii," 109–10.

excessive fees or carrying out official duties corruptly, judges and officials were to be punished with fines, "great disgrace (*velikaia opala*)" or were to await the tsar's further decree. But for similar offenses, lesser people suffered the lash. For taking a bribe and other official corruption, secretaries were imprisoned and undersecretaries and lesser officials knouted in the marketplace and often fined or imprisoned. Similarly, monetary compensation for insult to honor was graduated according to social status.[37] A court case of 1599/1600 shows deference in practice: when a local judiciary staff was found guilty of bribery, governor Prince Ivan Deev and his secretary were sentenced to disgrace, but their undersecretary was corporally punished.[38] Such provisions continued into the seventeenth century, as before, drawing the line (eventually) at felony crime. One norm held that if a gentryman and his people were accused of felony crime, his people were to be tortured first. Only if they implicated their master were they to be tortured. A decree of 1628 allowed a high-ranking person who had given surety to an absconded criminal to substitute one of his own slaves or peasants for a torture session aimed at finding the criminal's whereabouts. A 1627 verdict, however, affirms that social deference was not absolute. The governor in Ustiug Velikii asked his Moscow chancery whether corporal punishment for the crime of lewd living could be given to a man who was a locally selected judge (*zemskoi sudeika*). Moscow affirmed that the judge could be beaten with bastinadoes. That corporal punishment was generally associated with lower social rank is evident in a ruling of 1647, which substituted merciless beating with bastinadoes for a cash fine if a person were too poor to pay.[39] Thus, on the eve of the 1649 Ulozhenie, Muscovite criminal law deployed corporal and capital punishment for a wide range of high crime, felonies and official corruption. But it also included graduated sanctions and social deference, and few limitations and much discretion to judges about degrees of severity. The law, in other words, even for punishment, allowed judges flexibility.

[37] 1550 Law Code, arts. 3–5, 7–11, 28, 32–4, 47, 53–4: RZ II: 97–9, 101–3, 105–7. 1550 Law Code on dishonor, art. 26: RZ II: 101. Corporal punishment for insult to honor is cited in a decree of 1582 (ZA no. 42), but it was not affirmed by the 1589 Law Code, which maintained fines (arts. 41–72: PRP IV: 419–21).

[38] *Opis' arkhiva 1626*, pt. 1, pp. 261–2 (1599/1600). Social deference in late sixteenth-century law: ZA no. 42 (1582); 1589 Law Code, arts. 3–4, 8, 102–3, 123, 126, 211, 217: PRP IV: 413–14, 425, 428–9, 440–1.

[39] Torture peasants first: 1616/17 Felony Handbook, arts. 16–17: PRP V: 192–3. PRP V: 205–6 (162). "Sud voevody nad zemskim"(1627). Timofeev, *Istoriia*, 67–8 (1647); similar ruling: PSZ II: no. 1238 (1687).

PUNISHMENT IN PRACTICE BEFORE 1649

The few surviving sixteenth-century cases show restraint in the use of corporal punishment. In an interesting case of 1503 in which a peasant was found guilty of starting a fire intentionally, he was punished only with a fine and reparations, rather than with the execution decreed by the 1497 Law Code for arson.[40] Similarly, although the 1497 code allowed the death sentence for homicide and no norms as yet mitigated punishment according to intent, in a case of death in a brawl in 1525, the grand prince's judges levied only a compensatory fine. A complex case in June 1547 involving a false suit, runaway slaves and theft resulted only in restoration of the runaway to his owner and payment of damages, while the 1497 Law Code would have prescribed a knouting for a first theft.[41] As detailed in Chapter 7, cases of homicide were settled despite laws against it.

Judges adhered to the outlines, if not the letter, of the law. In a 1503 case of a felony theft (*tat'ba*) of hay, the defendant testified that he had already been found guilty in a previous theft and had been knouted for that offense. The judge then sentenced him to be punished "according to the law code" (*sudebnik*), not specifying the punishment (if the court followed the 1497 Law Code for a second theft, the punishment should have been execution).[42] With regard to bribery, corporal punishment was threatened (when the 1550 Law Code prescribed fines) in a case of plundering, robbing and murder of 22 people in autumn 1572 in Kolomna province. Here the Felony Chancery warned the officer in charge that he would suffer "great disgrace and corporal punishment" if he took bribes or favored any suspects during the investigation. A case in 1623 used corporal punishment in defending the tsar's dignity: a musketeer in Oskol mentioned the tsar in conversation without using his full name and title. The musketeer's punishment was in line with the 1550 Law Code on official corruption: a merciless marketplace knouting and prison time. Conversely, for falsely accusing someone of treason in 1629, a foreigner in Russian service was ordered to be beaten with bastinadoes "mercilessly, with his shirt off," to deter others, plus to be imprisoned for a week, while the 1550 law decreed execution for false accusation. Even more leniently, a non-Russian and cossack community in Borisov – 100 men in all – in 1636

[40] A collection of twenty-five memos from Moscow to the governor of Novgorod from 1555–6 includes theft, assault, homicide and debts, but none with resolution: DAI 1: no. 51, pp. 72–85. 1503 arson: AIu no. 10 (1503).

[41] AIu nos. 17 (1525) and 22 (1547). On first theft, see Appendix.

[42] Kashtanov, *Ocherki russkoi diplomatiki*, 409–14 (1503).

accused a village administrator (*prikaznoi*) of extortion, beatings and inappropriate demands. Their complaints elicited a surprisingly mild response: the administrator was only warned not to oppress the people.[43]

As these cases would lead one to suspect, even when judges punished homicide and major felonies, they took their own course with the law. So, for example, in a case of 1613, a peasant who was found guilty of killing another peasant with no premeditation was sentenced "according to the tsar's order and according to the law" to a marketplace knouting and to having his hand cut off. He was also ordered to pay cash compensation to the family and court fees and to gather signatories for a bond guaranteeing his future good behavior. What norm the judge was using is unclear, since none of the previous "Law Codes" (1497, 1550, 1589, 1606) prescribed bodily mutilation for homicide; perhaps not surprisingly, in the end, the judge canceled the bodily mutilation, announcing the tsar's "favor."[44]

Similarly flexible was the Beloozero governor's verdict in a 1620 case in which a Beloozero townsman was stabbed to death by a peasant of the St. Cyril Beloozero Monastery. Apparently judging it unintentional even before the 1625 decree on that issue, the governor sentenced the man to marketplace knouting. The 1625 law cited drunkenness as a likely justification for unintentional homicide; this was probably the norm applied by judges of the Siberian Chancery in a 1643/4 case involving the slave of a local cossack who had killed his wife. Under torture he admitted the crime, but testified that he had been so drunk that he did not remember anything. The Chancery ordered a merciless marketplace knouting and imprisonment "until the tsar's order." In this case the issue of compensation for the dead laborer would not apply, as the murder was done within the same landlord's community.[45] Conversely, a case of 1647 applied that provision of the 1625 law: when a peasant in Livni killed his landlord's cousin, a gentryman, the Military Service Chancery ruled that the killer should be given with his wife, children and all his property to the brother of the dead man as compensation; his landlord was told to pay the tsar's fine (*pennye dengi*).[46]

[43] AIuB II: no. 230 (II) (1572); 1550 Code, art. 3: RZ II: 97. AMG I: nos. 161 (1623) and 236 (1629); 1550 Law Code, art. 59: RZ II: 108. AMG II: no. 58 (1636).

[44] RGADA f. 1107, no. 19 (1613). Perhaps this judge had in mind the 1555 Medyn Charter that decreed knouting and cutting off a hand for a second theft, a ruling repeated in a "Law Code of Tsar Fedor Ivanovich" cited after 1605 and in the 1616/17 Felony Handbook; for references, see Appendix.

[45] RGADA f. 1107, no. 514 (1620). Siberia: "Uboistvennye dela," no. 3 (1643–4).

[46] RGADA f. 210, Prikaznyi stol, no. 182, fols. 398–9 (1647).

In addition to brigandage felonies, many (twenty-four) of a group of approximately seventy resolved criminal cases surveyed here concern state's interests construed broadly from treason to shirking military service. This is not surprising, since following the Time of Troubles (1598–1613) the Muscovite state engaged in repeated conflicts with Sweden and the Grand Duchy of Lithuania to regain lost territory. Tremendous anxiety was expressed about the security of the border in the 1620s and 1630s. In several instances of flight across the border, individuals were punished with sanctions ranging from Siberian exile to hanging; for giving false information to border governors, knouting was ordered in cases of 1622 and 1627.[47]

Corporal punishment was liberally dispensed in cases involved with mobilizing the army. Even men of gentry status were flogged for not reporting for service: two men of fairly high Moscow rank (*zhil'tsy*) in Kolomna were ordered beaten with bastinadoes mercilessly in 1615; two gentrymen in Voronezh were ordered beaten in 1622 with bastinadoes – one to be beaten "*bol'no*" (painfully) and the other "so harshly that it would be as if by knout" – in front of people to deter others from doing likewise.[48] In 1633 a marketplace knouting was decreed for local gentrymen who had fled service from Galich and Belaia, but any official who had not effectively chased down these no-shows would suffer only three days in prison or "great disgrace" – social deference again. These patterns continued during and after the Smolensk War (1632–4). In 1634, for example, gentrymen who failed to show for service were ordered beaten with a knout in the marketplace; bastinadoes were decreed for the governor of Rzhev, Prince Vasilii Fedorovich Mortkin, for not making an effort to collect and send these men to service – a harsh punishment for a man of high status. "Great disgrace and corporal punishment" were also threatened to the governor sent to replace Mortkin for failure to act.[49]

Military service was also at issue in cases against peasants who failed to perform labor services and pay fees for provisioning troops. A wide range of offenses that impeded the state's fiscal interests also called forth

[47] 1621 fleeing border: AAE I: nos. 310 (1581); AMG I: nos. 137 (1621), 144 (1621), 145 (1621), 147 (1622), 155 (1622), 197 (1627).

[48] AMG II: no. 102 (1615). AMG I: no. 148 (1622). Other punishments for fleeing service: musketeer bastinadoed: AMG I: no. 168 (1623); gentrymen bastinadoed and knouted: AMG I: nos. 222, 233, 247 (all 1629).

[49] AMG I: nos. 593, 596 (1633) and 604–5 (1634). Other punishment for fleeing service (all in AMG 2): Kolomna gentryman absent four years: no. 83 (1637); serving peasants knouted: no. 110 (1637); Smolensk soldiers sell selves to slavery, bastinadoed: no. 184 (1640); cossacks bastinadoed: no. 312 (1648).

corporal punishment: not paying customs fees, cutting down the tsar's forest reserves, not performing swornman duties, claiming to be a high-born man's servant rather than a tax-paying serf.[50] In the first reference to bastinadoes in our cases, a representative group of peasants of Cherdyn′ in 1614 were ordered bastinadoed mercilessly and imprisoned for a month since the whole village had refused to carry out its service obligations to the tsar. Meanwhile the neighboring governor of Perm, Lev Il′ich Volkov, who was found to have supported this community in its disobedience, lost his job, forfeited two years of pay and was put "in great disgrace."[51] Thus common patterns persisted: corporal punishment for lower-class individuals and serious but not corporal sanctions for officials in the fight against state crime.

M. A. Lipinskii's publication of a register listing the resolutions of about 158 cases that involved corporal "punishment" (*nakazanie*) in Tobol′sk from 1639 to 1643 provides a fascinating glimpse of the law in practice.[52] The entries are brief, but they identify the crime, the social status of plaintiff and defendant and the punishment. These cases were done on site by a collegial team of two governors (Prince Peter Ivanovich Pronskoi and Fedor Ivanovich Lovchikov) and two secretaries (Ivan Trofimov and Andrei Galkin). They include misdemeanors, official corruption, insult to the court, witchcraft, even allegations of treason. Since for many of the cases statutes did not provide an exact guide, the judges used their judgment, taking into consideration factors such as social rank, severity of the crime and recidivism; they never cite the law they applied.

Tobol′sk's judges used the knout most often, in about half of their verdicts (82 in a collection of 167 individual verdicts in 158 cases). In another thirty-five cases bastinadoes were used. Fines were the sole verdict in another thirty-three instances, as well as being the general punishment for not declaring and paying taxes on homebrew (section 2 of Lipinskii's cases). Prison terms of a day to several days were ordered in fifteen cases; in two more cases, people were banished from town. In assigning knoutings, judges often specified the degree of severity: in eighteen cases knouting was to be done "on the rack," but the most common form was flogging as the

[50] Customs fees: AAE III: no. 132 (1623); forest reserves: AMG II: no. 135 (1638); swornman: AAE III: no. 313 (1642); false status: AMG II: no. 193 (1642).

[51] AAE III: nos. 40 and 48 (1614). Other examples of non-gentry punished (all in AMG I): Riazhsk peasants bastinadoed for not doing siege duty and fortifications repair: no. 372 (1632); Rzhev peasants knouted for fleeing service: no. 623 (1634); Riazhsk official bastinadoed and imprisoned for not delivering orders: no. 278 (1630).

[52] Lipinskii (ed.), "Rospis′."

prisoner was being led through a public place. Bastinadoes were used as a mercy "instead of the knout," but often wielded "mercilessly." The judges sentenced men and women, Tatars and Russians, peasants and gentrymen, to knouting and bastinadoes, discriminating by the severity of the offense rather than by gender, ethnicity or social status. So, for example, a wife of a Tobol′sk infantry cossack was knouted in the marketplace for leaving her husband; a wife of another infantry cossack was knouted being led through the rows of shops for prostitution.[53]

About forty of these cases protect the dignity of the court: undersecretaries who incorrectly wrote the tsar's title in a document were beaten with bastinadoes "instead of by knout mercilessly." False allegations of "word and deed" (the 1550 Law Code prescribed execution for slander) called for various harsh punishments: merciless beating with bastinadoes for an unregistered man; knouting on the rack for a Tobol′sk infantry cossack (who said he made the allegation while drunk), for a peasant and for a slave.[54] For the "impoliteness" of calling the judge's court a "Shemiakin court," that is, corrupt, beating with bastinadoes was ordered for a sharecropper of a Tobol′sk gentryman, while two officers of the infantry cossacks were sent to prison for a day for bursting into the governor's office "rudely with great noise and petitioning to the Sovereign about guard service."[55]

As noted elsewhere, higher-ranking officials generally were given less harsh sanctions for minor crimes. For example, a Tobol′sk gentryman was imprisoned for a day for using troops to do personal work for him. A group of more than thirty officers and serving men – "men from the Grand Duchy of Lithuania, mounted cossacks and newly converted and serving Tatars from the yurts" – were imprisoned overnight (*na sutki*) for returning from an assignment without a formal report. But men of higher ranks did suffer corporal punishment if the crime affected state authority or income. A Tobol′sk gentryman and two servitors were beaten with bastinadoes for taking a bribe from a woman not to report her illegal tobacco sale, while for bribery a group of four – the leader (*ataman*) of the infantry cossacks, a swornman who was a Tobol′sk townsman and two infantry cossacks – were ordered to repay the money and knouted through the rows of shops (until the punishment was commuted through the

[53] Cossack wife: Lipinskii (ed.), "Rospis′," no. 39, p. 23; prostitute: no. 67, p. 27.

[54] Undersecretaries and title: Lipinskii (ed.), "Rospis′," no. 10, p. 19 and no. 24, p. 21; word and deed: no. 45, p. 24. Knoutings: infantry cossack: no. 102, p. 33; peasant: no. 53, p. 25; slave: no. 82, p. 30.

[55] Shemiakin: Lipinskii (ed.), "Rospis′," no. 116, p. 35; rudely: no. 19, p. 20.

intercession of the Archbishop; then, they paid only fines). These rulings for bribery were in line with the 1550 Law Code.[56]

Tobol′sk judges also corporally punished gentrymen and other servitors if their crime had to do with military service. A group of four Tatars who had fled service were beaten with bastinadoes, and a musketeer and infantry cossack were both knouted in the marketplace for fleeing service. Several infractions concerned prison and its staff, who were not high-ranking men. Three prison guards who released convicts without permission were knouted on the rack, as was a prison swornman who allowed prisoners to gamble in prison.[57] Judges punished sexual crime harshly. Although rape was traditionally included in church law codes, in Muscovite practice it was handled by secular courts, most likely because rape involved physical assault; Petrine law formally legislated this practice. Tobol′sk judges treated it as serious assault. For the forcible kidnapping and rape of a Tatar woman by a Tobol′sk gentryman, they prescribed bastinadoes; for rape of a slave girl by two other slaves, a marketplace knouting; for kidnapping and rape of a servant girl, a servitor of the Ketskoi fortress was sentenced to knouting on the rack and in the marketplace (*na kozle i po torgom*).[58]

Tobol′sk's judges considered several cases of homicide insufficient for the death penalty; they levied corporal punishment and fines, but rarely more compensation than that. A peasant who killed another peasant in 1640 paid the tax for a dead body and was ordered knouted while being led through the rows of shops and the marketplace; he also was put on surety bond. According to the 1625 law, he and his family should have been given as compensation to the landlord of the dead peasant, but this was not mentioned. The same resolution is seen in another case of a peasant killing a peasant of 1641.[59] Tobol′sk's judges dealt with misdemeanors and felony theft somewhat more leniently than did sixteenth-century codes. For misdemeanor robbery (*grabezh*) by two men of another (all three were of the "unregistered" status), they appropriately ordered marketplace beating. But in a case of recidivist felony theft, two men – a

[56] Using troops: Lipinskii (ed.), "Rospis′," no. 75, p. 29; not filing report: no. 78, pp. 29–30; tobacco bribe: no. 5, p. 18; leader, swornman: no. 28, pp. 39–40. 1550 Law Code on bribery, arts. 32, 53: RZ II: 102, 107.

[57] Tatars fled: Lipinskii (ed.), "Rospis′," no. 101, p. 33; musketeer, cossack: no. 20, p. 20; prison guards: no. 1, p. 17 and no. 12, p. 19; gamble in prison: no. 22, p. 21.

[58] Levin, *Sex and Society*, ch. 5, 212–46; Kollmann, "Women's Honor" and *By Honor Bound*, 72–5. Rape as secular crime in 1715 Military Articles, nos. 167–8: RZ IV: 359. Tatar woman: Lipinskii (ed.), "Rospis′," no. 3, p. 17; slave girl: no. 38, p. 23; servant girl: no. 51, p. 25.

[59] Peasants 1640: Lipinskii (ed.), "Rospis′," no. 33, p. 22; peasants 1641: no. 46, p. 24.

blacksmith of the archbishop's properties and an unregistered man – were spared the worst of sixteenth-century codes (execution according to the 1550 Law Code or knouting, bodily mutilation or execution in brigandage charters). Instead they were ordered tortured and knouted while being led through rows of shops; the unregistered man was put on surety bond, but the blacksmith was imprisoned "because he had been involved in previous crimes, in felony theft already."[60]

Tobol′sk's judges did not shirk from using the knout in non-felony crime, deploying it for fighting in prison, gambling, attacking, oppressing and harming a tribute-paying Tatar community.[61] Knouting in the marketplace or in the stalls was decreed for such crimes as tobacco use and sale, regardless of social rank: cases include musketeers, townsmen, cossacks, merchants, men and women. In one case of the illegal sale of tobacco, two men were knouted not only being led through the marketplace and the stalls, but also on the rack in front of the governor's office; this is probably because the guilty men were indentured servants of two of the judges themselves – Governor Prince Pronskoi and secretary Galkin.[62] Tobol′sk's judges, however, deployed bastinadoes for a range of crimes or circumstances that they considered less serious, including stealing a boat and fishing for sturgeon (a tsarist monopoly) and taking in stolen goods (which should have brought a knouting or execution, according to one brigandage charter).[63]

Tobol′sk's judges treated leniently a handful of very serious cases – church theft and witchcraft. Regarding a sexton of the Ascension church who had been arrested for stealing undisclosed items from the Trinity church, they put him through torture, followed by a month in prison. He was then released on surety bond, after being knouted while led through the stalls, despite the fact that since the 1497 Law Code church theft had been a capital crime. Similarly, regarding the potentially capital crime of witchcraft, they chose lesser sentences: a widow was tortured in suspicion of having hexed a slave of the Stroganov family and was ultimately sentenced to exile to Tara; an unregistered man was knouted in the stalls and in the marketplace for having "sorcerous (*volshebnoe*)" letters.[64]

60 Unregistered men: Lipinskii (ed.), "Rospis′," no. 12, p. 19; blacksmith: no. 59, p. 26. 1550 Code and brigandage charters, see Appendix.
61 Lipinskii (ed.), "Rospis′," no. 14, p. 19; no. 16, p. 20; no. 22, p. 21; no. 25, p. 21.
62 Tobacco use: Lipinskii (ed.), "Rospis′," no. 41, p. 24; no. 55, p. 26; no. 56, p. 26; no. 61, p. 27; judges' servants: no. 62, p. 27.
63 Lipinskii (ed.), "Rospis′," no. 114, p. 35; no. 99, p. 32. Stolen goods in 1539 Beloozero Charter, art. 3: RZ II: 214.
64 Sexton: Lipinskii (ed.), "Rospis′," no. 30, p. 22; widow: no. 64, p. 27; letters: no. 118, p. 35.

Conversely the Tobol′sk judges' punishments for insult to honor and minor injury went beyond the fines that the 1550 and 1589 Law Codes allowed. A public scribe assaulted the governor's undersecretary as he was inspecting illegal brewing, beating him and ripping his clothing, "by which he insulted [judges] governor Prince Peter Ivanovich Pronskoi and colleagues." The scribe was ordered knouted among the stalls, fined the undersecretary's dishonor fee and told to reimburse him for the cloak. This ruling of November 1641, with its combination of corporal punishment and fine calculated on the annual salary, parallels the norms of the future 1649 Ulozhenie.[65]

All in all, in the Tobol′sk collection of cases by the same judicial team over a compact set of years, the same flexible patterns of corporal punishment seen in more geographically scattered cases recur. Tobol′sk's judges' frequent resort to the knout was supported by the law, which to this point had barely mentioned other punishments. They discriminated among sanctions, often ruling more leniently than written law. Even as far away as Tobol′sk (about 1,400 miles by road from Moscow), Felony Chancery norms were applied with respect but flexibility.

Clearly physical violence was one of the tools with which the Muscovite state governed. But one should recall that many of the sources discussed in this chapter are laws threatening violence, and previous chapters have suggested the many considerations that kept local judges from implementing the full force of the law (as Tolbol′sk judges show). The state continued, however, to rely on violence and perhaps the deterrent effect of the threat of violence, as the seventeenth century presented more challenges. Even without the uprisings that broke out in several cities in 1648, the state would probably have issued something like the immense 1649 Conciliar Law Code (Ulozhenie) to assert its power. In accomplishing its primary goals – codifying social discipline (enserfment and other social restrictions) and defining judicial procedure – the Ulozhenie was permeated with corporal and capital punishment.

65 Public scribe: Lipinskii (ed.), "Rospis′," no. 79, p. 30; Ulozhenie ch. 10, arts. 27–99: RZ III: 106–12.

CHAPTER 10

Corporal punishment, 1649–1698

The story of corporal punishment in Muscovite law in the second half of the seventeenth century is the story of the expanding empire and bureaucratic state. In these fifty years the state ratcheted up military reform, territorial expansion and the mobilization of resources, enserfing the peasantry, tying townsmen to their social status, dragooning more people to serve. All this demanded more bureaucracy to control social groups from townsmen straining under taxation, to resistant colonial peoples, to gentry reluctant to serve in new model military units. At the same time church and state encountered fierce resistance to its confessionalizing project of religious reform. The 1649 Ulozhenie and subsequent legislation sharply accelerated punishment of the body to pursue this ambitious project of social disciplining; at the same time countervailing pressure from the spread of empire somewhat mitigated the violence.

THE 1649 CONCILIAR LAW CODE

The compilation of the 1649 Ulozhenie was dramatic.[1] In the spring and summer of 1648 during riots in Moscow and provincial towns protesting taxation and corrupt government, collective petitions flooded to the tsar, complaining, among other things, about the legal system – its arbitrariness, the confusing melange of laws, and the ability of large landholders and well-connected people (*sil'nye liudi*) to manipulate the legal system. Tsar Aleksei Mikhailovich and his entourage responded in July 1648 by establishing a commission to compile a new law code. They called a meeting of the collected estates – known as a Council of the Land (*zemskii sobor*, the term a nineteenth-century historians' invention) – to prepare and ratify the new code.

[1] Hellie, "Muscovite Law and Society," ch. 1, "*Ulozhenie*: Preamble" and "Early Modern Russian Law."

The speed with which the commission did its work suggests that legal compilation was already under way. Richard Hellie estimates that the working handbooks of about ten of the approximately forty chanceries went into the Ulozhenie, notably for the criminal law, those of the Felony Chancery. The committee also deployed foreign law, available in part from the Orthodox Church that itself was engaged in legal compilation, publishing in 1653 an updated *Nomokanon* (*Kormchaia kniga*) that paralleled the Ulozhenie in size and ambition.[2] The Ulozhenie was immense: at 967 articles, it was almost ten times as long as the 1550 Law Code (100 articles).

While in earlier centuries law and legal practice had rejected the harsher sanctions of Byzantine law, the 1649 Ulozhenie and subsequent criminal law embraced them. Richard Hellie denounces the 1649 Code's "perfectly barbarous criminal law" with its ample use of torture and knout and its new chapter on capital punishment (ch. 22); he and other scholars have identified Byzantine and Lithuanian law as sources for these more brutal punishments. With the establishment of the Patriarchate in 1589 that brought educated Greeks to Muscovy and with an influx of reforming Orthodox clerics from Ukraine and Belarus since the 1620s, Byzantine codes spread in Muscovy. Byzantine law also entered through the 1588 Lithuanian Statute, whose regime of punishments had been influenced by the *Procheiros Nomos* (Byzantine criminal law, called in Muscovite codes *gradskie zakony* or "laws of the [Imperial] city," i.e., Constantinople). The 1588 Statute had been available in Moscow chanceries in a Russian translation since the 1630s.[3] The 1588 Statute also provided military and political norms where previous Russian law lacked specificity: granting travel documents across the border (ch. 6), the behavior of military personnel on campaign (ch. 7), laws on forgery (chs. 4, 6) and in particular the problem of threats to the state (chs. 1–3). The Ulozhenie's first three chapters presented for the first time an articulated definition of state crime, carving out as sacred spaces the church and the person, home and presence of the tsar (see Chapter 15). State power was also energetically asserted by the code's stringent penalties for official corruption, especially by judicial staff,[4] and

[2] Chancery Handbooks: Hellie, "Early Modern Russian Law," 160. Ulozhenie and *Nomokanon*: Pozdeeva, "Activity," 50–2.

[3] Hellie, "Early Modern Russian Law," 164–8 (167–8), "*Ulozhenie*: Preamble," "Commentary on Chapters 3 Through 6" and "Commentary on Chapters 7–9." Man'kov, *Ulozhenie*, 294–310; Benemanskii, *Zakon gradskii*, 161–2, 184; Lappo, *Litovskii statut*.

[4] Judicial corruption: Ulozhenie ch. 10, arts. 5–7, 12, 13, 123, 129, 143, 146, 148; ch. 11: art. 24; ch. 15: art. 5; ch. 17: art. 53; ch. 21: arts. 83–4, 104: RZ III: 102–3, 117–19, 123–4, 155, 163, 183, 244, 247.

by greater legal protection for courts, their officers and procedures. Even the death penalty was ordered for homicides done in court or in association with legal proceedings. An important new provision punished those who sued the tsar directly, bypassing the proper local or chancery venue, at the same time that litigants were forbidden (on pain of prison) to approach the tsar or patriarch with a petition during the liturgy, for this, the code notes, is a time and place of prayer, not "earthly matters."[5] These two prohibitions on approaching the tsar reflect the Ulozhenie's abiding tension regarding state power, which is depicted both as personal, founded on the righteousness of the ruler at prayer, and as abstract, founded on the tsar as pinnacle of a rational judicial hierarchy.

This more assertive state law was enforced by liberal prescriptions of corporal punishment, moderated, as before, with discrimination of guilt; lawmakers employed what Hellie calls "graded sanctions," adjusting punishment to the circumstances of a crime. So, for example, it maintained the 1625 law distinguishing intent in homicide, and limited corporal punishment for harm committed through carelessness. If, for example, a man injured a pregnant woman, he was to be knouted, or executed if she died, even if he had no prior intent; but, such unintentional homicides as when a runaway horse killed someone or a bullet went astray were not to be punished. The biblical norm that allowed killing an intruder in one's home was maintained. Other clauses also considered a crime's context: if a slave killed or injured someone in defense of his master, he was not culpable of homicide. On the other hand, instigation as well as execution of a crime was punished, as in slaves plotting their master's murder or in instigation of rebellion or murder.[6]

The code's two criminal law chapters, as well as punishments scattered through the text, demonstrate the state's broader claims to control. Its unprecedented chapter on capital punishment is particularly harsh, since much of it is devoted to family law, traditionally covered by canon law with harsh Roman-law sanctions. Introduced here are execution for a child who kills a parent or a sibling; burying alive for women who kill their husbands; burning to death for a Muslim converting an Orthodox to

[5] Death penalty: Ulozhenie ch. 10, arts. 105–6, 133, 135, 142: RZ III: 112–13, 120–1, 123. Corporal punishment, dishonor fee: ch. 10, arts. 9, 14, 17, 105–6, 141–2, 170, 186, 191, 252; chs. 11: art. 27 and 14: art. 9; ch. 21: arts. 44, 55, 81: RZ III: 103–4, 112–13, 122–3, 130, 132–3, 145–6, 156, 161, 237, 239, 243. Not sue tsar directly: ch. 10: art. 20: RZ III: 104–5. Not approach in church: ch. 1, arts. 8–9: RZ III: 86.

[6] Hellie, "*Ulozhenie*: Preamble," 207. PRP V: 204–5 (1625); Ulozhenie 21: arts. 69, 71–3: RZ III: 241–2. Carelessness: Ulozhenie ch. 21, arts. 8, 12–13, 17–19, 20–1, 26, 88: RZ III: 231–3, 244–5.

Islam. Patriarchy is upheld in the provision that a parent who kills a child is punished with prison and public repentance, not corporal punishment.[7] Chapter 21 on brigandage felonies added prison terms and bodily mutilation to previous law.

After the Time of Troubles (1598–1613), church and state had begun to intensify social disciplining, issuing prohibitions against tobacco use, folk processions, public gatherings to drink, mass fist fights and the like. In 1648, for example, a decree forbade consorting with minstrels in public festivals and games.[8] The Ulozhenie continued such moral legislation, assigning corporal and capital punishment for Russians serving as slaves in the households of non-Christian foreigners, for pandering, and for poisoning, a crime that evokes witchcraft. Finally, the Ulozhenie introduced corporal punishment as sanctions for insult to honor, where there had previously been only monetary fines.[9]

Alongside its discrimination of sanctions and attention to such issues as intent, accident and incaution, the Ulozhenie deployed greater coercive force to defend the tsar's dignity and his instruments of governance and to police felonies and moral crime. But the code's hyper-specificity and reluctance to generalize prevented it from providing much guidance to judges on the use of force. Judges thus continued to use their judgment in the spirit of a now more coercive law.

CRIMINAL LEGISLATION AFTER THE ULOZHENIE

The 1649 Ulozhenie established a benchmark that lasted into the eighteenth century. But it was immediately supplemented with a cacophony of decrees responding to new challenges, of which there were many in the second half of the seventeenth century. As new model army regiments were recruited from lower social classes and provincial gentry, flight from service increased. As the state enforced enserfment, peasants fled. Social and economic rebellions flared up in 1648, 1662 and most notably in 1670–1, when the Stepan Razin uprising on the Middle Volga definitively earned this time period its sobriquet of "insurrectionary century" (*buntiashchii vek*), paralleling social unrest across Europe at the time. Resistance broke out to the state's enforcement of the church's Counter-Reformation-style reforms of service books, liturgy and church life.

[7] Ulozhenie ch. 22, arts. 1–3, 7, 14, 24: RZ III: 248–50.

[8] Morality prohibitions: PRP V: 340 (1627), 342 (1627), 359–60 (1640). PRP V: 399 (1648).

[9] Moral crimes: Ulozhenie ch. 20, art. 70, ch. 22, arts. 23, 25: RZ III: 220–1, 233. Dishonor: Ulozhenie ch. 10, arts. 27–99: RZ III: 106–12.

The brutality of threatened sanctions increased as the post-1649 state confronted such resistance. Enserfment – the state's boldest move to mobilize resources – generated tremendous stress on the judicial system. From the Thirteen Years War (1654–67) well into the 1680s, decrees attacked the problem of runaway serfs: for harboring runaway peasants, for example, according to a 1661 decree, if estate officials could prove that they had been ordered to do so by their landlord, they were not punished; they could also avoid punishment by yielding one of their own serfs if the officials themselves owned land. But estate officials who harbored peasants knowingly suffered merciless knouting. Enforcement proved to be difficult, and conflicting interests so challenged the policing of enserfment that laws of the 1680s mitigated some of these sanctions. In recognition of the shortage of peasant labor, a January 1683 decree imposed a fine instead of a person in compensation for a runaway, while an order of March 1683 instructed investigators no longer to knout estate officials who took in runaways.[10]

The state threatened military men who fled service with even more dire consequences than before. A decree of 1654, for example, punished with knouting even men of high Moscow ranks (*striapchie, stol'niki*) who resisted service in the increasingly modernized army. Numerous decrees threatened the knout or even hanging for gentrymen who refused to serve and threatened "disgrace and exile" for officers who did not carry out these punishments. Those who harbored or abetted men absconding from service were culpable as well: a decree of 1661 to the Vladimir area threatened "on pain of death" those who harbored runaway servitors. Military men who burned village property, killed villagers or otherwise pillaged while on campaign were to be hanged on the spot, according to a 1655 decree.[11]

People below gentry rank continued to be corporally punished in military settings: serfs sent by their landlords to military service (*datochnye liudi*) who fled the army were threatened with harsh punishment; those who had also stolen while in flight were ordered executed in 1654; in 1656

[10] PSZ I: no. 307 (1661); PSZ II: no. 985 (1683). Investigator instruction, arts. 4–5: PRP VII: 187–77 (1683).

[11] PSZ I: no. 128 (1654). Corporal punishment of gentry: PSZ I: nos. 144, 154 (1655), 297 (1661); AMG II: nos. 655, 657, 692 (1655), 1157 (1659); AMG III: no. 503 (1661). Hanging gentry: PSZ I: no. 253 (1659). Carol Stevens chronicles the provincial gentry's unwilling integration into new model units over the century: *Russia's Wars*, chs. 4–7. PSZ I: no. 302 (1661). PSZ I: no. 131 (1654). PSZ I: no. 166 (1655); similar decree: AMG II: no. 713 (1655). Other decrees also named corporal punishment or death for soldiers who attacked civilians: AMG II: nos. 660 (1655) and 851 (1656).

townsmen who refused to do carpentry work for the army were ordered mercilessly beaten with bastinadoes. A decree of 1679 deprived of their lands landlords whose bailiffs took in such runaway serf soldiers, if the landlord knew of it; if he did not, only the bailiff was to be punished with a merciless knouting and exile. Anyone who failed to report such runaways appearing in Moscow were themselves to be enrolled as infantrymen (*soldaty*).[12] The laws differentiated degree of guilt and social status, but threatened corporal punishment readily.

As new forms of taxation were introduced, land surveys became points of conflict between state and local interests. Harsh corporal punishment was decreed for those who obstructed land surveying in the 1670s and 1680s, regardless of social class: anyone – "gentry, cossacks, the people and peasants of service tenure landholders and private landholders" – interfering with surveyors was sentenced to a marketplace knouting on the rack and while being led around "to deter others." Decrees affirming that landlords themselves could be corporally punished for obstruction of a survey followed in 1681 and 1686. In typical state-building fashion, laws also punished challenges to the mobilization of natural resources: corporal, even capital, punishment protected the state's forests, increasingly valuable from now through the Petrine period for shipbuilding and construction as well as for firewood. According to a 1678 decree, landlords who cut down forest preserves suffered a fine, but their people and peasants were to be knouted in town on market days to deter others; for a second offense, they were to be executed. Officials who looked the other way and/or took bribes to allow this were fined and lost their lands and jobs.[13]

Anxiety about flight from serf and military status spilled over into anxiety about mobility in general. As in contemporary early modern Europe, an individual outside his home community was regarded as suspect. Although the literal phrase for people without fixed social status had always been "wandering men" (*guliashchie liudi*), the term seems to have taken on explicit meaning in the second half of the seventeenth century in Muscovy, when law after law forced communities to register and report strangers and punished those who harbored newcomers. Anxiety was particularly high in Moscow, a bustling metropolis that capaciously swallowed up newcomers, be they innocent traders and peasant artisans or

[12] PSZ I: no. 127 (1654). AMG II: no. 805 (1656). PSZ II: no. 756 (1679).

[13] Anyone knouted: PSZ II: no. 734 (1678). PSZ II: nos. 866 (1681) and 1192 (1686). Forest: PSZ II: no. 728 (1678).

hardened criminals and runaway serfs. Thus, for example, for major crime and arson in Moscow, immediate execution without reference to higher authorities was ordered in 1654. The decree concludes "and in the future no one in Moscow is to keep free people who have come to the city in their homes without showing them and registering them in the chanceries." An extensive order of November 1692, making reference to earlier ones of 1690/1 and 1691/2, discussed the problem of landlords and neighborhoods taking in unregistered people, falsifying surety bonds for them and sitting by while the new arrivals led a life of crime in Moscow. It sentenced such landlords to harsh corporal punishment, exile and paying compensation to victims. Similarly, an order of 1695 instructed city officials to keep lists of newcomers to Moscow, under threat of harsh punishment and a fine, and punished unrecorded people with merciless corporal punishment and exile "so that the chanceries know about all people in Moscow."[14]

Also typical of the early modern "police state," Moscow threatened harsh sanctions to regulate daily behavior in a more intrusive manner, already evident in the Ulozhenie. Punishment for illegal sale of spirits intensified: a decree of 1654 punished the illegal sale of homemade alcoholic drinks with a fine, a "merciless" knouting in the marketplace and five or six days in prison "depending upon the person [i.e., on social status]." A decree of 1660 to the Perm′ area threatened the death penalty or disgrace and exile for not enforcing prohibitions on alcohol sale. For servitors, their lands were to be confiscated; for peasants and serfs, they were to have their hands cut off and be exiled to Siberia; for townsmen and monastic people, they were to have corporal punishment, confiscation of property and exile to Siberia.[15]

Some of these harsh norms are attested in practice, often in an exemplary way. The Tobol′sk governor was ordered in 1626 to punish an entire village for murdering an administrator on the tsar's estates. He was to execute the ringleader, knout and exile others involved and fine the entire village. This sort of collective and differentiated punishment was deployed frequently during the Thirteen Years War (1654–67). For example, a 1659 decree ordered three levels of punishment for criminal bands who were attacking peasant villages in the Kashira and Kolomna areas: death penalty for the leaders (*pushchie zavodchiki*), knouting for band members and the hanging of one man in each town as a deterrent against others joining

[14] PSZ I: no. 126 (1654); similar decree: PSZ I: no. 150 (1655). PSZ III: nos. 1454 (1692) and 1509 (1695).

[15] PSZ I: nos. 130 (1654) and 285 (1660); similar decree: AAE IV: no. 166 (1669).

such robber bands. A similar provision is found in a verdict of June 1656 for a group of runaway serfs of Polish noblemen who were marauding in the Minsk province. Fifty-six were caught, then thirty escaped, leaving about twenty-six in prison. Twenty of them, regardless of individual guilt, were ordered hanged to deter others. Exemplary collective punishment is also cited in a March 1655 decree regarding runaway serfs and slaves: if a boyar's slave convinced others to join him in flight, once they were caught, four to six of the band were to be hanged as an example to others, the others knouted, and five to ten men in the village where they came from were also to be punished.[16]

The 1669 Criminal Articles, not surprisingly, escalated state-sanctioned violence. They expanded the Ulozhenie's two chapters on criminal law, explicitly citing Byzantine norms including beheading (art. 79). They shifted the Ulozhenie's punishments to rely less on prison and more on bodily mutilation and exhibited a more stringent approach to intent. If a person fights with another and on the same day plans an ambush and kills him, then that person is to be executed for the premeditated murder (art. 81); if someone guilty of unintentional murder then robs the corpse, he is to be knouted and his left hand and right foot are to be cut off (art. 82). Conversely, from Roman law the Articles also introduced mitigating elements, such as the concept that minor age (under 7) or insanity excuse a killer from guilt (arts. 79, 108).[17] The Criminal Articles' explicit references to Byzantine codes (*gradskie zakony*) demonstrate that Muscovy in the second half of the seventeenth century found in Roman law the coercive judicial power needed to pursue its increasingly intense state-building project. Whether the state through its officials could follow through on such threats is another question.

DEFERENCE TO SOCIAL STATUS IN SANCTIONS

Seventeenth-century regimes of punishment would seem, on the surface, to accord no place to social deference. The state stood ready to punish all to achieve its most important goals – taxation, military reform, policing officialdom, enserfment, criminal justice. But social status continued to affect a person's vulnerability to punishment, even though wholesale immunity from corporal punishment was not granted to any social

[16] "Uboistvennye dela," 1 (1626). PSZ I: no. 256 (1659). AMG II: no. 829 (1656). PSZ I: no. 151 (1655).
[17] 1669 Criminal Articles, arts. 79, 81–2, 108: PRP VII: 423–4, 429.

group.[18] This seeming contradiction can be resolved by reflecting on a key aspect of Muscovite concepts of justice. Ostensibly, the 1649 Ulozhenie asserted justice for all: "for people of all ranks of the Moscow state, from great to small ranks, trial and justice are to be in all cases the same to all." In only one place did the Ulozhenie even hint at the tsar's ability to bend the letter of the law with pardons. But this declaration should not be taken to imply the very modern concept of equal justice to all. Rather, it intends that all subjects of the tsar could expect justice and services from the state, but that each person's access to the tsar was determined by collective social markers – social class, religion, ethnicity or combinations thereof. Jane Burbank has called this Russia's "Imperial rights regime"; George Weickhardt has called it a socially differentiated form of "due process"; Valerie Kivelson has demonstrated this policy at work in Muscovy's interactions with Siberian natives.[19]

Thus, the 1649 Ulozhenie intended that judging should be done according to the law, but the law itself was differential. Like earlier codes, the Ulozhenie amply reinforces social hierarchy, most explicitly in its provisions regarding insult to honor, now deploying corporal punishment in addition to the sixteenth-century norm of fines. Corporal punishment was applied to lesser social groups – lower merchants, contract servitors, taxed townsmen and peasants, and slaves – when they insulted someone high above them on the social scale. Corporal punishment for people of relatively high ranks (the non-conciliar Moscow or provincial gentry ranks or merchants) was prescribed only when they insulted the highest-ranking individual in the society, the patriarch; insulting the tsar merited, of course, death. Otherwise, insults between social peers, whether peasants, gentry or boyars, continued to merit fines.[20]

Other provisions in the Ulozhenie also protected high social status, sometimes quite explicitly. The Ulozhenie's article that mandated bastinadoes for submitting a petition directly to the tsar allowed that if such a litigant were "more honorable" (*pochestnee*), he would merely be imprisoned for a week. Similarly, men in highest court ranks, which even in the seventeenth century were filled to a great extent by heredity within elite clans, were accorded protection from corporal punishment. For example, if a judge took a bribe and ruled corruptly, he was to pay

[18] Lack of legal exemptions from corporal punishment for privileged classes: Timofeev, *Istoriia*, 61. Social deference in Ulozhenie: Man'kov, *Ulozhenie*, 309–10.

[19] Justice the same: RZ III: 84. Sole reference to pardon: Ulozhenie ch. 2, art. 11: RZ III: 88. Burbank, "Imperial Rights"; Weickhardt, "Due Process"; Kivelson, *Cartographies*, chs. 7–8.

[20] Ulozhenie ch. 10, arts. 27–99: RZ III: 106–12; Kollmann, *By Honor Bound*, 55–8.

threefold damages to the victim and court fees, lose his job and suffer marketplace knouting, *unless* he were of conciliar (*dumnyi*) rank. If the latter, he merely suffered loss of "honor" and paid the damages and fees.[21]

Punishments for official corruption became harsher for less high-ranking officials; now even secretaries (*d'iaki*) suffered the lash. For intentionally delaying a case, a secretary was to be beaten with bastinadoes, but an undersecretary with a knout (both also paid fines). A governor in Vologda was instructed in 1669 that, should he favor people who brewed spirits illegally, he would pay fines and be in "great disgrace," but if the secretary in his office were guilty of such behavior, he would suffer marketplace knouting.[22]

Nevertheless, the Ulozhenie continued to allow high-ranking people to be corporally punished for grave offenses. People of "eminent" (*znatnye*) ranks, as well as provincial gentry or merchants, for example, could be tortured if a community survey labeled them criminal; if they were found guilty, they were to be executed. Similarly, if a master instructed his slave to physically beat or mutilate someone, both slave and master were to be beaten in the marketplace publically and imprisoned for a month. The master was also to pay double dishonor fine to the injured party.[23] While a 1678 decree imposed only a fine on men of higher ranks who obstructed the work of land surveyors (although they would suffer bastinadoes if they could not pay the fine), a 1686 revision decreed merciless knouting on the rack and being led through the marketplace for all, including gentrymen, for this offense. Even governors faced "harsh corporal punishment" for dereliction of duty.[24] Thus, in the seventeenth century the seriousness of the crime trumped social rank and official dignity.

CORPORAL PUNISHMENT IN PRACTICE, 1649–1698

Because the 1649 Ulozhenie was widely distributed as a printed book, judges and their staffs had better guidance than before on the law, but its hyper-specificity left unanswered questions. Also, the myriad decrees

21 Ulozhenie ch. 10, art. 20: RZ III: 105. Hereditary succession in politics: Kollmann, *Kinship and Politics*; Pavlov, *Gosudarev dvor*; Crummey, *Aristocrats and Servitors*; LeDonne, "Ruling Families." Judge bribed: Ulozhenie ch. 10, art. 5: RZ III: 102. Social deference in giving witness: Ulozhenie ch. 10, arts. 158–9: RZ III: 126–7.

22 Ulozhenie ch. 10, art. 16: RZ III: 104. AAE IV: no. 166 (1669).

23 Ulozhenie ch. 21, art. 39: RZ III: 236; ch. 22, art. 12: RZ III: 249. Another punishment for gentry: ch. 21, art. 47: RZ III: 238.

24 PSZ II: no. 1192 (1686). Threats to governors: AMG II: no. 817 (1655); PSZ I: nos. 220 (1658), 297 (1661); AAE IV: no. 237 (1679); PSZ III: no. 1526 (1695).

surveyed here because most are available in modern publications were not necessarily evenly distributed in their own day. Different chanceries issued decrees to governors under their own supervision; even if all decrees had been sent out to all governors, they could have been recorded in ledgers (*zapisnye knigi*) and then forgotten. There are undoubtedly decrees buried in those prolix ledgers in archives that have escaped historians' attention to this day. Thus, what seems to be judicial inconsistency was intrinsic to the system: judges followed the law as they and their scribes knew it, but their decisions inevitably differed.

A cluster of resolved homicide cases from the 1680s demonstrates the myriad considerations judges and their expert scribes dealt with. For example, Military Service Chancery judges dealt with a case from the regiment of Prince Grigorii Romodanovskii in which a foreigner in Russian service – *maeor* Osip Lorents Linenbek – admitted to accidentally killing his brother-in-law, a Russian, in a sword fight in May 1679. Using the law on unpremeditated homicide, Chancery judges ordered that, instead of death, he be exiled with his family, and in April 1680 the Linenbeks were sent to Moscow to be shipped out to Siberia. But to avoid exile, *maeor* Osip petitioned that they all be converted to Orthodoxy and his bishop conveyed the request to the patriarch. This was apparently done, as in May 1680 the tsar granted mercy, sending Linenbek back to the regiment but adding the proviso that, should he be arrested in crime again, there would be no more mercy.[25]

In a case of homicide in 1684 the Iakutsk governor initially ruled for execution but was dissuaded. Governor and General Matvei Osipovich Krovkov found a man guilty of killing his brother, even though the defendant testified that he was defending himself and his mother from the brother's attacks. The governor did not accept that story and initially sentenced him to execution, citing the Ulozhenie and "*gradskie zakony*" on killing a sibling. But at the place of execution the man's mother appealed for mercy, confirming her son's plea of self-defense. Upon further investigation (and bribery as well?), Krovkov changed his verdict and sentenced the man to be knouted and released on surety bond. This is in line with unpremeditated homicide, but harsher than the law for killing in self-defense (no punishment), perhaps showing the judge's misgivings in the case.[26]

[25] RGADA f. 210, Prikaznyi stol, no. 1037, fols. 44–74 (1680).

[26] DAI XI: no. 11 (1) (1684). Killing a sibling: Ulozhenie ch. 22, art. 7: RZ III: 248; 1669 Criminal Articles, art. 88: PRP VII: 425–6. Self-defense: Ulozhenie ch. 20, art. 200: RZ III: 134; 1669 Criminal Articles, art. 85: PRP VII: 424–5 (citing *gradskie zakony*).

The Ulozhenie's norms on accidental death came to bear in a case of May 1654. This involved a slave of Prince Ivan Romodanovskii found guilty of accidentally killing a captain of a gentry unit by shooting off his pistol during a muster. He was to be knouted in the marketplace mercilessly, so that others would be deterred from "shooting pistols . . . in the gentry units (*sotni*)."[27]

Unpremeditated homicide came in forms not always covered by the law. In Beloozero in February 1692, Governor Grigorii Artem′ev investigated the death of a woman killed by her husband's beatings; she lay ill for two weeks before succumbing. In July Artem′ev ruled that the husband should be knouted and put on firm surety bond to kill no more. A case of felony theft in October 1677 prompted a generous ruling for reasons unclear. A Mordvinian in Russian service had sued a peer for theft of the valuable commodity of honey; the case went to trial with torture. The accused and another man admitted to the theft as well as to slandering others under torture and were found guilty. According to either the 1649 or 1669 law, for a first theft the penalty should have been at least bodily mutilation and a knouting (followed by prison and exile according to the Ulozhenie, and surety bond according to the Articles); they were sentenced instead to bastinadoes and surety bond. The judge's reasons for mitigation (a bribe or community entreaties, perhaps) are not expressed, but his resolution was generous.[28]

Through the century judges enforced the law as they saw fit for insubordination by military servitors. In August 1661, the governor of Smolensk informed Moscow that he had punished eight men of relatively high Moscow rank (*zhil′tsy*) because they had fled service. They were beaten with bastinadoes and demoted to provincial service, assigned to whatever town their fathers had served in. A more serious punishment was levied for more serious misbehavior in June 1662. In a long memo about the persistent problem of runaway recruits, Governor Prince Boris Repnin described how ten to twenty soldiers fled per day from Great Novgorod into the forests, and how a group of infantrymen refused to obey the inspector sent to summon them to service. They had insulted him, beat three of the musketeers sent in his party, and chased them away with axes and bludgeons (*oslopy*). The group proved hard to catch, since, as the

[27] RGADA f. 210, Prikaznyi stol, no. 286, fol. 260 (1654). Accidental death: Ulozhenie ch. 22, art. 20: RZ III: 250.

[28] RGADA f. 1107, no. 3904 (1692); Kollmann, "Extremes of Patriarchy," 135 and "Judicial Autonomy," 63. AIuB I: no. 100 (1677). The law: see Appendix.

governor noted, they were from Olonets, while the inspector and the men sent with him were "all from the Novgorod area, they are all friends and clients of each other." He was instructed to punish them harshly, with knouting, to deter others from refusing service.[29] All these punishments are in line with the Ulozhenie on military service and with subsequent decrees intensifying corporal punishment during wartime.

Sometimes punishments were harsher than the law. In May 1682 a musketeer colonel who had abused his men – beating them, taking bribes, extorting money and labor services – was sentenced to lose his rank and lands to compensate victims, and to be beaten with bastinadoes. A commander in a new model cavalry unit was knouted "before the whole regiment" in 1687 for dishonor and disobedience to his colonel and for drunkenness. For dishonor alone between these two men of similar rank, the penalty would have been a cash fine, but in the grand project of creating a disciplined army, insult and insubordination to one's commanding officer merited corporal punishment.[30]

Judges loosely enforced the Ulozhenie's harsher sanctions in the realm of judicial and bureaucratic procedure and respect for the court. As before, for scribes making errors in documents, the punishment was harsh, often corporal, and socially discriminatory. For example, when a brigandage elder and brigandage secretary from Orel traveled to Moscow in 1663 to pursue a case, the secretary read aloud an incorrect version of the tsar's title in the Felony Chancery. For this insult, the elder, a gentryman, was imprisoned in Moscow for a week, while the scribe was beaten with bastinadoes, without a shirt, mercilessly, but the verdict spared him the knout. A combination of prison for the presiding official and bastinadoes for the scribe was ordered in similar cases in 1666, 1677 and 1685. A mid-level officer, filling in for a governor in 1685, was merely imprisoned for a day for inappropriately writing his name with patronymic in documents, as if he were of high enough rank to do so. Even invoking bastinadoes, these sentences were more lenient than the written law.[31]

29 AMG III: nos. 503 (1661) and 582 (1662).

30 AAE IV: no. 254 (1682). RGADA f. 210, Prikaznyi stol, no. 1064, fols. 10–13 (1687); relevant article in Ulozhenie ch. 10, art. 91: RZ III: 110.

31 PSZ I: no. 351 (1663). Differential punishments (all RGADA f. 210, Prikaznyi stol): no. 985, fols. 507–9 (1666) (official, two days in prison; scribe, merciless bastinadoes); no. 872, fols. 293–4 (1685) (same); no. 898, fols. 188–9 (1685); closest clause in Ulozhenie is ch. 10, art. 12 (RZ III: 103) ordering knouting for secretary or bodily mutilation for undersecretary for feloniously writing a document. RGADA f. 210, Belgorod stol, no. 854, fols. 97–100 (1677) (official, one day in prison; scribe, merciless bastinadoes instead of knout).

Harsher sanctions were inflicted where the state's dignity or income was involved. For disorder in the tsar's presence, in his quarters or on the Kremlin grounds, even higher-ranking people were beaten. For example, in January 1644 a *stol'nik* was ordered beaten mercilessly with bastinadoes, "wearing only a shirt," for insulting another *stol'nik*'s mother and sisters at the palace while the tsar was walking by. This was very harsh: even the Ulozhenie would have levied only fines for the dishonor and the insult to the palace. In October 1674 a *striapchii* was beaten with bastinadoes, instead of a knout, and suffered a four-fold dishonor fee for hitting another *striapchii* in the head with a stone in the sovereign's palace in the sovereign's presence. The Ulozhenie, meanwhile, mandated only a two-fold dishonor fee and six weeks in prison for drawing blood in the tsar's home. For cheating the state alcohol monopoly sanctions were made harsher from the 1649 Ulozhenie's knoutings to hanging in a March 1655 law. A group of six soldiers in Smolensk in July 1655 ran afoul of the new strictness: found to be selling wine illegally, based on confessions through testimony and torture, the leader was ordered hanged and the others beaten by the knout in front of the Chancery and in the marketplace, as was the single purchaser who had been identified.[32]

Judges also made common-sense rulings that were not so harsh. In the late seventeenth century, access to the Kremlin was greatly restricted and punishment was draconian. In March 1680, for example, a servant of a gentryman was caught riding a horse on the Kremlin grounds and resisting arrest when challenged – he hit and yelled at the musketeer arresting him. In the Military Service Chancery, he testified that his master had ordered him to bring the horse around to the stables (while the master walked on foot through the Trinity Gates) and that the servant had not understood that his social rank did not allow him to even enter, let alone ride a horse, in this privileged place. The Military Service Chancery judges informed him that they would spare him the death sentence he deserved and order only a merciless beating with bastinadoes. He was then returned to his master.[33]

Local knowledge often inspired flexibility in sanctions. For example, in Dobroe two gentrymen, Aleksei Shalov and Ivan Kuznetsov, gave testimony on June 28, 1681 before Governor Timofei Grigor'evich Argamak

[32] Zabelin, *Domashnii byt*, 354–8 (1644); Ulozhenie ch. 3, art. 1: RZ III: 89–90; ch. 10, art. 93: RZ III: 111. *Dvortsovye razriady*, III: col. 1079 (1674); Ulozhenie ch. 3, art. 2: RZ III: 90. AMG II: no. 684 (1655).

[33] Within the Kremlin: Kollmann, *By Honor Bound*, 189. RGADA f. 210, Prikaznyi stol, no. 1039, fols. 11–13 (1680).

regarding suspected runaway serfs on their properties. Shalov denied taking in a particular peasant, but the man in question himself testified that Shalov had settled him on his service tenure estate, but that he had never been properly registered. Kuznetsov argued that the man he was accused of harboring was not a runaway but a legally hired worker whom he had simply failed to register. Receiving from court scribes relevant sources regarding treatment of runaways, Governor Argamak ruled that both these landlords should be beaten with bastinadoes for taking in and not registering these people. But, indicating how desperate frontier governors were for manpower, he mitigated the sentence, ordering instead that the first runaway be given his own service tenure land and be enrolled in Dobroe as a gentrymen, while the other man was to be returned to Kuznetsov.[34]

Moral disciplining brought out harsh sanctions. Gambling, for example, is cited in the Ulozhenie only as a stimulus to crime – those people who entice other people to play cards and dice often get into theft. When confronted with such cases, judges were told to apply the rules for felonies. Iakutsk Governor and General Matvei Osipovich Krovkov in 1684, for example, was presented with a public scribe accused of gambling, drinking and general rowdy living and of paying for it with the fees paid for his work (his *ploshchadnye dengi*). The scribe was brought by two men who said they were his guarantors, liable for those funds. The scribe said in testimony that on the days of the alleged incidents (June 29–30), he was so drunk that he could not recall whether he gambled or not. But he insisted that he had not spent his fees, which were safe in the chest in the Chancery. Krovkov then ordered him to produce the funds (relieving the guarantors of that burden) and ordered him beaten with bastinadoes instead of the knout; he improvised a punishment for gambling since no theft was proven.[35]

As with gambling, legislation did not directly address sexual license, citing it indirectly in a statute on infanticide; in practice judges reacted to it with corporal punishment. For example, in Iakutsk in early August 1684, Governor Krovkov was presented with a gentryman who worked for the Tobol′sk Cathedral and a woman, wife of a local undersecretary, who were said to be living in sin. They denied it, as did another woman

[34] RGADA f. 210, Prikaznyi stol, no. 793, fols. 252–60 (1681). Labor shortages on the frontier: Stevens, *Soldiers on the Steppe.*

[35] Gambling, Ulozhenie ch. 21, art. 15: RZ III: 232. 1669 Criminal Articles (art. 14) drop reference to gambling: PRP VII: 400–1; commentary in PRP VII: 452–5. DAI XI: no. 11 (VI) (1684).

who was brought into the story. Nevertheless, the governor rejected their stories and ordered the two women beaten with bastinadoes to deter others, and he informed the man's superior, the Tobol′sk metropolitan, presumably so that he would summon the guilty man for moral instruction. All were to be put on surety bond to behave better. Thus, the judge responded with a lighter sentence than the knouting the Ulozhenie prescribed for pandering, and he also referred to the church, the traditional overseer of moral crimes.[36]

Litigations over insults to honor illustrate the full range of the patterns seen in this chapter: deference to social rank, mitigation of the law, harsh corporal punishment to those who obstructed the state's serious business. In the routine practice of dishonor litigation, the majority of suits were brought between people of the same social rank, or by someone suing someone lower on the social hierarchy, and judges assigned the cash fines called for in the law. So, for example, a gentryman paid a dishonor fee to a peer in March 1683, and in June 1684 an infantryman paid a fine to a peer. When a lower person insulted a very high social superior and corporal punishment was prescribed, verdicts often lessened the Ulozhenie's rules. For example, in February 1666 a peasant who was an elected town elder was sentenced to bastinadoes and a week in prison for insulting and disobeying the governor of Suzdal. The law would have required a knout and two weeks in prison.[37]

In a particular version of dishonor suits, men in the highest ranks had the right to appeal to the tsar directly when they felt that he had slighted their family and personal honor in a service assignment. Called precedence (*mestnichestvo*), the practice emerged in the first third of the sixteenth century, when the elite became more socially differentiated – old boyar families dating from the fourteenth century had splintered into multiple lines and new families, usually princes from northeast principalities who were descendents of Kiev Rus′ rulers, were joining the court, upsetting the prestige hierarchy. Analysis of suits into the seventeenth century, however, shows that the state was able to accomplish its goals undeterred by precedence disputes: on the one hand, virtually no litigant who challenged another family for "place" won his suit, thus maintaining

[36] DAI XI: no. 11 (VIII) (1684); Ulozhenie ch. 22, art. 26: RZ III: 250–1; 1669 Criminal Articles, art. III: PRP VII: 430.

[37] Kollmann, *By Honor Bound*, 96–104. RGADA f. 210, Prikaznyi stol, no. 1086, fols. 88–150 (1683); cf. Ulozhenie ch. 10, art. 93: RZ III: 111. RGADA f. 210, Prikaznyi stol, no. 1161, fols. 13–24 (1684); cf. Ulozhenie ch. 10, art. 94: RZ III: 111. RGADA Prikaznyi stol, no. 993, fols. 1–107 (1666); cf. Ulozhenie ch. 10, art. 92: RZ III: 111.

the social status quo. On the other hand, very few cases came to fruition. Romanov tsars manipulated the system to avoid disruption in military campaigns: they routinely declared assignments "without place," summarily dismissed a suit as groundless, reassigned both parties or promised a suit in the future. Such strategies also gave servitors face-saving alternatives. Punishment was swift and often symbolic, however, when servitors stubbornly insisted on their status.[38]

Precedence brought high servitors face to face with the tsar, who did not take kindly to his bureaucrats' service assignments being refused. Assignments were announced to high-ranking men in audiences with the tsar; in some precedence cases, the litigants so angered Tsar Aleksei Mikhailovich with their status pretensions that he personally levied harsh sanctions for disobedience to him. Often, sources were quite graphic: the tsar "showed his anger" (*kruchinilsia*) at the servitor. In 1655, for example, Aleksei Mikhailovich was so "brought to anger" by Prince Nikita L′vov's insistence on suing for "place," even though the campaign had been declared "without place," that the tsar told him he was behaving like a lowly field worker (*stradnichaia vina*), called his petition "senseless" and sentenced him to confiscation of all his lands and demotion to gentry service in exile. Then, he pardoned Prince L′vov, as was usually the case with high servitors, but substituted for confiscation a knouting, done in front of the Military Service Chancery so that his peers could see, a very humiliating corporal punishment. In another suit, a captain of the Tatar forces from Sviazhsk by the name of Naumov was ordered in June 1655 beaten with bastinadoes and sent back to serve as ordered, since the campaign was declared "without place" and he had still sued. But Naumov responded with the impudent declaration "Even if the tsar wants to cut off my head, I will not serve with him." This so angered Tsar Aleksei Mikhailovich that he ordered Naumov knouted, exiled to the Lena River to be enrolled in cossack service, and his lands confiscated. From this, no mercy saved him. Similarly, in December 1684 a member of the Moscow court ranks, Ivan Menshoi Dashkov, was imprisoned for speaking rudely in the palace. Imprisonment was the punishment for insult to the tsar's palace, but Dashkov stubbornly avoided arrest, angering the tsars, who ordered him demoted to gentry service in Aleksin and beaten mercilessly with bastinadoes. Subsequently the beating was pardoned, but not the demotion.[39]

[38] Precedence: Kollmann, *Kinship and Politics*, 26, 69 (origins) and *By Honor Bound*, ch. 4; Eskin, *Ocherki istorii mestnichestva.*

[39] AMG II: nos. 681, 710 (both 1655). PSZ II: no. 1097 (1684); Ulozhenie ch. 3, art. 1: RZ III: 89–90.

Such cases could come to the death penalty, even for high servitors. In the summer of 1684, Tsars Ioann and Peter Alekseevich and their sister regent Sofia reacted as had their father with righteous anger at a stubborn litigant. Gentryman Stepan Osipov syn Sukhotin had the insolence to ask them to reconsider a dishonor suit they had already resolved. For insubordination, they ordered him executed, then bestowed mercy, levying a fine instead. But in September, he sued again, "forgetting the fear of God and despising their copious and surpassing mercy." To this they responded with fury, ordering him executed to deter others from behaving this way. Only at the last minute on the execution spot on Red Square in early October did they reprieve him, bestowing mercy. Finally, when particularly high-ranking men were particularly recalcitrant, a formal ritual of humiliation was imposed: instead of corporal punishment, it involved humiliating supplication by the loser to his social superior. At the same time the ritual was designed so as to restore equilibrium between the two parties.[40] These many cases suggest the range of punishments available to judges and the range of their judgment in applying them.

There was a calculated hierarchy of punishments, ranging from symbolic to painful violence, but it did not add up to a guaranteed immunity from corporal punishment for any group. As the state deployed corporal punishment in the seventeenth century, Muscovites of all ranks were more vulnerable to the terrible knout. One might suggest that in its liberal use of corporal punishment Muscovy engaged in a version of the European "spectacle of suffering," ruling by terrifying display. Nevertheless, again and again judges demonstrated the imbrication of formal, centralizing law with flexible adjudication. Furthermore, this evidence does not tell the whole story. At the same time that the state was threatening more and more corporal punishment, other considerations contributed to an opposite trend. As the empire grew, the desire to use convict labor to serve the state was great. The state backed off from levying the death penalty on all but the most serious offenders, turning to bodily mutilation as a marker more than a sanction to control its growing population of exiles.

40 RGADA f. 210, Prikaznyi stol, no. 876, fols. 1–29 (1684). Rituals of humiliation: Kollmann, "Ritual and Social Drama" and *By Honor Bound*, 161–3.

CHAPTER 11

To the exile system

A horrific decree of 1663 announced that:

> for thieves, robbers and murderers ... sentenced to death: the Great Sovereign has ordered that instead of death, both their legs and the left arm should be cut off, but they should not be killed. Having done this punishment, the severed legs and arms are to be nailed on trees3 on the great highways and a description of their crimes is to be nailed up there ... so that people of all ranks will know their crimes.

Such bodily mutilation – in essence quartering – so exceeded corporal punishment that it was rescinded three years later. By contrast, in September 1691 Muscovite law changed centuries of graduated penalties for felony theft by allowing not two, but three, thefts before execution: "those criminals in the future who are arrested and admit to three thefts, but not to robbery or murder, are to be punished with the knout and, having been branded, exiled to Siberia. For three thefts, do not execute." Meanwhile, Tsar Aleksei Mikhailovich's doctor, Samuel Collins, who lived at and observed the Kremlin court for several years in the 1660s, remarked on Muscovy's use of the death penalty: "On the Saturday after Good Friday, [the tsar] goes into some of the Prisons, examines the Prisoners crimes, and delivers many of them. An English man put in for coyning, was lately releas'd. They put very few to death here, only whip them, which is worse than the pains of death."[1] These three different sources indicate that seventeenth-century criminal law in some cases was moving away from capital punishment ("they put very few to death here") towards exile, essentially using the bodies of criminals to serve the state and display its power.[2]

[1] PSZ I: nos. 334 (1663) and 383 (1666). PSZ III: no. 1413 (1691); verb used is *zapiatniav* (indicating hot-iron branding: SRIa XXI: 98). Collins, *Present State*, 59.

[2] European countries were also using exile and hard labor: Weisser, *Crime and Punishment*, 140–2; Briggs et al., *Crime and Punishment*, 80–2. Move away from capital punishment: Schmidt, *Sozialkontrolle*, 385–6.

THE LADDER OF RECIDIVISM

Graduated punishments for felony theft and robbery chart the criminal law's evolution regarding exile and corporal punishment. As discussed in Chapter 9, going into the seventeenth century punishments for felonies constituted a sort of ladder in three-step progression (see Appendix) like that seen for centuries in European common law; change came slowly. A decree of 1637 would have extended the ladder by distinguishing between "small and medium" crimes and proposing three thefts before execution, but the compilers of the 1649 Ulozhenie did not adopt this terminology or extend the ladder. The Ulozhenie did, however, add exile to punishment for felony theft or robbery. After knouting, a felon was to have an ear severed, be imprisoned for between two and four years depending upon the crime, and then to be sent to eternal exile. The severed ear would serve to identify the felon as such in exile (for references, see Appendix).

After the Ulozhenie, decrees chart a contradictory course regarding capital punishment and exile. A decree of 1653 specified that thieves and robbers sentenced to death should be spared that sentence, knouted, mutilated with the loss of a finger on the left hand and exiled to the frontier. The left hand might have been chosen because of a "sinister" association of the left side, or because it was assumed that most labor was done with the right hand. The death penalty was then specified for repeated robbery in exile, the mutilated hand proof of recidivism.[3] On the other hand, a decree of 1659 prescribed the death penalty even for a first instance of robbery in the turbulent Middle Volga region; contrasted to that, however, can be one of 1661 on forgery that replaced the death penalty with a horrific scale of bodily mutilation (see Appendix). The 1669 Criminal Articles kept the three-step ladder, but dropped the 1649 Ulozhenie's prison sentences and exile. It continued to use bodily mutilation to identify felons: the Articles sent home on surety bond felons guilty of up to two thefts or one robbery (without more serious crime involved), marking them with severed fingers. Exile was ordered only if the criminal had no registered home. Subsequent law tended to follow the Ulozhenie in sending capital felons into exile, but vacillated on whether to mark their bodies. Continuing the trend to limit capital punishment, a decree of March 22, 1683 replaced the death penalty for uttering treasonous words with knouting and exile without bodily mutilation, and one of May 1691

[3] PSZ I: no. 105 (1653). Symbolism of the left side: Ryan, *Bathhouse at Midnight*, 54–5.

replaced the death penalty for thieves with exile and branding. The first real extension of the "ladder of recidivism" came in September 1691: four thefts were now required for capital punishment, with exile for only three thefts. Capital punishment continued, of course, for premeditated homicide, political crime and recidivist felony: a decree of January 1692, for example, specified that if an exile who had been bodily marked (indicating felony crime) were caught in capital crime, he would be executed (for references, see Appendix).

EXILE AS PUNISHMENT

In the modern era the Russian empire became infamous for what George Kennan in 1891 called "Siberia and the exile system."[4] Russia's dependence on exile as judicial punishment was epitomized by several generations of Russian revolutionaries, from the Decembrists to Vladimir Ilich Ul'ianov, who reportedly derived his sobriquet "Lenin" from the Lena River in Siberia. The vast Soviet GULAG was heir to this tsarist tradition. But in the seventeenth century the "system" was just being established.

Historians trace the punishment of banishment to the Rus' Law, and sixteenth-century chronicles are full of reference to elite exile.[5] The imprisonment in monasteries discussed in Chapter 3 was a common method of dispensing with enemies in court political struggles, short of murder, and might be considered a form of exile. As discussed in Chapter 14, boyars sent away their enemies in the minority struggles of the 1530s–40s; Ivan the Terrible exiled boyars and metropolitans; Boris Godunov sent to monasteries and to far corners of the empire his Romanov rivals.[6] At the same time, the church banished misbehaving clerics, religious dissidents and individuals guilty of moral crimes to monasteries for repentance, amounting for some to life imprisonment. Even landlords, secular and lay, could practice a form of exile: a 1549 charter to the St. Cyril Beloozero Monastery prescribed banishing from the monastery's lands anyone caught in two felony thefts, along with corporal punishment, as did a 1595 administrative charter for the lands of boyar Dmitrii Ivanovich Godunov.[7] Early

[4] Kennan, *Siberia and the Exile System.* Recent survey: Gentes, *Exile to Siberia.*

[5] In the Rus' Law, *potok* (exile) parallels banishment in other such early European codes: Kaiser (trans. and ed.), *Laws of Rus'*, 136.

[6] Sixteenth-century beginnings: Safronov, *Ssylka*, 10–12; Gentes, *Exile to Siberia*, 34–6. Exile as judicial punishment: Shtamm, "Ugolovnoe pravo," in Nersesiants (ed.), *Razvitie*, 197–8; Shtamm, "Ugolovnoe pravo," in Skripilev (ed.), *Razvitie*, 206–7.

[7] Iakovlev (ed.), *Namestnichie*, 67 (1549), 90 (1595).

modern European cities commonly banished felons from their sovereign territory, but Russia was vast; its exiles stayed within the empire, serving the state in exile on the periphery.[8]

Exile used as judicial punishment is not mentioned in Muscovite law codes until the late sixteenth century; it is not in the 1397–8 Dvina or 1488 Beloozero administrative charters, nor in church law up through and including the 1551 Stoglav, nor in the 1497, 1550, 1589 or 1606 Law Codes, nor in brigandage charters or sixteenth-century Felony Chancery handbooks. When it appears in 1582, it is not associated with felony crime. At a time when territorial expansion to the steppe was heating up, those guilty of a range of judicial slander and misrepresentation were sentenced to knouting in the marketplace and being exiled to serve as cossacks in the "frontier towns, Sevsk and Kursk." From the 1590s the state forcibly transported communities of peasants to Siberia to farm and to serve. By the 1620s this flow of people was joined by exiles – people sentenced in crimes less than felonies – in a policy that Andrew Gentes describes as "economic rationalism." By the Time of Troubles, exile was being used enough to be cited in agreements by the militias in June 1611: they promised not to apply without consultation the death penalty or corporal punishment, or "to send anyone into exile among the towns."[9]

Case law of the 1620s is replete with convicts exiled to service and labor for serious crime. Several cases concern individuals on the western border suspected of spying. A townsman of Putivl' accused of spying was exiled to Siberia in 1621 to be enrolled in a town commune "or whatever service is appropriate"; a peasant accused of spying for the Tatars was sent to the Kazan region to be enrolled in an appropriate service category in 1622, while a slave who had fled across the western border in 1632 was sent to Siberia for lifetime exile in whatever service category "is appropriate." In the same year a Pole who had been in Russian service was exiled for unidentified offenses to the Kazan region for service. Finally, exile was the alternative to the death penalty in 1638, when the tsar, on the intercession of the patriarch, pardoned a group of convicted felons. The creation of the Siberian Chancery in 1637 reflects a quickening pace of populating Siberia with exiles.[10]

[8] Jason Coy describes how banished felons in early modern Germany often returned: *Strangers and Misfits*, 28–46, 97–8, 124–9.

[9] Gentes, *Exile to Siberia*, 49. ZA no. 42 (1582). 1611 agreement, art. 19: RZ III: 48.

[10] AMG I: nos. 137 (1621), 151 (1622), 171 (1623), 403 (1632). PRP V: 225–6 (1638).

The 1649 Ulozhenie demonstrates a broad range of non-felony crime for which exile was deployed: for an undersecretary who for a second time fails to register a case in order to pocket the fees himself; for the accomplices of a man who invades a house to commit murder (the perpetrator himself is to be executed); for townsmen who have indentured themselves to avoid paying taxes (repeating a 1642 norm); for people arrested for a fourth time for selling spirits in an illegal tavern; for more than three arrests for selling tobacco. All these norms specify that the exiles be assigned to work: "send him in fetters to work on whatever labor project the sovereign decrees." The Ulozhenie, however, also adds exile to punishments for brigandage felonies, and requires bodily mutilation as well.[11]

Bodily mutilation was used differentially and only for the most serious of exiles. It was, for example, threatened in 1653 and 1657 for thieves and robbers, with no social distinction made; conversely, when it was threatened for illegal sale of alcohol in the 1660s, it applied only to peasants and slaves, not higher ranks. Mutilation was not threatened in 1655 to military men when exile was specified for burning grain in fields, nor for those exiled for taking in runaways or schismatics.[12] In a whole range of other exile sentences, bodily mutilation was not required as, for example, in 1681 for anyone of any social rank who obstructed the work of surveyors; in 1683 for slaves who fled their owners, are recovered but are not wanted back; for those who spread treasonous ideas; for people falsely posing as cripples and begging; for living unregistered in Moscow; for musketeers who desert service in Azov.[13] Mutilation joined exile in association with felony crime.

EXILE AS LABOR AND COLONIZATION

Exile promised to provide the state with something it desperately needed – labor to populate and construct. As Russian control moved east and south, the state could not support its troops and bureaucracy with provisions sent from the heartland; it used exiles and forcibly moved peasants as servitors or as farmers to feed them, although the numbers were relatively

[11] Ulozhenie ch. 10, arts. 129, 198 (home invasion); ch. 19, art. 13; ch. 21, arts. 9, 10, 16; ch. 25, arts. 3, 16: RZ III: 119, 134, 204, 231–2, 252–3, 256.

[12] PSZ I: nos. 105 (1653), 203 (1657) and 285 (1660). AAE IV: no. 166; AMG II: no. 692 (both 1655). Schismatics: PSZ I: no. 302 (1661); PSZ II: no. 1102 (1684); Barsov, "Sudnye protsessy," no. 6 (1685); PSZ III: no. 1454 (1692).

[13] PSZ II: nos. 866 (1681) and 992 (1683). Treasonous ideas: PSZ II: no. 1002 (1683); false beggars: PSZ III: no. 1424 (1691); unregistered: PSZ III: no. 1509 (1695); Azov: PSZ III: no. 1552 (1696).

small in the seventeenth century.[14] Although as early as 1668 the reformer Andrei Vinius proposed using exiles (criminals and Muslim prisoners of war) to build and man galleys for a new Caspian fleet, exile as a source of labor took off in the late 1690s when Peter I directed convict labor to populate his newly conquered port of Azov. In 1696 he ordered runaway servitors and all exiled criminals to be sent to Azov, with their families, for hard labor (with no mention of bodily mutilation). Brian Boeck has chronicled this massive effort to build docks, buildings and infrastructure in a hostile natural environment. (The term *katorga* for "hard labor" emerged in 1701 in reference to Azov labor.) In 1699 Peter specified that convicts "who are from the skilled artisan ranks or townsmen, and not deserving of the death penalty" shall be exiled to Azov with families, but he specifically barred unmarried men. As much as the new harbor at Azov needed skilled artisans, it did not need restless young men. Boeck estimates that in one decade around 3,000 convicts and prisoners of war were exiled to Azov, but the ambitious port was a complete failure, decimated by disease, hunger and massive flight. The settlement would have been abandoned had it not been regained by the Ottomans in 1711. The Azov experience demonstrates some of the logistical difficulties in populating the empire with exiles expected to work.[15]

As the empire grew, exiles were sent to all possible destinations. In the second half of the sixteenth century, when exile was primarily for disgraced political figures, towns and monasteries in the heartland (Iaroslavl′, Uglich) and the Far North, Perm′ and Viatka lands hosted exiles. By the seventeenth century Siberia was the preferred destination: Tomsk, Ufa and Tobol′sk, "the far Siberian towns" or "on the Lena." But other destinations were also used – the southern frontier towns from Belgorod to Kiev, Kazan and Middle Volga towns to Astrakhan; the Dvina and far northern towns such as Pustoozero, Kholmogory, Kol′skii ostrog; and to the south, the northern Caucasus (the Terek). A decree of February 1683, for example, required that if a landlord did not want to take back slaves who had fled, then they were to be exiled to "the Siberian and Middle Volga and southern frontier towns and regions around Ufa."[16]

14 Exiles' occupations and colonization: Safronov, *Ssylka*, 21, 37–51; Gentes, *Exile to Siberia*, ch. 2. Statistics vary widely: Safronov, *Ssylka*, 27–36; Wood, "Siberian Exile," 42–3; Gentes, *Exile to Siberia*, 37.

15 AI v: no. 80, art. 5 (1668). PSZ II: no. 1552 (1696). Boeck, "When Peter I Was Forced to Settle." PSZ III: no. 1690 (1699). Azov exiles: Gentes, *Exile to Siberia*, 90–1. Family tracked down to join husband/father exiled to Siberia: RGADA f. 210, Sevsk stol, no. 147, fols. 209–26 (1653).

16 Destinations: Safronov, *Ssylka*, 18–22; Gentes, *Exile to Siberia*, 28, 51; ZA nos. 290 (1642), 338 (1648); AMG II: no. 710 (1655); PSZ II: nos. 992 (1683), 1552 (1696).

Whatever the destination, exile presented huge logistical problems for state agencies. Demands on resources were made at every stage of the journey. Some of the earliest decrees provided upkeep to the criminals on their journey – in 1632, "an *altyn*" and food each day.[17] Paying for transport to Siberia was always a challenge. A decree of 1696 announced that putting the burden of such payment on the Siberian Chancery was inappropriate, because exiles traveled in the summer, at which time the Siberian Chancery had no money to pay costs: it received its income in furs from native peoples in the winter. From then on, it decreed, food and upkeep costs of sending a convict to Siberia, at least to the town of Verkhotur′e, were to be paid by the chanceries that had sentenced the convict. It also instructed the Verkhotur′e governor to construct a "household with a standing fence and as many cottages as necessary" for the exiles. Communities complained of the burdens of exile transport: in September 1682 the northern townsmen and peasant communities of Sol′ Vychegodsk and Iarensk petitioned to be relieved of providing boats for exiles. Moscow granted their request to shift the exiles' route to the Kama River.[18]

A handful of cases from the 1680s show the complexity of logistics. In 1685 a serf from Pereiaslavl′ Riazanskii was sentenced to eternal exile to the Terek (Caucasus) for unspecified criminality; his journey went from Pereiaslavl′ to Nizhnii Novgorod to Astrakhan to the Terek area and involved the Musketeer Chancery (which initiated the suit and oversaw transport to Nizhnii Novgorod) and the Novgorod Chancery (which had resolved the suit and took over subsequent transport). Similarly, in 1687 a townsman of the Kola Peninsula was convicted in Moscow of corruption – stealing grain reserves and customs money, abusing his sworn man. The verdict sending him into exile in Pustoozero painstakingly details his route into exile: from Moscow to Pereiaslavl′ Zalesskii, to Iaroslavl′, to Vologda, to Tot′ma, to Ustiug, to Dvina, to Kevrol, to Mezen′, finally arriving in Pustoozersk, a journey of over 1,000 miles to the White Sea. A 1692 decree to the Musketeer Chancery describes the challenges of guarding exiles en route: they were to be transported in leg irons and handcuffs "with great care." Negligent escorts whose exiles fled in transit were to be knouted and themselves exiled to the towns to which the escapees had been headed;

[17] Safronov, *Ssylka*, 22–6, 30–6. Arduousness of transports: Gentes, *Exile to Siberia*, 51–5. AMG I: no. 403 (1632). Related decrees: AMG I: nos. 137 (1621), 151 (1622), 666 (1634); AIuB I: no. 55 XIX (1666).

[18] PSZ III: no. 1534 (1696). In 1728 the *gubernia* that sent exiles became responsible for transport costs: PSZ VIII: no. 5354. AAE IV: no. 259 (1682).

their wives and children were to be summoned to join them.[19] In all these cases the energies of several chanceries and several local communities were taxed along the way.

So arduous were these journeys that Safronov estimates that only about 70–75 percent of exiles destined for Eastern Siberia actually arrived there. Along the way people fell ill and lagged behind, they died or ran off, or were commandeered by local governors to work for them. Once exiles did arrive at their destinations, they had to be supervised. An October 1673 order to the governor of Turinsk details the challenges. He was informed of the disposition of groups of exiles in his area. In 1671/2 and 1672/3, Zaporozhian Cossacks had been exiled to Tobol′sk (approximately 1,400 miles northeast of Moscow), from which they were to be dispersed to various towns and enrolled as infantry cossacks. But in October 1673 one group fled Tobol′sk, so the orders were revised to keep the remaining Zaporozhians in irons in prison, rather than in service. As for groups considered more trustworthy – exiles from Astrakhan, Voronezh – they were to be put on surety bond, or if no bond could be raised, then local officials were to check on them weekly to make sure they did not flee. If any of those gained a reputation for criminality, then they were to be imprisoned as well. The Turinsk governor was specifically instructed to chase down any exiles in his charge who fled, and when they were caught, to send them to Tobol′sk. There the governor would knout and exile them to farther Siberian towns. The governors were told to make a register of any exiles who had arrived after 1661/2 and to confirm that they had remained in their assigned places.[20]

Two memos to Siberian governors of July 1698 depict the tensions inherent in this system. The governor of Irkutsk in eastern Siberia was instructed to remind the exiles that many of them were there only because of the tsar's mercy, having been spared the death penalty, and that they had been given land and benefits. He was told to enjoin them, therefore, to live humbly, support their families and pay their taxes to support the local servitors without resistance. At the same time the governor was told not to use exiles on assignments that would send them out of town, certainly not back to Moscow, and not to transfer them from farming to other roles. He was to present exiles who live decent Christian lives as examples to others and treat them with kindness. At the same time, the governor of Tiumen′ in western Siberia struggled with a surplus of exiles.

[19] RGADA f. 159, op. 3, nos. 2221, fols. 146–7 (1685) and 2470 (1687). PSZ III: no. 1449 (1692).
[20] Exile organization: Safronov, *Ssylka*, 30–6. PSZ I: no. 562 (1673).

He reported that he had neither enough land nor enough service roles to assign to them, and that many were committing crimes and could not be controlled. The Siberian Chancery merely instructed him to step up surveillance, making sure exiles stayed in their places and did their assigned service; in this he was to enlist the elders and residents of towns and villages to watch over exiles. Exiles who refused to farm were to be branded "with hot iron" prominently and told to "live humbly," on pain of execution for further disobedience.[21]

Only the most eminent of exiles were given relatively comfortable surroundings, servants and sufficient food. Such men were often exiled to towns within the traditional heartland of Muscovy and were not enrolled in service, as was the case with a group of boyars and kinsmen associated with the executed general Mikhail Borisovich Shein (see Chapter 15). Their exiles were short-lived: Prozorovskii and Izmailov were pardoned and allowed to return to Moscow – Prozorovskii in late September 1634, Izmailov in early October.[22] In September 1689 Prince Vasilii Vasil′evich Golitsyn was exiled with his son Aleksei and their wives and children to Iarensk in the northern Dvina province; although he died in exile, Golitsyn was provided with generous daily upkeep, to be paid from the customs income of Pustoozero; great detail was given to defining the carts and escorts taking them into exile.[23] Numerous less high-ranking individuals associated with the disgraced Regent Sofiia and the Shaklovitye were exiled in 1689 with less generous terms. Most were sent to Siberian towns, some to the Volga, a laywoman and an undersecretary to Kargopol′ and several clerics to monastery prisons. Men of relatively high status and clan caught up in the Tsykler affair of 1697 were demoted to provincial service ranks: boyar Matvei Pushkin was sent to serve in Eniseisk (2,000 miles away in Siberia) and boyar Fedor Sokovnin was allowed to go to his "farthest villages," both for their sons' treason. Sons of the executed *okol′nichii* Aleksei Sokovnin were demoted and sent to serve in Sevsk (some 335 miles overland southwest of Moscow).[24]

For lesser exiles, policy promoted populating Siberia with families. The 1669 code had said not to send a man into exile without his wife; a decree

[21] Irkutsk: AI v: no. 280; Tiumen′: DAI xii: no. 91 (both 1698).

[22] Provisions for eminent exiles: Safronov, *Ssylka*, 24–7; Vorotynskie princes: AI i: no. 174 (1562). Prozorovskii: AAE iii: nos. 336–7, 342–3, 346–7. Shein: AAE iii: nos. 338–9, 344–5. Izmailov: AAE iii: nos. 340–1, 348–9.

[23] Golitsyn: PSZ ii: nos. 1348 (1689), 1395 (1691); Hughes, *Russia and the West*, 77–84.

[24] RGADA f. 371, op. 2, delo 485, l. 103; PSZ ii: nos. 1349, 1352, 1359, 1362 (1689). PSZ iii: no. 1577 (1697).

in 1680 defined more exactly which family members were required to go into exile with a male criminal. His wife and children under three were to accompany; presumably older children would be left with kinsmen. A 1682 decree confirms that only the family living together with the criminal, not separately, would accompany.[25] But, exile was an unreliable form of colonization. In May of 1679 the governors of Eniseisk wrote to the governor of Iakutsk to detail the progress of a group of exiles who were being sent from Tobol′sk to Iakutsk via Eniseisk and Ilimsk. The Eniseisk governors had just dispatched the exiles, but reported that the group was changing as the trip progressed. Two men had become so ill en route that they had stayed behind with their families, one in Tobol′sk and one in Eniseisk. A woman who had been traveling alone had married another exile in Eniseisk, so he was added to the group. A man being sent to be enrolled in cossack service had died on the road between Tobol′sk and Eniseisk; another man had enrolled in the Tobol′sk town commune. New labor was moving east, but in depleted numbers and often not arriving at intended destinations.[26]

The seventeenth-century exile system was hardly a sure thing as a source of labor and colonization. Furthermore, the vast expanse of Siberia made controlling exiles particularly challenging. Not surprisingly, the state turned to bodily marking to identify and monitor the exiles guilty of the most serious crimes.

BODILY MUTILATION AND BRANDING

Bodily mutilation as judicial sanction appeared in a few secular and church codes before the mid seventeenth century but was rarely, if ever, applied in practice.[27] There are famous examples of reciprocal blinding in the fifteenth-century Muscovite dynastic war, but this was outside of the judicial sphere. Bodily mutilation is generally not cited in law before 1649: not in the 1488 charter to Beloozero, nor in the 1497, 1550, 1589 or 1606 Law Codes; the 1589 Law Code explicitly forbade using it. Reflecting Roman law, however, brigandage charters order severing a hand for a second felony theft, and a 1637 decree, never put into effect, prescribed

25 1669 Criminal Articles, art. 61: PRP VII: 419. PSZ II: no. 846 (1680). PSZ II: no. 970 (1682).

26 AIuB II: no. 201 (1679).

27 Bodily mutilation in Russian practice into eighteenth century: Timofeev, *Istoriia*, pt. 3, ch. 1; Evreinov, *Istoriia*, 26–55. The 1397–8 Dvina Charter (art. 5) cites branding for theft, and a church code of the late fifteenth or early sixteenth century mandates “cutting off a limb” for murder, but neither norm was used in practice: RZ II: 181. *Pravosudie mitropolichie*, art. 12: PRP III: 427.

facial branding for felons: letters or words would have been stamped on the face with a hot iron so that a criminal's crime could be read: R on the right cheek, Z on the forehead, and B on the left cheek for "*razboinik*" (robber); similarly, T on the right cheek, A on the forehead and T on the left cheek for "*tat'*" (thief).[28]

The brigandage charter's reference to severing a hand apparently had influence in early seventeenth-century cases of serious crime, as this is cited in cases of 1613 and 1644.[29] The 1649 Ulozhenie marks a more systematic introduction of bodily mutilation, used as debilitating sanction or as marker of identity as a felon. In some cases this took a form of talion: the body part that did the crime is itself punished. Thus, for drawing a weapon or wounding someone in the tsar's presence, or stealing from the palace, an unspecified hand is to be cut off, while the hand that steals a horse from a servitor on campaign should be cut off. A general principle for such talionic punishment is expressed in a clause whereby anyone who physically mutilates another should be punished with the same sort of mutilation.[30] In other clauses the 1649 Ulozhenie associated the severing of body parts with exile as an identifying mark. For a first theft or robbery, the left ear was to be severed, the right ear for someone caught in a second theft. The code explicitly states that if someone appears in a community with one or two mutilated ears and no letter of free passage, they are to be arrested as a runaway exile and "known criminal." For more than three instances of selling tobacco the Ulozhenie prescribes a particularly brutal form of mutilation: knouting and having nostrils slit before being sent into exile. Practice followed the law: in a 1653 case the punishment exactly matches these Ulozhenie norms, including a prison term preceding exile.[31] John Keep calls 1663 the "peak" of brutality in judicial sanction, for good reason. In contrast to the 1649 Ulozhenie and 1650s decrees that ordered fingers or ears severed for purposes of identification, mutilation began in the 1660s to be more debilitating. A decree of

[28] Reciprocal blinding: Kollmann, *Kinship and Politics*, 154. 1589 Law Code, art. 4: PRP IV: 414. 1555 Medyn Charter, art. 11; RZ II: 222; 1616/17 Felony Handbook, arts. 38–40: PRP V: 197. Letters: PRP V: 223–4 (1637) (*piatnati*). Another 1637 decree burned the word "*vor*" on counterfeiters' cheeks: AAE III: no. 266 (*napiatnati, rozzhegshi*). The British traveler Richard Chancellor reported in the mid sixteenth century that a thief caught for the second time "is burnt in the forehead with a hot iron," but no other sixteenth-century sources cite this: "Voyage," 35.

[29] RGADA f. 1107, no. 19 (1613) (the mutilation was ultimately pardoned). 1644: "Uboistvennye dela," 3 (1644).

[30] Ulozhenie ch. 3, arts. 4, 5, 9; ch. 7, art. 29; ch. 22, art. 10: RZ III: 90–1, 94, 248–9.

[31] Ulozhenie ch. 21, arts. 9–10, 16, 19, 90: RZ III: 231–2, 245. RGADA f. 210, Sevsk stol, no. 147, fols. 227–30 (1653).

1660 sentenced peasants guilty of selling wine illegally to have their hands cut off and be exiled to Siberia. Here the convict's mutilation destroyed his labor capacity. A decree of 1661 about forgery provided a terrifying graduated scale of mutilation involving severing feet, left hands or fingers as a substitute for the death penalty. The horrific 1663 decree cited at the beginning of this chapter almost amounted to quartering, as did many of the punishments meted out to rebels in the 1662 Kolomenskoe unrest, where some were mutilated and others branded with the letter B for rebel (*buntovshchik*) on their left cheek (see Chapter 16). This use of a semiotic symbol, rather than bodily mutilation, harkens back to the dormant 1637 law and presages practices of branding that appear in the 1690s.[32]

The 1669 Articles, written at a time of social stress and unrest marked by urban riots in Moscow in 1662 and culminating in the Stepan Razin rebellion of 1669–71, made the Ulozhenie's bodily mutilation more debilitating. For example, while the 1649 code had mandated cutting off a left ear for a first theft, the 1669 Articles specified "two small fingers from the left hand." For a second crime, it mandated cutting off a left hand at the wrist, while the 1649 code had specified only the second, or right, ear. Criminals are then to be given a letter allowing them to return to their previous homes, and they are to be allowed back "without prejudice." But should such a mutilated man engage in further crime, he would be mutilated further, losing a hand and a foot. For the serious crime of theft of church objects, for which the 1649 Ulozhenie had prescribed the death penalty, the Articles mandated severing a left hand and right foot for the first such crime (for references, see Appendix).

Muscovite legislators backed off such brutality to an extent after the 1660s. Already in 1666, the horrific 1663 decree had been rescinded. Later, two laws eliminated mutilation altogether for exiles: those who admitted to serious crime and who would have had their feet and hands severed (the 1669 norm) were now to be exiled to Siberia with no mutilation (September 1679), while the mutilation (severing "hands, feet and two fingers") that had been decreed for those who committed one or two thefts was replaced with eternal exile to Siberia (1680). But a decree of 1682 intensified the 1669 norm for the first stage of criminality by severing the mandated two small fingers of the left hand *and* the left ear, as well as ordering a knouting and eternal exile to Siberia; a decree of March 30, 1683

[32] Keep, "Bandits," 213. PSZ I: no. 285 (1660). AI IV: no. 158 (1661). PSZ I: no. 334 (1663). *Vosstanie 1662 g.*, 39–52, 84–5, 141–5, 176–80, 208–11, 232–4, 243–4, 247–50, 265–6. Letter B also cited by Kotoshikhin, ch. 7 art. 9: *O Rossii*, 103.

limited but did not eliminate mutilation, mandating that "ears" be severed instead of fingers. Although these laws were said to have come from the "tsars and boyars," they suggest that multiple chanceries were issuing often contradictory laws.

Nevertheless, the trend was towards bodily marking that preserved a convict's labor power; branding began to take the place of bodily mutilation in the law to mark exiles and criminals. It had been cited before, in 1637 and in the 1662 punishments, but by the 1690s the practice took off.[33] A decree of May 1691, for example, cancelled the bodily mutilation (severing ears or fingers) for those who had been convicted of a capital crime, but had been pardoned and sentenced to exile; instead, they were to be hot-iron branded with the letter V for "*vor*" (criminal) on the left cheek. The decree explicitly states that the brand would allow them to be recognized should they flee their exile. A January 1692 decree orders that if someone had been exiled for a capital crime and had not yet been branded, then it should be done to him. Similarly, if individuals exiled for a lesser crime were convicted while in exile for a capital crime, they were then to be branded. The decree also notes that if an exiled criminal who had been branded fled his exile, he was to be caught, re-branded with the letter R for "*razboinik*" (robber) on the other (right) cheek and returned to the place of exile; if he escaped again, the two brands alone were sufficient to mandate the death penalty, even if the runaway had not engaged in crime. This decree illustrates the role facial branding came to play by the 1690s: it documented the criminal as guilty of capital crime and identified the degree of recidivism. This is echoed in a July 1698 decree to the Irkutsk governor. He was told to execute without mercy any branded exile who was caught in crime, not even capital crime, since the criminal had already been once pardoned a capital crime by the tsar – this is evident, the decree noted, in his having been branded (for references, see Appendix).

In addition to letters, Russian officials turned to other customs of branding when regarding their human possession. One brand cited from the 1660s took the shape of an eagle (*orel*), like stamps used for taxable state merchandise. In 1698 an infantryman who had been sent into exile for raucous living "unbefitting an infantryman" – gambling, playing

[33] Decrees of 1637 and 1698 specifically describe branding done by hot iron: PRP v: 223–4 (1637); DAI xii: no. 91 (1698). So do others cited in this chapter; footnotes indicate the vocabulary of hot-iron branding (forms of the verb *zapiatnat'*); references to tattooing with gunpowder occur in the early eighteenth century; both methods might have been used; see Chapter 12.

cards, drinking – appealed to be allowed to return. He admitted that he had been eagle-stamped (*zaorlen*) before being exiled to Astrakhan.[34] A more explicit approach, which helped to identify and track the mobility of exiles, is found in decrees of the late 1690s to Siberia: criminals were to be branded with the name of the town to which they had been exiled. A 1698 decree to the governor of the Siberian town of Tiumen′, for example, instructs him to brand on the back any exiles who were caught in crime; the brand, to be done with hot iron, was the name of the city Tiumen′. For this task, he was provided with a model that he was to replicate at twice the size; similar brands were distributed to other Siberian towns as noted in a decree of 1698 to Irkutsk (see Appendix).

Not only Russia used pictorial symbols or city names to label exiles; in early modern Europe municipalities often branded criminals with their town symbol before banishing them. Van Dülmen notes, for example, that "the symbol of the gallows or the coat of arms of the city – in Frankfurt, for instance, an eagle – was often used." In other cases, the city of Frankfurt would brand a criminal with the letter F, Lucerne with an L. In sixteenth- and seventeenth-century France, brands could take the form of a fleur-de-lis, while in Amsterdam, three crosses from the city seal.[35] Early modern states marked bodies as communication and control.

EXILE, CRIME AND MUTILATION

This brutal litany of mutilations and branding demonstrates mounting violence in the positive law. But in practice, most sentences to exile did not include such physical harm. Of a group of about thirty-four resolved cases in the present study that sentenced people to exile, only around ten specified bodily mutilation or branding. Who then suffered these horrible physical markings?

As already suggested, crime and social status determined susceptibility to bodily marking. For felony crime, social rank should not have been taken into account, but for other crimes, bodily mutilation in practice was often limited to lesser classes. A decree of 1660 regarding illegal alcohol sales, for example, determined a range of punishments from land confiscation for gentrymen to corporal punishment and exile for social groups

[34] RGADA f. 210, Prikaznyi stol, no. 965, fols. 23 and 26–33 (1698). 1660s references to exiles being "branded" and even stamped with "eagle" insignia: ODB xvi: no. 975. "*Zaorlennyi*": SRIa v: 254; PSZ iv: no. 1893 (1701).

[35] Frankfurt: van Dülmen, *Theatre of Horror*, 49. Lucerne: Schneller, "Das Hexenwesen." France: Greenshields, *Economy of Violence*, 204. Amsterdam: Spierenburg, *Spectacle*, 70.

associated with trade and service on the tsar's lands or church lands. But private serfs and slaves guilty of the crime were to be bodily mutilated and exiled. A verdict on military men arrested in the 1662 Moscow "copper riots" reveals similar discrimination: the higher-ranking military men – provincial gentry, *zhil'tsy* and new model cavalrymen – "who had not undergone torture" were to be exiled without corporal punishment or branding to Astrakhan and enrolled as gentrymen (*deti boiarskie*), unless they hailed from the Volga region, in which case they should be sent to Siberia. Of the men of lesser ranks, the twenty most guilty were to be knouted, and the entire group, except the above-mentioned higher ranks, were to be branded on the left cheek with the letter B for rebel (*buntovshchik*) and exiled as farmers to other areas, not the Volga or Astrakhan.[36] Clearly, torture, corporal punishment and branding tainted the recipient, and men of the higher military ranks were spared such humiliation.

In practice laws associating bodily mutilation with brigandage crime and its degrees of punishment were observed. In 1666 a peasant guilty of robbery and highway robbery was sentenced to a knouting and exile in Astrakhan with his right ear cut off, since his left one already had been. For one theft in 1671 two peasants were sentenced to a knouting and the severing of two small fingers of the left hand, above the first joint, without exile; this follows the 1669 Criminal Articles norms.[37] In 1676, similarly, a case of theft of customs revenues and icons by a townsman in Putivl′ followed the 1669 code in mandating the severing of a hand and a foot. A second 1676 case for arrest on a first theft by a townsman in Belev was referred to a central chancery, seeking a ruling on whether the 1649 Ulozhenie was to be followed (severing a left ear) or the 1669 norm (two left fingers), along with knouting and exile. The Chancery ruled for the 1669 norm. In the end, the defendants in this case successfully appealed the mutilation and knouting, but they were still exiled.[38]

Bodily mutilation continued to the end of the century, even as branding became more common. For example, in 1689 the governor of Sol′ Kamskaia in the Urals reported that a man was punished for one robbery with no murder involved, using the 1669 norms, namely, his left hand and right foot were severed. Unfortunately, he reported, the man died of the wounds. Apparently the officials in this far-flung post did not

[36] PSZ I: no. 285 (1660). RGADA f. 210, Prikaznyi stol, no. 959, fols. 68, 267 (1662); excerpts in *Vosstanie 1662 g.*, 243–4.

[37] AIuB I: no. 55 (XIX) (1666); cf. PSZ I: no. 105 (1653). AIuB II: no. 245 (I) (1671).

[38] Customs: RGADA f. 210, Sevsk stol, no. 294, fols. 311–30 (1676). Chancery: RGADA f. 210, Sevsk stol, no. 294, fols. 182–212 (1676).

know of a 1682 decree changing that punishment to a less life-threatening mutilation, that is, a left ear and two fingers were to be severed. A peasant of the patriarch's lands convicted of murdering a slave was sentenced in 1695, "according to the New Articles," to eternal exile to the Belgorod frontier, preceding by a knouting on the rack and having his left ear severed. According to the 1669 Articles he should have been executed for intentional murder or knouted for unintentional homicide, but perhaps the judge had in mind a May 1691 decree that ordered a blanket substitution of exile for capital punishment.[39] By the late seventeenth century judges used exile whenever possible.

Bodily mutilation also was used in a variety of ways for other crimes, some symbolic of social rank, some of the crime. Branding with the letter B in 1662 labeled those men as rebels and of lower social status. Mutilation often signified a crime: a musketeer and a townsman guilty of reading aloud a letter and urging people to join the 1662 Moscow uprising, for example, lost their tongues (as well as both feet).[40] Such severing of tongues, although rarely cited in formal law, was particularly symbolic, commonly used in cases of seditious speech. So, for example, a townsman convicted of saying "inappropriate things" about the tsar's wife in 1651 was sentenced to exile to Great Novgorod with his tongue cut out; similarly, in 1667 Avvakum and others in his circle of schismatics were sentenced to exile and to having their tongues severed to prevent them from preaching their heretical views (Avvakum was ultimately pardoned the mutilation). Three musketeer officers sentenced to death in the Shaklovityi conspiracy were pardoned in 1689 at the last minute and sentenced instead to knouting and Siberian exile, with their tongues cut out, symbolic of their having spread evil words and ideas. Others convicted in this conspiracy were exiled without mutilation. A worker found guilty of speaking against Peter I was sentenced in 1697 to having his tongue cut out, as well as a merciless knouting and exile to a monastery.[41] Most people, even of the lower social ranks, however, were sent into exile without mutilation or branding. The majority of verdicts did not involve severing body parts, even when the law allowed it, and it was associated with exile, serving as a means to mark a criminal and control his mobility.

39 DAI XII: no. 56 (1689). PSZ II: no. 970 (1682). RGADA f. 210, Belgorod stol, no. 1604, fol. 147 (1695). Criminal Articles and 1691 decree: see Appendix.

40 Tongue, hands, feet 1662: RGADA f. 210, Prikaznyi stol, no. 959, fols. 30, 60 (1662); excerpt in *Vosstanie 1662 g.*, 266.

41 AAE IV: no. 51 (1651). Avvakum et al.: Barskov, *Pamiatniki*, no. xxiv, pp. 146–53. PSZ III: nos. 1349 and 1352 (1689). Golikova, *Politicheskie protsessy*, 51 (1697).

Russia was not alone in branding and mutilating criminals or in using the exile system. Branding, tattooing, scarring the body and other forms of bodily disfigurement were old methods of punishment and penal marking. In Greco-Roman antiquity, words were tattooed with ink and brands seared on skin to label runaway slaves and criminals with signs of their misdeeds. Tongues were cut out to indicate a crime of speech and hands were cut off to indicate theft. Such marks were "defamatory in the highest degree" – in early modern Europe branded individuals were barred from taking oaths and were humiliated; as van Dülmen notes, "a branded person would never again be able to find 'honest' work." Elsewhere, as in early modern Japan, tattooing of criminals developed into an underground semiotic system.[42]

Among Muscovy's contemporaries in early modern Europe, these practices were declining by the seventeenth century. Jason Coy observed that municipal officials in the city of Ulm in the sixteenth century threatened bodily mutilation to those they banished from the town, but rarely inflicted it. Similarly, Ulinka Rublack noted a 1551 Imperial law that forbade branding and observed that it was still done, but rarely. Van Dülmen concurs: "it was not as frequently imposed as we may think ... It was mainly members of the lower ranks of society ... who were punished in this way." In the mid sixteenth century in France, judicial practice began to shift from bodily mutilation to branding, and branding on the face gave way to branding on the shoulder. But in seventeenth-century Polish cities governed by Magdeburg law, branding was used, particularly for those expelled from the city. Into the eighteenth century branding and to a lesser extent bodily mutilation were occasionally cited in Europe, but as a rule their use declined as European sensibilities turned against them, and different forms of punishment, such as prison, emerged.[43] But in Muscovy, where exiles lived in the contiguous lands of a sprawling empire, branding served the state's purpose of identifying and controlling exiles, while a decline in bodily mutilation preserved their labor power.

[42] Jones, "Tattooing and Branding"; Peters, "Prison before the Prison," 9, 10, 31–2, 37; van Dülmen, *Theatre of Horror*, 49; Botsman, *Punishment and Power*, 27–8.

[43] Coy, *Strangers and Misfits*, 45, 49–50; Rublack, *Crimes of Women*, 80–1. Van Dülmen, *Theatre of Horror*, 49. Greenshields, *Economy of Violence*, 204–5. Poland: Laszkiewicz, "Kary vymierzone" and Kamler, "Penalties." Spierenburg, *Spectacle*, 69–77, 200.

CHAPTER 12

Peter I and punishment

In 1718 Peter the Great railed against street crime in Petersburg.

> From the many runaway soldiers and sailors and other criminals, crime and murder happens; they live in taverns and public baths and markets and pothouses . . . Therefore we decree to all . . . that no one is to allow such a person to stay with them overnight or to hire them without a surety . . . or they too will be punished harshly, knouted and sent to forced labor . . . If someone does not run to catch a criminal when the alarm is sounded and it is shown that from their failure to respond a murder or some other evil has occurred – from which God save us! – they are . . . to answer for this crime in the same way as those murderers and evildoers.[1]

Petrine laws are often didactic and emotional. "May God save us from crime," Peter muses. As ruler, he did not fail to punish those who brought crime upon his people and his state.

Historians have been critical of the Petrine legacy on judicial punishment. Some have argued that early eighteenth-century administrative and judicial reforms introduced a culture of denunciation and brutality.[2] As European public opinion turned against corporal punishment in the eighteenth century, its endurance made Russia appear then and to modern historians as backward. This chapter assesses how reforms towards "the well-ordered police state" applied to corporal punishment. It uses a group of seventy-five cases already examined for judicial procedure in Chapter 8. Dating from 1699 to approximately 1727, they come from around the realm, but a particularly rich group of about fifty-five cases (most of them resolved) stems from the provincial court in Arzamas and other Middle Volga venues. They show that, when it came to most crime, Petrine judges were no more, and no less, brutal than the preceding era. If Peter deserves his reputation for cruelty, it is in how he punished

[1] PSZ v: no. 3212 (1718).

[2] Anisimov, *Dyba i knut*, 567–72; Eroshkin, *Ocherki*, 115–17. Rogov disagrees: *Istoriia*, 224–7.

highest crime, as discussed in Chapter 18. Since the Ulozhenie remained the presiding law code, not surprisingly, regimes of punishment generally perpetuated Muscovite patterns.

PETRINE LEGAL CONCEPTS ABOUT PUNISHMENT

Petrine reforms gave extensive attention to the criminal law, but regarding forms of punishment, they did not change as much as it might seem.[3] The 1715 Military Articles create the impression of a shift to more coercive sanctions. They introduced new forms of corporal and capital punishment: execution by shooting squad, running the gauntlet (technically not a death penalty, it was used primarily for military crimes such as runaway recruits and fisticuffs or for serious religious crime) and even hanging by the ribs. Borrowing a European practice, they introduced public rituals of penance for certain crimes. But neither these new punishments nor penance were applied to secular judicial practice. There are even cases of lessening of punishment, as in a 1723 decree that changed the penalty for coin forgery. Rather than pouring molten ore down the throat, those convicted were now to be beheaded "for a fast death."[4]

In addition, the Military Articles continued many familiar ideas and practices. They maintain the view that punishment deters crime (nos. 24, 137) and provide different penalties for murder, unintentional homicide and death from carelessness or accident (nos. 158–9); they exonerate killing in self-defense, but set a higher standard for proving it (no. 157). They follow the 1669 Articles regarding the mitigating effect of minor age and mental incapacity (no. 195), and continue their trend (in comparison to the Ulozhenie) of punishing crime committed during drunkenness more harshly (no. 43). The Military Articles explicitly discuss practices that had been implicit before: they give judges flexibility to determine punishment based on the circumstances of the crime and the social status (*sostoiane*) of the guilty (nos. 145, 154, 164, 167–70, 176, 202–3) and discretion in the severity of quartering and torture (no. 124). They raise

[3] Romashkin cites 392 new criminal laws: *Osnovnye nachala*, 16; survey of Petrine legislation, 3–31. New legal concepts: ibid., 32–61. Scholars track the introduction in Russian law of a more sophisticated legal vocabulary over the eighteenth century: Wirtschafter, *Russia's Age of Serfdom*, 124, 138; Serov, *Sudebnaia reforma*, 201–5, 257–60, 446–7. Petrine punishments: Shtamm, "Ugolovnoe pravo," in Skripilev (ed.), *Razvitie*, 201–14.

[4] Shooting squad 1715 Military Articles, no. 6: RZ IV: 329. Gauntlet: PSZ IV: no. 2566 (1712); 1715 Military Articles, nos. 1, 141, 143, 170, 185, 189: RZ IV: 329, 353, 359, 362; PSZ V: no. 3136 (1717). Hanging "by the ribs": PSZ V: no. 3477, art. 4 (1719). PSZ VII: no. 4157 (1723). Penance: 1715 Military Articles, nos. 1, 6, 8, 157–8, 198: RZ IV: 328–30, 356–7, 363.

new issues, such as the difficulty of proving rape and the degree of male responsibility for unwed pregnancies (nos. 167–8, 176); they introduce more generalized terms for "crime" and "criminal" (*prestuplenie, prestupnik*) (nos. 189–90).[5] Although the Military Articles were not applied in secular courts, they demonstrate a higher level of judicial expertise at court in the early eighteenth century.

Other early eighteenth-century decrees also perpetuated seventeenth-century trends of punishment. On the one hand, the list of capital offenses was expanded, particularly to include crime against state revenue.[6] On the other hand, energetic state-building projects required labor, so exile continued to be applied in place of execution, even for capital crime. P. S. Romashkin even declares that Peter de facto abolished the death penalty except for the highest crime, seeing this as compassionate. He cites an anecdote according to which Peter, in conversation in 1715, responded with shock to being told about the liberal use of the death penalty in Charles V's 1532 *Carolina*:

> Is that really true? I would think that Great Sovereign would show more intelligence and perception in this issue. If it is true, then perhaps he believed that he had more extra people in his state than I have in mine. One must punish disorder and crimes, of course, but one should also preserve the lives of one's subjects as much as possible.[7]

With the harsh conditions of exile and forced labor and the suffering created by escalating taxes and recruitment quotas, Peter the Great can hardly be called humanitarian, and Romashkin's effort to read him in this light suggests some wishful thinking in the Stalinist context in which he was writing (1947). But whatever Peter's motivation, he presided over a significant limitation of the death penalty.

Extension of the ladder of recidivism continued: a 1703 decree increased the number of incidents of the serious crime of robbery (*razboi*) to an astounding ten before capital punishment was decreed, as long as no murder accompanied the crimes. Recidivist robbers were to be knouted, branded on the cheek and exiled eternally to forced labor. Similarly, in the

[5] 1715 Military Articles: RZ IV: 327–65.

[6] New capital crimes: illegal import of goods (1704: PSZ IV: no. 1967), harboring runaway soldiers (1712: PSZ IV: no. 2499), fleeing military service (PSZ IV: no. 2566 [1712], PSZ VI: no. 3599 [1720]), taking bribes (PSZ V: no. 2871 [1714], PSZ VI: no. 4007 [1722]), fleeing exile or harboring criminals (PSZ IV: nos. 2026 [1705], 2499 [1712]; PSZ V: no. 2823 [1714]), cutting down forests (PSZ IV: nos. 2026 [1705], 2499 [1712]; PSZ V: no. 2823 [1714]), judicial corruption (1720: PRP VIII: 102); petitioning the tsar's courtiers (1720: PRP VIII: 102).

[7] Romashkin, *Osnovnye nachala*, 64–70. Anecdote: Golikov, *Deianiia Petra Velikogo* V: 97–8.

state's eagerness to recruit labor, decrees excluded traditional felony crimes (theft and robbery) from the death penalty. For example, decrees of 1703, 1704 and 1705 mandated execution only for those guilty of "treason, rebellion, intentional murder and poisoning"; all other "criminality" was to be punished with exile to forced labor (references in Appendix).

Even facing massive flight from military service, Petrine legislators occasionally relented when the demand for manpower was intense. A 1700 law had decreed that runaway soldiers were to be hanged, but one of January 1705 modified it: only one in three was to be hanged, before the regiment; the others were to be knouted and eternally exiled to hard labor. A decree of 1711 allowed runaway "dragoons, soldiers, recruits, sailors and serving men of all ranks" to return to their units without punishment, even if they had committed crime deserving of corporal or even capital punishment while in flight. But if they failed to return within six months, they were to be executed "without any mercy." In 1712 and 1715 decrees mandated the death penalty for fleeing military service, but such stringency was soon relaxed: a decree of 1717 held that a recruit who flees service in his first year was to be punished by running the gauntlet three times; for a second flight, or if he flees after a year of service, then he was to be knouted, his nostrils slit before the whole regiment and he was to be exiled to eternal labor in the galleys. These are not insignificant punishments, but they avoid the death penalty and preserve the person's labor power.[8]

In non-military areas early eighteenth-century legislation also lessened punishment to capture labor. A decree of March 7, 1721 pardoned even murderers who voluntarily surrendered; spared execution, they would be punished by running the gauntlet and being exiled for ten years of hard labor. In the same year criminal legislation backtracked from the "ten robberies" of 1703 but settled on a ladder of felony recidivism longer than the three-step fifteenth-century original: three thefts and two robberies were allowed before execution (see Appendix). During Peter's reign, the threshold of felony crime requiring the death penalty was raised significantly in favor of exile or forced labor. Capital punishment was saved for murder, serious recidivist felony and political crime (see Chapter 18).

[8] PSZ IV: nos. 1820, art. 18 (1700), 2019 (1705) and 2318 (1711). PSZ V: nos. 2499 and 2566 (1712), 2900 (1715) and 3136 (1717).

SHAME AND SOCIAL HIERARCHIES OF PUNISHMENT

Some early eighteenth-century reforms introduced a new, European attitude to corporal punishment based on a more individualized concept of honor. As discussed in Chapters 9 and 10, a de facto exemption from corporal punishment for privileged social ranks (clergy and landed gentry) permeated seventeenth-century law codes; it continued into Peter I's era. Instructions to the governor of Astrakhan in 1700, for example, allowed torture on all Russian suspects and lower-class non-Russians, but exempted non-Russian elites (*murzy*) from torture except for "major state affairs and great treason." A charter in 1705 regarding illicit alcohol trade required that people of high social rank not be punished without consultation with higher courts.[9] As before, people of higher social status or officialdom paid fines when lesser classes received corporal punishment. Thus a decree of 1715 concerning submitting poll tax books on time punished negligent scribal staff "mercilessly" with bastinadoes but levied a fine on governors and judges. The Military Articles excused from torture various categories of people – pregnant women, the elderly over age 70, minors and, significantly, people who were "like nobility (*shliakhta*), servitors in high ranks." Similarly in 1719 Peter declared that people of higher ranks (*znatnye*) who submitted petitions to him, bypassing the proper lower venues, would lose their "honor and property," but petitioners of lower class (*nizhnie i podlye chiny*) would get "harsh corporal punishment."[10]

As before, however, the law did not hesitate to inflict corporal punishment on higher-ranking individuals for harm to state interests. Governors who failed to deliver recruits on time were threatened in 1711 with execution as traitors; landlords who sheltered a runaway soldier or did not report one, or *landraty* who failed to track them down, also suffered corporal punishment in a decree of April 1715. In 1720 Peter sentenced two governors, a "corrupt clerk" and five other officials to knouting, branding, exile or running the gauntlet for cutting down valuable timber on forest preserves. The Military Articles of 1715 are replete with corporal punishment for all ranks, as is the General Regulation of 1720.[11]

9 PSZ IV: nos. 1792, art. 23 (1700) and 2064, art. 3 (1705).

10 PSZ V: nos. 2912 (1715) and 3006, pt. 2, ch. 6, art. 10, p. 407 (1716). ZA Petra 378 (1719).

11 PSZ IV: no. 2315 (1711). PSZ V: nos. 2900 (1715) and 3509 (1720). General Regulation: PRP VIII: 101, ch. 50 (1720).

Peter's new concept of "political death" or "disgrace" (*oshel'movan'e*) introduced an explicitly European discourse of shame; it provided humiliating punishment in place of physical death for a person of high rank guilty of major crime.[12] "Political death" appears in laws by 1710; in 1714 it deprived the guilty of property and "exclusion from the company of good people," while the 1715 Military Articles declared that someone who had suffered political death or had been "in the hands of the executioners" could not rejoin the army, even while clarifying that "soldiers and officers guilty of great crimes can be tortured like any other evildoer." The General Regulation of 1720 explicitly forbade those who had been either "in public punishment" or "disgraced" (*oshel'movan*), to serve the tsar, to bear witness in court, to litigate for personal injury (this right is not denied to those who have suffered public punishment but not disgrace) and to associate in polite society. Anyone who entertained a disgraced person was to be sentenced to loss of rank and a term in forced labor. The Table of Ranks explained these harsh strictures: "No other incentive inclines people to the good better than love of honor, as in the same way no other punishment so terrifies as its loss."[13]

In distinguishing the upper classes, "political death" joined other efforts to create a European-style nobility. Decrees and terminology explicitly addressed this goal. A collective name (first *shliakhetstvo*, derived from Polish, gradually displaced by *dvorianstvo*) was introduced, along with new forms of etiquette and dress to create a new collective sense of identity; an increase in military service requirement gave men in the elite common life experiences.[14] The founding document of the new nobility was the 1722 Table of Ranks: it introduced the idea of hereditary noble status, awarding it to those who worked up to the highest ranks; it deployed shame by declaring that anyone who had been "publically punished on the square or had even only been [reprieved on the gallows while] bared for whipping [*obnazheny*] or tortured" would be dismissed from rank. It defined nobility with a sumptuary law: "Since such

[12] Political death: Shtamm, "Ugolovnoe pravo," in Skripilev (ed.), *Razvitie*, 212–13; Anisimov, *Dyba i knut*, 545–7, 549–50; Schrader, *Languages*, 28–9.

[13] Instruction to Navy: PSZ IV: no. 2267, art. 10 (1710). PSZ V: no. 2871 (1714). 1715 Military Articles, art. 209: RZ IV: 365. General Regulation, ch. 53: PRP VIII: 102 (1720). Table of Ranks: PSZ VI: no. 3534, ch. 53 and PRP VIII: 102 (1722). Honor and political death: Kollmann, *By Honor Bound*, 236–7. "Political death" for other crimes: strike someone in court: PSZ VII: nos. 4337 (1723); recruits who flee: PSZ VIII: no. 5611 (1728). Cited as parallel to "natural death": PSZ VII: nos. 4460 (1724), 4655 (1725), 4964 (1726), 5026 and 5218 (both 1727).

[14] Emergence of the nobility: Mironov, *Sotsial'naia istoriia* I: chs. 2, 4, 6–7; Raeff, *Origins*, ch. 4; Kollmann, "Etiquette for Peter's Time" and "Beginning a Civilizing Process."

eminence and worthiness of each rank can diminish when its dress does not match it . . . each person should use the clothing, carriage and livery that their rank and character demand."[15]

Numerous Petrine decrees reiterated the association of corporal punishment with shame. A decree of March 15, 1721, for example, allowed knouting for officers and soldiers sentenced to eternal exile or hard labor but spared those who were being sent for a fixed term. Instead, they were to run the gauntlet and not be knouted, since, if they had been "in the hands of the executioner, it would be impossible to use them in their prior service." Similarly, a decree of February 20, 1722 asked "officers and nobles and people of other ranks" who had been "in public punishments and in a term of hard labor, but who had no marks branded on them and had been released," to seek official pardon. By the end of the eighteenth century this consciousness had become entrenched; in criminal cases high-ranking individuals sentenced to corporal punishment were first deprived of all ranks and of gentry status before receiving the knout.[16]

EXILE AND BRANDING

At the other end of the social spectrum, early eighteenth-century laws intensified the use of exile and the marking of some exiles' bodies to provide forced labor for new harbors and canals, textile and munitions factories and mines. Women were exiled to textile manufacturing; those too feeble for hard labor were sent to monasteries to work. Demand for labor was everywhere, as revealed in a decree of 1722 that ordered schismatics no longer to be sent to Siberia, since they had become so numerous there that they were a bad influence. Rather, schismatics should be sent to Rogervik (modern-day Paldiski on the Baltic Sea) to construct the new harbor.[17]

As the exile and forced labor system grew, so did strategies for marking capital criminals. As detailed in Chapter 11, the eagle shape, words such as "*vor*" and "*tat'*," even the names of Siberian towns were used in brands by the late 1690s. A decree of 1703 simply says to "brand on the cheek,"

[15] PSZ VI: no. 3890, arts. 18–19 (1722). It also noted, however, that if a false accusation causes a nobleman to be tortured, that torture would not be considered dishonoring.

[16] Hands of executioner: PSZ VI: no. 3760 (1721); PSZ VIII: no. 5434 (1729). PSZ VI: no. 3909 (1722). End of century cases: PSZ XX: no. 15,032 (1780); PSZ XXI: no. 15,336 (1782); PSZ XXIII: no. 17,262 (1794).

[17] Women: PSZ V: nos. 3306, 3313 and 3336 (1719); PSZ VI: no. 3808 (1721). Feeble: PSZ IV: no. 2179 (1707). PSZ VI: no. 4109 (1722).

without specifying which cheek or what brand; a decree of 1704 cites "new brands." Terminology continues to evoke burning the skin with a hot iron, but some descriptions depict tattooing by rubbing gunpowder into a pricked place on the skin. Brands were disfiguring but not debilitating; they marked the bearer as a capital criminal. That branding served as a semiotic system is clear from Ivan Pososhkov. He recommended for false witness severe corporal punishment and branding "not only on the arm but also on the face so that all may know that he bore false witness and that no one may trust him." Similarly, for a criminal who admits to crime, he prescribed branding on arm and cheek "so that all may know that he was a most notorious malefactor but has now repented".[18]

Bodily disfigurement by the slitting of nostrils to replace or pair with brands joined Muscovite mutilations. This practice, found in Byzantine law, had been prescribed in the 1649 Ulozhenie for tobacco offenses, but it is cited in use only from Peter's time. Korb reported that some musketeers arrested in the 1698 uprising were spared death because of their youth; instead, they were exiled with their ears cut off and nostrils slit. Similarly, a February 1705 law spared from death individuals convicted of capital crimes other than murder and rebellion (who would be executed); they were sentenced to eternal exile to hard labor instead. As exiles, they were to be branded "with the new brand" and have their nostrils slit. For those exiled for a fixed term, their brand would be V for "*vor*" but no slit nostrils.[19]

Slitting nostrils became the Petrine bodily marking of choice. Slitting of nostrils and exile was the threat in 1718 for those who chopped down forests suitable for shipbuilding; a decree of February 23, 1720 replaced the Military Articles' severing of fingers for false oaths with cutting of nostrils; the 1720 General Regulation mandates it with exile for taking bribes, falsifying a report or stealing documents, even for highly placed officials.[20] The 1715 Military Articles included some talion-like bodily mutilation, but it was rarely applied to civilian crime.[21]

[18] Verb and noun (*piatnat', piatno*) for hot-iron branding continued to be used even when rubbing in gunpowder is being described. PSZ IV: nos. 1924 (1703) (*zapitanav*) and 1957 (1704) (*novymi piatnymi*). Gunpowder specified: RGADA f. 1135, no. 400 (*piatno*) and PSZ IV: no. 2026 (*novym piatnom*) (both 1705); PSZ V: no. 2876 (1715). Pososhkov, *Book of Poverty*, 214, 216–17, 296. See notes of Chapter 11 on terminology for branding in seventeenth-century decrees.

[19] Ulozhenie ch. 25: art. 16: RZ III: 256. Korb, *Diary*, I: 185. PSZ IV: no. 2026 (1705).

[20] PSZ V: no. 3149, pt. 3 (1718). PSZ VI: no. 3531 (1720). General Regulation, art. 50: 1729: PRP VIII: 101 (1720).

[21] A blasphemer's tongue pierced (no. 3); the hand that holds the knife in a knife fight was pierced (no. 143); two fingers with which a man made a false oath cut off (no. 196) (see also arts. 4, 144, 146,

Petrine decrees devoted attention to the challenge of making disfigurement enduring – a decree of February 1705 stressed the necessity of rubbing tattooed brands dark with gunpowder, so that they will last "for life." A particularly gruesome law of January 15, 1723 mandated that slitting the nostrils be done to the bone so that the skin did not grow back to obscure the marking. The explicit intent of all these laws was to control the mobility of convicts. If a branded man with slit nostrils were arrested in major crime, his criminal past was clear to all on his face. Disturbingly, amnesties of November 1721, 1725 and 1726 refused to allow exiles mutilated with a brand or slit nostrils to return to European Russia; they were to be freed but had to remain in Siberia. These unsatisfactory amnesties may reflect the state's inability to protect such disfigured individuals from arrest, or they might express revulsion towards the criminals' appearance. They certainly allowed Russians outside of areas of exile to avoid confronting the brutality of their own legal practices. Meanwhile, in the seventeenth and eighteenth centuries European governments were eliminating such practices, urged by humanitarian and sentimental attitudes, and Russia's use of bodily disfigurement into the nineteenth century contributed to its being labeled "backward" by Europeans. Russian law made timid steps in this direction after Peter I's reign. As early as 1728 the propriety of torture and eventually corporal punishment for minors was being questioned; in 1757 women sentenced to exile were exempted from both branding and the slitting of nostrils because "they do not flee or get involved in crime" as did male exiles. Ultimately in 1785 the Russian nobility and townsmen were exempted from corporal punishment.[22]

Nevertheless, Russia's continued reliance on the exile system forced it to devise ways of keeping track of hardened criminals. Thus, branding continued through the eighteenth century with expanded semiotic meaning. In 1762 V (*vor*) was stamped on a forger's face, in 1780 U (*ubiitsa*) on the forehead of a murderer, in 1782 L (*lzhets*) on a right arm of a "liar" or corrupt official. In 1794 the first letters of the phrase "criminal and composer of false banknotes" (*vor i sochinitel' fal'shivykh assignatsii*) was to be stamped on both arms. The criminal code of 1845 called for new

188–9): Military Articles 1715: RZ IV: 329, 353, 362–3. Anisimov on cutting off two fingers for oaths: *Dyba i knut*, 501.

22 PSZ IV: no. 2026 (1705). PSZ VII: no. 4417 (1723). Amnesties: PSZ VI: no. 3842 (1721); PSZ VII: nos. 4655 (1725) and 4871 (1726). Changing laws: Schrader, *Languages*, ch. 4. Not torture minors: PSZ VIII: no. 5323 (1728). End corporal punishment for minors: PSZ XI: no. 8140 (1740). No death penalty before age 15: PSZ XI: no. 8152 (1740). Age raised to 19: PSZ XI: no. 8601 (1742). PSZ XIV: no. 10,686 (1757).

branding stamps: KAT for *katorzhnyi* (hard labor), B for *brodiaga* (vagrant), SK for *ssylno katorzhnyi* (exiled to hard labor) and SP for *ssylno poselenets* (exiled to settlement). Bodily marking ended only gradually in the first half of the nineteenth century, urged on by debates in the bureaucracy, intelligentsia and medical community over its ethics and utility. Slitting of nostrils was banned in 1817, branding continued until 1863.[23]

Russia's judicial practice of bodily mutilation was initially very crude – the severing of hands and feet in the 1660s, by the late seventeenth century, less debilitating fingers and ears. By the turn of the century another semiotic leap took place as faces were disfigured to identify the criminal wherever he went and stamped with letters so that beholders could "read" his crime; nostrils could also be slit as a marker. This brutal semiotic system responded to the challenge of controlling the most dangerous prisoners in exile. The work of judges in Peter I's time, particularly that of a stable group in Arzamas, shows competent and consistent application of the criminal law with little reference to marking bodies.

THE LAW IN PRACTICE IN ARZAMAS: SETTLING SUITS

As in Muscovy, a classic way in Petrine criminal judicial practice of dealing with punishment was to settle felony suits, even though the law did not formally allow it for felonies.[24] Compensation was one motive for settling; another was suggested by Iu. V. Got′e, who found in a study of post-Petrine local government that more than half of the cases after 1727 were settled. Got′e suggests that litigants did so for fear of corruption costing them money or stretching out cases endlessly; settling allowed litigants to remain "masters of their own cases." An anecdote related by the Austrian diplomat Johann-Georg Korb displays the tensions of the issue. A German named Urban got into a drunken brawl with a Russian

[23] Timofeev, *Istoriia*, 145 (1762). PSZ xx: no. 15,032 (1780). PSZ xxi: no. 15,336 (1782). PSZ xxiii: no. 17,262 (1794). Other decrees: PSZ xii: no. 9293 (1746); PSZ xiv: no. 10,305 (1754). PSZ xxxiv: no. 27,197 (1817). Schrader, *Languages*, chs. 5–6; Anisimov, *Dyba i knut*, 577–84.

[24] Settling misdemeanors: 1497, art. 53: RZ ii: 61; 1550 Law Code, art. 31: RZ ii: 102; 1649 Ulozhenie ch. 10, art. 121: RZ iii: 117. Not settling felonies: August 1556 Decree, art. 17: PRP iv: 367; Ulozhenie 21: arts. 31 and 71: RZ iii: 234, 241–2. Settlements of misdemeanors: theft: RGADA f. 210, Stolbtsy Pomestnogo stola, no. 215, fol. 164 (1701); bride abduction: RGADA f. 1103, no. 509 (1701); injury from fight: RGADA f. 1103, no. 499 (1704) and RGADA f. 1381, no. 13 (1706); beehive disputes: RGADA f. 1381, nos. 126 and 129 (both 1713); RGADA f. 409, op. 4, no. 396 (1732).

and grazed the man's head with a pistol shot. The two sobered up and reached an amicable agreement, whereby Urban paid the man off. Peter the Great, hearing of this, declared it a capital crime that could not be privately settled. Urban was imprisoned for several months, tried and sentenced to a knouting, which he was ultimately spared on the intervention of the Austrian legate. But, Korb notes, he had to pay stiff "fees" (bribes, in Korb's view) to court scribes and officials. "Nothing is safe in Muscovy from these harpies," he fumed.[25]

Peter's insistence reflected his desire that judges rule according to the law. [26] But Petrine judges used their own judgment, accepting settlement even for very violent crimes. In a felony case of 1701, for example, a group of new model cavalrymen in service on the Belgorod front settled a case that involved highway robbery ending in a death, much injury and theft of property; more day-to-day violence was at stake in a settlement in a homicide case in Kerensk in 1714. A peasant had gone to his neighbor to buy fish and the neighbor and his drunken sons allegedly attacked and killed him. The widow nevertheless settled with the men, saying that she did not want "the bones of her husband to cause harm and yielding it all to God's judgment now." She made no reference to compensation (but one suspects it), nor did the court impose a *penia* in the name of the tsar.[27] This settlement in a case of spontaneous violence seems more understandable than that for highway robbery.

Even while allowing settlements, judges more often than in Muscovite times acted on the state's option to punish; as litigants acknowledged, "the tsar is free to punish the crime." In 1718, for example, a *iasak*-paying peasant reported on June 14 to Kerensk *landrat* Andrei Iur′evich Chikhachov that his brother had been attacked and badly wounded while on the way to the Shatsk market. That day the *landrat* investigated the wounds and interrogated the accused man, also a *iasak*-paying peasant, who testified that the wounded man had insulted him and they began to fight. The injured man testified that he recalled no details since they were both drunk. On June 28, they settled, with the defendant paying the court fees. The *landrat*, however, ordered punishment: the defendant was beaten before the Chancery with bastinadoes, instead of the knout, mercilessly, since he admitted that he had hit the plaintiff.[28]

[25] Got′e, *Istoriia oblastnogo*, 408–9. Korb, *Diary*, I: 172–4, II: 13.
[26] Rule according to the law: PSZ VI: no. 3510 (1720); PSZ VII: no. 4436 (1724).
[27] RGADA f. 210, Belgorod stol, no. 1790, fol. 7 (1701). RGADA f. 1441, op. 2, no. 245 (1714).
[28] RGADA f. 904, no. 443 (1718).

Similarly, on January 24, 1724, a Mordvinian man reported the murder of his father Dorofei. Interrogation revealed that the defendant Petr Matveev and a companion had encountered Dorofei in a tavern and that they had all drunk together. The three men continued to drink as they set out on the road to market. They fell to fighting when Dorofei refused to share the rest of his brew, and Matveev testified that he killed Dorofei in the melee. His companion rode off, Matveev hid the body in the forest, then fell asleep (drunk) on Dorofei's sled. Dorofei's horse turned around and went home, bringing a bloody sled loaded with a dead body and an unconscious murderer. Matveev came to to find all the villagers gathered around; he promptly confessed. After a torture session of thirty-five blows in early February, Dorofei's son and Matveev approached Arzamas judges majors and assessors Mikhail Timofeevich Kishkin and Fedor Vasil′evich Zasetskoi to settle the case. The judges treated the case as unintentional homicide, ordering excerpts from law codes on that topic, and ruled that Matveev should be knouted as punishment. He was released on recognizance (*rospiska*); acknowledging the settlement, the judges waived court fees other than the dead body fee and did not impose the compensation of a peasant family or fine required by the law.[29]

Judges apparently considered settlement of non-intentional homicide routine. Such appears to have been the case two decades later, when a conscientious judge allowed such a settlement. In 1740 in Ustiuzhna Zheleznopol′skaia two peasants had gotten into a drunken brawl at a feast on Easter Day in April; one was killed. The defendant argued that the death was unintentional, done in drunkenness, and the court identified appropriate citations from the Ulozhenie punishing this with knouting. But the landlords of the two peasants came to an agreement. In his verdict the judge thoroughly examined legislation from 1649 to the early eighteenth century regarding distribution of court fees in a settlement, and he explicitly cited the Ulozhenie in sentencing the defendant to thirty blows of the knout for unintentional homicide. He made no reference to the Ulozhenie's stricture against settling felony cases.[30] Petrine judges accommodated local subjects but even in settlements often imposed corporal punishment.

[29] RGADA f. 419, op. 1, pt. 1, no. 1511 (1724). [30] RGADA f. 596, no. 345 (1740).

THE LAW IN PRACTICE IN ARZAMAS: TORTURE AND PUNISHMENT

In the use of torture for felony crime Petrine judges paralleled Muscovite practice: they exonerated individuals who withstood multiple torture sessions; they followed rules about probable cause; they focused torture on the primary suspect, rather than indiscriminately; they tortured at quick intervals of a few weeks or a month, or in other cases gave defendants more time to recuperate. They tortured women as well as men; they used torture for homicide cases and only the most severe of theft cases. While the form had not changed, their use of torture seems done with more oversight than in Muscovite times.[31]

Formal presentation changed significantly. Judges more consistently entered into the transcript citations from the Ulozhenie justifying the use of torture before they embarked on it. In one case of 1719, for example, the judge ordered his staff to "make excerpts about interrogation at the site of torture" (*rozysk v zastenke*). Petrine judges also recorded more systematically the number of blows administered, a practice seen in Muscovy rarely and generally only for the highest crime.[32] By the mid 1720s, cases also record the names of judicial officials or others witnessing the torture. When they went to a third torture session, fire was used more frequently (in Muscovite cases, torture by fire is encountered generally in cases of the highest crime; see Chapter 6). But third sessions were relatively rare among Petrine judges.

Judge Iakov Gavrilovich Chertkov in Arzamas in 1719, for example, promptly resolved a case with only one torture session. This was a sexual crime, treated as seriously as felony assault. In July 1719 Vasilii Mikhailov, a peasant "man" of Lieutenant Colonel Prince Vasilii Ivanovich Gagarin, brought in the carpenter Petr Ievlev, who had been residing in his master's home to help build a church. Ievlev admitted that he was a runaway peasant and that, while working for Gagarin, he had sodomized three boys, ages five and six, and raped two little girls as well. He had given his landlord a handwritten note about this, which prompted his being turned in. *Stol'nik* Ivan Lavrent'evich Simanskoi "with colleagues" questioned him and he affirmed his confession; he also admitted to other instances of the same crime, naming nine more boys in three other homes where he

31 Weickhardt, "Probable Western Origins." Rare case of misdemeanor theft using torture: RGADA f. 1380, no. 63 (1719).

32 RGADA f. 1404, no. 668, fol. 2 (1719).

had tutored. He specifically denied that he held any heretical ideas. By September 20 Simanskoi turned to the governor of Nizhnii Novgorod *guberniia*, asking for guidance and underlining the man's denial of heresy. Their response is not recorded; the case resumes in July 1720, when judge *stol'nik* Iakov Gavrilovich Chertkov followed up on the confession with torture. First, he ordered excerpts from the Ulozhenie justifying the use of torture for those who admit guilt or for peasants brought in by their landlords. Then he submitted Ievlev to a remarkably high number (fifty) of blows of torture. Ievlev admitted all and added that as a youth in Moscow he had raped many women, seducing them by getting them drunk. Chertkov ordered more excerpts, receiving from his undersecretary the Ulozhenie's sole reference to sexual crime (which punished procurement with knouting). The clerk cited neither the Military Articles nor any church codes on sodomy, either of which would have been more helpful. Following his instincts, Chertkov on August 11 sentenced the defendant to be knouted mercilessly on the rack before many people in Arzamas, so that other people would neither commit sexual crime nor flee their masters.[33]

In a spectacular case of murder, judge Chertkov also ordered fewer than three sessions, since he obtained confession promptly. The case involved Andrei and Tatiana, a pair of lovers accused of murdering her husband in 1720. In initial interrogation, Andrei confessed but Tatiana denied any involvement. Andrei's first torture session, however, revealed all the lurid details. They had attacked the man while he was sleeping, drunk; the wife sat on her husband's chest while her lover strangled him with a belt she had given him. Under torture Andrei also volunteered details about other criminals and criminal activity in the area, about which Chertkov promptly informed neighboring governors. After this session Chertkov brought the wife and her lover to the place of torture for interrogation, where Tatiana continued her denials. So Chertkov ordered them both tortured. Andrei held to his previous version, but recanted an accusation against a third party; Tatiana confessed after twenty blows of the knout. Chertkov had no further witnesses, no implicated parties, and no need to prolong the trial. After two torture sessions, for murder Chertkov sentenced them both to death: for Andrei he did not specify the form, but for Tatiana, burial. He ordered that it should be done in Arzamas in the marketplace with a written description of her crime posted "so that to all

[33] RGADA f. 1380, no. 61 (1719). Peasants brought by landlords: Ulozhenie ch. 21, arts. 48 and 58: RZ III: 238–39; procurement: ch. 22, art. 25: RZ III: 250. Sodomy: 1715 Military Articles, no. 166: RZ IV: 358–9.

it would be known about her murdering her husband and so that other wives will, in the future, not murder their husbands." His verdict cited the Ulozhenie, apparently not knowing or disregarding the 1689 law that abolished burial as a judicial punishment.[34]

Another Arzamas case also stopped at two tortures and demonstrates equally professional adjudication. On September 2, 1722 Petr Kirilov, an Arzamas peasant, visited another man to collect his debt and was found robbed and stabbed. Kirilov soon died of his wounds, but not before revealing who had attacked him. The accused man responded that Kirilov had attacked him and it was self-defense. Seeking a confession and having no other witnesses or evidence, the judges turned to torture. Under torture on September 7, the accused man received fifteen blows and did not change his story; the same for his second session of twenty-five blows on November 1. The judges then ordered excerpts from the Ulozhenie and the 1669 Criminal Articles on self-defense and unintentional murder. On December 21, the triumvirate of governor Chelishev and majors and assessors Kishkin and Zasetskoi accepted the defendant's version. Ruling the murder unintentional, they sentenced the defendant to knouting before the Chancery. The verdict is notable for detailing the defendant's version of events, affirmed in two torture sessions.[35]

Petrine judges took the evidence of torture seriously; they occasionally exonerated defendants who withstood its rigors. In 1722 judge Chertkov took up a suit that was continued in the autumn by the triad of Chelishev, Kishkin and Zasetskoi. The case concerned the allegation that a man had been poisoned by his wife, Anissia; in an attempt to shift blame, in her initial oral interrogation Anissia claimed that her aunt and daughter-in-law had put her up to it, giving her poison. Under interrogation the two women vehemently denied that poison had been used at all, calling this slander. Lacking medical personnel to verify cause of death, Chertkov pursued the truth through torture. He ordered excerpts from the Ulozhenie justifying torture for Anissia, since she had been accused by multiple people. In her first encounter (April 1722), Anissia was only presented the instruments of torture; she held to her story. The two women, interrogated orally again, also stuck by their story. Anissia was then tortured on May 25; receiving ten blows, she recanted and admitted she had fabricated the tale of poison and that her husband had died of

[34] Lovers murder husband: RGADA f. 1380, no. 197 and 163 (1720), quote at no. 163, fol. 10. PSZ III: no. 1335 (1689). Execution by burial: see Chapter 13.

[35] RGADA f. 419, op. 1, pt. 1, no. 765 (1722).

natural causes. Since this story contradicted her earlier testimony, the judges subjected her to two more sessions of fifteen blows each (September 19 and 28). She held to her recantation; the three judges accepted the evidence of these three torture sessions and apparently accepted the argument that the death had indeed been by natural causes. Citing the Ulozhenie, they ruled that since the accused had withstood three tortures, Anissia was to be freed without punishment, along with the two women whom she had vindicated.[36]

An unresolved case of the mid 1720s demonstrates the new Petrine documentary style of numbered "points," new forms of address ("Father of the Fatherland") and the recording of torture sessions. The case involved a brawl over landownership. A peasant reported that men from their village had been in the forest cutting firewood when they were attacked by peasants from the neighboring village claiming the same land. In the melee a peasant was killed. Majors and assessors Kishkin and Zasetskoi summoned one of the accused men, Sergei Semenov, to interrogation, where he admitted that he had done the killing while drunk (intending to establish lack of premeditation); he absolved the others. Seeking to affirm and find conspirators, the judge went to torture. In his first torture session, on March 17, Semenov received thirty blows and said the same. On March 23 at his second torture, with twenty-seven blows, he repeated his story. At each of these torture sessions, witnesses were listed – an elder of the local forest district and elders of the administration of the Chancery of the Tsar's Palace (*Prikaz bolshogo dvortsa*).[37]

Torture was used on both men and women, but very few defendants were noble – only two in the cases surveyed here. They are split evenly on whether noble status could protect one from torture. In the lurid case of Andrei Lopatin in the 1720s, he was accused and convicted without recourse to torture for killing ten of his peasants, men and women. But when he resorted to claiming "word and deed" cases to escape the execution to which he had been sentenced, he was subjected to three torture sessions and knouted for the false claim. On the other hand, a Shatsk landlord, Afanasei Nikiforov, escaped not only torture but conviction and punishment. Nikiforov was a master manipulator of trials. Charged with killing one of his peasant girls in April 1717, he was interrogated and imprisoned, but the court transcript ruefully notes that he

[36] RGADA f. 419, op. 1, pt. 1, no. 766 (1722). Accusation by many: Ulozhenie ch. 21, art. 48: RZ III: 238; resisting torture, ch. 21, art. 100: RZ III: 246.

[37] RGADA f. 419, op. 1, pt. 1, no. 1512 (1724).

managed to get released by June without any surety bond or other guarantors, and that the undersecretary who should not have allowed this to happen would be investigated. Bribery seems likely. In January 1723 Nikiforov was arrested again and secured his release by February. He managed to escape justice for the next twenty years, when in 1745 the case was reopened by peasant petitioners outraged that he was still at large. The judges, in tortured logic, reviewed the case and determined that, although he had never been convicted of the murder, he should be forgiven under the amnesties of 1725 and 1726. Other charges were pending, however, for which the court pardoned him on the grounds of ill health: he was found to be completely incapacitated, paralyzed and having lost his senses. So Nikiforov was released on recognizance, still not convicted.[38]

THE LAW IN PRACTICE IN ARZAMAS: INDEPENDENT JUDGMENT

As several of these cases show, torture helped judges resolve a case locally, without reference to higher venues. They used familiar corporal punishments. In a case filed on October 7, 1719, for example, Arzamas *landrat* Stepan Afanas′evich Nesterov heard a case of felony theft (*tat′ba*); a peasant was caught with a stolen kaftan and a woman's sheepskin coat. He testified that he had been on the road to the market and had stopped at a tavern to drink. While drunk, he wandered into the next village and stole the items. Consistent with the Ulozhenie's article that criminals brought in with material evidence should be tortured, Nesterov brought the defendant to torture on October 9, where he received thirty blows. In torture, he affirmed the theft, but no other crime or helpers in crime. The case languished until August 5, 1720, by which time the judge was Iakov Gavrilovich Chertkov. His scribes provided him with excerpts from both the 1649 Ulozhenie and the 1669 Criminal Articles regarding first theft, whose sanctions differed slightly (see Appendix). Chertkov then crafted his own resolution, dispensing with the Ulozhenie's bodily mutilation, prison, exile and compensation. He ordered the defendant to be knouted in the marketplace mercilessly so that onlookers would be deterred and he released the defendant with a letter "according to the decree" (the Ulozhenie). He justified his decision by reference to the defendant's

[38] Lopatin: RGADA f. 419, op. 1, pt. 1, no. 21, fol. 7 (1726) and RGADA f. 1380, no. 768 (1722); fuller account: Kollmann, "Change," 383–4. Nikiforov: RGADA f. 904, no. 261 (1717).

confession in interrogation and torture and to the fact that he had sat in prison ten months without further accusation.[39] Chertkov shaped the verdict by the spirit, not letter, of the law.

Showing similar independence of mind, in February 1716 Matvei Lukianovich Ermolov, the *landrat* of Shatsk near Arzamas, resolved a case of horse theft. Two bandits had set upon a man who was watering his horse and had stolen the horse. He sounded the alarm in his village and a group tracked the thieves and recovered the horse. They brought both the horse and one of the accused men to judge Ermolov. Citing the Ulozhenie, he carried out oral interrogation (where the defendant admitted the theft) and torture. The defendant did not change his story, so, after he had sat in prison as required by the Ulozhenie to await more accusations, Ermolov sentenced him to knouting for first theft, following the Ulozhenie but not applying its stipulations about mutilation, prison and exile. In 1727 Arzamas judges similarly applied the law in their own way. On February 20, 1727 the peasant Fedor Stepanov was brought into Arzamas by the man of a local landlord because he had returned from a trip to sell grain in Moscow with the dead body of the peasant with whom he had been traveling. At first he said that they had been attacked by criminals, but eventually admitted that he killed the man in a drunken fight over money. Citing the Ulozhenie, major and assessor Zasetskoi subjected him to three torture sessions, where he held to his story. On March 24, Zasetskoi sentenced Stepanov to merciless knouting for unintentional homicide "in front of a gathering of people in public so that others will find it inappropriate to do the same." Zasetkoi justified the verdict by reference to oral testimony, three torture sessions, the Ulozhenie and the 1669 Criminal Articles. Stepanov was sent off on surety bond, following the 1669 code. The case was amply signed by the judge as well as by senior secretary Karapov and undersecretary Savastianov. That same day the convicted man was beaten and released on recognizance.[40] Simple knouting usually sufficed for such local crimes.

A case of a prison break in 1729 presents a rare use of bastinadoes as judicial sentence. A convict in the stone prison of the Dudin Monastery in Nizhnii Novgorod reported that he had learned of a plot by a group of about eighteen inmates to escape. In questioning, the accused men admitted that they had planned to flee by attacking their guards when they were let out

[39] RGADA f. 1380, no. 63 (1719).

[40] RGADA f. 904, no. 6 (1716). Stepanov: RGADA f. 419, op. 1, pt. 2, no. 242 (1727); torture sessions: Feb. 21, twelve blows; March 6, fifteen blows; by March 24, twenty-five blows.

to get water or do laundry. Perhaps because they did not actually escape, the men were sentenced to merciless beating with bastinadoes instead of the knout, in a public place, to deter others. Otherwise, the knout was used regularly, often "mercilessly": in a case of 1719, Chertkov sentenced a man to be beaten with the knout "while being led through the marketplace" – a common sentence in Muscovite cases, but rarely cited in Petrine cases.[41]

Instructions to governors in 1719 and 1721 required that all capital cases be referred to the Superior Courts (see Appendix), but these decrees did not immediately make an impression in Arzamas. There judges confidently applied and executed the law in a spirit of judicial autonomy. Judge Iakov Gavrilovich Chertkov, for example, was particularly busy rendering judgments in 1719–22. In one case, he decreed graduated sentences according to the crime. In May 1717 a girl was found dead in a field outside Arzamas. Investigation identified her as Stefanida, a runaway peasant girl. In early June *landrat* Chertkov questioned a driver, Leontii, and a woman Fedora about the allegation that they had lured the girl for prostitution. Fedora vehemently denied all and said she simply hired a driver to take Stefanida home. Leontii in turn confessed that he had indeed taken the money to drive the girl but then, being drunk, he had feared being found with her, strangled her and threw her body into the field. He absolved Fedora of the charge of procurement. Hearing this testimony, Chertkov ordered Leontii brought to "severe torture" (*krepkaia pytka*). In three brutal sessions of fifty-three, twenty-seven and thirty-two blows between June 1717 and September 1719, he held to his story. Thus Chertkov could consider the case against Fedora closed. He ordered up excerpts on murder from the Ulozhenie and made his verdict in February 1721: he summarized the investigative procedure (testimony and three torture sessions), referred to the relevant law (Ulozhenie ch. 21, art. 72), exonerated Fedora and sentenced Leontii to death by hanging.[42] For murder, exile was inappropriate; Chertkov did fail, however, to send this capital sentence on to referral.

A 1720 case shows similar local autonomy.[43] In September 1718 a noblewoman reported that her husband's father had been found dead after visiting a family with whom he had long-standing "neighborly village feuds." She blamed a peasant Oparin and a vagabond in that household. The investigation was started by Arzamas *landrat* Nesterov.

41 RGADA f. 409, op. 4, no. 336 (1729). RGADA f. 1380, no. 63 (1719).
42 RGADA f. 1380, no. 17 (1717). 43 RGADA f. 1380, no. 29 (1720), posted text on fol. 51v.

Oparin testified that two other men had enticed him to join in the murder; Nesterov proceeded to torture them. They denied all, leading Oparin to admit that he had slandered them and had committed the crime himself. By then, in June, judge Chertkov was in charge and he subjected Oparin to three more torture sessions to test his recantation. Then he ruled on the case. "Hearing the original transcript of the investigation and excerpts from the laws," he sentenced Oparin to hanging for the intentional murder of his landlord; he released a second accused man on surety bond since Oparin had exonerated him. Chertkov cited the relevant laws, including the 1649 Ulozhenie on murder, on recanting during torture and on dragging out the judicial process (ch. 21: arts. 72, 100 and 30). Chertkov ended his verdict with further instructions to investigate others implicated in the case. After the verdict was read aloud, Oparin was hanged "that same hour," with an extensive written text posted on the gallows explaining his crime for all to see. Again, a professionally conducted case, save for any higher review.

Arzamas judges did refer to higher courts for other reasons: in 1719 seeking advice from the Superior Court in Voronezh and in 1722 and 1723 working with the Bishop's judicial office in Nizhnii Novgorod. But not until 1728 is referring a capital sentence encountered, in a case that initiated in 1724: a dragoon was sentenced to beheading for intentional murder, and since the case was resolved after the new Instruction to Governors had affirmed referral of capital sentences, it was sent to the Nizhnii Novgorod Superior Court for review. Their decision is not recorded.[44]

For cases below the highest crime that went to the death penalty, Arzamas judges used the punishment that fit the crime. For most, it was hanging, as in a case of a killing that occurred during a theft and in three rulings of intentional murder. More brutal capital punishments – beheading, burial – were encountered, but they parallel Muscovite practice. A case that began in 1715 shows superior court judges wrestling with sentencing standards. Peasant Denis Demin was accused in Elat′ma in 1715 of fleeing service and committing as many as four robberies and five thefts. His case was judged so serious that he was sent to Tambov to be questioned in the Governor's office. There he was tortured in the case for the first time, admitting the robbery and thefts. By February 1720 he had been transferred to the Voronezh Superior Court. His case did not move

[44] RGADA f. 1380, no. 61, fols. 4–5v (1719). RGADA f. 419, op. 1, pt. 1, nos. 579 (1723), (1722), 1508 and 1509 (1724).

quickly. On November 14, 1721, he was sent to torture, and he admitted all as before. On December 18 he was tortured for the second time in Voronezh, but in April he appealed that he was still recovering from the first two tortures and that he had, in any case, already been tortured three times. The case includes excerpts from the Ulozhenie regarding execution for three thefts, contrasting it to the November 1721 decree whereby three thefts merited exile to galley labor with slit nostrils, but three robberies merited execution (see Appendix). The existing record is a draft; the scribe wrote, but crossed out, a verdict of knouting and exile with slit nostrils, leaving the ruling that, according to the Ulozhenie and the November 1721 law, Demin was to be executed by beheading.[45]

A 1738 case demonstrates reference to legal precedent. A case decided in Ustiuzhna Zheleznopol'skaia in the governor's office concerned a young peasant who had tried to escape military recruitment. He grabbed a knife and stabbed the recruiter, killing him. The case knowledgeably compares the Ulozhenie regarding unintentional murder with more recent decrees regarding resistance to recruiting. Those decrees, which primarily discuss self-mutilation and flight, imposed sentences ranging from the gauntlet to knouting and eternal exile to hanging, depending upon the circumstances. The judge, weighing the alternatives, opted for the death sentence since the man had murdered while resisting. The verdict was affirmed by the Novgorod governor and the sentence was carried out in Ustiuzhna Zheleznopol'skaia.[46]

Unlike Muscovite cases, however, "mercy" was awarded relatively rarely in these Arzamas cases. This might be an accident of the surviving sources or the personal predilection of judges Chertkov, Chelishev and so on. Meanwhile, mercy had not disappeared from Russian justice. Eighteenth-century Russian rulers continued to play the role of benevolent, patrimonial autocrats outside of the courtroom by bestowing gifts of land and new honorifics, medals and titles. Peter the Great, for example, made a show of announcing his "mercy" in welcoming runaway troops back to the ranks without punishment; he lavishly promised favor (*milost'*) to those who reported political crime; he awarded officers guilty of minor crimes forgiveness in honor of major military triumphs.[47] Like his predecessors, Peter and subsequent empresses liberally bestowed amnesties on

[45] RGADA f. 978, no. 17 (1715). [46] RGADA f. 596, no. 343 (1738).

[47] Invite runaways back: PSZ IV: no. 2318 (1711); PSZ V: nos. 2728 and 2755 (both 1713), 2813 (1714); PSZ VI: no. 3597 (1720); PSZ VII: nos. 4226 (1723) and 5122 (1727). Denunciations: ZA Petra 361 (1713), 362 (1714); PSZ V: no. 2877 (1715); PSZ VI: nos. 3648 (1720) and 3984 (1722). Officers: PSZ V: no. 2755 (1713).

prisoners on occasions such as military victories, Peter's recovery from ill health or Catherine I's accession. Catherine I promised forgiveness to counterfeiters who turned themselves in. Peter I even decreed in August 1720 that a special place should be set up before the Senate Chancery for the announcement of pardons.[48] Arzamas judges from about 1714 through the 1720s, however, avoided such florid displays, churning out orderly cases in notebook form and numbered questions, with extensive excerpts of the law and thorough verdicts outlining their procedure and legal rationales. They walked the fine line observed throughout this study of early modern Russian justice, combining personalized and formalized elements to produce justice that fit the law and the community.

The trend to favor exile over capital punishment did not make much impact in Arzamas for felony crimes in these years. Most people guilty of homicide were knouted; those convicted of premeditated murder were summarily executed in simple ceremonies. Settlements were accepted for unintentional homicide. Eighteenth-century reforms had improved judicial record-keeping, had apparently (judging by Arzamas judges' work) encouraged judges to adhere to the law in the use of punishment and mercy, but they had not undermined the informal qualities of Russian legal culture. Judges allowed settlements and mitigated sentences according to their judgment. But, as noted in Chapter 8, subsequent government policy undermined these good beginnings and also unbalanced the traditional blending of formal and informal elements in adjudication. Russia awaited Catherine II's judicial reforms for improvements, and those of the 1860s for a decisive move towards the more functional judicial system that Petrine judges presage.

[48] Amnesties: PSZ VI: no. 3842 (1721); PSZ VII: nos. 4638, 4645, 4655, 4767 (1725), 4871 (1726). Counterfeiters: PSZ VII: no. 5089 (1727). PSZ VI: no. 3635 (1720).

CHAPTER 13

Capital punishment: form and ritual

Beyond knouts and bastinadoes, beyond exile and branding, stood execution. In Muscovy as elsewhere, state and society deemed some crimes so heinous as to deprive a criminal of life. Capital punishment was a root of sovereignty, central to a ruler's legitimacy as protector of his society and sole possessor of the means of violence. Rulers balanced violence with other strategies of governance – co-optation, ideology, benign neglect – and also carefully managed how they used violence, especially capital punishment. Here not only protections in the law established legitimacy; so also did the ritual with which the execution was carried out. How executions were carried out – location, methods of death, surrounding ritual – "demonstrates sovereignty."[1]

In early modern Europe "spectacles of suffering" – shrouded in a Christian idiom of repentance, sacrifice and the purifying power of pain, involving brutal tortures and killings, often of multiple criminals at a time, and theatrically orchestrated in public spaces before assembled crowds – broadcast a particular image of authority of European rulers.[2] From London and Amsterdam to small German and Swiss towns, public executions used symbolism to underscore the authority of the court, the justice of sentence and the righteousness of the punishment. In Germanic lands, for example, the presentation of the verdict and execution were meticulously staged. Because the inquisitorial trial had been concluded behind closed doors, pronouncement of the verdict became its public face. Staged in the town square, attended by officials and the panel of judges, the announcement involved what John Langbein terms a theatrical restaging of the trial. Denunciations were made of the accused, speakers presented accusations and defenses, and judges went through the motions

[1] Garland, *Peculiar Institution*, 77.

[2] Van Dülmen, *Theatre of Horror*; Spierenburg, *Spectacle*; Evans, *Rituals*; Linebaugh, *London Hanged*; Foucault, *Discipline and Punish*.

of deliberation. The enactment culminated in formal reading of the verdict, citing excerpts from law codes. In some jurisdictions, the judge ritually broke his staff as he pronounced the sentence.[3]

Elaborate preparations for execution followed. Platforms and viewing stands were constructed, soldiers surrounded the gallows in case the crowd became unruly. Town dignitaries attended; priests comforted the condemned in the days before execution and escorted him or her to the gallows. The condemned was urged to confess and repent if he or she had not already done so, thus experiencing a "good death" and affirming the legitimacy of the whole process. To that end, torture was inflicted before execution as priests stood ready for confession and absolution.[4]

The criminal's sufferings resonated on multiple levels with the assembled populace. They could have a terrifying deterrent effect, but could also bring relief. Richard Evans reminds us that, given the early modern state's reliance on local communities to track down criminals, both onlookers and officials were usually complicit in bringing a criminal to justice. For the community an execution often represented a festive moment – rejoicing in the criminal's pious repentance or celebrating its own good fortune in expiating evil. Evans calls such festival moments "ceremonies of expulsion and reintegration." Karl Wegert developed this idea: calling early modern German concepts of justice a symbiotic "mixture of nature-bound custom and filtered Christianity," he argues that painful punishments mobilized the forces of nature itself to rid the community of the evil released by crime. Execution by fire and water, the breaking of bones ("the source of life"), hanging and exposing the body to decay in the elements – all conquered evil spirits in spiritual ways. Esther Cohen further suggests that in medieval Europe Catholics considered pain purifying; witness medieval Catholicism's emphasis on the passion of Christ and martyr saints. Inflicting painful tortures on a criminal before a horrendous execution was not mere vengeance or rule by terror; it also symbolically purified the condemned and expunged the evil he or she had committed. With such association with evil spirits, it is not surprising that executioners and their instruments were stigmatized.[5]

[3] Langbein, *Prosecuting*, 188–92.

[4] Illustrations: Paas, *German Political Broadsheet*, II: nos. 239 (1616), 392 (1619); III: 804 and 507 (1621), VIII: no. 2565 (1661). Descriptions: van Dülmen, *Theatre of Horror*, chs. 4–5; Evans, *Rituals*, ch. 2.

[5] Evans, *Rituals*, 37, 104. Wegert, "Social Context," 27–35. Cohen, "Symbols of Culpability." Shame of executioners: Spierenburg, *Spectacle*, ch. 2; Stuart, *Defiled Trades*. Folk symbolism of drowning and dismembering: Bulychev, *Mezhdu sviatymi i demonami*, 43–151.

By the eighteenth century in Europe such spectacles were less frequent but more elaborate – "the full execution ritual, with its elaborate procession and ceremonial procedures at the scaffold, was a phenomenon of the late seventeenth and eighteenth century."[6] As they mastered public display as a strategy of social control, early modern states were also developing others: more intensive bureaucracy, laws and policing; public education, prison and asylum; better means of communication with an increasingly literate society. Elite public opinion was taking a humanitarian turn, rejecting physical violence; Michel Foucault would say that individuals were internalizing new "discourses" of conformity that were more effective than a more overt praxis of violence.

This bleak Foucauldian vision of the role of public violence in the early modern state provides a powerful comparative model; one might assume at first glance that Muscovy, given the tropes of its "despotism" and "brutality", would have followed suit. As discussed in Chapter 10, law codes threatened more violence in judicial sanctions over the course of the seventeenth century; how the state used symbolic and coercive power to execute is the concern here.

FORMS OF CAPITAL PUNISHMENT

Muscovite sources are maddeningly laconic about how capital punishment was actually done. Perhaps they did not need to specify. Esther Cohen suggests that forms of execution "from Scandinavia to Spain" were so deeply embedded in folk culture that communities knew instinctively what to do. Certain kinds of crimes and certain kinds of criminals merited specific punishments, particularly for the most heinous crimes. Muscovy generally follows the pattern she sketches out for late medieval Europe.[7]

Executions for felony crime provided the model for those for highest crime (treason, heresy, witchcraft; see Chapters 14–16), but were less elaborate. One of the most common forms of execution for felony crime was hanging. While hanging itself might seem straightforward, the act could have symbolic significance. In early modern Germany, for example, the gallows were to be built from scratch of "clean oak, without knots or nails, and the body was to be left hanging until decomposed, consumed by the elements and the birds"; a Swiss judge prescribed that a "new rope"

[6] Evans, *Rituals*, 50; also Weisser, *Crime and Punishment*, 141.

[7] Cohen, "Symbols of Culpability." Forms of execution in Russia: Anisimov, *Duba i knut*, 551–61; Shtamm, "Ugolovnoe pravo," in Skripilev (ed.), *Razvitie*, 203–5.

was to be used.[8] No such instructions for the construction of gallows are found in Muscovy and cases make no mention of particular concern with such things. But given that hangings were done at places of maximum publicity, authorities seem to have assumed that they had emotional impact. The few Muscovite law codes and decrees that specify a mode of execution generally cite hanging, and foreign travelers from the early sixteenth century comment on it. Herberstein wrote: "They have no other form of execution unless the culprit is guilty of grave crimes."[9]

Case law shows that hanging was common and not limited to a particular social group. Decrees cite hanging for "Russian people and foreigners," for all "criminals," for runaway slaves and for "military men of all ranks."[10] Resolved cases attest to it: in Briansk a slave who falsely accused another person and who tried to flee over the border in 1621 was hanged; so also was a peasant who had fled over the border and assaulted two men in the process. A case of May 1684 in Iakutsk involved a man who had been in and out of trouble. In 1681/2 Kuzka Mikhailov, a hired laborer, had been tried for falsely alleging a "word and deed" case against a local bailiff; he testified that he falsely accused the bailiff because the latter had been demanding bribes and beating him. For this he was ordered knouted mercilessly both on the rack and while being led around the marketplace and was sent off to join the tsar's service. On the way he falsified travel documents and organized people for a rebellion, which he admitted when caught and questioned under torture. So, "for his many past and present crimes, his flight from service, for rebellion and falsified, evil letters," Iakutsk Governor Prince Ivan Priklonskii ordered this laborer hanged.[11]

Women, however, were generally not hanged, either in Europe or in Muscovy, although no Russian law explicitly bans it. Where laws and verdicts specify the form of execution for a female, they prescribe

8 Wegert, "Social Context," 30; Cohen, "Symbols of Culpability," 411.

9 The 1397–8 Dvina Charter (art. 5: RZ II: 181) and the 1589 Law Code (art. 108: PRP IV: 426) specify hanging for felony, as do some sixteenth-century brigandage charters: Iakovlev (ed.), *Namestnichie*, 67 (1549), 90 (1595). Herberstein, *Description*, 49; other sixteenth-century comments include Chancellor, "Voyage," 35 (*c*.1553); Fletcher, "Of the Russe," 176 (1580s).

10 Russian people: PSZ I: nos. 126 (1654) and 256 (1659). Runaway slaves: PSZ I: nos. 127 (1654) and 150 (1655). "Military men": PSZ I: no. 166 (1655). Hanging: Rogov, *Istoriia*, 135; Sergeevskii, *Nakazanie*, 100–2.

11 AMG I: nos. 144, 145 (both 1621). DAI XI: no. 38 (1684); verdict cites Ulozhenie on rebellion: ch. 2, art. 1: RZ III: 86. Other cases: AMG I: no. 147 (1622 peasant); RGADA f. 210, Prikaznyi stol, no. 36, fols. 467–76 and 485–91 (1628 musketeers); RGADA f. 159, op. 3, no. 1618, fols. 53–6 (1682 no social class identified); RGADA f. 1380, no. 17 (1717 peasant); PSZ V: no. 3477, art. 7 (1719 gentrymen); RGADA f. 1380, nos. 29 and 53 (1720 peasants).

beheading or forms other than hanging. Grigorii Kotoshikhin, in enumerating the ways in which women were executed for various crimes, does not include hanging.[12] Historians have argued that this had to do with propriety, following the lead of jurists. Sir William Blackstone in England explains "the decency due to the sex forbids the exposing and publicly mangling their bodies." In the rare occasions when women were hanged, as in medieval France, officials bound a woman's skirts around her legs on the gallows for decency. But Esther Cohen argues that modesty had little to do with a prohibition against hanging women; after all, in medieval Europe, women could be flogged in procession around the town while naked. Rather, she argues, communities either considered some crimes associated with women as so heinous (infanticide, witchcraft), or considered women so spiritually powerful and dangerous, that a more definitive form of death was required, lest the evil spirits they and their crimes embodied endure or return from the dead.[13] Whether Muscovite folk belief was the same is difficult to say, but the law followed the same prohibition.

In early modern Russia as well as Europe, therefore, women were burned or buried, forms selected to ensure that the women, their bodies, and their spiritual essences would be exterminated. Women (and men) found guilty of religious crime (see Chapter 15) were burned; in addition, women, and only women, were buried alive in Muscovy. A woman found guilty of killing her husband (also occasionally for witchcraft or infanticide) would be buried in a particularly cruel way: she was interred vertically up to the neck to die a slow, agonizing death by hunger and attrition. The law specified that no mercy could mitigate such a sentence, even if the family of the dead man interceded on her behalf. A husband who murdered his wife, on the other hand, was simply hanged or beheaded for murder. Burial was cited in practice in 1637 for a Kursk townswoman who admitted under torture to conspiring together with two other men to murder her husband.[14]

[12] A 1637 law says to execute a condemned woman "according to the *gradskii zakon*" (ZA no. 244), suggesting beheading, inasmuch as that phrase elsewhere indicates that: 1669 Criminal Articles, art. 79: PRP VII: 423. The Ulozhenie and the 1669 Criminal Articles do not define mode of execution for pregnant women: Ulozhenie ch. 22, art. 15: RZ III: 249; 1669 Criminal Articles, art. 101: PSZ VII: 428. A 1718 decree specifies beheading: PSZ V: no. 3154. Kotoshikhin, *O Rossii*, ch. 7, art. 34, p. 116.

[13] Blackstone cited in Hill, *Eighteenth-Century Women*, 150; Dolan, *Dangerous Familiars*, ch. 1; Burford and Shulman, *Of Bridles and Burnings*, ch. 6. Binding skirt: Naish, *Death Comes to the Maiden*, ch. 1. Cohen, "Symbols of Culpability." Rublack confirms that women were executed usually by beheading or burning: *Crimes of Women*, 82–3.

[14] Kotoshikhin associates burial with infanticide: *O Rossii*, ch. 7, art. 34, p. 116. RGADA f. 210, Belgorod stol, no. 83, fols. 258–67 and 708–9 (1637); Kollmann, "Extremes of Patriarchy" and "27 October 1698: Peter Punishes."

Law codes first mention it in the 1649 Conciliar Law Code; burial was affirmed in 1663 and in the 1669 Criminal Articles. Although an edict of 1689 abolished it, to be replaced with beheading, the punishment continued into the eighteenth century.[15]

Burial as judicial sanction was indeed horrific. John Perry, an engineer who served in Russia constructing canals from 1698 to 1712, described it thus:

They are set alive in the Ground, standing upright, with the Earth fill'd about them, and only their Heads left just above the Earth, and a Watch set over them, that they shall not be relieved till they are starved to Death; which is a common Sight in that Countrey, and I have known them live sometimes seven or eight Days in this Posture.

Jacob Reutenfels, writing in the early 1670s, witnessed such an execution of two women side by side and adds more details: "during the day a priest read prayers and gave comfort, and around these living dead they burned wax candles; at night another guard stood by." Later writers describe guards preventing passers-by from giving food and drink to the interred woman, but allowing them to toss coins, to be used for candles or subsequent burial. Occasionally such women were forgiven, disinterred and allowed to join a convent, as was the case with the two women Reutenfels saw. But usually they perished, quickly in the winter, as Collins reminds us, or lasting longer in many cases. Sergeevskii cites cases of women living twelve and even twenty-three days in the ground.[16]

The extraordinary character of this punishment can be explained in two ways. First, it consigned the women to the elements (earth) to die.[17] Second, it fit the severity of the crime. Here the European parallel is helpful. Early modern English law equated the murder of husbands by wives with treason:

if the feme kills her baron, it is regarded by the law as a much more atrocious crime; as she not only breaks through the restraints of humanity and conjugal affection, but throws off all the subjection to the authority of her husband.

[15] 1649 Ulozhenie ch. 22, art. 14: RZ III: 249. PSZ I: no. 335 (1663). 1669 Criminal Articles, art. 100: PRP VII: 428. PSZ III: no. 1335 (1689). Burial: Sergeevskii, *Nakazanie*, 108; Zagoskin, *Ocherk*, 55.

[16] Perry, *State of Russia*, 201. Reitenfels, *Skazaniia*, 118; also Collins, *Present State*, 37. Coins: Sergeevskii, *Nakazanie*, 109–10 cites DeBruin (de Bruyns), *Puteshestvie cherez Moskovoiiu* (1718) (unavailable to me). Endurance: Sergeevskii, *Nakazanie*, 108–9.

[17] Rogov, *Istoriia*, 190.

And therefore the law denominates her crime a species of treason, and condemns her to the same punishment as if she had killed the king.

The Englishman John Wing in 1632 called such a woman "a home-rebel, a house-traitor."[18]

In England, such "house-traitors" were burned at the stake instead of the punishment for men of being quartered; in Muscovy, burial in the ground. Where exactly Muscovy derived this punishment is unclear. There are no precedents for it in East Slavic codes from the Rus′ Law onward, nor in the Byzantine secular law that was influential in Muscovy in the seventeenth century. But women have been punished by burial in one form or another since classical times. In antiquity Vestal Virgins who broke their vows of chastity were buried alive; more pertinent to Muscovy as a possible influence is the burial of women cited in sixteenth-century France and in the 1532 *Carolina.* There, the procedure was somewhat different: a woman was interred alive in an open coffin, but was usually mercifully killed before being completely covered.[19] Suggestions of a procedure similar to Muscovy's crop up in Shakespeare,[20] but how this exact form emerged in Muscovy is a mystery.

In addition to the 1637 case, this punishment is attested several times in the seventeenth century. In 1676, for example, a woman who had been buried for the murder of her husband was pardoned, dug up and sent to exile at the Resurrection Convent associated with the St. Cyril Beloozero Monastery. The famed Old Believer Avvakum reported that his wife was buried alive with his sons in the 1670s; in 1677 a women was buried for killing her husband but, after "days" in the ground, the abbess and sisters of a local convent successfully interceded to allow her to join their ranks. In 1682 two women were condemned for a series of crimes – each for poisoning her husband, and one in addition for a murder committed

[18] Blackstone cited in Hill, *Eighteenth-Century Women,* 150. English law for this crime: Dolan, *Dangerous Familiars,* ch. 1; quote on 21.

[19] Evans says the woman was laid in a grave, covered with thorns and dirt and killed with a stake driven through her heart "perhaps to prevent the body from returning from the dead, in a reflection of old beliefs about vampirism": *Rituals,* 29–31, 48 (31). Others say the woman was strangled: Naish, *Death Comes to the Maiden,* 9. Polish urban practice: Kamler, "Penalties," 172. George Weickhardt argues for Muscovite borrowing of some norms of the *Carolina*: "Probable Western Origins."

[20] In *The Merry Wives of Windsor* (III.4.85–6) a woman rejecting a suitor declares: "Alas, I had rather be set quick i' th' earth And bowl'd to death with turnips!" In *Titus Andronicus* (V.3.178) the verdict on Aaron the Moor is to "Set him breast deep in earth and famish him." But commentary on neither play identifies what model Shakespeare might have had in mind, and Burford and Shulman, surveying punishments for women in English history, do not mention burial at all: *Of Bridles and Burnings.*

while fleeing prison. The two women were buried for three days and then pardoned, allowed to be tonsured at the Tikhvin Convent.[21]

Despite its 1689 abolition, the practice of burying women as a punishment continued – evidence that knowledge of the law was not uniform across the realm in the eighteenth century. Johann-Georg Korb reports a conversation in which Peter the Great himself declared this extreme punishment fitting for "the greatness of the crime." One case of 1720 involved a peasant woman in Arzamas who was found guilty, along with her lover, of intentionally murdering her husband. She was sentenced to death by burial in an "appropriate place in Arzamas at the market"; her conspirator was sentenced to death, in a way not specified. The case gives no indication that the judge knew of the 1689 decree outlawing burial; he might have been following the Ulozhenie in accordance with a 1714 decree that made it the overriding criminal law. Burial was also used in 1730 in Briansk, when a peasant woman survived in the ground from August 21 until September 22. As late as 1752, a verdict noted that even though the 1649 Ulozhenie would order burial for murdering a husband, decrees of Empress Elizabeth in 1744 and 1745 requiring review of capital sentences overrode that penalty. The guilty woman in that case was sentenced instead to eternal exile to Siberia.[22]

Historians consider beheading the most common type of execution in Muscovy[23]; it had long been used for political crime: witness the 1379 beheading of the thousandman of Moscow, Ivan Vel′iaminov, the beheading of rebellious Novgorodian mayors in 1471, numerous examples in the Oprichnina and in the seventeenth century.[24] For felony crime, beheading is cited frequently from the 1660s on: Grigorii Kotoshikhin, writing *c.*1666, for example, cites hanging and beheading as the most common forms of execution; Doctor Samuel Collins, working at court in the 1660s, says "hanging has not been in use but of late years," attributing the hiatus to a folk superstition against the practice.[25] In 1666, a decree distinguishes beheading from hanging according to the crime, not social

21 RGADA f. 1441, op. 5, no. 71, 6 fols. (1672). Avvakum: *Pamiatniki literatury drevnei Rusi. XVII vek*, II: 386. AI v: nos. 14 (1677) and 80 (1682).

22 Korb, *Diary*, I: 215. RGADA f. 1380, no. 197 and no. 163 (1720). PSZ v: no. 2828 (1714). Skinder, "Zhivaia zhenshchina," 398 (1730). RGADA f. 596, no. 361, 20 fols. (1752).

23 Zagoskin, *Ocherk*, 53; Sergeevskii, *Nakazanie*, 99.

24 1375: PSRL XI: 45 (6887). 1471: PSRL IV, pt. I: 510 (6979).

25 Beheading is not explicitly cited in the Law Codes of 1497, 1550, 1589 or 1606 or in decrees from 1550 to 1649, nor in the Felony Chancery administrative books. It is cited, however, in a fifteenth-century Byzantine-based church law: *Pravosudie metropolichie*, art. I: PRP III: 426. Kotoshikhin, *O Rossii*, ch. 7, art. 34, p. 116. Collins, *Present State*, 75.

rank, mandating that condemned thieves and robbers were to be hanged, but that murderers were to be beheaded. The influence of Byzantine law might account for the more frequent mention of legal beheading: the 1669 Criminal Articles cite Byzantine secular law in assigning death "by sword" for premeditated murder; a decree of 1689 and the Military Articles of 1715 follow suit.[26]

In Western Europe beheading was typically associated with social distinction. Van Dülmen suggests that in Western Europe it was a more honorable punishment that allowed for a Christian burial; Wegert suggests that it symbolically suggested self-sacrifice and thus an expiatory ritual; Garland notes that it was associated with the military heritage of noblemen. Russian scholars N. D. Sergeevskii and V. A. Rogov have said the same about Muscovy, but neither cites firm sources on this.[27] As detailed in subsequent chapters, the vast majority of executed criminals were eligible for Christian burial, regardless of their form of execution. As for social status relating to beheading, no Muscovite source theoretically makes this distinction. Some cases before the 1660s do associate beheading with gentry and higher-ranking people. In 1648, for example, a gentryman was found guilty of killing his father: even though on his deathbed father forgave son, still the court sentenced him to beheading; similarly, another gentryman was sentenced to beheading for killing a fellow gentryman in 1650.[28]

Perhaps not coincidentally, after the 1669 Criminal Articles specified beheading for murder, it is encountered for all social groups. In 1674, for example, a young hired laborer in Kadom was convicted of killing a Tatar woman during a robbery and sentenced to beheading, with specific reference to the "*gradskie zakony* and New Articles"; in June 1683 three townsmen in the Perm′ area were sentenced to beheading for raping, robbing and killing a woman; in 1686 a peasant was beheaded for the murder of two peasants in a fight.[29]

In Peter the Great's era beheading was used for felony as well as political crime. An anecdote about Peter reported that he expressed regret

[26] PSZ I: no. 383 (1666). 1669 Criminal Articles, art. 79: PRP VII: 423. PSZ III, no. 1335 (1689). 1715 Military Articles, art. 204: RZ IV: 364. This clause abrogated the custom of freeing a condemned man if the executioner's first blow or attempt to hang him failed to kill him.

[27] Van Dülmen, *Theatre of Horror*, 78–81, 97–101. Wegert, "Social Context," 31; Garland, *Peculiar Institution*, 83. Rogov, *Istoriia*, 135; Sergeevskii, *Nakazanie*, 101.

[28] RGADA f. 210, Prikaznyi stol, no. 567, fols. 159–64 and 276 (1648). RGADA f. 210, Belgorod stol, no. 298, fols. 342–3 (1650).

[29] RGADA f. 1122, op. 2, pt. 2, no. 1629, fol. 11 (1674). DAI X: no. 87 (1683). RGADA f. 159, op. 3, pt. 2, no. 2466, fols. 77–83 (1686) (cites the 1669 Criminal Articles).

about lady-in-waiting Mary Hamilton's being beheaded for the infanticide of three illegitimate children, but that he declared he could not save her without breaking church and secular law. Courts in early eighteenth-century Russia sentenced people of all ranks to beheading: a runaway soldier found guilty of murder and theft in March 1723; in 1724 a peasant convicted of murder; a landlord in 1729 who murdered several of his peasants; a townsman from Arzamas found guilty of incest. In making the latter verdict, the Senate declared that beheading should be the punishment for all cases of that heinous crime.[30]

Judicial practice for felony crime, then, generally limited the forms of execution to hanging and beheading. Other forms of execution – impaling, the wheel, quartering – were not invoked for less than highest crime. The burial of women – with attendant guards, priests and candles – suggests, however, that executions were not devoid of solemnity and sacrality. The interesting question is how elaborate and theatrical such rites may have been.

RITUALS OF EXECUTION

No Muscovite source explicitly prescribes a ritual for executions and the only extant descriptions involve celebrated political cases generally depicted by visiting foreigners. For felony crime in local courts, one can only piece together an impression of what transpired from scattered sources. Those sources reveal several ritual aspects: publicity – the act was witnessed by others; symbolism – the method of execution evoked a connection with the crime; sacrality – some religious intervention was present. All these elements contributed to the political legitimacy of the act and attempted to help the condemned achieve a good death, involving repentance, forgiveness and sacrament; these elements might also be construed as purging the community of the taint of the crime or of the criminal. But at the same time Muscovite sources present executions with minimal theatricality and minimal gratuitous violence. Ritual seems in tension with the pursuit of efficiency and dispatch.

The typical execution done in a local court for felony crime started with a verdict that mandated publicity for the explicit goal of deterrence: "so that others looking on this will not do the same." The 1649 Ulozhenie

[30] Hughes (*Russia in the Age*, 130) cites "anecdotes" of J. Stählin. RGADA f. 978, no. 17 (1723). RGADA f. 419, op. 1, pt. 1, nos. 1508 and 1509 (1724). Landlord murders: RGADA f. 1380, no. 768 (1722) and RGADA f. 419, op. 1, pt. 2, no. 21 (1729). PSZ VII: no. 5181 (1727).

cites this phrase in several articles.[31] Accordingly, local officials gathered a crowd. As observed with corporal punishment, often the verdict specified that the execution be carried out "on market day" to maximize the audience. In 1670 the Voronezh governor was ordered to gather together a crowd at his office in the square and to construct a platform for an execution.[32] He was also to "read the crimes" (the "*skazka*") to the condemned man before execution to instruct the crowd. When Ivan IV executed the eminent bureaucrat Viskovatyi in 1570, a later register of court cases says his "crimes" were read aloud to him; an early such instance in case law dates to January 1622, when a governor reported that he had hanged a peasant, "having said to him his crimes and treason." A detailed example is from a capital verdict from 1637 in Kursk: the Military Service Chancery ordered the governor

> at the execution to announce aloud to all the people in the tsar's name that all servitor and lesser servitors and local people are to live in peace, that there should be no robbery and murder and theft and no other criminality among them and that those who did engage in crime, robbery, theft and killing or other criminality would be executed by the same death penalty and that all people should know our [the tsar's] order and the verdict of the boyars and that, looking on such executions, they would avoid all manner of evil.[33]

By the Petrine era public announcements were widely disseminated beyond the site of execution: in 1699, for example, a capital verdict for corrupt customs officials included the instruction that it should be announced in towns and villages to "fiscal and customs and tavern officials and officers of communes" that they, too, would receive the death penalty for corruption. In a detailed verdict of 1726, according to which two commissars and an undersecretary were hanged for graft, the judge instructed not only that the verdict be read aloud to the condemned and nailed to the gallows, but that the verdict should be distributed to all fiscal offices of all the *gubernii* and provinces and be read aloud and posted in all "towns, major villages and hamlets."[34] The moment of execution provided the state an opportunity to broadcast its laws as broadly as possible.

[31] Quote from Ulozhenie ch. 10, art. 154: RZ III: 126; also ch. 11, art. 27: RZ III: 156; ch. 20, art. 22: RZ III: 211; ch. 10, arts. 143, 154, 171, 217, 251–2: RZ III: 123, 126, 130, 139, 145–6.

[32] KV II, pt. 2: no. 73, p. 93 (1670).

[33] Viskovatyi: *Opis' arkhiva 1626 goda*, pt. 1, p. 257 (1570); same in 1584 to Petr Golovin: ibid., pt. 1, p. 259. On Viskovatyi: Schlichting, 260. AMG I: no. 145 (1622). RGADA f. 210, Belgorod stol, no. 83, fol. 267 (1637).

[34] PSZ III: no. 1722 (1699). PSZ VII: no. 4826 (1726).

The locations of an execution were carefully chosen: town squares on market day for maximum publicity, outside of city walls to separate the town from the pollution inherent in both the criminal and the punishment, by city gates to strike awe in all who entered, or in places symbolically associated with the crime.[35] In late fifteenth- and sixteenth-century Moscow, people were executed in various places: "on the river below the bridge" in 1492; a later account added "on the ice." In 1547 a man was executed "on the meadow beyond the Moscow river opposite the fortress" and in 1555 men were executed "at the fire" (*na pozhare*) and "by the moat (*na rvu*) where churches now stand, between the Frolov bridge and Nikol'skii."[36] In February 1685 a decree changed the place of "marketplace knoutings" in Moscow from the square before the Judicial Chancery in the Kremlin to a spot "outside the Kremlin Spasskii Gates in the Kitai district on the square opposite the market stalls," in other words, essentially the same place as cited in 1555, on current-day Red Square. Thus executions took place around the *Lobnoe Mesto*, a circular platform that served for proclamations and religious ceremonies.[37]

Laws frequently specified that executions be done at symbolically charged sites associated with the crime. As early as 1537, Prince Andrei of Staritsa's gentrymen were hanged along the Novgorod highway along which they had fled in what was construed as a treasonous plot. Brigandage charters of the second half of the sixteenth century specified that a recidivist thief be hanged "where he had been caught with material evidence"; in 1615 Prince D. M. Pozharskii was ordered to hang Lithuanian spies along the road to the Grand Duchy of Lithuania; in 1631 the Pskov governor was instructed to hang anyone arrested for illegally selling or possessing salt in the spot where they were selling or were captured. The 1669 Criminal Articles said not to stage hangings in empty places but where the culprits had committed crime. Petrine decrees similarly

[35] Anisimov, *Dyba i knut*, 535; Sergeevskii, *Nakazanie*, 94–6; Shtamm, "Ugolovnoe pravo," in Nersesiants (ed.), *Razvitie*, 190.

[36] 1492: PSRL IV, pt. 1: 530–1 (7000) and 531 (7001); Shmidt (ed.), "Prodolzhenie," 266 (7001). 1547: Shmidt (ed.), "Prodolzhenie," 291 (7055). In the meadow 1547: Shmidt (ed.), "Prodolzhenie," 291 (7055). *Na pozhare*: PSRL XXXI: 133 (7063); Frolov and Nikol'skii refer to the modern Spasskii and Nikol'skii gate towers (thus the execution location is approximately that of today's Lenin Mausoleum); by the mid sixteenth century this Red Square side of the Kremlin was edged with a moat, so there were also bridges leading to these gates. "At the fire" refers to Red Square: PSRL XXXI: 161 (1634); Tikhomirov, "Zapiski prikaznykh liudei," 446 (1671).

[37] PSZ II: no. 1110 (1685). Snegirev, "Lobnoe mesto."

ordered that criminals be executed in the community where they committed the crime or kept their camps.[38]

In other ways as well, laws and legal practice directly associated punishment with the crime. The Ulozhenie, for example, mandated that those who had moved a land marker were to be punished at the place of the marker, and that a soldier who had defected to the enemy should be hanged within sight of enemy troops. In an interesting case from Iakutsk in 1649, a Russian laborer who had killed a Tunguz prince was sentenced to be knouted "in front of the son of the man who died." In 1699 a decree regarding fire safety in Moscow specified that anyone who looted buildings instead of helping to fight a city fire was to be "knouted without any mercy, being led by the place of the fire."[39] In 1682 the governor of Viatka informed his presiding Novgorod Chancery that he had hanged criminals found guilty of murder "each along the road by which he came to town," and in 1689 the governor of Sol′ Kamskaia informed the tsars and tsarevna that he had hanged the criminal Fedka Nevolin on the shores of the Kama River where Nevolin had committed his crimes. In 1696 two murderers, both peasants, were hanged on "the great Novgorod highway." A Petrine law of 1705 included elements of deterrence and symbolic location: runaway soldiers who are captured should be punished in front of the regiment they had fled, with the soldiers standing in array "with weapons and banners and drums": one in three, chosen by lot, was to be hanged and the other two were to be knouted and exiled.[40]

That executions were construed as evoking negative spiritual power might be inferred from decrees that forbade executions at times associated with religious events. A decree of April 25, 1559 banned executions and corporal punishments on a day of General Requiem (*bol′shaia ponakhida*); a 1653 decree allowed executions on all days but Sunday; decrees of the 1690s similarly prohibited "executions and corporal punishments" for the forty days of commemoration of deceased members of the ruling family.[41]

[38] 1537: PSRL XIII: 97 (7045). Brigandage charters: Iakovlev (ed.), *Namestnichie*, 67 (1549), 90 (1595). SGGD 3: no. 28 (1615). AAE III: no. 195 (1631). 1669 Criminal Articles, art. 123: PRP VII: 433; same instruction in 1679 to Arzamas governor: Iakovlev (ed.), *Namestnichie*, 98. Petrine decrees: PSZ IV: no. 2373 (1711); Military Articles, art. 137, *Tolkovanie*: RZ IV: 352 (1715); PSZ VI: no. 3847 (1721).

[39] Ulozhenie ch. 10, art. 231: RZ III: 141; ch. 7, art. 20: RZ III: 95. DAI III: no. 52 (1649). PSZ III: no. 1693 (1699).

[40] RGADA f. 159, op. 3, Novgorod chetvert′ no. 1618, fols. 53–6 (1682). DAI XII: no. 56 (1689). AAE IV: no. 313 (1696). PSZ IV: no. 2019 (1705).

[41] 1559 decree cited in 1606 Law Code, ch. 159: PRP IV: 539. PSZ I: no. 105 (1653). PSZ III: no. 1451 (1692); PSZ III: nos. 1483, 1488 (1694); SGGD 2: no. 217 (1694).

Even the laconic court cases surveyed here suggest that Muscovite executions were accorded spiritual significance. They report, for example, processions to the place of execution, which journey could evoke religious processions. Some sources describe the condemned walking to the place of punishment, while notorious criminals were often depicted as driven in carts, perhaps the better to be visible to onlookers or perhaps, as was the theory in early modern England, because the convict was not worthy to "to tread upon the face of the earth."[42] It might have been customary that the condemned wore a robe: one source describes how twelve people sentenced to death for their role in uprisings in Ustiug Velikii in 1648 were "dressed in execution clothes" (*smertnaia plat'e*). The condemned might have carried a candle, indicating a hallowed moment, as seen in a rare case from around 1636. Here a group of condemned robbers processed from the jail to the gallows with candle in hand. Giles Fletcher, in Russia in the 1580s, reports the same: "The prisoner is carried to the place of execution with his hands bound and a wax candle burning held betwixt his fingers." So also does Johann-Georg Korb, who adds the detail that some of the musketeers being executed in 1698 "covered their eyes and faces with a piece of linen (which is a national custom)." His dramatic portrayal of Peter's execution of the musketeers is immortalized in Vasilii Surikov's 1881 painting.[43]

Condemned criminals were accorded spiritual comfort before death, despite Olearius's claim to the contrary: "Certain people, for example those who have broken a vow, committed a murder and confessed to it, or perpetrated other gross sins, are not given communion before they reach the point of death." In laws and practice, the expectation of spiritual comfort and sacraments is widespread: sixteenth-century chronicles make a point of noting that Kubenskii and two Vorontsov men executed in boyar struggles did not have their father confessors with them at death; a 1637 decree regarding the execution of a pregnant woman mandates that she is to have confession and communion before being executed.[44]

42 Walking: 1555 Medyn Charter, art. 3: RZ II: 219–20; brigandage charters from 1556, 1571 and 1586: Iakovlev (ed.), *Namestnichie*, 70, 75, 84; 1616/17 Felony Handbook, arts. 20–1: PRP V: 194; Ulozhenie ch. 21, art. 93: RZ III: 245–6; 1669 Criminal Articles, art. 69: PRP VII: 420. Walking and being driven in eighteenth-century sources: Anisimov, *Dyba i knut*, 531–3. Not worthy: Garland, *Peculiar Institution*, 84.

43 Chistiakova, *Gorodskie vosstaniia*, 199 (1648). RGADA f. 141, no. 25 (1636); Kollmann, "Lynchings". Fletcher: "Of the Russe," 176. Korb, *Diary*, II: 103, 105. Surikov: State Tretiakov Gallery, Moscow.

44 Olearius, *Travels*, 273–4; Sergeevskii, *Nakazanie*, 90–3. 1546: Postnikov, 286 (7054). ZA no. 244 (1637).

The 1649 Ulozhenie developed the provision of religious comfort at executions more formally: a new clause prescribed that "thieves and robbers" sentenced to death be held for six weeks in prison in a hut (*izba*) "for repentance." A harsher 1653 decree regarding exiled criminals who had already been spared the death penalty still maintained sacrality: such recidivists should be executed "without mercy" on any day of the week except Sunday, without communion and without time in a "hut of repentance" unless the convict specifically requests the latter. Execution could be delayed only a week if the convict implicated others; otherwise it was to be immediate.[45] Subsequent legislation balanced spiritual comfort with speed of execution. Like the 1653 decree, the 1669 Criminal Articles allowed only a week to the condemned criminal for repentance, after which he could receive the last sacrament and be executed three days later. In extenuating circumstances the 1669 Law Code allowed at most a month before execution, urging officials to carry out executions "immediately" (*vskore*), not writing to Moscow for affirmation. It also depicts judges, not priests, accompanying the condemned on the scaffold, not for particularly spiritual goals. They were instructed to question the condemned rigorously at the moment of execution for information on accomplices, exhorting them to tell the truth, "recalling the fear of the Lord, so that they might free their souls of sin." A decree of 1683 affirmed the month's maximum time allotted by the 1669 code. Petrine laws that dealt with the endemic problem of runaways urged prompt and local execution.[46]

Spiritual counsel continued to be mandated by law before an execution, if not on the scaffold. The Eastern Patriarchs at the Church Council of 1666–7 soundly criticized Patriarch Nikon for forbidding condemned prisoners last rites, and affirmed that such convicts were to be visited by a priest for confession, communion and spiritual counsel a day or two before execution. A church law in 1669 affirmed this provision.[47] Instructions to priest elders of December 26, 1697 prescribed that if men or women condemned to death requested priests for confession, then they were to be given the sacrament if the cleric deemed it appropriate. A May 1722 Supplement to Peter the Great's Spiritual Regulation (1721) declared

[45] Ulozhenie ch. 21, art. 34: RZ III: 234. PSZ I: no. 105 (1653).

[46] 1669 Criminal Articles, arts. 20, 86, 123: PRP VII: 403, 425, 433. PSZ II: no. 1000 (1683). PSZ IV: no. 2373 (1711); PSZ VI: no. 3847 (1721); 1715 Military Articles, art. 137, *Tolkovanie*: RZ IV: 352; PSZ V: no. 3445 (1719).

[47] 1666–7 Council: Subbotin (ed.), *Materialy*, II: 280–5. PSZ I: no. 442, art. 14 (1669). Tumins and Vernadsky (eds.), *Patriarch Nikon*, 99–100.

that one of a priest's most solemn duties was "to support those who have been sentenced and are being led to death, and reassure them of God's mercy," and a decree of October of that same year required the Police Master to provide financial support for priests doing this pastoral service of confession and communion. The expectation that priests should counsel convicts continued through the century.[48]

These provisions were put into practice. In 1637 in Kursk when a townswoman and two men were condemned for murder, the verdict specified that they be given a priest before execution. In two cases of 1647, similarly, death sentences for witchcraft and fortune-telling specified that the condemned was to be given a priest (in one case communion was mentioned) before execution by burning.[49] A murder case of 1648 specifies that a priest be provided before execution, as does a case of 1676 about witchcraft. A verdict also specifies providing a priest before execution in a case from 1729 in Arzamas in which a gentryman was executed for killing several of his serfs.[50] Such access to the sacraments allowed a Christian burial, regardless of crime.

Further ritual is not attested in Muscovite executions for felony crime, in contrast to the elaborately staged spectacles of Western Europe. In a very few cases, torture-like beatings before the execution are cited, as in a few sixteenth-century brigandage charters that decree knouting before execution for a third conviction for theft or in a 1628 verdict for two musketeers of Briansk guilty of murder, who were ordered to be given a marketplace knouting before being hanged "to deter others."[51] But as a rule, extra tortures were not ordered or inflicted.

Muscovite graphic art left little record of executions – only a few chronicle miniatures. Foreigners who returned from Muscovy with ample engravings of political and religious events – Olearius, Meyerberg – included none of executions before Korb witnessed Peter the Great's extraordinary punishment of the musketeers. By contrast, in early modern Europe illustrated broadsheets were everywhere, in English, French,

[48] PSZ III: no. 1612, art. 23 (1697). May 1722 Supplement, art. 7: PSZ VI: no. 4022; English translation: Muller, *Spiritual Regulation*, 59. PSZ VI: no. 4119 (1722). Catherine II in August 1763 decreed that priests should see condemned convicts for "admonition and confession": *Politsiia Rossii*, 90.

[49] RGADA f. 210, Belgorod stol, no. 83, fols. 258–67 and 708–9 (1637). RGADA f. 210, Prikaznyi stol, no. 564, fol. 231 (1647); Novombergskii, *Koldovstvo*, no. 11, pp. 64, 73 (1647).

[50] RGADA f. 210, Prikaznyi stol, no. 567, fols. 159–64 and 276 (1648). Novombergskii, *Koldovstvo*, no. 28 (1676). Gentryman murders: RGADA f. 1380, no. 768 (1722) and RGADA f. 419, op. 1, pt. 2, no. 21 (1729).

[51] Iakovlev (ed.), *Namestnichie*, 67, 90. RGADA f. 210, Prikaznyi stol, no. 36, fol. 468 (1628).

Dutch and German, depicting and commenting on noteworthy events of the day, including many executions. Their political discourse was lively, both critical and approving of brutal punishments and executions.[52] That foreigners did not depict or describe executions in Muscovy until 1671 (Stepan Razin) and 1698 (musketeers) affirms what the source record suggests, namely, that all executions but those for the most notorious criminals were done with dispatch and minimal ceremony.

Muscovite law codes urged that executions be done "promptly" and the ritual elements observed here would not have significantly delayed the process. Delay might come from the need to recruit an executioner or from the necessity to wait for a market day (typically Fridays, but sometimes more often), but time for elaborate staging and gathering of officialdom was not taken. Officials moved quickly to enforce their verdicts or to carry out an order received from the center, even for corporal punishment short of execution. In 1622 in Krapivna, for example, the governor received orders from the Military Service Chancery to carry out a knouting immediately (*totchas*); in 1630, similarly, the governor of Riazhsk was ordered to carry out a beating with bastinadoes "right away," on pain of himself being put into "great disgrace with no mercy whatsoever" if he caused harm (*motchanie*) to the tsar's work by delay. In two separate cases of 1669, corporal punishment was carried out that same day. One case involved a gentryman who was ordered beaten with bastinadoes for shirking service, while the other involved a tradesman in Moscow sentenced to a beating for unknowingly wrapping goods in discarded official documents.[53]

Similarly, executions were done expeditiously. As seen in Chapter 7, decrees of the sixteenth and seventeenth centuries boldly instructed criminal law officials to execute without referring to the center, and they did so. In 1635, a local governor in Kursk received the order to execute three defendants in a murder case. He reported to Moscow that, after sending a priest to give them communion, he had carried out the sentence on March 3, that is, within a week of receiving the order. Similarly, in the

[52] Chronicle miniatures of punishments: Kazakov et al. (eds.), *Litsevoi letopisnyi svod*, XVII: 17–19, 81–2, 132, 170–2, 229–30, 253, 358, 385–6, 489–90; XVIII: 43–5, 147, 262–3; XIX: 133, 386–7, 553–7, 566. Korb: Kollmann, "Pictures at an Execution." Kunzle, *History of the Comic Strip*, I: ch. 6; artists' points of view, 163. Reproductions: Paas, *German Political Broadsheet.*

[53] AMG I: no. 155 (1622). AMG I: no. 278 (1630). Shirking service: RGADA f. 210, Prikaznyi stol, no. 786, fols. 67–70 (1669). Documents: RGADA f. 210, Prikaznyi stol, no. 786, fols. 305–12 (1669). Another case of punishment same day as sentencing: RGADA f. 210, Prikaznyi stol, no. 793, fols. 236–40 (1681).

1648 case cited above of a man beheaded for killing his father, the order was received in April and the local governor reported that he carried out the execution on April 11, again a delay of less than two weeks. By contrast, in July 1628 the Military Service Chancery queried the governor of Briansk with some consternation on why an execution ordered in March "had not been carried out promptly"; the condemned men were still in jail.[54]

After 1649, officials made efforts to accord the requisite time for repentance, but not always fully. A verdict given in October 1650 specified the full six weeks of repentance before the execution of a gentryman of Livni for murder, and the governor of Livni affirmed that he had provided the man six weeks. In another case resolved in 1650, this one in Kozlov, the governor received orders to execute two criminals who had languished three years in prison. Although the orders do not specify a time for repentance, the governor might have had that in mind in delaying a month before execution (he received the order to execute on June 29 and carried out the executions on August 2). Or he might simply have had other pressing tasks. In the same case, he delayed about the same amount of time (between receipt of orders on June 29 and July 31) for corporal punishment of two other criminals who did not merit time for repentance.[55]

A case of May 1659 in Suzdal conveys a spirit of efficient execution of orders. Here the criminal law elder Vasilii Shapilok reported that on May 15 he had been ordered to execute "on a market day in the square" four peasants who had killed their landlord and his wife. Describing the execution day, he reported that when the first of the condemned men had been led to the block, an unruly prisoner yelled out from the prison window that he and the condemned man had a case of treason to report. The elder stopped the execution, questioned and tortured the two men on the spot and determined that neither of them had any such valid report. He continued with the execution that same day. The case describes verdict and execution in the month of May, with no reference to time for repentance. Provision for repentance was also unremarked in a case of 1677. Here, a long enduring murder case in Kadom was finally brought to

[54] RGADA f. 210, Belgorod stol, no. 83, fols. 258–67 and 708–9 (1635). RGADA f. 210, Prikaznyi stol, nos. 567, fols. 159–64 and 276 (1648). RGADA f. 210, Prikaznyi stol, no. 36, fols. 467–76 and 485–91 (1628).

[55] Six weeks: RGADA f. 210, Belgorod stol, no. 298, fols. 342–3 (1650). Kozlov: RGADA f. 210, Prikaznyi stol, no. 172, fols. 253–8 and RGADA f. 210, Prikaznyi stol, no. 265, fols. 59–60 and 67–9 (1650).

a close by the governor, who handed down a guilty verdict in a case of a laborer accused of killing a Tatar woman. On November 30, 1677 he made his verdict and the very next day the young man was executed by beheading. The 1669 Criminal Articles' provision of execution by "sword" for murder was followed; its allowance of about a week for spiritual counsel was not.[56]

Particularly in cases of highest crime, executions were speedy. In 1662 and 1671 rebels were executed the same day as sentenced. Executions of condemned schismatics in 1684 followed within two weeks. In one case, a woman was condemned on January 11 and executed on January 29; in another, Moscow's order to execute was received in Murom on February 14 and the execution was done by February 26, with three days provided for repentance. In 1676 a condemned witch was sentenced to death with provision of a priest being provided to her. Still, the order was sent from Moscow on October 29 and the execution took place on November 3.[57] The Petrine practice of executions also moved with dispatch. Anisimov concluded that the "hut of repentance" fell out of use in the eighteenth century and that most executions took place within one or two days. Few verdicts for execution on the local level made any provision for a time for repentance.[58] In July 1720, for example, a peasant who was found guilty of intentionally killing his landlord was hanged "at the very same hour" that the verdict was read aloud by the presiding judge. Similarly, later that year: on the day the verdict was announced, a peasant found guilty of murder and robbery was hanged "that same hour before many people of all ranks . . . in Arzamas beyond the town commune near the stone *ubogii dom*" (a wintertime morgue when it was impossible to bury corpses). No mention was made of spiritual sustenance given to the condemned. Such practice continued after the Petrine era – in 1738 a man found guilty of intentionally killing a man who was trying to take him off as a recruit was hanged "that same day" with no reference to spiritual sustenance.[59]

56 SIDG no. 268, pp. 499, 502 (1659). RGADA f. 1122, op. 2, pt. 2, no. 1629, 12 fols. (1677).

57 RGADA f. 210, Prikaznyi stol, no. 959, fols. 7–20 (1662). KV II, pt. 1: no. 311, p. 395 (1671). Rumiantseva (ed.), *Dokumenty Razriadnogo*, sect. 5: nos. 58–66 (Jan. 1684); sect. 4: nos. 53–7 (Feb. 1684). Novombergskii, *Koldovstvo*, no. 28 (1676).

58 Anisimov, *Dyba i knut*, 524–5. Corporal punishment was also carried out promptly: knoutings "the same day" as the verdict: RGADA f. 1380, no. 164 (1720); RGADA f. 419, op. 1, pt. 2, no. 242 (1727).

59 Peasant: RGADA f. 1380, no. 29, fol. 51 (1720). *Ubogii dom*: RGADA f. 1380, no. 53, fols. 13–13v (1720). *Ubogii dom* as morgue for unidentified corpses: SRIa IV (1977): 306; Collins, *Present State*, 21–2; Sparwenfeld, *Diary*, 157 and n. 429 on 297. As winter storage place: Fletcher, "Of the Russe," 235. With spring thaw, priests buried these remains on the Seventh Sunday after Easter. By

The above case histories suggest that Muscovite executions for felony crime proceeded with minimal ritual. Two cases in particular show us the typical scene. In 1650 in Livni, the governor reported that he had been ordered to execute a gentryman for murder. After keeping the man in the hut of repentance for six weeks, the condemned man was brought out, his crimes and the verdict were read to him "before many people at the governor's office and on the square," and he was beheaded for murder, "so that, looking on this, other people will not commit such evil crimes." Instructions to the governor of Irkutsk in 1698 also sketch out a typical scene: he was told to hang before many people some exiled criminals who had committed capital crimes, "having read their crimes to them," and to leave their bodies hanging on the gallows "to strike terror in others." Before death they "should be given time as is customary for repentance." The ceremony was prompt and minimal, emphasizing deterrence through speed more than religious ritual.[60]

Several reasons for emphasizing speed over ritual or repentance might be cited. First, as Ivan Pososhkov argued in his memo to Peter I in 1724, swift justice was the best deterrent: "For if such summary justice be meted out to criminals it will inspire more terror in them than any horrible manner of death." Second, governors feared being disciplined themselves for failure to act. Recall the 1630 admonition to a governor to carry out a knouting promptly on pain of "disgrace" should he dally.[61] Finally, the degree of ritual in the typical execution was sufficient to make the point to the assembled crowd and to the condemned alike. Neither court culture nor religious ritual seemed to press to develop more elaborate staging, at least for felony crime.

A final part of the ritual involved what to do with the body. Those who died with confession and communion could receive a Christian burial, so most executed criminals could be buried. In a case of 1610, the Siberian Chancery ordered the governors of Berezov to take down six men who had been hanged as traitors and release their remains to their families for proper burial. In a case of 1696, a governor was instructed to release the bodies of two hanged criminals to relatives or, lacking them, to the winter morgue; similarly, a 1697 church law code allowed an executed criminal's body to be sent to the morgue, while a suicide should be cast into the

contrast, at this time in Europe bodies were in demand for anatomical theaters or illicit medicinal purposes: Rublack, *Crimes of Women*, 85–6. RGADA f. 596, no. 343 (1738).

60 RGADA f. 210, Belgorod stol, no. 298, fols. 342–3 (1650). AI v: no. 280 (1698).

61 Pososhkov, *Book of Poverty*, 215. AMG 1: no. 278 (1630).

forest or field.[62] The majority of our cases of execution for felony crime do not specify what to do with the body, in contrast to the fate of those executed for highest crime, whose remains were often desecrated, left for the dogs, burned to ashes and otherwise denied proper burial (see Chapters 14–18).

A 1698 verdict cited above that required that hanged bodies be left on the gibbet reveals another ritual aspect of executions, intended to terrify as well as to destroy the body to its essence. Such display of the executed was common in Europe, as Jason Coy remarks about early modern Germany: "The body was left hanging from the gallows until it decayed and fell, a grisly scene."[63] This practice was regularly used for highest crime. For felony crime such grotesque display fits the trend of brutalization of punishments exemplified by a 1663 decree on the displaying of severed body parts of a condemned criminal. Political criminals were routinely left hanging: in 1662, for example, the hanging bodies of rebels occasioned a sympathetic comment from a passer-by, for which he was arrested; in 1698 Peter the Great left the corpses of executed musketeers hanging for months around town and outside the windows of his sister Sofiia's convent.[64]

For felony crime, such references come relatively late, which does not mean that the practice did not exist earlier. In 1696 a central chancery scolded a governor in the Novgorod region for not having removed two bodies from the gallows for two months, despite being ordered to do so. The governor was accused of taking bribes from local peasants to keep the men hanging. In 1698 Johann-Georg Korb reported that two women who had hired accomplices for murdering the husband of one of them were found guilty. The two male accomplices were hanged and the women buried in the ground; when the women died, after three and six days, they were hanged, upside down, next to the corpses of the already hanged men. How long the gruesome display continued Korb does not report. Similarly, numerous decrees stipulated that hanged bodies be left for display: one in 1705 related to runaway soldiers; another of 1726 to corrupt customs officials.[65]

62 RIB II: no. 86 (1610). AAE IV: no. 313 (1696). PSZ III: no. 1612, arts. 23 and 21 respectively (1697).

63 AI V: no. 280 (1698). Coy, *Strangers and Misfits*, 51.

64 PSZ I: no. 334 (1663). RGADA f. 210, Prikaznyi stol, no. 959, fol. 21 (1662); the offender was ordered knouted "in the place where he had made his remarks." Korb, *Diary*, II: 211 (1698).

65 AAE IV: no. 313 (1696). Korb, *Diary*, I: 212 (1698). PSZ IV: no. 2019 (1705). PSZ VII: no. 4826 (1726).

Perhaps the most theatrical that Muscovite executions for felony crime got was in last-minute reprieves at sentencing or on the gallows. Such dramatic interventions in the name of the tsar's mercy fulfilled the sovereign's role as benevolent patriarch. A noted case of such a reprieve on the chopping block involved the future Tsar Vasilii Shuiskii: convicted of treason under the First False Dmitrii, he was pardoned at the moment of death; later commentators observed that Dmitrii lived to regret such benevolence. Such dramatic encounters occur in a wide variety of cases involving people of all social ranks; they often involved extenuating circumstances that explain the reprieve. In 1646, for example, the Military Service Chancery informed the governor of Belgorod of its resolution of a murder case involving a lower ranked military man accused of killing a musketeer. Moscow ordered the governor to gather a crowd of many people on a market day and before them to announce a verdict of death. He was then immediately to mitigate the sentence, substituting a marketplace knouting. The mercy was attributed to the memory of Tsar Aleksei Mikhailovich's parents, but the case also notes that the condemned man was ordered to pay off the debts of the deceased. This de facto settlement might explain the reprieve.[66]

Such reprieves occurred not only at sentencing, but even as the axe was brandished. In 1650 a verdict specified such drama: the Military Service Chancery ordered the Kozlov governor to gather a crowd and lead a man convicted of murder to the execution place. There, the governor was to read to him the verdict of death and he was to be placed on the block (*k plakhe klast'*). Immediately, then, he was to be lifted up from the block and given mercy – a merciless marketplace knouting in place of execution. Here the reason for the verdict was that guilt was in doubt; the judge apparently believed the crime to have been done unintentionally. Another Moscow verdict of 1683 to a local governor made the same stipulation: lead the condemned criminals to the block, read them the verdict, lay them on the block, and then immediately grant the reprieve. In this case, the mercy was attributed to the memory of the recently deceased Tsar Fedor Alekseevich as well as the intervention of the Annunciation Cathedral archpriest Nikita Vasil'evich. Similarly, in a case of November 1699, a verdict for several corrupt customs officials in Venev provided that the death penalty should be read to them on the gallows, their heads should be placed

[66] Shuiskii pardon: Petreius, *Relatsiia Petra Petreia*, 98; Margeret, *Russian Empire*, 68–9; PSRL xxxiv: 207 (7113). RGADA f. 210, Prikaznyi stol, no. 162, fols. 264–72 and 416–18 (1646).

on the chopping block, and then the tsar's mercy should be announced to them. Reprieved, instead of death, they should be beaten with a knout, mercilessly, and exiled eternally to hard labor at Azov.[67]

Executions for felony crime suggest a modicum of sacrality and ritual. Spiritual sustenance was provided. People were gathered, the public and the criminal were instructed in his or her crimes. Officials did not always provide the full measure of time for repentance and sources give no indication of elaborate ritual staging. Local officials seemed keenly aware of the peril of causing "harm to the sovereign's work" through delay and they favored efficient execution of orders over ritual invention.

And perhaps therein lay the terror of Muscovite executions. That a judge could render a verdict and execute within a day, a week, a few weeks, might have provided in Muscovy the "terror" that European "spectacles of suffering" transmitted with elaborate ritual. Given the state's tenuous grip on society with a skeletal bureaucracy and vast empire, the fast and cruel slash of the tsar's righteous sword of justice was perhaps the best messenger of state power and the best way to ensure that governors did their jobs. But for criminals of the highest order – traitors, witches, heretics and dissenters – Muscovite courts staged executions with more cruelty and with increasing ritual over the seventeenth century, both to act out state legitimacy and to demonstrate the tsar's benevolent work of purging the community of evildoers and malevolent spirits.

[67] RGADA f. 210, Prikaznyi stol, no. 592, fols. 1–4 (1650); Kollmann, "Quality of Mercy," 11–12. DAI X: no. 87 (1683). See also a 1684 case in which a mother's intervention when her son was on the gallows stopped the execution and reopened the case: DAI XI: no. 11 (1). PSZ III: no. 1722 (1699).

CHAPTER 14

Punishing highest crime in the long sixteenth century

In 1379 Moscow's leading boyar, Ivan Vasil′evich Vel′iaminov, was executed for treason: "He was slain by sword on the Kuchkov field near the fortress at Moscow by the order of Grand Prince Dmitrii Ivanovich. And a multitude stood by, and many cried over him and grieved over his noble birth and eminence." In 1474 boyar prince Daniil Kholmskoi promised to serve loyally, acknowledging "my Sovereign the Grand Prince and his sons have the right to punish me for any crime." Around 1589 the English diplomat Giles Fletcher related a tale he had been told about Ivan IV, later known as "the Terrible": Ivan was once said to have arrested a corrupt secretary (*d′iak*) for accepting a bribe of a goose full of money. He had the man brought "to the marketplace in Moscow" and asked "his *palachi* or executioners who could cut up a goose. He commanded one of them first to cut off [the secretary's] legs about the middle of the shin, then his arms above his elbows . . . in the end to chop off his head that he might have the right fashion of a goose ready dressed."[1]

These three quotations shift the focus from capital punishment for felony crime to that for highest crime and shift the nature of the argument a bit as well. A more interpretive mode is necessary, since the source basis changes for this topic. For the long sixteenth century (from Ivan III [ruled 1462–1505] through the Time of Troubles, approximately 1598–1613), trial transcripts do not exist; a few documentary sources such as surety deeds, loyalty oaths and an inventory of the tsar's archive are available, but most sources are narrative, in the form of chronicles and travel accounts. Chronicles are a problematic source, full of literary tropes and tendentiousness; but they often provide glimpses of judicial procedure and punishment. As noted already, travel accounts should be used critically, but the testimony of eyewitnesses can be revealing. This chapter suggests

[1] 1379: PSRL XI: 45 (6887). SGGD I: no. 103, p. 250 (1474). Fletcher, "Of the Russe," 165; goose tale in Rosovetskii, "Ustnaia proza," 74–5.

that in the long sixteenth century, violence under Ivan the Terrible and in the Time of Troubles stands as exceptions that prove the rule: capital punishment in normal times, like regimes of corporal punishment, however horrific in form, was wielded according to accepted legal norms, following orderly procedure, delivering legitimate violence and sometimes providing mercy.

HIGHEST CRIME IN THE LONG SIXTEENTH CENTURY

Ivan the Terrible (ruled 1533–84) has so dominated accounts of the sixteenth century that it is easy to miss how exceptional he and his violence were. Until Ivan took power into his own hands in the early 1560s, Muscovite rulers had addressed highest crime with judicial procedure and had punished it with a graduated range of sanctions. Like all rulers, the grand princes of Moscow (the title "tsar" was adopted in 1547) did not hesitate to punish what they considered treason, using the death penalty where deemed appropriate. The first quote cited above, from a sixteenth-century chronicle, records a beheading in 1379. While earlier chronicle verses are laconic ("On Kuchkovo field they killed Ivan Vasil′evich in Moscow"), the version quoted above adds the details that he was executed "by the order of the grand prince" and that "a multitude stood by."[2] These added details perhaps reflect sixteenth-century perceptions of the legitimate use of execution (on the order of the ruler) and its format (witnessed by a crowd).

From the late fifteenth century sources make reference to proper judicial procedure regarding highest crime. In trials of heretics, investigation and adjudication were done collectively by councils involving the grand prince, metropolitan, bishops and other hierarchs; extant transcripts (*sudnye spiski)* of some heresy trials show accusatory procedure and no torture, although David Goldfrank notes that torture could also be used. Verdicts in such church/state councils were often justified with reference to the "canons of the holy fathers" and to Byzantine law (*gradskii zakon*).[3] In secular courts as well, investigation and trial were done by proper procedure. Chronicles frequently precede reports of

[2] Fifteenth-century chronicle: PSRL xv, pt. 2: col. 440 (6887). Sixteenth-century: PSRL xi: 45 (6887).

[3] Church judicial councils include Novgorod 1490: Shmidt (ed.), "Prodolzhenie," 261–2 (6999); PSRL iv, pt. 1: 529 (6999); Gusev 1498: Zimin, "Kratkie letopistsy," 36 (7006) and Shmidt (ed.), "Prodolzhenie," 263–4 (7006). Kuritsyn 1505: Shmidt (ed.), "Prodolzhenie," 276 (7013). Bashkin 1553: Zimin, "Kratkie letopistsy," 18 (7061); *Opisi Tsarskogo arkhiva XVI v.*, 42, box 222; PSRL xiii: 232–3 (7061). Goldfrank, "Theocratic Imperatives." 1525, 1531 trials: *Sudnye spiski Maksima Greka*;

punishments for high crime with the phrase "having carried out an investigation" (*syskav*); they depict suspects being sent to Moscow for an audience with the grand prince or his men, resulting in a sentence in the name of the grand prince.[4] Sixteenth-century additions to an earlier chronicle cite proper procedure to legitimize the 1490s executions involved in the political fray between Ivan III's son and grandson: "hearing of and investigating this, their evil intent, Grand Prince Ioann Vasil'evich ordered the traitors executed." Ivan III is depicted interviewing rebellious Novgorod leaders in 1471; he punished Viatka rebels after interviewing them in 1489. Vasilii III in 1510 summoned rebellious Pskovians to his court for judgment; Ivan IV is depicted having Prince Semen Rostovskii interviewed by the boyars about his attempt to flee to the Grand Duchy of Lithuania in 1554 and rendering a verdict after discussion with the boyars "according to the trial transcript and his [Rostovskii's] testimony."[5]

Murderous violence erupted among the boyars in the 1530s and 1540s as they jockeyed for power and for the prize of Ivan's eventual marriage. Several boyars were killed, a rash step in a clan-dominated politics where endless vendetta could have erupted. Such violence shows that the system had spun out of control; it was brought back to equilibrium only by the reconciling distribution of benefits (boyar rank and its emoluments, intermarriage with the ruling clan, etc.) when Ivan came of age.[6] Regarding these chaotic decades, chronicles struggled to maintain the illusion that history was unfolding according to God's plan (alleging that the boyar murders were ordered by the sovereign or his regent) or blamed seductions by the Devil.[7] Revealing the norms the boyars were breaking,

Pliguzov, "Sudnyi spisok." 1556/7: *Opisi Tsarskogo arkhiva XVI v.*, 37, box 190. 1582/3: *Opis' arkhiva 1626 g.*, pt. 1, pp. 258–9.

4 "Syskav": 1488: PSRL VI: 238 (6996); 1491: PSRL XII: 263 (7000) and PSRL IV, pt. 1: 530, 531 (7000); 1504/5: Shmidt (ed.), "Prodolzhenie," 276 (7013); 1528: Nasonov (ed.), *Pskovskie letopisi*, I: 105 (7036); 1547: PSRL IV, pt. 1: 621 (7055) and PSRL XIII: 154–5 (7056); 1553: PSRL XIII: 233 (7061). Suspects sent to the grand prince and/or to Moscow: 1470/1: Nasonov (ed.), *Pskovskie letopisi*, II: 55 (6979), and *Novgorodskie letopisi*, 298 (6979); 1489: Shmidt (ed.), "Prodolzhenie," 260 (6997); 1514: PSRL XIII: 21 (7022) and PSRL XIII: 23 (7023); 1537: Postnikov, 284 (7045); 1538: PSRL XIII: 118 (7045). Grand prince meets for verdict: Nasonov (ed.), *Pskovskie letopisi*, I: 93 (7018); 1533: PSRL XIII: 79 (7042); PSRL IV, pt. 1: 570 (7043); 1554: PSRL XIII: 237 (7062).

5 1490s: PSRL XII: 263 (7000). 1471: *Novgorodskie letopisi*, 298 (6979) and Shmidt (ed.), "Prodolzhenie," 260 (6997). 1510: Nasonov (ed.), *Pskovskie letopisi*, I: 93–7 (7018). 1554: PSRL XIII: 237 (7062).

6 Rogov, *Istoriia*, 152; Kollmann, *Kinship and Politics*, ch. 5; Krom, *'Vdovstvuiushchee tsarstvo'*.

7 By order of grand prince, regent Elena or metropolitan: Nasonov (ed.), *Pskovskie letopisi*, I: 108, 109 (7046); *Novgorodskie letopisi*, 69, 127 (7045); PSRL XIII: 79 (7042), 83 (7042), 97 and 118 (7045); Postnikov, 283 (7042), 284 (7045); Zimin, "Kratkie letopistsy," 13 (7043); Shmidt (ed.),

chronicles criticized boyars for taking the law into their own hands – arresting, beating, exiling or killing opponents "without the grand prince's knowledge" or "by their own willfulness (*samovol'stvo*)." Boyars in 1538 were accused of caring about their own family interests and not "those of the sovereign and state (*a ne gosudar'skim ni zem'skym*)." A boyar was criticized for not participating in the tsar's councils, underscoring the centrality of counsel and advice-giving. One chronicler wrote ominously: "The boyars began to keep counsel among themselves and there was great unrest (*miatezh*)."[8] Chroniclers expected state-sanctioned violence to be carried out by proper procedure and the grand prince's law.

Indeed, behind the internecine quarrels of the 1530s and 1540s, judicial procedure for political crime churned on. Trials and investigations for political crime were carried out; records speak of testimony in cases against boyars, investigation into defections to Lithuania, a trial for a "word and deed" accusation and church–state heresy trials. In an intriguing but problematic source, Ivan IV is depicted personally conducting the interrogation of Russians freed from captivity in the Crimea. His questioning follows inquisitory norms: first oral interrogation, then questioning before instruments of torture, then threatening their use, then interrogation during torture. The source is, however, undated and its provenance is unknown.[9] Mikhail Krom demonstrates that, during the minority, boyars and chancery staff maintained judicial functioning in the ruler's name.[10]

Treason and heresy were punished variously according to social status and degree of guilt. For opposition to Moscow in 1471 in Novgorod, for example, ringleaders were executed, but lesser participants were resettled into the heartland or imprisoned. In a case of treason in 1491, some were executed, while others imprisoned. Heretics were burned in 1504/5.[11] When

"Prodolzhenie," 288 (7045); PSRL IV, pt. 1: 616 (7046). Blame boyars: PSRL XIII: 123 (7046) and PSRL XXXIV: 178 (7046); PSRL XXXI: 130 (7047); Postnikov, 283 (7042), 285 (7046); Shmidt (ed.), "Prodolzhenie," 285 (7042), 288 (7047); Zimin, "Kratkie letopistsy," 12 (7042).

8 *Samovol'stvo*: PSRL XIII: 123 (7046). Without the tsar's knowledge: PSRL XIII: 126 (7047), 140 (7050); PSRL XXXIV: 178 (7046); Shmidt (ed.), "Prodolzhenie," 288 (7047); PSRL XXXI: 130 (7047). Family interests: PSRL XIII: 126 (7047). Tsar's councils: PRSL XIII: 133 (7048). Boyar counsel: PSRL XXXI: 130 (7047); see also PSRL XXXIV: 178 (7046).

9 Trials cited in registers (*opisi*) of the tsar's archive, not the transcripts themselves: *Opisi Tsarskogo arkhiva XVI v.*, 23, box 42 and 40, box 214 (cases against boyars); 41, box 215 and 44, box 229 (defections); 44, box 231 ("word and deed"); 42, box 222 and 37, box 190 (heresy). Ivan's interrogation: Bogoiavlenskii, "Dopros tsarom Ioannom Groznym"; the publication does not name the document's archival location.

10 Krom, *'Vdovstvuiushchee tsarstvo'*, 412–28; see also Kollmann, *Kinship and Politics* and "Muscovite Russia, 1450–1598."

11 1471: *Novgorodskie letopisi*, 298–9 (6979). 1491: PSRL XII: 263 (7000) and PSRL IV, pt. 1: 530–1 (7000). 1504/5: Shmidt (ed.), "Prodolzhenie," 276 (7013); Zimin, "Kratkie letopistsy," 36 (7013).

Prince Andrei Staritskii was arrested in 1537, he and his family were imprisoned, his boyars were sentenced to death (then forgiven and knouted and imprisoned) and his gentrymen (*deti boiarskie*) were hanged.[12] David Goldfrank has argued that punishment of heresy over the sixteenth century moved from execution to penitential imprisonment, as was done to Matvei Bashkin, the elder Artemii, diak Ivan Viskovatyi and others in 1553–4.[13]

Even in Ivan's minority (1530s–40s), amid shocking boyar murders, factions avoided violence by using monastic exile or prison. Such banishments had been tried-and-true methods of medieval rulers across Europe, used by Frankish kings, for example.[14] In Muscovy, deposed church hierarchs were often sent to monastic exile, rather than being executed: Novgorod Archbishop Feofil in 1480, Metropolitans Daniil in 1538 and Ioasaf in 1542.[15] The sister of Prince Ivan Ovchina Obolenskii was forcibly tonsured in 1538, while many boyars were imprisoned in the Kremlin or sent off to Beloozero; some died there, others were released when fortunes reversed at court.[16] Similarly Tatar princes who displeased Moscow were imprisoned at the St. Cyril Beloozero Monastery and released when politics in Kazan made them useful again. Prince Ivan Mikhailovich Vorotynskii, directly implicated in the flight of two other boyars to the Grand Duchy of Lithuania, was not executed but imprisoned in 1534; he died there a year later. Prince Semen Lobanov Rostovskii, who admitted trying to flee to the Polish king "from poverty and stupidity," was sentenced to death in 1554, then forgiven and exiled to Beloozero.[17] All these strategies limited state-sanctioned violence.

A taboo against killing kinsmen of the ruler explains the most poignant examples of state-sanctioned violence in this era. Rather than kill such

[12] 1537: PSRL IV, pt. I: 576–8 and 616 (7045); *Novgorodskie letopisi*, 69 (7045); PSRL XIII: 91–7 and 118 (7045); Postnikov, 284 (7045); Tikhomirov, "Maloizvestnye," *Istoricheskie zapiski*, 85–6 (7045).

[13] 1553–4: Goldfrank, "Theocratic Imperatives"; *Opisi Tsarskogo arkhiva XVI v.*, 42, box 222; PSRL XIII: 232–3 (7061); AAE I: no. 239. See also Zhuchkova, "'I . . . derzhati ego v velitsei kreposti'."

[14] De Jong, "Monastic Prisoners," 291–2; Innes, "Charlemagne's Government," 80–2.

[15] Feofil: *Novgorodskie letopisi*, 309 (6988). Daniil: PSRL XIII: 127; Postnikov, 285 and Nasonov (ed.), *Pskovskie letopisi*, I: 109 (all 7047). Ioasaf: ibid., I: 111; Postnikov, 285; PSRL XIII: 141 (all 7050).

[16] Forcible tonsure: PSRL XXXIV: 178 (7046). Boyars imprisoned: Kholmskoi in Beloozero 1508: "Novoe o vosstanii Glinskogo," 72 (7017). Glinskii 1514: PSRL XIII: 21 (7022). Glinskii 1533, died 1536: Zimin, "Kratkie letopistsy," 13 (7042) and 14 (7045); PSRL XIII: 79 (7042) and 115 (7045); Postnikov, 283 (7042). Prince Ivan Ovchin Obolenskii in 1538: Postnikov, 285 (7046); PSRL XXXIV: 178 (7046). I. P. Fedorov in Beloozero 1546: PSRL XIII: 149 (7054); Postnikov, 286 (7054). Bel'skii 1539: PSRL XIII: 126 (7047); Bel'skii in Beloozero 1542: PSRL XIII: 141 (7050). Prisoners released and returning to favor: de Jong, "Monastic Prisoners."

[17] 1502 Abdul Letif, Beloozero: Shmidt (ed.), "Prodolzhenie," 275 (7010). 1533 Shigalei, Beloozero: PSRL XIII: 67 (7041); Nasonov (ed.), *Pskovskie letopisi*, I: 106 (7042). Vorotynskii: PSRL XIII: 79 (7042). Lobanov: PSRL XIII: 237–8 (7062).

potential rivals, the ruling elite imprisoned a ruler's uncles and cousins. A practice at least since the 1490s, in the vulnerable years of Ivan IV's minority it was systematic. These captives died in conditions of "great suffering," as chronicles describe it, sometimes weighted down with heavy irons or starved to death, but such imprisonment avoided killing. It also, however, pruned the dynastic family tree too much, leading to political crisis in the next generation.[18]

Similarly, high-ranking people caught in court struggles or found guilty of treason were often spared death. Two Patrikeev princes were forgiven execution and tonsured in 1499; when in 1511 Vasilii III arrested his brother Semen for trying to defect to the Grand Duchy of Lithuania, he forgave him and simply replaced his appanage and retinue with new men and new lands. In 1538 at the death of regent Elena, the leading boyar Prince Ivan Ovchin Obolenskii was imprisoned (where he died) but was not executed. Prince Ivan Ivanovich Turuntai Pronskoi was arrested for trying to defect in 1547; at the intercession of the metropolitan he was forgiven "for his foolishness" and put on surety bond.[19] As mentioned above, both Prince Vorotynskii and Prince Lobanov Riapolovskii were spared the death penalty for attempting to defect to the Grand Duchy in 1534 and 1554; they were imprisoned instead. Mercy tempered the passions that would have arisen from the capital punishment of such grandees.

An important strategy to minimize violence was the use of oaths accompanied by surety bonds (*poruka*). In numerous cases of proven or suspected treason (flight to Lithuania, correspondence with the Polish king) by eminent boyars, the grand prince forgave them punishment and

[18] These imprisonments: Kollmann, *Kinship and Politics*, 152–9, 168–77; Krom, *'Vdovstvuiushchee tsarstvo'*, 83–99 and ch. 4. Grand-princely kin who died in prison, with years of imprisonment: Prince Andrei Vasil'evich 1491–d. 1493: Shmidt (ed.), "Prodolzhenie," 263, 269 (7000, 7002). Prince Dmitrii Ivanovich "Vnuk" 1502–9: Shmidt (ed.), "Prodolzhenie," 275 (7010) and PSRL XIII: 11 (7017). Prince Vasilii I. Shemiachich 1524–30: Shmidt (ed.), "Prodolzhenie," 281 and 284 (7032, 7038); *Novgorodskie letopisi*, 124 (7037). Prince M. L. Glinskii 1534–6: Zimin, "Kratkie letopistsy," 13 and 14 (7042, 7045); PSRL XIII: 79 and 115 (7042, 7045); Postnikov, 283 (7042). Prince Iurii Ivanovich 1533–6: Shmidt (ed.), "Prodolzhenie," 285 and 287 (7042, 7044); Zimin, "Kratkie letopistsy," 14 (7044). Prince Andrei Staritskii April–Dec. 1537: Shmidt (ed.), "Prodolzhenie," 288 (7045, 7046); PSRL XIII: 97 and 121 (7045, 7046); Postnikov, 284 (7045). Most poignant example: Dmitrii, son of Prince Andrei of Uglich, imprisoned at age seven in 1491, released months before his death in 1540: Shmidt (ed.), "Prodolzhenie," 263 (7000); Postnikov, 285 (7049). See Chapter 3 on Kremlin locations of these incarcerations. Similarly, Empress Elizabeth's rival Ivan VI languished in prison from November 1741 until his murder in July 1764: Anisimov, *Elizaveta Petrovna*, 13–14, 40, 65, 77–83.

[19] 1499: PSRL XII: 264 (7030 [*sic*]) and Shmidt (ed.), "Prodolzhenie," 273 (7006). 1511: PSRL XIII: 13 (7019). 1538: PSRL XIII: 123 (7046); Postnikov, 285 (7046). 1547: PSRL XIII: 155 (7056); Shmidt (ed.), "Prodolzhenie," 293 (7056).

demanded an oath of loyalty. These oaths underscore the legality of the situation by sternly warning of the consequences of breaking the oath. Of twenty late fifteenth- and sixteenth-century oaths, all threaten the signatory with a spiritual sanction should he default: he will eternally lose the grace of God and that of the Mother of God, and of the Metropolitans and Saints Peter and Aleksii and numerous other named miracle-workers and other saints. Most also include a more tangible sanction, as noted in beginning the chapter: the subject acknowledges the grand prince's right to corporally punish him: "the grand prince is free" to punish.[20] Significantly, in only four cases is that acknowledgment missing; they involve close kinsmen of the ruler, respecting the taboo against corporal punishment within the ruling family.[21]

V. A. Rogov has forcefully argued that Russia's use of executions and corporal punishment from the mid fifteenth century into the 1530s was "typical for the feudal Middle Ages . . . In the activity of state power one cannot see ingrained unbridled harshness or heightened fanaticism. In the use of punishment one sees elements of sound judgment, political tact and a great portion of patience." He concludes that contemporaries in Europe used the death penalty far more frequently than Muscovy. Sixteenth-century foreigners' accounts before the Oprichnina (1564–72) suggest the same. So attuned to the tsar's "plaine despotism" and so fascinated by Russia's legal system, they describe floggings in ample detail, but about executions they are almost silent.[22] One can never be sure in a situation of absence, but one explanation is that in sixteenth-century Muscovy, executions were so simply done that they did not attract attention.

When executions were done, they follow patterns seen with felony crime. Modes of execution were hanging and beheading, with some

[20] Political *poruka*, all in SGGD 1: 1474 Kholmskoi: no. 103, p. 250; 1506 Ostrozhskii: no. 146, pp. 403–4; 1522 Shuiskii: no. 149, p. 415; 1524 Belskie: nos. 152–3, pp. 422, 424; 1525 Vorotynskii: no. 154, p. 427; 1529 Mstislavskii: no. 157, p. 435; 1531 Mstislavskii: no. 159, p. 443; 1532 Pleshcheev: no. 162, p. 450; 1546 Pronskoi: no. 165, p. 457; 1561 Glinskii: no. 172, p. 473; 1562 Bel'skii: no. 177, pp. 486–7; 1565 I. P. Iakovlev-Fedorov: no. 182, pp. 505–6; 1566 Vorotynskii: no. 189, p. 536. H. W. Dewey found thirty such charters from the late fourteenth century to 1568: "Political *Poruka*."

[21] Kinsmen, all in SGGD 1: 1505 Tsarevich Peter, married to Vasilii III's sister: no. 145, p. 402. *c.*1537 Prince A. I. Staritskii, Ivan IV's uncle: no. 163, pp. 451–2. 1553–4 Prince V. A. Staritskii, Ivan IV's cousin: no. 167, p. 461; no. 168, p. 464; no. 169, p. 468. 1571 Prince I. F. Mstislavskii, Ivan IV's first cousin once removed: no. 196, pp. 563–4 and no. 201, pp. 588–9. The latter's father, who married Grand Prince Vasilii III's niece *c.*1529, was forced to sign loyalty oaths in August 1529 and February 1531 and was not given this "kinsman's" exemption: nos. 157 and 159.

[22] Rogov, *Istoriia*, 121. The judicial system: Herberstein, *Description*, 43–52; Fletcher, "Of the Russe," 132–5, 149–53. Even Jerome Horsey, fascinated as he was by tales of Ivan IV's "torments, tortures and deaths," did not describe any judicial executions: "Travels."

symbolic features. "Traitors" in Novgorod in 1488 were hanged and beheaded; thirty gentrymen of Prince Andrei Ivanovich Staritskii in 1537 were strung up on the Novgorod road along which they had been fleeing with their prince.[23] For some men of higher social rank, such as rebellious city leaders in Novgorod in 1471, beheading was used.[24] It is perhaps more than idiom that, when especially eminent men vouchsafed for a peer in a surety bond, they not only pledged to pay a fine in case of the subject's default but also agreed that "in place of his head, our heads" can be taken in punishment.[25]

For those accused of spiritual crimes – heretics and witches – execution drew on elements of nature to purge society of their evil. Some heretics were drowned: three were thrown off a bridge in Novgorod in 1375, and witches were also cast into water to drown.[26] Burning for political criminals was rare, but it is mentioned for traitors in 1493, heretics in 1505 and arsonists and rioters in 1547.[27] A few references suggest even more brutal forms of execution: quartering in 1491 and impaling (*na kol*) in 1547, all for traitors. Humiliating spectacle is even attested. Typically for Novgorod, the punishment of so-called Judaizer heretics in 1490 seems patterned on Catholic models, such as the execution of Czech free-thinker Jan Hus in 1430: the convicted men were paraded through town, seated backwards on horses with their clothing on backwards, wearing conical hats stuffed with straw and tar that were then set on fire.[28] Muscovite

[23] 1488: PSRL XXXI: 117 (6996). 1537: PSRL IV, pt. 1: 616 (7046); PSRL XIII: 97 (7045); PSRL XXXIV: 172 (7045).

[24] 1379: PSRL XI: 45 (6887). Novgorod 1471: *Novgorodskie letopisi*, 298–9 (6979). Pskov 1471: Nasonov (ed.), *Pskovskie letopisi*, II: 55 (6979). 1491: PSRL XII: 263 (7000). 1493: Shmidt (ed.), "Prodolzhenie," p. 266 (7001). 1498: PSRL IV, pt. 1: 531 (7001); PSRL XII: 264 (7030 [*sic*]); Shmidt (ed.), "Prodolzhenie," 273 (7006). 1538: Postnikov, 285 (7046); PSRL XIII: 126 (7047). 1546: PSRL XIII: 149 (7054); Postnikov, 286 (7054). 1547: Postnikov, 287 (7055); Shmidt (ed.), "Prodolzhenie," 291 (7055).

[25] This phrase occurs only with the most eminent principals and guarantors: SGGD I: nos. 175, p. 476 (1562); 178, p. 488 (1563); 180, p. 496 (1564); 185, p. 517 (1565); 190, p. 538 (1566); 194, p. 559 (1566); 195, p. 560 (all 1566); 197, p. 566 (1571). Phrase does not occur: SGGD I: nos. 104, 155, 156, 166, 176, 179, 181, 184, 186, 191 and 198 (1474–1571).

[26] Symbolism of burning and drowning: Rogov, *Istoriia*, 168–77; Bulychev, *Mezhdu sviatymi i demonami*, 48–82. 1375: *Novgorodskie letopisi*, 241–2 (6884). Witches 1491: PSRL IV, pt. 1: 531 (7000).

[27] 1493: Shmidt (ed.), "Prodolzhenie," 266 (7001). 1505: Shmidt (ed.), "Prodolzhenie," 276 (7013). 1547: Postnikov, 288 (7055).

[28] 1491: PSRL IV, pt. 1: 531 (7000); PSRL XII: 263 (7000). 1547: Shmidt (ed.), "Prodolzhenie," 291 (7055); Postnikov, 287 (7055); Postnikov, 288 (7055). Another reference to impaling: SRIa VII (1980): 231 (1517). With impaling, one suspects the influence of the Dracula tale, popular in sixteenth-century Russia. 1490: PSRL XXXI: 118 (6999); Goldfrank, "Theocratic Imperatives," 34; Kazakova and Lur'e, *Antifeodal'nye ereticheskie*, 129–30.

criminal law in the sixteenth century deployed graduated sanctions for highest religious and political crime.

IVAN IV'S OPRICHNINA

In Ivan IV's Oprichnina, a bizarre state within a state, from 1564 to 1572, he and his men (*oprichniki*) led dozens of killing raids, ostensibly to wipe out treason. These killings were not judicial executions; they were spontaneous and indiscriminate. In the context of Muscovite judicial culture before and after Ivan's time, the Oprichnina was an anomaly.

Hundreds died in the Oprichnina. *Sinodiki* (commemorative lists commissioned by Ivan IV of people who had been killed) are chronologically inconsistent, but they indicate the extent of the carnage. What is more difficult to assess is how the victims died. Sources are hugely problematic: a handful of diplomatic and documentary records; a few chronicles, written anywhere from a few decades later to the early and even late seventeenth century; and accounts of foreigners, constituting the majority. All these narrative sources are, according to Hugh Graham, predisposed to sensationalize, to plagiarize and to pass on hearsay; he calls their authors "special pleaders" for their own personal gain.[29]

Therefore, three accounts of the Oprichnina by German-speaking foreigners resident in Muscovy for at least some of the years they describe in their accounts are used here with caution. Taube and Kruze, Livonian noblemen, served as Oprichnina diplomats from 1567 to 1571 before attempting an abortive revolt against Ivan and fleeing around 1572; they describe the Oprichnina's earlier years from hearsay. Heinrich von Staden, whom Graham calls a "conscienceless opportunist," was a mercenary and underling in the Oprichnina army who was in Russia until about 1576. Albert Schlichting was translator to Ivan's court doctor from May 1568 to October 1570, but was not an eyewitness to the sack of Novgorod or other events he so luridly describes.[30] Because these foreign accounts were written sensationally to lure readers or to win the patronage of foreign leaders, the problem of literary exaggeration is real. Prince Andrei Kurbskii's *History* provides many details about Oprichnina horrors but is a very dubious source. Supposedly written in 1573 in the Grand Duchy of Lithuania, nine years after Kurbskii left Russia in 1564, the account must be based on

[29] Veselovskii analyzed the *sinodiki*: *Issledovaniia*, 323–478; Skrynnikov published them: *Tsarstvo terrora*, Appendix, 529–45. Graham, "How Do We Know?"

[30] Taube and Kruze; Staden, *Land and Government*; Schlichting.

hearsay at best. It often contradicts other accounts on details such as how a person was killed, presenting a more lurid version.[31]

The luridness and questionable accuracy of most sources make it difficult to analyze the violence of the Oprichnina (1564–72). Taking the most bird's-eye view, one can perceive parallel processes at work in these years, one continuing judicial process for highest crime, and the other breaking all the rules. Through the 1560s, investigations for treason of eminent boyars and their kin continued. As the Livonian War (1558–83) heated up, the Grand Duke of Lithuania actively solicited Muscovite boyars to defect and some with ancestral and property connections with the Grand Duchy of Lithuania were sorely tempted. Such treason was real: trials and investigations were done; perfidy was uncovered; punishments and pardons followed as before.

In 1561, for example, three Muscovite commanders were suspected of colluding with the Grand Duchy; investigated, they were imprisoned for a year. In the same year Prince V. M. Glinskii (of an old Grand Duchy princely line) was suspected of flight there (for which his father had been imprisoned in 1533) and put on surety bond. He died *c.*1564 or 1565, avoiding an Oprichnina execution. In 1562 a group of eminent boyars and other elite men was embroiled in suspected treason: boyar Prince I. D. Bel′skii was arrested with letters of safe passage from the Polish king in his possession. Investigated, on the intercession of boyars and the metropolitan he was released on surety bond while three lesser compatriots were corporally punished. He survived Oprichnina violence but perished in the 1571 Moscow Tatar attack and fire.[32] Two Vorotynskie brothers were punished for treason. Accused of intending to flee in 1562, they were investigated and found guilty. Their property was confiscated and each imprisoned. Prince Alexander Ivanovich Vorotynskii was released in April 1563; he took tonsure at the end of 1564 and died soon thereafter. His brother Mikhail was kept in exile in Beloozero until being pardoned in the spring of 1566 and put on surety bond. In 1573 he was executed in post-Oprichnina violence.[33]

[31] Kurbskii, *History*; Fennell's footnotes show factual discrepancies. Edward L. Keenan has challenged its authenticity: "Putting Kurbskii in His Place." K. Iu. Erusalimskii assumes its authenticity and explores its manuscript history, which starts in the late seventeenth century: *Sbornik Kurbskogo.*

[32] 1561: Skrynnikov, *Tsarstvo terrora*, 156–7. 1563–4: SbRIO LXXI: 235; *Opisi Tsarskogo arkhiva XVI v.*, 41, box 217. Glinskii 1561: SGGD I: no. 172; Korsakova, "Glinskii." Bel′skii 1562: SGGD I: no. 177; PSRL XIII: 339–40; Skrynnikov, *Tsarstvo terrora*, 149; his death: Zimin, *Oprichnina*, 455.

[33] Vorotynskii investigation: *Opisi Tsarskogo arkhiva XVI v.*, 50. Their exile: *Opis′ arkhiva 1626 goda*, pt. 1, 256 and *Opisi Tsarskogo arkhiva XVI v.*, 40, box 214; AI I: no. 174. Prince A. I. Vorotynskii 1563: SGGD I: nos. 178–9; Skrynnikov, *Tsarstvo terrora*, 150–2, 273; PSRL XIII: 344 (7071). Prince

Prince Dmitrii Kurliatev was also investigated in 1562 for trying to flee to the Grand Duchy of Lithuania and he, as well as his wife and children, were all forcibly tonsured. Kurbskii's *History* says that the whole family was strangled a few years later, but that is not corroborated in other sources. Also in 1562 Ivan Bolshoi Sheremetev fell under suspicion of treasonous dealings with the Grand Duchy; in late 1563 his brother Nikita and he were arrested on suspicion of treason. In March 1564 Ivan was pardoned and put on surety bond. He lasted as a boyar until 1571, when he was tonsured, perhaps forcibly.[34]

Even once the Oprichnina had started up in late December 1564, high-ranking boyars and commanders suspected of treason were investigated, tried, punished or put on surety bond. Some then managed to escape death in the Oprichnina. They included two men put on surety bond for suspicion of treason in 1565. Boyar Prince V. S. Serebrianyi served as a boyar until his death in 1568, while Prince I. P. Okhliabnin joined the Oprichnina. In the waning year of the Oprichnina after the devastating 1571 Tatar attack on Moscow, Prince I. F. Mstislavskii was put on surety bond, accused of consorting with the Crimean Tatars. But he was not executed and survived until his arrest in court struggles in 1591.[35] Others who were put on surety bond early in the Oprichnina later perished. In March 1565, for example, Ivan Petrovich Iakovlev fell under suspicion and was put on a surety bond. In July 1571 he was executed in the wake of the Tatar attack on Moscow.[36] Also in 1565 Lev Andreevich Saltykov and his sons were put on surety bond for suspicion of treason. An Oprichnina boyar, he was disgraced, forcibly tonsured and executed *c.*1571. Similarly, Zakharii Ivanovich Ochin Pleshcheev was put on surety bond in 1566 and ended up killed in the Oprichnina; his name is in the *sinodik*.[37]

M. I. Vorotynskii 1566: SGGD I no. 189; Skrynnikov, *Tsarstvo terrora*, 476; his death: Veselovskii, *Issledovaniia*, 370.

34 Kurliatev 1562: PSRL XIII: 344 (7071); *Opisi Tsarskogo arkhiva XVI v.*, 36, box 187; his exile: *Opisi Tsarskogo arkhiva XVI v.*, 40, box 214; Skrynnikov, *Tsarstvo terrora*, 152; Kurbskii, *History*, 182–3. Sheremetev 1562: Skrynnikov, *Tsarstvo terrora*, 176 and 476; 1564: SGGD I: nos. 180–1; his tonsure: Zimin, *Oprichnina*, 439.

35 Serebrianyi 1565: SGGD I: no. 186; his death: Bogatyrev, *Sovereign*, 267; Zimin, *Oprichnina*, 391. Okhliabnin 1566: SGGD I: no. 194; his joining Oprichnina: Zimin, *Oprichnina*, 152. Mstislavskii 1571: SGGD I: no. 196; Skrynnikov, *Tsarstvo terrora*, 429–30; his arrest 1591: PSRL XXXIV: 197 (7099).

36 Iakovlev 1565 March 28: SGGD I: no. 182; in the *sinodik*: Veselovskii, *Issledovaniia*, 476–7. See also Taube and Kruze, 54; A. G., "Iakovlev-Chiron, I. P."

37 Saltykov 1565: SGGD I: no. 185; Skrynnikov, *Tsarstvo terrora*, 434; Taube and Kruze, 54; Kurbskii, *History*, 220–1; in the *sinodik*: Veselovskii, *Issledovaniia*, 441–2. See also Bogatyrev, *Sovereign*, 171, 268. Ochin Pleshcheev 1566: SGGD I: no. 195; Veselovskii, *Issledovaniia*, 429.

Trials and executions also continued. In the summer of 1564 Prince P. I. Gorenskii Ovchina was caught fleeing; he was tried and hanged. In 1567 a Grand Duchy spy who infiltrated Russia with letters inviting boyars to defect was caught, investigated and executed by impaling.[38] Also in 1567 Ivan IV in diplomatic correspondence to the Grand Duchy of Lithuania and Crimea explained that he had executed Prince V. F. Rybin Pronskoi and Ivan Karamyshev for "great treason," although historians suggest that they were executed for their critique of Oprichnina violence in 1566. In his missive to the Grand Duchy Ivan underscored judicial process: he had "investigated and found that they had made evil plans against him and his state and that he [Ivan], having investigated, had ordered them executed for their guilt."[39]

Thus, even as Oprichnina murders raged, courts were doing investigations, interrogations, verdicts, exiles and pardons. Old patterns of restraint in punishment also surfaced during the Oprichnina years, although they were not sufficiently vigorous to halt the violence. So, for example, metropolitans followed earlier custom by retreating to monasteries when their protests against Oprichnina violence went unheeded. Metropolitan Afanasii (appointed in March 1564) did so in May 1566; Metropolitan Filipp, appointed in his place, after protesting continually to Ivan IV, departed his post for a monastery in July 1568. Ivan responded by trumping up a council to depose him by November 1568 and having him killed in December 1569. Mercy and pardon continued as well. Ivan IV's cousin, Prince Vladimir Andreevich Staritskii, had been disgraced in 1563; three years later he was forgiven and given a new palace in Moscow.[40]

When Ivan IV began to obsess over his boyars' loyalties around 1564, he could have used proper judicial procedure against them, as his government was doing for some. He did not. Especially at the height of the Oprichnina (1568–71) Ivan, or Oprichnina henchmen acting in his name, abandoned restraint. Judicial procedure was ignored or turned into farce.

[38] Gorenskii 1564: Zimin, *Oprichnina*, 138; 1565–6: SbRIO LXXI: 322. Schlichting (245) says Prince Gorenskii was impaled where Taube and Kruze (35) say he was hanged. Gorenskii in the *sinodik*: Veselovskii, *Issledovaniia*, 375. Grand Duchy spy 1567: Skrynnikov, *Tsarstvo terrora*, 308–11.

[39] Zimin, *Oprichnina*, 202–7; Veselovskii, *Issledovaniia*, 432; SbRIO LXXI: 465. Taube and Kruze suggest they were beheaded: 43. To Grand Duchy 1567: SbRIO LXXI: 465; similar assurances 1565–6 (SbRIO LXXI: 322) and in 1563 (cited by Zimin from archival sources: *Oprichnina*, 110).

[40] Afanasii: Skrynnikov, *Tsarstvo terrora*, 203–4, 290; PSRL XIII: 401 (7074). Filipp: Skrynnikov, *Tsarstvo terrora*, 291, 323–8, 334–5, 339–41, 362; *Novgorodskie letopisi*, 98 (7077); Taube and Kruze, 42–4, 48; Bushkovitch, "*Life of Saint Filipp*"; Rozhdestvenskii, "Filipp"; Fedotov, *St. Filipp*. Staritskii 1563: PSRL XIII: 368 (7071); 1566: PSRL XIII: 401 (7074).

Heinrich von Staden describes the *oprichniki* in 1568 killing boyars in their homes or on the streets with no trial and leaving the bodies behind with tags to describe their "crime." Chronicles describe Ivan IV arriving in Novgorod in 1570, announcing his displeasure and proceeding to executions with no trials.[41]

In some cases judicial procedure was trumped up to give the guise of legality. When Prince Vladimir Staritskii was disgraced in 1563, for example, an investigation and church council condemned him. Accused of treason, he was exiled to his appanage and his mother was forcibly tonsured. As noted, a commission of boyars condemned Metropolitan Filipp in 1568 and a church council in 1570 affirmed it. Similarly a lengthy judicial "investigation" with torture into the "treason" of the city of Novgorod and of its Archbishop Pimen in 1570 was prepared, listing a range of punishments according to guilt (execution, prison, those "who were not guilty were freed"), in stark contrast to accounts of chaos and thousands of murders.[42]

The Oprichnina also occasionally inverted judicial procedure. Taube and Kruze's account of the demise of Prince Vladimir Andreevich Staritskii includes a farcical legal process in which a cook in Staritskii's service was suborned to accuse him of trying to poison Ivan IV. The accuser was subjected to a sham torture session to confirm his testimony and then he and Prince Staritskii were put to a face-to-face confrontation as in a usual trial. According to this account, the prince, understanding that he was doomed, took poison. Similarly, Schlichting describes a mock trial of boyar I. P. Fedorov in 1568, where Ivan told Fedorov to dress in the tsar's clothing and sit on the throne as a judge. Ivan allegedly bowed to him, then ordered him killed on the spot.[43]

The sack of Novgorod in 1570 depicts Ivan's violence gone wild. Muscovite chronicles describe people being beaten, tortured and thrown off the bridge, being pushed under if they surfaced. The town was overrun, property destroyed and treasuries confiscated. Foreign accounts – Schlichting, Taube and Kruze – are even more lurid. They describe Ivan running people through with a spear, chopping bodies in pieces; they allege that famine and cannibalism came in the wake of Ivan's destruction. Several

[41] Tags on bodies: Staden, *Land and Government*, 36. Novgorod: *Novgorodskie letopisi*, 338–45, 393–404 (7078); PSRL XXXI: 140 (7078).

[42] Staritskii: Skrynnikov, *Tsarstvo terrora*, 160–1; PSRL XIII: 368 (7071). Novgorod: *Opis' arkhiva 1626 goda*, pt. 1, 257–8 and 315–16.

[43] Staritskii: Taube and Kruze, 45–7; PSRL XXXIV: 191 (7077); Staden, *Land and Government*, 28. Fedorov: Schlichting, 223–4; Zimin, *Oprichnina*, 274–82.

years later eyewitnesses reported to Danish emissary Jacob Ulfeldt that corpses had been so numerous that they had clogged the river and caused flooding.[44] Organized butchery continued after the sack of Novgorod with mass executions in Moscow. Foreign accounts describe a special area being prepared in a market square in Kitai-Gorod called *Poganaia luzha*: musketeers surrounded the square and constructed poles, gallows and pots of boiling water in advance. When the tsar and his son Ivan arrived in battle dress with hundreds of men, Ivan allegedly exhorted people to gather around and watch. He began by issuing pardons to about half of the 300 men accused; they were put on surety bond. Pardons were a normal part of the judicial process; the brutal apparatuses and mass executions that followed were not. A. A. Zimin commented that "what occurred in Moscow on July 25 [1570] exceeded anything that had occurred before in its brutality and sadistic intensity." The remaining prisoners were accused of treason and without a trial or interrogations of any kind were condemned. As if in a proper trial, State Secretary V. Ia. Shchelkalov read out the "crimes" of the accused, and executions started, focusing on leaders of the bureaucracy – Ivan Viskovatyi, Nikita Funikov, Vasilii Stepanov, G. F. Shapkin. According to lurid, mostly foreign reports, the condemned were subjected to unspeakably cruel forms of execution: Viskovatyi, stripped naked, was tied to crossbars and cut to pieces; Funikov suffered having boiling water alternating with freezing cold water poured on him. Between 115 and 130 people were killed over several hours that day.[45]

Oprichnina violence was unprecedented. Late sixteenth-century Muscovite sources do not present quite as lurid a picture as do the foreign accounts, but they are hardly benign. The late sixteenth-century Novgorod chronicles, for example, describe a bear being sicced on a chancery official in 1571. The Piskarev chronicle, compiled in the early seventeenth century, can also be lurid: it accounts how Prince Vladimir Staritskii was poisoned, how Funikov was boiled in water and Viskovatyi cut to pieces and how decapitated heads of boyars were sent in 1572/3 to be displayed at the homes of other boyars.[46] Nevertheless, the foreign accounts and

[44] 1570: *Novgorodskie letopisi*, 338–44, 393–404 (7078); Taube and Kruze, 48–51; Schlichting, 232–7; Ulfeldt, *Puteshestvie v Rossiiu*, 300–1.

[45] 1570 Moscow: Schlichting, 259–65; Taube and Kruze, 51; Staden, *Land and Government*, 28; Skrynnikov, *Tsarstvo terrora*, 402–3; PSRL xxxiv: 191 (7078); Zimin, *Oprichnina*, 437–9. Schlichting reports 122 dead (264); Piskarev chronicle cites 120 (PSRL xxxiv: 191 [7078]); Staden cites 130 (*Land and Government*, 28).

[46] Bear sicced: *Novgorodskie letopisi*, 107 (7080). Staritskii: PSRL xxxiv: 191 (7077); Staden says the same: *Land and Government*, 28. Funikov, Viskovatyi: PSRL xxxiv: 191 (7078). 1572/3: PSRL xxxiv: 192 (7081).

Kurbskii's *History* are the locus of the most bestial violence, rarely if ever seen before or again in Muscovite politics. They are written in a rhetorical style that emphasizes lurid violence, with particular emphasis on such themes as bodily mutilation and sexual depredation. Quartering, almost unheard as a form of Muscovite execution to this date, is cited: Schlichting describes a man quartered by having his limbs pulled apart by fifteen executioners, with Ivan observing. Men were impaled and poisoned; bears were sicced on people; many were thrown into a river, stuffed under the ice.[47] Men are killed by being fried in a frying pan, tortured with needles under the nails or burned over hot coals. They are blown up with gunpowder in barrels or huts. Schlichting depicts Tsar Ivan forcing Prince Dmitrii Ovchina Obolenskii to drink huge beakers of mead, then having him assassinated in the wine cellar.[48]

Foreign narrative accounts stress the desecration and display of bodies. Schlichting reports that when Prince S. V. Lobanov Rostovskii was beheaded in 1565 by assassins, they shoved his body under the ice but brought his head to Ivan in a bag, whereupon Ivan scolded it. Several accounts describe people being killed in their homes and their bodies being hung there for family members to walk past and neighbors to see.[49] Sexual violence is also marked; both Schlichting and Taube and Kruze report that Ivan IV himself personally sexually humiliated and raped women, as did his men and his son Ivan.[50]

Foreigners and the Kurbskii *History* also depict Tsar Ivan as personally involved in the violence. The Kurbskii *History* depicts Ivan personally killing Shakhovskoi in 1563 in the town of Nevel; Taube and Kruze depict him personally impaling a man in 1567 and ordering the body cut up and left for display; they depict him in 1570 devising specific forms of execution for individual defendants. Schlichting depicts Ivan enjoying seeing a man being quartered and enjoying being splashed with blood, Ivan

47 Quartering: Schlichting, 229, 249. Impaled: Kurbskii, *History*, 182–3; Taube and Kruze, 35, 40, 54. Schlichting (245) says Prince Gorenskii was impaled where Taube and Kruze say he was hanged (35). Poison administered by Ivan: Taube and Kruze, 54. Bears sicced on people: Schlichting, 228, 249, 255–6; *Novgorodskie letopisi*, 107 (7080). Thrown into a river, under ice: Schlichting, 242–3; Taube and Kruze, 49–50; Staden, *Land and Government*, 26.

48 Frying pan, needles: Kurbskii, *History*, 188–9; Taube and Kruze say he was flogged: 41. Hot coals: Kurbskii, *History*, 198–9. Blown up: Kurbskii, *History*, 228–31; Schlichting, 225. Mead: Schlichting, 214–15.

49 1565: Schlichting, 221. Bodies mutilated, left in the street: Taube and Kruze, 36, 40, 41; Schlichting, 230, 265. Bodies at homes: Schlichting, 229, 240, 246, 247, 256–7; Taube and Kruze, 41; Staden, *Land and Government*, 35.

50 Sexual violence: Schlichting, 225, 246–7, 266; Staden, *Land and Government*, 21, 28, 35; Taube and Kruze, 41–2, 55.

running people through with a pike or shooting them with arrows, Ivan pouring boiling soap on a man and stabbing him when he pulled away, and Ivan and his son stabbing numerous people numerous times. Even the usually circumspect Giles Fletcher a generation later reported the lurid tale cited at the beginning of the chapter about Ivan personally directing a man to be quartered as if he were a roast goose.[51]

The violence attributed to Ivan IV is unprecedented in the Muscovite judicial or literary record and is more bloodthirsty than the tortures visited upon the condemned in early modern Europe's "spectacles of suffering" which were, after all, legal proceedings. Accounts of it, indeed, should be looked at very critically. The particular group of foreigners who reported to Europe about Ivan would be predisposed to emphasize or invent violence for popular appeal; their narratives should be analyzed in the context of early modern European literary tropes of violence.[52] But even if their forms of execution are sensationalized, hundreds, perhaps thousands, of people died. Taboos were broken: previously untouchable categories of people – Ivan's kinsman and the metropolitan – were killed, not to speak of numerous men in high clans whose fathers and grandfathers would likely have been offered a loyalty oath had they transgressed in their times. The mass scale is unprecedented. Even if these accounts' specific violence is discounted by half, Ivan's violence surpassed anything seen before.

Ivan's executions during the Oprichnina were truly horrific, but why he and his men did them is obscure. There is little agreement here. Efforts to see the Oprichnina as a rational institution and its violence as motivated by social class or political policy have foundered on the randomness of the violence. Some scholars have therefore argued that Ivan was irrational, because of factors from physiological pain to psychological paranoia to insanity.[53] Another approach holds that Ivan's violence was rational in a mystical, irrational sort of way; it was "sacred violence," inspired by his vision of himself as an arm of God in the apocalyptic end time.[54] That argument links Ivan with the apocalyptic sensibility evident in writings

[51] 1563: Kurbskii, *History*, 190–1. 1567: Taube and Kruze, 40. Devising forms: Taube and Kruze, 51. Blood splashed: Schlichting, 229–30. Pike and arrows: Schlichting, 250–1 (1569), 234 (1570). Boiling soap: Schlichting, 254. Stabbing: Schlichting, 258 and 264. Goose: Fletcher, "Of the Russe," 165.

[52] Kappeler describes the image of Ivan but not literary tropes: *Ivan Groznyj im Spiegel.*

[53] Historiography: Pavlov and Perrie, *Ivan the Terrible*, 118–25; Crummey, "Ivan the Terrible."

[54] Panchenko and Uspenskii, "Ivan Groznyi i Petr Velikii," 66–78; de Madariaga, *Ivan the Terrible*, 376–82; Pavlov and Perrie, *Ivan the Terrible*, 159–61; Bogatyrev, "Ivan the Terrible Discovers" and "Heavenly Host"; Dvorkin, *Ivan Groznyi kak religioznyi tip*; Bulychev, *Mezhdu sviatymi i demonami.*

and a few visual sources at the Muscovite court in his day. Excerpts from texts such as the Book of Revelation were included in some of the vast historical-theological works compiled under Metropolitan Makarii (1542–63); icons and frescoes produced then in the Kremlin depict, often in arcane symbolism, apocalyptic themes.[55]

The connection between Ivan's often bizarre and violent behavior and this body of very esoteric ideas has been made by reference to literary compositions attributed to him (such as his will and letters, some of which are very problematic sources), and to symbolic, religious and mystical connotations of Oprichnina actions and artifacts. A. L. Iurganov and A. A. Bulychev, for example, link Ivan's favored forms of execution – drowning, cutting bodies into pieces, throwing victims to dogs or bears – with popular concepts of righteous retribution. Bulychev grounds his study even more broadly than Iurganov, drawing eclectically on sources from ancient Rome to the Old and New Testaments to folk traditions recorded as late as the early twentieth century in Russia. They show that water and wild beasts were widely associated with devils and evil spirits; demolishing the body so that it could not be buried in a Christian burial consigned the victim to the status of unclean dead. Other scholars have seen the Oprichinina as a carnivalesque effort to create an anti-society from which to punish evil with Christ's avenging sword.[56]

On its surface, one might construe Ivan's violence as Christian apocalyptic vengeance simply because of the ubiquity of apocalyptic sensibility in theological writings of his time. And those writings were violent to be sure, deriving from the Book of Revelation. But Muscovy's interaction with apocalyptic thought is very complex; visual representations of the apocalypse in Ivan's time, for example, were remarkably unviolent. The famous "Church Militant" icon depicts not the Battle of Armaggedon but the triumph of Christ and the heavenly host. Other icons referenced eschatological thought from wisdom theology in complex and esoteric symbolism, as in a mid-sixteenth-century four-part icon championed by Metropolitan Makarii against critics of its rare and controversial iconography. Sergei Bogatyrev has argued that frescoes and a royal banner done

[55] Flier, "K semioticheskomu analizu" and "Till the End of Time"; Hunt, "Ivan IV's Personal Mythology"; Bulychev, *Mezhdu sviatymi i demonami*; Iurganov, *Kategorii*. Visual representations: Podobedova, *Moskovskaia shkola*, 40–58; Bogatyrev, "Ivan the Terrible Discovers" and "Heavenly Host." An early sixteenth-century Novgorodian apocalyptic icon: Flier, "Semiotics of Faith."

[56] Bulychev, *Mezhdu sviatymi i demonami*, pt. 2, 43–151; Iurganov, *Kategorii*, 356–404. Panchenko and Uspenskii, "Ivan Groznyi i Petr Velikii"; Likhachev and Panchenko, *"Smekhovoi mir"*; Hunt, "Ivan IV's Personal Mythology."

in the late 1550s and early 1560s represent a turn towards a "straightforward reference to apocalyptic violence," but that reference was primarily textual, represented in blood-curdling excerpts from the Book of Revelation embroidered (in difficult to parse ceremonial script – *viaz'*) on the banner. The imagery itself was hardly graphic or violent, particularly in comparison to the apocalyptic woodcuts from Albrecht Dürer and other north European artists that Bogatyrev himself cites. Last Judgment frescoes and icons do indeed depict sinners suffering in hell, but in cartoon-like sketches compared to the blood and gore of, for example, contemporary European religious art. One might make the argument that in the absence of graphic representations of violence, even subtle changes in iconography were shocking to beholders, but what they thought cannot be known. Not until the seventeenth century did apocalyptic imagery depict violence more realistically, and in secular painting one awaits nineteenth-century social realism. In other words, the triumphalist message about the apocalypse promoted in visual imagery to which Ivan IV would have been exposed at Makarii's court stands in jarring contrast to the violence attributed to him in the Oprichnina.[57]

Certainly Ivan's violence was symbolic; at its root, all violence by sovereign figures is sacrificial and sacred; they occupy a space of "exception," possessing the right to kill to maintain social stability. In ancient societies, ritual sacrifices (human or animal) by sovereign figures (priests, kings) channeled violence in this way; in modern societies judicial systems and legal punishments assume this role. But a sovereign's obligation is to avoid excess. Their violence – in warfare, in elaborate rituals of animal or human sacrifice, in capital punishment – should be measured and orderly, designed to protect society, not to predate upon it. That is the proper link between sovereign power and violence. Ivan IV's violence transgressed this space of exception. Surely his violence took forms that were popularly recognized as purifying (fire, water, dismemberment). But it was also humiliating and sadistic and, most importantly, indiscriminate. He went far beyond identified traitors or criminals and killed en masse. Not only did such behavior violate Christian expectations of avenging angels; from a theoretical point of view, it also destabilized his society, doing what Giorgio Agamben argues that twentieth-century mass violence did –

[57] Church Militant: Rowland, "Biblical Military Imagery"; Bogatyrev, "Heavenly Host," 79–80. Esoteric icon: Podobedova, *Moskovskaia shkola*, 40–58. Bogatyrev, "Heavenly Host" and "Ivan the Terrible Discovers." European graphic art: Merback, *Thief, the Cross*. Later illustrated apocalypses: *Litsevye apokalipsisy*; Bogatyrev notes that some illuminated apocalypses dated to the sixteenth century might have been produced later: "Heavenly Host," 87–8.

turning the exception into a horrific norm. Even D. S. Likhachev and A. M. Panchenko, who placed Oprichnina violence in the context of the unique "humor" wielded by autocrats, acknowledge that prolonged joking quickly stops being funny and collapses into its opposite – in this case, into indescribable cruelty.[58] If Ivan were guided by a sense of apocalyptic destiny, he had church and secular courts to turn to. If he were inspired by the apocalyptic thinking of his time to kill, he killed too indiscriminately. His violence was not sacred in either a Christian or theoretical framework; it was irrational, if not insane.

But for the purposes of this book, the important point is that Oprichnina violence far exceeded the norms of sixteenth-century judicial practice. Even Bulychev admits that legal practice did not use many of Ivan's symbolic forms (e.g., execution by animals) or excesses.[59] Even during the Oprichnina, behind the scenes boyars and bureaucrats proceeded with trials and investigations, surety bonds and pardons, corporal and capital punishment. When the Oprichnina was over, the system remained.

FROM GODUNOV TO THE TIME OF TROUBLES

Perhaps the best indication that Oprichnina violence did not represent the norm is that prosecution and punishment of highest crime reverted to pre-1560s patterns in the reigns of Fedor Ivanovich and Boris Godunov (1584–1604). V. A. Rogov argues that precisely because of the horrors of the Oprichnina, elites were eager to restore judicial procedure and prevent excesses. When the documents affirming Boris Godunov's ascension to the throne in 1598 asserted that the goal of his rule should be to create "justice through proper trials" and "peace and quiet," these traditional platitudes spoke to contemporary anxieties.[60]

Narrative sources about the reign of Boris Godunov – foreigners and chronicles – are permeated with anti-Godunov sentiments disseminated by all the governments that followed him in the chaos of the Time of Troubles, principally in works by the camps of the First False Dmitrii (1604–6), Tsar Vasilii Shuiskii (1606–10; the chronicle *Inoe skazanie*) and the Romanovs (came to throne 1613, *Novyi letopisets* and other sources). Within a generation of his death, allegations of his assassination of

58 Likhachev and Panchenko, "*Smekhovoi mir*," 48. Agamben, *Homo sacer*. Modern judiciary taking the place of primeval sacrificial rites: Girard, *Violence and the Sacred*, 15–24.

59 Bulychev, *Mezhdu sviatymi i demonami*, 47, 93, 114.

60 AAE II: no. 8, p. 56 (1598); Rogov, *Istoriia*, 158–60.

Tsarevich Dmitrii and his ruthless ambition were widespread, ready for future development by poets, historians and composers. Thus it is all the more striking that contemporary sources – even hostile ones – are almost unanimous in praising Godunov for his competence at "the art of ruling." Prince Ivan M. Katyrev-Rostovskii's biographical sketch, for example, praises Godunov for his intelligence, his generosity to the poor, his fortifications – before faulting him for his "insatiable desire for power." Isaac Massa, who scathingly condemns Boris and his "cruel" wife as constantly scheming for power, concludes by praising Boris for having given Moscow "good laws and fine privilege," for having improved security in city streets and, most of all, for restoring law and order: "he was the declared enemy of those who had been guilty of extortion, accepting presents and bribes."[61]

Even Jacques Margeret and Conrad Bussow, both of whom favored the pretender (the First False Dmitrii) in their accounts, credit Boris with benevolent rule until the late years of his reign, when his anxiety over the pretender Dmitrii brought out his cruelty. Margeret stated that "for not ten persons were publicly executed during his reign before Dmitrii's arrival in Russia, except for some thieves who had assembled in a band of up to 500." Some contemporaries assert that upon becoming tsar, Boris took an oath not to use the death penalty for five years. No such document exists, but the idea fits the general assessment of Godunov, exemplified by Bussow: "This Boris Fedorovich exercised his office with such devotion and skill that almost every one was amazed, and it was still said by all that there was not his equal in Russia, in that he had rectified many injustices, and many abuses had been curtailed, and many widows and orphans had obtained justice through him."[62]

Sources do not ignore the fact that Boris Godunov did punish his rivals. There was plenty of strife among boyar factions in the reign of Fedor Ivanovich (1584–98), when Godunov was the leading boyar, and during his reign as tsar (1598–1605). But in the 1580s and 1590s the Godunov faction practiced court politics as usual – no boyars were killed in the night as in Ivan's minority nor killed en masse as in the Oprichnina. Rather, Boris Godunov used time-honored strategies of

[61] Katyrev-Rostovskii, "Povest′," cols. 620–1; Massa, *Short History*, 95.

[62] Anxiety: Margeret, *Russian Empire*, 16–64 *passim*; Bussow, *Disturbed State*, 7–35 *passim*. Rogov follows this two-stage interpretation: *Istoriia*, 158–63. Five years: Margeret, *Russian Empire*, 61; Massa, *Short History*, 44; Bussow, *Disturbed State*, 13 and 26, quote on 7.

political death, as enumerated by eyewitness Giles Fletcher. He described how the tsars keep the noble "houses from rising again":

> many of their heirs are kept unmarried perforce that the stock may die with them. Some are sent into Siberia, Kazan and Astrakhan' under pretense of service ... Some are put into abbeys and shire themselves friars by pretense of a vow to be made voluntary ... but indeed forced unto it ... These and such like ways begun by the Emperor Ivan Vasil'evich are still practiced by the Godunovs.

Godunov indeed forcibly tonsured Fedor Nikitich Romanov and exiled other Romanovs and rivals on trumped-up charges; he sent them off as governors to far-flung posts that kept them out of the Kremlin power elite. He refused to let the scion of the Mstislavskii family marry.[63] Such non-lethal means controlled political struggle short of bloody violence.

Modern historians also conclude that court politics of Boris's time was remarkable in its stability and general leniency.[64] Andrei Pavlov, the most assiduous student of Boris's reign, argues that Godunov's bloodiest years were the first six or seven after Ivan IV died in 1584, when boyar clans were jockeying for power. The Shuiskie, many of whom were exiled or died in suspicious circumstances, were the major losers. During his years as tsar (1598–1604), Godunov maintained equilibrium by the traditional strategy of distributing benefits to the elite. Also following tradition, he expanded the number of boyars, including not only his extended clan and faction but also members of rival families such as the Romanovs and the Belskie. Pavlov concludes that Boris Godunov, "unlike Ivan the Terrible, did not resort to widespread terror against the elite. Only a relatively small number of boyars and gentry suffered direct disgrace and repression under him. For the entire period when he was in power, there was not one public execution of a boyar."[65] Judicial and administrative procedures returned to regular patterns. A law code was compiled for the northern lands in 1589 on the basis of the 1550 Law Code; military muster books continued to be compiled; Kremlin chanceries issued numerous decrees on land, taxation, slavery and serfdom. Transcripts do not survive, but

[63] Fletcher, "Of the Russe," 140. Romanovs and others in late 1600: Pavlov, *Gosudarev dvor*, 73–6. Exiles: Massa, *Short History*, 35–6, 44–5; Bussow, *Disturbed State*, 26–7; PSRL XIV: 52–4; *Razriadnye knigi 1598–1638 gg.*, 133, 152, 175 (Golovins, Nagie, Sitskie). Mstislavskii: Margeret, *Russian Empire*, 53; Massa, *Short History*, 45.

[64] Dunning makes this remark and cites supporting historians: Margeret, *Russian Empire*, 115, n. 38.

[65] Pavlov, *Gosudarev dvor*, 79 and *Praviashchaia elita*, pt. 3, ch. 3. Equilibrium was restored after the minority ended in 1547 also by bestowal of boyar rank and benefits to winners and losers: Kollmann, *Kinship and Politics*, ch. 5.

registers of documents in Kremlin archives list numerous trials, including of public officials.[66]

After Boris Godunov's death in 1605, Russia was thrown into the maelstrom of dynastic crisis, social uprising and foreign invasion, a period known as the Time of Troubles. Foreign invasion, cossack uprisings, peasant rebellions, a succession of self-declared pretenders to the throne, and boyar factions vying for power – all created a situation in which unbridled violence raged. V. A. Rogov marks it as a setback for legality:

> "The Time of Troubles" destroyed the developing conception of sanctions and punishment for crime as categories pertaining to the central authority. The old understanding of punishment lost its meaning, inasmuch as sanctioning functions were centered not only in the hands of the central authorities but also with all the opposing sides, including invaders and pretenders. The gradations of punishment that had existed before were destroyed.

Chester Dunning has argued that this long chaotic period accustomed Russians to greater violence thereafter, while Laura Engelstein counters that the violence of the Time of Troubles was a weapon of a "weak state," not a stable one. She argues, complementing the interpretation presented here, that after this stage of excessive violence, the Romanovs' increasing stability over time allowed it to be measured in the use of judicial violence.[67]

Almost all surviving sources on violence in the Time of Troubles are tendentious and exaggerated in various ways – vilifying one side or the other, making more lurid the types of punishments, inflating statistics of losses to what Skrynnikov calls "exemplary (*primernye*) numbers" up to five times higher than reality.[68] Nevertheless, there was much shedding of blood, killing on the battlefield and plundering of peasant villages. This was war and civil rebellion, a crisis of sovereign authority. Little of it qualified as judicial violence, as judgments and penalties meted out by a legitimate authority with established procedure.

[66] The number of laws from 1584 to 1604 (eleven) included in a definitive collection was close to the number issued from the 1560s to 1582 (nine), although that entire 40-year span paled in comparison to the energetic pace of the 1550s (thirty-three): ZA nos. 1–53. Military service books: *Razriadnaia kniga 1475–1605 gg.*; *Razriadnaia kniga 1495–1598 gg.*; *Razriadnaia kniga, 1559–1605 gg.* Documents in archives include a 1584 verdict against Petr Golovin and several corruption cases in 1599–1602: *Opis' arkhiva 1626 goda*, pt. 1, 259–62.

[67] Rogov, *Istoriia*, 169–70, 178. Dunning, "Terror"; Engelstein, "Weapon of the Weak," 680–1. The Time of Troubles is variously dated beginning at the end of the dynasty (1598, preferred here) or the invasion of the First False Dmitrii (1604).

[68] Skrynnikov, *Smuta*, 114.

One should, for example, exclude the punishment of captives after battle, by both sides, from legal process. While war was still raging and its outcome unsure, executing captive soldiers made sense – it reduced the opposing forces and intimidated the enemy. There are many notorious examples: in January 1605 Tsar Boris Godunov's troops at Dobrynichi immediately executed all their captives except for the Poles, whom they kept as trophy prisoners. According to Isaac Massa, one of the few sources that mention such executions, in 1606 and 1607 Tsar Vasilii Shuiskii's army drowned their captives after the battles at Gremiachii and Vyrka River and after the siege of Moscow; throughout his reign, captives were summarily executed.[69]

The violence perpetrated by the pretender "Tsarevich Peter" at Putivl′ in 1606 followed cossack traditions that will be seen again in the Stepan Razin uprising (see Chapter 16). As a chronicler noted, "much blood was spilled" in daily mass executions. Diabolical punishments are alleged by hostile sources: in addition to tossing from towers and bridges, men were quartered, hanged upside down and shot. Hostile sources also suggest that female family members of victims were raped and enslaved. Memory remained long after the fact among servitors loyal to Moscow.[70]

R. G. Skrynnikov tries to depict Tsarevich Peter's executions as a "legal" process by a "tsar" supported by a boyar council as in traditional Muscovite judicial process. But he demonstrates that the executions were run in cossack "democratic" style: executions were on the public square; occasionally the crowd would be invited to shout their approval or disapproval of a given victim.[71] This lent legitimacy to the act and shared the collective responsibility. Scholars have drawn parallels between this violence and that attributed to Ivan IV. They cite the gruesome variety of forms of execution alleged to Ivan and to the various pretenders, even including being mauled with bears. They note the similarity of Ivan IV asking an assembled crowd to approve his executions to cossack spectacles of "participation."[72] The parallels are fascinating, but difficult to unravel.

[69] Margeret, *Russian Empire*, 63 says hanged; Massa, *Short History*, 85 says hanged, shot and drowned. On Dobrynichi, Massa adds that after the siege prisoners were given a blow to the head before being drowned (by plunging under the ice of the river): *Short History*, 156, 163, 167–8. Prisoners executed later: ibid., 174. Two contemporary accounts reported that many cossacks blew themselves up on their own kegs of gunpowder rather than be captured at the battle of Vyrka River: VBDM 106; PSRL XIV: 74.

[70] Blood spilled: PSRL XXXIV: 211, 214. Diabolical: PSRL XXXIV: 214, Belokurov, *Razriadnye zapisi*, 10; VBDM 110; PSRL XIV: 74. Women: VBDM 104; PSRL XIV: 74. Memory: Skrynnikov, *Smuta*, 158–9; VDBM 318–19.

[71] Skrynnnikov, *Smuta*, 156–7.

[72] Dunning, *Russia's First Civil War*, 337–8; Perrie, *Pretenders*, 125, 137–8, Skrynnikov, *Smuta*, 158, Perrie, *Image*, 31–2, 62–5. Bears: VBDM 227 (1607).

Cossacks did not have to learn these tactics from Ivan IV; they were intrinsic to cossack communities beyond the Muscovite state through the sixteenth century. Nevertheless, scholars make a good point that oral tradition about Ivan IV meting out purifying and legitimate violence took on a life of its own, regardless of its historical accuracy. We cannot say how widespread such folk traditions were among the cossacks of Muscovy's southern borderlands through the seventeenth century or in the communities that joined in their violence, but they might have helped provide a justification for wielding communal violence.

During the Troubles, rulers dealt with traitors expeditiously. In 1604 Isaac Massa depicts Boris Godunov torturing and drowning anyone "who had even pronounced Dmitry's name" in a lawless way: "people were condemned without being heard." While the First False Dmitrii as Tsar famously pardoned Prince Vasilii Shuiskii for plotting against him, as Tsar himself, Shuiskii ordered a hetman who had spread letters in favor of the pretender to be impaled in 1606; in 1607 he ordered a priest who had done the same to be beheaded. A courier sent from a rebel stronghold died under torture by fire in 1607.[73] Even when constituted governments, however short-lived, punished those whom they considered the greatest threats to themselves, their justice was more arbitrary than orderly. The First False Dmitrii, for example, was assassinated by a group organized by Vasilii Shuiskii in May 1606. His body was dragged to Red Square for display; contemporaries Jacques Margeret and Peter Petreius relate the version that his buried body so angered the earth that an unseasonal killing frost was visited on the land. So he was exhumed, the body burned and the ashes cast to the wind. No judicial procedure was involved here.[74] Successive pretenders killed rivals and suffered at the hands of their own men. For example, the Second False Dmitrii executed a "cossack tsarevich" in 1607 and two other pretenders in summer 1608; he himself was assassinated by one of his own guards, Petr Urusov, in December 1610.[75]

Neither Tsar Vasilii Shuiskii nor the early Tsar Mikhail Romanov observed much procedure in the use of judicial violence against rivals.

[73] 1604: Massa, *Short History*, 73. Pardon: PSRL XIV: 67; Palitsyn, *Skazanie*, 111. Dunning underscores the First False Dmitrii's clemency: *Russia's First Civil War*, 173, 199, 207–8, 215. Shuiskii's executions: Massa, *Short History*, 163, 166; Smirnov, *Vosstanie Bolotnikova*, 555; PSRL XIV: 76.

[74] Margeret, *Russian Empire*, 73; Petreius, *Relatsiia Petra Petreia*, 96–7. Treatment of Dmitrii's corpse: Dunning, *Russia's First Civil War*, 226–38, 243–5.

[75] Second Dmitrii executes: Dunning: *Russia's First Civil War*, 395; Tikhomirov, "Novyi istochnik," 127; PSRL XIV: 77, 89 (*Novyi letopisets*); VBDM 229–31; Smirnov, "Kogda byl kaznen?" 116–17. Second Dmitrii assassinated: Dunning, *Russia's First Civil War*, 414; PSRL XIV: 104–5; Bussow, *Disturbed State*, 147–51.

In 1606 the rebel Ivan Bolotnikov and the pretender "Tsarevich Petr" surrendered to Shuiskii's forces in Tula and were brought to Moscow. Conrad Bussow reports that Shuiskii accepted their surrender and promised to allow Bolotnikov to serve him, then perfidiously broke his word. He sent Bolotnikov to Kargopol in secrecy, where he was ordered killed. Tsarevich Petr (real name Ileika Muromets) was treated with somewhat more proper procedure. After months of interrogation, torture and imprisonment, he was publically hanged on the Serpukhov road outside of Moscow. One chronicle reports that Shuiskii convened a council to condemn him ("*po sovetu vsei zemli*") and disseminated the pretender's confession widely. A German observer, Elias Gerkman, described the execution: the False Peter was driven to a scaffold set up outside of Moscow. He addressed the crowd before death, recanting his confession and claiming to be the true son of Tsar Fedor Ivanovich. The executioner hanged him on a rope too thick to draw tight enough and the condemned hanged until the executioner finished him off with a blow to the head.[76] Under Tsar Mikhail Romanov, a similarly public execution was the fate of rebel Ivan Zarutskii, arrested in June 1614 outside of Astrakhan with Tsaritsa Marina (wife of the First False Dmitrii) and her son, the "little Brigand." Taken to Moscow, Zarutskii was impaled and the boy was hanged, but no reference to a trial remains. The Piskarev Chronicle simply reports that "the tsar ordered" them all executed.[77] These accounts are as problematic and laconic as sixteenth-century chronicles, but they suggest that Shuiskii and Mikhail Romanov disregarded procedure in the heat of war. This should not be surprising, after all.

Nevertheless, rule by law remained an ideal. In their pursuit of the throne several leaders – Vasilii Shuiskii, Polish King Sigismund, commanders of the national militia – signed agreements promising to rule lawfully. In the spring of 1606 as Prince Vasilii Shuiskii rushed to seize the throne, he declared that he would not "without a proper trial with my boyars execute any man nor confiscate hereditary estates or homes and property from their brothers or wives or children who were not together in crime with them." Later Romanov thinking, chronicled in the *Novyi letopisets*, depicts the boyars as objecting that Shuiskii need not make such promises, as they were not in Muscovite tradition; such an argument

[76] Bolotnikov's death: Bussow, *Disturbed State*, 103–4. Council: PSRL XXXIV: 215. Muromets: Gerkman cited at length in Smirnov, "Kogda byl kaznen?" 108. The *Inoe skazanie* refers to the "many tortures" that Muromets suffered before hanging: RIB XIII: col. 115; his confession: VBDM 222–6. Other versions: VBDM 118, 174–5, 182–3; PSRL XIV: 77 (*Novyi letopisets*).

[77] Zarutskii and Little Brigand: PSRL XIV: 134; PSRL XXXIV: 218–19.

played into Romanov claims to autonomous power in contrast to the traditional consultation promised here. Polish King Sigismund made similar promises on behalf of himself and his son as candidates for the Russian throne in February and August 1610: he agreed to punish and to confiscate property and rank only according to guilt proven by "first judging fairly with the boyars and Council members"; he also agreed not to punish innocent kin nor to confiscate land without a trial, and to consult the boyars in all things.[78]

In June 1611 the leaders of the militia that routed the Poles from the Kremlin – Prince D. T. Trubetskoi, Ivan Zarutskii and P. P. Liapunov – promised even more. Like the others, they vowed not to execute or exile anyone without guilt and without a verdict, but they specified it would come from the "whole land." They went on to vow that legal process would be followed for anyone accused of treason and that no vigilante vengeance would be allowed. "If someone kills someone else without a verdict of the whole land, he himself will be executed." Who exactly constituted the "whole land" as a judicial instance was not clarified, but their vision of an orderly judicial process is unambiguous. Kotoshikhin asserted that Mikhail Romanov also agreed to such limitations in 1613, but he is the sole source.[79]

Tempting though it has been for historians to construe these agreements as "constitutional" limits on autocratic power, most historians agree that they did not break with pre-Romanov custom.[80] Muscovite rulers had traditionally defined the judicial world as one in which the sovereign worked in consort with the boyars. The 1497 and 1550 Law Codes begin by declaring that the grand prince "with his brothers and boyars" had issued the code. The 1550 Law Code associates boyars with lawmaking when it mandates: "As for any new cases about which it is not written in this law code, they are to be resolved by being presented to the sovereign and with the verdict of all the boyars, and then those cases are to

[78] Shuiskii 1606: Iakovlev (ed.), *Pamiatniki*, no. 6, p. 18; also published AAE II: no. 4; PSRL XXXIV: 213 (Piskarev); PSRL XIV: 69 (*Novyi letopisets*). Feb. 1610: Iakovlev (ed.), *Pamiatniki*, no. 14, p. 48 (art. 11); SbRIO CXLII: 72 (art. 11). Aug. 1610: Iakovlev (ed.), *Pamiatniki*, no. 16, p. 55; SbRIO CXLII: 98.

[79] Militia agreement: Karamzin, *Istoriia gosudarstva rossiiskogo*, III: footnotes to vol. 12, ch. 5, note 793, cols. 138–43; Iakovlev (ed.), *Pamiatniki*, no. 21, p. 69; RZ III: 48. See a similar assertion in a 1611 oath to the Second False Dmitrii by some of these same leaders: AAE II: no. 170. Kotoshikhin, *O Rossii*, 126; Crummey, "'Constitutional' Reform," 33.

[80] Rogov, *Istoriia*, 181; Dunning, *Russia's First Civil War*, 406 and 580, n. 5; AAE II: no. 44; Crummey, "'Constitutional' Reform"; Tel'berg, *Ocherki*, ch. 2.

be written into this law code."[81] These were not constitutional rights, but traditional expectations of counsel. In promising to consult with boyars or "the Land" in rendering justice, Shuiskii, King Sigismund and the militia leaders were not innovating. They were upholding tradition, separating themselves from the wanton violence of recent years and seeking touchstones of legitimacy. Their focus on ending killing, vengeance and destruction of property suggests how extraordinary the violence of the Time of Troubles was.

"WORD AND DEED"

V. A. Rogov argues that the legacy of the Time of Troubles was a determination to return to "legality" (*zakonnost'*), a dominant theme in post-Time of Troubles historical works by Avraamii Palitsyn, Ivan Timofeev and others. In the decades that followed the Time of Troubles, the Romanovs followed through on these expectations, executing virtually no boyars in court political disputes through the entire century.[82] Even their efforts to prosecute enemies played into public sensibilities and ended up stabilizing the realm.

The Romanovs' assiduous prosecution of "sovereign word and deed" (*slovo i delo*) cases of lese-majesty at first glance might seem ludicrous. Governors were ordered to arrest, interrogate and punish any whiff of disrespect for the tsar; hundreds of such cases were brought and prosecuted, but real treason was rarely uncovered. More often, the treasonous "words" amounted to indiscreet moments of drunken abandon. But the Romanovs benefitted from these prosecutions far more than simply by deterring others. Angela Rustemeyer has argued that the zeal of the system came not from the top, but from society upwards. Muscovites of all social ranks accepted the concept of the tsar's honor and willingly turned in those they suspected of treasonous views; their identification with the realm endured through the eighteenth century. Governors processed these cases harshly (see Chapter 6), but punished them in familiar ways – with graduated sanctions according to degree of guilt. Thus, according to Rustemeyer, "word and deed" prosecutions had a stabilizing effect, affirming popular engagement with the terms of autocracy and providing

[81] RZ II: 54 (1497) and 97 (1550). Verdict of boyars: 1550 Law Code, art. 98: RZ II: 120. Krom underscores this clause: *'Vdovstvuiushchee tsarstvo'*, 596–9.

[82] Rogov, *Istoriia*, 179–80. Robert Crummey counts five boyar executions in the century: *Aristocrats and Servitors*, 225, n. 46; Paul Bushkovitch speaks of "more than a generation of peace (1613–71)" in court politics: *Peter the Great*, 49–51.

a venue for the rulers to demonstrate a balanced and benevolent use of power. Rustemeyer goes so far as to argue that the "relative stability" of the early modern Russian state was linked to "the mobilization of most of society on behalf of the tsar's honor."[83]

Mark Lapman's study of 209 cases up to 1649 in which the punishment for a "word or deed" case is known affirms Rustemeyer's findings that cases of lese-majesty were not punished excessively. Lapman found that about a quarter of his cases resulted in no corporal punishment at all; in about 60 percent, punishment was no worse than bastinadoes with brief jail time. In only 5 percent were the accused sentenced to death and, of those eleven defendants, only five in the end were executed and six pardoned. The harshest punishments went to people found guilty of serious treason – conspiracy, defection or rebellion, disrespectful words about the sovereign by high-ranking officials, even witchcraft.[84] The Romanovs' assiduous prosecution of "word and deed" cases has been taken as evidence of a foundation for a more cruel and coercive state after the Time of Troubles. But Rustemeyer and Lapman have shown that state-sanctioned violence in these prosecutions was meted out judiciously and that the Romanovs moved into the seventeenth century supported by a social consensus that inextricably engaged them in an "unautocratic balancing act" to maintain stability.[85]

From the late fifteenth to the early seventeenth century the Muscovite state did not hesitate to defend itself from perceived threat, whether in the form of rebellion, defection to the enemy, sorcery or heresy. Although laconic, chronicle sources describe a judicial culture that deployed execution when merited and dispensed mercy where fitting. Only in moments of political chaos – Ivan IV's minority, the Oprichnina and Time of Troubles, periods when legitimate and/or stable government was absent – are arbitrary violence and killing encountered.

Whether or not the Time of Troubles is responsible for the increase of brutal punishments in seventeenth-century law – one can also cite the influence of Byzantine canon law and Lithuanian Statutes – the issue is

[83] Rustemeyer, *Dissens und Ehre*, 422 and Conclusion.

[84] Lapman, "Political denunciations in Muscovy," 178–81 and Table 20. Breakdown: 21 percent of cases were dismissed "with a reprimand"; 5 percent imprisoned; 31 percent bastinadoes, some with prison time; 19 percent knouting, often with jail; 8 percent exile with knouting; 11 percent "harsh"; 5 percent capital sentence. Rustemeyer on punishment: *Dissens und Ehre*, 244–54, 358–60, 426.

[85] Dunning, "Terror," 512–13. Rustemeyer, *Dissens und Ehre*, 258, 434.

how violence was used. Michael Geyer reminds us that violence is "an inevitable and paradoxical effect of the search for security and its prerequisite, social harmony." Christoph Schmidt similarly remarked that "As tyrannical as power is without legality, so powerless is legality without executive power."[86] The seventeenth-century state wielded violence as one of several strategies to maintain control and it used it deliberately and judiciously. For highest crime the state used brutal torture to ferret out guilt; it levied sentences graduated according to the crime; it deployed capital punishment on those who most threatened the state. It mobilized violence differently for different crimes: for members of the boyar elite caught up in court struggles, executions were kept subdued and straightforward. For witches and schismatics, executions were horrific, intended to accomplish their complete destruction.

[86] Geyer, "Some Hesitant Observations," 695; Schmidt, "Von Gottes und Rechts wegen," 565.

CHAPTER 15

Factions, witchcraft, and heresy

When Fedor Shaklovityi was executed for treason in 1689, he said nothing "to justify himself" as his sentence was being read. But a musketeer executed later that day spoke from the gallows. "As he was walking to the execution, Obros'ka Petrov acted very honorably: he declared his repentance before all the people with tears in a loud voice, admitting that he deserved this shameful death for his criminal deeds and warning others watching his execution to avoid such evil deeds and so harrowing a death." By contrast, in 1677 two condemned schismatics did not address the crowd but "leaped headfirst" into the cage that would confine them in the fire.[1] These vignettes sketch out the terrain of this chapter – executions for certain highest crime and their attendant rituals.

The seventeenth century was indeed the "rebellious century" (*buntiashchii vek*). Muscovite authorities were challenged from many sides: church and state were intertwined in the prosecution of witchcraft and religious dissent; governors tracked down "word and deed" against the ruler; in succession crises of the 1680s boyar rivals traded charges of "treason" as political tables spun. How the law dealt with such crime reflects the high stakes involved – prosecution balanced proper procedure and graduated sentences with brutality in interrogation and execution. This chapter examines the punishment of three kinds of highest crime in the seventeenth century – alleged treason within court politics, witchcraft and religious dissent. It focuses on how such crimes were judged and how they were punished, starting with a look at how the law defined highest crime.

DEFINING HIGHEST CRIME IN THE SEVENTEENTH CENTURY

Since the fifteenth century Muscovite courts had had no problem dealing with highest crime – treason, witchcraft, heresy. The term "*izmena*" for

[1] Petrov: Matveev, "Zapiski," 56. Leap headlong: Filatov, *Arzamas v XVII veke*, 80.

treason was long attested in chronicles and appeared in Muscovite documents by the mid sixteenth century, but law codes contained only brief enumerations of crimes punished by death.[2] Only in the 1649 Ulozhenie, taking inspiration from foreign codes, did the state attempt to define crime against the state, in a move that G. G. Tel′berg called a stabilizing reaction to the violence of Ivan IV, the Time of Troubles and mid-century urban uprisings and that Richard Hellie considered an assertion of autocratic power.[3] The Ulozhenie, however, was not systematic: rather than introducing a collective noun for "state crime" or enunciating overarching principles, it detailed discrete crimes.

Tel′berg defined state crime narrowly as secular threats, citing Chapter 2 of the Ulozhenie, which cites threats to the tsar, attempts to overthrow the ruler or state, mass uprisings and plots (*skop i zagovor*) and even threats to the ruler's spiritual well-being (meaning that sorcery against the ruler was a political crime). One should point out that the third chapter complemented the second; it punishes with death homicide in the tsar's presence, palace or courts of law and mandates lesser penalties for insults, assaults or theft in those settings. Furthermore, Tel′berg's definition of state crime should be expanded to include the Ulozhenie's very first chapter, which addresses crime against religion and the church. It prescribes execution for blasphemy, for disrupting the liturgy and for homicide in church, and details corporal punishment for lesser misbehavior in church. Accordingly, most scholars consider serious religious dissent crime against the state;[4] judicial practice justifies this broad definition. Church and state cooperated in prosecutions of dissent and schism, heresy, witchcraft and sorcery. After having deposed Patriarch Nikon for his opposition to the tsar, for example, the state all the more

[2] *Izmena*: SRIa VI (1979): 172. Tel′berg finds the term's first judicial use in a 1562 loyalty oath: *Ocherki*, 69–72. Of twenty loyalty oaths from the late fifteenth century to the 1580s, the root *izmena* occurs as noun or verb for three men: Prince I. D. Bel′skii in 1562 (SGGD I: no. 177, pp. 484–5), I. P. Iakovlev in 1565 (SGGD I: no. 182, p. 504) and Prince I. F. Mstislavskii in 1571 and 1581 (SGGD I: no. 196, pp. 563–4 and no. 201, pp. 588–9). All other oaths use terminology such as "guilt," "evil," "evildoer" (*vina, likhoe, likhodei*) or "good" (*dobroe*): SGGD I: nos. 103, 145–6, 149, 152–4, 157, 159, 162–3, 165, 168–9, 172, 189 (1474–1566). *Izmena* also cited in a Muscovite diplomatic report in 1567: SbRIO LXXI: 465. It was common in the seventeenth century: *Opis′ arkhiva 1626 goda*, 257; RZ III: 48 (1611), 86, 88–9 (1649). Earlier, brief lists of capital crime: Pskov Judicial: Kaiser (trans. and ed.), *Laws of Rus′*, art. 7, p. 88 (it uses the term "*perevetnik*" for traitor); 1497 Law Code, art. 9: RZ II: 55 and 1550 Law Code, art. 61: RZ II: 108 (both use "*kromolnik*," as does a 1582 decree: ZA no. 42).

[3] Tel′berg, "Politicheskii sud" and *Ocherki*. Hellie, "*Ulozhenie*: Preamble" and "Commentary on Chapters 3 through 6."

[4] Ulozhenie chs. 1–3: RZ III: 85–91. Tel′berg, "Politicheskii sud" and *Ocherki*. More expansive definition: *Narodnoe antitserkovnoe dvizhenie*, 18–19; Golikova, "Organy," 246–7.

assiduously prosecuted Old Believers (whom it labeled schismatics) for similar disobedience as well as for heresy.

Not only was state crime not defined systematically in the Ulozhenie, neither was it distinguished by venues of prosecution. Some have considered the tsar's Privy Chancery (*Prikaz tainykh del*) as focusing on this, but it did far more – its primary task was to administer the tsar's properties. I. Ia. Gurliand pointed out that the Privy Chancery lacked the staff to carry out criminal investigations on its own and worked with other chanceries on cases of state crime in which the tsar was particularly interested, such as the prosecutions of Patriarch Nikon and Stepan Razin. Throughout the seventeenth century, highest crime was prosecuted in a variety of venues, including the Military Service, Foreign Affairs, Patriarchal and other chanceries as the crime and social status of the accused dictated. N. B. Golikova adds that from Aleksei Mikhailovich's time onwards, special commissions investigated particular disturbances, such as urban uprisings and musketeer rebellions.[5]

Procedure is perhaps the best distinguishing characteristic in defining state crime before Peter the Great's time. Tel′berg noted that the Ulozhenie introduces a procedural exception for political crime, in that it allows the tsar to resolve a case "according to his judgment" (*po razsmotreniiu*) when eyewitness or material evidence was lacking (often the case in allegations of witchcraft or intent against the tsar).[6] Given that torture was used in such cases, their resolutions rarely depended solely on the tsar's discretion, but the point is significant. In the end, what distinguished state crime from felony in Muscovy was not institutional setting or positive law as much as the harshness of interrogation and the brutality of punishment meted out for treason, sorcery, witchcraft and other perceived threats to the state.

POLITICAL EXECUTIONS AMONG BOYAR FACTIONS

The Romanovs came to power in 1613 and presided over a decades-long era of "peace" among boyar factions, undoubtedly a welcome respite for clans that nurtured memories of the Oprichnina and Time of Troubles. Paul Bushkovitch noted that during Aleksei Mikhailovich's reign there

[5] Gurliand, *Prikaz velikogo gosudaria*, 301–13; see also Brown, "Muscovite Government Bureaus," 321; *Narodnoe antitserkovnoe dvizhenie*, 17–28; Tel′berg, *Ocherki*, ch. 7. Golikova, "Organy," 248–50, 255, 275–7.

[6] Ulozhenie ch. 2: art. 12. Tel′berg, "Politicheskii sud," 18. Man′kov details differences in procedure for common felony and political crime: *Ulozhenie*, 306–7, 330–4.

were no executions of boyars at all; Robert Crummey cited only five in the entire century.[7] The few executions that did occur were justified by the charge of treason, but they reveal a tension between proper procedure and arbitrary violence not so evident for prosecutions of heresy, witchcraft or rebellion. These intense, face-to-face struggles among the ruling boyars teetered precariously on the line between internecine violence and legal prosecution.

The execution of General Mikhail Borisovich Shein in 1634 was the only execution of a boyar in the first half of the century, and it cannot be fully attributed to struggles among factions, although some have argued this. Others argue that Shein, who surrendered his troops to the Polish king in the disastrous Smolensk campaign of 1632–4, fell as a scapegoat for the humiliating defeat.[8] Permitted by the king to depart in dignity with the majority of his army in February 1634, Shein was met in Moscow as a traitor and tried by a court of boyars. On May 18, 1634, he, his second in command Artemii Vasil′evich Izmailov and Izmailov's son Vasilii were sentenced to death; their property was to be confiscated and several others received lesser sentences. Trial transcript does not survive, but the lengthy judgment verdict and ritual of execution follow tradition.

On May 28 a brief version of the sentence was read to the condemned men at the Kremlin Criminal Chancery (*Prikaz sysknykh del*); they were driven to Red Square accompanied by two officials and two scribes, with no reference to priests as confessors. At the place of "the fire," sometimes cited in Red Square executions, a scribe read aloud a very long indictment to the men; they were then beheaded. There is no reference to the disposition of their bodies. The German scholar Olearius, in Russia August–December 1634, alleged that the execution was carried out duplicitously: the condemned were led to believe that they would be reprieved at the last minute, but they were not. Olearius also described how Shein's son, who had been sentenced to exile, was knouted.[9]

At the same time, mercy softened the blow of their deaths to affected boyar factions. Lesser commanders in the Smolensk debacle were pardoned at the sentencing: Prince Semen Prozorovskii and Ivan

[7] Bushkovitch, *Peter the Great*, 49–51; Poe, "Central Government," 442–5; Crummey, *Aristocrats and Servitors*, 225, n. 46.

[8] Zertsalov, "M. B. Shein pod Smolenskom"; Korsakova, "Shein"; Solov′ev, *Istoriia Rossii*, bk. v, vol. IX: 169–73; Stevens, *Russia's Wars*, 131–2. Olearius reported that Shein's execution was intended to avert an uprising over the Smolensk defeat: *Travels*, 153–4.

[9] AAE III: no. 251 (1634). PSRL XXXI: 161 (1634). Olearius, *Travels*, 153–4. "The fire" as Red Square: 1554/5: PSRL XXXI: 133 (7063); Tikhomirov, "Zapiski prikaznykh liudei," 446 (1671).

Mikhailovich Shein were informed that they merited death but that, upon the intercession of various members of the tsar's family, they were forgiven and sentenced only to exile and confiscation of lands. Prince Mikhail Belosel'skii was similarly forgiven because he had been sick during the campaign; he was sentenced only to exile and property confiscation; in the end he was kept under house arrest since he was ill and near death. Four other men were exiled, two were imprisoned and two secretaries were released. Ivan Mikhailovich Shein died on the road into exile, and by September the remaining two exiles (Prozorovskii and Timofei Izmailov) were forgiven and allowed to return. Such a combination of measured violence and magnanimity had been typical of boyar political struggle since the sixteenth century.[10]

These executions were not elaborate or theatrical, perhaps in deference to the eminence of the victims, perhaps because court politics was an in-house affair. They followed the bare-bones ritual for felony crime. The event was legitimized by the usual gathering of a crowd and the reading of the verdict, but no reference is made to provision of religious comfort. Later executions of boyars in similar circumstances were similarly low-key. With the rise of the Matveev faction in the early 1670s around Aleksei Mikhailovich's second wife Nataliia Naryshkina, tensions mounted over succession. Aleksei Mikhailovich's heir Fedor Alekseevich (ruled 1676–82) was known to be sickly; beyond him awaited two potential heirs, both minors – Ioann, son of the first wife (Mariia Miloslavskaia), and Peter, son of Naryshkina. When Fedor Alekseevich died, rivalries between the Miloslavskie and Naryshkiny erupted in a musketeer-led rebellion (discussed in Chapters 16 and 17) and deadly struggle among boyars.

The Miloslavskii faction emerged victorious in May 1682, although technically both heirs, Ioann and Peter, shared the throne with the oversight of their older sibling, Tsarevna Sofiia Alekseevna, child of Tsar Aleksei Mikhailovich's first marriage. Prince Ivan Andreevich Khovanskii, chief of the Moscow musketeers, fell afoul of the Miloslavskii faction in the summer of 1682. He had not led the Musketeer Chancery at the time of the May rebellion, but had taken charge immediately thereafter and waxed in power. Musketeers so controlled the city in the summer months that the royal entourage had remained in the safety of the Trinity St. Sergius Monastery after its annual August pilgrimage. A showdown

[10] Prozorovskii: AAE III: nos. 336–7, 342–3, 346–7; Korsakova, "Prozorovskii." Ivan Mikhailovich Shein: AAE III: nos. 338–9, 344–5. Timofei Izmailov: AAE III: nos. 340–1, 348–9. Others: Solov'ev, *Istoriia Rossii*, bk. v, vol. IX: 171–2. Boyar political struggle: Kollmann, *Kinship and Politics*, ch. 5.

between the Miloslavskie and the Khovanskie came on September 17, when Khovanskii and his son Andrei were charged with treason. In his account the pro-Miloslavskii Sil'vestr Medvedev cited Khovanskii's impudence and sympathy for the church schism, even alleging that he had tried to lure Sofiia into personal danger, while the official verdict charged corruption, insubordination and treason. But historians agree that the charges were trumped up and the execution was an expedient move by a faction consolidating power.[11]

The Khovanskie were condemned, apparently, in closed-door session among the boyars, with legal procedure evoked after the fact. Regent Sofiia summoned Khovanskii and his son to Trinity St. Sergius Monastery on the excuse of an impending diplomatic reception. Along the way, her troops intercepted them. One source says that Khovanskii brought seventy men with him, while the Danish diplomat von Gorn reported 150 and added that Khovanskii was confronted by 4,000 of Sofiia's men. Father and son were bound, placed on horseback and brought to the Trinity Monastery. Although Military Service Chancery records assert that Khovanskii's death sentence was the result of "proper investigation and clear evidence and a completed case" and include a traditional phrase that the "tsars had ordered and the boyars agreed" (here adding Regent Sofiia as well), there is no evidence of investigation and court procedure, "as there should have been," the pro-Naryshkin Andrei Matveev wrote a generation later. An anonymous denunciation of September 2 alleging that the Khovanskie had plotted against the tsars was cited as proof. The Khovanskie were given no opportunity for oral interrogation, interrogation under torture, or face-to-face confrontation with their accusers, even though Prince Ivan specifically requested the latter as the death penalty was being read.[12]

The physical location of the proceedings underscored their irregularity. As the two men were led to the monastery on horseback, the officer in charge, Prince Mikhail Ivanovich Lykov, was instructed to stop in front of the monastery. All the boyars walked out and sat on benches before the

[11] Pro-Miloslavskii Medvedev: "Sozertsanie kratkoe," 76–91. Pro-Naryshkin Zheliabuzhskii depicts the musketeers wavering in support of Khovanskii ("Zapiski," 2–7), while Neuville presents him as scheming for power (*Curious and New Account*, 18–20). Verdict: *Vosstanie v Moskve 1682 g.*, nos. 86 and 63. Hughes, *Sophia*, 82–5; Buganov, *Moskovskie vosstaniia*, 272–9; Pogodin, *Semnadtsat' pervykh let*, Appendices, 136–48. Thorough analysis: Lavrov, *Regentstvo*, 24–47.

[12] Quantities of troops: PSRL XXXI: 178 (Mazurin chronicle); Bogdanov, "Glazami," 87 (von Gorn). Matveev, "Zapiski," 45. Denunciation: *Vosstanie v Moskve 1682 g.*, no. 67. Khovanskii requests confrontation: Matveev, "Zapiski," 45–6.

gates to hear the reading of the already-decided verdict. The Khovanskie were not allowed to enter the monastery, to see a judge or to meet with the co-tsars or Regent Sofiia. State secretary Fedor Shaklovityi immediately read the verdict: beheading for treason. This was promptly done, off to the side "by the great Moscow road." Sil′vestr Medvedev, eager to present the event as legal and proper, notes that the reading of the sentence and the execution were witnessed by many boyars and an assembled crowd.[13] But the entire affair was kept as low-key as the Miloslavskie could manage, most likely not to risk riling up the Khovanskie's supporters.

The execution of Fedor Shaklovityi in 1689 was similar in form and in purpose. Political tables had turned, and now the Naryshkiny were forcing Sofiia and the Miloslavskii faction out of power. In the summer of 1689 Peter was in a strong position. He had amassed independent military power, building upon his boyhood "play" regiments; he had been married in January 1689, which demonstrated his having achieved maturity and called the question about succession. At the same time, political support for Sofiia and Prince V. V. Golitsyn was waning after a disastrous Crimean campaign and as Sofiia's plans for her own coronation were creating a sense of urgency. In the late summer of 1689, Sofiia tried to mobilize Moscow musketeers against Peter and he retreated to the Trinity St. Sergius Monastery. From that bastion he called the hand of Moscow's elite. Over several tense weeks Sofiia's support eroded as, one by one, Moscow's boyars made the trek out to the monastery to join Peter's side. Ultimately the musketeers abandoned Sofiia and mass violence was averted.[14]

By ousting Sofiia, Peter did not reject the legitimacy of his elder stepbrother and co-tsar Ioann, a Miloslavskii. But he crushed Sofiia's support. Prince V. V. Golitsyn was arrested and sent with his family into exile, charged with the failure of the Crimean campaign and with bypassing the tsars and ruling with Sofiia. But Golitsyn was not charged with treason, saved apparently by the intervention of his cousin and Peter's confidant, Prince Boris Golitsyn. Other close supporters of Golitsyn were also exiled, and Peter confined his half-sister to a convent for the rest of her life.[15]

[13] Outside gates: Matveev, "Zapiski," 45; *Vosstanie v Moskve 1682 g.*, no. 63, p. 86 and no. 207, p. 280. Execution: *Vosstanie v Moskve 1682 g.*, no. 207, p. 280; no. 204, p. 265 and no. 63, p. 86; Matveev, "Zapiski," 46; PSRL XXXI: 178 (Mazurin). Matveev reports that, lacking an executioner at the monastery, they recruited a musketeer: "Zapiski," 45. Medvedev, "Sozertsanie kratkoe," 111.

[14] Hughes, *Sophia*, ch. 9; Bushkovitch, *Peter the Great*, 149–69.

[15] Boris Golitsyn's intervention: Bushkovitch, *Peter the Great*, 166–8; Hughes, *Sophia*, 238. Golitsyn's exile: PSZ III: nos. 1348, p. 33 (Sept. 9, 1689) and 1395, pp. 89–91 (March 7, 1691). Golitsyn's

These sentences, lacking any extant court record, resemble the "disgrace" (*opala*) visited upon boyars in the sixteenth century; they came from the collective boyar elite and in the name of the sovereign.

The blame for the abortive "uprising" went to Sofiia's commander of the musketeers, Fedor Shaklovityi. Charged with plotting to kill Peter and his mother to ensure Sofiia's coronation, he is called by Paul Bushkovitch the "scapegoat for Sofia and Golitsyn." Shaklovityi and two compatriots were interrogated and tortured at the Trinity Monastery on September 7 and on September 11 all three were beheaded near the monastery. Numerous others implicated with him were punished – Sil′vestr Medvedev was sentenced to death a month later for his role in advising Shaklovityi and planning Sofiia's coronation, but his execution was delayed until February 1691 while he was subjected to a church trial for heresy and sorcery. Along with Shaklovityi, four musketeers were sentenced to death and then pardoned on the block, the sentence reduced to knouting and eternal Siberian exile (for three, their tongues were also ordered cut out). About forty other musketeers or monastic servitors associated with Medvedev were exiled with knouting or bastinadoes.[16]

The Shaklovityi affair resulted in four weighty published volumes of court transcripts, but they record only interrogations and verdicts, not the execution. An eyewitness account fills in the picture. Andrei Matveev informs us that Shaklovityi was executed near the monastery on the square that faces the great Moscow road. He reported that Shaklovityi said not a word before death as the state secretary who read the verdict and a boyar looked on. Beyond them a crowd had gathered and another condemned man, as noted above, spoke tearfully.[17]

Perhaps because of the eminence of the victims in 1634, 1682 and 1689, in these cases the authorities did not stage theatrical public executions. All these men were killed almost immediately upon verdict. For the Khovanskie, proper procedure was feigned, while the Shein and Shaklovityi affairs were carried out with speedy interrogation and verdict. Moscow's rulers, perhaps unsure of public response and eager to present a facade of stability, saw no advantage in dramatizing these executions.

confiscated property: *Rozysknye dela*, III and IV. Sofiia in captivity depicted by Ilya Repin (1879): State Tretiakov Gallery, Moscow.

16 Lavrov, *Regentsvo*, 168–82. Neuville describes torture by knouting and water: *Curious and New Account*, 43–4. *Rozysknye dela*, I: cols. 266–70, 715–22, 931–8, 983–4, 1011–12, 1277–80. PSZ III: nos. 1349, 1352 and 1359 (1389).

17 Matveev, "Zapiski," 56. Neither Neuville, P. N. Krekshin nor I. A. Zheliabuzhskii provide details: Neuville, *Curious and New Account*, 45; Krekshin, "Zapiski," 87; Zheliabuzhskii, "Zapiski," 10.

Such was the moral economy of court politics, in which conflict was concealed behind a facade of stability.[18] When it came to the punishment of spiritual threats to state and society from heretics, rebels and witches, however, publicity was a conscious strategy.

PUNISHING WITCHCRAFT

Witchcraft – practicing it or possessing magical books, herbs or potions – was prosecuted and punished as a spiritual assault on the godly foundations of society itself. Witchcraft had always been considered a grave crime in the East Slavic world. Church law codes from the times of Kiev Rus′ had condemned witchcraft and sorcery, prescribing punishments from fines to burning. In 1227 in Novgorod four male witches were burned to death for practicing sorcery, while in Pskov in 1411 twelve female witches were executed by burning.[19]

In Muscovy jurisdiction on witchcraft was shared by church and state. In 1551, the Stoglav Church Council associated witchcraft with heresy, declaring that "sorcerers, fortune-tellers, astrologers" and others with malevolent spiritual power should be turned over to secular authorities for execution; the Ulozhenie's article punishing with death evil intentions against the ruler's health has been taken to refer to witchcraft. Grigorii Kotoshikhin reported that the Felony Chancery dealt with sorcery, forbidden books and black magic, punishing such crimes with burning for men and beheading for women. Russia's confessionalization project of the mid seventeenth century included decrees against witchcraft, some of which lumped witches in with "thieves, robbers and brigands," while others associated witchcraft with immorality and heresy. Punishments were harsh: in a decree of 1653, witches and their materials for soothsaying or hexing were to be burned and their homes razed; a decree of 1689 also prescribed burning and beheading for witchcraft.[20]

18 Keenan, "Muscovite Political Folkways"; Kollmann, *Kinship and Politics*, ch. 5.

19 Russell Zguta ("Witchcraft Trials," 1190) surveys Kievan-era law on witchcraft, such as the Byzantine *Nomokanon* (which prescribes death by sword) and Charters of Vladimir (arts. 9 and 14) and Iaroslav (art. 40) (which impose fines: Kaiser [trans. and ed.], *Laws of Rus′*, 43, 48). Mikhail Benemanskii points out that these fines rejected Byzantine corporal punishment: *Zakon gradskii*, 145. Thus, Will Ryan considers early East Slavic law on witchcraft "relatively mild": *Bathhouse at Midnight*, 410. 1227: *Novgorodskaia pervaia letopis′*, 65; 1411: Nasonov (ed.), *Pskovskie letopisi*, II: 36 (6919).

20 1551: Emchenko, *Stoglav*, ch. 41, question 22, pp. 312–13; Stoglav ch. 2, art. 1: RZ III: 86. Tel′berg, *Ocherki*, 67. Kotoshikhin, *O Rossii*, 116. Novombergskii, *Koldovstvo*, 78–80 (1653). PSZ III: no. 1362 (1689). Laura Stokes analyzes the link between witchcraft prosecutions and confessionalization and social disciplining in fifteenth-century German towns: *Demons of Urban Reform*.

Charges of sorcery often emerged in the midst of criminal suits of other sorts. The ruling family was particularly sensitive to such threats; as Valerie Kivelson has analyzed, when things went wrong at the court, or when peasants were arrested for speaking ill of the sovereign, sorcery was immediately suspected. Even in the long sixteenth century, for which case law is not available, evidence of this sensitivity is widespread. Oaths of allegiance to rulers included a vow not to use sorcery against the ruler. Ivan III's celebrated falling-out with his wife Sofiia Palaiologa in 1497 focused on fear that she was plotting to poison him with malevolent potions; women suspected of providing her such poisons were drowned at night in the Moscow River.[21] Solomoniia Saburova, Vasilii III's rejected wife, was accused of consulting sorcerers to conceive, and Boris Godunov is said to have suspected his Romanov rivals of sorcery against him. Conversely, rumors spread that the First False Dmitrii had bewitched the state even posthumously, bringing frost and famine on the realm. In 1643 a man was sentenced to death by burning for hexing the tsar's bride, Evdokiia Lukianovna, and in 1676 the Miloslavskie contrived accusations of witchcraft against a key rival, A. S. Matveev; the same accusation surfaced in the heat of the 1682 succession crisis, when Matveev, Ivan Mikhailovich Naryshkin and European court physicians were charged with using magic to harm the heirs to the throne.[22]

In the seventeenth century some case law reveals the Kremlin's obsession with sorcery in its ranks. Chapter 6 reviewed a case of 1638 in which two court seamstresses denounced each other for trying to bewitch the tsaritsa. Accusations grew until about ten women were involved. They suffered numerous rounds of torture and interrogation; none was found guilty enough to merit execution; most were punished with exile. Russell Zguta also details other Kremlin witchcraft scares: in 1635 a Kremlin servant girl and her husband, along with an accused witch and her husband, were exiled to Kazan, while in the 1640s a man who had boasted in prison of intending to bewitch the tsaritsa was investigated as well.[23]

Even when the ruling family was not implicated, witchcraft trials were serious business. As Valerie Kivelson, Eve Levin and others have argued,

[21] Sorcery associated with criminal suits: Kivelson, "Patrolling the Boundaries," 322; Smilianskaia, *Volshebniki*, 188. Sorcery and treason: Kivelson, "Political Sorcery." Oaths: Zguta, "Witchcraft Trials," 1193–4; Ryan, *Bathhouse at Midnight*, 411–14. Ivan III and Sofiia: PSRL XII: 263 (7000).

[22] Saburova: AI I: no. 130; Kivelson, "Political Sorcery," 271. Godunov: Solov′ev, *Istoriia Rossii*, bk. IV, vol. VIII: 395. False Dmitrii: Petreius, *Reliatsiia Petra Petreia*, 97; *Pamiatniki literatury drevnei Rusi. Konets XVI–nachalo XVII vekov*, 328, 332 (Chronograph of 1617). Evdokiia: MDBP pt. 5, no. 18, pp. 275–6 (1643). Matveev 1676, 1682: Sedov, *Zakat*, 260–6; Löwe, "Der Strelitzen-Aufstand von 1682," 180–1.

[23] Novombergskii, *Koldovstvo*, no. 33 (1638). Zguta, "Witchcraft Trials," 1194.

the focus in Muscovite witchcraft trials was generally on healing gone awry, rather than on pacts with the Devil, a more common concern in Western Christendom. Perhaps because of that, the witch crazes that rampaged through sixteenth-century Europe were as a rule absent in Russia; individual cases were dealt with by the criminal law, as neighbors accused neighbors and kin accused kin of hexing them and causing death, illness, infertility and the like.[24]

When cases came to resolution, only a small minority of accused witches were executed. Valerie Kivelson, working with a collection of over 200 cases, estimates 10 percent, while Russell Zguta found a similar percentage in forty-seven cases; both were working with seventeenth-century trials. The remaining 90 percent of cases were disposed of in the same ways as other criminal cases – with varying punishments according to the severity of the offense.[25]

Witches in Muscovy were executed as in Europe – by burning, based on the biblical injunction (John 15: 16) "if a man not abide in me, he is cast forth as a branch that is withered; and men gather them and cast them into the fire and they are burned." Burning completely destroyed the malevolent spiritual power a witch represented.[26] Otherwise, such executions followed the same patterns as those for common felonies. In 1647, for example, the governor of Shatsk was ordered to execute a married couple found guilty of witchcraft. He was to provide them with a priest and order them to take communion in a worthy manner, although the order does not specify an amount of time for repentance. Then he was to drive them to the town square, announce to them and an assembled crowd their sacrilegious crimes and burn them in a cage "stuffed with straw." In 1676 the governor of Sokol′sk received a similar order to execute an artilleryman and his wife for poisoning people with magic roots: they were to have a priest provided and then were to be executed on a market day before a crowd, burned along with their evil roots and

[24] Kivelson disputes Ryan's argument that Muscovite witchcraft included a strong focus on satanism: Kivelson, "Male Witches," 609–11; Ryan, *Bathhouse at Midnight*, 38, 411–16 and "Witchcraft Hysteria." See Kivelson, "Desperate Magic," "Through the Prism," "Patrolling the Boundaries," "Political Sorcery" and "Male Witches."

[25] Kivelson finds that women were slightly over-represented among those executed, while the majority of accused witches were men: "Male Witches," 607–8, 617 and n. 5; Zguta, "Witchcraft Trials," 1196. She finds exile the most common penalty for convicted witches, while Zguta found in a total of ninety-nine accused witches in forty-seven cases, twenty-one were acquitted and released, ten were sentenced to burning, five were exiled, three died under torture, one escaped jail and one priest was handed over to the church.

[26] Biblical quote: Levack, *Witch-Hunt*, 90. Burning was used for heresy and occasionally for other crime, as for peasants who killed their masters: AMG 1: no. 259 (1629).

grasses. The governor received the order on October 29 and carried out the execution six days later on November 3.[27] Note that in both cases the condemned were allowed spiritual comfort; had their bodies not been reduced to ash, they could have had a Christian burial. Exclusion from the church was a rare and shameful sanction.

Decrees of the mid seventeenth century ordered that both the tools of black magic and the sorcerers who used them were to be burned. In 1628 in a case of a monastic deacon in Nizhnii Novgorod found with books of divination, the books were ordered burned and the deacon held in monastic confinement, without sacraments, for at least a year. Adam Olearius reported instances in which Russians accused two foreigners of witchcraft because they possessed a skeleton and a skull, not understanding that they used these items professionally, one being a doctor, the other an artist. Olearius reported that the men were reprieved but that "the skeleton was dragged out beyond the Moscow River and burned."[28]

Not all condemned and convicted witches were burned. In a unique case of witch hysteria in 1656 in the town of Lukh, four men accused of witchcraft were beheaded, while a convicted woman was buried in the earth. In other cases, the punishment took a bizarre form of bodily mutilation: in 1648, for example, a peasant was brought in by his landlord in Belev with incriminating evidence – a magic spell written on paper. The peasant testified that he had never used this evil spell, but he was found guilty of sorcery. He was sentenced to have the writing burned on to his back and to be knouted, "so that no one will write such evil spells." A case of 1694 also imposes this punishment.[29]

Such executions were as susceptible as others to the tsar's mercy. In 1647, for example, the death sentence on a man who had consulted a fortune-teller was reversed, replaced with a marketplace knouting; the fortune-teller herself, however, despite the fact that she was elderly and had suffered three horrific torture sessions, was executed. In 1689 *stol'nik* Andrei Il'ich Bezobrazov was implicated in the case against Fedor Shaklovityi, charged with recruiting healers from among his peasants to

[27] Novombergskii, *Koldovstvo*, no. 11, pp. 63–4, 73 (1647); no. 28 (1676). A witch was also convicted and burned in Temnikov in 1671: Popov (ed.), *Materialy dlia istorii*, 107–8. Other cases: Solov'ev, *Istoriia Rossii*, VII: 132–5; AAE IV: no. 31.

[28] Burn materials: Kivelson, "Through the Prism," 80. AAE III: no. 176, p. 259 (1628). Other examples: Novombergskii, *Koldovstvo*, nos. 16 and 17 (both 1653). Olearius, *Travels*, 132–3.

[29] 1656: Kivelson, "Through the Prism," 78 and Kivelson personal communication. RGADA f. 210, Prikaznyi stol, no. 567, fols. 193, 206 (1648). RGADA f. 210, Prikaznyi stol, no. 679, fols. 297–300 (1694).

bewitch Tsar Peter and his mother. The trial resulted in multiple sentences: on execution day, January 8, 1690, Bezobrazov was beheaded on Red Square, while the two healers found guilty of witchcraft were burned, along with their sack of herbs and potions, "at the Swamp" opposite the Kremlin across the river. Bezobrazov's wife was sentenced to be tonsured for not revealing the plot, and four of Bezobrazov's people were knouted and exiled to Siberia. One conspirator, Ivashko Shcherbachev, was dramatically pardoned on the execution block (sentencing him instead to a knouting and Siberian exile), while the exile sentence of three minor figures was also pardoned.[30]

Witchcraft was more harshly prosecuted in the eighteenth century as Peter I introduced a European satanic conception. The Military Articles of 1715, drawing on Swedish military law, put "black magic" and consorting with the Devil in the first chapter, to be punished with death by burning or by running the gauntlet. The church actively prosecuted witchcraft in the eighteenth century, but gradually the law began to treat witchcraft as fraud and superstition, rather than religious crime. By Catherine II's era, it was not tried as a criminal offence.[31] In the seventeenth century, by contrast, witchcraft merited a more public and brutal mode of execution than that for felony crime. So also for religious dissent.

SCHISM IN THE CHURCH

Like witchcraft, crime against the church, including heresy and religious dissent, was treated as state crime. From fifteenth-century law on, secular codes had considered "theft from a church" a capital crime.[32] Other crimes against religion were also included in secular codes: both the 1649 Ulozhenie and the 1715 Military Articles give pride of place (Chapter 1) to blasphemy, heresy and other insults to faith and church, and prescribe execution by burning for blasphemy and for converting

[30] RGADA f. 210, Prikaznyi stol, no. 564, fols. 154–234 (1647). PSZ III: no. 1362 (1689). *Rozysknye dela*, II; the entire volume is devoted to this case; verdict on cols. 291–316.

[31] Military Articles ch. 1, arts. 1–2: RZ IV: 328–9 (1715). Ryan (*Bathhouse at Midnight*, 416–17) traces these articles to the 1683 edition of the 1621–2 Swedish military code, which derived from the 1532 *Carolina*. The 1720 Naval Ordinance dropped the reference to satanism, but maintained the harsh punishment: *Morskoi Ustav*, bk. IV, ch. 1: PRP VIII: 485. Eighteenth-century witchcraft persecutions and changing attitudes: Ryan, *Bathhouse at Midnight*, 418–28; Freeze, "Institutionalizing Piety," 230; Smilianskaia, *Volshebniki*, pt. 1, 27–200; Lavrov, *Koldovstvo i religiia*, 347–93; Zguta, "Witchcraft Trials," 1200–1.

[32] Theft in church: 1497 Law Code, arts. 9, 10: RZ II: 55; 1550 Law Code, art. 61: RZ II: 108; 1616/17 Felony Handbook, art. 41: PRP V: 197; Ulozhenie ch. 21, art. 14: RZ III: 232; 1669 church criminal code: PSZ I, no. 442, art. 13; 1669 Criminal Articles, art. 12: PRP VII: 400.

Orthodox believers to Islam. Through the sixteenth century church courts worked with secular officials to punish heretics, although, as David Goldfrank has argued, monastic exile and other penances were preferred to execution.[33] In the seventeenth century the proliferation of religious dissent by Old Believers (schismatics) occasioned a heightening of procedure and punishment.

Prosecution of schismatics charted a different course than that for accusations of witchcraft. While accused witches were treated harshly from the outset, officials were always hopeful of bringing dissenters to see the error of their ways. As rejection of Nikonian reforms proliferated in the 1650s and 1660s, the church's initial response was to contain the prosecutions in its own courts, using oral interrogation and avoiding torture.[34] The Church Council of 1666 provides a good example in its treatment of dissidents as wayward fellow brethren, not as criminals. In 1666 the Council interviewed major dissidents – Bishop Alexander of Viatka, Ivan Neronov, Avvakum and his circle, Nikita Dobrynin and many others – with oral interrogation that often turned into spirited debate. With a few exceptions, notably Avvakum and his close followers, many accused recanted and embraced the faith; their punishment was mild, at worst being sent to a monastery for spiritual oversight. Those who persisted were anathematized and punished. But the Council's summary documents at its second year of meeting (1667) drastically changed the legal landscape. The Council not only anathematized schismatics, but declared them liable to corporal punishment and trial by secular courts. Such harshness convinced Old Believers in their expectation of impending apocalypse and resulted in their more radical opposition; the 1667 Council constituted an "irrevocable break" in the old vision of Russian Orthodoxy as an integral community.[35]

After 1667 the state was increasingly drawn into prosecution of religious dissent. While Robert Crummey has characterized prosecution of Old Believers under Aleksei Mikhailovich (ruled 1645–76) as "haphazard and hesitant," it intensified in the late years of the reign.

[33] Ulozhenie ch. 1 and ch. 22, art. 24: RZ III: 85–6, 250; 1715 Military Articles ch. 1, arts. 1–2: RZ IV: 328–9. Goldfrank, "Theocratic Imperatives."

[34] Church court investigation without torture: Subbotin (ed.), *Materialy*, I: 192–8, 203–8, 361–5, 427–31, 458–63; II: 26–34; III: 106–17.

[35] Council proceedings: Subbotin (ed.), *Materialy*, II. PSZ I: no. 412 (1667). Radicalized Old Belief: Lupinin, *Religious Revolt*, 177–9. Irrevocable break: ibid., 169; similar comments in Crummey, *Old Believers*, 15 and Michels, *At War*, 66, 112–14. Zen'kovskii, *Russkoe staroobriadchestvo*, I: 217–31.

A characteristic interchange occurred in 1672, when Nizhnii Novgorod Metropolitan Filaret requested that secular authorities participate in the hunt for Old Believers, since he had insufficient police forces; he specified that the arrested should be tried by secular courts, as the 1667 Council decree had specified. Government forces became more involved after the 1666–7 Councils in part because the focus of prosecution shifted to schismatic communities in the borderlands, where criminal elements often intermingled. Georg Michels has shown how an Old Believers' occupation of the Paleoostrov Monastery in the 1680s and their self-immolation were led by criminal bands for whom religious dissent was merely a convenient rallying point.[36] Similarly, the siege of the Solovetskii Monastery that began in 1666 was initially fueled by the monastery's rejection of Nikonian books, reforms and central control, but by the time the siege was broken in January 1676, the stand-off had devolved from the state's point of view into armed treason. Virtually all of the more than 200 rebels were summarily executed after interrogations in which the investigating commander was explicitly instructed to use torture.[37] State forces were also drawn into more and more frantic identification and dispersal of Old Believer communities in the 1670s and 1680s as dissenters resorted to the horrific practice of self-immolation. Its apex was in these decades; even as self-immolation gradually lost support within the community, it continued sporadically thereafter.

Church and state responded to the expanding schism with condemnations such as the "*Uvet Dukhovnyi*" of 1682 but maintained a mixed approach. It prescribed corporal, not capital, punishment for those who taught anti-Orthodox ideas, sending the guilty for repentance to a monastery or imprisoning them, depending upon the degree of their remorse. It also prescribed exile for those who harbored schismatics. One foreign traveler in March 1684 gives such an approach a particular spin: J. G. Sparwenfeld wrote that "many hundreds have been burned alive and, when this did not help, decapitated, for the Russians are more afraid of seeing blood . . . As it has become apparent that such methods do not help, they do not persist with them anymore, but instead send them to monasteries on water and bread."[38]

[36] Crummey, *Old Believers*, 39. Barsov, "Sudnye protsessy," no. 3 (1672). Michels, "Violent Old Belief."
[37] Subbotin (ed.), *Materialy*, III: 353–8, esp. 358. Michels, "Solovki Uprising"; Crummey, *Old Believers*, 16–21.
[38] Self-immolations through the eighteenth century: Sapozhnikov, "Samosozhzhenie"; Lupinin, *Religious Revolt*, ch. 10; Crummey, *Old Believers*, ch. 3. *Uvet Dukhovnyi*: Lupinin, *Religious Revolt*, 183; *Staroobriadchestvo. Litsa, sobytiia*, 285.

As self-immolation terrified onlookers, a decree of 1684 addressed it and the schism with draconian harshness. Capital punishment was prescribed for those "who convince others to burn themselves" and for "anyone who wants to re-baptize children, even if they otherwise observe Orthodoxy."[39] It went into great detail regarding the prosecution of committed Old Believers, defined in the decree as "a heretic or schismatic who speaks against the church, does not go to church, does not let the clergy into his home, and does not go to confession, does not take communion." Such a person "creates among Christians seduction and uprising." These people were to be questioned with torture about where they learned their ideas; those they informed on were to be questioned in face-to-face confrontation until the full circle of schismatics was identified. The goal here, however, was still to bring the heretic back into the fold, if possible. Those who repented were to be examined by the archbishop and set free on surety bond if their repentance were true. Punishments followed a range: those who requested re-baptism were to be corporally punished and sent to their local hierarchs for instruction. Those who stood firm for the Old Belief three times under torture, refused to recant, or whose repentance was found to be false, were to be executed by burning.

Milder punishments were decreed for those who might have been misled by heretical teachings: "if some simple-minded people have been brought into mild disbelief," they were to be punished according to their degree of guilt, and also freed on surety bond. Similarly, those who opposed the new Nikonian books and rituals "lacking sound mind or of minor years" were to be corporally punished, given on surety bond and watched over by their father confessors and communities so that they maintained a pious life thereafter. The law decreed corporal punishment for those who harbored schismatics, harsher for those who did it knowingly than those who did not know. The 1684 decree ended with an unusual and unprecedented clause: the property of anyone exiled as an Old Believer was to be sold at a premium to reimburse the state for the "not insignificant cost" of "chasing them down." Thus even with draconian punishments for leaders of the opposition, church and

39 The 1682 setting: Pascal, *Avvakum et les débuts*, 540–4; Kartashev, *Ocherki*, 234–7; Zen′kovskii, *Russkoe staroobriadchestvo*, 1: 292–301; Sparwenfeld, *Sparwenfeld's Diary*, 85. 1682 decree: Barsov, "Sudnye protsessy," 20. 1684 decree: PSZ II: no. 1102 (n.d.; variously dated 1684, 1685); printed in Barsov, "Sudnye protsessy," no. 6 (dated April 7, 1685). Dated 1685 and called the "document of 12 points": *Staroobriadchestvo. Litsa, sobytiia*, 85.

state held out hope of recapturing the errant soul and thereby applied a range of prosecution and punishments.

Several cases preceding the Councils of 1666–7 show the church striving to rehabilitate sinners, but punishing where necessary. In the 1650s and 1660s several dissenting clerics were interviewed and recanted, or were punished lightly in hopes of future repentance, such as a priest who was declared "insane" for questioning the new books. Some early dissenters showed the wisdom of this policy. Ivan Neronov, for example, had first been judged by a 1656 church council as an apostate and sent to a monastery to repent; he fled the monastery and continued preaching the new faith. In 1666 he was brought before the Council, where he repented and was pardoned; he died in 1670 in good graces. Prosecutions of less highly placed leaders of the schism often turned harsher. The investigation of an accused schismatic, Sila Bogdanov, in Rostov in 1657 tracked a progression from oral interrogation in the metropolitan's court to torture in secular courts in Moscow. Neither Bogdanov nor two other accused men recanted; Sila Bogdanov called the tsar and Patriarch Nikon "Antichrists." But none was sentenced to death. Rather, they were all exiled for life to a monastery.[40]

A similar policy to use only as much coercive force as necessary is evident in the prosecution of followers of the ascetic monk Kapiton in the spring of 1666. The musketeer unit that tracked them down in the forest by Pereiaslavl' Zalesskii destroyed their settlement, but not before a small group, calling the tsar "Antichrist," chose self-immolation. Investigating, the governor of Vologda interrogated the survivors and reported that he did not put in chains those who had recanted, while he sent those who refused to recant in chains to local monasteries to attend church, work and return to the faith. Peasant families who had joined the schismatic community in the forest were sentenced to exile to Kazan to serve as musketeers. Only the accused leaders, on the orders of the Privy Chancery, were tortured (by knout and fire). Monk Vavilo was unrepentant and was sentenced to death, accused not only of irreverence to the church and its hierarchs but also of leading Christians astray: "From

[40] 1650s–60s: Michels, *At War*, 73 and ch. 2 *passim*. Neronov: Subbotin (ed.), *Materialy*, I: 124–33, esp. 128–31, 220–43; Michels on Neronov: *At War*, 53–63. Sila Bogdanov: Rumiantseva, *Narodnoe antitserkovnoe dvizhenie*, appendix nos. 1–2; Rumiantseva (ed.), *Dokumenty Razriadnogo*, II: 29–58; Michels, *At War*, 33–8.

your senseless (*neistovye*) preaching in your forest encampments many people died without confession and communion." Monk Leonid recanted, blaming his schismatic beliefs on his "simplicity," but he too was ordered executed by fire for proselytizing. Others less identified with leadership were interrogated, tortured and sent to monasteries to be rehabilitated.[41]

Gradually the church abandoned hope of redeeming the most stubborn. Several dissenters who recanted at the 1666 Church Council had by the 1680s returned to dissent. Nikita Dobrynin "Pustosviat," for example, had been prosecuted repeatedly for his opposition to Nikon's reforms and had been defrocked in 1660. When brought before the Council in 1666, he had repented, but he resurfaced in the Old Belief in July 1682, engaging in a public disputation with the patriarch and Regent Sofiia. Calling his beliefs "shameful, putrid, blasphemous" and "impossible to understand," Sofiia pronounced him a "heretic" and sentenced him to death. He was promptly executed.[42] Unlike Dobrynin, Avvakum never recanted; already by 1653 Avvakum had been exiled to Siberia. He had returned to Moscow in 1664 but refused to recant and was soon exiled again. Even from exile he persisted in his opposition and in May 1666 he refused to repent at the 1666 Church Council. When brought back to the 1667 session, Avvakum, Nikifor, Lazar and Epifanii were tried by the Tsar's Privy Council; one source reports that during this trial, Avvakum suffered seventy knout blows of torture. In August all four were sentenced to exile to Pustoozero, with the tongues of Lazar and Epifanii being severed to prevent them from preaching (Avvakum was spared this by the tsar's mercy). After continued stubborn opposition in exile, Avvakum and his fellow Pustoozersk Old Believers were sentenced to execution by fire in 1681.[43]

Social class protected dissenters only so much. An eminent boyar's wife Feodosiia Morozova, a stubborn opponent of the reforms, was prosecuted repeatedly through the 1660s and 1670s and refused to recant. Because of her personal connections with Tsar Aleksei Mikhailovich, she was not executed but suffered exile and death in prison. Other elite female

[41] Vavilo and Leonid: *Narodnoe antitserkovnoe dvizhenie*, 67–72, 114, 162–202; Rumiantseva, *Narodnoe antitserkovnoe dvizhenie*, appendix nos. 3–4.

[42] Dobrynin: Subbotin (ed.), *Materialy*, I: 393–6; Michels, *At War*, 93–8; *Polnyi pravoslavnyi bogoslovskii*, II: cols. 1642–3. Disputation depicted by Vasilii Perov (1880–1): State Tretiakov Gallery, Moscow.

[43] 1667 trial: Subbotin (ed.), *Materialy*, II: 21–34. Torture: Esipov (ed.), *Raskol'nichie dela*, I: 116; Barskov, *Pamiatniki*, no. 24, no. 1.

supporters of the Old Belief, including Morozova's sister Evdokiia and Elena Khrushcheva, also died in captivity after refusing to recant.[44]

In the spirit of decrees of 1667 and 1684, harsh punishment was visited on the most recalcitrant through the rest of the century. In 1671, for example, an undersecretary accused of writing heretical books was tortured and sentenced to beheading and in 1683 elder Varlaam was investigated by state courts as he had been in 1677. The Novgorod governor sent him to Moscow, where he was repeatedly questioned, apparently without torture, but refused to recant. Varlaam was sentenced to be executed in his home town of Klin, unless he should recant at the last minute. He did not and was burned on October 24, 1683.[45]

Torture was used in Novgorod in 1682–3 in a case initiated by the metropolitan regarding the production of Old Believer books; oral interrogation of several people drew attention to Iakov Kalashkinov. The church court interrogated him and, after consulting with Moscow, sent him to the secular court of the Novgorod Chancery in Moscow. There he unrepentantly admitted to schismatic beliefs; records of his interrogation show no indication of torture. He was sentenced by the tsars, Regent Sofiia and the boyar council to death by burning, but their verdict specified that Iakov was to be tortured at the place of execution to find out about other schismatics. Returned to his home town of Dmitrov, he underwent the ordered torture, with knouting and weights with shakes of the body (*vstriaski*) before being executed by burning. He revealed no new information. Similarly in Pskov in 1683 the church court began with oral interrogation of two Pskov townsmen for dissent. It then transferred the men to the governor for torture. The two townsmen were subject not only to 100 blows but also to multiple applications of fire and weights. Upon the governor's report to Moscow, one of the two was ordered executed and the other, who had recanted, was sent to a monastery for repentance and confinement. The full harshness of the 1684 legislation is witnessed in a case of late 1684 of a woman who had been exiled to the Kola Peninsula for schismatic belief. Accused of refusing to attend Orthodox services, blaspheming, insulting priests and religious objects, she was subjected to torture by twenty-five blows with three episodes of weights and

[44] Michels, "Muscovite Elite Women." Morozova's husband's brother Boris was Tsar Aleksei Mikhailovich's tutor; his fate, see Chapter 17. Morozova immortalized by Vasilii Surikov (1887): State Tretiakov Gallery, Moscow.

[45] Barskov, *Pamiatniki*, no. 23 (1671). Rumiantseva, *Narodnoe antitserkovnoe dvizhenie*, appendix nos. 13–20 (1683).

shaking, but she did not recant. She was sentenced to execution by fire before many people "to deter them."[46]

In a case that started out as a criminal investigation of treason, the Don Cossack Kuzma Kozoi was interrogated with torture by Prince V. V. Golitsyn and several other prominent boyars on September 19, 1687; the testimony quickly turned to Kozoi's adherence to the Old Belief. Under torture by beating, weights, shaking and fire, he informed on others who shared his beliefs and those who had taught him. On September 25, on the verge of death from torture, he recanted his beliefs and requested confession on his deathbed. But interrogation continued on September 30, this time with no torture mentioned. The same investigation also yielded prosecution of others accused of dissent, including a past ataman of the Don Cossacks and five others. They were interrogated with torture and executed in Moscow in May.[47]

Prosecution of religious dissent shows that church and state would have liked to preserve souls where possible. In 1689 Moscow ordered the governor of Pskov not to use torture on a defendant "if he turns out to have truly left the schism."[48] Repentance, forgiveness and rehabilitation were the church's desired outcomes. But for stubborn heretics, horrific capital punishment was ordered, and it was rendered with conscious symbolism.

RITUALS OF EXECUTION FOR RELIGIOUS CRIME

Executions for crime that had an element of evil spiritual power (witchcraft, religious dissent) mobilized more dramatic ritual than for felony crime. Sentences to execute a schismatic, as expected, included the usual instruction to assemble people so that others would be deterred from the crime. In 1671 the undersecretary found guilty of writing heretical books was sentenced to be executed by beheading "on a market day before many people, having announced to him his guilt." The decree sentencing Nikita Pustosviat in July 1682 similarly mandated that his death be an example to deter others; he was beheaded in Red Square. Conversely, a decree mandating a public execution of schismatics specified that their heretical books should be burned "in secret." Some cases describe the witch or

[46] Rumiantseva, *Narodnoe antitserkovnoe dvizhenie*, appendix nos. 6–11 (1682–3). Barsov, "Sudnye protsessy," no. 4 (1683). Another case that used torture and culminated in a capital sentence: Barsov, "Sudnye protsessy," no. 5 (1683). Rumiantseva (ed.), *Dokumenty Razriadnogo*, v: nos. 58–66 (1684).

[47] Kuzma: Druzhinin, *Raskol*, 276–83 and chs. 5–6 *passim* (1687). Ataman: Pushkarev, "Donskoe kazachestvo," 25; Druzhinin, *Raskol*, 284–312 and chs. 4–5 *passim*.

[48] Barsov, "Sudnye protsessy," no. 8, p. 34 (1689).

dissenter being brought to the place of execution in a cart, perhaps for greater exposure. Executions are mentioned in Red Square and across the river from the Kremlin in "the Swamp."[49]

Despite laws providing time for repentance, it is rarely encountered in spiritual crimes. A case of 1672 provided brief respite of this sort. The governor of Murom was instructed to burn a Polish elder who was accused of spreading anti-Orthodox teachings; he was told that if the man recanted upon being sentenced and sought a father confessor, the governor was to send the priest and then delay the execution for three days. The elder did recant and the governor provided him the three days before sending him to the fire. Brutality was occasionally ratcheted up, as in the case of a male witch who was ordered quartered before being thrown into the fire in 1643; he was accused of bewitching the tsar's bride. As noted above, in 1682–3 dissenter Iakov Kalashkinov was ordered to be tortured at execution to obtain information on others.[50]

Burning was the punishment that most witches and dissenters suffered, even though drowning was also historically associated with spiritual crime, and beheading was also used. In addition to the cases of an undersecretary in 1671 and Nikita Dobrynin in 1682, cited above, the German traveler Georg-Adam Schleussing wrote in 1684 that Old Believers were beheaded daily and that he had witnessed such an execution of a schismatic who refused Sofiia Alekseevna's offer to spare him if he repented.[51] But burning was most common, done not at the stake, but with the condemned person in a cage, the cage stuffed and surrounded with hay. Johann Frisch in 1677 described it: "according to Muscovite custom, made of wood, hay and other flammable materials." The condemned apparently climbed into the cage through an opening at the top, or "leaped," as noted in beginning the chapter. Traveler Jacob Reutenfels in 1680 observed that those condemned for heresy "are locked into small wooden huts and are burned while they are alive and looking out of the

[49] Barskov, *Pamiatniki*, no. 23 (1671). Subbotin (ed.), *Materialy*, I: 393–6 (1682). Execution of a woman on the Kola Peninsula also cites deterrence: Rumiantseva (ed.), *Dokumenty Razriadnogo*, V: no. 65 (1684). Burn books secretly: Barsov, "Sudnye protsessy," no. 4. Witch in cart: Novombergskii, *Koldovstvo*, no. 11, p. 73 (1647). Red Square or "Swamp": MDBP pt. 5, no. 18, p. 276 (1643). Swamp *(boloto)*: there is still a "Bolotnaia Square" on the island across from the Kremlin. Neuville cites the humiliation of being taken away "in a common cart" when Fedor Shaklovityi was arrested in 1689: *Curious and New Account*, 43.

[50] Rumiantseva (ed.), *Dokumenty Razriadnogo*, IV: 73–86 (1672), quote on 77. MDBP pt. 5, no. 18, p. 276 (1643). Kalashkinov: Rumiantseva, *Narodnoe antitserkovnoe dvizhenie*, appendix nos. 7–11.

[51] In 1375 heretics were "hurled to their deaths from the bridge connecting the two sides of Novgorod": Goldfrank, "Burn, Baby, Burn," 18. Schleussing: Lapteva (ed. and trans.), "Rasskaz ochevidtsa," 117–18.

structure." J. G. Sparwenfeld, traveling in Russia in 1685, claimed to have observed at least two such executions.[52] Here the symbolism was stark: burning destroyed the evil spirits embodied in the condemned.

Whether a practice observed in Europe, namely, that those condemned to die by burning were mercifully killed before the fire consumed them, occurred in Muscovy as well cannot be established. Lyndal Roper writes that "in late seventeenth-century Augsburg, most witches were given the 'merciful' and honourable punishment of execution by the sword, which at least spared them the executioner's touch. But their bodies were still burnt in public for all to see at the place of execution." Brian Levack and others find the practice of killing a condemned witch (by garroting or sword) before burning from the Spanish and Italian territories, to France, Scotland, the Germanies and Sweden.[53] In Muscovy no references to this occur in the few descriptions of such executions.

As in Europe, Muscovite executions for spiritual crime went to great lengths to eradicate every trace of the heretic, to avoid leaving relics for future veneration and to destroy evil spirits. In October 1683, for example, the governor of Klin reported that he had burned a schismatic and had, as ordered, "scattered the ashes and stamped them into the ground."[54] While the bodies of those executed for secular treason were often defiled and/or left on display for humiliation, witches and heretics were to be reduced to dust and scattered to the winds.

Old Believers embraced this logic in their practice of self-immolation. When making the eschatological choice of death over capture by the forces of "Antichrist," they turned the state's burning cage into their own blessed, fiery coffins. For self-immolation they locked themselves in small wooden buildings (churches, homes, barns, bathhouses) that observers called by the same word used for the cage that confined condemned heretics in the fire (variously called *srub* and *strub*). In preparation for self-immolation communities packed these chapels with

[52] Early reference to a cage (*kletka*) 1493: Shmidt (ed.), "Prodolzhenie," 266 (7001). Leaping: Frisch: Filatov, *Arzamas v XVII veke*, 80. Filling the cage with straw: Novombergskii, *Koldovstvo*, no. 11, p. 64 (1648). Other foreigners remark on this: Tikhonravov, *Sochineniia*, II: 373. Some verdicts use interchangeably with "in a wooden cage" (*v srube*) the phrase "in a pile of wood" (*v kostre*): Barsov, "Sudnye protsessy," no. 4, p. 14 (1683), no. 5, p. 21 (1683); Rumiantseva, *Narodnoe antitserkovnoe dvizhenie*, appendix nos. 18–20; SRIa VII: 368. Zagoskin on burning as judicial sanction: *Ocherk*, 56–7. Reitenfels, *Skazaniia*, 118; Sparwenfeld, *Sparwenfeld's Diary*, 219.

[53] Roper, *Witch Craze*, 65; Levack, *Witch-Hunt*, 90–3; Harvey, "Burning Women at the Stake"; Campbell, "Sentence of Death," 44–5.

[54] Klin: Rumiantseva, *Narodnoe antitserkovnoe dvizhenie*, appendix nos. 18–19 (1683). Same phrase: Barsov, "Sudnye protsessy," nos. 4 (1683) and 6 (1685).

hay and tar, just as executioners filled their cages. In several instances Old Believer communities prepared structures for self-immolation by placing "straw and hay at appropriate points" or even "gunpowder, tar and dry hay."[55]

In early modern Europe in expectation of a "good death," the behavior and "last words" of the condemned on the gallows or at the stake were widely reported.[56] This might have been a practice in Russia, but until now only a few references to it can be found. In 1606 the "False Tsarevich Peter," for example, spoke eloquently to the crowd until he was silenced by his executioner; somewhat differently, the 1669 Criminal Articles urged judges to question the condemned on the gallows for more information.[57] For Old Believers, cases often include instructions to governors to note whether the heretic spoke to the crowd and, if so, to record what he or she said. This might reflect the state's hope of gathering accusations against others, the church's hope of capturing a recantation or a more general expectation that people being executed should speak. In some executions of schismatics, speaking is mentioned. Old Believer accounts assert that on April 1, 1682, when Avvakum and others were being burned, Avvakum made a two-fingered sign of the cross and began to preach; he also comforted a fellow sufferer as people watching took off their hats. This mythic version may parallel communities' expectations for such moments.[58]

When the elder Varlaam was executed in Klin in 1683, as noted above, the governor was explicitly ordered to give him a final chance to repent at the point of death. The Moscow undersecretary sent to Klin to observe the proceedings added details: as the accused was being led to the execution spot, he was apparently presented with an icon, but he did not pray to it; he did not bid goodbye to the gathered people but turned and prayed in the direction of the east. The scribe reported that he said nothing at his death. The execution of the mystical preacher Quirin Kuhlmann, a devotee of Jacob Boehme, in May 1689 provides a little

[55] *Srub/strub*: SRIa XXVII: 158; *Narodnoe antitserkovnoe dvizhenie*, 164. *Srub* refers both to the first four logs laid down to form the foundation of a squared chamber of a log structure, and to the walled room or chamber built upon that foundation. Structures prepared: Crummey, *Old Believers*, 47, 51, 166, 174; Sapozhnikov, "Samosozhzhenie," 10, 18–20, 27–9, 31, 34 (18, 36). Self-immolation in barn and bathhouse: Filatov, *Arzamas*, 73–5 (1675).

[56] In England: Royer, "Dead Men Talking."

[57] Smirnov, "Kogda byl kaznen?" 108–9; VBDM 182–3, 222–6 (1606). 1669 Criminal Articles, arts. 20, 86, 123: PRP VII: 403, 425, 433.

[58] Avvakum: Esipov, *Raskol'nichie dela*, I: 117. Old Believer tradition places Avvakum's execution on Good Friday, but documents do not confirm this: Pascal, *Avvakum et les débuts*, 544–6.

more detail. After lengthy interrogations involving torture by knout and fire, he and a compatriot Kondratii Norderman were found guilty of heresy. A sympathetic eyewitness reports that the men in prison were told that they were to be freed the following morning, but instead were brought to a large square where had been prepared a small hut filled with straw and barrels of tar. The men were led to the site with no accompanying priest; both began to pray and Kuhlmann's last words were addressed directly to God. The men spoke no more from the hut once the fire began. Another report adds that Kuhlmann's "blasphemous books and letters" were burned with him.[59]

Execution scenes of witches and dissenters provide us tiny glimpses into the ritual moment of public death. The convicted person was subjected to a horrific death and sometimes to additional tortures. He or she was allowed, perhaps, to speak to the crowd, or to his Maker, in the last minutes. At least one account suggests that some were given the opportunity to pray to an icon as they approached the scaffold. Perhaps the viewing public and officials hoped to see the convicted go to his or her death well, with acceptance and repentance, thereby legitimizing the execution in the public's eyes. The moment of execution was infused both with hope of repentance and a desperate desire to destroy evil, capturing the state's own balancing act between violence and mercy. In this turbulent century, the state had to respond in a way that honored its legitimizing ideology as communities used violence to oppose injustice. Violence – judicial or popular – had its languages, rules and limits, demonstrated and tested as the "century of rebellion" unfolded.

[59] Rumiantseva, *Narodnoe antitserkovnoe dvizhenie*, appendix nos. 19–20 (1683). Tikhonravov, *Sochineniia*, II: 305–75, trial and execution on 363–73 (1689); *Polnyi pravoslavnyi bogoslovskii*, I: col. 1499.

CHAPTER 16

Riot and rebellion

Bookended by cossack-peasant uprisings in 1606 and 1670 and punctuated by urban revolts in 1648, 1662 and 1682, the seventeenth century presented the tsar's subjects with ample cause for unrest. As the government pursued aggressive state-building, enserfment was fully codified in law by 1649, followed by constant campaigns to track down runaways; Russian authority extended to borderlands resistant to central control; wars on the western and southern frontiers in the 1630s, 1650s–60s and 1680s strained resources; bureaucratization and taxation squeezed the populace. With regularity, aggrieved populations petitioned for redress and, when pushed to extremes, revolted. Their behavior in riot often mimicked judicial procedure, and thus offers telling perspectives on Muscovite judicial culture; the state for its part was challenged to observe legalities in the midst of what has been called the "century of rebellion."

PUNISHMENT OF URBAN RIOTERS AND REBELS

In the second half of the seventeenth century Moscow and other cities erupted in violence over abusive officials and crippling taxation. The disorders were carried out, however, according to Muscovy's ideology of legitimacy. Righteous subjects were expected to advise the tsar on injustice in his realm; as a just ruler, he was expected to protect his people from iniquity. The culture and practice of petitioning was so deeply legitimized that, as Valerie Kivelson has written, people had lawful claim to address the state in escalating forms of protest: "consultation, supplication, indignation, and riot." Brian Davies underscores that Muscovites, when pushed as far as riot and murder, invoked this ideology by representing themselves as "all the community" (*ves' gorod, ves' mir*), rather than as rebellious individuals. When addressing the tsar directly, they petitioned humbly and respectfully, putting the state in a position where it had to respond. The state's response epitomizes the ambiguities of "legality" in such moments: the state claimed the "legal" power to punish rebels, labeling them traitors, but implicitly recognized a riot's moral authority by exercising that power in restrained ways; restoring stability was more important than punishing all offenders.[1]

In 1648 riots broke out in Moscow and several provincial towns over excessive taxation, especially an increased salt tax, and the corruption of boyar Boris Ivanovich Morozov's clique. In Moscow, disturbances erupted on June 1–2, sparked by the tsar's refusal to accept petitions from the "common people" about these abuses. Some musketeers and gentry eventually joined in the riots, motivated by complaints over salary arrears and abuse by superiors. For twelve days the crowd rampaged through the Kremlin and town, demanding the heads of officials and plundering homes of targeted boyars, other high-ranking officials, bureaucrats and wealthy merchants. On June 2 "in a furious driving & running," they streamed into the home of Nazarii Chistoi, a wealthy merchant and state secretary detested for introducing the salt tax; they beat him to death and threw his naked body on a trash heap, where it lay for two days before his servants dared collect it. On June 3 fire broke out; half the city burned, with great loss of property and life.[2] The violence in Moscow subsided only when the crowd was satisfied in its demands for the blood of corrupt officials – Pleshcheev, Trakhaniotov and Morozov – as discussed in the next chapter.

Official prosecution of the 1648 uprisings in Moscow was relatively muted. Valerie Kivelson observes, "The state itself, in an astonishing admission of its own impropriety and the legitimacy of the rebels' actions, exacted almost no direct retribution from the mutineers." The Swedish envoy Pommerening suggests that the tsar had "promised" not to prosecute the rioters, giving what S. V. Bakhrushin called an "amnesty." Certainly, Moscow was not blanketed with executed rioters hanging from gibbets. Pommerening reported that thirty-five men were beheaded and that "hundreds" of musketeers were exiled on trumped-up charges of gaming or illegal alcohol sale, rather than rile up the town with reference to the riots.[3] The state also rewarded with cash,

[1] Davies, *State Power*, ch. 5; Kivelson, "Muscovite 'Citizenship'," 474. See also Rowland, "Problem of Advice," "Did Muscovite Literary Ideology" and "Muscovy." "The whole community" cited in 1648 Tomsk uprising: Pokrovskii, *Tomsk*, 356.

[2] Driving and running: Loewenson, "Moscow Rising," 153–4 (Leyden pamphlet). Other accounts: Bazilevich (ed.), *Gorodskie vosstaniia*, 56 (Anonymous Swede); 36 (Pommerening). Summary of events: Roller-Assfalg, "Der Moskauer Aufstand."

[3] Kivelson, "Devil Stole His Mind," 748. Promises and amnesty: Bazilevich (ed.), *Gorodskie vosstaniia*, 39 (Pommerening); Bakhrushin, "Moskovskoe vosstanie 1648 g.," 57. Behead and exile:

land and peasants gentry and musketeers who had served loyally.[4] The government's interest was more in establishing calm than in punishing each guilty party to the maximum.

After the immediate threat had died down, punishment was used to prevent further disturbances. In January 1649, for example, two trials investigated men accused of loose talk about the uprisings. An indentured servant of boyar N. I. Romanov, Savva Korepin, was denounced for predicting new uprisings in conversations between January 8 and 18. By January 19 he and numerous witnesses were being interrogated and put in face-to-face confrontation; on January 19 and 20 Korepin suffered two sessions of torture, each with fire, the first with thirty-three blows of the knout, the second with sixteen. After that session Korepin was so debilitated he requested his father confessor. On January 29 boyar judges sentenced him to death and he was beheaded that same day. Another man implicated in loose talk and sentenced to exile with his tongue severed was also punished on January 29; whether any sort of dramatic ceremony was done with them is not recorded.[5] Thus, in the aftermath of urban riot in Moscow, punishments from execution to knouting to mutilation were used, but not mass executions. The state's justice system acknowledged the moral economy of the crowd by being restrained in punishment, at the same time that the crowd, presumably, understood that some punishment would follow but so also would satisfaction of some of their demands.

Some provincial towns also erupted in violence in 1648, spurred by the same causes as in Moscow and often exacerbated by knowledge of the June Moscow events. Here too the state responded in a restrained manner. Kozlov on the southern frontier was the first; servitors had filed petitions against a notoriously corrupt governor, Roman Boborykin, at least twice in 1647, getting minimal satisfaction, and scores of Kozlov gentrymen had traveled to Moscow to petition personally against Boborykin in May and early June 1648. The Kozlov delegation that arrived in Moscow on June 1 witnessed the uprising. Returning home on June 11,

Bazilevich (ed.), *Gorodskie vosstaniia*, 40, 45 (Pommerening); see also Chistiakova, *Gorodskie vosstaniia*, 101.

[4] Reward loyalty: Bazilevich (ed.), *Gorodskie vosstaniia*, 42 (Pommerening), 75 (Tolstoi *sbornik*); Chistiakova, *Gorodskie vosstaniia*, 96–101. Petitions seeking restitution after the uprisings: Zertsalov, "O miatezhakh v gorode Moskve," 3–116 and docs. 6, 8; Zertsalov, "K istorii Moskovskogo miatezha 1648 g.," docs. 1–2. Rustemeyer comments on the importance of compensation: *Dissens und Ehre*, 240–54.

[5] Korepin: Bazilevich (ed.), *Gorodskie vosstaniia*, 86–92. Cut tongue: ibid., 83–6.

their reports sparked an immediate uprising, driving the governor and those who supported him out of town. The rioters released prisoners, ravaged shops and homes of the wealthy, but committed no murders. The unrest spread to villages (where one murder was recorded) and lasted until early July, when musketeers arrived from Moscow with a newly appointed governor and an investigator, E. I. Buturlin. They subdued the rioters, primarily local cossacks, and Buturlin embarked on investigations. Of eighty-four arrested individuals, only a handful was corporally punished: a musketeer was beaten with bastinadoes, a boyars' slave with a knout, ten musketeers implicated in the murder were not executed but knouted. Three ringleaders – the men who had instigated the riots by spreading word of the Moscow uprising – were hanged. Harsh but measured, this response prevented a rekindling of revolt in a testy frontier situation; far harsher punishments could have been visited upon the rioters.[6]

A 1648 uprising in Kursk was similarly fueled by economic grievances, rebuffed petitions and knowledge of events in Moscow. In the spring of 1648 a Muscovite investigator, Konstantin Teglev, had arrived to track down peasants and servitors who had fled landlords or service by indenturing themselves (*zakladnichestvo*); Teglev was enforcing a new law against such flight. Representatives of a local monastery that had accepted many indentured people set off for Moscow with a petition against Teglev; when they returned in July 1648 with news of the Moscow uprisings, peasants, townsmen and servitors (musketeers, cossacks) swarmed the governor's office, demanding Teglev. After a siege of four hours on July 5, they stormed the office, seized and killed Teglev and another official. The governor and others fled to a church for safe haven as the riot churned around them for two more days. On July 7 the governor was able to regain control of the city.

Again in the face of murder and mayhem, the state responded with rigorous investigation, judicial procedure and harsh but limited punishment. In August a Moscow investigator, V. V. Buturlin, questioned 1055 people, using torture with fire, imprisonment and face-to-face confrontation. Five ringleaders – four peasants and one musketeer– were hanged as examples along the roads into town. Forty-three, including two women, were exiled after knouting. Many were put on surety bond; a priest and nun were sent to Moscow for trial and eventually sent into

[6] Kozlov: Chistiakova, *Gorodskie vosstaniia*, 126–32; Bazilevich (ed)., *Gorodskie vosstaniia*, 93–108; Zertsalov, "K istorii miatezha 1648 goda v Moskve," 4; Zertsalov, "K istorii Moskovskogo miatezha 1648 g.," 11–12; Davies, *State Power*, 218–42.

monastic exile.[7] The majority of townsmen who joined the riots were not punished. Such responses tacitly acknowledged the justice of the community's complaints even though the violence had, as in other towns, escalated to murder.

An uprising in Ustiug Velikii in 1648 paralleled that in Kursk. Grievances were rife over the tax burden, sparked by the visit of a Moscow tax collector, Anisim Mikhailov, in the spring of 1648. When a merchant arrived from Moscow on July 8 with tales of the uprisings, discontent mobilized. Revolt broke out on July 9, directed at Mikhailov, the governor and his staff, including undersecretaries who had been sued for corruption in previous years. As in other towns, the crowd surged through the city, seeking its targets. They seized and killed Mikhailov at his home, throwing his body into the river; two undersecretaries fled the town for safety. One later reported that as he identified the peals of successive church bells, he realized that the crowd was heading in his direction. He fled across the river and spent days hidden in the forest.

In investigations starting in September 1648, over 4,817 people were interrogated in 31 peasant communes and in towns. More than 100 were brought to torture so harsh that five died of it in prison. Four of the identified leaders of the riots were executed in December 1648, hanged, as in Kursk, at spots of symbolic value and maximum publicity: one at the confluence of the Iuga and Sukhona rivers, another along the Sukhona and a third along the main highway out of town. The fourth was hanged at the spot where the crowd had thrown Anisim Mikhailov's body into the river. Twelve other people were sentenced to death, brought to the gallows, forgiven and exiled. In all, over fifty families of townsmen and thirty of musketeers were punished and exiled for their participation. Again, sanctions were harsh, but they encompassed only a fraction of the rioters, and executions were few. Reviewing these and other urban disturbances in the provinces in 1648, D. A. Liapin notes other conciliatory gestures, such as the state's granting a Council of the Land and instructing governors in 1649 and 1651 to rule by the law and not to mistreat or oppress the populace.[8]

N. N. Pokrovskii, similarly, labeled the state's response to 1648 unrest in Tomsk "pacifying." The pattern is familiar: the rioting community

[7] Kursk: Chistiakova, *Gorodskie vosstaniia*, 118–26; Bazilevich (ed.), *Gorodskie vosstaniia*, 109–34.

[8] Ustiug Velikii: Chistiakova, *Gorodskie vosstaniia*, 190–202; Bazilevich (ed.), *Gorodskie vosstaniia*, 135–65; Zertsalov, "K istorii miatezha 1648 goda v Moskve," 32–3. Liapin, "K voprosu," 151. Liapin suggests that incidents in several other towns in 1648 have been exaggerated by historians to depict the unrest as "national" in scope.

petitioned "as one" against an abusive governor, investigations were made and punishments were few. Pokrovskii explains Moscow's response by reference to three elements: its fear of further uprisings, the community's skillful use of customs of petitioning and the state's acknowledgment of their right to do so.[9] Another example of the state's restrained hand in punishing rebellions occurred in Novgorod and Pskov in 1650, where the populace protested precipitous rises in grain prices associated with a settlement of war debt with Sweden. Both cities, even as late as the mid seventeenth century, enjoyed certain autonomies, with parallel offices of governor and elected town elders. In Pskov discontent erupted in February 1650, ending in a virtual takeover of the governor's office by the elders. They held off a three-month siege (June–August) by the tsar's troops. Meanwhile, Novgorod had erupted in mid March; the governor's home was seized and homes of the wealthy sacked. In both cities, property damage was great, but murders were few. In July the Pskov elders tried as traitors and executed ten gentrymen charged with conspiring with the tsar's besieging troops.

The Novgorod uprising was put down readily in April, perhaps because it lacked as broad a base of support as the Pskov rebels enjoyed. Most of the Novgorodian rebels were released on surety bond. But the government's forces only managed to quell the Pskov uprising with greater conciliation. A delegation led by Kolomna Bishop Rafail was dispatched to Pskov in July, offering amnesty in return for turning over uprising leaders. Rebuffed in that, in August the state offered full amnesty without handovers of leaders. On August 24 after long negotiations with Bishop Rafail, most of Pskov had sworn allegiance to the tsar and the rebels released the governor and gentry whom they had imprisoned. Despite the promised amnesty, by autumn in Pskov Moscow was carrying out an investigation, arresting major instigators of rebellion and sending them to Novgorod for trial. In the end a few ringleaders were hanged and a few exiled, but mass numbers were not punished.[10]

In 1648–50, then, these many uprisings challenged the government to deal with violence in ways that did not undermine state power. However violent, urban rioters consistently acted according to a rhetoric of legitimacy: they addressed the tsar humbly for redress of grievances and expected

[9] Pokrovskii, *Tomsk*, 333. Tomsk uprising: Chistiakova, *Gorodskie vosstaniia*, 214–29; Pokrovskii, *Tomsk*, ch. 7; Zertsalov, "K istorii miatezha 1648 goda v Moskve," 33–6.

[10] Novgorod and Pskov: Tikhomirov, "Pskovskoe vosstanie," "Novgorodskoe vosstanie" and "Vosstaniia"; Olearius, *Travels*, 214–17.

protection. Acting out its role, the tsar's government responded by sending investigators, carrying out extensive interrogations and punishing with swift and measured justice, balancing its right to use violence with its respect for community concepts of justice. Rioters were pacified, stability was restored and force was balanced with accommodation.

This is not to say that the tsar's government was instinctively benevolent; when it could catch a rebellion before it acquired the moral authority of righteous petitioning, it was more forceful, as in 1662. On July 25, 1662 the Moscow populace erupted over devalued copper coins, rampant counterfeiting and, again, official corruption. Here, the government put down the unrest and plundering after only one day. The events took place in Moscow (where incendiary letters were posted and plundering broke out) and in Kolomenskoe (where the tsar was at his suburban summer residence on the Moscow River). There, a crowd from Moscow approached Tsar Aleksei Mikhailovich with noise and anger; evoking the traditional right of petitioning, one man showed the tsar one of the incendiary letters and demanded the punishment of corrupt officials. The tsar dispersed the crowd calmly and firmly, in the words of General Patrick Gordon, "reprehending them for comeing in such a tumultuary way and in such numbers." Later that day, swelled with new arrivals from Moscow, they returned, more angry and threatening and demanding boyars, but by then troops had arrived. They dispersed the crowd, capturing many and chasing others to the river and into the water to their deaths. Gordon provides a revealing detail that at word of the unrest, the entire population of the German Quarter (foreign mercenaries and merchants who were beholden to the tsar) armed itself and rushed "some to horse and others afoot" to the tsar's defense. Kotoshikhin, writing four years later, reports that the tsar, "seeing that they had not come in good faith and were speaking impolitely and threatening," himself ordered the soldiers to "beat, strike to death and arrest" the rioters. His angry reaction fits the model of the "righteous anger" of a patrimonial tsar. By approaching the tsar with threats to take things into their own hands and with high emotion, they risked undermining their moral authority, and in this case, the state's military ability to suppress the uprising more quickly than in 1648 or later in 1682 sealed their fate.[11]

[11] Gordon, *Diary*, II: 160–1; Russian translation: Gordon, *Dnevnik*, 119–20. Kotoshikhin, *O Rossii*, 103. Summary of events: Löwe, "Der Moskauer Kupfergeldaufstand." The Ulozhenie punished "impolite" behavior in the presence of the tsar or in presenting petitions: chs. 2–3 and ch. 10, art. 105: RZ III: 86–91, 112–13. Righteous anger: Kollmann, *By Honor Bound*, 162–5. Approaching tsar or

In 1662 investigations began immediately, with orders to use "multiple forms of harsh torture severely" and to execute "by all manner of punishments, quartering and hanging." Bazilevich is undoubtedly right that the first punishments were intended to terrorize the population – on the very day of the uprising the tsar ordered his commanders to execute "ten to twenty" of the Moscow rioters; a decree of July 26 mandated that rioters be "hanged along all the roads around Moscow." Without much interrogation and investigation, on that day Prince A. N. Trubetskoi hanged ten men in Lubianka Square and ten more along the Moscow River at the Swamp, both places where the uprising had broken out. When all the investigations were over, a peasant who hailed from a village outside Moscow was hanged "on the Gzhelskaia Road" that led to his home; Kuzma Nagaev, a musketeer who had incited the crowds, and Luchka Zhitkoi, the peasant who had handed the tsar a letter, were in effect quartered, their left hands, both feet and tongues severed (the intent was likely to kill, as it was recorded that Nagaev died of his wounds on August 12; Zhitkoi's survival is unknown). Recall that in the next year a horrific decree ordered virtual quartering for felons guilty of capital crime.[12]

Others were mutilated by the loss of a hand or foot, which was not, apparently, intended to kill. One man, for example, was sentenced to severing of a hand, another, a hand and a foot; they were then to be released to their homes "until they heal." Most mutilation was a prelude to exile; in addition, exiles of low social rank were branded on the cheek with the letter B for "*buntovshchik*" (rebel). Heinz-Dietrich Löwe remarked on the gruesomeness of the interrogations; Buganov estimated that in all, over 1,700 people were questioned in three venues (Moscow, Kolomenskoe and the nearby Nicholas Ugreshskii Monastery) well into September. Only 196 were tortured (7.6 percent of those arrested), but those who were suffered greatly. They suffered an average of twenty-five knout blows, with some receiving far more. All in all, the punishment for this single day of uprising, plundering and insolent approach to the ruler resulted in an exemplary execution of twenty-two, the execution or near-fatal mutilation of several more, and the exile of almost 1,500

his officials with respect: Davies, *State Power*, 222–3. "German Quarter": a suburban district in Moscow where foreigners, mostly Europeans, lived, at first by choice, then by law from 1652.

[12] All manner of punishments: Buganov, *Moskovskoe vosstanie 1662 g.*, 99. Terrorize: Bazilevich, "Vosstanie v Moskve v 1662 g.," 263. July 26: *Vosstanie 1662 g.*, no. 81. Gzhelskaia road: Zertsalov, "O miatezhakh v gorode Moskve," 301–5; RGADA f. 210, Prikaznyi stol, no. 959, fols. 7–20 (1662). Nagaev and Zhitkoi: *Vosstanie 1662 g.*, nos. 13 and 15; Zertsalov, "O miatezhakh v gorode Moskve," 298–9. PSZ 1: no. 334 (1663).

participants from Moscow.[13] The violence was swift, harsher and in greater quantity than seen before, reflecting that the balance of moral authority in 1662 did not shift from tsar to crowd. Here, as at most times, the state's sovereign right to punish opposition trumped popular concepts of justice. But extraordinary moments like those in 1648 and 1682 demonstrate the state's equal obligation to affirm that moral economy when pushed to the wall.

On April 17, 1682 Tsar Fedor Alekseevich died without heirs and Moscow was soon paralyzed by a rebellion of musketeers and soldiers who were initially discontented with abusive commanders and then manipulated by the Miloslavskii faction to favor the succession of Tsar Fedor's brother Ioann Alekseevich (age sixteen) (from Tsar Aleksei Mikhailovich's first marriage to Mariia Miloslavskaia) over Peter Alekseevich (age ten) (son of Nataliia Naryshkina, the tsar's second wife).[14] The musketeers marauded for three days, May 15 to May 17, murdering dozens of hated colonels, corrupt bureaucrats and Naryshkin insiders. After the worst violence died down, the half-brothers Ioann and Peter ruled as co-tsars, overseen by their Miloslavskaia sister Sofiia Alekseevna. But the musketeers de facto ruled Moscow, dispatching into exile Naryshkin associates and executing criminals. The pro-Miloslavskii Sil′vestr Medvedev derided them: the musketeers "behaved proudly and haughtily to the tsars everywhere, as if they were eminent people, and they associated with the boyars and treated people of all ranks with no respect." He also observed that no one was running the government, most of the chancery bureaucrats having fled their offices.[15]

[13] Until heal: *Vosstanie 1662 g.*, no. 158. Branded with B: ibid., nos. 234, 241; Kotoshikhin, *O Rossii*, 103 (ch. 7 art. 9). Twenty hanged: *Vosstanie 1662 g.*, no. 82. Investigation: Buganov, *Moskovskoe vosstanie*, 131–2, 116; Zertsalov, "O miatezhakh v gorode Moskve," 244–5; Löwe, "Der Moskauer Kupfergeldaufstand," 116. Hanged on roads: *Vosstanie 1662 g.*, nos. 81, 120–55.

[14] 1682 uprisings: Buganov, *Moskovskie vosstaniia*, 87–347; Hughes, *Sophia*, ch. 3; Löwe, "Der Strelitzen-Aufstand von 1682." Contemporary sources: narratives by the Military Service Chancery written by Oct. 3, 1682 (no. 63), by Nov. 3, 1682 (no. 171), not before Sept. 1683 (no. 204) and not before end 1683 (no. 207): *Vosstanie v Moskve 1682 g.* Resident foreigners report eyewitness and hearsay: Bogdanov, "Moskovskoe vosstanie 1682 g."; Keep, "Mutiny in Moscow, 1682"; Belov, "Pis′ma." Eyewitness narratives by two men resident in the Kremlin – pro-Miloslavskii Sil′vestr Medvedev (written by end 1684) and pro-Naryshkin Andrei Matveev (written 1720s): Medvedev, "Sozertsanie kratkoe"; Matveev, "Zapiski." Russian eyewitness accounts of 1682: Bogdanov, "Podennye zapisi"; Buganov, "Novyi istochnik"; PSRL xxxi: 174–6 (Mazurin Chronicle), also published in Tikhomirov, "Zapiski prikaznykh liudei." Chronicle written by a cleric *c.*1691: PSRL xxxi: 187–203.

[15] Exile enemies May–Sept. 1682: *Vosstanie v Moskve 1682 g.*, nos. 16, 30–2, 72, 124–5; PSRL xxxi: 175 (Mazurin). Musketeers torture and execute: *Vosstanie v Moskve 1682 g.*, no. 207, p. 279. Medvedev, "Sozertsanie kratkoe," 97 (quote), 58.

The Miloslavskii faction proceeded cautiously in consolidating authority and, like its predecessors in 1648, avoided large-scale executions. Rather, they played a cat-and-mouse game as the balance of power shifted. Even during the rioting and into early September, Tsarevna Sofiia rewarded loyal supporters and appeased musketeers with cash bonuses paid for by extraordinary taxes on church and private property.[16] Almost immediately after the bloodshed abated, the musketeers began to shore up their position by demanding in late June that a pillar be constructed in Red Square with plaques on which would be inscribed an immunity charter labeling their killings lawful. They also requested higher salaries. Although Sil′vestr Medvedev later called this petition "stupid," Sofiia granted their demands for salary, pillar and exoneration.[17]

As the Miloslavskii faction stabilized, the balance of power shifted. When the royal family left town on August 20 on its annual summer pilgrimage, nervous musketeers asked them to return and denied plans to rekindle the insurrection. In early September the government took the bold move of sending four musketeer regiments to Kiev to disperse trouble-makers.[18] But not until September 17 were the Miloslavskie emboldened to move against their rivals, including Princes Ivan and Andrei Khovanskie (see Chapter 15) and their adjutant Boris Odintsov. The Military Service Chancery summary written a year later records that "in the months to the end of the year there was apprehension in all the regiments; the known ringleaders were executed, and others, having been tortured, were exiled."[19] Indeed, many were arrested and in mid October two musketeers were executed in Red Square "for criminality, murder, inappropriate words and uprising."[20] Other members of the Khovanskii clan and faction, including Prince Ivan's wife and second son Ivan, were arrested and exiled, avoiding execution. In December 1682, Regent Sofiia issued an order threatening execution without mercy for anyone fomenting rebellion.[21]

16 Buganov, *Moskovskie vosstaniia*, 347–59; Bogdanov, "Podennye zapisi," 36; Medvedev, "Sozertsanie kratkoe," 59; *Vosstanie v Moskve 1682 g.*, nos. 26, 70, 76 and no. 207, p. 279.

17 *Vosstanie v Moskve 1682 g.*, nos. 20–1; no. 207, p. 280; Medvedev, "Sozertsanie kratkoe," 67–75; PSRL XXXI: 176 (Mazurin); Lavrent′ev, "Moskovskoe 'stolpotvorenie'," 132–6.

18 *Vosstanie v Moskve 1682 g.*, nos. 63, 68, 71, 74a, 130.

19 Matveev, "Zapiski," 46. Lavrov reports that five were executed the same day as the Khovanskie and Odintsov, disputing Buganov's claim of thirty-seven: *Regentsvo*, 41 and n. 103; Buganov, *Moskovskie vosstaniia*, 278. Chancery report: *Vosstanie v Moskve 1682 g.*, no. 207, p. 282.

20 Arrested: *Vosstanie v Moskve 1682 g.*, nos. 109, 126, 142, 156–9, 163–4, 168–9, 173, 192–3, 199. Two executed: ibid., no. 160.

21 Prince Ivan and Khovanskii kin: *Vosstanie v Moskve 1682 g.*, nos. 91, 101, 104, 128, 131, 139, 144, 145, 150, 207, p. 281. PSRL XXXI: 179 (Mazurin). PSZ II: no. 978 (Dec. 31, 1682).

At the same time, the government and the musketeers negotiated to end the tensions, using the familiar pattern of petition and mercy. After the Khovanskie's execution, frightened musketeers enlisted the patriarch to intercede with the tsars on terms of surrender. By September 22, the Miloslavskie were confident enough to release those imprisoned by the rebels. By September 25, groups of musketeers and soldiers were submitting declarations of loyalty to the tsars, and on October 3 twenty representatives of the musketeer regiments arrived at the Trinity Monastery (about 50 miles outside of Moscow where the co-tsars were staying for their safety) with a petition for forgiveness. The tsars granted their request with terms that assured the musketeers protection from abusive officials but also threatened "execution with no mercy" should they foment rebellion in the future.[22]

Thereafter, the Miloslavskii faction rehabilitated some of the musketeers' detested colonels, even while reminding them not to abuse their men. On October 28, before the tsars returned to Moscow, the musketeers requested that the pillar be destroyed. It and its plaques were razed, its plinth taken off to the Moscow Administrative Chancery. With all this accomplished, the tsars' entourage returned to the Kremlin in formal procession on November 3.[23]

Here, as in the 1648 uprising, the government's reaction focused on re-establishing order, punishing a few, rewarding many, regaining moral authority and moving forward. Angela Rustemeyer observes that in punishing rebels in these various urban uprisings, the state missed an opportunity to enhance its power by public commemoration. Comparing Muscovy to the Habsburg realm, where "liturgies of commemoration" shaped the memory of uprisings to favor the regime, she notes that in Russia no positive effort to dictate interpretations of the events was made, leaving the construction of memory to popular tales often sympathetic to rebels.[24] One wonders what that might have looked like. Popular memory undoubtedly privileged the moral economy of the crowd; the state's commemoration should by rights have been more complex, reflecting

[22] Negotiations: Lavrov, *Regentsvo*, 47–56; Buganov, *Moskovskie vosstaniia*, 347–59; *Vosstanie v Moskve 1682 g.*, nos. 119, 120, 122, 132, 134. Patriarch intercedes: ibid., no. 63, p. 94 and no. 112. Release rebels' prisoners: ibid., no. 106. Declarations of loyalty: ibid., no. 111 and no. 207, p. 281. Forgiveness: ibid., no. 63.

[23] Rehabilitate colonels: *Vosstanie v Moskve 1682 g.*, nos. 127, 143, 166, 202 (September to June 1683). Dismantle pillar: ibid., nos. 172 and 174. Plinth: PSRL XXXI: 179 (Mazurin). Entourage returns: *Vosstanie v Moskve 1682 g.*, no. 171, p. 224.

[24] Rustemeyer, *Dissens und Ehre*, 254–6.

not only the state's right to resist oppression but also its patrimonial interaction with its people's grievances.

THE STEPAN RAZIN REBELLION

Because these urban uprisings were acted out according to a rhetoric of advice-giving and petitioning, they posed more nuanced dilemmas to Moscow's rulers than did the cossack-peasant rebellion led by Stepan Razin in 1670–1. This was mass armed rebellion suppressed by out-and-out war. Violence was horrific on both sides. While Paul Avrich asserted that "the brutality of the repressions by far exceeded the atrocities committed by the insurgents," the opposite could equally be argued. Across a huge territory the rebels killed tsarist officials, merchants, landlords and clerics; they burned peasant villages.[25] But even in this charged wartime situation, each party observed its own moral economy. For the state, that meant following patterns of criminal justice observed already – investigatory procedure, record-keeping, differentiated punishments, ample provision of mercy and exemplary brutality for the worst offenders. Everything was more intense – the speed of trial, the intensity of torture, forms of execution – but the government put down mass uprising in a way that balanced exemplary punishment with restoration of stability.

Military commanders and local governors fighting the rebellion were ordered to observe the full range of judicial procedure. An order of October 9, 1670 to Field Commander Ivan Vasil'evich Buturlin is an excellent example: he was told that if any rebel cossacks petitioned for mercy, he was to reprimand them for their guilt but forgive them in the name of the tsar who "does not want to shed Christian blood." Buturlin was ordered to have them turn in their leaders and to question these men "severely," torturing with fire; he was to execute the guilty, not writing to the tsar before doing so, and to read aloud their crimes before a crowd "so that those looking on will not do such crime or lead others into treason and criminality." Buturlin was further ordered that people who had been "led into crime and treason" by the rebels and who now sought the tsar's mercy should be forgiven, made to take a loyalty oath and released to their homes, without punishment or destruction of their houses and villages. Another such order of September 1670 sent to Field Commander Prince G. G. Romodanovskii told him to execute ringleaders "according to the

[25] Avrich, *Russian Rebels*, 109. Summary of events: ibid., ch. 2; Schleuning and Tuchtenhagen, "Der Kosaken-Aufstand."

tsar's order and Ulozhenie." Moscow explicitly instructed Don and Ukrainian Cossacks who joined them against the rebels to judge the guilty "by their military law codes"; various documents attest that they did so.[26] Orders were explicit that commanders should investigate (*syskat'*) before rendering judgment.[27] This is traditional judicial procedure in microcosm.

In wartime conditions, things moved quickly. As in the order to Buturlin, some commanders were ordered to execute the ringleaders immediately, without corresponding with Moscow. In September 1670 Moscow gave permission to Field Commander Romodanovskii to execute Colonel Dzinkovskii (who had joined the rebels) and advised him to execute other such traitors in the future without consulting Moscow. The Military Service Chancery gave the same permission to the Kozlov governor in November 1670.[28] Across the theater of war such prompt punishment occurred. In a report of late September or early October 1670, Field Commander Dolgorukov confirmed that he had been ordered to send back only reports from eyewitnesses and oral interrogations and to execute any ringleaders by quartering and hanging their bodies "at prepared places (*po primetnym mestam*) in the towns and provinces where they committed crimes." He duly reported that he had captured many rebel cossacks, questioned them and found them guilty of killing tsarist officials in Temnikov. These he did not hang, however, but beheaded, exercising discretion on punishment. Repeatedly, generals report to the center that they had captured many rebels, investigated them by community survey, oral interrogation and torture, and executed the ringleaders. Less guilty captives they corporally punished, sometimes with mutilation. Other commanders reported that they had executed ringleaders without consultation, as ordered. Often commanders were helped in their investigations by communities who brought forward alleged ringleaders in a bid for leniency for themselves.[29]

Prior investigation was mandated: Dolgorukov reported in November 1670 that he had investigated and executed rebels sent to him by his field

[26] Buturlin: KV II, pt. 1: no. 103, pp. 121–2. Romodanovskii: KV II, pt. 2: no. 28, p. 37. Ukrainian Cossacks: KV II, pt. 2: no. 98, p. 133 (Dec. 70); KV III: no. 74, p. 79 (May 71). Don Cossacks: KV III: no. 1, p. 6; no. 103, p. 112 (June 71) and no. 199 (July 71).

[27] Orders to investigate: KV II pt. 1: no. 272, p. 334 (Nov. 1670); nos. 300 and no. 315 (both Dec. 1670); KV III: no. 82, p. 90 (June 1671).

[28] Dzinkovskii: KV II, pt. 2: no. 32, p. 42. Kozlov: KV II, pt. 1: no. 196, p. 234.

[29] Dolgorukov: KV II, pt. 1: no. 79. Execute without consult: KV II, pt. 2: no. 24, p. 33 (Sept. 70). Communities aid: KV II, pt. 1: no. 265, p. 325 (Nov. 1670); no. 294, p. 369 (Dec. 1670); no. 342, p. 432 (Dec. 1670).

commanders: twelve peasants and cossacks from Kurmysh. Field Commander F. I. Leont′ev reported in October 1670 that he had captured and investigated many cossacks who, on interrogation and torture, admitted killing the governor and officials of Alatyr′. He ordered some beheaded in the rebel camp and others hanged in Arzamas and outside towns "in prepared places."[30] Commanders took procedure seriously. Field Commander Daniil Bariatinskii reported on November 5, 1670 that since he had not yet completed his investigations in Kozmodemiansk, he could not identify trustworthy locals. By November 17 he was able to report that he had "conducted among the priests and townsmen and people of all ranks an investigation about the criminals and traitors" in Kozmodemiansk and as a result he had corporally punished 400 rebels (100 with bodily mutilation), executed 60 ringleaders and brought 450 Russians and 505 Cheremisy to loyalty oaths. The Tot′ma governor reported that he had captured Ataman Iliushka Ivanov in mid December 1670 and that, after torture and interrogation, he had executed him "according to the Ulozhenie and *gradskie zakony*" as well as in response to the petition of the assembled community. The Tambov governor in June 1671 sought instruction on what to do with men in prison who had been freed by the rebels but had remained loyal to the tsar; Moscow advised referring major criminal cases to the center and recommending accusatory format trials for those incarcerated for lesser issues. In late 1671 an inspector was sent to Userda to investigate the rebellion; at least ten men were executed and several others knouted as a result.[31]

Following procedure was so stringently prescribed that, in early 1671, in the wake of the rebellion, a group of Smolensk officers was punished for taking rebels home with them as slaves; the captives were returned to their Volga homes. Similarly the boyar and tsar's in-law, Ivan Bogdanovich Miloslavskii, was investigated for taking in rebels as domestic slaves in Astrakhan.[32] Conscientiousness about judicial procedure is evident in other ways as well. A bureaucrat in the newly captured town of Kadom reported that the rebels had destroyed most documents, but that the governor's office still had a copy of the 1649 Ulozhenie. The Kerensk governor wrote to Moscow in February 1671 that the rebels had destroyed

[30] Don Cossacks: KV III: no. 108, p. 117. Arzamas elder: KV IV: no. 42 (by Feb. 71). Dolgorukov: KV II, pt. 1: no. 218 and no. 229, p. 277. Leont′ev: KV II, pt. 1: no. 91, p. 108.

[31] Bariatinskii: KV II, pt. 1: no. 202, p. 245; no. 232, p. 281. Tot′ma: KV II, pt. 1: no. 324, p. 410. Tambov: KV III: no. 96. Userda: KV III: no. 139. Other commanders doing investigations: KV II, pt. 1: no. 310, p. 391; no. 312, p. 398; no. 321, p. 405 (all Dec. 1670).

[32] Smolensk: KV III: nos. 11, 15 and 31. Miloslavskii: KV III: nos. 188 and 205–6 (all July 1672).

the Ulozhenie along with all other important documents, so that he "had nothing according to which to render justice." Others reported to Moscow that they needed further instructions before reaching a verdict for a particular crime or social group, as their official instructions did not cover that issue. Field Commander Narbekov reported in November 1670 that he did not have specific instructions on what to do with monks or priests found to be ringleaders.[33] The governor of Kozlov requested orders on how to punish the arrested wives of rebels in March 1671, while the Kadom governor reported that he had no instructions on what to do with suits brought by neighbors against neighbors for crime during the uprising; the Temnikov governor reported that his prisoners were petitioning for resolution of their cases "according to the Ulozhenie."[34]

Commanders reported sentencing the guilty to a range of corporal and capital punishment, according to guilt. A list of rebels punished in the Vetluga campaign from December 1670 notes that in one village four men were hanged and eleven knouted and bodily mutilated. In another village, five were hanged, one knouted and mutilated, while in another fifty-four men were knouted. After Astrakhan was retaken, dozens of trials took place in the autumn of 1672; punishments ranged from execution to exile to release on surety bond. The Kadom governor also reported in February 1671 a variety of hangings, knoutings and mutilations that he administered after investigation, interrogation and torture. In one case a peasant was spared death, receiving a knouting instead, because his landlord testified that the man had been forced to serve the rebels and had meanwhile sheltered and saved his landlord from death.[35]

In the wake of the uprising, the tsar's commanders extended mercy generously, as instructed. Commanders and governors sent lists to Moscow of how many dozens and hundreds of Russians, Cherkassy, Tatars, Mordva and others had taken loyalty oaths. In November 1670, for example, Field Commander Bariatinskii reported that he had given the oath to several Chuvash men and sent them off to convince their villages to surrender. They did so and Bariatinskii brought 549 more

[33] Kadom: KV II, pt. 1: no. 276, p. 339 (Nov. 1670). Kerensk: KV IV: no. 39. Narbekov: KV II, pt. 1: no. 242, p. 292.

[34] Kozlov: KV III: no. 30, p. 38. Kadom: KV III: no. 137 (Aug. 1671). Temnikov: KV III: no. 157 (Nov. 1671). Other officials seeking orders: KV II, pt. 1: no. 299, p. 376 (Dec. 1670); KV II, pt. 2: no. 133 (Oct. 1670); KV III: no. 63 (May 1671) and no. 137 (Aug. 1671).

[35] Vetluga and another village: KV II, pt. 1: no. 342. Astrakhan: KV III: no. 232. Kadom: KV III: no. 17. Other cites to a range of punishments being employed: KV II, pt. 1: no. 174 (Oct. 1670); no. 255 (Nov. 1670); KV II, pt. 2: no. 70 (Nov. 1670).

people to the loyalty oath, swearing according to their *shert'* (oath of allegiance to the tsar). At the same time he executed more than twenty Chuvash and at least two Russians and ordered several knouted. All in all, in November 1670 Field Commander Dolgorukov reported that over 5,000 peasants in Nizhnii Novgorod province were forgiven without punishment.[36]

Such mercy was both shrewd and pragmatic. Ideologically, it demonstrated the tsar's benevolence and attempted to rebuild trust. Documents rationalized such mass forgiveness by explaining that the people had been foolishly tricked by the "seductions" of Razin's "seditious" letters. Pragmatically, the rebellion was so extensive that the state could not execute everyone who participated. Furthermore, it did not want to risk inflaming passions further, which risk was clear in November 1670. The Kadom governor reported that he had been sending emissaries throughout the region to seek surrender, promising the tsar's mercy. But the governor of Kasimov had ignored his instructions to give this process time and had executed four peasant rebels. The community was so outraged that they killed the Kadom emissaries when they arrived.[37]

All this judicial procedure and forgiveness, however, should not obscure the violence of the process. Russian officers themselves described gruesome scenes of battle. Prince Iurii Nikitich Bariatinskii reported about an encounter at Ust' Urenskaia on November 12, 1670 in which "we cut down so many of these rebels, mounted and on foot, that in the field and in their camps and in the streets it was impossible to ride through on horseback because of the corpses, and so much blood ran that it flowed in great rivers as during rain." He noted that he had beheaded the ringleaders but released on loyalty oath the majority of 323 captives. Commanders destroyed as they went, as when Field Commander Iakov Timofeevich Khitrovo's forces pursued rebel cossacks into the Shatsk area village of Sasov in October 1670. He chased many off, killed many in battle, hanged captured ringleaders and torched the village. He then brought the remaining villagers to loyalty oath, urging them to find their compatriots who had fled and convince them also to abandon the uprising, for which they could expect "the tsar's mercy." Field Commander Fedor Ivanovich Leont'ev captured a group of rebels in the

[36] Bariatinskii: KV II, pt. I: no. 202, pp. 241–3. Dolgorukov: KV II, pt. I: no. 235. More oath-taking: KV II, pt. I: no. 258 (Nov. 1670) and no. 294, p. 369 (Dec. 1670).

[37] Foolishly tricked: KV II, pt. I: no. 277, p. 342 (Nov. 1670); KV III: no. 15, p. 16 (Feb. 1671); Schleuning and Tuchtenhagen, "Der Kosaken-Aufstand," 160–1. Kasimov: KV II, pt. I: no. 237.

Nizhnii Novgorod area in November 1670. He executed twenty men after interrogation and torture by fire, destroyed their forest encampments and burned the "villages and hamlets" of peasants who had joined the rebels. But he also accepted the repentance of at least four villages, bringing almost 1,200 people to loyalty oaths.[38]

The government intended the violence to be exemplary. In late November 1670, for example, it sent a report to Hetman Mnogogreshnyi in Left Bank Ukraine about Field Commander Dolgorukov's success in vanquishing the rebels, detailing the army's bloody march down the Volga from late September, punctuated by group executions of ringleaders at each site of battle. As usual, deterrence was a goal (commanders' orders include the familiar phrase "so that those looking on would not commit such crimes"), but rule by terror was also intended. In September 1670, for example, Field Commander Prince G. G. Romodanovskii was ordered to execute ringleaders wherever he captured them "to strike fear in many people."[39]

A curious form of exemplary execution occurred in the winter of 1670–1. Cossack leader Iliushka Ivanov had been captured on December 11 and hanged in Tot′ma on December 12. The governor of neighboring Galich, Semen Nesterov, upon hearing the news, requested that the dead body be sent to him to convince local followers that Ivanov was really dead. Receiving the (undoubtedly frozen) body on December 25, Nesterov reported that Ivanov's sympathizers had identified the body and "I ordered the dead body hanged at the town marketplace and I ordered it proclaimed on market days to all the people that they should not commit rebellion in the future and I posted on the gallows a broadsheet describing his crimes." Hearing of this, another governor requested the corpse for the same purpose, and it was shipped from Galich to the Vetluga area on January 15.[40]

Moscow's army was on the move and executions were not elaborate or theatrical; time was of the essence. But they were used to good effect. Rebels were hanged or quartered at the most visible spots. A November 1670 account of the progress of battle in the Northern Donets region notes dozens of men hanged, several by the feet, some quartered, the

[38] Rivers of blood: KV II, pt. 1: no. 251, p. 303. Sasov village: KV II, pt. 1: no. 173. Leont′ev: KV II, pt. 1: no. 244, pp. 293–4.

[39] Mnogogreshnyi: KV II, pt. 1: no. 264. Deterrence: KV II, pt. 1: no. 103, p. 121 (Oct. 70); no. 155, p. 184 (Oct. 70); no. 196, p. 234 (Nov. 70); no. 315 (Dec. 70). Strike fear: KV II, pt. 2: no. 28.

[40] Galich: KV II, pt. 1: no. 374, p. 475. Vetluga: KV II, pt. 1: no. 350, p. 446; no. 374 (quote on 475); nos. 402 and 405.

mother of Stepan Razin beheaded, and others hanged, all along the Donets River and roads of the region. A nun who had led a rebel contingent was arrested in Temnikov in December 1670 and accused of heresy and witchcraft; under torture she claimed she had taught a cossack commander the arts of witchcraft. She was condemned and burned in a cage along with writings and roots that she had in her possession.[41]

An anonymous English account from 1672, contemporary but not necessarily an eyewitness, painted a dire picture of Commander Dolgorukov's "severe judgment" at Arzamas.

> The place was terrible to behold, and had the resemblance of the Suburbs of Hell. Round about it were Gallows, each of which was loaded with forty or fifty men. In another place lay many Beheaded and covered with Blood, Here and there stood some impaled, whereof not a few lived unto the third day, and were heard to speak. Within the space of Three Moneths, there were by the Hands of Executioners put to death Eleven thousand Men, in a legal way, upon the hearing of Witnesses.[42]

This account's number of 11,000 dead may be exaggerated, but his last comment confirms our findings; punishment was levied with procedure "in a legal way, upon the hearing of Witnesses." The tsar's troops used brutal violence consciously to punish, to strike fear and to deter, but they were not arbitrary.

The rebels were equally violent. Virtually all foreign accounts were written by sympathizers to the tsar, often men in the tsar's service; not surprisingly, they stress the brutality of the rebels; so also do state documents.[43] But Razin's cossacks, like cossack rebels in the Time of Troubles and like cossacks across the Eurasian steppe, used violence as a conscious strategy to strike terror. In the Razin rebellion, violence was directed against those who benefitted from enserfment and high taxes on the peasants and cossacks of the wild frontier. The guilty were the tsar's governors, musketeers and foreign troops; the bureaucrats who kept tax, land and indenture records; wealthy merchants; all manner of landholders, clerical and secular. Razin himself justified social rebellion by a rhetoric of naive monarchism: he was fighting not against the tsar but against corrupt boyars in Moscow and rapacious local landlords. While

41 Northern Donets: KV II, pt. 2: no. 70. Witch: KV II, pt. 1: no. 293, p. 367; Man'kov (ed.), *Zapiski*, 99 (Anonymous English).

42 Man'kov (ed.), *Zapiski*, 98 (Anonymous English) and 100.

43 Man'kov (ed.), *Zapiski* (Anonymous English); Konovalov, "Ludvig Fabritius's Account"; Konovalov, "Razin's Execution," 94–7 (Martius), 97–8 (Hebdon); *Moskoviia i Evropa*, 315–70 (Jan Struys); Man'kov (ed.), *Inostrannye izvestiia*, 70–130 (Martius, foreign newspapers).

the tsar had been hijacked by evil advisers, Razin argued, the church had been perverted by corrupt bishops who had deposed the legitimate Patriarch Nikon (half Mordvinian, Nikon was a native son of the Middle Volga). To this end Razin devised a pretender strategy, claiming to be escorting to Moscow both the tsar's son Aleksei, miraculously saved from the plots of evil boyars, and Patriarch Nikon. In his entourage he set up a false tsarevich and a false Nikon, displayed in luxuriously outfitted barges. In reality, Tsarevich Aleksei Alekseevich had died at age sixteen in January 1670, as Moscow repeatedly explained in proclamations to the Volga, and Patriarch Nikon was in monastic captivity at the time.[44]

Razin's movement quickly morphed from typical cossack plundering in 1667–9 to social rebellion as he moved up the Don and Volga in the summer and autumn of 1670. Peasants eagerly jumped in, often before cossacks had arrived in their town to organize them; historians speak of two parallel rebellions – cossack and peasant. Local communities who joined were those most recently settled, often through forcible population transfer, and those most heavily oppressed by service and taxation obligations. The cossacks' rage turned against governors and their chancery staffs, as well as the officers (many of them foreign) and troops who remained loyal to the tsar; local communities targeted local officials, secular and clerical landlords and their estate staffs. In November 1670, for example, cossacks and rebellious villagers captured the bailiffs of several local landlords, but the men escaped and organized resistance.[45] Governors and their staffs were killed in almost every town the rebels captured: Astrakhan, Chernyi Iar, Tsaritsyn, Korsun, Alatyr′, Ostrogozhsk, Ol′shansk, Penza, Kozomodemiansk, Insar, Murashkin, Saransk, Upper Lomov, Lower Lomov, Kurmysh and others.

The rebels' methods of violence in many ways mimicked state judicial process. Much of their killing occurred in the heat of battle, but when they paused to prosecute, they followed some familiar procedures and rituals. They used the same formats of torture – knouting and fire; they carried out mock executions, bringing people to the chopping block, then

[44] Cossack violence: Gordon, *Cossack Rebellions*, 66–7, 80. Proclamations on Aleksei: KV II, pt. I: no. 119, p. 141 (Oct. 70); no. 171, p. 203 (Oct. 70); no. 277, p. 341 (Nov. 70); no. 327, p. 412 (Dec. 70). Arrested rebels mention tsarevich and patriarch: KV II, pt. I: no. 64, p. 75 (Sept. 70); no. 83, p. 101 (Oct. 70); no. 92, p. 109 (Oct. 70); no. 121, p. 144 (Oct. 70); no. 124, p. 149 (Oct. 70). Barges: Avrich, *Russian Rebels*, 95; Man′kov (ed.), *Zapiski*, 97–8 (Anonymous English). On the false Aleksei: Perrie, *Pretenders*, 237.

[45] Two rebellions: Romaniello, *Elusive Empire*, ch. 6; Schleuning and Tuchtenhagen, "Der Kosaken-Aufstand," 157–61. Bailiffs: KV II, pt. I: no. 241, p. 290.

excusing them. This happened in 1670 to a Temnikov undersecretary once, and twice to a priest. Another undersecretary on an embassy caught by the rebels in Astrakhan was led to the gallows but reprieved by petition of the prisoners of war whom he had been escorting home. But government troops later executed him for collaborating with the rebels.[46]

The rebels beheaded victims and hanged people upside down, just as the tsar's troops did; the latter was the fate of the two sons of the murdered governor of Astrakhan in July 1670. Rebels also had their own forms of execution; drowning was a typical method for these cossacks so intimately tied to the river. One foreigner reports that they weighted down a bound victim by pulling his shirt over his head and filling it with sand. Sometimes in the heat of battle they simply tossed people in the water and beat them back when they surfaced.[47] The rebels executed for maximum publicity and symbolic effect. Defenestration of a sort (*raskat*) was common, as it had been in the Time of Troubles. Then, for example, in Putivl′ in 1606 a local hegumen, Dionisii, implored the population to stay loyal to Tsar Vasilii; Tsarevich Peter had him thrown from the city tower. In Razin's rebellion, hated governors (such as Prince I. S. Prozorovskii in Astrakhan in July 1670) were also thrown from city towers in a symbolic expulsion from the community. Another governor was burned with his staff and family while taking refuge in the cathedral in Alatyr′, the burning aimed at purifying community. Other governors were simply drowned or cut down with swords.[48]

The cossacks also followed their own customs of rough justice. Known for government by acclamation in assemblies (*krugi*), in several instances they gathered the community for advice on the fate of tsarist officials. In Ostrogozhsk in September 1670, townsmen declared the governor and the undersecretary cruel and corrupt – both were executed. Rebels instituted cossack government by assembly in place of murdered governors, as in Kurmysh in November 1670. They also maintained their custom of dividing their plunder among themselves; Ludwig Fabritius, captive in Astrakhan and passing as a cossack, was forced to accept a share in the

[46] Rebel torture: KV II, pt. 1: no. 100, p. 116 (Oct. 1670). Temnikov: KV III: no. 223. Priest: KV II, pt. 1: no. 124, p. 149. Embassy undersecretary: KV I: nos. 182–3, pp. 249–52 (Sept. 70). His execution: KV II, pt. 2: no. 73, pp. 93–4 (Dec. 70).

[47] Prozorovskii sons: Tikhomirov, "Zapiski prikaznykh liudei," 445. Drowning: Avrich, *Russian Rebels*, 78; eyewitness letter of Sept. 24, 1669: *Moskoviia i Evropa*, 471. Beat them back: KV I: no. 171, p. 236 (Aug. 70).

[48] 1606: Koretskii, "Aktovye i letopsnye," 57–8; same in Gremiachii 1606: Skrynnikov, *Smuta*, 225. Symbolism of *raskat*: Schleuning and Tuchtenhagen, "Der Kosaken-Aufstand," 149; Löwe, "Der Strelitzen-Aufstand von 1682," 184–5; Perrie, *Pretenders*, 131, 138. Representative account of taking Astrakhan: KV I: no. 183 (Sept. 1670); Alatyr′: KV II, pt. 1: no. 79, p. 92.

plunder, which he was loath to take. After the rebellion, investigators considered receiving a share of booty proof of being a rebel.[49]

The execution of Metropolitan Iosif in Astrakhan in May 1671 reveals a fascinating symbolic discourse involving the power of the written word. Cossacks had allowed the metropolitan and deposed town governor Prince Semen L'vov to live in Astrakhan since June 1670, but they distrusted them (rumor, probably false, had it that the two were in correspondence with the Don Cossack Horde loyal to the tsar). They beheaded Prince L'vov at the same time that they moved against Metropolitan Iosif, which was after months of tolerating his opposition.[50] Ultimately, Iosif's bold remonstrances and powerful use of tsarist documents pushed them to the ultimate violence.

Throughout the uprising both sides used proclamations and letters to solicit support or discredit opponents and to appeal to local communities.[51] In physical form and in oral proclamations such documents created charged moments for rebels and populace alike. The law itself treated them as embodiments of the tsar: desecration of tsarist documents was punished as harshly as dishonor to the ruler himself. Accordingly, they were heeded as if the voice of the tsar himself were being heard; incidents around official documents occurred frequently. Rebels often ripped up official proclamations rather than allow them to be read aloud, as happened in Nizhnii Novgorod province in October 1670 when emissaries of Field Commander Dolgorukov were captured. Similarly, in October 1670 a priest reported that he had been taken to the rebels' camp and told to join the rebellion. In response, he read aloud a proclamation he had received from Moscow, urging his parishioners to resist. The cossacks and peasants refused to obey the letter, at which he pronounced anathema on them as he had been instructed. At this, they raised an outcry, threatened to kill him and he barely escaped.[52]

[49] Ostrogozhsk: KV II, pt. 2: no. 20, p. 28. Kurmysh: KV II, pt. 1: no. 218, p. 268. Fabritius says that Stepan Razin called an assembly to judge his captives in Astrakhan: Konovalov, "Ludvig Fabritius's Account," 81–2. Fabritius' share: ibid., 87. Booty is proof: KV III: no. 232, docs. 1, 15, 19, pp. 257, 262–3 (all by Oct. 1672).

[50] Prince L'vov's death: KV III: no. 166, p. 183 (Jan. 1672). Captured at Chernyi Iar in July 1670, Prince L'vov had been pardoned by Razin: KV I: no. 157; no. 162, p. 226 (both July 1670); no. 183, pp. 250–1 (Sept. 1670). On L'vov: Konovalov, "Ludvig Fabritius's Account," 78–9, 82.

[51] Proclamations denying the pretender: KV II, pt. 1: no. 119, p. 141 (Oct. 70); no. 171, p. 203 (Oct. 70); no. 277, p. 341 (Nov. 70); no. 327, p. 412 (Dec. 70). Notifications of Razin's capture and execution June–October 1671: KV III: nos. 53–5, 70, 90, 103, 104 and 117; KV IV: no. 99.

[52] Ulozhenie punishes desecration of tsarist documents: ch. 4 and ch. 10, arts. 11–13: RZ III: 91, 103–4. Nizhnii Novgorod: KV II, pt. 1: no. 100, p. 116. Priest: KV II, pt. 1: no. 124, p. 149. Deference to written documents by the illiterate: Boskovska, "'Dort werden wir'," 365, 385.

The rebels themselves also relied upon the power of oral proclamations from their charismatic leader, Stepan Razin, letters that Moscow labeled "seductive." Razin urged communities to join his battle against the evil boyars, justifying it in the name of the Christian God or the Muslim Allah depending upon the community. Rebels read these proclamations aloud, as in Ostrogozhsk in September 1670 after having killed the town governor and undersecretary, or in November 1670 in the Galich area where sympathetic priests "read aloud on many days" Razin's proclamations. State forces took pains to gather up such letters from conquered territory and send them back to Moscow.[53]

Documents were among the major targets of rebels whenever they took a town. Georg Michels distinguished the violence of the Razin rebellion from more religiously inflected "rites of violence" in the European Reformation by noting that in Muscovy rebellious peasants refrained from ritualistic violence against the bodies of landlords and churchmen or against religious objects. Rather, they focused on the destruction of government and estate records, killing relatively few. Rebels certainly wanted to destroy the information contained in records of indenture, slavery, debts, land purchase and the like. But in view of the particular fear rebels and state troops evince at documents from their enemies, one is tempted also to see here the authority of the embodied voice of power. It is not coincidental that in Muscovy court transcripts and verdicts were read aloud; in uprisings, verdicts on key rebels were also posted and declaimed (Razin's stretches to several pages). All this public proclamation embodied the presence of the tsar.[54]

The power of official words shaped the drama of Astrakhan Metropolitan Iosif's killing. The rebels had controlled the city since July 1670 with great blood-letting, but had not harmed the metropolitan until his fate was caught up in that of documents he possessed. In late 1670 Iosif had received official proclamations addressed to him, to the community and to the rebels, which he was instructed to have read aloud, exhorting all to surrender to the tsar.[55] Iosif ordered at least three copies be made and sent

[53] Ostrogozhsk: KV II, pt. 2: no. 20, p. 28. Galich area: KV II, pt. 1: no. 242, p. 291. Letters collected: KV II, pt. 1: no. 53, p. 65 (Sept. 1670); no. 78, p. 91 (Sept. 1670); no. 207, p. 252 (Nov. 1670); no. 221, p. 270 (Nov. 1670). Letters sent to Moscow: KV II, pt. 1: no. 335 (Dec. 1670); Avrich, *Russian Rebels*, 89, 92–3.

[54] Michels, "Rituals of Violence." Razin verdict: KV III: no. 81 (June 6, 1671); its English version: Man'kov (ed.), *Zapiski*, 102–6 (Anonymous English). Verdicts to others: KV II, pt. 2: nos. 33 and 42–3.

[55] Accounts of his death: KV III: no. 192 (July 1672); nos. 195 and 200–1 (all July 1672); no. 219 (Aug. 1672).

the one addressed to the rebel commanders to them. They refused to accept it. Then Iosif summoned the community and ordered his sacristan to read aloud the proclamation. Hearing it, the rebels raised an outcry and grabbed it from the sacristan, but only after he had finished the reading. To this the metropolitan reacted in anger, calling them traitors and heretics, at which they insulted him, threatening him with death, but in the end only walking off with the document. The next day the rebels arrested and tortured the sacristan, demanding to find all copies of the documents, to no avail.

A few months later, the metropolitan and the rebels had another testy stand-off in Holy Week of April 1672, this time at the marketplace, where the rebels shouted down the metropolitan as he exhorted people to surrender to the tsar's approaching army, citing but not reading the tsar's decrees. The next day, Holy Saturday, the rebels visited the metropolitan several times, demanding that he turn over the copies of the decrees; he countered by reading them aloud in the cathedral. The rebels refused to listen and ran out to the cossack assembly. The feisty Iosif pursued them with a large entourage and ordered two proclamations read aloud, the one addressed to them and the one addressed to him. During this reading at their assembly the cossacks yelled in protest, threatening the metropolitan with arrest and death, while he in turn exhorted the city people to arrest the cossacks instead. The cossacks took one of the proclamations from him, but Iosif refused to yield the one addressed to him personally. On this holy day, the encounter ended up in a stand-off; Iosif returned to hide his document in the cathedral.

During the week after Easter, the cossacks arrested and tortured Iosif's sacristan and staff, demanding to find the hidden documents and their copies. Ultimately they killed the sacristan without finding the documents, and they followed up by demanding that the metropolitan sign a letter of loyalty to Razin. Iosif refused. On May 11 they interrupted him at liturgy and when he chastised them, they withdrew. Typically, Iosif followed them to their assembly, where the rebels, having crossing a line they had not before, taunted him, seized him and dragged him off to torture and eventually to his death. Throughout, Iosif's authority multiplied as he embodied the voice of the tsar; the physical document and its oral declamation struck fear in this oral culture. Iosif's stubborn insistence on speaking the tsar's words sealed his fate.

The rebels observed some cossack tradition in their treatment of Iosif: they gathered in assembly to discuss whether to arrest him or not. But this was only pro forma: a cossack who protested killing a churchman was himself summarily killed. The audacity of the metropolitan's execution is striking; he was the highest-ranking church official killed by the rebels. The eyewitness description by two cathedral priests who stood by Iosif's side in these fateful days is full of poignant detail: when the metropolitan realized that the cossacks would not back down, he took steps to protect the dignity of his office. He removed his sacred garments and cross, to the anguish of the accompanying priests. Dressed in a simple robe, he was led to horrible torture – suspended on a spit over a fire. The rebels badgered him to reveal the location of the letters and of his treasure. After torture, the rebels pushed Iosif off the tower to his death. Sympathetic eyewitnesses record that when his body fell, a hush fell over the whole town and even rebel cossacks were speechless, hanging their heads in silence. The rebels soon thereafter dragged the remaining priests of the cathedral to their assembly and forced them to sign loyalty notes to them; frightened, they did so. Written documents embodied their authors, and their proclamation by charismatic figures like Iosif brought the tsar to life, making the bearers of these words too threatening.

Iosif's shocking execution perhaps did not have the effect that the rebels expected – there was neither rejoicing nor improvement in the rebels' weakening grasp on Astrakhan. Executions could alienate communities as well as reassure or strike fear, and Muscovite officials worked to ensure that their executions of rebels produced the latter effects. In the heat of repression, mass numbers were killed to strike terror in local communities. After hostilities waned, some rebel leaders were executed with more attention, locally and in Moscow. In September 1670, for example, a priest and several cossack ringleaders from Ostrogozhsk were sent to Moscow for trial; they were convicted and executed there by quartering on October 3. The record notes laconically that some were executed at "the Swamp" and others by the Iauza gates to the Vladimir road. The verdict read aloud at the execution is preserved; in it the convicted men were pointedly reminded that their compatriots were being executed in the same way at the same time on the Volga.[56] By executing some in Moscow, the state broadcast to the political classes and foreigners its ability to put down rebellion. Even greater theatrical effect was used for the most dangerous rival of all, the rebellion's leader, Stepan Razin.

[56] Ostrogozhsk rebels: KV II, pt. 2: nos. 33 and 42–3.

CHAPTER 17

Moral economies: spectacle and sacrifice

When Stepan Razin was brought to Moscow in 1671 after two years of leading a bloody insurrection, an English eyewitness recorded the sight:

> today hee was brought to the place of execution where after a long scrowle read of all his Roguerry from the yeare 1663 to his being taken, sentence of death was pronounced against him, and soe presently brought to the blocke which was in the open place beefore the castle, and there hee had his armes, his leggs, and then his head cut off which were presently sett up upon 5 poles, the trunke of his body left upon the earth to bee eaten by the doggs – a fitt death for such a villaine.

In 1682, on the other hand, the violence was in the hands of the people, as bloodthirsty crowds of musketeers streamed into the Kremlin:

> They seized boyar Artemon Sergeevich Matveev from the tsar himself and threw him to the ground, and catching him on pikes, they cut him up into pieces with their halberds. Boyar Prince Grigorii Grigor′evich Romodanovskii they found at the patriarch's palace and took him out on the square in front of the chanceries and cut him up with halberds and stabbed him with pikes. Boyar Prince Mikhail Iur′evich Dolgorukov, caught in the vestibule, they cut up on the Beautiful Staircase.[1]

This chapter examines these obverse sides of violence – the exemplary violence of state-sanctioned executions and the rough justice of the crowd – for each type of violence not only demonstrates legal practices and principles common to all, but also exposes the very foundations of the legitimacy of the state.

EXEMPLARY EXECUTIONS

When Muscovy had the highest of criminals to execute, it staged horrific ceremonies. The ceremonies paralleled executions for felony crime in their

[1] Konovalov, "Razin's Execution," 98 (Martius). PSRL XXXI: 174 (1682). The "Beautiful" or "Red" (*krasnyi*) Staircase led down one flight from the palace to Cathedral Square.

speed and efficiency, but all was intensified: publicity, pain and violence. Less theatrical than their European counterparts, they nevertheless communicated both the tsar's awesome power to punish and his solicitous ability to protect his people from harm. Three executions of the highest traitors in the mid seventeenth century demonstrate how Muscovy mobilized symbolic violence.

The pretender Timoshka Ankudinov was brought to the block in Moscow in 1653. He had initially claimed to be an eminent Russian boyar and ultimately to be the son (sometimes grandson) of Tsar Vasilii Shuiskii (who in reality had no surviving sons). Ankudinov had led a storied and adventurous life, fleeing Russia in 1643 when charged with theft of state funds and the murder of his wife; he traveled among the courts of Poland, Moldova, Wallachia, Constantinople, Rome, Khemelnytskii's Hetmanate, Sweden and elsewhere, seeking patrons and favor. His compatriot Konstantin Koniukhovskii was captured in 1652 in Revel (Estonia), Timoshka himself in Holstein in 1653. Koniukhovskii was brought to Moscow in grotesque procession. He walked at the head of a long parade, bound in chains; an iron ring circled his neck, from which hung a heavy chain to his waist, which was belted in iron. His hands were tied behind his back and thick ropes were attached to his neckpiece and hands, dragging behind him. Alongside him an armed guard walked and a chancery secretary on a white horse rode, calling out "Orthodox people! Look here! Here is the traitor to the sovereign, to the grand prince, to his tsarist eminence. Here is the evildoer and betrayer of the Russian land, our beloved fatherland. Here is the accursed heretic, a pagan. Here is the abominable and evil heretic." Crowds lined the streets and followed the procession. Koniukhovskii was led to the Foreign Affairs Chancery, where he was subjected to harsh interrogation and torture including knouting with excruciating weights and shaking, fire and hot pincers. Ultimately, he was confined to the Kremlin Chudov Monastery, on the promise of forgiveness if he confessed, which he ultimately did.

Within a year, the pretender Timoshka was captured. Sent to Moscow, Timoshka Ankudinov played the role of Tsar Shuiskii's son to the hilt. Immediately brought to torture, he refused to talk unless in the presence of the highest boyars. After two days of torture with no result, he was taken to Red Square, where five wheels elevated on posts had been prepared in advance. After his sentence was read aloud, he was quartered: they removed most of his clothing, axed off his right arm to the elbow and left leg to the knee; then the left arm and right leg in the same way, then the head. These five body parts were mounted on the wheels for a day, while the torso was cast to the ground for the dogs. The next day all the bodily remains were gathered, the wheels dismantled and all was taken off to a garbage trench outside of town; Ankudinov was declared an anathema and went to his grave unblessed. Koniukhovskii was brought to witness the execution and then sent into exile with three fingers cut off his left hand. Olearius reported that on the day of the execution a Polish diplomat was driven by the site to ensure that he would report back to Poland and Europe that the "false Shuiskii" had been killed.[2]

Here, Moscow's spectacle of execution terrorized the populace in ways different from such executions in Western Europe – all was done promptly, only a single victim was executed, the physical space was not as elaborate, there is no mention of viewing stands for city fathers and other dignitaries. But the government's goals were accomplished: some of the few foreign diplomats in Moscow at the time assured Europe of Russia's stability, while the Russian public was informed of the capture of a perfidious traitor. His humiliating treatment dispelled sympathy for Ankudinov; the reading of the sentence legitimized state justice; the exposure of body parts delegitimized the pretender. The spectacle was frightening in its brutality (no more brutal than its European counterparts) and speed.

This spectacle was particularly violent because quartering – severing limbs and head – had rarely been cited in Muscovy; when it had been used, it was applied to treason broadly defined. Chronicles report that in 1491/2 of a group of six men, "traitors," some were quartered, some beheaded. Foreign accounts report quartering during the Oprichnina, and it is also cited in 1629 as punishment for the "treason" of killing one's landlord.[3] Just after Ankudinov's execution, in June 1654 another traitor was quartered. Tsar Aleksei Mikhailovich himself reported the incident in letters home from the Smolensk campaign. A Smolensk gentryman Vasilii Mikhailov syn Neelov had been caught on the border; he admitted in interrogation that he was headed to the Polish king with information about Russian troops. The tsar himself arrived on the scene and personally ordered "the traitor Vaska Neelov quartered"; the execution is not described. As noted above, punishments amounting to quartering abounded in response to the 1662 rebellion and its aftermath; it was used in the reprisals against Razin's rebels in 1670–1.[4] It appears to have

2 Solov'ev, "Timoshka Ankidinov," 14: 20–1; Olearius, "Podrobnoe opisanie," 253–6 (1656 edn.); Longworth, "Ankidinov, Timoshka"; S. Tr., "Ankudinov, Timoshka"; Perrie, *Pretenders*, 233.

3 1491/2: PSRL IV, pt. 1: 530–1 (7000). AMG 1: no. 259 (1629).

4 Neelov: *Pis'ma russkikh gosudarei*, II, pp. 2–3. 1662 and Razin: see Chapter 16. Brutal decree: PSZ 1: no. 334 (1663); rescinded PSZ 1: no. 383 (1666).

been limited to men of lower rank: in the seventeenth century five men of boyar clan or similarly high rank – Shein, two Khovanskie, Bezobrazov and Shaklovityi – were beheaded, not quartered (see Chapter 15).

Stepan Razin's execution in 1671 and that in 1674 of another pretender (Ivashko Vorob′ev, an adolescent captured in the restive Don–Volga area who claimed to be Tsarevich Semen Alekseevich) expanded on Ankudinov's 1653 ritual. Familiar elements were included – speedy torture, humiliating procession, reading of verdict, public quartering, display of body parts. In the 1670s cases, theatricality was heightened. The sparse commentary in Russian documents that Razin was "sentenced and executed with an evil death, quartering . . . before all the people on the Square" is supplemented by European eyewitness accounts, as well as the lengthy verdict read to him. European witnesses noted not only the violence of the execution but also the emotional behavior of the condemned. Even more interestingly, the official Russian description of Vorob′ev's 1674 execution survives – unique in its detail before the time of Peter I.[5]

Stepan Razin was hunted down in the Don region by cossacks loyal to Moscow; Ataman Kornelei Iakovlev brought him up the Don and Volga with heavily armed escorts provided by Aleksei Mikhailovich, reaching the capital in April 1671. Razin and the pretender Ivashko in 1674 were each met outside the city and brought into Moscow in procession in a cart so high that "all could see." One Russian eyewitness account of Razin describes that they "brought him . . . along Tver′ Street in a cart, fixed with a raised platform where he was standing, tied up in a cross form, his arms and legs shackled, and above his head opposite his face hung a hangman's noose." In the cart also "sat many musketeers armed with halberds." Razin's brother Frol, in chains and tied to the cart, walked alongside. There is no mention of their carrying candles or of a priest on the scene.[6]

One contemporary English account says that when Razin was transferred to the cart at the gates of Moscow, he was forced to disrobe from

[5] Russian sources: KV III: no. 81, p. 87 and no. 103 (both June 1671). Foreign accounts: Man′kov (ed.), *Zapiski* (Anonymous English); Konovalov, "Razin's Execution." Razin verdict: KV III: no. 81 (June 1671); its English version: Man′kov (ed.), *Zapiski*, 102–6 (Anonymous English). Pretender execution: KV III: no. 273 (1674); also published AI IV: no. 247. Vorob′ev: Perrie, *Pretenders*, 237–8.

[6] Razin to Moscow: KV III: no. 57 and nos. 71–3, p. 76 (all May 1671). Razin's cart: KV IV: no. 66 (May 1671); Man′kov (ed.), *Zapiski*, 100 (Anonymous English); Reitenfels, *Skazaniia*, 119; Konovalov, "Razin's Execution," 95 (Martius), 97–8 (Hebdon). Vorob′ev's procession: KV III: no. 273, p. 337.

his "silken" clothing and don "an old ragged sute"; in 1674 the pretender Vorob′ev was clothed in a rough black wool robe, white stockings and soldier's boots. In neither case are special robes for the occasion mentioned. Each man was accompanied by hundreds of armed guards, regiments of cossacks, and musketeers with "flying colors." Crowds lined the streets to watch. No words by Razin are recorded; in 1674 Vorob′ev was accompanied in the cart by four armed musketeers who forbade him to talk at all.[7]

Razin was brought immediately to a brutal torture session on June 2; rumor had it that he revealed nothing and showed no pain. Tsar Aleksei Mikhailovich himself contributed interrogation questions for the boyar judges on three topics: the taking of Astrakhan, Patriarch Nikon and Razin's contacts with foreign rulers. The pretender Vorob′ev's torture in 1674 was described as less brutal, and he readily admitted to his imposture. All men of conciliar rank had been ordered to attend the session; they compiled a report that was immediately taken to the tsar. He handed down a death sentence and that same day Vorob′ev was executed. In 1671 Razin was also condemned the same day as his first torture but was kept for four more days of interrogation.[8]

In each case, preparations for execution had been made in Red Square. Sharpened poles had been erected for display of severed body parts for Razin and his brother; for the pretender, a podium for the reading of the sentence. Several foreign accounts of Razin's execution report that foreigners were specifically invited to watch; Reutenfels observed that the common people were held at bay by three rows of soldiers and that only foreigners were allowed near the execution spot. A contemporary German newspaper account, perhaps with poetic license, alleges that they stood so close they were "splashed with blood."[9]

Both executions were preceded by reading of a lengthy verdict legitimizing state justice. Russian accounts do not describe the condemned men's behavior, and foreign accounts differ on that of Razin. An anonymous English account reports that Razin gazed at a nearby church, bowed three

[7] Razin's clothing, demeanor: Man′kov (ed.), *Zapiski*, 100 (Anonymous English); Man′kov (ed.), *Inostrannye izvestiia*, 122 (German newspaper). Pretender's clothing: KV III: no. 273, p. 337.

[8] Razin's torture: Man′kov (ed.), *Zapiski*, 100 (Anonymous English); Reitenfels, *Skazaniia*, 119; Konovalov, "Razin's Execution," 96 (Martius), 98 (Hebdon). Tsar's questions: KV III: no. 77 (June 1671); Buganov, *Razin i razintsy*, 117–30. Pretender's verdict: KV III: no. 273, p. 338. Four days: Konovalov, "Razin's Execution," 98 (Hebdon); KV IV: no. 66, p. 61 (May 1671).

[9] Poles: KV IV: no. 66 (May 1671). Podium: KV III: no. 273, p. 338. Foreigners attend: Reitenfels, *Skazaniia*, 119; Man′kov (ed.), *Inostrannye izvestiia*, 123 (German newspaper).

times to the crowd, said "forgive me" and submitted to quartering, uttering no cries of pain. Reutenfels also reports that he crossed himself and submitted to the axe. But, contradicting these accounts of a "good death," Martius says that Razin did nothing to prepare himself for his death and made hateful gestures in anger and resistance. A German newspaper colorfully put defiant words in his mouth: "You think that you killed Razin but you did not seize the real one and there are many more Razins who will avenge my death."[10] No description mentions religious counsel, which Russian criminal law prescribed and which foreigners would have expected, indicating most likely that the state intended this criminal to a die an anathema.

Frol Razin, Stepan's brother, was spared execution by claiming to have further knowledge of treason (claiming a "word and deed" case); he was eventually executed in May 1676. Stepan Razin and the pretender were both quartered. A Russian eyewitness account reports that "they led him from the Moscow Administrative Chancery and executed him at the fire on the square, they quartered him."[11] Their five severed body parts were displayed on pikes; sources indicate that eventually Stepan Razin's were moved across the river to "the Swamp" and kept on display – "for a year" in one account, "until they rotted away" in another. They stayed on display for at least two years; the verdict for pretender Vorob′ev in 1674 specified that after three days his displayed body parts were to be moved to "the Swamp" to join those of Razin. Razin's torso was tossed "to the dogs," while Vorob′ev's was tossed in a ravine outside of town. Absent the usual mention of confession and communion and with such desecration and display of the body, these men went to their deaths anathematized.[12]

These executions from 1653 to 1674 are as theatrical as any observed so far in Muscovy. The judicial process was done with terrifying speed, the execution rituals with publicity and symbolism in the center of the capital city. Crowds were assembled along the path of the victims and at the place

[10] Razin faces death: Man′kov (ed.), *Zapiski*, 101 (Anonymous English); Reitenfels, *Skazaniia*, 119; Konovalov, "Razin's Execution," 96 (Martius); Man′kov (ed.), *Inostrannye izvestiia*, 130 (German newspaper).

[11] Frol's fate: Avrich, *Russian Rebels*, 113; Man′kov (ed.), *Inostrannye izvestiia*, 74, n. 43; KV III: no. 85, p. 94 (June 1671). Tikhomirov, "Zapiski prikaznykh liudei," 446; "the fire" refers to Red Square in 1554/5: PSRL XXXI: 133 (7063) and 1634: PSRL XXXI: 161.

[12] Razin's body: KV III: no. 291, pp. 365–6 (*c.*1676); Tikhomirov, "Zapiski prikaznykh liudei," 446. Foreigners report seeing Razin's body parts still on display in February 1676: Buganov, *Razin i razintsy*, 319. Pretender's body: KV III: no. 273, p. 339 (Sept. 1674). Capture and execution of Razin in Russian documents: KV III: nos. 52–7 (April–May 1671), 70–3 (May–June 1671), 90 (June 1671), 103 (June 1671), 104 (June 1671), 117 (July 1671); KV IV: no. 99 (Oct. 1671).

of execution, the condemned were presented in chains in carts whose equipment was redolent of the terror of execution, bodies were desecrated, their parts displayed for years. It was a conscious and violent display of expulsion from the community.

Not only the state wielded violence to punish righteously. When Muscovy's populace believed the government had been so abusive as to require the tsar's personal intervention, it responded by calling him to act on the moral economy implicit in Muscovy's patrimonial ideology. The crowd's public and symbolic use of violence, sanctioned by a sense of righteousness, led to bloody suffering and heart-rending sacrifices.

SYMBOLIC VIOLENCE AND MORAL ECONOMY

Moscow's seventeenth-century urban uprisings unfolded as a ritual drama between the ruler and the people, a drama that acted out and tested the tsar's legitimacy. As powerful as the tsar claimed to be, his legitimacy was based on popular expectations that he be pious, render justice, succor the poor and respond to his people. In normal times the tsar took advice from churchmen and boyars; in normal times people submitted petitions seeking his "favor"; normally, the tsar's government was responsive enough, and the people sufficiently accepting of their dependent status, that violence did not erupt.[13] Violence bubbled up when abuse was too great, taxation and service too burdensome, and government too unresponsive. At such times the tsar himself could be compelled to interact with the people, playing the role of mediator and judge, as the crowd invoked traditional rights to petition and claim face-to-face interaction with the sovereign as father figure. He responded in kind, in several instances meeting directly with the crowd, chiding the people, reassuring them, acquiescing to their demands, as events unfolded in each case.

Such symbolic drama played out in the 1662 "copper riots," when the crowd streamed from Moscow to Kolomenskoe, the tsar's suburban estate, demanding relief from hard times and presenting a list of corrupt officials and merchants in quasi-legal petitionary interaction. But the crowd, according to Patrick Gordon (on the scene and perhaps an eyewitness), violated the implicit pact of petitioning by being noisy and impatient as it approached Tsar Aleksei Mikhailovich as he was "comeing

[13] Petitionary order: Kivelson, "Muscovite 'Citizenship'," "Devil Stole His Mind" and *Cartographies*; Rowland, "Problem of Advice," "Did Muscovite Literary Ideology" and "Muscovy"; Pokrovskii, *Tomsk*; Davies, *State Power*, ch. 5; Kollmann, *By Honor Bound*, 199.

out of the church and getting to horseback." A Moscow townsman, Luchko Zhitkoi, handed him a letter humbly tucked into his hat. (This motif also appears in the satirical Tale Shemiaka's Judgment, where a crafty peasant presents his hat in such a way that the judge believes a bribe is enclosed in it.) Kotoshikhin even reports that "the people were talking with the tsar and grabbed the buttons of his robe and asked 'whom should we believe?' And the tsar promised them before God and gave his hand to them on his word, and many in the crowd clasped the tsar's hand."[14] The tsar rebuked the crowd for its unruliness, but "told them that their grievances should be redressed." No other source gives such a remarkable detail as a commoner seizing a tsar by his buttons, doubting his word and shaking his hand; the image crystallizes the tsar's deep embeddedness in the terms of the ideology. The tsar met his people face to face in other instances of political crisis as well. Fourteen years earlier, in 1648, crowds had also walked right up to Tsar Aleksei Mikhailovich in the Kremlin as he was walking to and from church; in 1682 they barged into the tsars' living quarters. All the while the charisma of the ruling family protected him from harm. Unruly crowds also treated the tsar's womenfolk as untouchable – in 1648 rioting crowds spared the tsar's sister-in-law from harm; in 1662 the tsar advised his boyars to hide in the women's quarters, presumably the safest place; in 1682 the mother and sisters of the young tsars repeatedly met in person with the mob and were not harmed.[15] The ruler's special status protected him and his immediate family, but imposed upon him the responsibility of response, even to heart-wrenching sacrifices.

Those sacrifices were first encountered in the heated days of June 2–5, 1648. After being rebuffed from petitioning to the tsar outside of Moscow on June 1, an angry crowd streamed into the Kremlin on June 2 demanding that the tsar meet personally with it – no substitutes would do. They were incensed at the corruption of the faction of Boris Ivanovich Morozov, Aleksei Mikhailovich's brother-in-law and his "former major-domo and tutor" (in Olearius's words). Typical for Muscovite politics, Morozov's clique was cemented by marriage: Petr Trakhaniotov, head of the Artillery Chancery, was married to Morozov's sister; Levontii Pleshcheev, head of the Moscow Administrative Chancery, was married

14 Hat motif: Bulgakova, *Povest' o sude Shemiaki*, 20. Crowd in Kolomenskoe: Gordon, *Diary*, II: 160; Russian translation: Gordon, *Dnevnik*, 119; Zertsalov, "O miatezhakh v gorode Moskve," 298; Kotoshikhin, *O Rossii*, 102; Löwe, "Der Moskauer Kupfergeldaufstand."

15 1648 sister-in-law: Olearius, *Travels*, 208. 1662 women's quarters: Kotoshikhin, *O Rossii*, 102.

to Trakhaniotov's sister; the tsar himself and Boris Morozov had married Miloslavskii sisters.[16] The crowd demanded all three – Morozov, Trakhaniotov and Pleshcheev.

Levontii Pleshcheev had been repeatedly petitioned against for corruption and abuse of power – false arrest, false torture, extortion – but he had always escaped punishment, protected by Morozov. When the crowd streamed into the Kremlin on June 2, they demanded Pleshcheev, accosting the tsar as he was leaving the palace for church, then again as he was walking back from church. During his dinner, as the crowd grew to "several thousand," Aleksei Mikhailovich sent out his boyars to calm them, but one was injured by the crowd's rough treatment. The tsar himself then stepped onto the "Beautiful Porch" attached to the palace overlooking Cathedral Square to meet with the crowd; it screamed for Pleshcheev. Aleksei Mikhailovich promised to investigate and punish the boyar if appropriate, requesting a day's time to investigate. (One foreign source suggests that the tsar was trying to save Pleshcheev's life by stalling.[17]) The crowd granted him a day, but it proceeded to rampage, plunder and kill throughout the afternoon and night, discovering and killing State Secretary Nazarii Chistoi at his home. The next morning, June 3, 1648, the crowd approached the Kremlin a second time, demanding Pleshcheev. Even though they were locked out at the gates, the threat was immense. The tsar released Pleshcheev to the crowd.

Clothing his action with legitimacy, Aleksei Mikhailovich sent Pleshcheev out accompanied by a few musketeers, a priest and an executioner, as if Pleshcheev were being escorted to Red Square for a legal execution. But the crowd pounced on Pleshcheev and "dracked him on the market place, where they cuggelld him so black and blew and with axes they cut him asunder like a fish, the pieces they let lye nacked here & there." Later that day, as arson spread through the town, someone severed the head and tossed it into a fire, while others dragged the remainder of the body into the flames.[18]

The tsar's yielding Pleshcheev was different from the riotous violence of the day and night. It followed rules understood better by the crowd and the tsar than by foreign observers. A Swedish eyewitness, for example, records that the tsar "yielded to the demand of the crowd unwillingly and

[16] Majordomo: Olearius, *Travels*, 203. Kinship links: Olearius, *Travels*, 205. Olearius, last in Russia in 1643, continued to gather information for the expanded 1656 edition of his *Travels*.

[17] Tsar stalls: Bazilevich (ed.), *Gorodskie vosstaniia*, 54 (Anonymous Swede).

[18] Pleshcheev's death: Bazilevich (ed.), *Gorodskie vosstaniia*, 54–6 (Anonymous Swede) and 36 (Pommerening). Quote from Leyden pamphlet: Loewenson, "Moscow Rising," 154.

against his own wishes," as indeed he probably did. But, however unwillingly, Aleksei Mikhailovich understood his obligations and acquiesced in this bloody drama, giving Pleshcheev to the crowd "by the head" (*golovoiu*) in the words of Russian sources. To give a person "by the head" was a legal transaction putting someone in complete subjugation to another; the phrase was used when a murderer of a serf was given to the victim's landlord in compensation, or when a person sold himself into slavery, or when a boyar underwent a ritual of humiliation.[19] Furthermore, Russian sources in this instance and repeatedly in their descriptions of the riots specify that the crowd acted "*mirom*," that is, as a whole community. Invoking the power of the community assembled to protest injustice, the crowd transformed this exchange from uncontrolled violence into righteous dialogue.[20]

Pleshcheev's death on the second day did not end this bloody ritual drama between tsar and people; the crowd continued to demand Trakhaniotov and Morozov. The tsar asked for two days longer, and while fires broke out all across town on the afternoon of the second day, June 3, the tsar attempted to save Trakhaniotov by sending him "in exile" to a low-level governorship. Trakhaniotov left on the night of June 3–4, but the situation became so threatening that the tsar sent for his return. Emissaries caught up with Trakhaniotov near the Trinity Monastery, where he had requested sanctuary. Frightened of bringing the crowd down on them, the monks offered him only confession and communion and sent him back to Moscow.[21]

The tsar again agreed to give his boyar to the crowd, but this time he achieved a greater semblance of legality. The tsar announced that Trakhaniotov had been sentenced to beheading for treason and for inciting the arson of June 3 (rumors had alleged this). The crowd escorted the party to Red Square, where an official executioner beheaded Trakhaniotov on June 5; his head was left "on his chest for all to see for a day," reminiscent of earlier displays of body parts by official courts and rebels alike. One Russian source treats this as a proper state-sanctioned execution, saying simply that Trakhaniotov "was executed." But another

19 Against his wishes: Bazilevich (ed.), *Gorodskie vosstaniia*, 56 (Anonymous Swede). *Golovoiu*: ibid., 74 (Tolstoi *sbornik*) and 77 (*Novyi letopisets*); SRIa IV: 62 and 3: 196–7. Rituals of humiliation: Kollmann, "Ritual and Social Drama."

20 *Mirom*: Bazilevich (ed.), *Gorodskie vosstaniia*, 74 (Tolstoi *sbornik*), 76 (Pskov I), 79 (*Letopis' o mnogikh miatezhakh*). As all the people (*vsem narodom*): ibid., 77.

21 Trakhaniotov leaves Moscow: Bazilevich (ed.), *Gorodskie vosstaniia*, 75 (Tolstoi *sbornik*). Trakhaniotov tracked down: ibid., 36 (Pommerening); 58 (Anonymous Swede); 79–81 (Azar'in).

Russian source sees this merely as crowd violence: "he was killed at the Moscow Administrative Office by the common people (*chernye liudi*)."[22] Twice already Tsar Aleksei Mikhailovich had acquiesced to the sacrifice of one of his own men to assuage the crowd.

The ritual drama was not complete, however, until the fate of Boris Ivanovich Morozov was settled. On June 2 his house was the rioting crowd's first target; on June 5 they demanded his head along with Trakhaniotov's. The dilemma was clearly excruciating for Tsar Aleksei Mikhailovich: Swedish Resident Pommerening reports that "it is said that the tsar told them it would be better to kill him [the tsar] than to kill Morozov."[23] On the third day, June 5, as the crowd demanded Trakhaniotov and Morozov, three times the tsar sent out the patriarch and his own father confessor and some boyars to plead for Morozov, but in vain. Finally Aleksei Mikhailovich appeared himself "with uncovered head and in tears" and beseeched the crowd to spare this man so beloved to him. The crowd was reaching the limits of its patience: a Swedish eyewitness reports that the crowd's mood was such that "they were ready to consider even his tsarist majesty a traitor" until he had satisfied them concerning Morozov. Several sources report that the tsar himself took an oath, kissing a cross or an icon (accounts differ) held by the patriarch, promising to banish Morozov from public life. Only then did the crowd accept his terms and the uprisings were calmed; Morozov was spirited out of the Kremlin in the early hours of June 12, exiled "according to the petitions of the common people."[24] The tsar bought peace with the sacrifice of two of his closest confidants, saving only one of the crowd's three targets.

Violence in 1648 in Moscow was replete with symbolism: the crowd's streaming into the Kremlin and accosting the tsar himself demonstrated the popular belief in the tsar's accountability to the people; the burning of Pleshcheev's body can be seen as a ritual purifying fire, the ransacking of boyar homes, a ritual expulsion from the community. The tsar's

[22] Beheaded by tsar's order: Bazilevich (ed.), *Gorodskie vosstaniia*, 75 (Tolstoi *sbornik*), 36 (Pommerening). Executed, using same terms as official sources (*kaznisha, kaznili*): ibid., 79 (*Letopis' o mnogikh miatezhakh*), 79 (Chronograph). Crowd violence: ibid., 81 (Azar'in).

[23] Pommerening: Bazilevich (ed.), *Gorodskie vosstaniia*, 6; see also Zertsalov, "K istorii miatezha 1648 goda," 33–6.

[24] Crowd's mood: Bazilevich (ed.), *Gorodskie vosstaniia*, 57–8 (Anonymous Swede). Interaction with the crowd on Morozov: ibid., 57 and 74 (Tolstoi *sbornik*); Loewenson, "Moscow Rising," 155 (Leyden pamphlet). Morozov spared: quote from *Novyi letopisets*: Bazilevich (ed.), *Gorodskie vosstaniia*, 77; see also ibid., 58–9 (Anonymous Swede), 37 (Pommerening), 75 (Tolstoi *sbornik*); Loewenson, "Moscow Rising," 155–6. Despite the tsar's promise, Morozov returned to power in October 1648.

astounding acquiescence in the sacrifice of his own men acted out the moral economy of patrimonial tsardom.[25] That this was not an isolated instance of senseless violence is confirmed by the repetition of this ritual drama in 1682.

In 1682 the situation unfolded in the tense days after Tsar Fedor Alekseevich died (April 27) and factions around Aleksei Mikhailovich's two wives (the Miloslavskie and Naryshkiny) jockeyed for power. Initially the Naryshkiny succeeded in declaring nine-year-old Peter the tsar, but others supported the Miloslavskii faction and the feeble-minded fifteen-year-old Ioann (represented by his sister Sofiia). As in 1648, the unrest was enabled in part by the absence of Kremlin guards, an indicator of how deeply the inviolability of the person of the tsar was inculcated. Even by the 1680s there was apparently no fixed palace guard; the responsibility was shared among various chanceries and overseen by the tsar's Privy Chancery.[26] In 1682, armed musketeers flooded into the Kremlin with minimal resistance. Danish diplomat von Gorn, reporting hearsay but well informed, declared that the guard on duty that day opened the gates to the musketeers, while Andrei Artamonovich Matveev, in the palace at the time, related that orders to lock the gates came too late. Contemporary eyewitness accounts eerily echo the 1648 events. All report that the musketeers – four regiments accompanied by as many as 4,000 soldiers, by one account[27] – entered the Kremlin heavily armed, with drumming and banners. Some depict them marching in disciplined battle formation, while others describe a chaotic scene. The German merchant Butenant reported that the musketeers brought a list of forty boyars and officials targeted for death; the Military Service Chancery's later report listed twenty individuals, all musketeer commanders or associates of the Naryshkin faction.[28] The worst of the rioting took place over three days, as in 1648.

[25] Symbolism of the riot: Stepan Roller-Assfalg, "Der Moskauer Aufstand."

[26] Peter was born May 30, 1672; Ioann on August 27, 1666. 1682 riots: see Chapter 16. Kremlin guard: Gurliand, *Prikaz velikogo gosudaria*, 221–2. Kotoshikhin, writing in 1666, related that the *Stremiannyi* musketeer regiment guarded the ruling family on trips out of town: Kotoshikhin, *O Rossii*, 90. Earlier associated with the palace, by the end of the seventeenth century, the musketeers (*strel'tsy*) were Moscow city police.

[27] Palace gates: Bogdanov, "Glazami," 86 (von Gorn); Matveev, "Zapiski," 19–20. 4,000 musketeers: Bogdanov, "Glazami," 86.

[28] Disciplined formations: Bogdanov, "Glazami," 86; Bogdanov, "Podennye," 35; Medvedev, "Sozertsanie kratkoe," 52. Chaotic scene: PSRL XXXI: 174 (Mazurin); Keep, "Mutiny," 422; PSRL XXXI: 193 (1691 chronicle); Matveev, "Zapiski," 19; *Vosstanie v Moskve 1682 g.*, no. 207, pp. 276–7. Butenant's list: Keep, "Mutiny," 423. Chancery list: *Vosstanie v Moskve 1682 g.*, no. 207, p. 277.

When they first stormed into the Kremlin on May 15, 1682, the musketeers secured the gates to prevent their boyar targets from leaving; informed in advance, they had arrived precisely when the boyars were assembled in the palace. Various regiments had been suing their colonels for abuse and corruption for several months, with unsatisfactory results; therefore, as the Dutch resident von Keller had reported in April 1682, the musketeers' anger was turning against the colonels' boyar protectors. Danish ambassador von Gorn depicts the musketeers sending emissaries to the boyars' meeting with complaints against their officers and, when they were put off, raising the call to "save Ioann Alekseevich." Their cry reflects rumors, likely spread by the Naryshkiny's rivals, that this faction was plotting to harm Tsarevich Ioann Alekseevich and may even have poisoned the recently deceased Tsar Fedor Alekseevich. Rioting for this reason would have seemed justified, since protecting the person of the tsar would be considered just cause for such popular uprising.[29]

As in 1648, those in charge ventured out to the porch at the "Beautiful Staircase" to speak to the crowd: various boyars, the patriarch and, most importantly, some of the women of the ruling family. Those female relatives included two daughters of Mikhail Fedorovich, seven daughters of Aleksei Mikhailovich by his two wives, his widow Tsaritsa Nataliia Kirillovna Naryshkina, her mother, and the widow of the recently deceased Tsar Fedor Alekseevich, Marfa Matveevna Apraksina.[30] Accounts differ on exactly who went out to placate the crowd – a late 1683 Military Service Chancery account lists four boyars (Prince M. A. Cherkasskii, Prince I. A. Khovanskii, P. V. Sheremetev Bol′shoi and Prince V. V. Golitsyn); Medvedev writing soon thereafter mentions only the patriarch; a 1691 chronicle cites in turn the boyars Prince I. A. Khovanskii and Petr Mikhailovich Saltykov and the patriarch.[31] But the musketeers insisted on seeing Tsarevich Ioann Alekseevich. Bravely, the Kremlin women walked out with fifteen-year-old Ioann and nine-year-old Peter. The German Butenant heard that Sofiia Alekseevna and the widow Marfa Apraksina took the lead, while the

[29] Informed in advance: Keep, "Mutiny" 82; Buganov, *Moskovskie vosstaniia*, 144–6. Musketeers sue colonels: Belov, "Pis′ma," 381 (von Keller); Bogdanov, "Glazami," 86 (von Gorn). Protect Ioann: Keep, "Mutiny," 422; Buganov, "Novyi istochnik," 323–4; Medvedev, "Sozertsanie kratkoe," 52–3; PSRL XXXI: 189–90, 193 (1691 chronicle); Matveev, "Zapiski," 19–20; *Vosstanie v Moskve 1682 g.*, no. 207, p. 277; Bogdanov, "Glazami," 86–7.

[30] Kremlin women enumerated in the Military Service Chancery's post-Sept. 1683 report: *Vosstanie v Moskve 1682 g.*, no. 204, pp. 256–7, 259.

[31] Boyars: *Vosstanie v Moskve 1682 g.*, no. 207, p. 277; Medvedev, "Sozertsanie kratkoe," 52–3; PSRL XXXI: 193 (1691 chronicle).

1691 chronicle reports that Nataliia Naryshkina led them out. The pro-Miloslavskii Sil′vestr Medvedev adds Tsarevna Sofiia Alekseevna and the patriarch. Boyars and officials followed, but it was Nataliia Naryshkina who engaged in conversation with the musketeers; Matveev, in the palace at the time, marveled at how impudently the crowd asked Tsarevich Ioann whether he had been harmed.[32]

Despite seeing Ioann and Peter alive and healthy and conversing with various boyars and the patriarch, the crowd was not appeased. Something set them off, although they were certainly already primed for violence; German merchant Butenant reports that the musketeers had rung the tocsin to summon others. Most sources suggest that the boyars' haughty attitude to the crowd angered it. These riots were more violent than those of 1648: the musketeers streamed all the way into the Kremlin palace searching for victims. Yet, as in 1648, they left the charismatic figures – rulers, clerics and women – unscathed. In several face-to-face encounters, Ioann and Peter, the patriarch and the royal women may have been terribly frightened, but they were not harmed. Medvedev even colorfully describes how the patriarch shooed the musketeers out of his palace and cathedral, declaring sternly that he was "harboring no traitors."[33]

Once the crowd was set off, it turned murderous. Musketeers stormed the group assembled on the veranda, grabbed and killed Artamon Sergeevich Matveev, childhood guardian of Nataliia Naryshkina, in full sight of Nataliia and her son Peter. They swarmed through the palace rooms and churches, discovering boyars and officials hiding under altars, in closets or caught unawares. They tossed them to the waiting halberds and pikes of the frenzied crowd. They killed at least nine men that day, most in the palace but some in offices and homes throughout the Kremlin and in Moscow. Victims included a brother of Nataliia Naryshkina, a musketeer colonel, boyars A. S. Matveev, Prince G. G. Romodanovskii, Prince Iu. A. Dolgorukov and his son Mikhail, State Secretary Larion Ivanov and his son, and Fedor, son of boyar Petr Saltykov. (In two cases of mistaken identity – the younger Saltykov and the younger Dolgorukov – the musketeers returned the bodies to their fathers, with apologies, without

[32] Women come out: Butenant: Keep, "Mutiny," 423; PSRL xxxi: 193 (1691 chronicle); Medvedev, "Sozertsanie kratkoe," 53. Impudent musketeers: Matveev, "Zapiski," 20.

[33] Ring tocsin: Butenant: Keep, "Mutiny," 422–3. Accounts differ on who was talking when the musketeers broke ranks. Military Service Chancery account does not name them: *Vosstanie v Moskve 1682 g.*, no. 207, p. 277. Butenant and Matveev list A. S. Matveev and Prince M. Iu. Dolgorukov: Keep, "Mutiny," 423; Matveev, "Zapiski," 21. Medvedev cites the patriarch: "Sozertsanie kratkoe," 53. Patriarch expels musketeers: ibid., 56.

desecrating them.[34]) That evening the homes of three hated officials – Prince Iurii Alekseevich Dolgorukov, Ivan Maksimovich Iazykov and State Secretary Larion Ivanov – were plundered, crowd violence symbolic of expulsion from the community.

The violence went on for two more days, also reminiscent of 1648. On Tuesday May 16 the musketeers returned and again streamed through the palace demanding the elder Naryshkiny – Kirill Poluekhtovich and his son Ivan – and the foreign Dr. Daniil von Gaden, accused of poisoning the late Tsar Fedor Alekseevich. Tsaritsa Nataliia Naryshkina, in some accounts accompanied by Peter, Ioann and the tsarevny, pleaded with the crowd for one more day. A Military Service Chancery report written after the end of 1683 alleges that "the Great Sovereign ordered that they give them to them: State Secretary Averkii Kirilov, the doctor Ian and the son of Dr. Stepan," but other accounts list different men – von Gaden's son and another foreign doctor Johann Gutmensch – seized forcibly, along with another Naryshkin, two musketeer colonels and others.[35] The musketeers granted the women's request for delay regarding the elder Naryshkiny, as had occurred in 1648.

On May 17, musketeers returned for their prime targets, the Naryshkiny and Dr. Daniil, just as they had in 1648 on the third day. The musketeers promised that with the deaths of these two men, the bloodletting would cease. Again the Kremlin women pleaded for mercy; Butenant describes the two widowed tsaritsy – Nataliia Naryshkina and Marfa Apraksina – and Tsarevna Sofiia falling to their knees in supplication. They won some mercy for the elder Naryshkin, Kirill Poluekhtovich, whose fate was deferred to the next day. But the musketeers were insistent on being given Ivan Naryshkin and Dr. Daniil. Events unfolded with heartbreaking drama. According to a Russian chronicle penned by a cleric around 1691, all the royal women pleaded with the rebels for mercy. When they realized their cause was hopeless, a chilling ritual ensued. The Miloslavskie daughters departed the scene, bowing to the rebels three times as they backed away, leaving only Naryshkiny – Tsaritsa Nataliia, her mother Anna and Peter. Crying, Nataliia stepped into the palace and

[34] Dolgorukov: Bogdanov, "Glazami," 87; Keep, "Mutiny" 426; Matveev, "Zapiski," 25. Saltykov: Keep, "Mutiny" 425; *Vosstanie v Moskve 1682 g.*, no. 207, p. 278; PSRL XXXI: 194 (1691 chronicle); Matveev, "Zapiski," 23.

[35] Women plead: Medvedev, "Sozertsanie kratkoe," 56; PSRL XXXI: 174 (Mazurin); PSRL XXXI: 196 (1691 chronicle). Tsar ordered: *Vosstanie v Moskve 1682 g.*, no. 207, p. 278. Other sources: Keep, "Mutiny," 429; Medvedev, "Sozertsanie kratkoe," 56.

emerged with her brother. She and her mother handed over their brother and son, "like a lamb to the slaughter," to certain death.[36]

As in 1648, ritual sacrifice was required – Nataliia Naryshkina, regent while her minor son Peter was tsar (Ioann became co-tsar on May 26), sacrificed her brother to quell the riots. Indeed, the violence thereafter began to abate. Only Andrei Matveev presents this moment as anything other than a voluntary offering of a sacrificial boyar. Writing in the 1720s about what he had witnessed in 1682, his account lionizes the Naryshkiny, for good reason. Orphaned on the first day of the riots, the sixteen-year-old Andrei Matveev was protected by Nataliia Naryshkina and was spirited out of the Kremlin in disguise by a court jester a few days later. Hidden in one of her distant estates, he grew up under her protection and later enjoyed a diplomatic career under Peter I. Recalling 1682, Matveev reports that Ivan Naryshkin prepared himself for death bravely and calmly by taking confession and communion. Then Nataliia Naryshkina and Sofiia Alekseevna placed in his hands a Mother of God icon and all three began to walk out to the howling crowd and sea of pikes. Undeterred by the holy icon, the crowd surged forward, seized Naryshkin and dragged him away. To Matveev, rather than a ritual sacrifice, the moment descended into chaotic violence.[37] But the moment, however chaotic and violent, was also a ritual: it played out the terrifying responsibility of any sovereign to kill to achieve social stability.

The next day the women won mercy from the rioters, just as Aleksei Mikhailovich had saved Boris Morozov in 1648. Interceding for mercy, as was their role in Muscovite ideology, the women secured the life of the elderly Kirill Poluekhtovich Naryshkin on May 18, the day after what the musketeers had said would be their last blood-letting. A contemporary eyewitness depicts Tsarevna Sofiia Alekseevna, a Miloslavskaia, in face-to-face conversation with the musketeers, while Naryshkin stood alongside, prostrating himself three times to the rebels. The musketeers allowed Kirill Poluekhtovich to be tonsured and exiled to the St. Cyril Beloozero Monastery; three minor sons were

[36] Women in supplication: Keep, "Mutiny," 432; see also PSRL xxxi: 175 (Mazurin). Ivan Naryshkin brought out: PSRL xxxi: 197 (1691 chronicle). Sil'vestr Medvedev passes quickly over the incident, but depicts Peter and his mother, "seeing the people's stubbornness," yielding Ivan Naryshkin: "Sozertsanie kratkoe," 56–7.

[37] Matveev, "Zapiski," 28–31, 36. Matveev admitted Sofiia Alekseevna's involvement but alleged she was doing so cynically: "as in Italian politics: they say one thing, they think another and in the end finally do the deed" ("Zapiski," 30). Matveev biography: Serov, *Administratsiia Petra I*, 56. Butenant also cites the icon: Keep, "Mutiny," 432.

also spared. The tonsuring was done the next day, and these four Naryshkiny were dispersed to separate places of exile.[38]

The crowd's violence in 1682 displayed the same harrowing mixture of bloodthirsty anarchy and ritual as that in 1648. Sources are unanimous on the gruesome fate that befell the victims. Those caught in the palace were brought to the veranda ("the Beautiful Porch") and tossed to the pikes and halberds of the crowd, just as Razin's cossacks had tossed their victims from on high. In 1682 in the Kremlin, those unfortunates tossed onto the assembled crowd were slashed, stomped and stripped naked. The bodies or body parts of most of those killed, whether in Cathedral Square or elsewhere in the Kremlin or around town, were hoisted on pikes and brought to the Lobnoe Mesto on Red Square for display and further desecration. Some bodies were cut into such tiny pieces or so "mashed like manure" that they were no longer recognizable.[39] In one particularly gruesome incident, on May 15 the elderly, bedridden Prince Iurii Dolgorukov was seized from his home, tossed from a landing to the courtyard where he was killed and dragged out to the street. His body was left overnight; no one dared to bury the crowd's victims. On the next day musketeers returned and desecrated his body unspeakably. They disemboweled it, smashing the internal organs and throwing them to the dogs; some men allegedly rubbed their boots with his body fat.[40]

The musketeers attempted to legitimize their violence with various stratagems. They tried to involve the entire community: ringleaders, upon killing a targeted official, would hold up the body or body part on a pike and shout to the crowd "do you like it? (*liubo li?*)," to which the crowd shouted out affirmation. Matveev reports that musketeers forced the onlookers "unwillingly to wave their hats and shout out agreement with them. If anyone in the crowd was quiet or sighed out of heartfelt pity, he

[38] Royal women as intercessors: Thyrêt, *Between God and Tsar*, ch. 4. Sofiia negotiates: PSRL xxxi: 175 (Mazurin). Military Service Chancery report and Sil'vestr Medvedev (both written a year or two later) and the 1691 chronicle depict all the women interceding: *Vosstanie v Moskve 1682 g.*, no. 207, p. 278; Medvedev, "Sozertsanie kratkoe," 57; PSRL xxxi: 197. Butenant depicts only Nataliia Naryshkina: Keep, "Mutiny," 430.

[39] Tossed on pikes: Keep, "Mutiny," 423–6, 429; Medvedev, "Sozertsanie kratkoe," 53–5; PSRL xxxi: 174 (Mazurin); PSRL xxxi: 194 (1691 chronicle); *Vosstanie v Moskve 1682 g.*, no. 207, p. 277. Bodies mashed: PSRL xxxi: 194 (1691 chronicle); Medvedev, "Sozertsanie kratkoe," 55.

[40] Dolgorukov: PSRL xxxi: 195–6 (1691 chronicle). Bodies lay for up to five days: Bogdanov, "Podennye," 36. Permission was given to bury bodies only on May 17: Keep, "Mutiny," 435. The remains of Ivan and Afanasii Kirillovichi Naryshkiny lay untouched until kinsmen dared to collect them from Red Square on May 20: PSRL xxxi: 176 (Mazurin). Matveev alleged that a brave family servant collected the remains of his father Artamon Sergeevich on the day he died, May 15, defying the ban: Matveev, "Zapiski," 32.

was beaten fiercely." Some scholars make a link to Ivan the Terrible's alleged similar behavior, asking the crowd to affirm the justice of his executions of Viskovatyi and others in 1570; cossacks in the Razin uprising also sought popular affirmation of punishing officials. The 1691 chronicle reported that in 1682 the crowds mimicked this behavior: "In the town squares everyone acted like wild animals to the dead bodies, mutilating them horribly, raising them up on the pikes – a head, an arm, a leg – and asking the people, "How do you like this? And the people, afraid, said, "We like it."[41]

Musketeers also emulated legal procedure in carnivalesque inversion. For example, bodies were carried to Red Square in mock procession, and, echoing the heralds in the 1653 execution (Chapter 16), Medvedev reported that "the stupid people said disgusting things, as if bestowing praise, calling out loudly, "Here is the boyar Artemon Sergeevich! Here is the boyar Romodanovskii! Here is Dolgorukii! Here comes a member of the Council! Step aside!" When they took Ivan Naryshkin from the Konstantinov torture chamber to Red Square, they processed through the Spasskii Gates – used for the tsars' religious processions – rather than simply walking out through the Konstantinov Tower's own gates.[42]

Another ploy for legitimacy was embodied in the musketeers' attitude to plundering. As in 1648, they vowed among themselves not to engage in plunder and they punished those who did. In looting Kirill Poluekhtovich Naryshkin's home, they allegedly found tsarist crowns and robes; the musketeers gathered such property in the Kremlin and in subsequent weeks sold it at cheap prices to their compatriots.[43] Thus the plundering that did occur was not intended as theft; the crowd may have been doing it as symbolic expulsion, but the musketeers tried to maintain order among themselves. Furthermore, in choosing Red Square for display and desecration of their victims, they were echoing the official executions of pretenders and traitors like Stepan Razin.

[41] *Liubo?*: Matveev, "Zapiski," 25, 11; PSRL XXXI: 195 (1691 chronicle). See also Medvedev, "Sozertsanie kratkoe," 55; Keep, "Mutiny," 433–4; Rosovetskii, "Ustnaia proza," 91–2. Legitimizing symbolism: Löwe, "Der Strelitzen-Aufstand von 1682," 184–96.

[42] Disgusting things: Medvedev, "Sozertsanie kratkoe," 55. Spasskii Gates: Matveev, "Zapiski," 31. The Konstantinov-Eleninskaia tower and gate stand to the south of the Tocsin Tower on the St. Basil's side: Tikhomirov and Ivanov, *Moskovskii Kreml'*, 49. Thanks to Jack Kollmann for information on Kremlin towers.

[43] Not to plunder: Medvedev, "Sozertsanie kratkoe," 57; Bogdanov, "Podennye," 36; PSRL XXXI: 175 (Mazurin). Crowns and robes: PSRL XXXI: 196 (1691 chronicle). Selling: *Vosstanie v Moskve 1682 g.*, nos. 17, 19, 22, 25, 29, 36–7, 136 and no. 207, p. 278; Bogdanov, "Podennye," 36.

In most cases victims were hunted down and killed on the spot, but one of the key targets – the foreign doctor von Gaden – was caught in the German suburb and brought back to the Kremlin palace to be kept under guard until his execution. Then he and Ivan Naryshkin were treated to a charade of judicial procedure. Taken to the Kremlin torture chamber in the Konstantinov Tower, the location of the Felony Chancery, Naryshkin was tortured for six hours and then quartered in Red Square, all as a common criminal would have been. Reminiscent of Stepan Razin, Naryshkin's head, arms and legs were hoisted on pikes, his head was paraded across the bridge over the Moscow River and back, and his torso was cut into pieces and hoisted repeatedly before the crowd. Later that day Dr. von Gaden suffered the same torture and Red Square execution.[44]

The musketeers' killing and desecration of bodies in the Kremlin and Red Square was accompanied by a steady, ominous drumming of their regimental drums (*barabany*), the great Kremlin signal bell (*nabat*) in the Tocsin Tower and even the bells of parish churches. Russian chronicles say the drumming was to "summon more musketeers," but others depict it as meant to be intimidating. The German merchant Butenant reported that

> when someone who was about to die was brought out, a sign was given in the palace: all the drums, which stood next to one another, more than two hundred of them, were struck, and also the tocsin was rung until such time as the murdered man was dragged from the palace and cast down in the bazaar or great market.

A Russian eyewitness reported "whenever they were cutting people up, in the citadel Kremlin they beat the signal bells."[45] Medvedev remarked on the drumming and Matveev recalled it as "ceaseless": "Oh, what a wild terror there was then."[46] Such drumming is not attested in 1648 or at state-sanctioned executions in 1653 or the 1670s; here it carried a portent of authority and community.

[44] Naryshkin and von Gaden's deaths: PSRL xxxi: 175 (Mazurin); PSRL xxxi: 197–8 (1691 chronicle); Keep, "Mutiny," 431–2; Medvedev, "Sozertsanie kratkoe," 56–7.

[45] Parish bells: Bogdanov, "Podennye," 35. Kremlin Tocsin or "*Nabatnaia*" tower was located opposite St. Basil's; its bell was struck in time of impending danger, particularly fire. Bell removed in time of Catherine II: *Po Kremliu*, 29; Tikhomirov and Ivanov, *Moskovskii Kreml'*, 54. Drumming: PSRL xxxi: 192 (1691 chronicle); Butenant: Keep, "Mutiny," 433. Russian eyewitness: PSRL xxxi: 174, 175 (Mazurin).

[46] Medvedev, "Sozertsanie kratkoe," 52; Matveev, "Zapiski," 25; see also Buganov, "Novyi istochnik," 323; *Vosstanie v Moskve 1682 g.*, no. 207, p. 278.

Another curious incident manipulating the symbols of legal judicial procedure occurred later in 1682, when men of the Bokhin regiment marched to the Kremlin, stopped before the palace and set down blocks and executioner's axes. Some of them lay down bodily, offering themselves for execution. State Secretary Fedor Shaklovtyi emerged to ask what crime they were doing this for, and they replied that they had been falsely accused of rekindling the insurrection and were seeking an investigation to clear their names. They were forgiven and dismissed.[47]

Suspicion of the supernatural permeated contemporaries' perception of evil. Even our most highly educated reporters – Sil′vestr Medvedev and Andrei Matveev – associated these events with disorder in the universe. Medvedev, calling it "the wrath of God," described how "a great windy tempest arose, with dark clouds," while Matveev, writing decades later from memory, echoed the image: the day had started out "sunny, quiet and breezy, but when the shedding of the blood of these boyars started, from the tyrannical tortures, suddenly a very dark tempest and ferocious gloom came up, without clouds, with a harsh wind."[48] Fear of witchcraft pervades, as in the rumors that the Naryshkiny had poisoned the late tsar Fedor Alekseevich or that Matveev was involved in sorcery; it is expressed in the rebels' desperate search to find and kill the foreign doctors. A strange discovery in the plundered home of State Secretary Larion Ivanov played into these fears.

In Ivanov's home rioters found some huge, grotesque fish: "ocean-going fish that had many fins that hung from them like mustaches, long and thin, like hair." They were cuttlefish. Musketeers immediately assumed the worst: these strange creatures must be poisonous, intended by Ivanov for a potion to kill the tsar and all the musketeers. One musketeer even tried to prove this by feeding a stray dog a bit of cuttlefish that he had secretly laced with poison – the dog promptly died, confirming popular fears. Even when the Greek merchants who had imported the cuttlefish testified that they were harmless, considered a delicacy in Mediterranean lands, no one believed them until later when another dog, fed some cuttlefish without a dusting of poison, survived and dispelled the rumors.[49]

[47] Bokhin regiment: *Vosstanie v Moskve 1682 g.*, nos. 189–90 (document dated not later than December 18, 1682); PSRL XXXI: 179 (Mazurin Chronicle puts it December 27, 1682); *Vosstanie v Moskve 1682 g.*, no. 207, p. 281 (chancery report mistakenly dates it October 1682).

[48] Medvedev, "Sozertsanie kratkoe," 52; Matveev, "Zapiski," 23. Clerical author of 1691 chronicle also mentions the weather: PSRL XXXI: 192.

[49] PSRL XXXI: 196, 198 (1691 chronicle). Thanks to Alexander Kamenskii for help with translation of cuttlefish passage. Cuttlefish are actually mollusks, not fish.

These grotesque creatures became symbols of the boyars' perfidy and instruments of humiliation for victims. Musketeers hung two of them on pikes on the bridge across the Moscow River and two on pikes by the body of Larion Ivanov with a placard saying "with these snakes the traitors wanted to destroy the tsar's clan and the musketeers." One contemporary eyewitness recounted how Ivan Naryshkin's head was paraded around town on a pike from which also hung "ocean fish with seven or five tails." Elsewhere dead meat was used to humiliate victims: musketeers placed alongside the body of Prince I. A. Dolgorukov, killed at his home and left to lie on a trash heap in the street, "a sturgeon fish and a carcass of meat." Matveev reports that they stuffed Dolgorukov's mouth with salted fish as if he were eating it.[50]

These horribly violent spectacles sought, with primeval symbolism, the same goal that the judicial system was also striving for – to maintain or re-establish social stability. The grotesque humiliations de-legitimized the crowds' enemies by associating them with fearful powers of magic and the unknown; the violence purged the evil represented by hated officials by destroying them with fire or dismemberment, leaving no trace. Crowd violence was both obverse and reflection of Muscovite concepts of justice and practice.

As in 1648, these events acted out the moral economy of the crowd. The rioters claimed to be defending the tsar, and they associated their actions with legal procedures, even if in carnivalesque inversion. They displayed their executions at a frequent place of execution, Lobnoe Mesto in Red Square, even though they killed on the run. They granted the royal family a day's respite, but demanded satisfaction on the third day, an interval replete with Christian symbolism. In each riot, in 1648 as well as 1682, they dispensed mercy to clan elders and minor sons. Their killings, arson and plundering of elite homes were as symbolic as profane, purifying the symbolic space of the city and expelling pernicious elements. Such symbolic violence was not unique to Muscovy; social theorists and philosophers have reflected on the social stabilizing effects of crowd violence. Mikhail Bakhtin, for

[50] Placard and fish on pikes: PSRL XXXI: 196 (1691 chronicle); Matveev reports rather that one was placed alongside Ivanov's corpse ("Zapiski," 24). Head and fish on pikes: PSRL XXXI: 175 (Mazurin); see also PSRL XXXI: 198 (1691 chronicle). Dolgorukov: PSRL XXXI: 195 (1691 chronicle); Matveev, "Zapiski," 26.

example, suggested that when rioting crowds dismembered the bodies of hated political figures, they were figuratively "carving up the body politic." In Edward Muir's application of Bakhtin, because people believed that "various social groups originated in the parts of God's body," their desecration of hated social groups would end the corruption and abuse perpetrated by them.[51]

But the most remarkable aspect of these events is the interaction between the ruler and his people. The deaths of Pleshcheev and Trakhaniotov in 1648 and of Ivan Naryshkin in 1682 conform to the theory of René Girard, Giorgio Agamben and others, who postulate that sovereign states and their rulers possess the obligation and right to kill to protect the body politic.[52] The sacrifices of Pleshcheev, Trakhaniotov and Naryshkin in 1648 and 1682 in the Kremlin at the hands of sovereign rulers add a deeper dimension to our understanding of Muscovy's legitimizing ideology. The ruler's patriarchal role of protecting his people from injustice required, in such extremes, that he sacrifice individuals to the good of the community, regardless of how unrepresentative, unreasonable and voracious that self-appointed community was in such instances. His status as sovereign put him in a "space of exception" with the authority to sacrifice a victim to unify and affirm community; his legitimacy depended upon his acting on that authority.

Intolerable to our modern sensibilities, to the moral economy of seventeenth-century Muscovy such blood-letting was necessary and acceptable. Both ruler and people understood the terms: the community spoke as one, "*mirom*," to the tsar, who was obliged to protect them. He was not protected from the people by police; note that in 1662 he was saved from having to yield boyars by the quick arrival of troops and of volunteers of the foreigners' suburb. Nor did Muscovite ideology lead the tsar to think he needed police – he was supposed to engage with his people. When petitionary order turned into riot in 1648 and 1682, the only way to stop the plundering, arson and killing was to re-establish the ideal balance between community and tsar. Doing so required, in essence, a ritual sacrifice.

Here was ground zero in this political system. The tsar was required to participate in social violence; he stepped into the exceptional space of

[51] Roller-Assfalg cites Manfred Gailus, Mary Douglas, Walter Burkert and René Girard, among other theorists: "Der Moskauer Aufstand"; Muir applies Bakhtin: *Ritual*, 107.

[52] Girard, *Violence and the Sacred*, ch. 1; Agamben, *Homo sacer*.

sovereignty, sacrificing to re-establish stability. In ideological terms, he was fulfilling his obligations as a pious tsar. So deep did the ideology of Orthodox autocracy go. The relationship of violence, autocracy and ideology in Muscovy is profound: precisely because the tsar was good, pious and benevolent – not a tyrant, not a despot – he was required to respond to his people, even to the point of killing.

CHAPTER 18

Peter the Great and spectacles of suffering

"It is a four-sided pillar of white stone . . . with iron sticks on the sides on which are hanged the heads of the executed; on the top of the pillar is a square stone on which are placed the corpses of the executed." Such a pillar, as described by the Habsburg resident Otto Pleyer in 1718, stood in Red Square since at least 1697; one had also been constructed in St. Petersburg outside the Peter–Paul Fortress. There the severed head of Peter the Great's former brother-in-law, Avraam Fedorovich Lopukhin, hung from 1718 to 1724, still visible when the corpse of Prince M. P. Gagarin was added to the display in 1721. These gruesome structures were only dismantled and replaced with others outside the city gates in 1727 after the reigns of Peter and his wife Catherine.[1]

When Peter set to the task of punishing the musketeers in 1698 and thereafter throughout his reign, he transformed the rules of public violence. No more the pious tsar morally obliged to heed the righteous petitions of his people, Peter transformed Russia's concepts of political power and legitimacy. Instead of piety, achievement and military victory justified Peter's rule. In place of godly community, Peter substituted a secular ideology of absolutism and well-ordered police state. Instead of leading his people to salvation, he vowed to improve life in the here and now.[2]

Peter would never have tolerated the negotiations with blood-thirsty crowds and ritual sacrifices that his father and mother had been forced into. Asserting government as impersonal bureaucracy, not patrimonial

[1] Perry, *State of Russia*, 155. Pleyer cited by Evfimov: "Evdokiia Lopukhina," 160. SbRIO LXIX: no. 21, p. 43; no. 25, p. 47. Lavrent'ev, "Moskovskoe 'stolpotvorenie'," 136–7; Anisimov, *Dyba i knut*, 586–7; Schrader, *Languages*, 46.

[2] New impersonal ideology since the mid seventeenth century: Kivelson, "Devil Stole His Mind." Petrine transformations of ideology: Wortman, *Scenarios of Power*, II: ch. 2; Raeff, *Understanding Imperial Russia*; Anisimov, *Reforms of Peter the Great*; Whittaker, *Russian Monarchy*, ch. 2; Kharkhordin, "What is the State?"

community, he allowed people to approach him with petitions only for the crimes of treason, rebellion and official corruption. Recall that his father, Aleksei Mikhailovich, had met face-to-face with an angry crowd three times in 1648 and was not hurt. No strong palace guard protected the Kremlin because according to Muscovite ideology the tsar would not need one. Peter the Great relied on no such charisma to protect him, creating in the late 1680s a palace guard from among the men in his famous "play regiments" (the future Preobrazhenskii and Semenovskii Regiments). The fact that Peter understood he needed police to protect him epitomizes how differently he envisioned his sovereign power.[3]

Ideologically Peter the Great asserted far broader claims of absolute power than his Muscovite predecessors. Borrowing a dictum from European absolutist thought – "for his Majesty is an autocratic monarch who is not obliged to answer for his acts to anyone in the world; but he possesses the force and the authority to rule his states and lands as a Christian sovereign, according to his will and best judgment"[4] – Peter claimed a power unlimited by traditions of Christian piety. Laws of his time projected an impersonal vision of the state, embodied in the concept of "state interest." Implicit in the law since 1497, it was specified in a decree of 1714 ("many do not realize that everything that can cause evil and losses [*vred, ubytok*] to the State is crime") and in the loyalty oath of the 1715 Military Articles ("And should I see or hear anything threatening and suspicious to the person of His Highness, or His armies, or the people of His state, or the state interest, I will ... ").[5] In adding official corruption as a "third point" to the issues about which people could approach the ruler (in addition to the first "two points" of threats to the monarch's health, and rebellion and treason), he not only asserted impersonal judicial hierarchy but also underscored "state interest."[6] In distinguishing crimes against "state interest" from "particular crimes" from which only private individuals suffer, Petrine law further asserted the state as impersonal. At the same time the theocratic grounding of state legitimacy

[3] Boltunova, *Gvardiia Petra Velikogo*, 40.

[4] PSZ v: no. 3006, ch. 3, art. 20, commentary: PRP viii: 325 (1716).

[5] State interests: PSZ v: nos. 2673 point 4 and no. 2726 (1713). Evil and losses: PSZ v: nos. 2871, 2786, point 2 (1714); see also PSZ vi: nos. 3586 and 3601 (1720). RZ iv: 328 (1715).

[6] Two points: PSZ iv: no. 1748 (1700); PSZ v: nos. 2726 and 2756 (1713); Serov, *Sudebnaia reforma*, 97. Third point: ZA Petra, 362–3 (Jan. 1715); PSZ v: nos. 2877 (1715), 3143 (1718). In Jan. 1718 the three "points" were maintained but only for the first two could one approach the ruler: ZA Petra, 366–8; PSZ v: no. 3143. More prohibitions against approaching the tsar: PSZ v: no. 2673, pt. 2 (1713); ZA Petra, 361–2 (1714); PSZ v: nos. 2879 (1715), 3261 (1718); PSZ vi: nos. 3838 (1721) and 3947 (1722); ZA Petra, 371–9 (1718), 385–6 (1724).

endured, and high religious crime continued to be prosecuted as state crime.[7] Rituals of execution for crimes against the state provided a stage to demonstrate such overweening state power. This chapter concludes the examination of capital punishment by examining execution for highest crime in the early eighteenth century; it does not analyze all possible cases in procedural detail, but tests Russia against the Foucauldian paradigm of "spectacles of suffering."

Even before he visited Europe, Peter enhanced the brutality and theatricality of public executions, perhaps informed by some of the European officers (including Bruce, Gordon and Lefort) whom he had befriended in his teenage years. For example, Peter presided over two brutal executions in the 1690s just before he left on his Grand Embassy to Europe. Trials for such eminent cases were done by boyar commissions, but Peter took personal interest, as in the case of Jacob Jansen, who had defected from Russian service to the Turks in the Azov campaign in 1696. After a harsh interrogation, in September of that year Jansen was sentenced to be broken on the wheel, the first time that this punishment is mentioned in Russian practice. The verdict specified that his bones were to be broken with a wheel, then he was to be beheaded and his head mounted on the wheel; body parts were to be sent to the storehouse for corpses of paupers, criminals and abandoned bodies, an anonymous and infamous death.[8]

Even more gruesome was the case of the *dumnyi dvorianin* and former musketeer colonel Ivan Tsykler in February and March 1697, found guilty of plotting against the tsar. Trial process, overseen in Preobrazhenoe by boyar Lev Kirillovich Naryshkin, Tsar Peter's uncle, was harsh: multiple torture sessions yielded more denunciations and in the end death sentences for six men. The execution of the most prominent – Tsykler and *okol'nichii* A. P. Sokovnin – was unprecedented in publicity and brutality:

[7] Particular crime: PSZ v: nos. 2673, point 4 and no. 2726 (1713); nos. 2871 and 2786, point 2 (1714); no. 2994, pt. 5 (1716); ZA Petra, 129–32 (1723); PSZ vii: no. 4460 (1724). Eighteenth-century prosecution of witchcraft and sorcery: Smilianskaia, *Volshebniki: Bogokhul'niki*; Lavrov, *Koldovstvo i religiia.* Military Articles ch. 1, arts. 1–2: RZ iv: 328–9 (1715); PSZ vii: nos. 4344, art. 5 (1723) and 4713 (1725).

[8] Golikova, *Politicheskie protsessy*, 42–4, 216; Zheliabuzhskii, "Zapiski," 44. Perry, *State of Russia*, 149–50. Bogoslovskii asserts that death by wheel was introduced in 1698, but this precedes it: *Petr I*, iii: 116. The usual process of the "wheel" was to shatter arm and leg bones with blows of a cartwheel, then to thread the broken limbs excruciatingly through the spokes and hoist the wheel horizontally on a pole; the victim died a painful death of exposure: Merback, *Thief, the Cross.*

proclamations were published two days in advance to summon a large crowd. The verdict from Tsar Peter in which "the boyars concurred" was handed down in Preobrazhenoe on March 4; the same day they were quartered and their heads taken to Red Square for display on a specially built stone pillar with iron slabs on which were written their crimes. John Perry's contemporary account notes that they remained there "till the Frost broke up, and the Scent became so nauseous to the Inhabitants, that they were order'd to be removed from thence, and cast into a Pit with common Rogues and Thieves." A description of their crimes was to be read aloud in the capital and all major towns.[9] The execution included highly symbolic violence. Since most of those condemned with Tsykler and Sokovnin were musketeers, their plot was linked with Miloslavskii-led musketeer uprisings of 1682 and 1689. Thus, Peter ordered the body of Ivan Mikhailovich Miloslavskii exhumed and placed under the blocks where Tsykler and Sokovnin were beheaded so that their blood poured out onto the face of the corpse. Then he ordered Miloslavskii's body cut in pieces and the pieces buried under the instruments of torture. A year later when informed in Europe of the musketeer uprising in Moscow, Peter declared "the seeds of Ivan Mikhailovich are sprouting."[10]

This was not the only time that Peter punished a corpse – he is said to have ordered hanged the dead bodies of two women who had been executed by burial for killing their husbands, and a 1716 decree forbidding dueling ordered the body of the slain duelist hanged alongside the successful duelist. Early eighteenth-century law also shamed the bodies of suicides by dragging them through the streets.[11] When Peter rushed back from Europe at news of the musketeer rebellion in 1698, he drew on what he had observed there to further develop spectacles of retribution.

In June 1698 four musketeer regiments, in league with or on behalf of the cloistered Tsarevna Sofiia Alekseevna, took the opportunity of Peter's sojourn to Europe to rebel; while Peter rushed back, Generals A. S. Shein and Patrick Gordon defeated them and proceeded to torture and execute many (to Peter's great displeasure). When Peter returned in late August,

[9] Thanks to Paul Bushkovitch for a copy of the trial transcript: RGADA, f. 371, op. 2, d. 485, 108 fols. The execution (not described in the transcript): Perry, *State of Russia*, 155; Golikova, *Politicheskie protsessy*, 87–101; Lavrent'ev, "Moskovskoe 'stolpotvorenie'," 136–7.

[10] Golikova, *Politicheskie protsessy*, 100; Schuyler, *Peter the Great*, 280–1; Zheliabuzhskii, "Zapiski," 48–51; Perry, *State of Russia*, 153–5. Matveev noted the irony of Tsykler having been involved in the construction of musketeers' pillar in 1682: "Zapiski," 35. Seeds: Bogoslovskii, *Petr I*, II: 540; see also II: 411–12.

[11] Burial: Korb, *Diary*, I: 212. Dueling: Military Articles ch. 49, point 15: PRP VIII: 460 (1715).

he oversaw intensive torture sessions and trials by judges in the Preobrazhenskii Chancery. Here, in contrast to the measured responses to the riots and rebellions of 1648, 1662, 1682 and 1689, all guilty parties were sought out for punishment. Here, vengeance more than the pursuit of social stability ruled the day. In all, 799 people were interrogated and executed (another 269 were flogged, branded and exiled) between September 30 and October 21, 1698 in what an eyewitness, Johann-Georg Korb, called seven "days" of executions.[12]

Almost all of the forms of torture and execution that Peter visited upon the musketeers had been practiced in Muscovite criminal law. Two women were buried alive; approximately 660 men were hanged and about 130 beheaded. Some punishments were new: a handful suffered breaking on the wheel and, halfway through the era of executions, Peter introduced the innovation of beheading by sword instead of by the traditional axe.[13] Nevertheless, the scale, brutality and publicity of punishment were unprecedented.

These were mass spectacles: on each "day" up to 200 individuals were executed, in groups dispersed throughout the city in places associated with the condemned (in front of the offices of musketeer regiments, or in front of a church administrative office for a priest, for example), or in locations calculated to have the greatest public impact (at all city gates or hanging from city walls) or intended to humiliate Peter's rival, Sofiia (by hanging men before her windows at the Novodevichii Convent). Bodies were left on display throughout the winter for all to see; when they were taken down in the spring of 1699, twelve graves were dug on twelve thoroughfares leading out of the city and the corpses were interred en masse. Over each was a pillar with tablets describing the men's crimes and spits to display severed heads.[14]

As with the 1697 Tsykler rituals, publicity was all-important. For the first "day" on September 30, for example, Peter personally sent invitations – delivered by Lefort's young nephew – to members of the European diplomatic corps. He had crowds assembled and addressed them as the executions took place. On another of the "days," Peter led a

[12] Korb, *Diary*; see also Perry, *State of Russia*, 180–5. Overview: Moutchnik, "Der 'Strelitzen Aufstand'"; Kollmann, "27 October 1698: Peter Punishes" and "Pictures at an Execution." Depicted by Vasilii Surikov (1881): State Tretiakov Gallery, Moscow.

[13] Korb, *Diary*, I: 251; Bogoslovskii, *Petr I*, III: 112.

[14] Bogoslovskii, *Petr I*, III: 68–9, 86–7, 91–2, 111–16; Korb, *Diary*, I: 182–4, 188, 192–6; II: 90, 101–12. Mass graves: Moutchnik, "Der 'Strelitzen Aufstand'," 219; Lavrent'ev, "Moskovskoe 'stolpotvorenie'," 138–48.

grotesque version of a religious procession through the town. After having five men beheaded at the suburban Preobrazhenskii Regiment office before all the other condemned men, Peter, accompanied by his entourage and foreign diplomats, escorted 196 condemned men (two each per wooden cart) to the Moscow city gates. There they paused while Peter, mounted on his horse and wearing his "green Polish cloak," admonished the crowd to listen to the reading of the men's crimes. Then smaller groups of the men were escorted in procession to several locations for hanging. That night Peter, reportedly in good spirits, entertained the foreign corps at a banquet. Similarly, at the October 10 execution of 235 men, Korb observed "the Czar, the foreign Ministers, and the Muscovite magnates, besides a vast multitude of Germans, being spectators of this horrifying tragedy."[15]

These executions were without question what scholars of early modern Europe call a "theater of horror." Although Muscovite executions in the 1670s and 1680s contained similar elements, nothing so theatrical had yet been staged in Russia. When Peter returned from Europe in 1698, he intensified the spectacle of executions for the highest crime, primarily for official corruption. Already perhaps instructed in this by his European advisers,[16] Peter also brought from Europe a model, for he had, indeed, witnessed such a thing. In Amsterdam on December 4, 1697 Peter had been invited to join the city fathers to witness a group execution: two murderers were beheaded, three criminals hanged and several others beaten and branded. The "Book of Ceremonies of the City of Amsterdam" records that "Tsar or Grand Prince of Moscow Petr Alekseevich was present at this sad ceremony, sitting in the tribunal of the town Ratusha. He stayed the entire time while the procedures took place, leaning out of the middle window and carefully observing the execution. He was about 26 years old, he is very tall." Regarding Peter's watching the whole ceremony without flinching, M. M. Bogoslovskii remarks: "This is the same trait of Peter's character that we can observe in his sending the gift of an axe to Romodanovskii." It was the old boyar Prince Fedor Iur′evich Romodanovskii whom Peter chose to head the trials, torture, investigation and punishment in 1698, liberally making use of that axe.[17]

[15] Bogoslovskii, *Petr I*, III: 67–9; Korb, *Diary*, I: 183; II: 101, 104–5.

[16] Another informant on European spectacles might have been diplomat Peter Tolstoi. On July 5, 1698 in Naples, Tolstoi saw a condemned murderer broken on the wheel, his corpse cut in quarters and cast into a field. The execution was accompanied by a procession of Catholic priests and dignitaries and attended by city notables. Tolstoi returned from his travels in January 1699 and remained through his career Peter's confidant: Okenfuss (trans.), *Travel Diary*, 202–4.

[17] Bogoslovskii, *Petr I*, II: 276–7. On the Dutch observation that Peter was "tall," he was 6 foot 8.

Peter's borrowing such gruesome displays of violence from Europe presents a nice irony about Peter's famous "window on Europe." There he not only opened Russia to the Europe of Enlightenment, political pluralism, prosperity, social mobility, printing and political dissent, all celebrated as the Western tradition. He also saw how polities mobilized symbolism to broadcast power. Having abandoned participation in the tsar's annual cycle of religious ritual (Epiphany, Palm Sunday and other rites) after his mother died in 1694, Peter actively imported secular symbols of sovereignty. Surrounding his elite with sculptures of Mars and Minerva, Peter inculcated in them a new European discourse of legitimacy based on conquest, wisdom and progress. He introduced European dress, architecture and secular art to transform the elite's visual world and daily lives. Richard Wortman argues that the "royal advent" replaced the coronation ritual as "the defining ceremony of his reign," but spectacles of punishment did the same.[18] Ironically, Russia, so often called by Europeans a "rude and barbarous kingdom," took from Europe not only Enlightenment but also practices of violence.

As noted, for the punishment of highest crime, especially official corruption, Peter introduced brutal forms of execution, such as breaking on the wheel and impalement; in his time breaking on the wheel was extended to common felony.[19] Early eighteenth-century rituals intensified theatricality by providing priests to condemned men on the gallows, following Western practice; they intensified publicity by gathering huge crowds. Laws echoed Muscovite goals of deterrence by terror: the Military Articles of 1715 advocated prompt and local executions to strike "terror" (*strakh*) in observers, while the General Regulation of 1720 decreed that all bureaucratic offices should have "a public place where at the ordered time all bodily punishments and executions should be done, so that all people, looking on it, can protect themselves from such sins and crimes." Grim symbols of the newly assertive state were dispersed through the realm: when plague ravaged the south in 1718, it was ordered that gallows be constructed throughout the affected area, threatening immediate hanging to anyone who disregarded the sanitary embargo.[20]

18 Wortman, *Scenarios of Power*, I: ch. 2 and 44; Vasil'ev, *Starinnye feierverki*; Cracraft, *Petrine Revolution in Russian Culture*, *Petrine Revolution in Russian Imagery*, *Petrine Revolution in Russian Architecture* and *Revolution of Peter the Great*.

19 Military Articles introduced running the gauntlet, but it was rarely cited in secular cases: ch. 1, arts. 1, 6: PSZ v: no. 3006 or RZ IV: 329 (1715). Wheel for common crime: PSZ v: no. 3154 (1718). Eighteenth-century modes of execution: Anisimov, *Dyba i knut*, 551–61.

20 1715 Military Articles, art. 137, *Tolkovanie*. RZ IV: 352; Romashkin, *Osnovnye nachala*, 62–90. General Regulation, art. 47: PRP VIII: 99 (1720). PSZ v: no. 3237 (1718).

In Peter's reign, separate institutions to prosecute highest crime were developed: the Preobrazhenskii Chancery in Moscow had been drawn into political cases as early as 1696; in prosecuting the rebellion of 1698, it became a sort of supra-chancery, empowered to enlist local governors in pursuit of highest crime. Later, a similar chancery for political crime was created in St. Petersburg (*Tainaia kantselariia*), as well as numerous commissions to investigate official corruption and other cases.[21]

Even while, as already observed, the death penalty for common felonies was declining in favor of forced labor and exile, courts continued to stage dramas of death for traitors and corrupt officials. Indeed, P. S. Romashkin argues that Peter de facto abolished the death penalty save for such high crimes.[22] So dramatic became public executions that foreigners took notice. Earlier travelers – Herberstein, Fletcher, Margeret, Olearius, Collins and others – had not mentioned public executions until the mid-century urban riots and Razin's execution in 1671 gave them something to describe. Travelers to Peter the Great's Russia had no difficulty finding incidents of state-sanctioned violence and describing them in lurid detail.

Soon after the musketeer executions in 1698, another spectacular execution was staged. In June 1700 Grigorii Talitskii was accused of heresy and treason. Under torture he admitted to having had an apocalyptic vision of Peter as Antichrist and confessed that he had plotted to murder Peter. Peter's trusted religious adviser, Stefan Iavorskii, was unable to get Talitskii to recant, and in November 1701 the court announced graduated sentences: Talitskii, two laymen and three defrocked priests were sentenced to death (their wives to Siberian exile). Another eight were sentenced to knouting and exile, while a defrocked bishop was exiled to the Solovetskii Monastery. The forms of execution of the three priests were not specified, but for Talitskii and two others, the method was horrific. They were to be smoked, that is, suspended over a fire prior to being quartered. One description says they were smoked for eight hours and then their bodies and the entire scaffold were consigned to flames, a deeply purifying symbolic punishment.[23] Nothing in the punishment of seventeenth-century traitors and dissenters compares to this.

[21] Golikova, "Organy," 255–63 and *Politicheskie protsessy*, ch. 1; Serov, *Sudebnaia reforma*, 94–5, 271–84.

[22] Romashkin, *Osnovnye nachala*, 70.

[23] One source suggests that Talitskii recanted during the smoking and was pardoned and exiled, but other sources do not confirm this: N. S., "Talitskii, Grigorii." See also Zagoskin, *Ocherk*, 57; Bushkovitch, *Peter the Great*, 222–3; Golikova, *Politicheskie protsessy*, 135–45; Esipov (ed.), *Raskol'nichie dela*, 1: 59–84.

Horrific violence was visited upon traitors, even for the tsar's own kin group. The prosecution of Peter's son Aleksei for treason is well known. Starting in February 1718 after Aleksei had been returned from his escape to Vienna, all the implicated were systematically investigated, including Peter's first wife and Aleksei's mother, the cloistered Evdokiia Lopukhina. Torture was the fate of her brother Avraam Fedorovich (he suffered three sessions and admitted plotting against Peter), her spiritual advisers, her female staff and her alleged lover Semen Glebov. On March 5 the court pronounced graduated sentences: Avraam Lopukhin was sent to St. Petersburg for further investigation; four men, including Glebov, were sentenced to death; another twenty-eight people, including two female servants, were sentenced to corporal punishment. Evdokiia herself was exiled to a far-off monastery in the north.[24]

On March 15, 1718 a huge crowd – Weber declared it to be "between two and three hundred thousand Souls" – gathered in Red Square for three executions. They took place near the wall with severed heads and body parts described at the beginning of this chapter. Semen Glebov was impaled, a practice nearly unprecedented in Russian judicial practice but historically associated with traitors. One foreign observer suggests that Peter hoped this excruciatingly slow death would encourage Glebov (who had denied all wrongdoing but the sexual liaison) to confess and reveal more information. But, the report goes, Glebov rebuked Peter. He died the next day and his body was piled on top of the stand. One or two other men were beheaded that day. Two days later the defrocked Archbishop of Rostov Dosifei, one of Evdokiia's spiritual advisers, was broken on the wheel, then beheaded. His body was burned, again a purifying punishment for someone once associated with spiritual power; his head was displayed on the pillar. Peter publicized the event by publishing in 1,940 copies a manifesto with the death sentence.[25]

At the same time (February to April 1718) Aleksei Petrovich's supporters were being investigated in Moscow. An early casualty was Aleksandr Vasil'evich Kikin. Peter's ally since the days of the "play" regiments, Kikin had joined the tsarevich's camp around 1713. He was arrested in early February 1718; tortured on February 11 and 18 and March 5, he admitted to helping plan Aleksei's flight to Vienna. Although it is said that Tsaritsa Catherine interceded for Kikin, the court sentenced him to breaking on the

[24] Bushkovitch, *Peter the Great*, 387–425; Hughes, *Russia in the Age*, 408–9.

[25] Evfimov, "Evdokiia Lopukhina"; Bushkovitch, *Peter the Great*, 399–400; Weber, *Present State*, I: 219–20.

wheel. This was done on the same day as former Archbishop Dosifei; the only mercy Kikin received was that he was beheaded on the second day of his suffering after, according to Pleyer, beseeching Peter for that mercy. Kikin's head was displayed on the wall on Red Square with the others.[26]

As investigations intensified in spring 1718, focus shifted to St. Petersburg. The tsarevich himself suffered repeated torture and the Senate sentenced him to death on June 24; he died two days later in prison before execution could be arranged. Prosecution continued of Avraam Fedorovich Lopukhin, Peter's former brother-in-law, who admitted in several torture sessions in June to hoping that a popular revolt would rise against the tsar. The Senate heard the case: on August 9 Lopukhin was given a face-to-face confrontation with an accuser before the Senate; on October 28 he was tortured in the presence of the Senators; another torture session followed on November 1. On the basis of this evidence the Senate rendered a guilty verdict and death sentence on November 19.

Lopukhin and four members of Aleksei Petrovich's household staff were executed in December 1718 by the Trinity Church outside the Peter–Paul Fortress. Weber describes a mass spectacle – "there being a concourse of an immense number of Spectators" – where five were executed and four others pardoned and knouted and disfigured instead. The five executed were given a mercy: sentenced to the wheel, they were beheaded instead. The German envoy Weber reveals something of the ritual, including the absence of "last words":

> One of them who was a Polander and had served the Czarewitz for Interpreter, underwent his Punishment with the utmost Reluctancy and Cowardice, nor could he even be brought to undress till they pulled off his Clothes by Force. But all the Russians submitted to their Fate with a great deal of Resignation, and those who suffered Death, expected their Turn in fervent Devotion without saying any thing to the Spectators.

After execution, display was gruesome and intentional. Weber again: "The Corpses lay for some days exposed to publick View in the Market-place with the Heads under the Arms, after which they were twisted upon Wheels." As in Moscow, in St. Petersburg a wall for displaying the body parts of traitors was erected "opposite the Crownwork," that is, a fortified bastion across the rivulet north of the fortress.[27] Lopukhin's head was displayed there, while his body was hoisted on a wheel and kept on display

[26] Pavlov-Sil'vanskii, "Kikin, A. V." Anisimov cites Pleyer: *Dyba i knut*, 558.

[27] Weber, *Present State*, 1: 243–4; Gel'vikh, "Lopukhin, A. F."; Bushkovitch, *Peter the Great*, 422–3. Dates differ: Bushkovitch gives Dec. 9, Gel'vikh Dec. 8, and Weber (whose dates are unreliable)

until March 21, 1719, when the family was allowed to bury it in Moscow. The head remained on display until five years later, when in March 1724 his widow petitioned that it be taken down.[28]

Not only in the capitals but around the realm, punishment of traitors was horrific and public. The soldier Aleksandr Semikov was arrested in Ukraine in late 1724, claiming to be Tsarevich Aleksei Petrovich. Tried in St. Petersburg, Semikov was sentenced to be punished in his home region of Pochep: he was beheaded and his head displayed for years, with a plaque describing his crime. The stone fixture erected for this purpose was still in place in the town square as late as 1860.[29] Petrine criminal law practice transformed the rituals of state-sanctioned executions, even while the same legal procedures as before were applied: panels of judges, harsh interrogations, graduated sentences, mercy.

Weber notes that immediately after Lopukhin's 1718 execution, Peter declared his intent to create a "High Court of Justice" to punish "those bloodsuckers who had enriched themselves with the Spoils of their Country." In the concluding years of his reign, official corruption became an especial focus of punishment, pausing only at the highest echelons of power. Peter's close friend Alexander Menshikov was never punished, although his enormous corruption was evident as early as 1711 and although several people involved in a 1714 investigation of corruption around Menshikov were corporally punished and exiled. Peter I's long-time adviser Petr Shafirov also escaped death in a corruption scandal that erupted in late 1722 in his jockeying with Menshikov for power. The Senate found Shafirov guilty and sentenced him to death; the tsar approved the order. Only on the chopping block did Shafirov receive a last-minute reprieve, being sentenced instead to eternal exile to Siberia. With his connections at court, the sentence was reduced to exile in nearby Novgorod, and in the waning days of Peter's reign Shafirov managed to return to the capital.[30]

Less privileged officials were subjected to exemplary execution, as in the 1721 case of the notorious governor of Siberia, Prince M. P. Gagarin. After investigation under torture in February and March into decades of abuse,

Dec. 20. Polander: Weber, *Present State*, 1: 244. Location of executions and display: map of St. Petersburg in ibid., 295, points 34 and 25.

[28] Von Bergholz, *Dnevnik*, 4: 37–8. Body parts left on display for years: Anisimov, *Dyba i knut*, 584–8.

[29] Troitskii, "Samozvantsy," 140; Lashkevich, "Istoricheskoe zamechanie."

[30] Weber, *Present State*, 1: 245. Menshikov: Bushkovitch, *Peter the Great*, ch. 8, esp. 321–3 and 432; Hughes, *Russia in the Age*, 432–9. Shafirov: Likhach, "Shafirov, Petr Pavlovich"; Bushkovitch, *Peter the Great*, 430–1; Serov, *Administratsiia Petra I*, 79–80, 87–103.

graft and corruption, on March 16 the court ordered him hanged. The Holstein diplomat Friedrich von Bergholz relates that Prince Gagarin was hanged before the windows of the Justice College, in the presence of the tsar, all of Gagarin's relatives and assembled crowds. His corpse was then taken to the same square near the Peter–Paul Fortress where other traitors' body parts were displayed. Bergholz saw his body still hanging there on July 18, 1721: "on the large square there stood many pikes with heads stuck on them, among whom, on a specially created scaffold, one could see the head of the brother of the widowed tsaritsa and four other eminent people" (referring to Avraam Lopukhin, Kikin and others executed in the Aleksei Petrovich affair in 1718). Gagarin's body was taken eventually down for the warm months, but hung up again on November 25, 1721.[31]

Similarly, in January 1724 Peter staged a mass execution of corrupt officials at the same square outside the Peter–Paul Fortress. The public was alerted on the day before by the beating of drums throughout town; rumors spread that the condemned would include one of Peter's highest officials, Chief Inspector (*Oberfiskal*) A. Ia. Nesterov, who had long been on trial for corruption. The condemned did indeed include Nesterov and over a dozen officials. Bergholz admired the stalwart behavior of the condemned: an inspector (*fiskal*) approached the block bravely, "kneeled down and boldly placed his head on the block." *Oberfiskal* Nesterov, whom Bergholz described as "a stout and eminent man with gray, almost white hair," had been accused of graft of more than 300,000 rubles; in multiple torture sessions he had denied all. On the scaffold, he was stoic. First he turned towards the fortress cathedral and crossed himself, then looked directly at the emperor in the windows of the Fiscal Office "from which the Emperor and many other grandees watched the execution." He bowed to Peter and "at the urging of the priest" seemed to mouth the words "I am guilty." Then his limbs were broken and he was positioned on the wheel, from which he refused the entreaties of a priest and an emissary from the emperor to formally admit his guilt. Refusing to speak further, eventually he was removed from the wheel and beheaded: "they placed him face down on the block in the blood of the three they had already beheaded." That same day, a dozen others were mutilated, flogged and sent into exile. Bergholz reported that only two of the victims were young people; all the rest were "gray old men," bureaucrats who had enriched themselves at the state's expense. Ensuring that the ceremony would have impact where it was needed the most, Peter had decreed that

[31] Korsakova, "Gagarin"; von Bergholz, *Dnevnik*, 1: 105–6; Gentes, *Exile to Siberia*, 76.

"all the officials from the chancelleries and offices were obliged to attend the execution as a warning to them."[32]

One could multiply these examples of theatrical public executions in Peter I's Russia. They bring this analysis of punishment in early modern Russian legal practice to a close, reflecting both continuity and change. Many of the practices of execution in Peter the Great's time had been used earlier: the gathering of a crowd, the intent of deterrence, execution by hanging and beheading, speedy movement from verdict to execution. But inspired by European models, Petrine criminal practice transformed Muscovite rituals of execution for the highest crimes in theatricality, publicity and impact. Huge crowds were summoned with drums and proclamations; priests accompanied victims on the scaffold; officials and diplomats were ordered or invited to attend; mass groups were executed or corporally punished at the same location; body parts remained on display for years; pamphlets were published describing and legitimizing the executions. When Muscovite courts used some of these techniques in 1671 and 1674, their intent had been as much to reassure onlookers of the tsar's victory over rebellion as to strike fear. For the "well-ordered police state," it was even more about inculcating in the observing populace respect for the state. In the first decades of the eighteenth century, the sovereign's authority to wield violence shed its Muscovite ideology of consultation and patrimonial interaction and emerged as bare coercive power, the acting out of the sovereign's right and obligation to use violence to protect the realm.

[32] Korsakova, "Nesterov"; von Bergholz, *Dnevnik*, 4: 12–14; Serov, *Administratsiia Petra I*, 60.

CONCLUSION

Russian legal culture

From 1500 to 1800, Russia developed a powerful early modern empire. It did so in ways common to its European and Ottoman peers, ways that balanced the rulers' claims to monopolize violence and resource extraction with opposing claims emanating variously from privileged nobilities and municipalities, tribal elites, religious establishments or popular concepts of justice. In all these states, legitimacy was grounded not only in the measured deployment of state-sanctioned violence, but also in the state's fulfillment, to a greater or lesser degree, of expectations that the ruler would respond to his people, respect tradition and provide security. Such expectations were expressed in religio-political discourses from France's increasingly secular royal absolutism to the Ottoman sultan's Sunni Islam, and delivered with mechanisms such as distribution of benefits to elites, preservation of local autonomies and flexibility in governance. Early modern states thrived on a bricolage of legal and institutional rationality and pluralistic informality. While often considered different from these patterns, Russia's combination of centralizing power and flexible strategies of governance fits early modern practice.

Russia succeeded in achieving an empire-wide centralized bureaucratic network in a setting of scarce resources, in part by fiercely asserting state control over people, productivity and trade to enrich the ruler and elites and to pay for expansion and administration. In the sixteenth century, the state distributed land to create a landed military elite, and by 1649 it had enserfed seigneurial peasants to ensure a labor force for that gentry; it registered tax-paying townsmen and other peasants to provide an immobile populace to tax and recruit. Moscow's rulers were careful never to divide sovereignty by allowing kinsmen, elites or officials to amass power; rulers never devolved power by selling offices or allowing local notables or merchants to coalesce. They created a single bureaucratic network, a single judicial hierarchy for important issues (landholding, slavery and serfdom, crime), a single judicial procedure and criminal law. They were able to centralize perhaps more efficiently than their European counterparts because they did not face entrenched local interest groups such as nobilities.

At the same time Russia's persistent dearth of population meant that a centralized government network rested relatively lightly on society. The state set itself minimal goals, concentrating on warfare, collecting revenue and manpower and providing highest justice. Even so, the state depended on communities for the manpower to staff even a skeletal central administration. Communities "selected" members to serve as brigandage elders, swornmen, bailiffs, prison guards, executioners, chiefs of alcohol and other monopolies. All able-bodied men joined in posses to chase down criminals. Villages, urban communes, seigneurial and monastic estates managed all manner of local governance below the criminal law; church, family and community provided such social services as existed. This, as argued here, forced local officials to be responsive to communities to some degree.

Ideology also mandated flexible interaction between state and people. Just as Habsburg emperors patronized Baroque Catholicism and Ottoman sultans espoused Sunni Islam, Russia's tsars asserted legitimacy with Orthodox Christian imagery and ideas. While tolerating the diverse religions and cultures of their varied subjects, Russia's rulers asserted a vision of church–state unity grounded in Christianity. Its touchstone was the piety of the tsar; his duty was to protect his people militarily against enemies and to bestow benevolence on them. He was to patronize the church, feed the poor and heed his people's grievances; he was to right injustice and set a moral example for all. Thus, in the courtroom individuals initiated suits by petitioning directly to the ruler, and in riots the crowd assumed the ruler was on its side. Moscow's rulers played out this ideology by patronizing saints' cults, churches and monasteries and by visually displaying power in imperial architecture and rituals such as cross processions, holyday celebrations and pilgrimages. In the seventeenth century church and state acted on this ideology by introducing confessionalizing reforms and moral disciplining, only to be rudely rebuffed by traditionalists who preferred the old ways.[1] Peter the Great maintained a claim to God-given legitimacy, but asserted a far more comprehensive claim to "absolute" power, borrowing Western models. He substituted European classical and martial symbolism for Orthodox iconography; he

[1] Confessionalizing: Michels, *At War*; Bushkovitch, *Religion and Society*, ch. 3. Europe: Evans, *Rituals*, 880–91; Sharpe, "Crime in England"; Breen, "Patronage, Politics."

aggressively deployed ritual (horrific executions, lavish processions) and the visual (European architecture, art, museums, dress, entertainment) to present his power as absolute and to transform his elite into a European-style nobility. But eighteenth-century Russian rulers, even espousing a European rhetoric of absolutism, continued to play the role of benevolent tsar, claiming to "serve the state" and bestowing gifts, favor and mercy. Ideology both legitimized claims of autocratic power and complicated that power with obligations and interconnections with society.[2] The hard edges of autocracy were also burnished by the "politics of difference." In this multi-ethnic, multi-religious empire, the state allowed colonial peoples to retain institutions, elites and petty jurisdiction according to their own traditions. These three strategies of governance – minimal goals, Christian ideology, toleration of difference – meant, as demonstrated here, that officials ruled with flexibility and discretion under the over-arching legal claim of autocracy.

Individuals and communities promoted such differential outcomes by using the courts as expediently as possible, seeking change of venue, appealing corruption, begging for mercy. They expected justice to match their sense of fairness. Building personal relations with officials with gifts and in-kind support (*kormlenie*), they expected and received flexibility in sentencing and the ability to settle even criminal cases. Individuals and communities stone-walled community surveys, evaded arrest en masse, laxly enforced prison routines and otherwise pushed the edges of the state's claims of control. Only beyond ordinary crime (recidivist theft, murder) in the sphere of highest crime – treason, heresy, witchcraft, egregious corruption – was central control more consistently and harshly imposed.

It is perhaps an unanswerable, even existential, question of how well this judicial system "worked" to satisfy community grievances and punish crime equitably, thereby enhancing social cohesion. What moderns would call corruption was by and large a gift-giving economy that greased the wheels in normal times for officials and litigants alike; but communities were always vulnerable to excessive demands transgressing popular concepts of fairness. Lacking full judicial records, we cannot know how often cases were filed, how many were resolved and other concrete data. Nevertheless, there are many indications that the system provided justice: people turned to the courts, they manipulated them knowledgeably, they

[2] Muscovite and Petrine ideology: Flier, "Political Ideas and Rituals"; Rowland, "Biblical Military Imagery" and "Two Cultures"; Wortman, *Scenarios*, I: ch. I; Marker, *Imperial Saint*.

cooperated with local brigandage offices and did their service as guards, bailiffs and members of arresting posses. This evidence complements Angela Rustemeyer's findings in a study of lese-majesty litigations through the eighteenth century. She demonstrated that seventeenth- and eighteenth-century Russian subjects willingly accepted the terms of autocracy, buying into the myth of the tsar's legitimacy and accepting the tsar's judicial system as their own. What resulted was a stable, integrated judicial culture.[3] Russia's early modern criminal justice system was not a one-way street.

A second existential question – this one posed by historiography about Russia – regards violence. As noted in the Introduction, by the sixteenth century tropes depicted Russia as more violent, barbaric and despotic than its supposedly more civilized European counterparts. This theme resurfaced in twentieth-century scholarship: some scholars argue that Russia from early modern times to the present day has been inordinately violent, more than contemporary European countries. Such a normative approach, however, is ill advised; overall societal violence cannot be quantified for early modern centuries and, furthermore, the approach blurs the distinction between societal and state violence. All states deploy violence to govern. The question posed here is not *how much* state violence, but *how it was used* – arbitrarily or according to rules and law; excessively or in balance with other strategies of governance; symbolically, pragmatically.[4]

This work has engaged with two bodies of thought about how states use violence. One, associated with René Girard, Giorgio Agamben and others, argues that all sovereign figures – ruling individuals or judicial systems – possess the sole right to kill for the sake of social stability. This is the basis of their claim to legitimacy. Such a perspective helps to explain Tsar Aleksei Mikhailovich's acquiescence to crowd demands for the heads of corrupt officials in 1648. Another broad theory sees changing uses of state-sanctioned violence as instrumental to the rise of the modern state. As sketched out in the Introduction, in contrast to older views that extolled early modern European states for parliamentary pluralism, rule by law and enlightenment, this theory looks at the coercion inherent in

[3] Rustemeyer, *Dissens und Ehre*, Conclusion. Others on how the courts "worked": Kollmann, *By Honor Bound*, 247–52; Kivelson, *Cartographies*, 50–4; Serov, *Sudebnaia reforma*, 232–3, 445–54. Russia's essential legality is a key theme for Boris Mironov: *Sotsial'naia istoriia*, II: ch. 9.

[4] Dunning, "Terror"; Hellie, "Late Medieval and Early Modern Russian Civilization." Crime statistics for early modern Europe can be compiled, but not for these centuries in Russia: see essays by Sharpe and Spierenburg in Johnson and Monkkonen, eds., *Civilization of Crime*.

state control. It sees early modern coercion as overt and physical, modern as internalized and psychological, but coercive nonetheless. It has sparked a response from scholars who emphasize rather that internalized discourses of civility obviated the need for rule by terror.[5]

These two approaches have been fruitfully expanded. The "civilizing" school has examined how confessionalization, social disciplining and civility improved social order; scholars show how states' creation of judicial systems provided good alternatives to intra-personal violence. Nevertheless, other historians remind us that violence never went away. Gerd Schwerhoff, for example, argued that early modern individuals and communities always used violence "as a means of social control" – to defend personal honor, to discipline neighbors and kin, to protest political policy. In a study of vindicatory violence by nobles in sixteenth- and seventeenth-century France, Stuart Carroll boldly challenges the argument for a "civilizing" effect: the modern state arose on the back of armies and warfare as much as on court etiquette and Enlightenment ideals: "civilization," he abruptly proclaims, "is built on violence."[6] Interpretations about the relationship of violence to early modern state-building and modernity in general stand divided between an evolutionary social, even biological, model (from violent to civilized society and individual) and a view of violence as constant in human social organization. The evidence presented here for Russia, however, perhaps undermines this opposition; it neither tracks the evolutionary change postulated for Europe nor demonstrates endemic brutality. Early modern Russia's deployment of state-sanctioned violence followed its own timing and suited its own circumstances.

If one defines social control broadly, then it must be said that violence permeated early modern Russia. Laura Benton argues that empires necessarily "delegate" sovereignty to local elites and officials, and in the process they delegate state-sanctioned violence. In this light, Russia was, through the period covered here, a very violent society, inasmuch as serfdom was based on coercion, no matter how much autonomy village communes had

[5] Foucault, *Discipline and Punish*, pt. 1, ch. 1. Statistical school, critique of Foucault: Spierenburg, "Long-Term Trends," "Violence and the Civilizing Process" and *Spectacle*, vii–xii and 183–207; Johnson and Monkkonen, "Introduction"; Evans, *Rituals*, Introduction; Sharpe, "Crime in England"; Rousseaux, "Crime, Justice and Society"; Schrader, *Languages*, 188–90; Muchembled and Birrell, *History of Violence*.

[6] Schwerhoff, "Criminalized Violence" and "Social Control of Violence." Carroll, *Blood and Violence*, 330. Spierenburg acknowledges the persistence of violence in modern society: "Violence and the Civilizing Process."

in practice. Landlords disciplined serfs with the knout; village elders exercised tyranny over the younger men and all women of their villages; the state chased down runaway serfs. This sort of delegated state-sanctioned violence was intrinsic to the Russian state-building project.[7]

The criminal judicial system surveyed here similarly used violence throughout. No Foucauldian internalized discourses here: no long-term prison sentences, no asylums or schools to inculcate self-restraint and conformity. Not until the nobility encountered European culture in the eighteenth century, and literacy, means of communication and public institutions proliferated in the nineteenth century, could the Russian state try to disseminate less coercive cultural norms. Like its European counterparts, early modern Russian courts used judicial torture, "marketplace" beatings and mass, exemplary violence to suppress rebellion. But its judicial violence was always balanced. Until the time of Peter I, Russia did not deploy executions as a "theater of terror" with the same degree of brutality and theatricality seen in Amsterdam, London and German cities. Russian executions meted out swift justice, unadorned with religious ritual save for confession and communion on the eve. They were pragmatically legitimized by reading of the sentence and by reference to the "tsar's order" and to laws justifying the verdict. Even when Peter I introduced European-style "spectacles," they were as a rule used on traitors and corrupt officials, not common felons. And, as argued here, local courts' use and threats of violence were often mitigated by their interdependencies with communities. Not only violence, but mercy and flexible adjudication defined the system.

Furthermore, eighteenth-century developments suggest further limitations in Russia's use of sovereign violence. Going into the eighteenth century, Russia moved more quickly than the leading European countries to decrease capital punishment and judicial torture. In Europe, only in the late eighteenth century with Enlightenment values, civility and the development of alternative institutions did significant penal reform begin, after Cesare Beccaria in 1764 mobilized Enlightenment philosophy against torture and the death penalty. Judicial torture was gradually phased out (Prussia, 1754; Saxony, 1770; Austria and Bohemia, 1776; France, 1780–8), but the death penalty endured. Executions were gradually sequestered into prisons out of the public's eye; abolition of the death penalty in Europe began only in the mid nineteenth century.[8]

[7] Benton, *Search for Sovereignty*, 31–2. Hoch, *Serfdom and Social Control*.

[8] Executions in public lasted in England and in Vienna until 1868, in France through the nineteenth century. Habsburg Emperor Joseph II tried to abolish the death penalty but it was reinstated soon

On torture Russia followed roughly this chronology. It was regulated by law from the 1740s and 1750s; Catherine II eliminated it for several categories of criminals and crime from the 1760s on; in 1801 torture was formally abolished.[9] As for capital punishment, however, from the early eighteenth century its use was declining. So energetically did Peter the Great send capital criminals off to exile that courts used the death penalty relatively rarely (if spectacularly); his mandatory review of capital sentences complemented this decline. In 1743 Peter's daughter Empress Elizabeth declared her intention to end capital punishment completely, replacing it with exile to hard labor. Although the Senate moderated her measure, capital punishment was rare thereafter. Only about a dozen executions of common criminals occurred into the 1820s, as well as those of political criminals such as peasant rebel Emelian Pugachev (1775) and the gentry Decembrists (1825).[10]

Why Russia led the way in limiting capital punishment in Europe is difficult to say. Empress Elizabeth herself did not make clear her motivations in abolishing the death penalty; they might have been, as Cyril Bryner argues, grounded in her religious belief. But a general rise in humanitarian sentiment did not accompany her move. After all, the alternatives to capital punishment were not benign. Knouting was brutal and the conditions of exile to Urals mines, swampy harbor sites and Siberian winters took great human toll. Not only was the Senate's ambiguous interpretation of the empress's abolition evidence of elite opposition, but Elizabeth's own legal codification commission (1754–66) maintained the death penalty (this code was not enacted). Some intellectuals, including Prince M. M. Shcherbatov, wrote in opposition to Beccaria, while others, including Catherine II and Alexander Radishchev, promoted humanitarian values in their plays and novels.[11]

after his death in 1790. Habsburg forms of execution and torture in 1787 included decapitation, burning, breaking on wheel, amputation of hands, quartering and impaling: Balázs, *Hungary and the Hapsburgs*, 236. Abolition of death penalty: Netherlands 1850, Belgium 1863, Norway 1875, Denmark 1892, Sweden 1910, France late twentieth century. See Weisser, *Crime and Punishment*, 133–42; Spierenburg, *Spectacle*, 183–207; Evans, *Rituals*, ch. 3; Kann, *History of the Habsburg Empire*, 178–80; Garland, *Peculiar Institution*, ch. 4.

9 Russian abolition of torture: Caroli, "La Torture dans la Russie," 824–45; Schrader, *Languages*, 13–14, 112–28, 196–7 n. 38. Catherine II's criminal policy: Babkova, "Politika Ekateriny II"; de Madariaga, "Penal Policy."

10 Abolition: Sergeevskii, "Smertnaia kazn'"; Schmidt, *Sozialkontrolle*, 386–8; LeDonne, *Absolutism*, 212–13. Dozen instances: Daly, "Russian Punishments," 161, 163–8.

11 Bryner, "Issue of Capital Punishment." Harshness of prison and exile: de Madariaga, "Penal Policy," 101; Schmidt, *Sozialkontrolle*, 388–93. Unpromulagated code: Omel'chenko, *'Zakonnaia monarkhiia'*, 48–51; Sergeevskii, "Smertnaia kazn'," 60. Anti-reform: Sergeevskii, "Smertnaia

It is clear, however, that Elizabeth's move was in step with the general evolution of Russian criminal law from the late seventeenth century wherein capital punishment was declining in favor of exile. Thereafter, through the first half of the nineteenth century, the empire was ruled by and large without recourse to capital punishment. Controlling the most hardened criminals in the exile system constantly posed challenges (executions were secretly reinstated in Siberia briefly in the 1830s–40s and exiles were marked with branding to mid century). But Jonathan Daly has found that judicial violence applied as a whole in Russian courts well into the nineteenth century was "comparatively lenient" compared to practices in England and Wales, France, Prussia and the United States. Capital punishment was used less often; France's system of penal exile suffered much higher mortality; Britain exiled a greater proportion of its population than did Russia; Russia incarcerated fewer than any of these other countries.[12] Even though urban crime rose in Russia in the nineteenth century when European crime rates were falling (Russia lagged in creating urban police forces), its judicial violence was not out of line in the European context.

Numerous factors contributed to Russia's different use of state-sanctioned violence than Europe from the sixteenth to the nineteenth centuries. Jonathan Daly suggests that in the nineteenth century it reflected both the difficulty of governing so large and diverse an empire with coercion alone and also the elite's growing commitment to prison reform. Two other aspects of Russia's historical heritage might also have predisposed the state to take a different attitude to judicial violence. One is Russia's relationship to Roman law. Relying on home-grown handbooks of judicial procedure and punishment, Russia's criminal courts never really absorbed the Roman law to which they were exposed, in which harsh corporal sanctions abounded. Upon receiving some Roman law from Byzantium in the wake of Christianization, Kievan-era canon and secular law changed bodily mutilation and corporal punishments such as beheading to compensatory fines. Later Muscovite law similarly balanced corporal punishment with fines and frequent mitigation. In the

kazn'," 59–60; Bryner, "Issue of Capital Punishment," 415; Adams, *Politics of Punishment*, 17–19. Pro-reform: de Madariaga, "Penal Policy"; Radishchev, *Journey*.

12 Endurance of corporal punishment, debates on abolition: Schrader, *Languages*, 30–8 and ch. 6; Daly, "Russian Punishments," *passim*; Adams, *Politics of Punishment*, ch. 1. Schrader describes jurists' struggles to manage population of exiles: *Languages*, 191, n. 3 and ch. 4. Comparatively lenient: Daly, "Russian Punishments," 176. Russian prison system: Adams, *Politics of Punishment*, chs. 2–5; Daly, "Russian Punishments," 173–8.

second half of the seventeenth century, when bodily mutilation and corporal punishment reappeared in Russian law with a new wave of church law, countervailing political tendencies checked their impact. The state revised laws to favor exile over capital punishment for all but the most heinous crimes; debilitating bodily mutilation was reduced in favor of branding. Roman law came to Russia incompletely and was less stringently applied even when it entered secular law.[13]

More speculatively, religious and cultural norms might also have shaped the judicial system's use of violence. The dominant culture of the ruling elite, despite the empire's multicultural composition, was Russian Orthodox, and Elise Wirtschafter and Cynthia Whittaker have shown that, even after Peter the Great's Europeanizing reforms, Russia's noble and educated elite approached political problems through a religio-moral lens. Rather than promoting pragmatic, rational or legal approaches in advice literature, plays and other political writings, the elite applied personal, moral solutions to public problems. They were taught not only in European universities and by European tutors, but also by enlightened Russian Orthodox bishops who, intermingling European trends, such as secular Enlightenment philosophy and Lutheran pietism, with Orthodoxy, preached a moral philosophy of individual perfectibility and ethical obligation.[14] When it came to violence, the message Orthodoxy offered was modulated.

As suggested in Chapter 14, Russian Orthodoxy never developed a rhetoric of religiously sanctioned violence like that of Latin Christianity. It had no medieval crusades; its language about non-believers was reticent compared to medieval Catholic theology. In the sixteenth to early eighteenth centuries, conversion of colonial subjects was a secondary priority of colonial policy; established religions and native religious traditions were tolerated.[15] Even its visual sensibility avoided depictions of violence: where late medieval and early modern European painting graphically depicted the passion and sufferings of Christ and other Christian martyrs, Orthodox iconography depicted saints as static and the crucified Christ as serene and beautiful in death. The visual world presented no realistic imagery of violence, save for a mid-sixteenth-century Illuminated

[13] Daly, "Russian Punishments," 176–8. Absence of Roman law: Feldbrugge, *Law*, ch. 3.

[14] Whittaker, *Russian Monarchy*; Wirtschafter, *Play of Ideas* and "Christian Rulership."

[15] Anti-Tatar rhetoric was common in Muscovite chronicles (Ostrowski, *Muscovy and the Mongols*, chs. 6–11); Bogatyrev shows anti-Protestant sentiment in compositions about the Livonian war ("Battle for Divine Wisdom"). But wars were not declared on theological grounds. Conversion in ideology and practice: Kivelson, *Cartographies*, ch. 6; Romaniello, *Elusive Empire*, ch. 5.

Chronicle (with many images of executions and battles) that existed in a single copy that never moved from Kremlin archives. In sixteenth-century Russia, apocalyptic sensibility penetrated religious writings, and some very violent texts, such as the Book of Revelation, were included in contemporary collections. But visual depictions of the apocalypse focused on the triumphant army of the righteous, not the bloody battle of Armageddon; they were esoterically symbolic, a far cry from the terrifyingly graphic sacred and secular imagery of contemporaneous European engravings. Imagery of violence was conspicuously absent even after secular painting developed in Russia in the eighteenth century.[16] The social impact of this visual world is difficult to parse, but it bears considering in light of eighteenth-century Orthodox moral philosophy, Empress Elizabeth's ban on capital punishment and nineteenth-century penal practice. Perhaps these many factors – imperial "politics of difference," shallow reception of Roman law, Orthodox moral philosophy (at least in the eighteenth century), preferences for beauty over violence, triumph over strife, in visual culture – contribute to why Russia deployed state-sanctioned violence differently than did its early modern European peers.

This book has argued that Russia essentially fit into the patterns of state-building, local governance and adjudication seen in some of its early modern peers in Europe and the Ottoman Empire. On the ground adjudication in early modern states had much in common. Centralizing states in Europe had to deal with established social groups and solidarities – nobilities and gentries, guilds, strong regional customs – and consequently local justice was often moderated to suit local needs. The same in Russia – for opposite reasons. In early modern Russia, the state had too few officials on the ground in its vast and sparsely populated empire to accomplish its needs without relying on local villagers to staff and support centrally assigned officials. Here too, justice could be modulated. Different circumstances – same outcome. This early modern interaction between state and society satisfied the needs of each side enough to maintain stability and promote the state's goals.

[16] European graphic depictions: Merback, *Thief, the Cross.* Beauty in Orthodoxy iconography: Pentcheva, "Containers of Power," 115; Lossky, "The Cross'; "Crucifixion," *Oxford Dictionary of Byzantium.* Apocalyptic imagery: Flier, "Till the End of Time"; Rowland, "Biblical Military Imagery." Bogatyrev considers Ivan IV's banner violent, but it pales in comparison to Dürer's apocalypse that he cites: "Heavenly Host."

This research also shows that Russia in the early modern period possessed a defined law and functional legal system. It was not excessively violent in the European context, nor was it arbitrary in applying the law. Justice could be slow in coming or suborned, but the system was not one of unbridled satrapies, vigilante justice or uncontrolled brutality; Russia was not a despotism.

For their part, people mobilized to defend individual or group interests in litigation and collective petitions. People accepted the terms of the state's legitimacy, turning in neighbors suspected of treason and doing their stints as selected officers of the court. They manipulated suits, appealed for change of venue, complained of corruption. In their interactions with the courts they created a robust legal culture. Modern-day Russians are perhaps too disparaging of their own legal heritage. They are fascinated with "the strappado and knout," the culture of denunciation, the endemic corruption of the bureaucracy. In day-to-day practice, Muscovy's legal legacy was nuanced, resilient and in keeping with contemporary strategies of state-building and governance.

APPENDIX

Punishment for felonies

PSKOV JUDICIAL CHARTER (1397–1467), ART. 8. KAISER (TRANS. AND ED.), THE LAWS OF RUS′, 88

For up to two thefts, spare his life, give corporal punishment according to guilt. For third time, execute.

1397–8 DVINA CHARTER, ART. 5. RZ II: 181

One theft: compensate victim value of property and brand the thief.
Two thefts: sell the thief into slavery and brand him.
Three thefts: hang him.

1497 LAW CODE, ARTS. 10–11, 13. RZ II: 55–6

One theft: marketplace knouting, compensate victim value of property or give thief to victim to work off the debt.

Two thefts: execution, compensate victim from thief's property.

On first arrest, if there is material evidence and testimony of criminal reputation, then execute and compensate victim from thief's property.

1550 LAW CODE, ARTS. 52, 55–6. RZ II: 106–7

For an arrest for one theft, with material evidence and testimony of criminal reputation, torture. If he confesses, execute. If he won't confess, then imprison until death and compensate from his property. If they say he is a good man, then give him an accusatory trial.

One arrest for theft with no prior thefts or worse crimes involved, then marketplace knouting, compensate victim the value of the property or give thief to victim to work off the debt; put thief on surety bond or imprison until bond is collected.

Two thefts: torture and execute if he admits, and compensate victim from his property; if he denies and is called criminal anyway, then imprison till death. If they call him a good man, then put him on surety bond or prison until bond is collected.

1555 MEDYN CHARTER, ART. 11. RZ II: 222

One theft: knout and put on surety bond or prison until bond can be collected.
Two thefts: knout, cut off hand and imprison.
Three or more: execute.

1589 LAW CODE, ARTS. 103, 107–8. PRP IV: 425–6

If he is brought in with material evidence, take a 30 ruble fine for the tsar. Then investigate and if they say he is criminal, torture with 100 blows and if he confesses, execute. If he doesn't confess, prison until death. Compensate the victim. If community says he is good, then there is no suit. If it is a false suit, pay him dishonor.
One theft: same as 1550 Law Code.
Two thefts: same as 1550 Law Code, except that if the man does not admit after torture but is still called criminal, he is to be hanged, not imprisoned.

LAW OF BORIS GODUNOV (RULED 1598–1604) IN 1616/17 HANDBOOK OF FELONY CHANCERY, ARTS. 9–11. PRP V: 191

If he refuses to admit guilt after torture, then imprison till death.
One or two robberies without worse crimes: imprison until the tsar's decree.
One robbery, with murder or arson: execute.
Three robberies: execute.

1616/17 HANDBOOK OF FELONY CHANCERY, ARTS. 38–40. PRP V: 197

One theft: knout, firm surety bond or failing that, prison; compensate victim.
Two thefts: knout, cut off hand and imprison; compensate by selling off property.
Three or more thefts: death penalty and sell off property to compensate.

1637 DECREE OF FELONY CHANCERY. PRP V: 223–4

Robbers are to be branded with R on the right cheek, Z on the forehead, B on the left cheek. Thieves: T on the right, A on the forehead, T on the left cheek.

A "small" crime is one robbery, one theft or two not large thefts, without homicide or arson. Medium crime is two robberies, three small thefts, with no homicide or arson. Both are punished with knout, branding and surety bond. Those guilty of medium crimes are also branded and exiled to Siberia.

FEBRUARY 10, 1637. ON FORGERY. AAE III, no. 266, pp. 406–8

Forgers of coins, instead of the death penalty, are to be branded on the cheeks with hot iron, with the word "*vor*" [criminal], "so that such criminals in the future will be known." If such criminals with a brand show up, without an immunity charter, they are to be arrested.

1649 ULOZHENIE. RZ III: 231–2, 256

Ch. 21, arts. 9 and 11. For one theft or for a swindler, torture; if no other worse crimes, then knout, cut off left ear, two years prison and after prison, eternal exile to southern frontier for hard labor and provide with letter of having served his term. Compensate the victim from thief's property.

Art. 10: two thefts, torture, knout, cut off right ear, four years prison and then eternal exile at labor for tsar on southern frontier; provide with letter of having served his term.

Art. 12. Three or more thefts: torture, then execute and compensate victim.

Art. 13. One theft with homicide: execute.

Art. 16. For one robbery, torture, cut off right ear, three years prison, then exile to labor on the southern frontier eternally. Provide with letter of having served his term. Compensate victim.

Art. 17. Two robberies with no homicide – torture, then execute and compensate victim.

Art. 18. One robbery with homicide or arson, execute.

Ch. 25: Art. 3. For first conviction selling alcohol illegally, marketplace knouting, five-ruble fine. For second, marketplace knouting, ten-ruble fine and surety bond. Third conviction: marketplace knouting, half-year prison.

Art. 16: for more than two arrests for selling tobacco, knout on the rack or in the marketplace. For more than three, slit the nostrils and nose, torture and knout, exile to distant lands to deter others.

OCTOBER 20, 1653. CAPITAL PUNISHMENT TO EXILE. PSZ I: no. 105

Thieves and robbers who are sentenced to death by the Ulozhenie and are in prison awaiting execution: replace capital punishment with knout, cutting off a finger of the left hand and exile to Siberia, Volga or southern frontier towns with wives and children. Subsequent arrests merit death penalty.

AUGUST 8, 1659. PSZ I: no. 255

For the Middle Volga area, "above the tsar's decrees and the Ulozhenie" execution for "robbery even without murder," even for a single robbery. The same also for peasants who fled masters and committed arson or robbery while in flight.

OCTOBER 16, 1660. ORDERS TO PERM VELIKAIA, CHERDYN′ AND SOL′ KAMSKAIA. PSZ I: no. 285

Servitors who own lands who are guilty of illegal alcohol sales are to suffer confiscation of their service lands and ancestral estates, but if their people or serfs are arrested on the same charge, the people or serfs are to have their hands cut off and are to be exiled to Siberia. If merchants or servants and serfs of the lands of the tsar, bishops or monasteries are so guilty, then they are to have corporal punishment and be exiled to Siberia, their property confiscated for the tsar. Any people entering Moscow and towns with undeclared wine are to be punished corporally and exiled.

SEPTEMBER 18 AND OCTOBER 21, 1661. ON FORGERY. AI IV, no. 158, pp. 304–7

Those sentenced to death for forgery of money now are subject to severing a left hand. A graduated scale of severing of fingers and hands for lesser acts of forgery.

MAY 11, 1663. MUTILATION. PSZ I: no. 334

For men sitting in prison awaiting death sentence for two or three robberies, or for murder or repeated theft: instead of death, they are to have severed both feet and the left hand. These limbs are to be displayed on roads, with a written notice announcing the victim's crimes.

JANUARY 24, 1666. RESCIND MUTILATION. PSZ I: no. 383

May 1663 law for threefold mutilation abrogated: death penalty re-instituted, with hanging for thieves and robbers, beheading for murderers.

1669 CRIMINAL ARTICLES. PRP VII: 398–9, 402, 424

Art. 8. For one theft: if an arrested man admits without torture, question him severely about other crime without torture and then two weeks in jail. If more accusations appear within two weeks, torture. If not, knout, cut two small fingers off left hand, put on surety bond and return him home with a letter identifying his crime and punishment. If he reappears in crime, cut off hand and foot and exile those who have harbored him. If he has nowhere to return to (unregistered), then send to Felony Chancery for exile to Siberia.

Art. 9. Two thefts: in first arrest, if in testimony and torture he admits to two, then beat with knout, cut off left hand at the wrist and free on surety bond; if no bond, then give over to his master with a letter as in art. 8. Compensate victim from his property.

Art 10. Three or more thefts: torture, execute even if he didn't do a murder, and compensate from his property.

Art 17. One robbery: torture, if he admits to one with no murder, then follow art. 8. Or follow a decree of 1662/3, which says for one robbery, cut off hand and foot and free even without surety bond; provide him a letter about his crime and punishment.

Art. 18. Two robberies: torture; if he admits only to two with no murder, execute; compensate for his property. If he is arrested for one robbery but admits to two, then execute.

Art. 19. Robbers in testimony and torture who admit to one robbery with murder or arson of homes or grain, then execute.

Art. 82. If someone, after killing someone without premeditation steals money from the corpse, or clothing, horses, etc., knout, cut off left hand and right foot, and release.

SEPTEMBER 10, 1679. EXILE. PSZ II: no. 772

Convicted criminals who were to be punished with cutting off hands and feet are now to be exiled to Siberia to farm, with wives and children, eternally.

NOVEMBER 17, 1680. RESCIND MUTILATION. PSZ II: no. 846

For those who committed one or two thefts, the previous mutilation of cutting off hands, feet or two fingers is abrogated; they are to be exiled to Siberia eternally with wives and children under four.

NOVEMBER 28, 1682. ADJUST LADDER. PSZ II: no. 970

For one robbery or one theft, not accompanied by homicide or arson: now the guilty party is to be beaten with the knout and have the left ear and two small fingers of the left hand cut off. Exile to Siberia eternally with wives and children under four.

Two thefts: same as Ulozhenie.
Three thefts: execute.

MARCH 22, 1683. CAPITAL PUNISHMENT TO EXILE. PSZ II: no. 1002

For saying rebellious words: instead of death penalty, knout and exile to various towns.

MARCH 30, 1683. MUTILATION. PSZ II: no. 1004

Convicts in prison awaiting sentence of having fingers cut off are now to have ears cut off instead; then exile to wherever is appropriate.

MAY 3, 1691. BRANDING. PSZ III: no. 1404

Instead of death sentence according to the Ulozhenie and 1669 Criminal Articles, exile instead and stamp their face with the letter "V" for "*vor*" [criminal] so that if they flee exile, they will be recognized. For crimes for which the Ulozhenie and 1669 Criminal Articles prescribe cutting off ears and exile, do so without the brand. Do not cut off ears or fingers.

SEPT. 8, 1691. EXTEND LADDER. PSZ III: no. 1413

Three thefts, with no robbery or murder: death penalty changed to knouting, branding and exile to Siberia.

JANUARY 22, 1692. BRANDING. PSZ III: no. 1430

If a convicted criminal who had been branded and had then been exiled flees his place of exile and is caught in Moscow or other towns, he is to be severely knouted, branded a second time on the right cheek and returned to the place of exile. If he escapes again and is caught in even minor crime, execute without informing the tsar. If someone is branded twice and appears from exile in Moscow and is caught, even not in crime, execute. If someone is exiled for a capital crime, and was not branded, brand and exile with harsh punishment.

Those criminals who are sent to Siberia and other towns, not for capital crimes [presumably not branded], and flee and are caught in Moscow but not in crime, are to be beaten severely with a knout and exiled to far-flung towns. If they become involved in crime, except capital crime, they are to be sentenced according to the Ulozhenie, the 1669 Criminal Articles and the Byzantine codes, as appropriate. For capital crimes, make verdict as written above, and exile once branded.

JULY 9, 1698. BRANDING. DAI XII: no. 91, pp. 395–6

Tiumen′ voevoda is told to brand any exiles who are caught in crime or fail to do their assigned task with a brand on their backs indicating the name of the city "Tiumen′" and to beat them mercilessly by knout, send them home to live lawfully and threaten them with death for a repeat occurrence. Similar brands were being sent to other Siberian towns. Model is provided here, and for all Siberian towns; the actual brand should be twice that size.

JULY 9, 1698. BRANDING. AI V, no. 280, pp. 509–10

Governor of Irkutsk is told to execute without mercy branded exiles who engage in crime in exile or leave their place of exile without permission, even if that crime is not a capital crime. Hang them and do not remove the body from the gallows. Their brand should indicate what town they are exiled to.

JANUARY 19, 1703. EXTEND LADDER. PSZ IV: no. 1924

For up to ten incidents of robbery (without murder) worthy of capital punishment according to the Ulozhenie: now such robbers are not to be executed, but are to be knouted, branded on the cheek and exiled eternally to work in Azov. But if they admit to even one robbery with murder, execute according to the Ulozhenie.

NOVEMBER 19, 1703. CAPITAL PUNISHMENT TO EXILE. PSZ IV: no. 1951

Execution is ordered for those guilty of "treason, rebellion, intentional murder and poisoning." All other crime is to be punished with exile to Azov for hard labor.

JANUARY 14, 1704. CAPITAL PUNISHMENT TO EXILE. PSZ IV: no. 1957

Capital punishment is decreed for murder, for taking a "leading role in crime," for treason or rebellion. For all other previously capital crimes, now punish with knouting, branding with new brands and eternal exile to hard labor. For those who would have received corporal punishment and exile, they are to be spared corporal punishment and exiled for ten years.

FEBRUARY 5, 1705. BRANDING. PSZ IV: no. 2026

Convicts held for capital crimes other than murder and rebellion are to be knouted severely and branded "with the new brand," to have their nostrils slit and to be eternally exiled to hard labor. For those sentenced to only a fixed term of exile, do not slit nostrils but brand "V" for "*vor*" on the forehead. All who are so branded or have nostrils slit will then be recognized if they flee.

JANUARY 1719. REFER CAPITAL SENTENCE. PSZ V: no. 3294, pt. 6, p. 625

Governors are to refer capital sentences to the Superior Court and provide annual reports of executions performed.

MARCH 3, 1719. REFER CAPITAL SENTENCE. PSZ V: no. 3316, p. 670

Military courts are to refer death penalties to the Military College, which will report them to the tsar for confirmation.

MARCH 7, 1721. EXTEND LADDER.
PSZ VI: no. 3755

Murderers who voluntarily turned themselves in are spared the death penalty, sentenced to gauntlet and exile for ten years of hard labor.

NOVEMBER 4, 1721. BRANDING, MUTILATION.
PSZ VI: no. 3842, pt. 1, p. 450

Exiles mutilated with a brand or slit nostrils receive amnesty but are not allowed to return to the Center; they must remain in Siberia.

NOVEMBER 10, 1721. ADJUST LADDER.
PSZ VI: no. 3847, pp. 452–3

For up to two thefts: corporal punishment and release on surety bond.
For a third theft: slit nostrils and exile to eternal hard labor.
For more than three thefts, execution.
For one or two robberies without murder: knouting, slit nostrils and exile to eternal hard labor.
For three robberies or one robbery with murder: execution.
For anyone with slit nostrils caught in serious crime: execution.
Any case deserving of capital punishment or exile to hard labor is to be sent to the Superior Court. Appeal is possible for unjust sentences from the Superior Court.

OCTOBER 9, 1726, MARCH 10, 1727. DECEMBER 31, 1727.
PSZ VII: nos. 4964, 5026, 5218

Sentences of death or "political death" are to be approved by the Supreme Privy Council (later the Senate) for cases arising in the Colleges and capitals, and by governors in the provinces.

SEPTEMBER 12, 1728. REFER CAPITAL SENTENCE.
PSZ VIII: no. 5333, art. 16, p. 100

Instruction to local governors: all sentences to death or exile are to be approved by the regional Governor General.

Glossary

batogi	Bastinadoes
boi	Misdemeanor assault
desiatskii	Decurion, village police official
d'iak	Secretary
dumnyi	Top four political ranks in seventeenth century; "of the Council," conciliar
dumnyi d'iak	State secretary
grabezh	Misdemeanor robbery
gradskie zakony	Byzantine criminal codes derived from *Procheiros nomos*
guba	Territory policed for brigands
gubernia	Large administrative unit instituted 1708
iasak	Tax/tribute paid by colonial subjects in steppe and Siberia
katorga	Exile to hard labor
knut	Knout
kormlenie	Support by community for tsarist officials
landrat	Locally elected gentry official, 1718–22
likhoi	Evil person, felon
mestnichestvo	Precedence: elite rank system
na kozle	[To knout] on the rack/trestle
nedel'shchik	Bailiff
ochnaia stavka	Face-to-face confrontation in trial
okol'nichii	High honorific court rank, second to boyars
osmotr	Inspection of physical evidence
palach	Executioner
piatidesiatskii	Fifty-man, village police official
pod'iachii	Undersecretary
pominki	Gifts
poniatye	Witnesses from community

poruka	Surety bond
posul	Bribe
poval'nyi obysk	Community survey
prikaznoi	Person employed by the state
pristav	Bailiff
pytka, pytochnyi	Torture; having to do with torture
raspros, dopros	Oral interrogation
razboi	Felony assault and robbery
Razboinyi Prikaz	Felony Chancery
Razriad	Military Service Chancery
rozsylshchik	Courier
rozysk, sysk	Inquisitorial trial format
sbornik	Collection of written documents
s'ezzhaia izba, prikaznaia izba	Governor's office
slovo i delo	Lese-majesty allegations
sotskii	Hundredman, village police official
ssylka	Exile
stol'nik	Honorific Moscow rank
sud	Accusatorial trial format; general term for court case
sudebnik	Law code (1497, 1550, 1589, 1606)
syshchik	Investigator
tat'ba	Felony theft
torgovaia kazn'	Knouting in a marketplace
tsarevich	Son of the tsar
tsarevna	Daughter of the tsar
tsaritsa	Wife of the tsar
tseloval'nik	Swornman
uezd	Province
Ulozhenie	Conciliar Law Code of 1649
voevoda	Local governor; military commander
vorovstvo	Felony crime
vstriaski	Placing weights on a person hanging in torture; shaking the weighted body
vybornyi	Official selected by community
"word and deed"	See *slovo i delo* above
Zemskii	Referring to community institutions
zhilets, zhil'tsy	Lowest rank of the Moscow-based upper service class

Bibliography

ARCHIVAL

Rossiiskii gosudarstvennyi arkhiv drevnikh aktov (RGADA), Moscow:

*Arzamas area collections (unless specified, each has one catalog/*opis'*)*
f. 409, Nizhnii Novgorod Gubernskaia kantseliariia, op. 1–4, 1709–27.
f. 418, Alatyr Provintsial'naia kantseliariia, 1720–80.
f. 419, Arzamas Provintsial'naia kantseliariia, op. 1, pts. 1–12, 1709–79.
f. 441, Sviazhsk Provintsial'naia kantseliariia, 1721–81.
f. 453, Shatsk Provintsial'naia kantseliariia, op. 1–2, 1719–79.
f. 495, Kadom Voevodskaia kantseliariia, 1727–79.
f. 515, Krasnoslobodsk Voevodskaia kantseliariia, 1727–80.
f. 519, Kurmysh Voevodskaia kantseliariia, 1726–79.
f. 585, Temnikov Voevodskaia kantseliariia, op. 1–4, 1725–79.
f. 672, Nizhnii Novgorod Nadvornyi sud, 1710–27.
f. 676, Arzamas Zemskaia izba, Ratusha and Provintsial'nyi magistrat, 1703–79.
f. 677, Nizhnii Novgorod Provintsial'nyi nizhnii sud, 1720–2.
f. 748, Nizhnii Novgorod Zemskaia izba, Ratusha and Gubnyi magistrat, 1713–75.
f. 782, Temnikov Zemskaia izba, Ratusha and Gorodovoi magistrat, 1715–79.
f. 882, Kasimov Landrat and Kantseliariia sudnykh i rozysknykh del, 1715–22.
f. 884, Kerensk Landrat, Kantseliariia sudnykh i rozysknykh del and Zemskii komissar, 1715–26.
f. 887, Kurmysh Landrat, Kantseliariia sudnykh i rozysknykh del and Zemskii komissar, 1717–34.
f. 901, Temnikov Landrat, op. 1–2, 1711–20.
f. 904, Shatsk Landrat, 1711–26.

f. 916, Alatyr Landrat and Kantseliariia sudnykh i rozysknykh del, 1714–20.
f. 974, Temnikov Kantseliariia sudnykh i rozysknykh del and Zemskii komissar, 1719–26.
f. 978, Voronezh Nadvornyi sud, 1709–27.
f. 994, Shatsk Provintsial′nyi sud, 1719–27.
f. 1006, Kadom Kantseliariia sudnykh i rozysknykh del, 1718–72.
f. 1071, Kantseliariia upravitelei dvortsovykh sel Alatyrskogo uezda, 1726–74.
f. 1103, Arzamas Prikaznaia izba, 1608–1715.
f. 1122, Kadom Prikaznaia izba, op. 1–2, 1623–1715.
f. 1124, Kasimov Prikaznaia izba, 1642–1715.
f. 1127, Kerensk Prikaznaia izba, 1657–1715.
f. 1132, Krasnoslobodsk Prikaznaia izba and Prikaz iasachnykh del, 1704–15.
f. 1135, Kurmysh Prikaznaia izba, 1662–1714.
f. 1143, Nizhnii Novgorod Prikaznaia izba, op. 1–3 in 5 pts., 1645–1714.
f. 1167, Temnikov Prikaznaia izba, op. 1 in 2 pts., 1604–1715.
f. 1175, Shatsk Prikaznaia izba, 1631–1715.
f. 1380, Arzamas Kantseliariia sudnykh i rozysknykh del, 1711–25.
f. 1381, Arzamas Iasachnyi prikaz and Kantseliariia upravitelia dvortsovykh sel Arzamasskogo uezda, 1703–76.
f. 1404, Arzamas Landrat, 1709–20.

Beloozero area collections
f. 410, Novgorod Gubernskaia kantseliariia, 1724–76.
f. 421, Beloozero Provintsial′naia kantseliariia, op. 1–3, 1706–76.
f. 498, Kargopol′ Voevodskaia kantseliariia, 1722–76.
f. 596, Ustiuzhna Zheleznopol′skaia Voevodskaia kantseliariia, 1728–76.
f. 663, Ustiuzhna Zheleznopol′skaia Landrat and Kantseliariia sudnykh i rozysknykh del, op. 1–2, 1714–26.
f. 921, Beloozero Landrat, Kantseliariia sudnykh i rozysknykh del, Kamerirskaia Kontora, Renteria i Polkovoi dvor, 1716–19.
f. 1048, Kargopol′ Landrat, Kantseliariia sudnykh i rozysknykh del and Zemskii komissar, 1712–25.
f. 1107, Beloozero Prikaznaia izba, 1599–1715.
f. 1123, Kargopol′ Prikaznaia izba, 1677–1715.
f. 1171, Ustiuzhna Zheleznopol′skaia Prikaznaia i gubnaia izba, 1614–1715.
f. 1441, Kirillo-Belozerskii muzhskoi monastyr′, op. 1–7, 1397–1930.
f. 1596, Beloozero Gubnaia izba, 1615–1714.

Military service chancery archive

f. 210, ODB XI, Moscow and Vladimir stol.
f. 210, ODB XII, Belgorod and Novgorod stol.
f. 210, ODB XIV, Belgorod stol.
f. 210, ODB XV–XVII, Prikaznyi stol.
f. 210, ODB XVIII–XIX, Sevsk stol.
f. 210, ODB XX, Stolbtsy Pomestnogo stola, Stolbtsy raznykh stolov, Stolbtsy iz Sobr P. F. Karabanova.

Other collections

f. 22, Gosarkhiv, Razriad XXII, Otdel fondov verkhovnogo upravleniia, Dela sudnye, pt. 1, Ugolovnaia chast′, 1712–65.
f. 141, Prikaznye dela starykh let, op. 1–2, 1505–1705.
f. 159, Prikaznye dela novoi rozborki, op. 1–4, 1572–1818.
f. 371, Preobrazhenskii and Semeonovskii prikazy, 1613–1729.

PRIMARY SOURCES

Akty istoricheskie, sobrannye i izdannye Arkheograficheskoiu kommissieiu, 5 vols., St. Petersburg: Tip. Ekspeditsii zagotovleniia gosud. bumag, 1841–2.

Akty iuridicheskie, St. Petersburg: Tip. 2-ogo Otd. sobstvennoi E. I. V. Kantseliiarii, 1838.

Akty Moskovskogo gosudarstva, 3 vols., St. Petersburg: Tip. Imperatorskoi Akademii nauk, 1890–1901.

Akty, otnosiashchiesia do iuridicheskogo byta drevnei Rossii, 3 vols. and index, St. Petersburg: Tip. Imperatorskoi Akademii nauk, 1857–1901.

Akty, sobrannye v bibliotekakh i arkhivakh Rossiiskoi imperii Arkheograficheskoiu ekspeditsieiu Imp. akademii nauk, 4 vols. and index, St. Petersburg: Tip. 2-ogo Otd. sobstvennoi E. I. V. Kantseliiarii, 1836, 1838.

Barskov, Ia. L., *Pamiatniki pervykh let russkogo staroobriadchestva*, St. Petersburg: Tip. M. A. Aleksandrova, 1912.

Barsov, E. V., "Akty, otn. k istorii Belozerskogo kraia," in *Chteniia* (1883), bk. II, pt. 4: 13–16.

"Sudnye protsessy XVII–XVIII v. po delam tserkvi," in *Chteniia* (1882), bk. III, pt. 5: 1–42.

Bazilevich, K. V. (ed.), *Gorodskie vosstaniia v Moskovskom gosudarstve XVII v. Sbornik dokumentov*, Moscow and Leningrad: Gosudarstvennoe sotsial′no-ekonomicheskoe izd., 1936.

Belokurov, S. A., *Razriadnye zapisi za smutnoe vremia (7113–7121 g.)*, Moscow: Tip. Shtaba Moskovskogo voennogo kruga, 1907.

Belov, M. I., "Pis′ma Ioganna fan Kellera v sobranii niderlandskikh diplomaticheskikh dokumentov," in Nosov (ed.), *Issledovaniia*, 374–82.

von Bergholz, F. W., *Dnevnik kammer-iunkera Berkhgol'tsa*, 4 pts., Moscow: Tip. Katkova, 1858–60.

Berry, Lloyd E. and Crummey, Robert O. (eds.), *Rude and Barbarous Kingdom: Russia in the Accounts of Sixteenth-Century English Voyagers*, Madison, Wis.: University of Wisconsin Press, 1968.

Bogdanov, A. P., "Moskovskoe vosstanie 1682 g. glazami datskogo posla," *Voprosy istorii* (1986), 3: 78–91.

"Podennye zapisi ochevidtsa Moskovskogo vosstaniia 1682 goda," *Sovetskie arkhivy* (1979), 2: 34–7.

Bogoiavlenskii, S. K., "Dopros tsarom Ioannom Groznym russkikh plennikov vyshedshikh iz Kryma," in *Chteniia* (1912), bk. II, pt. 3: 26–33.

Buganov, V. I., "Novyi istochnik o moskovskom vosstanii 1682 g.," in Nosov (ed.), *Issledovaniia*, 318–24.

Bulatov, S. Ia. (ed. and trans.), *Karolina. Ugolovno-sudebnoe ulozhenie Karla V*, Alma-Ata: Izd. Nauka Kazakhskoi SSR, 1967.

Bulgakova, F. I., *Povest' o sude Shemiaki*, St. Petersburg: Tip. V. S. Valasheva, 1879.

Bussow, Conrad, *The Disturbed State of the Russian Realm*, Orchard, G. Edward (trans. and ed.), Montreal: McGill-Queen's University Press, 1994.

Chancellor, Richard, "Voyage," in Berry and Crummey (eds.), *Rude and Barbarous Kingdom*, 9–41.

Chteniia v Imp. obshchestve istorii i drevnostei rossiiskikh pri Moskovskom universitete. Sbornik, 264 vols., Moscow: Universitetskaia tip., 1845–1918.

Collins, Samuel, *The Present State of Russia: In a Letter to a Friend at London, Written by an Eminent Person Residing at the Great Czars Court at Mosco for the Space of Nine Years*, London: Printed by John Winter for Dorman Newman, 1671.

Coxe, Willam, *Travels into Poland, Russia, Sweden and Denmark*, 4th edn., 5 vols., London: T. Cadell, 1792.

Crull, Jodocus, *The Ancient and Present State of Muscovy*, London: A. Roper and A. Bosvile, 1698.

"Dela ob opredelenii gubnykh starost . . . ," in *Vremennik*, III (1849): 32–52.

Dewey, Horace W. (comp., ed. and trans.), *Muscovite Judicial Texts, 1488–1556*, Michigan Slavic Materials, 7, Ann Arbor, Mich.: Dept. of Slavic Languages and Literatures, 1966.

Dopolneniia k Aktam istoricheskskim, 12 vols. and index, St. Petersburg: Tip. Ekspeditsii zagotovleniia gosud. bumag, 1846–75.

Dvortsovye razriady, 4 vols., St. Petersburg: Tip. 2-ogo Otd. sobstvennoi E. I. V. Kantseliarii, 1850–5.

Emchenko, E. B., *Stoglav. Issledovanie i tekst*, Moscow: Indrik, 2000.

Esipov, G. (ed.), *Raskol'nichie dela XVIII stoletiia. Izvlechennye iz del Preobrazhenskogo prikaza i Tainoi rosysknykh del kantseliarii*, 2 vols., St. Petersburg: Tip. Tov. Obshchestvennaia Pol'za, 1861.

Fennell, John L. I. (ed. and trans.), *Prince A. M. Kurbsky's History of Ivan IV*, Cambridge University Press, 1965.

Filatov, N. F., *Arzamas v XVII veke. Ocherk istorii. Dokumenty*, Arzamas: Arzamasskii gosud. ped. institut im. A. P. Gaidara, 2000.

Fletcher, Giles, "Of the Russe Commonwealth," in Berry and Crummey (eds.), *Rude and Barbarous Kingdom*, 109–246.

Gordon, Patrick, *Diary of General Patrick Gordon of Auchleuchries: 1635–1699*, Fedosov, Dmitry (ed.), 2 vols., Aberdeen: AHRC Centre for Irish and Scottish Studies, 2009–10.

Dnevnik. 1659–1667, Fedosov, D. G. (trans. and ed.), Moscow: Nauka, 2002.

Graham, Hugh F. (trans. and ed.), "'A Brief Account of the Character and Brutal Rule of Vasil'evich, Tyrant of Muscovy' (Albert Schlichting on Ivan Groznyi)," *Canadian-American Slavic Studies* 9 (1975), 2: 204–72.

Hellie, Richard (trans. and ed.), *The Muscovite Law Code (Ulozhenie) of 1649*. Part 1. *Text and Translation*, Irvine, Calif.: Charles Schlacks Jr. Publisher, 1988.

Herberstein, Sigismund von, *Description of Moscow and Muscovy, 1557*, Picard, Bertold (ed.) and Grundy, J. B. C. (trans.), New York: Barnes and Noble, 1969.

Horsey, Sir Jerome, "Travels," in Berry and Crummey (eds.), *Rude and Barbarous Kingdom*, 262–369.

Iakovlev, A. I. (ed.), *Namestnichie, gubnye i zemskie ustavnye gramoty Moskovskogo gosudarstva*, Moscow: Izd. Istoriko-filologicheskogo fakul'teta Imp. Moskovskogo universiteta, 1909.

Pamiatniki istorii Smutnogo vremeni, Moscow: Izd. N. N. Klochkova, 1909.

Kaiser, Daniel H. (trans. and ed.), *The Laws of Rus': Tenth to Fifteenth Centuries*, Salt Lake City, Ut.: Charles Schlacks Jr. Publisher, 1992.

Katyrev-Rostovskii, I. M., "Povest'," in *Russkaia istoricheskaia biblioteka* XIII (1909): 561–623.

Kazakov, E. N. et al. (eds.), *Litsevoi letopisnyi svod XVI veka. Russkaia letopisnaia istoriia*, 24 vols., Moscow: Firma AKTEON, 2009–10.

Keep, John, "Mutiny in Moscow, 1682: A Contemporary Account," *Canadian Slavonic Papers* 23 (1981): 410–42.

Khoziaistvo krupnogo feodala-krepostnika XVII v., Leningrad: Izd. Akademii nauk SSSR, 1933.

Kleimola, Ann M., *Justice in Medieval Russia: Muscovite Judgment Charters (pravye gramoty) of the Fifteenth and Sixteenth Centuries*, Philadelphia: American Philosophical Society, 1975.

Konovalov, S., "Ludvig Fabritius's Account of the Razin Rebellion," *Oxford Slavonic Papers* (old series) 6 (1955): 70–101.

"Razin's Execution: Two Contemporary Documents," *Oxford Slavonic Papers* (old series) 12 (1965): 94–8.

Korb, Johann-Georg, *Diary of an Austrian Secretary of Legation at the Court of Czar Peter the Great*, MacDonnell, Count (trans.), 2 vols., London: Frank Cass & Co. Ltd., 1968; reprint of English trans. London: Bradbury & Evans, 1863.

Koretskii, V. I., "Aktovye i letopsnye materialy o vosstanii I. I. Bolotnikova," *Sovetskie arkhivy* (1976), 5: 45–58.

Kotoshikhin, Grigorii, "'On Russia in the Reign of Alexis Mikhailovich': An Annotated Translation," Uroff, Benjamin (trans., notes and intro.), unpublished PhD dissertation, Columbia University, 1970.

O Rossii v tsarstvovanie Alekseia Mikhailovicha, 4th edn., St. Petersburg: Tip. Glavnogo upravleniia udelov, 1906.

Krekshin, P. N., "Zapiski," in Sakharov (ed.), *Zapiski russkikh liudei*, 1–128.

Krest'ianskaia voina pod predvoditel'stvom Stepana Razina. Sbornik dokumentov, 4 vols. in 5 pts., Moscow: Izd. Akademii nauk SSSR, 1954–76.

Lappo, I. I., *Litovskii statut v moskovskom perevode-redaktsii*, Iur'ev: Tip. K. Mattisena, 1916.

Lapteva, L. P. (ed. and trans.), "Rasskaz ochevidtsa o zhizni Moskovii kontsa XVII veka," *Voprosy istorii* (1970), 1: 103–26.

Lipinskii, M. A. (ed.), "Rospis' komu imianem i za kakuiu vinu kakoe nakazane bylo . . . ," in *Chteniia* (1883), bk. 1: 17–41.

Loewenson, Leo, "The Moscow Rising of 1648," *Slavonic and East European Review* 27 (1948/9): 146–56.

Man'kov, A. G. (ed.), *Inostrannye izvestiia o vosstanii Stepana Razina. Materialy i issledovaniia*, Leningrad: Nauka, Leningradskoe otd., 1975.

Sobornoe ulozhenie 1649 goda. Tekst, kommentarii, Leningrad: Nauka, Leningradskoe otd., 1987.

Zapiski inostrantsev o vosstanii Stepana Razina, Leningrad: Nauka, Leningradskoe otd., 1968.

Margeret, Jacques, *The Russian Empire and Grand Duchy of Muscovy: A 17th-Century French Account*, Chester S. L. (trans. and ed.), Pittsburgh, Pa.: University of Pennsylvania Press, 1983.

Massa, Issac, *A Short History of the Beginnings and Origins of These Present Wars in Moscow . . . 1610*, Orchard, G. Edward (trans. and intro.), University of Toronto Press, 1982.

Matveev, A. A., "Zapiski," in Sakharov (ed.), *Zapiski russkikh liudei*, 1–67.

Medvedev, Sil'vestr, "Sozertsanie kratkoe . . . ," in *Chteniia* (1894), bk. IV, sect. 2: i–lii, 1–198.

"Mirskoi vybor zemskogo sudeiki, 1659 g.," in *Chteniia* (1883), bk. 1: 5–9.

Moskoviia i Evropa. G. K. Kotoshikhin. Patrik Gordon. Ian Streis. Tsar' Aleksei Mikhailovich, Moscow: Fond Sergeia Dubova, 2000.

Moskovskaia delovaia i bytovaia pis'mennost' XVII veka, Moscow: Nauka, 1968.

Muller, Alexander V., *The Spiritual Regulation of Peter the Great*, Seattle and London: University of Washington Press, 1972.

Narodnoe antitserkovnoe dvizhenie v Rossii XVII veka. Dokumenty Prikaza tainykh del o raskol'nikakh 1665–1667 gg., Rumiantseva, V. S. (ed.), Moscow: AN SSSR, Institut istorii, 1986.

Nasonov, A. N. (ed.), *Pskovskie letopisi*, 2 vols., Moscow and Leningrad: Izd. Akademii nauk SSSR, 1941–55.

Neuville, Foy de la, *A Curious and New Account of Muscovy in the Year 1689*, Hughes, Lindsey (ed.), London: School of Slavonic and East European Studies, University of London, 1994.

Nosov, N. E. (ed.), *Issledovaniia po otechestvennomu istochnikovedeniiu. Sbornik statei, posviashchennykh 75-letiiu professora S. N. Valka*, Moscow and Leningrad: Nauka, 1964.

Novgorodskaia pervaia letopis' starshego i mladshego izvodov, Tikhomirov, M. N. and Nasonov, A. N. (eds.), Moscow and Leningrad: Izd. Akademii nauk SSSR, 1950.

Novgorodskie letopisi, St. Petersburg: Tip. Imp. Akademii nauk, 1879.

"Novoe o vosstanii Mikahila Glinskogo v 1508 godu," *Sovetskie arkhivy* (1970), 5: 68–73.

Novombergskii, N. Ia., *Slovo i delo gosudarevy*. Vol. I. *Protsessy do izdaniia Ulozheniiia Alekseiia Mikhailovicha 1649 g.* Moscow: Iazyki slavianskoi kul'tury, 2004.

Slovo i delo gosudarevy. Vol. II. *Materialy. Prilozhenie. Koldovstvo v Moskovskoi Rusi XVII-go stoletiia*, Moscow: Iazyki slavianskoi kul'tury, 2004.

Okenfuss, Max J. (trans.), *The Travel Diary of Peter Tolstoi*, DeKalb, Ill.: Northern Illinois University Press, 1987.

Olearius, Adam, "Podrobnoe opisanie puteshestviia Golshtinskogo posol'stva v Moskoviiu . . . ," Barsov, P. P. (trans.), in *Chteniia* (1868), bk. I: 1–76, bk. II: 1–102, bk. III: 103–226, bk. IV: 227–388; (1869), bk. I: 389–530, bk. II: 531–692, bk. III: 693–796, bk. IV: 797–920.

The Travels of Olearius in Seventeenth-Century Russia, Baron, Samuel H. (trans. and ed.), Stanford University Press, 1967.

Vermehrte Newe Beschreibung. Der Muscowitischen und Persischen Reyse. Schleswig [Holstein] 1656, Lohmeier, Dieter (ed.), Tübingen: Max Niemeyer, 1971.

"O miatezhakh v gorode Moskve i v sele Kolomenskom v. 1648, 1662 i 1771 gg.," in *Chteniia* (1890), bk. III: 3–116.

Opisanie dokumentov i bumag, khran. v Moskovskom arkhive Ministerstva iustitsii, 21 vols., St. Petersburg and Moscow: Tip. Pravitel'stvuiushchago Senata, 1869–1921.

Opis' arkhiva Posol'skogo prikaza 1626 goda, 2 pts., Moscow: Glavnoe arkhivnoe upravlenie pri SM SSSR, 1977.

Opisi Tsarskogo arkhiva XVI veka i arkhiva Posol'skogo prikaza 1614 goda, Shmidt, S. O. (ed.), Moscow: Izd. Vostochnoi literatury, 1960.

Palitsyn, Avraamii, *Skazanie Avraamiia Palitsyna*, Derzhavina, O. A. and Kolosova, E. V. (eds.), Moscow and Leningrad: Izd. Akademii nauk SSSR, 1955.

Pamiatniki delovoi pis'mennosti XVII veka. Vladimirskii krai, Moscow: Nauka, 1984.

Pamiatniki drevnei pis'mennosti, 190 vols., St. Petersburg: Izdanie Obshchestva liubitelei drevnei pis'mennosti i iskusstva, 1878–1925.

Pamiatniki literatury drevnei Rusi. XVII vek, vol. I, Moscow: Khudozhestvennaia literatura, 1988.

Pamiatniki literatury drevnei Rusi. XVII vek, vol. II, Moscow: Khudozhestvennaia literatura, 1989.

Pamiatniki literatury drevnei Rusi. Konets XVI–nachalo XVII vekov, Moscow: Khudozhestvennaia literatura, 1987.

Pamiatniki russkogo prava, 8 vols., Moscow: Gosudarstvennoe izd. iuridicheskoi literatury, 1952–63.

Perry, John, *The State of Russia under the Present Czar*, London: Cass, 1967; reprint of London: for Benjamin Tooke, at the Middle Temple-Gate in Fleetstreet, 1716.

Petreius, Peter, *Relatsiia Petra Petreia o Rossii nachala XVII v.*, Limonov, Iu. A. (ed.), Moscow: AN SSSR, Institut istorii, 1976.

Pis'ma russkikh gosudarei i drugikh osob tsarskogo semeistva, 5 vols., Moscow: Tip. E. Lissnera i Iu. Romana, 1861–96.

Politsiia Rossii. Dokumenty i materialy, 1718–1917 gg., Saratov: Ministerstvo vnutrennikh del Rossiiskoi Federatsii, Saratovskii iuridicheskii institut MVD Rossii, 2002.

Polnoe sobranie russkikh letopisei, 43 vols. to date, St. Petersburg and Moscow: Akademiia nauk SSSR, 1841– .

Polnoe sobranie zakonov Rossiiskoi imperii, Series 1, 1649–1825, 45 vols., St. Petersburg: Tip. II Otd. Sobstv. Ego Imp. Vel. kantseliarii, 1830.

Popov, A. (ed.), *Materialy dlia istorii vozmushcheniia Stenki Razina*, Moscow: Tip. L. Stepanovoi, 1857.

Pososhkov, Ivan, *The Book of Poverty and Wealth*, Vlasto, A. P. and Lewitter, L. R. (eds. and trans.), Stanford University Press, 1987.

Razriadnaia kniga 1475–1605 gg., Savich, N. G. (ed.), 4 vols. in 10 pts., Moscow: AN SSSR, Institut istorii, 1977–94.

Razriadnaia kniga 1495–1598 gg., Buganov, V. I. (ed.), Moscow: Nauka, 1966.

Razriadnaia kniga 1559–1605 gg., Kuz'mina, L. F. (ed.), Moscow: AN SSSR, Institut istorii, 1974.

Razriadnye knigi 1598–1638 gg., Buganov, V. I. (ed.), Moscow: AN SSSR, Institut istorii, 1974.

Reitenfels, Iakov [Reutenfels, Jacob], *Skazaniia svetleishemu gertsogu toskanskomu Koz'me Tret'emu o Moskovii. Padua 1680*, in *Chteniia* (1905), no. III: 1–128; (1906), no. III: 129–228; (1906), no. IV: 3–24.

Roginskii, M. G., "Poslanie Ioganna Taube i Elerta Kruze," *Russkii istoricheskii zhurnal* 8 (1922): 29–59.

"Ros'pis' voevodam v tekh gorodakh . . . ," in *Vremennik*, III (1849): 608.

Rossiiskii gosudarstvennyi arkhiv drevnikh aktov. Putevoditel' v chetyrekh tomakh, 4 vols., Moscow: Drevlekhranilishche, 1991–9.

Rossiiskoe zakonodatel'stvo X–XX vekov, 9 vols., Chistiakov, O. I. (ed.), Moscow: Iuridicheskaia literatura, 1984–94.

Rozysknye dela Fedore Shaklovitom i ego soobshchnikakh, 4 vols., St. Petersburg: Tip. Tov. Obshchestvennaia pol'za, 1884–93.

Rumiantseva, V. S. (ed.), *Dokumenty Razriadnogo, Posol'skogo, Novgorodskogo i Tainogo prikazov o raskol'nikakh v gorodakh Rossii. 1654–1684 gg.*, Moscow: AN SSSR, Institut istorii, 1990.

Russkaia istoricheskaia biblioteka, 39 vols., St. Petersburg and Leningrad: Arkheograficheskaia komissiia, 1872–1929.

Sakharov, N. (ed.), *Zapiski russkikh liudei. Sobytiia vremen Petra Velikogo*, St. Petersburg: Tip. Sakharova, 1841.

Sbornik Imp. Russkogo istoricheskogo obshchestva, 148 vols., St. Petersburg and Petrograd: Imp. Russkogo istoricheskogo obshchestva, 1867–1916.

Semevskii, M. I., *Istoriko-iuridicheskie akty XVI–XVII veka*, St. Petersburg: Tip. V. Balasheva, 1892.

Shemiakin, A. N. (trans.), "Rossiia pri Petre Velikom," in *Chteniia* (1874), bk. II: 1–120.

Shmidt, S. O. (ed.), "Prodolzhenie khronografa redaktsii 1512 goda," *Istoricheskii arkhiv* 7 (1951): 254–99.

Skinder, A. I., "Zhivaia zhenshchina, vrytaia v zemliu," *Russkaia starina* (1879), 6: 398.

Slovar' Akademii rossiiskoi, 7 vols., St. Petersburg: Pri Imp. Akademii nauk, 1789–94.

Slovar' russkogo iazyka IX–XVII vv., 29 vols. to date, Moscow: Nauka, 1975– .

Sobranie gosudarstvennykh gramot i dogovorov, 5 pts., Moscow: Tip. N. S. Vsevolozhskago, 1813–94.

Sparwenfeld, J. G., *J. G. Sparwenfeld's Diary of a Journey to Russia 1684–87*, Birgengard, Ulla (ed. and trans.), Slavica Suecana, Series A Publications, 1. Stockholm: Kungl, 2002.

Staden, Heinrich von, *The Land and Government of Muscovy: A Sixteenth-Century Account*, Esper, Thomas (ed. and trans.), Stanford University Press, 1967.

Subbotin, N. I. (ed.), *Materialy dlia istorii raskola za pervoe vremia ego sushchestvovaniia*, 9 vols., Moscow: Tip. T. Ris, 1875–86.

Sudnye spiski Maksima Greka i Isaka Sobaki, Pokrovskii, N. N. and Shmidt, S. O. (eds.), Moscow: GAU pri SM SSSR, 1971.

"Sud voevody nad zemskim sudeikoi, 1627 g.," in *Chteniia* (1883), bk. I: 9.

Tikhomirov, M. N., "Maloizvestnye letopisnye pamiatniki," *Istoricheskii arkhiv* 7 (1951): 207–53.

"Maloizvestnye letopisnye pamiatniki XVI v.," *Istoricheskie zapiski* 10 (1941): 84–94.

"Novyi istochnik po istorii vosstaniia Bolotnikova," *Istoricheskii arkhiv* 6 (1951): 81–130.

"Zapiski o regentstve Eleny Glinskoi i boiarskom pravlenii 1533–1547 gg.," *Istoricheskie zapiski* 46 (1954): 278–88.

"Zapiski prikaznykh liudei kontsa XVII veka," *Trudy Otdela drevnerusskoi literatury* 12 (1956): 449–56.

(ed.), *Zakon sudnyi liudem prostrannoi i svodnoi redaktsii*, Moscow: Izd. Akademii nauk SSSR, 1961.

Tikhonravov, N. S., *Sochineniia*, 3 vols., Moscow: Izd. M. i S. Sabashnikovykh, 1898.

Titov, A. A. (ed.), *Kungurskie akty XVII veka. 1668–1699 g.*, St. Petersburg: Tip. Ministerstva vnutrennykh del, 1888.

Tobol'skii archiereiskii dom v XVII veke, Novosibirsk: Sibirskii khronograf, 1994.

Tumins, Valerie A. and Vernadsky, George (eds.), *Patriarch Nikon on Church and State: Nikon's "Refutation,"* Berlin, New York and Amsterdam: Mouton Publishers, 1982.

"Uboistvennye dela i nakazaniia za nikh v Sibirskikh gorodakh 1626–44," in *Chteniia* (1909), no. III, Miscellany: 1–5.

"Ukaz, 29 noiabria 1714, o sozhenii . . . ," *Pamiatniki drevnei pis'mennosti* 38 (1882): 264–65.

Ulfeldt, Jacob, *Puteshestvie v Rossiiu*, Moscow: Iazyki slavianskoi kul'tury, 2002.

Veselovskii, S. B., "Arzamasskie pomestnye akty, 1578–1618," in *Chteniia* (1916), bk. 1, no. 178, p. 238.

Voskoboinikova, N. P. (ed.), *Opisanie drevneishikh dokumentov arkhivov moskovskikh prikazov XVI-nach. XVII vv. (RGADA f. 141. Prikaznye dela starykh let)*, 3 books to date, Moscow: Arkheograficheskii tsentr, 1994– .

Vosstanie 1662 g. v Moskve. Sbornik dokumentov, Moscow: Nauka, 1964.

Vosstanie I. Bolotnikova. Dokumenty i materialy, Moscow: Izd. Sotsial'no-ekonomicheskoi literatury, 1959.

Vosstanie v Moskve 1682 g. Sbornik dokumentov, Buganov, V. I. and Savich, N. G. (eds.), Moscow: Nauka, 1976.

Weber, Friedrich Christian, *The Present State of Russia*, 2 vols., reprint edn., London: Cass, 1968.

Zakonodatel'nye akty Petra I, Voskresenskii, N. A. (ed.), Moscow: Izd. Akademii nauk, 1945.

Zakonodatel'nye akty Russkogo gosudarstva vtoroi poloviny XVI-pervoi poloviny XVII veka, Leningrad: Nauka, Leningradskoe otd., 1987.

Zheliabuzhskii, I. A., "Zapiski," in Sakharov (ed.), *Zapiski russkikh liudei*, 1–112.

Zhuchkova, I. L., "'I . . . derzhati ego v velitsei kreposti': Sobornaia gramota o ssylke Matveia Bashkina – vol'nodumtsa XVI veka," *Istoricheskii arkhiv* (1993), 2: 186–88.

Zimin, A. A., "Kratkie letopistsy XV–XVI vv.," *Istoricheskii arkhiv* (1950), 5: 3–39.

SECONDARY SOURCES

Absoliutizm v Rossii (XVII–XVIII vv.), Moscow: Nauka, 1964.

Adams, Bruce F., *The Politics of Punishment: Prison Reform in Russia, 1863–1917*, DeKalb, Ill.: Northern Illinois University Press, 1996.

A. G., "Iakovlev-Khiron, I. P.," in *Russkii biograficheskii slovar'*, xxv ("Iablonovskii-Fomin"): 88–9.

Agamben, Giorgio, *Homo sacer: Sovereign Power and Bare Life*, Heller-Roazen, Daniel (trans.), Stanford University Press, 1998.

A. K., "Torture," in *Oxford Dictionary of Byzantium*, III (1991): 2098–9.

Akishin, M. O., *Politseiskoe gosudarstvo i sibirskoe obshchestvo. Epokha Petra Velikogo*, Novosibirsk: AVTOR, 1996.

Akishin, M. O. and Remnev, A. V. (eds.), *Vlast' v Sibiri, XVI-nachalo XX veka: Mezharkhivnyi spravochnik*, Novosibirsk: ANO "Mass-Media-Tsentr," 2002.

Aleksandrov, V. A. and Pokrovskii, N. N., "Mirskie organizatsii i administrativnaia vlast' v Sibir' v XVII veke," *Istoriia SSSR* (1986), 1: 47–68, *Vlast' i obshchestvo. Sibir' v XVII v.*, Novosibirsk: Nauka, 1991.

Alekseev, Iu. G., *Sudebnik Ivana III. Traditsiia i reforma*, St. Petersburg: Dmitrii Bulanin, 2001.

"'Zapis' chto tianet dushegubstvom k Moskve.' Nekotorye voprosy datirovki i soderzhaniia," in *Rossiiskoe samoderzhavie i biurokratiia*, 50–63.

Anan'ev, D. A., "Voevodskoe upravlenie Sibiri XVIII veke. Osobennosti protsessa biurokratizatsii," *Rossiiskaia istoriia* (2007), 4: 3–15.

Anisimov, E. V., *Dyba i knut. Politicheskii sysk i russkoe obshchestvo v XVIII veke*, Moscow: Novoe literaturnoe obozrenie, 1999.

Elizaveta Petrovna, Moscow: Molodaia gvardiia, 2005.

Gosudarstvennye preobrazovaniia i samoderzhavie Petra Velikogo v pervoi chetverti XVIII veke, St. Petersburg: Dmitrii Bulanin, 1997.

The Reforms of Peter the Great: Progress through Coercion in Russia, Alexander, John T. (trans.), Armonk, NY: M. E. Sharpe, Inc., 1993.

Russkaia pytka. Politicheskii sysk v Rossii XVIII veka, St. Petersburg: Norint, 2004.

Russkii zastenok. Tainy tainoi kantseliarii, Moscow and St. Petersburg: Tsentrpoligraf, 2010 (republication of Anisimov, *Russkaia pytka*, 2004).

"Samoderzhavie XVIII veka. Pravo pravit' bez prava," in Torke et al. (eds.), *Russische und Ukrainische Geschichte*, 53–61.

Antonov, A. V., "K voprosu o sudebnom immunitete svetskikh zemlevladel'tsev v seredine XVI veka," *Russkii diplomatarii* 5 (1999): 197–206.

Arakcheev, V. A., "Zemskaia reforma XVI veka. Obshcherossiiskie tendentsii i regional'nye osobennosti," *Rossiiskaia istoriia* (2006), 4: 3–11.

Avrich, Paul, *Russian Rebels, 1600–1800*, New York: Schocken Books, 1972.

Avtokratov, V. N., "K istorii zameny stolbtsovoi formy deloproizvodstva – tetradnoi v nachale XVIII v.," *Problemy istochnikovedeniia* 7 (1959): 274–86.

Babich, M. V., *Gosudarstvennye uchrezhdeniia XVIII veka. Komissii petrovskogo vremeni*, Moscow: ROSSPEN, 2003.

"Komissii kak gosudarstvennye uchrezhdeniia petrovskoi epokhi," in *Rossiiskoe samoderzhavie i biurokratiia*, 182–201.

"Landratskaia kantseliariia," in *Gosudarstvennost' Rossii*, III (2001): 12–14.

Babkova, G., "Politika Ekateriny II v oblasti ugolovnogo prava i sudoproizvodstva v 1762–1767 gg.," *Themis. Ezhegodnik istorii prava i pravovedeniia* 4 (2003): 41–76.

Bakhrushin, S. V. "Moskovskoe vosstanie 1648 g.," in Bakhrushin, *Nauchnye trudy*, II (1954): 46–91.

Nauchnye trudy, 4 vols. in 5 pts., Moscow: Izd. Akademii nauk SSSR, 1952–9.

Balakireva, L. M., "Sozdanie Krepostnoi kontory pri Iustits-kollegii (1719 g.)," in *Rossiiskoe samoderzhavie i biurokratiia*, 202–18.

Balázs, Éva H., *Hungary and the Hapsburgs, 1765–1800: An Experiment in Enlightened Absolutism*, Wilkinson, Tim (trans.), Budapest: CEU Press, 1997.

Bardach, Juliusz et al., *Historia państwa i prawa polskiego*, 3rd edn., Warsaw: Państwowe Wydawnictwo Naukowe, 1979.

Barkey, Karen, *Empire of Difference: The Ottomans in Comparative Perspective.* Cambridge University Press, 2008.

Baron, Samuel H. and Heer, Nancy Whittier (eds.), *Windows on the Russian Past: Essays On Soviet Historiography since Stalin*, Columbus, OH: American Association for the Advancement of Slavic Studies, 1977.

Baron, Samuel H., and Kollmann, Nancy Shields (eds.), *Religion and Culture in Early Modern Russia and Ukraine*, DeKalb, Ill.: Northern Illinois University Press, 1997.

Bartlett, Roger and Lehmann-Carli, Gabriela (eds.), *Eighteenth-Century Russia: Society, Culture, Economy: Papers from the VII International Conference of the Study Group on Eighteenth-Century Russia, Wittenberg 2004*, Münster: LIT-Verlag, 2007.

Bazilevich, K. V., "Vosstanie v Moskve v 1662 g.," in *Ocherki istorii SSSR. XVII vek*, 256–64.

Beik, William, *Absolutism and Society in Seventeenth-Century France: State Power and Provincial Aristocracy in Languedoc*, Cambridge University Press, 1985.

Bellomo, Manlio, *The Common Legal Past of Europe, 1000–1800*, Cochrane, Lydia G. (trans.), Washington, DC: Catholic University of America Press, 1995.

Benemanskii, M., *Zakon gradskii*, Moscow: Moskovskii Arkheologicheskii institut, 1917.

Benton, Lauren A., *A Search for Sovereignty: Law and Geography in European Empires, 1400–1900*, Cambridge University Press, 2010.

Berelowitch, André, "De modis demonstrandi in septidecimi saeculi Moschovia," in Torke, Hans-Joachim (ed.), *Von Moskau nach St. Petersburg. Das russische Reich im 17. Jahrhundert*, in *Forschungen zur osteuropäischen Geschichte* 56 (2000): 8–46.

Bérenger, Jean, *A History of the Habsburg Empire 1273–1700*, Simpson, C. A. (trans.), London and New York: Longman, 1994.

Bobrov, A. G. and Vasil'eva, O. V., "Povest' o Shemiakinom sude," in *Slovar' knizhnikov*. vol. III. *XVII vek*, Pt. 3, *P-S* (1998): 245–7.

Boeck, Brian J., *Imperial Boundaries: Cossack Communities and Empire-Building in the Age of Peter the Great*, Cambridge University Press, 2009.

"When Peter I Was Forced to Settle for Less: Coerced Labor and Resistance in a Failed Russian Colony (1695–1711)," *Journal of Modern History* 80 (2008): 485–514.

Boes, Maria R., "Public Appearance and Criminal Judicial Practices in Early Modern Germany," *Social Science History* 20 (1996): 259–79.

Bogatyrev, Sergei, "Battle for Divine Wisdom: The Rhetoric of Ivan IV's Campaign against Polotsk," in Lohr and Poe (eds.), *Military and Society*, 325–63.

"The Heavenly Host and the Sword of Truth: Apocalyptic Imagery in Ivan IV's Muscovy," in Kivelson et al. (eds.), *New Muscovite Cultural History*, 77–90.

"Ivan the Terrible Discovers the West: The Cultural Transformation of Autocracy during the Early Northern Wars," *Russian History* 34 (2007), 1–4: 161–88.

"Localism and Integration in Muscovy," in Bogatyrev (ed.), *Russia Takes Shape*, 59–127.

The Sovereign and His Counsellors: Ritualized Consultations in Muscovite Political Culture, 1350s–1570s, Helsinki: Academia Scientiarum Fennica, 2000.

Bogatyrev, Sergei (ed.), *Russia Takes Shape: Patterns of Integration from the Middle Ages to the Present*, Helsinki: Academia Scientiarum Fennica, 2004.

Bogoiavlenskii, S. K., "Prikaznye d'iaki XVII veka," *Istoricheskie zapiski* 1 (1937): 220–39.

Prikaznye sud'i XVII veka, Moscow and Leningrad: Izd. AN SSSR, 1946.

"Raspravnaia palata pri Boiarskoi dume," in *Sbornik statei, posviashchennykh V. O. Kliuchevskomu*, Moscow: Pechatnia S. P. Iakovleva, 1909: 409–26.

Bogoslovskii, M. M., *Oblastnaia reforma Petra Velikogo. Provintsiia 1719–27*, reprint edn., The Hague and Paris: Mouton, 1970.

Pamiatniki zakonodatel'stva Petra Velikogo, Moscow: Izd. N. N. Kochkova, 1910.

Petr I. Materialy dlia biografii, 5 vols., Moscow: OGIZ, Gos. sotsial'no-ekon. izd., 1940–8.

"Zemskie chelobitnye v drevnei Rusi," *Bogoslovskii vestnik* (1911), I: 133–50; II: 215–41; III: 403–19; IV: 685–96.

"Zemskoe samoupravlenie na russkom Severe v XVII veke," 2 vols., in *Chteniia* (1910), bk. I, pp. i–viii, 321 pp., and 105 pp. of Addenda; (1912), bk. II, pp. i–iv and 311 pp.

Boltunova, E. M., *Gvardiia Petra Velikogo kak voennaia korporatsiia*, Moscow: RGGU, 2011.

Bonney, Richard, *The Rise of the Fiscal State in Europe, 1200–1815*, Oxford University Press, 1999.

Boskovska, Nada, "'Dort werden wir selber Bojaren sein'. Bauerlicher Widerstand in Russland des 17. Jahrhunderts," *Jahrbücher für Geschichte Osteuropas* 37 (1989): 345–86.

Botsman, Daniel B., *Punishment and Power in the Making of Modern Japan*, Princeton and Oxford: Princeton University Press, 2005.

Bouwsma, William, "Lawyers and Early Modern Culture," *American Historical Review* 78 (1973): 303–27.

Brackett, John K., "Crime and Punishment," in Dewald (ed.), *Europe, 1450 to 1789*, II: 79–89.

Breen, Michael P., "Patronage, Politics, and the 'Rule of Law' in Early Modern France," *Proceedings of the Western Society for French History* 33 (2005): 95–113.

Brewer, John, *The Sinews of Power: War, Money and the English State, 1688–1783*, Cambridge, Mass.: Harvard University Press, 1988.

Brewer, John and Hellmuth, Eckhart (eds.), "Introduction," in Brewer and Hellmuth (eds.), *Rethinking Leviathan*, 1–21.

Rethinking Leviathan: The Eighteenth-Century State in Britain and Germany, Oxford and New York: Oxford University Press, 1999.

Briggs, John, Harrison, Christopher, McInnes, Angus and Vincent, David, *Crime and Punishment in England: An Introductory History*, London: University College London Press, 1996.

Brown, Peter, *Power and Persuasion in Late Antiquity: Towards a Christian Empire*, Madison, Wis.: University of Wisconsin Press, 1992.

Brown, Peter B., "Bureaucratic Administration in Seventeenth-Century Russia," in Kotilaine and Poe (eds.), *Modernizing Muscovy*, 57–78.

"Early Modern Russian Bureaucracy: The Evolution of the Chancellery System from Ivan III to Peter the Great, 1478–1717," 2 vols., unpublished PhD dissertation, University of Chicago, 1978.

"Guarding the Gate Keepers: Punishing Errant Rank-and-File Officials in Seventeenth-Century Russia," *Jahrbücher für Geschichte Osteuropas* 50 (2002), 2: 238–43.

"How Muscovy Governed: Seventeenth-Century Russian Central Administration," *Russian History* 36 (2009), 4: 459–529.

"The Military Chancellery: Aspects of Control during the Thirteen Years War," *Russian History* 29 (2002), 1: 19–42.

"Muscovite Government Bureaus," *Russian History* 10 (1983): 269–330.

"Neither Fish nor Fowl: Administrative Legality in Mid- and Late-Seventeenth-Century Russia," *Jahrbücher für Geschichte Osteuropas* 50 (2002): 1–21.

"The Service Land Chancellery Clerks of Seventeenth-Century Russia: Their Regime, Salaries and Economic Survival," *Jahrbücher für Geschichte Osteuropas* 52 (2004), 1: 33–69.

"With All Deliberate Speed: The Officialdom and Departments of the Seventeenth-Century Muscovite Military Chancellery (*Razriad*)," *Russian History* 28 (2001), 1–4: 137–52.

Bryner, Cyril, "The Issue of Capital Punishment in the Reign of Elizabeth Petrovna," *Russian Review* 49 (1990): 389–416.

Buganov, V. I., *Moskovskoe vosstanie 1662 g.*, Moscow: Nauka, 1964.

Moskovskie vosstaniia kontsa XVII veka, Moscow: Nauka, 1969.

Razin i razintsy, Moscow: Nauka, 1995.

Bulgakov, M. B., *Gosudarstvennye sluzhby posadskikh liudei v XVII veke*, Moscow: Izd. IRI RAN, 2004.

"Struktury posadskogo samoupravleniia na gosudarstvennoi i mirskoi sluzhbakh v XVII veke," *Otechestvennaia istoriia* 2005, 4: 94–108.

"Zemskoe sudoproizvodstvo v Ustiuzhne Zheleznopol′skoi v 20-kh godakh XVII v.," *Arkhiv russkoi istorii* (2007), 8: 619–28.

Bulychev, A. A., *Mezhdu sviatymi i demonami. Zametki o posmertnoi sud′be opal′nykh Tsaria Ivana Groznogo*, Moscow: Izd. Znak, 2005.

Burbank, Jane, "An Imperial Rights Regime: Law and Citizenship in the Russian Empire," *Kritika: Explorations in Russian and Eurasian History* 7 (2006), 3: 397–431.

Burbank, Jane and Cooper, Frederick, *Empires in World History: Power and the Politics of Difference*, Princeton and Oxford: Princeton University Press, 2010.

Burbank, Jane and Ransel, David L. (eds.), *Imperial Russia: New Histories for the Empire*, Bloomington, Ind. and Indianapolis: Indiana University Press, 1998.

Burford, E. J. and Shulman, Sandra, *Of Bridles and Burnings: The Punishment of Women*, New York: St. Martin's Press; London: Robert Hale, 1992.

Burkert, Walter, *Homo necans: The Anthropology of Ancient Greek Sacrificial Ritual and Myth*, Bing, Peter (trans.), Berkeley: University of California Press, 1983.

Burns, Kathryn, "Notaries, Truth and Consequences," *American Historical Review* 110 (2005), 2: 350–79.

Bushkovitch, Paul, "The *Life of Saint Filipp*: Tsar and Metropolitan in the Late Sixteenth Century," in Flier and Rowland (eds.), *Medieval Russian Culture*, 29–46.

Peter the Great: The Struggle for Power, 1671–1725, Cambridge University Press, 2001.

Religion and Society in Russia: The Sixteenth and Seventeenth Centuries, New York and Oxford: Oxford University Press, 1992.

Butler, W. E., "Foreign Impressions of Russian Law to 1800: Some Reflections," in Butler (ed.), *Russian Law*, 65–92.

Butler, W. E. (ed.), *Russian Law in Historical and Political Perspective*, Leyden: A. W. Sijthoff, 1977.

Campbell, Ruth, "Sentence of Death by Burning for Women," *The Journal of Legal History* 5 (1984): 44–59.

Caroli, Dorena, "La Torture dans la Russie des XVIIIe et XIXe siècles," in Durand and Otis-Cour (eds.), *La Torture judiciare*, II: 809–45.

Carroll, Stuart, *Blood and Violence in Early Modern France*, Oxford University Press, 2006.

Chekunova, A. E., "Vidovye osobennosti i terminologiia pis'mennykh istochnikov kontsa XVII–pervoi chetverti XVIII veka," *Otechestvennaia istoriia* (2001), 4: 162–70.

Cherepnin, L. V., *Russkaia paleografiia*, Moscow: Gosudarstvennoe izd. politicheskoi literatury, 1956.

Chicherin, Boris, *Oblastnye uchrezhdeniia Rossii v XVII veke*, Moscow: Tip. Aleksandra Semeva, 1856.

Chistiakova, E. V., *Gorodskie vosstaniia v Rossii v pervoi polovine XVII veka (30–40-e gody)*, Voronezh: Izd. Voronezhskogo universiteta, 1975.

Chteniia v Imp. obshchestve istorii i drevnostei rossiiskikh pri Moskovskom universitete. Sbornik, 264 vols., Moscow: Universitetskaia tip., 1845–1918.

Clements, Barbara Evans, Engel, Barbara Alpern and Worobec, Christine D. (eds.), *Russia's Women: Accommodation, Resistance, Transformation*, Berkeley: University of California Press, 1991.

Clements, Barbara Evans, Friedman, Rebecca and Healey, Dan (eds.), *Russian Masculinities in History and Culture*, Basingstoke: Palgrave Macmillan, 2002.

Cohen, Esther, "Symbols of Culpability and the Universal Language of Justice: The Ritual of Public Executions in Late Medieval Europe," *History of European Ideas* 11 (1989): 407–16.

Collins, Daniel E., *Reanimated Voices: Speech Reporting in a Historical-Pragmatic Perspective*, Amsterdam and Philadelphia: John Benjamins, 2001.

"Speech Reporting and the Suppression of Orality in Seventeenth-Century Russian Trial Dossiers," *Journal of Historical Pragmatics* 7 (2006), 2: 265–92.

Cook, Alexander, "Unsettling Accounts: The Trial of the 'Gang of Four': Narratives of Justice and Humanity in the Aftermath of China's Cultural Revolution," unpublished PhD dissertation, Columbia University, 2007.

Coy, Jason P., *Strangers and Misfits: Banishment, Social Control, and Authority in Early Modern Germany*, Leiden and Boston: Brill, 2008.

Cracraft, James, *The Church Reform of Peter the Great*, Stanford University Press, 1971.

The Petrine Revolution in Russian Architecture, University of Chicago Press, 1988.

The Petrine Revolution in Russian Culture, Cambridge, Mass. and London: Belknap Press of Harvard University Press, 2004.

The Petrine Revolution in Russian Imagery, University of Chicago Press, 1997.

The Revolution of Peter the Great, Cambridge, Mass.: Harvard University Press, 2003.

Crews, Robert D., *For Prophet and Tsar: Islam and Empire in Russia and Central Asia*, Cambridge, Mass.: Harvard University Press, 2006.

"Crucifixion," in *Oxford Dictionary of Byzantium*, 1: 555.

Crummey, Robert O., *Aristocrats and Servitors: The Boyar Elite in Russia, 1613–1689*, Princeton University Press, 1983.

"'Constitutional' Reform During the Time of Troubles," in Crummey (ed.), *Reform in Russia*, 28–44.

"Ivan the Terrible," in Baron and Heer (eds.), *Windows on the Russian Past*, 57–74.

The Old Believers and the World of Antichrist: The Vyg Community and the Russian State, 1694–1855, Madison, Milwaukee and London: University of Wisconsin Press, 1970.

Crummey, Robert O. (ed.), *Reform in Russia and the U.S.S.R.*, Urbana, Ill. and Chicago: University of Illinois Press, 1989.

Daly, Jonathan, "Russian Punishments in the European Mirror," in McCaffray (ed.), *Russia in the European Context*, 161–88.

Davies, Brian L., *Empire and Military Revolution in Eastern Europe: Russia's Turkish Wars in the Eighteenth Century*, London: Continuum, 2011.

"Local Government and Administration," in Perrie (ed.), *Cambridge History of Russia*, 1: 464–85.

"The Politics of Give and Take: *Kormlenie* as Service Remuneration and Generalized Exchange, 1488–1726," in Kleimola and Lenhoff (eds.), *Culture and Identity*, 39–67.

State Power and Community in Early Modern Russia, Basingstoke and New York: Palgrave Macmillan, 2004.

Davies, Norman, *God's Playground: A History of Poland*, 2 vols., New York: Columbia University Press, 1982.

Davis, Natalie Zemon, *Fiction in the Archives: Pardon Tales and Their Tellers in Sixteenth-Century France*, Stanford University Press, 1987.

The Gift in Sixteenth-Century France, Madison, Wis.: University of Wisconsin Press, 2000.

Demidova, N. F., *Sluzhilaia biurokratiia v Rossii XVII v. i ee rol' v formirovanii absoliutizma*, Moscow: Nauka, 1987.

Devereaux, Simon and Griffiths, Paul (eds.), *Penal Practice and Culture, 1500–1900: Punishing the English*, London: Palgrave Macmillan, 2004.

Dewald, Jonathan (ed.), *Europe, 1450 to 1789: Encyclopedia of the Early Modern World*, 6 vols., New York: Charles Scribner's Sons, 2004.

Dewey, Horace W., "The 1550 *Sudebnik* as an Instrument of Reform," *Jahrbücher für Geschichte Osteuropas* 10 (1962), 2: 161–80.

"The Decline of the Muscovite *Namestnik*," *Oxford Slavonic Papers* 12 (1965): 21–39.

"Muscovite *Guba* Charters and the Concept of Brigandage (*Razboj*)," *Papers of the Michigan Academy of Science, Arts and Letters*. Pt. 2. *Social Sciences* 51 (1966): 277–88.

"Political *Poruka* in Muscovite Rus'," *Russian Review* 46 (1987), 2: 117–34.

"Trial by Combat in Muscovite Russia," *Oxford Slavonic Papers* 9 (1960): 21–31.

Dewey, Horace W. and Kleimola, Ann M., "Coercion by Righter (*Pravezh*) in Old Russian Administration," *Canadian-American Slavic Studies* 9 (1975): 156–67.

Dmitriev, F., *Istoriia sudebnykh instantsii i grazhdanskogo appelliatsionnogo sudoproizvodstva ot sudebnikia do uchrezhdeniia o guberniiakh*, Moscow: Universitetskaia tip., 1859.

Dobroklonskii, A. P., "Solotchinskii monastyr', ego slugi i krest'iane v XVII veke," in *Chteniia* 1888, 1: 1–130.

Dolan, Frances E., *Dangerous Familiars: Representations of Domestic Crime in England, 1550–1700*, Ithaca, NY and London: Cornell University Press, 1994.

Druzhinin, V. G., *Raskol na Donu v kontse XVII veka*, St. Petersburg: Tip. I. N. Skorokhodova, 1889.

Dukes, Paul, *Catherine the Great and the Russian Nobility: A Study Based on the Materials of the Legislative Commission of 1767*, London: Cambridge University Press, 1967.

Dülmen, Richard van, *Theatre of Horror: Crime and Punishment in Early Modern Germany*, Neu, Elisabeth (trans.), Cambridge: Polity Press, 1990.

Dunning, Chester S. L., "The Legacy of Russia's First Civil War and the Time of Troubles," in Torke, Hans-Joachim (ed.), *Von Moskau nach St. Petersburg. Das russische Reich im 17. Jahrhundert* in *Forschungen zur osteuropäischen Geschichte* 56 (2000): 133–55.

Russia's First Civil War: The Time of Troubles and the Founding of the Romanov Dynasty, University Park, Pa.: Pennsylvania State University Press, 2001.

"Terror in the Time of Troubles," *Kritika: Explorations in Russian and Eurasian History* 4 (2003), 3: 491–513.

Dunning, Chester S. L. and Smith, Norman S., "Moving beyond Absolutism: Was Early Modern Russia a 'Fiscal-Military' State?," *Russian History* 33 (2006), 1: 19–43.

Durand, Bernard and Otis-Cour, Leah (eds.), *La Torture judiciare: approches historiques et juridiques*, 2 vols., Lille: Centre d'Histoire Judiciare, 2002.

Dvorkin, Aleksandr, *Ivan Groznyi kak religioznyi tip. Stat′i i materialy*, Nizhnii Novgorod: Izd. Bratstva vo imia Sv. Aleksandra Nevskogo, 2005.

Eder, Markus, *'At the Instigation of the Devil': Capital Punishment and the Assize in Early Modern England, 1670–1730*, Hilgertshausen-Tandern: Markus Eder, 2009.

Eeckaute, Denise, "Les brigands en Russie du XVII au XIX siècle: mythe et realité," *Revue d'histoire moderne et contemporaine* 12 (1965): 161–202.

Efremov, N. N. and Shtamm, S. I., "Osnovnye istochniki prava," in Nersesiants (ed.), *Razvitie russkogo prava*, 17–44.

Engelstein, Laura, "Weapon of the Weak (Apologies to James Scott): Violence in Russian History," *Kritika: Explorations in Russian and Eurasian History* 4 (2003), 3: 679–93.

Enin, G. P., *Voevodskoe kormlenie v Rossii v XVII veke (Soderzhanie naseleniem uezda gosudarstvennogo organa vlasti)*, St. Petersburg: Rossiiskaia natsional′naia biblioteka, 2000.

"Voevodskoe prazdnichnoe kormlenie v nachale 60-kh godov XVIII v.," *Vspomogatel′nye istoricheskie distsipliny* 25 (1994): 103–16.

Eroshkin, N. P., *Ocherki istorii gosudarstvennykh uchrezhdenii dorevoliutsionnoi Rossii*, Moscow: Gosud. uchebno-pedagog. izd., 1960.

Eroshkina, A. N., "Landrat," in *Gosudarstvennost′ Rossii*, V (2005), 1: 486–7.

"Prikaz sysknykh del [articles nos.] 1–5," in *Gosudarstvennost′ Rossii*, III (2001): 403–6.

Erusalimskii, K. Iu., *Sbornik Kurbskogo*. Vol. 1. *Issledovanie knizhnoi kul′tury*, Moscow: Znak, 2009.

Eskin, Iu. M., *Ocherki istorii mestnichestva v Rossii XVI–XVII vv.*, Moscow: Kvadriga, 2009.

"Raspravnaia palata," in *Gosudarstvennost′ Rossii*, IV (2001): 18–19.

"Razboinyi prikaz," in *Gosudarstvennost′ Rossii*, IV (2001): 11–12.

"'I Vasilei skazal, to de Artemei zamyslil vorovski . . . '," *Istoricheskii arkhiv* 1993, 2: 189–209.

Evans, Richard J., *Rituals of Retribution: Capital Punishment in Germany, 1600–1987*, Oxford and New York: Oxford University Press, 1996.

Evans, Robert John Weston, *The Making of the Habsburg Monarchy, 1550–1700: An Interpretation*, Oxford: Clarendon Press; New York: Oxford University Press, 1979.

Evfimov, S. V., "Evdokiia Lopukhina – posledniaia russkaia tsaritsa XVII veka," in Lobachev and Lavrov (eds.), *Srednevekovaia Rus′*, 158–61.

Evreinov, N. N., *Istoriia telesnykh nakazanii v Rossii*, New York: Chalidze, 1979.

Evremova, N. N., "Sudoistroistvo i protsessual′noe pravo," in Skripilev (ed.), *Razvitie russkogo prava*, 215–39.

Fedotov, George P., *St. Filipp, Metropolitan of Moscow: Encounter with Ivan the Terrible*, Belmont, Mass.: Notable & Academic Books, 1978.

Feldbrugge, Ferdinand, *Law in Medieval Russia*, Leiden and Boston: Martinus Nijhoff, 2009.

Fichtner, Paula Sutter, *The Habsburg Monarchy, 1490–1848: Attributes of Empire*, Basingstoke and New York: Palgrave Macmillan, 2003.

Flier, Michael S., "K semioticheskomu analizu Zolotoi palaty Moskovskogo Kremlia," in *Drevnerusskoe iskusstvo. Russkoe iskusstvo pozdnego srednevekov′ia. Shestnadtsatyi vek*, Batalov, Andrei (ed.) et al., St. Petersburg: Dmitrii Bulanin, 2003: 178–87.

"Political Ideas and Rituals," in Perrie (ed.), *Cambridge History of Russia*, I: 387–408.

"The Semiotics of Faith in Fifteenth-Century Novgorod: An Analysis of the Quadripartite Icon," *Canadian-American Slavic Studies* 25 (1995), 1–4: 125–58.

"Till the End of Time: The Apocalypse in Russian Historical Experience before 1500," in Kivelson and Greene (eds.), *Orthodox Russia*, 127–58.

Flier, Michael S. and Rowland, Daniel (eds.), *Medieval Russian Culture*. Vol. II. California Slavic Studies, XIX, Berkeley and Los Angeles: University of California Press, 1994.

Floria, B. N., "S. Nemoevskii o Russkom gosudarstve i obshchestve XVI-nachala XVII vv.," *Russia Medievalis* 9 (n.d.), I: 105–14.

Ford, Franklin L., *Robe and Sword: The Regrouping of the French Aristocracy after Louis XIV*, Cambridge, Mass.: Harvard University Press, 1962.

Foucault, Michel, *Discipline and Punish: The Birth of the Prison*, Sheridan, Alan (trans.), New York: Vintage Books, 1979.

Franklin, Simon, "On Meanings, Functions and Paradigms of Law in Early Rus′," *Russian History* 34 (2007), 1–4: 62–82.

Freeze, Gregory L., *From Supplication to Revolution*, New York and Oxford: Oxford University Press, 1988.

"Institutionalizing Piety: The Church and Popular Religion, 1750–1850," in Burbank and Ransel (eds.), *Imperial Russia*, 210–49.

Freeze, Gregory L. (ed.), *Russia: A History*, Oxford and New York: Oxford University Press, 1997.

Garland, David, *Peculiar Institution: America's Death Penalty in an Age of Abolition*, Cambridge, Mass.: Harvard University Press, 2010.

Gaskill, Malcolm, *Crime and Mentalities in Early Modern England*, Cambridge University Press, 2000.

"Reporting Murder: Fiction in the Archives in Early Modern England," *Social History* 23 (1998): 1–30.

Gatrell, Vic, Lenman, Bruce and Parker, Geoffrey (eds.), *Crime and the Law: The Social History of Crime in Western Europe Since 1500*, London: Europa Publications, 1980.

Gel′vikh, A., "Lopukhin, A. F.," in *Russkii biograficheskii slovar′*, X ("Labzina-Liashenko"): 648–9.

Gentes, Andrew A., *Exile to Siberia, 1590–1822*, Basingstoke: Palgrave Macmillan, 2008.

Gernet, M. N., *Istoriia tsarskoi tiur'my*. Vol. 1. *1762–1825*, Moscow: Gosud. izd. iuridicheskoi literatury, 1951.

Gerth, H. H. and Mills, C. Wright (eds. and trans.), *From Max Weber: Essays in Sociology*, New York: Oxford University Press, 1946.

Geyer, Michael, "Some Hesitant Observations concerning 'Political Violence'," *Kritika: Explorations in Russian and Eurasian History* 4 (2003), 3: 695–708.

Giddens, Anthony, *The Nation-State and Violence: Volume Two of A Contemporary Critique of Historical Materialism*, Berkeley and Los Angeles: University of California Press, 1987.

Girard, René, *Violence and the Sacred*, Gregory, Patrick (trans.), Baltimore and London: Johns Hopkins University Press, 1977.

Givens, Robert D., "Eighteenth-Century Nobiliary Career Patterns and Provincial Government," in Pintner and Rowney (eds.), *Russian Officialdom*, 106–29.

Glaz'ev, V. N., *Vlast' i obshchestvennost' na iuge Rossii v XVII veke. Protivodeistvie ugolovnoi prestupnosti*, Voronezh: Izd. Voronezhskogo gosud. universiteta, 2001.

Goffman, Daniel, *The Ottoman Empire and Early Modern Europe*, Cambridge University Press, 2002.

Goldfrank, David M., "Burn, Baby, Burn: Popular Culture and Heresy in Late Medieval Russia," *Journal of Popular Culture* 31 (1988): 17–32.

"Theocratic Imperatives, the Transcendent, the Worldly, and Political Justice in Russia's Early Inquisitions," in Timberlake (ed.), *Religious and Secular Sources*, 30–47.

Golikov, I. I., *Deianiia Petra Velikogo, mudrago preobrazitelia Rossii; sobrannye iz dostovernykh istochnikov i raspolizhenniia po godam*, 12 vols., Moscow: Universitetskaia tip. u N. Novikova, 1788–9.

Golikova, N. B., "Organy politicheskogo syska i ikh razvitie v XVII–XVIII vv.," in *Absoliutizm v Rossii*, 243–80.

Politicheskie protsessy pri Petre I. Po materialam Preobrazhenskogo prikaza, Moscow: Izd. Moskovskogo universiteta, 1957.

Gorchakov, M., *O zemel'nykh vladeniiakh vserossiiskikh mitropolitov, patriarkhov i sv. Sinoda (988–1738 gg.)*, St. Petersburg: Tip. A. Transhilia, 1871.

Gordon, Linda, *Cossack Rebellions: Social Turmoil in the Sixteenth-Century Ukraine*, Albany, NY: State University of New York Press, 1983.

Gosudarstvennaia Tret'iakovskaia Galereia. Iubileinyi al'bom k 850-letiiu Moskvy, Moscow: Krasnaia ploshchad', 1997.

Gosudarstvennost' Rossii. Slovar'-spravochnik, 5 bks. in 6 pts., Moscow: Nauka, 1996–2005.

Got'e, Iu. V., *Istoriia oblastnogo upravleniia v Rossii ot Petra I do Ekateriny II. Reforma 1727 goda. Oblastnoe delenie i oblastnye uchrezhdeniia 1727–1775 gg.*, 2 vols.; vol. I, Moscow: Tip. G. Lissiera i D. Sobko, 1913; vol. II, Moscow and Leningrad: Izd. Akademii nauk SSSR, 1941.

Graham, Hugh, "How Do We Know What We Know About Ivan the Terrible? (A Paradigm)," *Russian History* 14 (1987), 1–4: 177–98.

Greenshields, Malcolm, *An Economy of Violence in Early Modern France: Crime and Justice in the Haute Auvergne, 1587–1664*, University Park, Pa.: Pennsylvania State University Press, 1994.

Grekov, B. D., *Izbrannye trudy*, 4 vols., Moscow: Izd. Akademii nauk SSSR, 1957–60.

"Novgorodskii dom sviatoi Sofii. (Opyt izucheniia organizatsii i vnutrennikh otnoshenii krupnoi tserkovnoi votchiny)," in Grekov, *Izbrannye trudy*, IV (1960), 484 pp.

Griffiths, Paul, "Bodies and Souls in Norwich: Punishing Petty Crime, 1540–1700," in Devereaux and Griffiths (eds.), *Penal Practice and Culture*, 85–120.

Groebner, Valentin, *Liquid Assets, Dangerous Gifts: Presents and Politics at the End of the Middle Ages*, Selwyn, Pamela E. (trans.), Philadelphia: University of Pennsylvania Press, 2002.

Gurliand, I. Ia., "Prikaz sysknykh del," in *Sbornik statei po istorii prava*, 87–109.

Prikaz velikogo gosudaria tainykh del, Iaroslavl: Tip. Gubernskogo pravleniia, 1902.

Halperin, Charles, "Administrative Discretion in Ivan IV's Muscovy," *Russian History* 33 (2006): 429–46.

Harding, Robert, "Corruption and the Moral Boundaries of Patronage in the Renaissance," in Lytle and Orgel (eds.), *Patronage in the Renaissance*, 47–64.

Hartley, Janet, "Russia as a Fiscal-Military State, 1689–1825," in Storrs (ed.), *Fiscal-Military State*, 125–45.

Harvey, A. D., "Burning Women at the Stake in Eighteenth-Century England," *Criminal Justice History* 11 (1990): 193–5.

Hellie, Richard, "The Church and the Law in Late Muscovy: Chapters 12 and 13 of the *Ulozhenie* of 1649," *Canadian-American Slavic Studies* 25 (1991), 1–4: 179–99.

"Commentary on [*Ulozhenie*] Chapter 11 (The Judicial Process for Peasants)," *Russian History* 17 (1990), 3: 305–39.

"Commentary on [*Ulozhenie*] Chapters 3 through 6," *Russian History* 17 (1990), 1: 65–78.

"Commentary on [*Ulozhenie*] Chapters 7–9," *Russian History* 17 (1990), 2: 179–226.

"Early Modern Russian Law: The *Ulozhenie* of 1649," *Russian History* 15 (1988), 2–4: 155–80.

The Economy and Material Culture of Russia: 1600–1725, Chicago and London: University of Chicago Press, 1999.

Enserfment and Military Change in Muscovy, Chicago and London: University of Chicago Press, 1971.

"Late Medieval and Early Modern Russian Civilization and Modern Neuroscience," in Kleimola and Lenhoff (eds.), *Culture and Identity*, 146–65.

"The Law," in Perrie (ed.), *Cambridge History of Russia*, I: 360–86.

"Muscovite Law and Society: The Ulozhenie of 1649 as a Reflection of the Political and Social Development of Russia Since the Sudebnik of 1589," unpublished PhD dissertation, University of Chicago, 1965.

"Russia, 1200–1815," in Bonney (ed.), *Rise of the Fiscal State*, 481–505.

"Russian Law from Oleg to Peter the Great," in Kaiser (trans. and ed.), *Laws of Rus'*, xi–xl.

Slavery in Russia, 1450–1725, Chicago and London: University of Chicago Press, 1982.

"The Structure of Modern Russian History: Toward a Dynamic Model," *Russian History* 4 (1977), 1: 1–22.

"Thoughts on the Absence of Elite Resistance in Muscovy," *Kritika: Explorations in Russian and Eurasian History* 1 (2000), 1: 5–20.

"*Ulozhenie* Commentary: Preamble and Chapters 1–2," *Russian History* 15 (1988), 2–4: 181–224.

Henshall, Nicholas, *The Myth of Absolutism: Change and Continuity in Early Modern European Monarchy*, London and New York: Longman, 1992.

Hill, Bridget (ed.), *Eighteenth-Century Women: An Anthology*, London: Unwin Hyman, 1984.

Hittle, J. Michael, *The Service City: State and Townsmen in Russia, 1600–1800*, Cambridge, Mass. and London: Harvard University Press, 1979.

Hoch, Steven L., *Serfdom and Social Control in Russia: Petrovskoe, a Village in Tambov*, University of Chicago Press, 1986.

Hughes, Lindsey A. J., *Russia in the Age of Peter the Great*, New Haven and London: Yale University Press, 1998.

Russia and the West: The Life of a Seventeenth-Century Westernizer, Prince Vasily Vasil'evich Golitsyn (1643–1714), Newtonville, Mass.: Oriental Research Partners, 1984.

Sophia, Regent of Russia, 1657–1704, New Haven and London: Yale University Press, 1990.

Hunt, Priscilla, "Ivan IV's Personal Mythology of Kingship," *Slavic Review* 52 (1993), 4: 769–809.

Iliushenko, M. P., *Istoriia deloproizvodstva v dorevoliutionnoi Rossii*, Moscow: RGGU, 1993.

Imber, Colin, *The Ottoman Empire, 1300–1650: The Structure of Power*, 2nd edn., Basingstoke and New York: Palgrave Macmillan, 2009.

Inalcik, Halil, *The Ottoman Empire: The Classical Age 1300–1600*, Itzkowitz, Norman and Imber, Colin (trans.), New York and Washington: Praeger, 1973.

Ingham, Norman, "Muscovite Law and the Tale of Ruff Son of Ruff," *Russian History* 34 (2007), 1–4: 303–14.

Innes, Matthew, "Charlemagne's Government," in Story (ed.), *Charlemagne. Empire and Society*, 71–89.

Issatschenko, Alexander V., "Russian," in Schenker and Stankiewicz (eds.), *Slavic Literary Languages*, 119–42.

Iurganov, A. L., *Kategorii russkoi srednevekovoi kul'tur*, Moscow: MIROS, 1998.

Ivanov, V. I., *Bukhgalterskii uchet v Rossii XVI–XVII vv. Istoriko-iuridicheskovedcheskoe issledovanie monastyrskikh prikhodo-raskhodnykh knig*, St. Petersburg: Dmitrii Bulanin, 2005.

Jennings, Ronald C., "Kadi, Court, and Legal Procedure in 17th c. Ottoman Kayseri: The Kadi and the Legal System," *Studia Islamica* 48 (1978): 133–72.

Johnson, Eric A. and Monkkonen, Eric H., "Introduction," in Johnson and Monkkonen (eds.), *Civilization of Crime*, 1–13.

Johnson, Eric A. and Monkkonen, Eric H. (eds.), *The Civilization of Crime: Violence in Town and Country since the Middle Ages*, Urbana, Ill. and Chicago: University of Illinois Press, 1996.

Jones, C. P., "Tattooing and Branding in Graeco-Roman Antiquity," *The Journal of Roman Studies* 77 (1987): 139–55.

De Jong, Mayke, "Monastic Prisoners or Opting Out? Political Coercion and Honour in the Frankish Kingdoms," in de Jong (ed.), *Topographies of Power*, 291–328.

De Jong, Mayke (ed.), *Topographies of Power in the Early Middle Ages*, Leiden: Brill, 2001.

Kaiser, Daniel H., *The Growth of the Law in Medieval Russia*, Princeton University Press, 1980.

Kamen, Henry, *The Spanish Inquisition: An Historical Revision*, London: Weidenfeld & Nicolson, 1997.

Kamler, Marcin, "Penalties for Common Crimes in Polish Towns, 1550–1650," *Acta Poloniae Historica* 71 (1995): 161–74.

Kann, Robert A., *A History of the Habsburg Empire, 1526–1918*, Berkeley, Los Angeles and London: University of California Press, 1974.

Kappeler, Andreas, *Ivan Groznyj im Spiegel der ausländischen Druckschriften seiner Zeit*, Berne and Frankfurt: Herbert Lang, 1972.

The Russian Empire: A Multiethnic History, Essex: Longman, 2001.

Kappeler, Andreas (ed.), *Die Geschichte Russlands im 16. und 17. Jahrhundert aus der Perspektive seiner Regionen*, Wiesbaden: Harrassowitz, 2004.

Karamzin, N. M., *Istoriia gosudarstva rossiiskogo*, 4 vols., reprint edn., Moscow: Kniga, 1989.

Kartashev, A. V., *Ocherki po istorii russkoi tserkvi*, 2 vols., Paris: YMCA Press, 1959.

Kashtanov, S. M., "Iz istorii poslednikh udelov," *Trudy Moskovskogo gosud. istoriko-arkhivnogo instituta*, 10 (1957): 275–302.

Ocherki russkoi diplomatiki, Moscow: Nauka, 1970.

Kavelin, K., *Osnovnye nachala russkogo sudoustroistva i grazhdanskogo sudoproizvodstva i grazhdanskago sudoproizvodstva, v period vremeni ot Ulozheniia do Uchrezhdeniia o guberniiakh*, Moscow: Tip. Avgusta Semena, 1844.

Kazakova, N. A. and Ia. S. Lur'e, *Antifeodal'nye ereticheskie dvizheniia na Rusi XIV-nachala XVI veka*, Moscow: Izd. Akademii nauk SSSR, 1955.

Keenan, Edward L., "Muscovite Political Folkways," *Russian Review* 45 (1986), 2: 115–81.

"Putting Kurbskii in His Place, or: Observations and Suggestions concerning the Place of the *History of the Grand Prince of Muscovy* in the History of Muscovite Literary Culture," *Forshchungen zur osteuropaïschen Geschichte* 24 (1978): 131–62.

Keep, John, "Bandits and the Law in Muscovy," *Slavonic and East European Review* 35, 84 (1956): 201–22.

Kennan, George, *Siberia and the Exile System*, 2 vols., London: J. R. Osgood, McIlvaine, 1891.

Kharkhordin, Oleg, "What is the State? The Russian Concept of *Gosudarstvo* in the European Context," *History and Theory* 40 (2001): 206–40.

Khodarkovsky, Michael, *Russia's Steppe Frontier: The Making of a Colonial Empire, 1500–1800*, Bloomington, Ind.: Indiana University Press, 2002.

Khoury, Dina Rizk, *State and Provincial Society in the Ottoman Empire. Mosul, 1540–1834*, Cambridge University Press, 1997.

Kim, Marie Seong-Hak, "Lawyers," in Dewald (ed.), *Europe, 1450 to 1789*, III: 459–64.

Kivelson, Valerie A., *Autocracy in the Provinces: The Muscovite Gentry and Political Culture in the Seventeenth Century*, Stanford University Press, 1996.

Cartographies of Tsardom: The Land and Its Meaning in Seventeenth-Century Russia, Ithaca, NY and London: Cornell University Press, 2006.

"Coerced Confessions, or If Tituba Had Been Enslaved in Muscovy," in Kivelson et al. (eds.), *New Muscovite Cultural History*, 171–84.

"Desperate Magic: The Moral Economy of Witchcraft in Seventeenth-Century Russia," unpubl. ms., 2010.

"The Devil Stole His Mind: The Tsar and the 1648 Moscow Uprising," *American Historical Review* 98 (1993), 3: 733–56.

"Male Witches and Gendered Categories in 17th-c. Russia," *Comparative Studies in Society and History* (2003): 606–31.

"Muscovite 'Citizenship': Rights without Freedom," *Journal of Modern History* 74 (2002), 3: 465–89.

"On Words, Sources, and Historical Method: Which Truth about Muscovy?," *Kritika: Explorations in Russian and Eurasian History* 3 (2002): 487–99.

"Patrolling the Boundaries: The Uses of Witchcraft Accusations and Household Strife in Seventeenth-Century Muscovy," *Harvard Ukrainian Studies* 19 (1997): 302–23.

"Political Sorcery in Sixteenth-Century Muscovy," in Kleimola and Lenhoff (eds.), *Culture and Identity in Muscovy*, 267–83.

"'Sovereign Have Pity on Me!': Anomalies in Muscovite Sentencing," *Russian History* (2007), 1–4: 331–40.

"Through the Prism of Witchcraft: Gender and Social Change in Seventeenth-Century Muscovy," in Clements et al. (eds.), *Russia's Women*, 74–94.

"Torture, Truth, and Embodying the Intangible in Muscovite Witchcraft Trials," in Marker et al. (eds.), *Everyday Life*, 359–73.

Kivelson, Valerie A. and Greene, Robert H. (eds.), *Orthodox Russia: Belief and Practice Under the Tsars*, University Park, Pa.: Pennsylvania State University Press, 2003.

Kivelson, Valerie A., Petrone, K., Kollmann, Nancy Shields and Flier, Michael S. (eds.), *The New Muscovite Cultural History*, Bloomington, Ind.: Slavica, 2009.

Kleandrova, V. M., "Istochniki prava," in Skripilev (ed.), *Razvitie russkogo prava*, 40–51.

Kleimola, A. M. and Lenhoff, G. D. (eds.), *Culture and Identity in Muscovy, 1359–1584*, UCLA Slavic Studies, New Series, 3, Moscow: ITZ-Garant, 1997.

Kliuchevskii, V. O., "Istoriia soslovii v Rossii," in Kliuchevskii, *Sochineniia*, VI (1959): 276–466.

Sochineniia, 8 vols., Moscow: Izd. Sotsial'no-ekonom. literatury, 1956–9.

Kolchin, M. A., *Ssyl'nye i zatochennye v ostrog Solovetskogo monastyria v XVI–XIX vv.*, in Tsepkov, A. I. (ed.), *Monastyrskie tiur'my v tsarskii Rossii: Sbornik*, Riazan': Aleksandriia, 2010: 173–330; reprinted from Moscow 1908 edn.

Kolesnikova, E. A., "Mestnye organy vlasti v Rossii posle Smuty (1613–1645 gg.)," unpublished Candidate dissertation, Moskovskii pedagog. gosud. Universitet im Lenina, 1995.

Kollmann, Nancy Shields, "27 October 1698: Peter Punishes the *Strel'tsy*," in Cross, Anthony Glenn (ed.), *Days from the Reigns of Eighteenth-Century Russian Rulers*, Cambridge: Study Group on Eighteenth-Century Russia, 2007, I: 23–36.

"Beginning a Civilizing Process: Handbooks of Morals and Behavior in Early Modern Russia," in Marker et al. (eds.), *Everyday Life*, 329–44.

By Honor Bound: State and Society in Early Modern Russia, Ithaca, NY: Cornell University Press, 1999.

"Change and Continuity in the Law under Peter I," in Bartlett and Lehmann-Carli (eds.), *Eighteenth-Century Russia*, 383–91.

"Concepts of Society and Social Identity in Early Modern Russia," in Baron and Kollmann (eds.), *Religion and Culture*, 34–51.

"Etiquette for Peter's Time: The Honorable Mirror for Youth," *Russian History* 35 (2008), 1–2: 63–83.

"The Extremes of Patriarchy: Spousal Abuse and Murder in Early Modern Russia," *Russian History* 25 (1998), 1–2: 133–40.

"Judicial Autonomy in the Criminal Law: Beloozero and Arzamas," in Kappeler (ed.), *Die Geschichte Russlands*, 252–68.

Kinship and Politics: The Making of the Muscovite Political System, 1345–1547, Stanford University Press, 1987.

"Law and Society in Seventeenth-Century Russia," in Perrie (ed.), *Cambridge History of Russia*, I: 559–78.

"Lynchings and Legality in Early Modern Russia," *Forschungen zur osteuropaïschen Geschichte* 56 (2002): 1801–6.

"Marking the Body in Early Modern Judicial Punishment," *Harvard Ukrainian Studies* 28, 1–4 (2006): 557–65.

"Muscovite Russia, 1450–1598," in Freeze (ed.), *Russia: A History*, 27–54.

"Pictures at an Execution: Johann Georg Korb's 'Execution of the *Strel'tsy*'," in Boeck, Brian, Martin, Russell E. and Rowland, Daniel (eds.), *Dubitando: Studies in History and Culture in Honor of Donald Ostrowski*. Bloomington, IN: Slavica Publishers, forthcoming 2012.

"Provincial Landowners as Litigants," in Ostrowski, Donald and Poe, Marshall T. (eds.), *Portraits of Old Russia: Imagined Lives of Ordinary People, 1300–1725*, Armonk, NY and London: M. E. Sharpe, 2011: 179–87.

"The Quality of Mercy in Early Modern Legal Practice," *Kritika: Explorations in Russian and Eurasian History* 7 (2006), 1: 5–22.

"Ritual and Social Drama at the Muscovite Court," *Slavic Review* 45 (1986), 3: 486–502.

"Russia," in Allmond, Christopher (ed.), *The New Cambridge Medieval History*. Vol. VII. *c.1415–c.1500*, Cambridge University Press, 1998, 748–70.

"Russian Law in a Eurasian Setting: The Arzamas Region, Late Seventeenth–Early Eighteenth Century," in Szvak (ed.), *Place of Russia in Eurasia*, 200–6.

"Torture in Early Modern Russia," in Kivelson et al. (eds.), *New Muscovite Cultural History*, 159–70.

"Women's Honor in Early Modern Russia," in Clements et al. (eds.), *Russia's Women*, 60–73.

Kollmann Jr., Jack E., "The Moscow Stoglav ('Hundred Chapters') Church Council of 1551," unpublished PhD dissertation, University of Michigan, 1978.

Kondratieva, Tamara, *Gouverner et nourrir: du pouvoir à la Russie, XVIe–XXe siècles*, Paris: Belles Lettres, 2002.

Korsakova, V., "Gagarin, Kniaz' Matvei Petrovich," in *Russkii biograficheskii slovar'*, IV ("Gaag-Girbel'"): 75–82.

"Glinskii, Kniaz' Vasilii-Prokopii M.," in *Russkii biograficheskii slovar'*, V ("Gerberskii-Gogenloe"): 319.

"Nesterov, A. Ia.," in *Russkii biograficheskii slovar'*, XI ("Naake-Nakenskii-Nikita Nikitich Starshii"): 252–3.

"Prozorovskii, Kniaz' Semen Vasil'evich," in *Russkii biograficheskii slovar'*, XV: 26–9.

"Shein, Mikahil Borisovich," in *Russkii biograficheskii slovar'*, XXIII ("Shebanov-Shiuts"): 41–59.

Kosheleva, O. E., *Liudi Sankt-Peterburgskogo ostrova Petrovskogo vremeni*, Moscow: OGI, 2004.

Kotilaine, Jarmo and Poe, Marshall (eds.), *Modernizing Muscovy: Reform and Social Change in Seventeenth-Century Muscovy*, London and New York: Routledge, 2004.

Kouri, E. I. and Scott, Tom (eds.), *Politics and Society in Reformation Europe*, Basingstoke: Macmillan Press, 1987.

Kozliakov, V. N., *Sluzhilyi gorod Moskovskogo gosudarstva XVII veka. (Ot Smuty do Sobornogo ulozheniia)*, Iaroslavl: Izd. Iaroslavskogo gosud. pedegog. universiteta im. K. K. Ushinskogo, 2000.

Krom, M. M., "Private Service and Patronage in Sixteenth-Century Russia," *Russian History* 35 (2008), 3–4: 309–20.

'Vdovstvuiushchee tsarstvo'. Politicheskii krizis v Rossii 30–40-kh godov XVI veka, Moscow: Novoe literaturnoe obozrenie, 2010.

Kunzle, David, *History of the Comic Strip*. Vol. 1. *The Early Comic Strip*, Berkeley: University of California Press, 1973.

Kuritsyn, V. M., "Pravo i sud," in *Ocherki istorii SSSR. Period feodalizma. XVII vek*, 394–411.

Langbein, John H., "The Criminal Trial before the Lawyers," *University of Chicago Law Review* 45 (1978): 263–316.

Prosecuting Crime in the Renaissance: England, Germany, France, Cambridge, Mass: Harvard University Press, 1974.

Torture and the Law of Proof, University of Chicago Press, 1977.

Lapman, Mark Charles, "Political Denunciations in Muscovy, 1600 to 1649: The Sovereign's Word and Deed," unpublished PhD dissertation, Harvard University, 1981.

Lapteva, T. A., *Provintsial'noe dvorianstvo Rossii v XVII veke*, Moscow: Drevlekhranilishche, 2010.

Lashkevich, S., "Istoricheskoe zamechanie o smertnoi kazni samozvantsa, Aleksandra Semikova . . . ," in *Chteniia* (1860), 1, pt. 2: 141–6.

Laszkiewicz, Hubert, "Kary vymierzone przez sąd miejski v Lublinie w drugiej połowie XVII wieku," *Czasopismo Prawno-Historyczne* 41 (1989): 139–51.

Lavrent'ev, A. V., "Moskovskoe 'stolpotvorenie' kontsa XVII veka (Pervye grazhdanskie pamiatniki v Rossii i politicheskaia bor'ba v epokhu Petra I)," *Arkhiv russkoi istorii* 2 (1992): 129–48.

Lavrov, A. S., *Koldovstvo i religiia v Rossii. 1700–1740 gg.*, Moscow: Drevlekhranilishche, 2000.

Regentstvo tsarevny Sof'i Alekseevny. Sluzhiloe obshchestvo i bor'ba za vlast' v verkhakh Russkogo gosudarstva v 1682–1689 gg., Moscow: Arkheograficheskii tsentr, 1999.

Lazutka, S., Valikonite, I. and Gudavichius, E., *Pervyi litovskii statut (1529 g.)*, Vilnius: Izd. Margi Rashtai, 2004.

LeDonne, John P., *Absolutism and Ruling Class: The Formation of the Russian Political Order, 1700–1825*, New York and Oxford: Oxford University Press, 1991.

"Ruling Families in the Russian Political Order, 1689–1825," *Cahiers du monde russe et soviétique* 28 (1987), 3–4: 233–322.

Lenman, Bruce and Parker, Geoffrey, "The State, the Community and the Criminal Law in Early Modern Europe," in Gatrell et al. (eds.), *Crime and the Law*, 11–48.

Leont'ev, A. K., *Obrazovanie prikaznoi systemy upravleniia v Russkom gosudarstve*, Moscow: Izd. Moskovskogo universiteta, 1961.

Levack, Brian B., *The Witch-Hunt in Early Modern Europe*, 2nd edn., London and New York: Longman, 1995.

Levin, Eve, *Sex and Society in the World of the Orthodox Slavs, 900–1700*, Ithaca, NY and London: Cornell University Press, 1989.

Lewis, Mark Edward,. *Sanctioned Violence in Early China*, Albany, NY: State University of New York Press, 1990.

Liapin, D. A., "K voprosu o 'gorodskikh vosstaniiakh' v Rossii v seredine XVII v. (po materialam iuzhnorusskikh uezdov)," *Rossiiskaia istoriia* (2010), 4: 142–54.

Likhach, E., "Shafirov, Petr Pavlovich," in *Russkii biograficheskii slovar'*, XXII ("Chaadaev-Shvitkov"): 553–63.

Likhachev, D. S. and Panchenko, A. M., *"Smekhovoi mir" drevnei Rusi.* Leningrad: Nauka, 1976.

Likhachev, N. P., *Razriadnye diaki XVI veka. Opyt istoricheskago issledovaniia*, St. Petersburg: Tip. V. S. Balasheva, 1888.

Linebaugh, Peter, *The London Hanged: Crime and Civil Society in the Eighteenth Century*, Cambridge University Press, 1992.

Litsevye apokalipsisy russkogo Severa. Rukopisi XVII–XIX vv. Iz fondov drevlekhranilishcha Pushkinskogo doma, St. Petersburg: Izd. Pushkinskogo doma, 2008.

Lloyd, Howell A., Burgess, Glenn and Hodson, Simon (eds.), *European Political Thought, 1450–1700: Religion, Law and Philosophy*, New Haven and London: Yale University Press, 2007.

Lobachev, S. V. and Lavrov, A. S. (eds.), *Srednevekovaia Rus'*, St Petersburg: Izd. Sankt-Peterburgskogo universiteta, 1995.

Lohr, Eric and Poe, Marshall (eds.), *The Military and Society in Russia, 1450–1917*, Leiden, Boston and Cologne: Brill, 2002.

Longworth, Philip, "Ankidinov, Timoshka," in *Modern Encyclopedia of Russian and Soviet History* 2 (1976): 2–4.

Lossky, Vladimir, "The Cross," in Ouspensky and Lossky (eds.), *Meaning of Icons*, 180–5.

Lovell, Stephen, Ledeneva, Alena and Rogachevskii, Andrei (eds.), *Bribery and "Blat" in Russia: Negotiating Reciprocity from the Middle Ages to the 1990s*, New York: St. Martin's Press, 2000.

Löwe, Heinz-Dietrich, "Der Moskauer Kupfergeldaufstand von 1662," in Löwe (ed.), *Volksaufstände in Russland*, 105–30.

"Der Strelitzen-Aufstand von 1682 in Moskau," in Löwe (ed.), *Volksaufstände in Russland*, 163–96.

Löwe, Heinz-Dietrich (ed.), *Volksaufstände in Russland. Von der Zeit der Wirren bis zur "Grünen Revolution" gegen die Sowjetherrschaft*, in *Forschungen zur osteuropäischen Geschichte*, 65 (2006).

Łożiński, Władysław, *Prawem i lewem. Obyczaje na Czerwonej Rusi w pierwszej połowie XVII wieku*, 4th edn., Lvov: Nakladem Ksiegarni Gubrynowicza i syna, 1931.

Lukashevich, A. A., "Vidy dokumentov v Rossiiskom gosudarstve pervoi chetverti XVIII v. (na materiale General'nogo reglamenta)," *Sovetskie arkhivy* 1991, 4: 38–46.

Lupinin, Nicholas, *Religious Revolt in the XVIIth Century: The Schism of the Russian Church*, Princeton, NJ: Kingston Press, Inc., 1984.

Lytle, Guy Fitch and Orgel, Stephen (eds.), *Patronage in the Renaissance*, Princeton University Press, 1981.

McCaffray, Susan (ed.), *Russia in the European Context, 1789–1914: A Member of the Family*, Gordonsville, Va.: Palgrave Macmillan, 2005.

McConville, Sean, "Local Justice. The Jail," in Morris and Rothman (eds.), *Oxford History of the Prison*, 266–94.

McIntosh, Marjorie Keniston, *Controlling Misbehavior in England, 1370–1600*, Cambridge University Press, 1998.

de Madariaga, Isabel, *Ivan the Terrible: First Tsar of Russia*, New Haven: Yale University Press, 2005.

"Penal Policy in the Age of Catherine II," in de Madariaga, *Politics and Culture*, 97–123.

Politics and Culture in Eighteenth-Century Russia, London and New York: Longman, 1998.

Maisel, Witold, "Torture in the Practice of the Poznań Criminal Court, 16th–18th Cent.," in Waltoś (ed.), *Humanitarian Traditions*, 11–22.

Mal'tsev, A. N., *Rossiia i Belorussiia v seredine XVII veka*, Moscow: Izd. Moskovskogo universiteta, 1974.

Man'kov, A. G., *Ulozhenie 1649 goda. Kodeks feodal'nogo prava Rossii*, 2nd edn., Moscow: Gosud. publichnaia istoricheskaia biblioteka Rossii, 2003.

Zakonodatel'stvo i pravo Rossii vtoroi poloviny XVII v., St. Petersburg: Nauka, 1998.

Mann, Michael, *The Sources of Social Power*. Vol. 1. *A History of Power from the Beginning to AD 1760*, Cambridge University Press, 1986.

Marker, Gary J., *Imperial Saint: The Cult of St. Catherine and the Dawn of Female Rule in Russia*, DeKalb, Ill.: Northern Illinois University Press, 2007.

"Literacy and Literacy Texts in Muscovy: A Reconsideration," *Slavic Review* 49 (1990), 1: 74–89.

Marker, Gary J., Neuberger, Joan, Poe, Marshall and Rupp, Susan (eds.), *Everyday Life in Russian History*, Bloomington, Ind.: Slavica, 2010.

Meny, Y. and de Sousa, L., "Corruption: Political and Public Aspects," *International Encyclopedia of Social and Behavioral Sciences* 4 (2001), 2824–30.

Merback, Mitchell B., *The Thief, the Cross and the Wheel: Pain and the Spectacle of Punishment in Medieval and Renaissance Europe*, University of Chicago Press, 1998.

Michels, Georg, *At War with the Church: Religious Dissent in Seventeenth-Century Russia*, Stanford University Press, 1999.

"Rituals of Violence: Retaliatory Acts by Russian and Hungarian Rebels," *Russian History* 35 (2008), 3–4: 383–94.

"Ruling Without Mercy: Seventeenth-Century Russian Bishops and Their Officials," *Kritika: Explorations in Russian and Eurasian History* 4 (2003): 515–42.

"Muscovite Elite Women and Old Belief," *Harvard Ukrainian Studies* 19 (1997): 428–50.

"The Solovki Uprising: Religion and Revolt in Northern Russia," *Russian Review* 51 (1992), 1: 1–15.

"The Violent Old Belief: An Examination of Religious Dissent on the Karelian Frontier," *Russian History* 19 (1992), 1–4: 203–30.

Mikhailov, M. M., *Russkoe grazhdanskoe sudoproizvodstvo v istoricheskom ego razvitii ot Ulozheniia 1649 goda do izdaniia svoda zakonov*, St. Petersburg: Tip. II Otd. sobstvennoi E. I. V. Kantseliarii, 1856.

Mikhailova, Yulia and Prestel, David K., "Cross Kissing: Keeping One's Word in Twelfth-Century Rus'," *Slavic Review* 70 (2011), 1: 1–22.

Miller, David B., *Saint Sergius of Radonezh, His Trinity Monastery, and the Formation of the Russian Identity*, DeKalb, Ill.: Northern Illinois University Press, 2010.

Mironov, Boris N., "Local Government in Russia in the First Half of the Nineteenth Century: Provincial Government and Estate Self Government," *Jahrbücher für Geschichte Osteuropas* 42 (1994): 161–201.

Sotsial' naia istoriia Rossii perioda imperii XVIII-nachalo XX v. Genezis lichnosti, demokraticheskoi sem' i, grazhdanskogo obshchestva i pravovogo gosudarstva, 2 vols., St. Petersburg: Dmitrii Bulanin, 1999.

Moore, Sally Falk, "Certainties Undone: Fifty Turbulent Years of Legal Anthropology, 1949–99," *Journal of the Royal Anthropological Institute* 7 (2001), 1: 95–116.

"Treating Law as Knowledge: Telling Colonial Officers What to Say to Africans about Running 'Their Own' Native Courts," *Law & Society Review* 26 (1992), 1: 11–46.

Morison, John (ed.), *Ethnic and National Issues in Russian and East European History*, London: Macmillan, 2000.

Morris, Norval and Rothman, David J. (eds.), *The Oxford History of the Prison*, New York and Oxford: Oxford University Press, 1998.

Mousnier, Roland, *Social Hierarchies, 1450 to the Present*, Evans, Peter (trans.), New York: Schocken Books, 1973.

Moutchnik, Alexander, "Der 'Strelitzen-Aufstand' von 1698," in Löwe (ed.), *Volksaufstände in Russland*, 197–222.

Mrochek-Drozdovskii, P., *Oblastnoe upravlenie Rossii XVIII veka do uchrezhdeniia o guberniiakh, 7 Noiarbria 1775 goda.* Pt. 1 *Oblastnoe upravlenie epokhi pervogo uchrezhdenii gubernii (1708–19 g.)*, Moscow: Universitetskaia tip., 1876.

Muchembled, Robert and Birrell, Jean, *A History of Violence: From the End of the Middle Ages to the Present*, Cambridge: Polity, 2012.

Muir, Edward, *Mad Blood Stirring: Vendetta and Factions in Friuli during the Renaissance*, Baltimore and London: Johns Hopkins University Press, 1993.

Ritual in Early Modern Europe, Cambridge University Press, 1997.

Naish, Camille, *Death Comes to the Maiden: Sex and Execution, 1431–1933*, London and New York: Routledge, 1991.

Nersesiants, V. S. (ed.), *Razvitie russkogo prava v XV-pervoi polovine XVII v.*, Moscow: Nauka, 1986.

Nevolin, K. A., "O prostranstve tserkovnogo suda v Rossii do Petra Velikogo," in Nevolin, *Polnoe sobranie sochinenii*, VI (1859): 251–389.

Polnoe sobranie sochinenii, 6 vols., St. Petersburg: Tip. Eduarda Pratsa, 1857–9.

Nexon, Daniel, "State and Bureaucracy," in Dewald (ed.), *Europe, 1450 to 1789*, v: 511–20.

Nikitin, P. E., *Istoriia goroda Smolenska*, Moscow: Tip. S. Selivanovskogo, 1848.

Nosov, N. E., *Ocherki po istorii mestnogo upravleniia Russkogo gosudarstva pervoi poloviny XVI veka*, Moscow: Izd. Akademii nauk SSSR, 1957.

Nosov, N. E. (ed.), *Issledovaniia po otechestvennomu istochnikovedeniiu. Sbornik statei, posviashchennykh 75-letiiu professora S. N. Valka*, Moscow and Leningrad: Nauka, 1964.

Novokhatko, O. V., *Razriad v 185 godu*, Moscow: Pamiatniki istoricheskoi mysli, 2007.

"Upravlentsy srednego zvena v XVII veke: neformal′nye kontakty sluzhilykh po otechestvu i prikaznykh," *Otechestvennaia istoriia* (2005), 3: 158–69.

Novosel′skii, A. A., "Praviashchie gruppy v sluzhilom 'gorode' XVII v.," *Uchenye zapiski RANION* 5 (1929): 315–35.

Votchinnik i ego khoziaistvo v XVII veke, Moscow and Leningrad: Gosudarstvennoe izdatel′stvo, 1929.

N. S., "Talitskii, Grigorii," in *Russkii biograficheskii slovar′*, XX ("Suvorova-Tkachev"), 274–5.

Ocherki istorii SSSR. Period feodalizma. XVII vek, Moscow: Izd. Akademii nauk SSSR, 1955.

Okenfuss, Max J., *The Discovery of Childhood in Russia: The Evidence of the Slavic Primer*, Newtonville, Mass.: Oriental Research Partners, 1980.

The Rise and Fall of Latin Humanism in Early-Modern Russia: Pagan Authors, Ukrainians, and the Resiliency of Muscovy, Leiden and New York: E. J. Brill, 1995.

Omel′chenko, O. A., *'Zakonnaia monarkhiia' Ekateriny Vtoroi. Prosveshchennyi absoliutizm v Rossii*, Moscow: Iurist, 1993.

Ostrowski, Donald G., *Muscovy and the Mongols: Cross-Cultural Influences on the Steppe Frontier, 1304–1589*, Cambridge University Press, 1998.

Ouspensky, Leonid and Lossky, Vladimir (eds.), *The Meaning of Icons*, Palmer, G. E. H. and Kadloubovsky, E. (trans.), Crestwood, NY: St. Vladimir's Seminary Press, 1999.

The Oxford Dictionary of Byzantium, 3 vols., New York and Oxford: Oxford University Press, 1991.

Paas, John Roger, *The German Political Broadsheet, 1600–1700*, 10 vols. to date, Wiesbaden: Harrassowitz, 1985–.

Panchenko, A. M., "Povest′ o Frole Skobeeve," in *Slovar′ knizhnikov*. vol. III *XVII vek*. Pt. 3. *P-S* (1998): 209–12.

Panchenko, A. M. and Uspenskii, B. A., "Ivan Groznyi i Petr Velikii. Kontseptsii pervogo monarkha. Stat′ia pervaia," *Trudy Otdela drevnerusskii literatury* 37 (1983): 54–78.

Pascal, Pierre, *Avvakum et les débuts du Raskol*, Paris: Centre D'Études Russes Istina, 1938.

Pashkova, T. I., *Mestnoe upravlenie v Russkom gosudarstve pervoi polovine XVI veka. Namestniki i volosteli*, Moscow: Drevlekhranilishche, 2000.

Pavlov, A. P., *Gosudarev dvor i politicheskaia bor′ba pri Borise Godunove (1584–1605 gg.)*, St. Petersburg: Nauka, St. Peterburgskoe otd., 1992.

Pavlov, Andrei and Perrie, Maureen, *Ivan the Terrible*, London: Longman, 2003.

Pavlov-Sil′vanskii, N., "Kikin, A. V.," in *Russkii biograficheskii slovar′*, VIII ("Ibak-Kliucharev"), 627–9.

Peck, Linda Levy, "Court Patronage and Government Policy: The Jacobean Dilemma," in Lytle and Orgel (eds.), *Patronage in the Renaissance*, 27–46.

Pentcheva, Bissera V., "Containers of Power: Eunuchs and Reliquaries in Byzantium," *RES: Anthropology and Aesthetics* 51 (2007): 108–20.

Perrie, Maureen, *The Image of Ivan the Terrible in Russian Folklore*, Cambridge University Press, 1987.

Pretenders and Popular Monarchism in Early Modern Russia: The False Tsars of the Time of Troubles, Cambridge University Press, 1995.

Perrie, Maureen (ed.), *The Cambridge History of Russia*, Vol. 1, Cambridge University Press, 2006.

Peters, Edward M., "Prison before the Prison: The Ancient and Medieval Worlds," in Morris and Rothman (eds.), *Oxford History of the Prison*, 3–43.

Torture, New York: Basil Blackwell, 1985.

Peterson, Claes, *Peter the Great's Administrative and Judicial Reforms: Swedish Antecedents and the Process of Reception*, Stockholm: Nord. bokh, 1979.

Pihlajmaki, Heikki, "Torture," in Dewald (ed.), *Europe, 1450 to 1789*, VI: 56–61.

Pintner, Walter M. and Rowney, Don Karl (eds.), *Russian Officialdom: The Bureaucratization of Russian Society from the Seventeenth to the Twentieth Century*, Chapel Hill, NC: University of North Carolina Press, 1980.

Pipes, Richard, *Russia under the Old Regime*, New York: Charles Scribner's Sons, 1974.

"Was There Private Property in Muscovite Russia?," *Slavic Review* 53 (1994), 2: 524–30.

Pisar′kova, L. F., *Gosudarstvennoe upravlenie Rossii s kontsa XVII do kontsa XVIII veka. Evoliutsiia biurokraticheskoi sistemy*, Moscow: ROSSPEN, 2007.

"Razvitie mestnogo samoupravleniia v Rossii do Velikikh reform: Obychai, povinnost′, pravo," *Otechestvennaia istoriia* (2001), 2: 3–27, and 3: 25–39.

"Rossiiskaia biurokratiia v epokhu Petra I," *Otechestvennaia istoriia* (2004), 1: 18–41, and 2: 3–19.

Plavsic, Borivoj, "Seventeenth-Century Chanceries and Their Staffs," in Pintner and Rowney (eds.), *Russian Officialdom*, 19–45.

Pliguzov, A. I., "Sudnyi spisok Maksima Greka," *Arkhiv russkoi istorii* (1992), 1: 32–85.

Podobedova, O. I., *Moskovskaia shkola zhivopisi pri Ivane IV. Raboty v Moskovskom Kremle 40-kh–70-kh godov XVI v.*, Moscow: Nauka, 1972.

Poe, Marshall, "The Central Government and Its Institutions," in Perrie (ed.), *Cambridge History of Russia*, 1: 435–63.

'A People Born to Slavery': Russia in Early Modern European Ethnography, 1476–1748, Ithaca, NY: Cornell University Press, 2000.

"The Truth about Muscovy," *Kritika: Explorations in Russian and Eurasian History* 3 (2002): 473–86.

"What Did Russians Mean When They Called Themselves 'Slaves of the Tsar'?," *Slavic Review* 57 (1998): 585–608.

Pogodin, M. P., *Semnadtsat' pervykh let v zhizni Imp. Petra Velikogo 1672–1689*, Moscow: Tip. V. M. Frish, 1875.

Po Kremliu. Kratkii putevoditel', 3rd edn., Moscow: Moskovskii rabochii, 1964.

Pokrovskii, N. N., *Tomsk. 1648–49 g. Voevodskaia vlast' i zemskie miry*, Novosibirsk: Nauka, Sibirskoe otd., 1989.

Polnyi pravoslavnyi bogoslovskii entsiklopedicheskii slovar', 2 vols., St. Petersburg: Izd. P. P. Soikina, 1913.

Potter, Cathy J., "Payment, Gift or Bribery? Exploring the Boundaries in Pre-Petrine Russia," in Lovell, Ledeneva and Rogachevskii (eds.), *Bribery and "Blat" in Russia*, 20–34.

Pozdeeva, I. V., "The Activity of the Moscow Printing House in the First Half of the Seventeenth Century," *Solanus* (new series) 6 (1992): 27–55.

Praviashchaia elita russkogo gosudarstva IX-nachala XVIII vv. Ocherki istorii, St. Petersburg: Dmitrii Bulanin, 2006.

Prest, Wilfrid, "Judicial Corruption in Early Modern England," *Past and Present* 133 (1991), Nov.: 67–95.

Pushkarev, S. G., "Donskoe kazachestvo i Moskovskoe gosudarstvo v XVII v.," *Zapiski Russkoi akademicheskoi gruppy v SSHA* 2 (1968): 5–28.

Radishchev, Aleksandr Nikolaevich, *A Journey From St. Petersburg to Moscow*, Thaler, Roderick Page (ed.), Weiner, Leo (trans.), Cambridge, Mass.: Harvard University Press, 1966.

Raeff, Marc, *Origins of the Russian Intelligentsia: The Eighteenth-Century Nobility*, New York: Harcourt, Brace & World, 1966.

Understanding Imperial Russia: State and Society in the Old Regime, Goldhammer, Arthur (trans.), New York: Columbia University Press, 1984.

The Well-Ordered Police State: Social and Institutional Change through Law in the Germanies and Russia, 1600–1800, New Haven: Yale University Press, 1983.

Rancour-Laferriere, Daniel, *The Slave Soul of Russia: Moral Masochism and the Cult of Suffering*, New York University Press, 1995.

Redin, D. A., *Administrativnye struktury i biurokratiia Urala v epokhu petrovskikh reform (Zapadnye uezdy sibirskoi gubernii 1711–27 gg.)*, Ekaterinburg: Izd. Volot, 2007.

Rogov, V. A., *Istoriia ugolovnogo prava, terrora i repressii v Russkom gosudarstve XV–XVII vv.*, Moscow: Iurist, 1995.

Ugolovnye nakazanii i repressii v Rossii serediny XV–seredina XVII vv., Moscow: A/O Rosvuznauka, Izd. VZPI, 1992.

Roller-Assfalg, Stefan, "Der Moskauer Aufstand von 1648," in Löwe (ed.), *Volksaufstände in Russland*, 69–104.

Romashkin, P. S., *Osnovnye nachala ugolovnogo i voenno-ugolovnogo zakonodatel' stva Petra I*, Moscow: Voenno-iuridicheskaia akademiia, 1942.

Romaniello, Matthew P., *The Elusive Empire: Kazan and the Creation of Russia, 1552–1671*, Madison: University of Wisconsin Press, 2012.

Roodenburg, Herman and Spierenburg, Pieter (eds.), *Social Control in Europe*. Vol. 1. *1500–1800*, Columbus, OH.: Ohio State University Press, 2004.

Roper, Lyndal, *Witch Craze: Terror and Fantasy in Baroque Germany*, New Haven and London: Yale University Press, 2004.

Rosovetskii, S. K., "Ustnaia proza XVI–XVII vv. ob Ivane Groznom – Pravitele," *Russkii fol' klor* 20 (1981): 71–95.

Rossiiskoe samoderzhavie i biurokratiia. Sbornik statei v chest' N. F. Demidovoi, Moscow and Novosibirsk: Drevlekhranilishche, 2000.

Rousseaux, Xavier, "Crime, Justice and Society in Medieval and Early Modern Times: Thirty Years of Crime and Criminal Justice History," *Crime, History and Societies* 1 (1997): 87–118.

Rowland, Daniel, "Biblical Military Imagery in the Political Culture of Early Modern Russia: The Blessed Host of the Heavenly Tsar," in Flier and Rowland (eds.), *Medieval Russian Culture*, 182–212.

"Did Muscovite Literary Ideology Place Limits on the Power of the Tsar (1540s–1660s)?" *Russian Review* 49 (1990), 2: 125–55.

"Muscovy," in Lloyd et al. (eds.), *European Political Thought, 1450–1700*, 267–99.

"The Problem of Advice in Muscovite Tales about the Time of Troubles," *Russian History* 6 (1979), 2: 259–83.

"Two Cultures, One Throne Room: Secular Courtiers and Orthodox Culture in the Golden Hall of the Moscow Kremlin," in Kivelson and Greene (eds.), *Orthodox Russia*, 33–57.

Royer, Katherine, "Dead Men Talking: Truth, Texts and the Scaffold in Early Modern England," in Devereaux and Griffiths (eds.), *Penal Practice and Culture*, 63–84.

Rozhdestvenskii, S., "Filipp," in *Russkii biograficheskii slovar'*, xxi ("Faber-Tsiavlovskii"), 116–21.

Rublack, Ulinka, *The Crimes of Women in Early Modern Germany*, Oxford: Clarendon Press, 1999.

Rumiantseva, V. S., *Narodnoe antitserkovnoe dvizhenie v Rossii XVII veka*, Moscow: Nauka, 1986.

Russkii biograficheskii slovar', reprint edn., 25 vols., New York: Kraus Reprint, 1962.

Rustemeyer, Angela, *Dissens und Ehre. Majestätsverbrechen in Russland (1600–1800)*, Wiesbaden: Harrassowitz, 2006.

"Systems and Senses. New Research on Muscovy and the Historiography on Early Modern Europe," *Kritika: Explorations in Russian and Eurasian History* 11 (2010): 563–79.

Ryan, W. F., *The Bathhouse at Midnight: An Historical Survey of Magic and Divination in Russia*, University Park, Pa.: Pennsylvania University Press, 1999.

"The Witchcraft Hysteria in Early Modern Europe: Was Russia an Exception?" *Slavonic and East European Review* 76 (1998), 1: 49–84.

Rybalko, N. V., *Rossiiskaia prikaznaia biurokratiia v Smutnoe vremia. Nachala XVII v.*, Moscow: Kvadriga, 2011.

Safronov, F. G., *Ssylka v vostochnuiu Sibir' v XVII veke*, Iakutsk: Iakutskoe knizhnoe izd., 1967.

"Samosozhzhenie," in *Staroobriadchestvo. Litsa, sobytiia, predmety i simvoly*, Moscow: Tserkov', 1996: 249–50.

Sapozhnikov, D. I., "Samosozhzhenie v Russkom raskole," in *Chteniia* (1891), bk. III: 1–171.

Sawyer, Jeffrey K., "Judicial Corruption in Early Seventeenth-Century France," *Law and History Review* 6 (1988), 1: 95–117.

Sbornik statei po istorii prava, posv. M. F. Vladimirskomu-Budanovu, Kiev: Tip. S. V. Kul'zhenko, 1904.

Sbornik statei, posviashchennykh Akeksandru Sergeevichu Lappo-Danilevskomu, Petrograd: Tip. M. M. Stasiulevicha, 1916.

Scarry, Elaine, *The Body in Pain: The Making and Unmaking of the World*, New York: Oxford University Press, 1985.

Schenker, Alexander M. and Stankiewicz, Edward (eds.), *The Slavic Literary Languages: Formation and Development*, Columbus, OH: Slavica Publishers, 1980.

Schleuning, Stefan and Tuchtenhagen, Ralph, "Der Kosaken-Aufstand unter Stepan Razin 1667–1671," in Löwe (ed.), *Volksaufstände in Russland*, 131–62.

Schmidt, Christoph, *Sozialkontrolle in Moskau: Justiz, Kriminalität und Leibeigenschaft, 1649–1785*, Stuttgart: F. Steiner, 1996.

"Von Gottes und Rechts wegen, oder zu einigen Charakteristika von Gerechtigkeit in Russland. Ein Kommentar," *Jahrbücher für Geschichte Osteuropas* 53 (2005), 4: 565–8.

Schneider, Zoe A., "Courts," in Dewald (ed.), *Europe, 1450 to 1789*, III: 447–56.

Schneller, Joseph, "Das Hexenwesen im sechszehnten Jahrhundert," *Der Geschichtsfreund* 23 (1868): 351–70.

Schrader, Abby M., *Languages of the Lash: Corporal Punishment and Identity in Imperial Russia*, De Kalb, Ill.: Northern Illinois University Press, 2002.

Schuyler, Eugene, *Peter the Great: Emperor of Russia*, 2 vols., New York: Charles Scribner's Sons, 1884.

Schwerhoff, Gerd, "Criminalized Violence and the Process of Civilisation: A Reappraisal," *Crime, History and Societies* 6 (2002): 103–26.

"Social Control of Violence, Violence as Social Control: The Case of Early Modern Germany," Hoffmann, Lukas (trans.), in Roodenburg and Spierenburg (eds.), *Social Control in Europe*, I: 220–46.

Scribner, R. W., "Police and the Territorial State in Sixteenth-Century Württemberg," in Kouri and Scott (eds.), *Politics and Society in Reformation Europe*, 103–20.

Sedov, P. V., "'On mne svoi ...' (Svoistvo pri Moskovskom dvore XVII v.)," *Nestor* 7 (2005): 190–9.

"Podnoshenia v moskovskikh prikazakh XVII veka," *Otechestvennaia istoriia* (1996), 1: 139–50.

"Sozdanie Raspravnoi palaty," in Torke et al. (eds.), *Russische und Ukrainische Geschichte*, 97–108.

Zakat moskovskogo tsarstva. Tsarskii dvor kontsa XVII veka, St. Petersburg: Dmitrii Bulanin, 2006.

Semiachko, S. A. and Smirnov, I. P., "Povest′ o Ershe Ershoviche," in *Slovar′ knizhnikov*. vol. III. *XVII vek*. Pt. 3. *P-S* (1998): 119–23.

Sergeevich, V. I., *Lektsii i issledovaniia po drevnei istorii russkogo prava*, 4th edn., St. Petersburg: Tip. M. M. Stasiulevicha, 1910.

Sergeevskii, N. D., *Nakazanie v russkom prave XVII veka*, St. Petersburg: Izd. Knizhnogo magazina A. F. Tsinzerlinga, 1887.

"Smertnaia kazn′ pri Imperatritse Elizavete Petrovne," *Zhurnal grazhdanskogo i ugolovnogo prava* (1890), 1: 51–60.

Serov, D. O., *Administratsiia Petra I*, Moscow: OGI, 2007.

Stroiteli imperii. Ocherki gosudarstvennoi i kriminal′noi deiatel′nosti spodvizhnikov Petra I, Novosibirsk: Izd. Novosibirskogo universiteta, 1996.

Sudebnaia reforma Petra I. Istoriko-pravovoe issledovanie, Moscow: IKD Zertsalo, 2009.

"Zabytoe uchrezhdenie Petra I: Vyshnii sud (1723–1726 gg.)," in *Rossiiskoe samoderzhavie i biurokratiia*, 219–37.

Shaffern, Robert W., *Law and Justice from Antiquity to Enlightenment*, Lanham, Md., Boulder, Colo., and New York: Rowman and Littlefield, 2009.

Sharpe, James A., "Crime in England: Long-Term Trends and the Problem of Modernization," in Johnson and Monkkonen (eds.), *Civilization of Crime*, 17–34.

"Enforcing the Law in the Seventeenth-Century English Village," in Gatrell et al. (eds.), *Crime and the Law*, 97–119.

Shoemaker, Robert B., *Prosecution and Punishment: Petty Crime and the Law in London and Rural Middlesex, c. 1660–1725*, Cambridge University Press, 1991.

"Streets of Shame? The Crowd and Public Punishments in London, 1700–1820," in Devereaux and Griffiths (eds.), *Penal Practice and Culture*, 232–57.

Shtamm, S. I., "Sud i protsess," in Nersesiants (ed.), *Razvitie russkogo prava*, 203–51.

"Ugolovnoe pravo," in Nersesiants (ed.), *Razvitie russkogo prava*, 157–202.

"Ugolovnoe pravo," in Skripilev (ed.), *Razvitie russkogo prava*, 158–214.

Shveikovskaia, E. N., *Gosudarstvo i krestiane Rossii. Pomor′e v XVII veke*, Moscow: Arkheograficheskii tsentr, 1997.

Silverman, Lisa, *Tortured Subjects: Pain, Truth and the Body in Early Modern France*, Chicago and London: University of Chicago Press, 2001.

Skripilev, E. A. (ed.), *Razvitie russkogo prava vtoroi poloviny XVII–XVIII vv.*, Moscow: Nauka, 1992.

Skrynnikov, R. G., *Smuta v Rossii v nachale XVII v. Ivan Bolotnikov*, Leningrad: Nauka, Leningradskoe otd., 1988.

Tsarstvo terrora, St. Petersburg: Nauka, St. Peterburgskoe otd., 1992.

Slatin, A., "Monastyrskii sud XVII-go veka," *Russkaia starina* 1878, 9–12: 119–21.

Slovar' knizhnikov i knizhnosti drevnei Rusi, 3 vols. in 7 pts., St. Petersburg: Dmitrii Bulanin, 1998.

Smilianskaia, E. B., *Volshebniki. Bogokhul'niki. Eretiki*, Moscow: Izd. Indrik, 2003.

Smirnov, I. I., "Kogda byl kaznen Ileika Muromets? (Neskol'ko khronologicheskikh sapostavlenii)," *Istoriia SSSR* (1968), 4: 108–19.

Vosstanie Bolotnikova. 1606–1607, Leningrad: Gosudarstvennoe izd. polit. lit., 1951.

Snegirev, I., "Lobnoe mesto v Moskve," in *Chteniia* (1861), bk. 1: 12–14.

Solov'ev, S. M., *Istoriia Rossii s drevneishikh vremen*, 29 vols. in 15 bks., Moscow: Izd. sotsial'no-ekonomicheskoi literatury, 1959–66.

Solov'ev, S., "Timoshka Ankidinov," *Finskii Vestnik. Ucheno-literaturnyi zhurnal* 13 (1847), 2: 1–38 and 14 (1847), 2: 1–34.

Spierenburg, Pieter, "The Body and the State. Early Modern Europe," in Morris and Rothman (eds.), *Oxford History of the Prison*, 44–70.

"Long-Term Trends in Homicide: Theoretical Reflections and Dutch Evidence," in Johnson and Monkkonen (eds.), *Civilization of Crime*, 63–105.

The Spectacle of Suffering: Executions and the Evolution of Repression: From a Preindustrial Metropolis to the European Experience, Cambridge and London: Cambridge University Press, 1984.

"Violence and the Civilizing Process: Does it Work?," *Crime, History and Societies* 5 (2001): 87–105.

Stadnikov, A. V., *Tserkovnyi sud v sisteme rossiiskogo pravosudiia v X–nachale XX vekov. Dokumenty i materialy. Krestomatiia*, Moscow: IPKgossluzhby, 2003.

Staroobriadchestvo. Litsa, sobytiia, predmety i simvoly, Moscow: Tserkov', 1996.

Starr, S. Frederick, *Decentralization and Self-Government in Russia, 1830–1870*, Princeton University Press, 1972.

Stevens, Carol B., "Belgorod: Notes on Literacy and Language in the Seventeenth-Century Russian Army," *Russian History* 1980, 7, 1–2: 113–24.

Russia's Wars of Emergence, 1460–1730, London: Pearson; New York: Longman, 2007.

Soldiers on the Steppe: Army Reform and Social Change in Early Modern Russia, DeKalb, Ill.: Northern Illinois University Press, 1995.

Stokes, Laura, *Demons of Urban Reform: Early European Witch Trials and Criminal Justice, 1430–1530*, Houndmills, Basingstoke and New York: Palgrave Macmillan, 2011.

Storrs, Christopher (ed.), *The Fiscal–Military State in Eighteenth-Century Europe*, Aldershot: Ashgate, 2009.

Story, Joanna (ed.), *Charlemagne. Empire and Society*, Manchester and New York: Manchester University Press, 2005.

S. Tr., "Ankudinov, Timoshka," in *Russkii biograficheskii slovar'*, II ("Aleksinskii-Bestuzhev-Rumin"), 152–4.

Stuart, Kathy, *Defiled Trades and Social Outcasts: Honor and Ritual Pollution in Early Modern Germany*, Cambridge University Press, 1999.

Suslova, E. D., "Severnoe dukhovenstvo kak istochnik popolneniia prikaznoi biurokratii XVII veka: Opyt lokal'nogo issledovaniia," *Rossiiskaia istoriia* (2009), 3: 123–27.

Szvak, Gyula (ed.), *The Place of Russia in Eurasia*, Budapest: Magyar Ruszisztikai Intézet, 2001.

Talina, G. V., *Vybor puti. Russkoe samoderzhavie vtoroi poloviny XVII-pervoi chetverti XVIII veka*, Moscow: Russkii mir, 2010.

Tel'berg, G. G., *Ocherki politicheskogo suda i politicheskikh prestuplenii v Moskovskom gosudarstve XVII veka*, Moscow: Tip. Imp. Moskovskogo universiteta, 1912.

"Politicheskii sud v Moskovskom gosudarstve XVII veka," *Voprosy prava* 7 (1911), 3: 1–35.

Thompson, E. P., "The Moral Economy of the English Crowd in the Eighteenth Century," *Past and Present* 50 (1971): 76–136.

Thyrêt, Isolde, *Between God and Tsar: Religious Symbolism and the Royal Women of Muscovite Russia*, DeKalb, Ill.: Northern Illinois University Press, 2001.

Tikhomirov, M. N., *Klassovaia bor'ba v Rossii XVII v.*, Moscow: Nauka, 1969.

"Novgorodskoe vosstanie 1650 g.," in Tikhomirov, *Klassovaia bor'ba*, 139–69.

"Pskovskoe vosstanie 1650 g.," in Tikhomirov, *Klassovaia bor'ba*, 23–138.

"Vosstaniia v Novgorode i Pskove v 1650 g.," in *Ocherki istorii SSSR. Period feodalizma. XVII vek*, 249–56.

Tikhomirov, N. Ia. and Ivanov, V. N., *Moskovskii Kreml'. Istoriia arkhitektury*, Moscow: Stroizdat, 1967.

Tilly, Charles, *Coercion, Capital, and European States, AD 990–1992*, rev. pbk. edn., Cambridge, Mass.: Blackwell, 1992.

Tilly, Charles and Ardant, Gabriel, *The Formation of National States in Western Europe*, Princeton University Press, 1975.

Timberlake, Charles E. (ed.), *Religious and Secular Sources in Late Tsarist Russia*, Seattle and London: University of Washington Press, 1992.

Timofeev, A. G., *Istoriia telesnykh nakazanii v russkom prave*, St. Petersburg: Tip. S-Peterburgskoi tiurmy, 1897.

Torke, Hans-Joachim, *Die staatsbedingte Gesellschaft im moskauer Reich. Zar und Zemlja in der altrussische Herschaftsverfassung, 1613–1689*, Leiden: E. J. Brill, 1974.

Torke, Hans-Joachim, Crummey, Robert O., Sundhaussen, Holm and Vulpius, Ricarda (eds.), *Russische und Ukrainische Geschichte vom 16–18. Jahrhundert*, in *Forschungen zur osteuropäischen Geschichte* 58 (2001).

Troitskii, S. M., *Russkii absoliutizm i dvorianstvo v XVIII v. Formirovanie biurokratii*, Moscow: Nauka, 1974.

"Samozvantsy v Rossii XVII–XVIII vekov," *Voprosy istorii* (1969), 3: 134–46.

Uruszczak, Wacław, "The Torture in Practice of the Wiśnicz Criminal Court in the Seventeenth Century," in Waltoś (ed.), *Humanitarian Traditions*, 23–8.

Ustiugov, N. V., "Evoliutsiia prikaznogo stroia russkogo gosudarstva v XVII v.," in *Absoliutizm v Rossii*, 134–67.

Vasil′ev, V. N., *Starinnye feierverki v Rossii, XVII-pervaia chetvert XVIII veka*, Leningrad: Izd. Gos. Ermitazha, 1960.

Velychenko, Stephen, "Local Officialdom and National Movements in Imperial Russia: Administrative Shortcomings and Under-government," in Morison (ed.), *Ethnic and National Issues*, 74–85.

Venkatappiah, B., "Misuse of Office," *International Encyclopedia of Social Sciences* II (1968): 272–6.

Vershinin, E. V., *Voevodskoe upravlenie v Sibiri, XVII vek.* Ekaterinburg: Razvivaiiushchee obuchenie, 1998.

Veselovskii, S. B., *Issledovaniia po istorii oprichniny*, Moscow: Izd. Akademii nauk SSSR, 1963.

Vlast′ v Sibiri XVI–nachalo XX veka. Mezharkhivnyi spravochnik, Novosibirsk: ANO MASS-Media-Tsentr, 2002.

Volkov, L. V., in "Chelobitnoi prikaz," in *Gosudarstvennost′ Rossii*, IV (2001): 408–9.

Volodikhin, D. M., *Ivan Groznyi. Bich bozhii*, Moscow: Veche, 2006.

Vremennik imp. Moskovskogo obshchestva istorii i drevnostei rossiiskikh, 9 vols., Moscow: Universitetskaia tip., 1848–57.

de Waele, Michael, "Officeholding," in Dewald (ed.), *Europe, 1450 to 1789*, IV: 20–2.

Waltoś, S. (ed.), *Humanitarian Traditions of the Polish Criminal Procedure*, Warsaw: Nakladem Uniwersytetu Jagiellońskiego, 1983.

Weber, Max, "Politics as a Vocation," in Gerth and Mills (eds.), *From Max Weber*, 77–128.

Wegert, Karl, "The Social Context of State Terror in Early Modern Germany," *Canadian Journal of History* 26 (1991): 21–41.

Weickhardt, George G., "The Canon Law Code of Rus′, 1100–1551," *Russian History* 28 (2006), 1–4: 411–46.

"The Composite Law Code of 1606," *Russian History* 33 (2006), 1: 1–18.

"Due Process and Equal Justice in the Muscovite Codes," *Russian Review* 51 (1992), 4: 463–80.

"Muscovite Judicial Duels as a Legal Fiction," *Kritika: Explorations in Russian and Eurasian History* 7 (2006), 4: 713–32.

"The Pre-Petrine Law of Property," *Slavic Review* 52 (1993), 4: 663–79.

"Pre-Petrine Law and Western Law: The Influence of Roman and Canon Law," *Harvard Ukrainian Studies* 19 (1995): 756–83.

"Probable Western Origins of Muscovite Criminal Procedure," *Russian Review* 66 (2007): 55–72.

"Response," *Slavic Review* 53 (1994), 2: 531–8.

Weisser, Michael R., *Crime and Punishment in Early Modern Europe*, Atlantic Highlands, NJ: Humanities Press, 1979.

"Crime and Punishment in Early Modern Spain," in Gatrell et al. (eds.), *Crime and the Law*, 76–96.

Whittaker, Cynthia H., *Russian Monarchy: Eighteenth-Century Rulers and Writers in Political Dialogue*, DeKalb, Ill.: Northern Illinois University Press, 2003.

Wirtschafter, Elise Kimerling, "Christian Rulership in Enlightenment Russia: Father Platon at the Court of Catherine II," in Lenhoff, Gail and Kleimola, Ann (eds.), *"The Book of Royal Degrees" and the Genesis of Russian Historical Consciousness*, Bloomington, Ind.: Slavica, 2011: 333–40.

The Play of Ideas in Russian Enlightenment Theater, DeKalb, Ill.: Northern Illinois University Press, 2003.

Russia's Age of Serfdom, 1649–1861, Malden, Mass. and Oxford: Blackwell Publishing, 2008.

Witzenrath, Christoph, *Cossacks and the Russian Empire, 1598–1725: Manipulation, Rebellion and Expansion into Siberia*, London and New York: Routledge, 2007.

Wolff, Larry, *Inventing Eastern Europe. The Map of Civilization on the Mind of the Enlightenment*, Stanford University Press, 1994.

Wood, Alan, "Siberian Exile in the Eighteenth Century," *Siberica* 1 (1990), 1: 38–63.

Wortman, Richard S., *The Development of a Russian Legal Consciousness*, Chicago and London: University of Chicago Press, 1976.

"Peter the Great and Court Procedure," *Canadian-American Slavic Studies* 8 (1974), 2: 303–10.

Scenarios of Power: Myth and Ceremony in Russian Monarchy, 2 vols., Princeton University Press, 1995–2000.

Yaney, George L., *The Systematization of Russian Government: Social Evolution in the Domestic Administration of Imperial Russia, 1711–1905*, Urbana, Ill. Chicago and London: University of Illinois Press, 1973.

Zabelin, I. E., *Domashnii byt russkikh tsarei v XVI i XVII stoletiiakh*. Bk. I. *Gosudarev dvor*, Moscow: Kniga, 1990.

Istoriia goroda Moskvy, Pt. 1, Moscow: Stolitsa, 1990; reprint of Moscow: Tipo-litografiia T-va I. I. Kushnerev, 1905.

Zagoskin, N. P., *Ocherk istorii smertnoi kazni v Rossii*, Kazan: Tip. Imp. Universiteta, 1892.

Zaozerskii, A. I., *Tsarskaia votchina XVII v.*, 2nd edn., Moscow: Gosud. sotsial'noi-ekonomicheskoe izd., 1937.

Zen'kovskii, S. A., *Russkoe staroobriadchestvo*, 2 vols., Moscow: Institut DI-DIK, 2006.

Zertsalov, A. N., "K istorii miatezha 1648 goda v Moskve i drug. gorodakh," in *Chteniia* (1896), bk. I: i–iv, 1–36.

"K istorii Moskovskogo miatezha 1648 g.," in *Chteniia* (1893), bk. III, docs. 1–2.

"M. B. Shein pod Smolenskom," in *Chteniia* (1897), bk. II, Smes': 18, 22, 24–7.

"O miatezhakh v gorode Moskve i v sele Kolomenskom v 1648, 1662 i 1771 gg.," in *Chteniia* (1890), bk. III: 3–116.

Zguta, Russell, "Witchcraft Trials in 17th-c Russia," *American Historical Review* 82 (1977), 5: 1187–1207.

Zhivov, V. M., *Iazyk i kul'tura v Rossii XVIII veka*, Moscow: Shkola "Iazyki russkoi kul'tury," 1996.

Zhukov, A. Iu., *Upravlenie i samoupravlenie v Karelii v XVII v.*, Velikii Novgorod: NovGU, 2003.

Zimin, A. A., *Krupnaia feodal'naia votchina i sotsial'no-politicheskaia bor'ba v Rossii: Konets XV–XVI v.*, Moscow: Nauka, 1977.

Oprichnina Ivana Groznogo, Moscow: Mysl', 1964.

"O slozhenii prikaznoi sistemy na Rusi," *Doklady i soobshcheniia Instituta istorii Akademii nauk* 3 (1955): 164–76.

Reformy Ivana Groznogo. Ocherki sotsial'no-ekonomicheskoi i politicheskoi istorii Rossii serediny XVI v., Moscow: Izd. sotsial'no-ekonomicheskoi literatury, 1960.

Rossiia na poroge novogo vremeni. (Ocherki polit. istorii Rossii pervoi treti XVI v.), Moscow: Mysl', 1972.

Rossiia na rubezhe XV–XVI stoletii. Ocherki sotsial'no-politicheskoi istorii, Moscow: Mysl', 1982.

Zlotnikov, M. F., "Podiachie Ivanovskoi ploshchadi. K istorii notariata Moskovskoi Rusi," *Sbornik statei, posv. Lappo-Danilevskomu*, 82–130.

Index

For EU product safety concerns, contact us at Calle de José Abascal, 56–1°, 28003 Madrid, Spain or eugpsr@cambridge.org.

www.ingramcontent.com/pod-product-compliance
Lightning Source LLC
LaVergne TN
LVHW102007210926
848483LV00009B/118
* 9 7 8 1 1 0 7 0 2 5 1 3 4 *